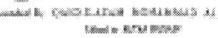

The front page of the last edition of *Dawn*, Delhi, on 15 August 1947. The management had hoped that the paper would continue to be published in Delhi as it prepared to move headquarters to Karachi, but the offices of the paper in Delhi were destroyed by a mob. It carried messages by Jinnah, King George VI, and Lord Mountbatten, the last Viceroy of India.

Dawn's issue of 25/12/1953. "When the truth cannot be spoken, and patriotism is held almost a crime, the editorial space is left blank on the Quaid-i-Azam's birthday, to speak more eloquently than words." Due to the government's several pressures, Editor Altaf Husain decided not to write an editorial as a protest and left the blank space with the above note.

A complete desk job: I was ill and at home the day that General Zia-ul-Haq died. A friend rang me from *Arab News*, Jeddah, asking me whether I could "report". I monitored radio and TV and filed the report on the phone. *From the author's personal collection.*

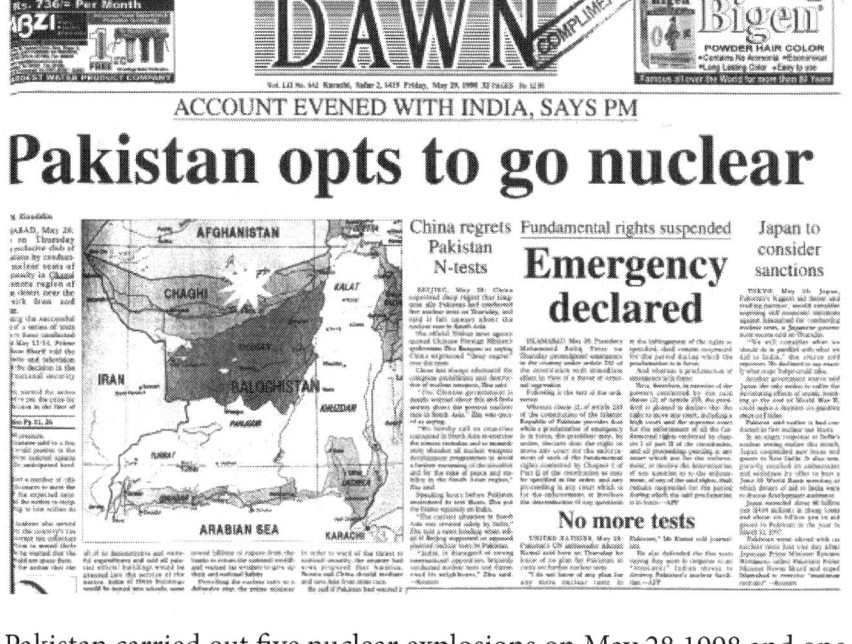

Pakistan carried out five nuclear explosions on May 28 1998 and one more on May 30 to become the world's seventh nuclear power.
Courtesy Dawn Library

PM reaffirms Pakistan stand

Changes in Pressler law being sought: Clinton

From Muhammad Ali Siddiqi

WASHINGTON, April 11: President Clinton said here on Tuesday he was working with Congress to seek changes in the Pressler Amendment because it was a law directed only against Pakistan.

"I do not think it is right for us to keep the money and the equipment," the President said while addressing a Press conference along with Prime Minister Benazir Bhutto in the Grand Foyer of the White House, following one hour of talks on bilateral relations and security issues.

Even though the President made no firm commitment that the Pressler amendment would be abolished, he kept no secret of his distaste for the law under which he said he could not transfer the equipment to Pakistan while the money had already been spent.

The law had placed Pakistan, he said, in "a no man's land."

Prime Minister Bhutto on her turn said she was "deeply encouraged" by President Clinton's attitude and the understanding he had shown of Pakistan's position on the Pressler amendment and the security situation in the area.

"I have no intention of dumping Pakistan," he replied when a questioner asked him whether or not the world would get a wrong signal if the United States dumped Pakistan, a country that had been America's ally for half a century.

Since he had been President, he said he had "done everything possible to broaden our ties with Pakistan," and deepen cooperation in other fields. When he became President, the Pressler amendment had already gone into effect. "That's what I found out when I became President."

He said he was the first President to declare that holding back both the money and the equipment was wrong. Therefore, he would "do my very best" to explore possibilities with Congress in a way "that's fair to Pakistan."

The President said he would not abandon Pakistan, because "the future of the entire part of the world where Pakistan is depends in some large measure on Pakistan's success."

A joint statement was later to be issued, and Ms. Robin Raphel, Assistant Secretary for South Asia, was holding a Press briefing for the media till our going to press.

On Kashmir, President Clinton said the United states was willing to play a mediatory role, and he believed many other Indo-Pakistan problems could be tackled if the Kashmir issue were resolved. He said he emphasised to Indian Prime Minister Rao when he was here the need for a solution to the Kashmir issue.

Related reports on Pp 14, 18

Prime Minister Bhutto said the Clinton administration regarded Kashmir as a disputed territory and welcomed President Clinton's mediation offer, but regretted that India was not willing to accept this.

President Clinton made it clear that an improvement in relations with Pakistan would continue along with a similar movement toward India.

However, the President repeatedly referred to Pakistan as a moderate, progressive Islamic country that was keen to combine the best of its Islamic tradition with democratic ideals. He quoted Quaid-i-Azam Mohammad Ali Jinnah and said he was glad that Pakistan rising to his ideals.

In her opening statement, Prime Minister Bhutto said:

"Since 1989, my last visit to Washington, both the world and Pakistan-US relations have undergone far-reaching changes.

"The Post Cold war era has brought into sharp focus the positive role that Pakistan, a moderate, democratic, Islamic country of 130 million people, can play from its strategic location at the trijunction of South Asia, Central Asia and the Gulf, a region of both political conflict and economic opportunity.

"Globally, Pakistan is active in UN peace-keeping operations. We are in the forefront of the fight against international terrorism, narcotics, illegal immigration and counterfeit currency. We remain

Continued on Page 6

WASHINGTON: US President Bill Clinton escorts Benazir Bhutto to the Rose Garden at the White House on Tuesday after their formal talks.—AFP

Benazir Bhutto overshadowed an equally charismatic Bill Clinton at their White House meeting in April 1995. Picture shows the Prime Minister and the President entering the rose garden.
Courtesy Dawn Library

The censorship period during Ziaul Haq's military regime was the longest in Pakistan's history — from October 1979 to January 1982. The blank space in Dawn's leader page of November 29, 1979, shows the top article censored by the military regime. Ziaul Haq's was the only regime which flogged journalists.

Dawn's page one of the same date — November 29, 1979 — showing blank space.

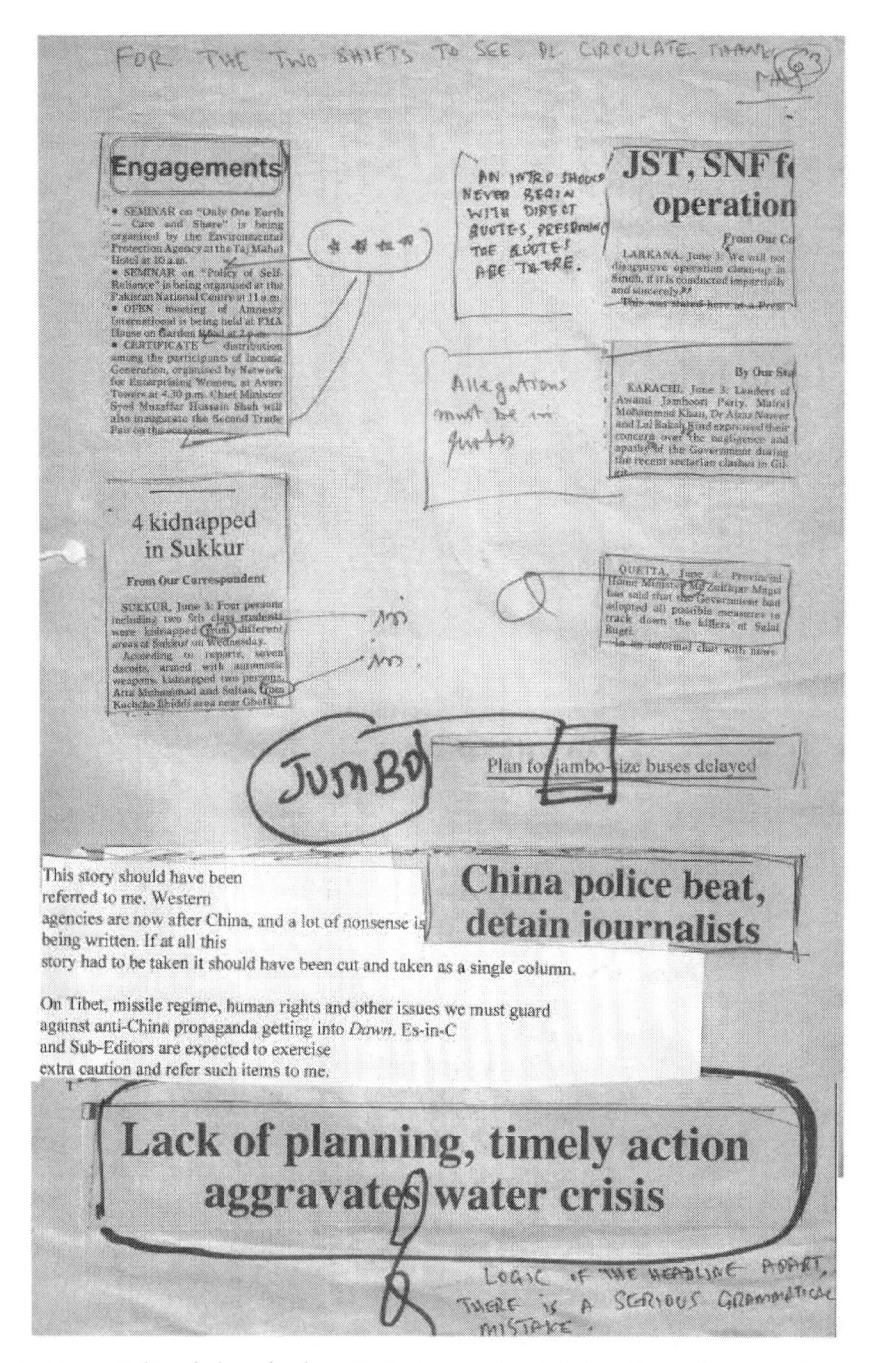

A News Editor's headache. Pointing out mistakes for subeditors' benefit the next day. Most subeditors never cared.
From the author's personal collection.

Baitullah Mehsud, one of the founders of Tehreek-i-Taliban Pakistan, seen here with two of his companions. This photo was taken just before the signing of a deal with security forces on February 7 2005, at Sara Rogha, South Waziristan.

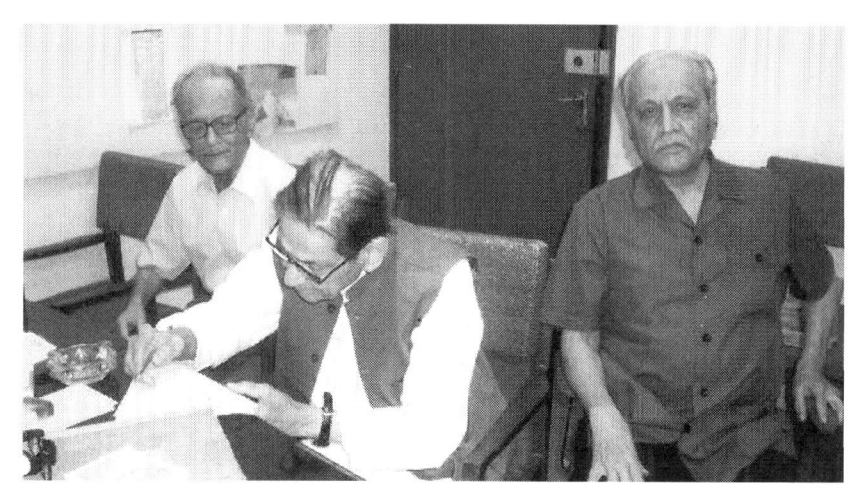

Meticulous checking of facts: Minhaj Barna poring over my account of his bio-data for this book. The other person is M.A. Majid. This picture was taken in my room in *Dawn* office.
From the author's personal collection

Ahmad Ali Khan, who believed that an editor should shun publicity and stay in the background. During his 28 years as *Dawn's* editor, chief editor and editor-in-chief, he attended only two diplomatic receptions: one by the Soviet General at a hotel in Karachi; the other, a reception on the eve of China's national day, by the Chinese Consul General at his Clifton home, Karachi on September 30, 1998.

Here he is shaking hands with Chinese Consul General An Qiguang, who spoke Urdu fluently. The author is in the centre.
From the author's personal collection

WAITING FOR
DAWN

Muhammad Ali Siddiqi

Filament Publishing

Published by
Filament Publishing Ltd
16, Croydon Road, Waddon, Croydon,
Surrey, CR0 4PA, United Kingdom
Telephone +44 (0)20 8688 2598
Fax +44 (0)20 7183 7186
info@filamentpublishing.com
www.filamentpublishing.com

© Muhammad Ali Siddiqi 2017

The right of Muhammad Ali Siddiqi to be identified as the author of this work has been asserted by him in accordance with the Designs and Copyright Act 1988.

ISBN 978-1-912256-30-3

Printed CreateSpace

This book is subject to international copyright and may not be copied in any way without the prior written permission of the publishers.

Originally published by Ushba Publishing International, Karachi
Original ISBN 978-9699154409

PREFACE TO INTERNATIONAL EDITION

The rise of fascism in Pakistan owes a great deal to its foreign connections, especially its involvement in the Afghan resistance movement after the Soviet Union invaded Pakistan's western neigbour on Christmas eve, 1979. That Pakistan chose to become a frontline state, with Islamabad playing Hanoi to Afghan Vietcong, was a dangerous and expensive undertaking that would not have been possible without support from many Western and Arab nations. The country leading the anti-Soviet crusade and determined to turn Afghanistan into the Soviet Union's Vietnam was the United States. The CIA's overt and covered aid to America's beloved guerilla – then called Mujahideen with fervor and now branded terrorists – sowed the seeds of a phenomenon that has turned Pakistan into what it is: a country mauled by terrorism.

Two Arab states, Saudi Arabia with its vast oil wealth, and Egypt with its Soviet arms, sustained anti-Soviet resistance. Most astonishingly, and unknown to the world, Pakistan became a conduit for arms for the anti-Soviet militants from a country it doesn't even have diplomatic relations with: Israel. President Jimmy Carter hated US arms being captured by the occupying Soviet forces, so Soviet arms captured by Israel in its many wars with Arab states started reaching the 'Mujahideen' in a big way through Pakistan. Thus a large part of the book covers world politics, including the part Islamabad played in the rapprochement between Washington and Beijing. As for my views about British and

American societies, I expect my Anglo-Saxon readers to be both amazed and amused. I have also cut out or accommodated only briefly some of my editorials contained in the Pakistani edition.

I am grateful to Mr Chris Day, Director, Filament Publishing Ltd., for his decision to publish my book. I like Filament's very original motto: 'changing the world, one book at a time.' My thanks to Ms Shahbano Alvi, MD of Ushba Publishing International, the publisher of my book, for giving permission to Filament, for printing this international edition. My thanks go to Dr Ahmad Ali Khan of Brain Trust International, for introducing me to Chris. Ahmad is not only my cousin Farhat's husband, he is my school buddy, so we have known each other for more than half a century, and his Chigwell, London, home provides me with five-star hotel services free of charge open-ended.

CONTENTS

Preface to International Edition … iii
Foreword … ix
Preface … xiii
Acknowledgment … xvii

Chapter One: The first time … 1
Chapter Two: A gentleman's martial law … 33
Chapter Three: Revanche! … 77
Chapter Four: Mobs are born … 115
Chapter Five: A nuclear sub … 141
Chapter Six: Mr Ramay's bill of indictment … 163
Chapter Seven: Terror comes to Dawn … 181
Chapter Eight: A hot country … 191
Chapter Nine: Flogging and hanging … 209
Chapter Ten: Fireworks and a wedding … 239
Chapter Eleven: On the Potomac … 279
Chapter Twelve: Benazir in Washington … 357
Chapter Thirteen: Society changes … 413
Chapter Fourteen: Priests … 435
Chapter Fifteen: 9/11 and Pakistan's domestic scene … 459
Chapter Sixteen: 2007 crisis … 477
Chapter Seventeen: Brother Arabs … 529

Postscript … 569
Appendices … 573
Index … 589

DEDICATION

I DEDICATE THIS BOOK TO the sacred blood of Pakistan's innocent men, women and children murdered by terrorists devoid of mercy, compassion and all those values which humans throughout history have considered holy. Out of their blood shall rise a new Pakistan shining in freedom and serenity, free from the scourge of hate and fanaticism and dedicated to the values Jinnah symbolised.

FOREWORD

No one could be more qualified to write a memoir on Pakistan's turbulent history than a grandstand viewer – and a journalist to boot. With more than half a century of experience in journalism – 49 years in *Dawn*, South Asia's best paper, – Muhammad Ali Siddiqi has been witness to events which have shaped today's Pakistan and Karachi. He lived history as a citizen, and reported and commented as a newsman – in Pakistan and abroad. This book is, thus, his record for posterity of a mauled, brutalised nation's history. The book is also a mirror to the life of a typical, self-made Karachian struggling to acquire education, while making two ends meet as a typist. This is a tribute as much to the author as to the city that threw open its doors to all those who chose to make it their home. Life for him was anything but a bed of roses, for he would sleep on the editing desk of the *Times of Karachi* to proceed in the morning to the new campus – located in what then was a wilderness of barren hills and brown land. That was 1960. In 1992 he was at the White House reporting on the Benazir-Clinton summit conference as *Dawn*'s Washington correspondent.

Because his entry in the profession coincided with the first military takeover in 1958, he like all Pakistani journalists worked within the oppressive atmosphere of a military dictatorship, though, strange as it appears, author Siddiqi mentions Ayub Khan all along with respect – a contradiction I cannot fathom. He makes no secret of his admiration for Z.A. Bhutto, who, he said, was murdered because of his reforms, especially the nationalization of industry, and quotes Machiavelli "A man forgets his father (*pater*) but not his patrimony."

The book describes in detail the impact the military rule had on the press, the muzzling of the media, draconian laws, the journalists' epic struggle for freedom, the historic 1970 strike, the flogging of journalists during Ziaul Haq's tyranny, and the freedom which finally came after great sacrifices. Simultaneously, we get a glimpse of the technological revolution in printing, for Siddiqi began with hot metal and journeyed through photo-offset to finally enter the computer era when *Dawn*'s page are sent to Islamabad and Rawalpindi by a click.

For a person like me, reading his book is a pleasure as he takes me through the vicissitudes of Pakistan's history of which I have often been part as a politician and constitutional lawyer. The sweep of his book includes the constitutional and political developments in the fifties of the last century to Musharraf days in this century with traumas of its own – the assassination of Benazir Bhutto, the Lal Masjid rebellion and its inept handling by the military government, leading to the unleashing of a new wave of terrorism. His theory about the degeneration of such a positive force as religion into fascism is simple. It began within two years of Pakistan's birth, for as a school boy he saw some religious posters that disseminated a subtle hatred against Pakistan in those formative years when the country was struggling to set up the infrastructure of a state. The seeds of Talibanism had been sown. He believes "the people of Pakistan have on the whole shown maturity of judgment and a remarkable degree of openness of mind and have seldom shown resistance to change. As results of the general elections held in 1970, 1977, 1985, 1988, 1990, 1993, 2002 and 2008 show, the people of Pakistan did not fail to realise that religious parties had nothing but empty rhetoric to offer."

I would recommend to the reader chapters one and 17. Titled 'The first time', chapter one captures some of Karachi's lost charm. Goans were part of Karachi's mainstream with exotic Portuguese names – D'Sica, D'Cruz, Rodriguez, Lobo, Menezes, D'Souza, Ignatius and Monteiro, some of them Siddiqi's colleagues. The scarf then was identified with Goans, and an average Karachiite considered it normal to see Goan families or a woman alone going to church, with Christian boys dressed as Santa Claus riding cycles late into night.

Chapter 'Brother Arabs' says something about us Pakistanis' romantic view of the Arabs, and the consequent blunders Pakistan has made in dealing with Arab countries. His thesis is that the Arabs are basically a secular people, they do not appreciate religion as a state's basis, their historical experience has been vastly different from South Asian Muslims', the Arabs have no concept of pan-Islamism and that they are often amused at Pakistanis' infantile concept of the ummah – the worldwide Muslim community. While the reader may not accept these rather radical views, I recommend the chapter for reasons of originality.

(Barrister) Kamal Azfar
Former Governor of Sindh
Karachi, Pakistan
February 24, 2015

PREFACE

JOURNALISTS REPORT ON THE DAY'S events, but the events eventually become history. Yes, the book in hand is my version of history as I saw it. If I appear subjective, and I concede I do, I would not be the first or last journalist to be so. Newspersons worldwide face a daunting task because they write for newspapers, which in most cases are commercial ventures geared to the tastes if not prejudices of their readers. They must sell or wind up. In Pakistan since the Ayub era, the press has stood acutely polarised – a reflection, of society itself. This polarisation acquired neurotic levels from the seventies onwards. Any research scholar has to go through the files of Pakistani newspapers since the seventies to see the absence of some of the basic norms of journalism in reporting and comments. In fact, there is evidence aplenty of attempts by reporters, columnists and editorial writers to arouse passions to animal levels. As I grew as a journalist in this era, I watched this phenomenon in horror. There are basically two reasons for this.

One: dictators banned or restricted political activity and muzzled the press. But when dictators fell, freedom exploded and came to the people of Pakistan in social and political chaos; it did not come through an evolutionary process. Thus neither politicians nor journalists knew how to use freedom, how to consolidate democracy, how to create a hate-free society, and how to build a milieu that accepted political, cultural and religious pluralism. Two, ignorant and semi-literate clerics acquired on society a hold that was out of proportion to their worth and their vote bank. As *Time* magazine put it (June 30, 2008, Internet edition), "It is almost like a bad joke. A bus driver, a ski lift operator and a gym rat have turned the Islamic world's only nuclear armed nation upside down" — a reference to Baitullah Mehsud, who was a trainer at a fitness centre, Fazlullah, a ski lift operator, and Mangal Bagh, a truck driver. The man who spawned this phenomenon was Ziaul Haq. I have dwelt at length on the pernicious effects on state and society of what came to be called the military-mullah alliance.

I flatter myself when I say that the sweep of my book covers the period from Pakistan's birth in 1947 to the middle of 2008, which I chose to be the cut-off point for my Pakistani edition. Recording and commenting on all events in these tragedy-filled six decades was beyond me. So I had to work within parameters in a way that gaps did not serve to distort the Pakistan story. I have specially chosen to dwell on the period between 1958, when I entered the profession of journalism, and the cut-off point. All tragedies — and triumphs, if any — occurred in this period. The reader may at places feel bored because I have quoted extensively from speeches, texts and vital treaty documents to preserve for posterity some important aspects of our history. I have also quoted from Dawn editorials — all of them not necessarily written by me — to record for history what Dawn thought of some of the most crucial political, constitutional and foreign policy issues in Pakistan's history.

I feel proud of my association with Dawn, spanning as it does more than four decades, for no newspaper in South Asia had been associated with Jinnah and with the struggle for Pakistan the way Dawn had been. For that reason, the book also gives the reader some glimpses into Dawn's history, its founding and the various phases through which it passed, not only editorially but also technologically and the changes in layouts. Personally for me it has been a journey through a technological revolution in a lifetime. When I began my career in the PPA (now PPI) news agency in 1958, news was sent to our newspaper-clients on the teleprinter; now it is the age of email and modem. I have attempted to catch this phenomenon to note at the same time that the revolution wasn't merely technological; during the same era the press bounced back to freedom — bounced back, because until 1958, when the military first took over, the press in Pakistan was as free as a press could be.

Writing a book while doing a fulltime job is a difficult if not impossible task, but if have achieved anything in this world it is time management. Chapter two explains why and how I developed this habit, which both helped and often tormented me. I had originally hoped to finish the book in three years; I was able to finish it in November 2009. Since the late Ahmad Ali Khan, who had been my editor for 28 years, finds repeated mention in this book I refer to him as AAK.

Finally, nostalgia is an intrinsic part of a memoir, but I have restricted it to just one topic that all readers should find fascinating — Karachi: what this 'British city' was when I landed at the harbour six decades ago as a boy and the phenomenon that it is today.

Karachi
Pakistan
December 21, 2009

ACKNOWLEDGMENT

I HAVE BEEN METICULOUSLY KEEPING the clippings of all my editorials, signed articles and news stories printed in Dawn over a period spanning more than four decades. Nasir Nayyer, my son, catalogued them in a way that I could have instant recourse to any piece even before the internet era. My immense thanks to him and to my family for their cooperation. My profound thanks go to Ms Sabahat Kaleem, Dawn librarian, for helping me with checking and verifying the mass of facts and figures this book contains, assisted by her deputy, Syed Azhar Ali. Above all, my gratitude to the Haroons and to the Dawn family for maintaining and encouraging at *Dawn* an ambience that has been conducive to reading, writing and research.

Sharif Al Mujahid is South Asia's leading authority on the freedom movement and is perhaps Pakistan's most quoted author abroad. He has been my mentor and teacher since I became his student at the Karachi University's journalism department in 1957. For half a century, thus, it has been a relationship that has always been to my advantage. As his student I used to be his voluntary typist, and that helped me a great deal in grasping the intricacies of writing. That I am still poor at this job is a reflection on me.

On the Indian leaders' commitments to a plebiscite in Kashmir, I have borrowed from: (1) the late Rasheed Ahmad Kidwai's booklet *Jammu and Kashmir Issue*; (2) the article by the late foreign minister Zain Noorani in *The Nation* of February 11, 1990, and (3) *Kashmir and the People's Voice*, published by Pakistan Publications, Karachi,

April 1964. For extracts from various UN resolutions and quotes from UN mediators Gunnar V. Jarring and Frank P. Graham I have relied on (1) *Reports on Kashmir by United Nations Representatives*, published by the Government of Pakistan, 1962, and (2) CSS website (cssforum.com.pk). Extracts from Z. A. Bhutto's speeches to the Security Council on September 22, 1965, and the General Assembly on September 28, 1965, have been taken from the full texts published by the Department of Films and Publications, Government of Pakistan, September 1965. I had managed to keep them with me since then.

1

THE FIRST TIME

"Does the roof leak?" I asked a colleague only a few days after joining Dawn in July 1960 as a trainee subeditor. The question was relevant. Karachi those days used to have its annual quota of monsoon rains, and sometimes it rained quite heavily. In 1960, it was especially heavy, and the roof of the offices of The Times of Karachi, the newspaper I worked for before joining Dawn, used to leak.

"No" replied my colleague, who if I remember correctly, was Manzoor Siddiqi, a reporter. "It does not leak; it falls!"

The offices of Dawn were then located in an old barracks which was once a godown – subcontinental English for a warehouse. The roof of red tiles rested on old, moth-eaten wooden beams, and bits of tiles and chunks of mortar sometimes fell during heavy downpours. Hence my colleague's rather amusing response. The newsroom consisted of one long hall, in the centre of which was the subeditorial desk. Instead of the standard horseshoe type in the centre of which sat the night-in-charge, or chief sub-editor, it was T-shaped, given this shape by putting several tables together. The desk always remained covered with sheets of newsprint, and the subeditors sat on both sides of the T's stem, while three men sat at the head of the T. One was the chief subeditor (called night shift-in-charge); to his left sat his deputy, and to his right some senior sub who made pages. Dummy sheets were seldom used, and in get-up Dawn's pages resembled those of The Times, London, though the make-up of the leader page was chaotic, and I often wondered how the seniors tolerated this. I think the primary reason was that Altaf Husain, who took up Dawn's editorship at Mohammad Ali Jinnah's urgings in October 1945, was not a professional journalist. But more about this remarkable man later.

Away from the end of the T stem were two desks, one on each corner of the hall – one for the reporters (where the roof used to "fall") and the other for the one-man commerce team. The commerce news occupied half a page and consisted mostly of commodity rates, stock market reports, State Bank statements, and company news, which was limited because industrialisation had not yet begun. The commerce man left early, and his place was occupied by the sports team consisting then of three men headed by Anwar Hussain, popularly known as Annoo Bhai. There is a park in Nazimabad named after him. A former doubles champion in tennis before independence, he was a strong-willed man, had his way and was feared for his bluntness. He wanted me on the sports desk and obtained the permission of the night shift-in-charge to have me on his staff. However, the next day other seniors overruled the chief subeditor's decision. When Anwar found me sitting on what was called the general desk he got up and went straight to the editor's room to complain. Fortunately, Altaf was out of the country, and I remained on the general desk. Till today I have wondered whether I would have been better off if Anwar had succeeded in getting me on the sports desk. What I miss till today is cricket reporting from abroad. I have no doubt if I were in the sports section I would have visited several cricket-playing countries, some of which I have never had the pleasure of visiting – like the West Indies, South Africa and the down under.

The offices of Dawn were then located in an area which most Karachiites today wouldn't know – New Chali. The name of the road was South Napier Road. The most horrible aspect of this name was that North Napier Road harboured Karachi's red light district. In general, the red light area was referred to without "North". So we in Dawn were very careful never to miss the word "South" when writing the newspaper's mailing address or talking to someone. I remember one swipe by Morning News, our contemporary and rival, though lagging far behind in circulation. Because Dawn was a mainstream paper, Morning News catered to the minorities and published news, pictures and comments that could interest its Christian, Parsi and Hindu readers. Published simultaneously at Dacca and Karachi, Morning News also used to print a crossword of sorts, entitled Get-a-Word. Those who entered the competition and won got a prize and lots of money. We in Dawn never took much notice of Morning News, and it had a low circulation because it made the fundamental mistake of copying Dawn in style and get-up. However, I do not remember now – more than four decades after the incident – what caused the provocation to Dawn. There was an editorial in it, which said, among other things, that it did not believe in increasing its circulation by crosswords and such means. Morning News was furious, retaliated and accused Dawn of kowtowing to every government (which till then was more or less true, because most federal governments then were led by the Muslim League, the party that created Pakistan, whose founder, Jinnah, was also the founder of Dawn). However, the unkind bit of humour came when Morning News referred to Dawn as "our Napier Road contemporary". Dawn quietly dropped the controversy.

In the '60s, New Chali was the centre of commodity trade in Karachi. The area smelled of spices, grains and oils, and lines of camel carts stood for their turn to carry the load. The Japanese had not till then invented the Suzuki carrier van, and donkey carts did the job. The traders were mostly Sindhis and people belonging to the Gujrati-speaking community, while Makranis were manual workers, who carried loads on their backs and owned donkey and camel carts. The Urdu-speaking, who by then constituted the city's majority, were mostly white collar workers, and it goes without saying that they ran Dawn, though editor Altaf himself was from East Pakistan, which means he was Bengali speaking. The pace of life in Karachi was easy, and people were "normal", unlike the abnormality that now characterises the collective behaviour of us Pakistanis. Even though independence was then 13 years old, Karachi still retained its British looks, despite the sudden rise in the population from half a million in August 1947, when independence came, to a million and a half. For a city which existed between Merewether Tower and P.I.B. Colony, there were enough parks and playgrounds. The very names of the cricket grounds gave an indication of Karachi's multi-religious, multi-cultural society – the Karachi Goans' Association ground, the Karachi Parsi Institute, the Hindu Gymkhana, the Abdullah Haroon Muslim Gymkhana, Patel Park (later named Nishtar Park), and Karachi Gymkhana, the club founded by British sahibs ruling "Scinde". Even a decade after independence, a KG membership still meant entry into the city's elite.

The Goans were then part of Karachi's mainstream life, and it was quite common to find Goans with their Portuguese names — Lobo, D'Sica, D'Cruz, Misquita, D'Souza, De'Souza, Perera, Rodriguez, Fernandez, Ignatius, Menezes, Barganza and Pinto — in government and commercial offices. The Goan men were in the professions also, while the women worked as teachers, secretaries and telephone operators. Generally, they wore the long Western dress without fear of being derided, much less attacked, and during Yuletide the so-called Christian district in Saddar came alive, with boys dressed as Santa Clause riding bicycles and families or women and girls in twos or threes going to church in scenes hard to visualise today. People wore overcoats. That was quite common in winter, because the Karachi I am talking about — early sixties — was much colder than it is today, with the minimum temperature in January falling to one degree centigrade. The Goans came to Karachi toward the end of the 18th century, and as a Goan booklet written in 2005 informs us, they "marched with the British troops to Afghanistan, and subsequently, on the annexation of Sind by the British in 1842, some of them remained in the country" — the country being Sind. Karachi was then, says the booklet, "a small fishing village, marshy and extremely malarious. Notwithstanding its proximity to the sea it was subject to extremes of heat and cold. In summer, the discomfort of the extreme heat of the day was aggravated by hot blasts of wind and thick clouds of dust. The nights were, however, cool and pleasant. In winter, a thin incrustation of ice in pails and tubs of water was not an infrequent sight." Among the Goan journalists I worked with were Michael Ignatius, sports editor of Morning News in the sixties, and Donald Menezes, who was my boss in Morning News and later colleague in Dawn. He now lives in Canada.

Also with me in Morning News was a fascinating character, Anthony Mascarenhas. To my knowledge Tony is perhaps the only Pakistani Goan journalist who finds a mention in Wikipedia. He was a reporter with wide contacts, and nothing about him was Goan. Tall and well built Tony was handsome, and I used to call him "Punjabi Muslim" because of his looks. He was Morning News's New Delhi correspondent when I reached there in May 1964 along with Mother and a beautiful girl, Razia. I did not wish to be in India a day longer than necessary and had to go to Aurangabad on Ammi's urgings to kidnap this lovely, little girl who was her niece. Nehru had died only a week ago, and I was madly in love with both Ayub and Bhutto and wanted to get away from India as quickly as possible. The way Pakistan was stable those days it has never been since. I wanted emergency nationality for Razia, and Tony with his connections at the Pakistan High Commission in New Delhi saw to it that I got it in a matter of hours. The feeling which I then had about Tony's involvement with Pakistan's intelligence services was subsequently strengthened. When he first came to my hotel to take us to the High Commission he told me that I was being watched. Journalists are watched by host governments worldwide, even if those intelligence agencies belong to democratic countries. The next day, when Razia, Ammi and I were leaving for Pakistan by train, Tony came to the station to say us goodbye. He told me again in whispers that I was being watched. But the way he told me did not seem to me a hint from a friend; he was a friend no doubt, and I am grateful to him till this day for that quick visa, but the way he told me and the way he operated — he did not tell us that he would be at the railway station and came there unannounced — had an air of professionalism about it. Seven years later, all this would change, and perhaps I would not blame Tony for what he did.

Born at Belgaum near Goa in 1928, Neville Anthony Mascarenhas came to Karachi as a boy and was educated at St Patrick's College before going to Bombay, where he worked for Reuters. With independence, Reuters sent him to Pakistan to establish the British news agency in the new country. Later, with his experience, Tony helped found the Associated Press of Pakistan, the government news agency. He left the Times of Karachi a year before I joined it in 1959 but was my colleague in Morning News when in 1964 I joined the paper, owned by Khawja Nooruddin — who belonged to Dhaka's Nawab family and was thus related to Prime Minister Khawja Nazimuddin. A year later, war broke out between Pakistan and India, and Tony — then Morning News's correspondent in New Delhi, and his family along with other Pakistanis were interned by India. I left Morning News in 1966 while he started working for the Sunday Times, London. We never met again. In March 1971, when the army began its crackdown in East Pakistan, and the whole world, except China, turned against Pakistan, Tony went to London and denounced the Yahya regime in the strongest possible terms in British newspapers. In fact, his story in the Sunday Times, London, was spread over three pages and constituted the first major disclosure in the international press of the slaughter that was going on in East Pakistan. Once the war was over, Tony lost all importance for the British press. That is how this world is. He then worked as a freelance journalist, but his heyday as a reporter was over. Of the way he was later ostracised by the British press, Tony wrote: "I have been too long a journalist not to know that a relative 'outsider' such as I was, even with the biggest story in the world, could be indefinitely knocking on the doors of Fleet Street". Till this day I do not know why Tony failed to get British nationality, and I felt deeply hurt when I learnt that he later became an Indian national, though he continued to live in Britain. He died on December 3, 1986 at a rather young age, 58, leaving behind his wife Yvonne Gertrude D'Souza, whom he had married in 1952. He wrote two books *The Rape of Bangladesh: A Legacy of Blood*. In its obituary, *The Times* said Tony's first story about the situation in East Pakistan created "a worldwide sensation"

The Pakistani Goans suffered a financial blow when India invaded the Portuguese colony in December 1961, annexed the tiny territory and confiscated the property of Pakistani Goans. One motive behind Tony's decision to seek an Indian nationality could be the possibility of getting his ancestral property in Goa back. The ban on alcohol in 1977 toward the fag end of Bhutto's rule also affected Goan social life, which revolved a great deal round the club life of the Karachi Goan Association. It is a pity that we have lost this enterprising community to migration, for very few Goans are left in Karachi, even though they contributed to the city's growth and its cosmopolitan culture. Goan women now avoid Western clothing for fear of being molested and, except for the older among them, most wear shalwar-shirt, the standard Pakistani dress for women. Decades later some Goans were still around. They included Noel Monteiro, who later left for Australia. Another Goan, Walter Fernandez, was a fine sports reporter and worked for two decades for Dawn. He quit Dawn under most unfortunate circumstances. Briefly, he had taken to the bottle.

The Parsis' contribution to Karachi's growth and to its culture is enormous. But there was very little interaction with them because the Parsis then, as now, belonged to the elite. Today, while writing these lines in the 21st century, I feel lucky that I should have talked to and interviewed in the late 20th century a Parsi who was born in the 19th. Jal Framji Khambatta came to Karachi from Pune (Poona) in 1909 when he was 12. I interviewed him 77 years later. I do not know when Khambatta died, because I had left for the US in 1992 and on my return found no trace of him. However, when I met him in 1986 he was 89 and appeared in full control of his mental faculties. The difference between the Karachi of his boyhood and that in his old age was perhaps as great and dramatic as that between the Karachi that I saw in 1949 when I landed on the Keamari harbour and the city that it is today. There were no cars and mechanical vehicles as Khambatta and his family trekked on a bullock cart from harbour to city in 1909 when the British rule over Sind was more than six decades old. All he saw on the road were beasts of burdens, and all carts were pulled by horses, camels, bullocks and donkeys. Even the tramcars were pulled by horses. On the watery edges of the road between the harbour and where Qamar House stands today were warehouses. His images of Karachi of those days included a conscientious municipal worker going up the ladder each evening to light street lamps, the roads being without tar coating, aerated water selling a dozen bottles a rupees, mutton six paisas a seer, wheat flour ten seers a rupee and doctors charging two rupee for home visits. He remembered the boom of the gun that announced the arrival of mail by sea once in a fortnight. The gun boomed basically for the news-starved white community, for the mail was brought by a small streamer from Bombay, the pier of Karachi being too small to handle big ships from England. And on Sundays people watched as troops marched from Napier Barracks to the Trinity Church. As I wrote in my write-up on Khambatta in Dawn's issue of January 24, 1986, "guns and soldiers signifying peace. That was something!"

It was in Karachi that Khambatta went to school (N.J.V. High School) and college (D.J.), proceeded to Bombay to become a doctor like his father, but fell ill and returned home to Karachi on a stretcher to begin a career in accountancy that was to span half a century. And what a half century it was! It meant World War II, the arrival of the Allied forces, the takeover by the Americans of the Karachi branch of the Yokohama Special Bank, where Khambatta worked, the South Asian people's epic struggle for freedom, the Muslim League's movement for a separate homeland for the Muslims of the subcontinent, India's partition and finally — Pakistan! Khambatta remembered the names of the various British firms whose one-story stone houses still dot the city but names most of which have been forgotten — Volkert, Forbes, Campbell, Ralli, Sasson, Graham and many more. "Those were Pax Britannica days," I wrote in the interview, "with gentlemen miners from the coal pits reigning with all the trappings and regalia of the British raj — bearer, butler, buggy, chota hazri, qui hi and all that. There were etiquettes to observe, and don't you dare forget you were a native." Since most bosses were Europeans, said Khambatta, no one could enter the boss's room bare-headed, though it was better to be bare-footed than to be wearing chappals, for the gora sahib positively despised the native version of slippers. And if you had a coat on, see to it that it was buttoned up, And of course, no cigarettes! Khambatta suffered these office etiquettes for a long time, for his own career in accountancy spanned nearly half a century (from 1925 to 1972) when he finally retired as Assistant Manager of the Karachi Race Club.

There were banks, too — banks which have now ceased to exist or have changed hands and names, like the National Bank of India, the Chartered Bank of India, China and Australia, the Imperial Bank of India, and so on. It was in the Yokohama Special Bank that Khambatta got a job in 1925 and thus began a love affair that was to survive the Second World War. It was also in 1925 that he married Jer, who unfortunately had become stone deaf when I met her and their daughter, Armaity, at the Khambatta apartment more than five decades later. The war wasn't important for the world alone; it was equally so for Khambatta, for the Japanese attacked Pearl Harbour in December 1941, and suddenly Khambatta found himself working for an enemy bank. He had some rough moments when the Americans took over the Yokohama bank, and he was in danger of becoming jobless because, when the Americans thought of employing him, the British suspected he was a security risk. The Americans, however, thought there was no proof of Khambatta being a spy and employed him in the US Army's engineering section. This situation lasted till the end of the war, when the Americans departed, so did the British a few years later, and a few years later still, the "enemy" came back to open the branch, this time in a Karachi that was Pakistan's capital. The bank, renamed Bank of Tokyo, re-employed Khambatta, made him chief of the Pakistan staff and on retirement in 1954 invited him to a month's grand tour of Japan, where the president of the bank personally read out a citation hailing him as their oldest employee. He did not conquer Everest, but said Khambatta "a job done with honesty and loyalty is its own reward".

As one of Karachi's oldest citizens, Khambatta missed a city that was once at peace with itself. "When I was a boy, the only trouble with the streets was the lack of tar coating. The roads were macadamised, and victorias and buggies kicked up dust. The only sensation was an occasional horse that ran amok." The city's first car belonged to "Sugar King" Abdullah Haroon, and when it came on the roads people lined up to watch it. "Now the streets are overflowing with vehicles, and the cars have become a nuisance — a threat to life." Sitting in the Khambatta apartment on Chaudhri Khaliquzzaman Road where the Iranian bridge pours cars and vehicles of all sorts coming from Hoshang Road's junction with Dr Ziauddin Ahmad Road, neither Khambatta nor I then had the vaguest idea of the kind of nerve-shattering traffic jams that would become Karachi's lot two more decades later. In his days, said Khambatta, the city clicked. "You wrote a letter to the municipality or the Telephone Department, and you got a reply. Now, you write dozens of letters of complaint and nobody bothers even to acknowledge". When I joined Dawn, there were no Parsis or Goans among the journalists, though there must be some on the management side. More astonishingly, none of our colleagues was a Sindhi, basically because there was hardly any Sindhi middle class. Decades later, Ahmad Ali Khan, who became editor in 1973, began a conscious policy of recruiting the Baloch and Sindhis for Dawn.

The journalists then working for Dawn in the sixties were a class of their own, and it was my good fortune to have worked with them. Those who ran Dawn those days, besides the editor, Altaf Husain, were Mohammad Ashir, the news editor, Assistant Editor Jamil Ansari, and Mohammad Ahmad Zubairi, who besides being Senior Assistant Editor, was also editor of Evening Star, the Dawn group's evening paper, which also happened to be Karachi's first evening English daily. Its price was one anna. Ahmad Ali Khan was not there when I joined the paper in

July 1960. He had left for Lahore in 1949 to join *The Pakistan Times*. Later he would be my boss in Dawn for 28 years, when he rejoined Dawn in 1962 and became editor in February 1973. In Ashir Dawn had a news editor the like of whom the paper would not have for decades. An M.A. in English from Allahabad University — and an earlier B.A. degree from the Aligarh University — Ashir began his career as a sports reporter in *Pioneer*, Lucknow, one of whose editors was Desmond Young, author of the celebrated book *The Desert Fox*. Soon Ashir became *Pioneer*'s news editor and later, as the subcontinent moved toward freedom, undertook a hazardous train journey with his family to Karachi three months before partition to start planning for Dawn's Karachi edition to coincide with the coming of independence. He was also a correspondent for London's Daily Telegraph and Daily Express, besides also working occasionally for Australia's Melbourne Age and Globe and Courier Mail of Canada. An indication of his humane nature came to me when, during my first meeting with him at his Mules Mansion residence at Keamari, where I had gone to probe the possibilities of a job with Dawn, he offered me a cigarette. This was unusual, because in our society, then and as now, young ones do not smoke in the presence of their elders.

My period of apprenticeship as subeditor was surprisingly short — perhaps 20 days, and I was soon regularised on a salary of Rs 275. But the payment I actually received was over Rs 300 depending upon how much money Evening Star received in ad revenues in a given month. Those days, Dawn's morning shift, beginning at 8am, used to bring out the evening paper. (The situation changed in 1971 when Evening Star was detached from Dawn with an editor and staff of its own. I was then Evening Star's edition-in-charge while Akhtar Adil Razwy was the editor.) So the Dawn subeditors were rewarded by an amount that varied between Rs 25 and Rs 30 depending upon the advertisement revenue. Work in the newsroom then was a sort of continuous activity in which the morning shift edited copy for Evening Star, the mid-shift, starting from 12 noon, worked to fill Dawn's inside pages, and the night shifts saw the edition through at 2am. There were two night shifts: an early night shift, which began at 6pm and ended at midnight, and the late night shift, which came at 8pm and worked till the front page was handed over to the printers at about 2am. However, once most copy was in by midnight we were not allowed any rest, for we were supposed to send copy for the inside pages of the next day's Evening Star. This came as crashing bore to us, because by midnight we were all terribly hungry and had no interest whatsoever in the next day's Star. The problem was with the system. If you were in the early night shift, then for reporting to the office at 6pm you had to leave home at 5.30pm, because Karachi, relatively speaking, was still quite small those days and it was possible to reach New Chali, from, say, PIB Colony or even Nazimabad in 20 to 25 minutes. But 5.30pm was no time for dinner. The late-night shift staff left their homes at about 7.30, but even that was no dinner time. So every subeditor had his own routine. When on night duty, the wisdom went, get up at 11.30 a.m. or so, have a mighty breakfast, skip lunch and then have an early dinner at 7pm. Some indeed practised this routine, but even they went hungry by midnight. One subeditor, Mahdi Jafar, came regularly at 8.30pm and when asked why he was late gave the standard answer: "I come to the newsroom after listening to Radio Pakistan's 8pm bulletin". Everyone knew, though, that this was his way of having a home dinner. Mahdi Jaffar was one of the nicest men I knew in the profession. He remained with Dawn until his death in the late eighties.

The copy we subbed for Evening Star's inside pages consisted of stuff from Daily Express, London, with which Dawn had a contract. The Gambols strip, which generations of Dawn readers have seen and enjoyed, and the crossword, chess and bridge features were then and in some cases still are from Daily Express. What Evening Star's inside pages were filled up with was sex and crime news, book reviews, which were of a very high quality, and a lot stuff from Chapman Pincher, Daily Express's legendary defence correspondent. We were told by our seniors that we were not supposed to merely edit the stories mechanically, we were to learn from the stuff we edited and pay attention to language, idiom and punctuation. Mistakes made were quickly spotted, and the subeditor was penalised in various ways. One standard form of punishment — if the mistake was grave — was to impose a one-rupee fine on the guilty subeditor. This was deposited with someone, and when a lot of money was collected we ordered things to eat. Ashir was particular about the Dawn style, even though there was no Dawn stylebook yet (Saleem Asmi, News Editor and later Editor, was to prepare one in the '90s). But till today I remember Ashir's insistence that per cent must be used as two words, with "cent" followed by a full-stop, that in the headline it should never be the percentage sign (%) but p.c., that there was no need for 'e' after 'g' in acknowledgment, judgment and abridgment, that it must be Soekarno not Sukarno, Rumania not Romania, Jakarta not Djakarta, Khrushchev and not the various spellings which the Western wire agencies followed, that there was no such thing as Red China (China pure and simple), and that in view of the controversy over the Gulf being Persian or Arab we were to cut out the adjective and reduce it to the Gulf. This holds good even today. One day some subeditor wrote "devaluated" in the headline. We do not know when editor Altaf barged into the newsroom. He must be fuming with rage. But in the evening we found written on the blackboard in the editor's handwriting in large letters: "Devaluated! Nonsense! Devalued".

Ashir's way of pointing out mistakes was to circulate advisories which all subeditors saw and signed. The circular was then pasted in the log book, and we were told to leaf through the log book in our spare time, which in fact was a rarity. If the mistake were serious, the subeditor would receive a white envelope, asking him to see the news editor in the morning. This was a harsh punishment because, after a night duty, we wished to sleep well into the morning. Seeing him in the morning meant we would rise relatively early, journey to the Dawn office, and return home for the long siesta to prepare ourselves for the night shift. We protested and said that we could see Ashir in his office in the evening. But the real reason for summoning us to the office in the morning, we were told, was to punish us by making us travel twice, and that would make us better subeditors. However, sometimes I did not think the siesta was worth four bus rides. So often I passed the afternoon in a library or a cinema house. After all I was young, and could do with a little less sleep.

My favourite library was the American Friends of the Middle East Library, located close to the Karachi Press Club. It was an absolutely wonderful library, and its location suited me. It was a tragedy of sorts for me when the library was moved to Islamabad. As for the movies, I believe the time and money spent in the cinema halls was well spent, because I saw only English movies, which were and are incomparably superior to anything movies in any other language. In fact, watching Hollywood movies became a way of life with me, for often — when I was on the early night shift — I would have lunch in a restaurant, spend the afternoon in a cinema house watching an English movie, and go to the Dawn office for the early night shift. The number of cinemas screening English movies grew in numbers later, but those days only Paradise, Capitol, Rex and Palace screened English movies. The passion for English movies has persisted with me in this old age, and I think I have seldom felt sorry. As is typical of all young people, I, too, quite often came to identify myself with the hero in a given movie and saw it several times over. Some of Hollywood's legendary heroes like Gregory Peck, Omar Sheriff, Peter O'Toole, Anthony Queen and Marlon Brando fascinated me, and — laughable as it may appear to the reader — I adopted their mannerisms and attitudes and sometimes used to good effect some of the dialogues I had come to memorise.

The Night of the Generals first came to Karachi when I was no more an unmarried "vagabond". I was married and Faisal, my first born, was perhaps two years old. But I continued to see it, if necessary alone. Later, when the age of the VCR advanced, I saw it on the video I do not know how many times. Still later, when I was Dawn's Washington correspondent in the '90s I missed The Night. But one day a channel showed it and I recorded it on the video on a VCR that was built into the TV set. On my return to Pakistan in 1995 I resumed seeing it on the

DVD. The other film that equally fascinated me because of Peck and Quinn was The Guns of Navarone. God alone knows how many times I have seen it. I think I remember most of the two movies' dialogues by heart and sometimes use them in daily conversation without being detected.

"We don't want to see any loose ends dangling, do we?" said Omar Sharif, playing the role of an intelligence officer in the German Army in occupied Poland. I have often used this sentence very appropriately in sophisticated company and impressed others. Also, Peck's outburst on David Niven, who as Corporal Miller had nagged him all along by challenging his leadership: "Well, son, your by-standing days are over! You are in it now up to your neck!" Or Gen Kahlenberg's remark to Lance Corporal Hartmann when the latter says he does not want to be an officer: "I am shattered. My world is toppling. What's the point of being a general when corporals prefer to remain corporals?" However, the most effective way of exiting out of an unwanted situation, where the other party was, otherwise, nice and polite, was shown by O'Toole as Lt.-Gen Tanz in The Night of the Generals. Eleanor, the wife of Gen Gabler, the corps commander, wanted Gen Tanz to marry their rebellious daughter, Ulrike, who hated war and the Junker class to which she belonged and was in love with Hartmann. Eleanor told Gen Tanz she was holding a soiree in his honour because "what an inspiration you have been to us all at home!" As Gen Tanz moved toward the door after saying that he looked forward to the soiree, where Hartmann was to conduct Wagner, Eleanor told the General that Ulrike would be there at the soiree. "You remember, Ulrike, don't you? In Berlin, at the garden party at Gen Jodl's house." Gen Tanz was not the sort who believed in what General Gabler called "domesticity", seemed non-plussed and said with a wooden face, "Yes, I remember her quite well." Then he clicked his heels, said "My compliments!" and left the room. Since then, saying "My compliments" has been a most effective way with me for getting out of awkward situations without hurting anyone's sentiments, and I recommend this to the reader.

The Night of the Generals has a drama that is relevant to Pakistan, or perhaps to any country where intelligence agencies and special forces loyal to the dictator inspire awe and fear in state institutions in a manner that serves to erode them. In this case, Gen Gabler is a corps commander but he is terribly afraid of Tanz, who is Lieutenant General but he belongs to the SS, "a pet of Hitler", as the Polish Inspector investigating a prostitute's murder calls him.

But back to Ashir and to my first stint with Dawn. Sometimes subeditors wrote "Bogra" in the headline to identify the ex-prime minister, and distinguish him from his namesake, Chaudhry Mohamed Ali. Ashir did not like it, because Bogra is the name of a place. One day we received an advisory which asked us not to use Bogra in the headline. Ashir's warning said: "Subeditor doing this again will come to grief". Headlines those days used to be written by subeditors in capital letters, and even changes and editing in the body were made in caps. One day I wrote U in a way that to the headline-maker appeared V. The mistake was detected in time, but I received a note asking me to see the news editor in the morning. When I did, Ashir, never wanting in dry humour, asked me what my academic qualification was. When I told him I was an M.A., he said, "You ought to know, my boy, V has two lines, U has three. Now don't you ever forget this. Good boy!" Ashir was the only journalist who attended diplomatic functions in black tie and white jacket with a red stripe running down his trousers. He remained associated with Dawn till his death in London on June 6, 1964. Ashir was also one of the founders of the Karachi Press Club, established in 1959, and remained its president up to 1962. Uzair Ashir, his son, also joined journalism and was my colleague in The Sun, Karachi, where he was commerce editor. Others who called the shots in Dawn then were Jameel Ansari, who was to be editor between March 1965 and February 1972 with varying titles (Acting Editor March 30, 1965 to April 12, 1966; Executive Editor April 13, 1966 to April 5, 1967, and Editor April 6, 1967 to February 1972), and Mohammad Ahmad Zubairi, who besides being Senior Assistant Editor was editor of Evening Star.

Among the subeditors, there were two unforgettable characters. One was Ibtisam Ahmad. Belonging to eastern Punjab's Khwaja family, he had inherited literary traditions and was well versed in Urdu and English poetry, and that showed in his writings. He used to write for The Statesman, a Karachi weekly. It had a very limited circulation, and very few Pakistanis had heard of it. It had high literary standards, and Bertrand Russell and Michael Foot were among those who wrote for it. Ibtisam was six feet plus, and was, for that reason, often referred to as single column top, the term journalists have for single column stories touching the top rule. He entered the world of journalism after resigning from what could have been a career in the police service. He had passed the civil service examination, was taken on the police service and was functioning as Assistant Superintendent of Police when he realised he was not temperamentally suited to the kind of police force we have in Pakistan. He resigned and joined The Statesman as a proof reader on a modest salary. Later he joined Dawn and was one of the shifts-in-charge when I first came to the paper. I worked with him in two other papers —Daily News, when it was launched by the Jang group in 1962 with Shamim Ahmad as its founder-editor, and Morning News, where I worked after resigning from Daily News in 1963. A sensitive man, he fell victim to the stress that is the lot of newspaperman and died rather young at age 50 in January 1976. The other person was Khawja Mohammad Zubair, who has remained one of my best friends till this day, though unfortunately he has retired from Dawn and now lives in America. Of him later.

What was the news those days? In brief, the country's placidity showed itself on Dawn's pages. The foreign news consisted mostly of the cold war, the unending diplomatic battles in the UN and outside between Nato and Warsaw pact, the frequent military coups in the Middle East and Latin America, Khrushchev and the post-Stalin Russia, the beginning of the Soviet-Chinese ideological polemics that would divide the world communist movement, the gradual hotting up of the war in Indo-China, the ferocious struggle by the Algerians under the banner of the National Liberation Front, and the countless anti-colonial wars in Africa. Palestine and all that associated with it — the Deir Yassin massacre, the Palestinian Diaspora, the total destruction of 400 Palestinian villages and Amin el-Husseini — had been forgotten. All that the world knew of was the question of Palestinian refugees. It would take Abu Ammar a.k.a. Yasser Arafat and the battle of Karameh in 1967 to put the Palestinian issue on the world's front pages.

On the home front, there was little opposition to Ayub Khan. The only criticism of the regime the people heard came from the Jamaat-i-Islami (JI), which till then was a Mohajir-Punjabi show. Couched in powerful language but with low intellectual contents it appealed to a microscopic minority among the urban Punjabi- and Urdu-speaking people. The British era politicians — some of them Jinnah's close associates — were too sophisticated to appeal to the people's religious sentiments or employ the religious idiom to attack Ayub personally or to discredit the military regime's policies. From the benefit of the hindsight I can say that what the JI rhetoric did was to introduce a new idiom that would later become popular even with newspapermen, "scholars" and religious elements not necessarily belonging to the JI. This marked the beginning of two negative and highly destructive processes: one was the erosion of the moral basis of the state of Pakistan; the other was the transformation of Islam into an exclusively political doctrine. Till then Pakistan and Islam were not something controversial; you could be loyal to one without being a traitor to the other. That would not be the case four decades later in the aftermath of 9/11 when Pakistan and Islam would be made to appear antithetical to each other, and you were forced to make a choice. You could be loyal either to Pakistan or to Islam; you could not be loyal to both. If you chose to be loyal to Pakistan, then you were a traitor to Islam and must be killed. Those believing in this philosophy then would wage war on the state of Pakistan, attack Pakistani soldiers and defence installations, carry out suicide bombings that would kill Pakistani civilians, too, occupy territory in the federal capital and raise the banner of armed revolt against the state of Pakistan.

As I reminisce about those days I feel nostalgic about an era when religion was practised peacefully, when religion was as it should always be — an affair between man and his God — and when, above all, Islam had not been turned into an instrument of fear and oppression, much less torture. There was only one Shia procession in a year, that on the 10h of Moharram, and no Sunni processions at all. It would be decades later that there would be Sunni processions, too, less to earn the Almighty's blessings and more as a counterpoise to Shia processions; and the absurd idea that there should be a Sunni party to safeguard Sunni rights in a Sunni-majority country had not yet been born. Music was not a bad word, and Radio Pakistan, especially its listeners' request programme, was a major source of music, which included classical and semi-classical music, ghazal singing and popular film songs. One could play music loud to the extent of being a nuisance, and restaurants outdid each other in blaring loud music to attract customers. Restaurants were then classified by their ethnic ownership, but such words as Malabari, Irani or Sindhi carried no prejudice. Irani restaurants were of two types: one served tea and snacks, the price of a cup of tea being one and a half annas. Later it became 10 paisas. The other category catered to a richer clientele. In Saddar, there were three famous Irani-owned restaurants noted for their cleanliness: Café George, Parisian and Cafeteria. Malabari restaurants served food to low-income groups. Sindhi "hotels" were essentially chai kahanas (tea shops), with customers sitting on benches, and the tea served in glasses. Sometimes dates were used as a sweetener, and that gave the Sindhi "hotel" tea a flavour of its own. There was no Pathan middle class then in Karachi, and the Pakhtoon-owned eateries served the labour class. However, the restaurant that the elite patronised was Shezan on Victoria Road opposite to the BVS Parsi School. Shezan has long disappeared along with a Karachi that was a middle-class city. The sartorial degeneration of the middle class had not yet begun, and the educated invariably wore shirts and trousers.

The literary scene was dominated by the progressive writers, and popular magazines were invariably entertainment-oriented, with considerable space devoted to films and the Nigar awards ceremony, which was the film industry's annual feature. The "lazy native" was very much there, but before the 20th century ended, the Pakistani nation would undergo an extraordinary transformation, for today Pakistanis are among the busiest people in the world, even if this busyness means rudeness, selfishness and utter heartlessness. No one has an extra minute to spare. The pace of life then was slow, peaceful and agreeable. Cycle rickshaws were still there, till they were abolished in the early sixties by Ayub. May God bless him! The bad among the students carried knuckledusters, the gangsters' main weapon was the knife, and even though Mr Mikhail Kalashnikov had invented the pistol-machine gun that fires 600 bullets a minute, Pakistanis had not still heard of it. (American M-249 fires 2,000 rounds a minute). Cricket Crazy Carachi hosted international matches without the visitors living in fear of being bombed, foreign tourists were a normal sight, no one questioned girls' right to education, there were all girls' colleges, no doubt, but co-education was something non-controversial, the sea breeze made Karachi's weather pleasant the year round, and an idyllic peace reigned.

Politically speaking, the middle class was "correct" and tolerated no nonsense against Pakistan. Only the Red Shirts and the remnants of the followers of Ghaffar Khan and the like whispered against Pakistan. Thoroughly discredited because the 1947 referendum had secured the North-Western Frontier Province for Pakistan, and regarded as Jinnah's and Pakistan's most implacable and hated enemies, the Red Shirts were a microscopic minority which had no influence beyond some limited pockets in the NWFP. They drew all Pakistanis' contempt when they referred to the Durand Line as an artificial line and considered Hindu India's agents when they demanded the creation of Pakhtoonistan. For the Pakistani nation, the Pushtoon heroes were Sardar Abdul Rab Nishtar and Qayyum Khan. Some four decades later, "mujahideen" claiming to be fighting for Islam would be in open revolt against Pakistan and attack its army and defence installations in a manner no Red Shirts would have dreamed of in his wildest imagination.

I was a happy man in *Dawn* for two reasons: one, I worked for a paper whose very name carried prestige and influence, founded as it was by Jinnah. Its editorials sometimes shook the government, and the policy-makers took its criticism and advice seriously. It also did not believe in printing a news item if it was not totally satisfied with the veracity of the facts mentioned. It did not mind missing a news item, but it would not report news which could turn out to be false and was denied the next day. For this reason, *Dawn* commanded respect. Two, I was happy in Dawn because the paper was till then "correct", and its policy and the political views of those with whom I worked conformed to my political philosophy. If you were in Dawn you must be "correct", you must not only conform to Dawn's policy as a journalist, as a citizen, too, you must have the same views. Dissent was unknown. If you had any other views, then leave Dawn, for it was not a place for non-conformists, dissidents, radicals, free thinkers or deviationists. And I was a conformist to the core. What pleased me most about Dawn were its patriotic fervour and the strong line it pursued on Kashmir and on Pakistan's security matters. One reason for this policy was Altaf's personality, the background to the founding of Dawn and the circumstances leading to his appointment as Dawn's editor. A very emotional man, and bubbling with energy, Altaf was moved by causes where injustice was involved. That was the reason why his anti-British activity annoyed his father, who was a "government servant". (Very few people in the English-speaking world would today approve of this term which is still used in Pakistan, India and Bangladesh to describe those who work for the state on a salary). In this case, "government servant" referred to the fact that Altaf's father, Khan Bahadur Syed Ahmadullah, worked in the bureaucracy of the British-ruled Bengal. He belonged to Bengal's zamindar family and was a lawyer before joining the judiciary. Born in 1900, Altaf, his eldest son, grew to be a brilliant student, had a degree from a Chittagong college, won a gold medal for English literature with his M. A. degree from the Dacca University, and initially opted for a career in education. However, his passion for Muslim causes led him to extensive political writings.

Controversy surrounds the name Dawn. In her book *From Mutiny to Mountbatten*, Zeba Zubair, Altaf's daughter, attributes the origin of the name to her father. As a student at Dacca University, Altaf used to write commentaries on the politics of the day from a Muslim point of view and used to distribute those commentaries on cyclostyled sheets bearing name Dawn. But it is doubtful that those who founded a weekly called Dawn in Delhi in October 1941 were aware of Altaf and his cyclostyled sheets.

Funded by private donors as a weekly in Delhi in October 1941, Dawn, as it proclaimed on its front page, was "published under the supervision of Nawabzada Liaquat Ali Khan, General Secretary, All-India Muslim League" with Mr Hassan Ahmad as editor. A trust managed its affairs, M. A. Jinnah being its managing director. The aim of the paper was to give tongue to the Muslims in an India in which the English press was entirely owned and staffed by non-Muslims. By 1942, the political situation in South Asia changed dramatically as the days of the Raj seemed numbered. The Germans were 60 miles from Alexandria, the Japanese were knocking on India's doors, and the only issue was whether the post-British India would be one country in which the Muslims – South Asia's rulers for a thousand years – would be consigned to the status of a permanent minority, or they would succeed in having a state of their own in a subcontinent they had enriched with their culture and civilization. Even though a weekly, Dawn was read by both friends and foes keen to know the Muslim League's point of view on vital political and constitutional issues as the battle for India's freedom hotted up. Finally, Liaquat Ali Khan decided to convert the paper into a daily, with the first issue hitting the news-stands on October 12, 1942. The editor was Pothan Joseph, a Christian from Kerala. The aim of the newspaper, in Jinnah's words, was "to mirror the views of Muslim India", while Pothan put it succinctly, "Dawn proposes to speak for a cause that has suffered very much from muzzled advocacy and perverted versions." True to his democratic ideals, Jinnah never interfered in the working of the paper. In a statement on November 15, 1945, he said it was wrong that Dawn was his paper or that whatever the paper wrote was "inspired by me or the Muslim League organization". He added, "No doubt Dawn follows the Muslim League policy. It is a Trust, it does not belong to the Muslim League. As a trustee, no doubt, I have to manage and direct the Trust, but I assure you I have never interfered with my Editor as a trustee or otherwise. If there was any serious, fundamental departure from Muslim League policy, then, naturally, I would interfere."

Since he worked for the British government, Altaf used to write for various British-owned newspapers under different pennames and highlighted the Muslim cause forcefully. He thought he had succeeded in keeping his name secret, but Jinnah had made discreet inquiries and came to know who the author was. The two first met in 1936, and in the following article that appeared in Pakistan Annual, edited by M. A. Majeed, who would be my boss and Dawn's leader page editor for more than two decades, Altaf himself tells us how he first met Jinnah, how the Leader came to know about the real identity of the man who was writing in newspapers under various pennames and how Altaf finally joined Dawn. For brevity's sake I have condensed the article, and Altaf's words are those which appear within quotes.

When he first met Jinnah in Calcutta, "he was going up and down the subcontinent re-organising the Muslim League and asking Muslims everywhere to contest next year's elections on the League's ticket. He was then plain Mr. Jinnah, and had not yet made that profound impact on the masses which was to come in later years. Bengal Muslim leaders were talking of a 'United Muslim Party', but Mr. Jinnah's coming changed all that." Altaf had his first glimpse of him was when Jinnah came to the Islamia College to address the students. "His speech had a tremendous effect on teachers and students alike. An unexpected opportunity to meet him face to face came the following day when I received a message that Mr. Jinnah wanted to see me at the Carmac Street residence of the Ispahanis where he was staying. I had not known until then that he was even aware of my existence." When he was ushered into Jinnah's presence the Leader sized him up and said he was doing a fine job, referring to Altaf's fortnightly column, 'Through the Muslim Eyes' in the Statesman for two years. Because he was a British government employee he wrote under the penname of Ainul Muluk and thought his identity was a closely guarded secret known only to three people. Jinnah told him that he had been greatly impressed by the column and had learned the real name of its author from Arthur Moore, the Editor of the Statesman. "Before I took leave of him he said things about my column which made me tread on air as I walked out into the street". He met Jinnah again in Bombay towards the end of 1938. He was now Director of Public Information, and Wordsword, the Statesman's acting Editor, was far less sympathetic to the Muslim cause than Moore, who had gone on leave. He terminated Altaf's column and replaced it by another one called Muslim Jehan by "Musafir" and entrusted it to Humayun Kabir, a Congressite Muslim, who after independence found a place in the Indian cabinet.

When Altaf met Jinnah again, the latter asked him why he had stopped writing for the Statesman. When Altaf gave him the reason, Jinnah said he would get in touch immediately with Moore, who had returned from leave. Shortly after his return to Calcutta Moore contacted him, and his column was resumed as Dar-el-Islam under the new penname of Shahed. This time it became a weekly feature. "From then until 1942 I had no personal contact with the Quaid, but this was renewed during 1942-43 when for about 14 months I was Press Adviser to the Government of India in Delhi. Those were extremely difficult days when the 'Quit India' movement of the Congress was at it height and civil disobedience had unleashed violence throughout the country. I had secretly continued my column and now I had the opportunity of receiving periodic inspiration and briefing from the Quaid."

Towards the end of 1943 Altaf was back in his post as Director of Public Information in Calcutta. It was there that in April, 1945 Khawaja Nazimuddin, Chief Minister of Bengal, called him to his house one day and handed him a letter from Liaquat Ali Khan conveying Jinnah's offer of Dawn's editorship. "I was thrilled, but it was a difficult decision to make. It meant throwing away a secure and well-paid government job without a pension, to earn which I had to put in another three years' service. But after a few days the Quaid-i-Azam wrote me again and said: 'Once more may I point out that as Editor of Dawn you will be occupying a unique position, and a man does not live on bread alone'. That settled it"

Altaf took over Dawn's editorship in October 1945 from Pothan Joseph, who was the paper's first editor when it became a daily on October 12, 1942. "From then on I had the privilege of knowing the Quaid-i-Azam at close quarters. He was not only my Leader but became also my employer. What sort of an employer did I find him? I do not think that anywhere else in the world there was, is or will be, another newspaper boss who left his Editor so completely free to write exactly as he liked. He never issued any directive, never said 'Do this' or 'Don't do that'. In fact, he told me to study a given situation and form my honest and independent opinion on it, and then to write fearlessly what I thought – 'no matter even if the Quaid-i-Azam is offended thereby'".

Of Dawn's popularity, Mr Hamid Zubairi, who was on its staff in Delhi and later joined it in Karachi, wrote, "Within months, Dawn became very popular and the demand was so great that we could hardly supply the required copies. The management used to supply 20 copies to the agents against a demand of 100. As a result, it was generally sold in the black market". As India headed towards freedom and the Muslims towards their destiny, Jinnah desired that Dawn should be published simultaneously in New Delhi and Karachi when independence came. (The Statesman of Calcutta, too, had hoped that after partition, it would be able to publish from both Calcutta and Karachi). But that was not to be, for all such pious hopes were drowned in the orgy of fire and blood that followed independence.

On September 6, 1947, the Dawn offices were attacked and burnt. The "provocation: was its headline, "Pakistan Zindabad!" Wrote Mr Zubairi, "We all were working when suddenly a Hindu mob raided our office. They ransacked and set it on fire. The office van was burnt and a driver killed. We were safe, but not before we had lost everything we had. Dawn never came out from Delhi again – it was closed forever. We all were scattered. I, with the members of my family, took refuge in Old Fort, and remained there for about a month and finally came to Pakistan in October".

At times it was doubtful whether Dawn would come out from Karachi on the day Pakistan came into being because of the partition holocaust, the chaos preceding the establishment of a functioning government and the absence of normality. However, the Delhi staff had already begun to move to Karachi. They included Ahmad Ali Khan, who would be Editor, Chief Editor and Editor in Chief of Dawn (1973 to 2000), M. A. Zubairi, who founded the Business Recorder and Aaj TV group. On August 15, 1947, the day after Pakistan came into being, Dawn's Karachi edition hit the streets. I was then a school boy in Hyderabad Deccan, the remnant of the Mughal Empire, which India would attack and dismember 13 months later. As a Class VII student I had heard about Dawn, but it was not available in Parbhani, the town where my father was Deputy Collector. In the Nizam's bureaucratic Persian jargon he was Madadgar-e-Maal. Fifty years later I would be a Dawn staff member, freshly back in Karachi after a stint as Dawn's Washington correspondent, to take part in its golden jubilee celebrations.

The supplement marking Dawn's 50 years was for some reason published 20 days ahead of the event on July 27, 1997. Entitled Landmark in a Paper's Odyssey my article described the paper's maiden issue thus: "It was a 16-page issue with a kind of front page that subeditors even in the classical mould would refuse to countenance. It carried just one story with the headline spread across seven columns. There was no other story, no double columns or single column 'tops', nor a 'bottom' or an 'anchor', as we journalists call it, to balance the page. The only other piece on the page was not even news; it was an article – a message by Beverley Nichols, the author of Verdict on India (with the celebrated chapter on Jinnah, Dialogue with a Giant). But a look at the lead story would convince the reader why it was and had to be the only story, for it announced the birth of the Islamic world's biggest state – Pakistan. This was Dawn's issue of Aug 15, 1947, a maiden one as far as its Pakistani readers were concerned. Its price was two annas.

"As its second editorial of the day, entitled 'About Ourselves', said on that 'historic and sacred day', Dawn was 'proud to be able to present its readers in Pakistan with an edition of their own. From today,' said the editorial, which no doubt must have been written by its legendary Editor, Mr Altaf Hussain, 'this newspaper is being published simultaneously from the capitals of Pakistan and Hindustan'. "Then it declared, and quite justly, 'Since it was brought into being through the efforts of the Quaid-i-Azam six years ago, Dawn has served the cause of the nation in its own humble way. Its difficulties have been many, its handicaps great and often it has had to be produced under almost impossible conditions. Those responsible for its conduct have throughout been sustained by the ungrudging support which they have received from its readers and from the Muslim public generally.'"

My first stint with Dawn was brief: it lasted from July 1960 to October 1962. A most shocking event was a fire in the Dawn office on January 17, 1961. We saw flames shooting as if from a nearby building. We went back to work in the newsroom, but within minutes it had spread to the roof of that part of the building which housed the printing machine. Altaf was roused from bed, Ashir was already there — he reverse drove his car at speed to get it out of the forecourt — and the fire engines controlled the fire quickly. But it was obvious that the printing machine would not be operational that day. But the paper had to come out in the morning. So arrangements were made for Dawn's publication at another press. If I remember correctly, it was the machine of the Times of Karachi, which by then had ceased publication.

The paper's lead story the next morning was "Fire in Dawn office". It was a banner headline in 120 point cap. The printers had used the wooden headline type for the 120 pt. Readers criticised this, and I remember friends telling me that a fire in the Dawn office was of no consequence to the reader. For nearly a fortnight then, work in the newsroom came to an end very early, and pages were handed over most probably at 10pm to be sent for commercial printing. Even worse was the case for Evening Star, for which we closed copy at 9.30am. As we used to say Dawn had become an evening paper while Evening Star a morning paper.

In my own family there was a stir when I seemed to attain the ultimate that Ammi wanted — an "HCS" officer. HCS meant the Hyderabad Civil Service, the equivalent in the Nizam state of the well-known Indian Civil Service, the British-crafted bureaucratic system, which was considered the steel frame of British rule in South Asia. Competitive exams were held for selection to this coveted service and the brightest ones were supposedly selected. Pakistan adopted the system of evaluating the candidates through written examinations and the feared viva voce tests. I remember that those in the panel who interviewed me included Dr Raziuddin Siddiqi, who had been recommended to the Nobel committee for a prize in physics, and Jamshed Marker, who later became a diplomat but was known throughout Pakistan as a cricket commentator.

Ammi never came round to calling it CSP, and always used to hope that her youngest son would become "an HCS officer". Relatives and friends saw my name in the list of successful candidate in the newspapers, and came to our modest home in Fatima Jinnah Colony off Jamshed Road to congratulate us. Nearly half a century has passed, but I still recall that pathetic but hopeful dialogue that took place between Ammi and Abbu as I lay slept, so they thought. Abbu said "If we are to have any happy days, he will soon receive the call-up notice". Alas, the call-up notice never came. My position was 98th among 150 successful candidates selected from all over Pakistan, which then included what is now Bangladesh. But I fell victim to the "quota system". God is my witness. Till today I have never spoken or written one word against "the quota system". If it was in the interest of Pakistan and that meant I should be out of the CSP lot so let it be. No complaint. I shared my parents' disappointment to that extent that their hopes for me were dashed. But as a Pakistani I have never had any grudge against the quota system. Those who had devised the system had a point. If the selection to the "superior services" were to be based on merit, then it is obvious that Urdu- and Punjabi-speaking people would have monopolised the upper echelon of Pakistan's civilian bureaucracy, since there was hardly any middle class in the other three provinces — Balochistan, the North-Western Frontier Province and Sindh. The Urdu-speaking middle class, with nearly 100 per cent literacy, would have been represented in state employment beyond its population ratio; that would also have been the case with Punjab. So it was decided quite early after Pakistan came into being that recruitment to the upper bureaucracy would be according to the quota assigned to each province so as to give equal representation to all provinces. Karachi was not a province and was part of Sindh. But for this purpose, Karachi was treated as a province and given two per cent of the seats. When the four provinces were amalgamated into one province, Karachi still had a two per cent quota. This has been a source of lot of bitterness in the Urdu-speaking community, but I have never, ever spoken against it.

From the benefit of hindsight I say how lucky I was that I was not trapped into the bureaucracy. In the first place, journalism has given me what a bureaucratic career would never have. The exposure to situations, personalities and the world at large that came to me as a journalist would never have been mine if I had been a babu. More important the amount of reading and writing I have done is a tremendous source of satisfaction for me, for over the decades hundreds of thousands of people have read my pieces in Dawn and foreign newspapers. The coming of internet has only added to that number. Besides, I wonder if there is any other bureaucracy in the world which has suffered ignominy of the kind the Pakistani officialdom has. Ayub Khan — and I have remained his admirer till this day — first carried out what would later become a shibboleth with every change of regime in Pakistan: screening. Ayub retired many top officials, including some old ICS hands who had crossed over to Pakistan. Some of them had not entered the newly created Pakistan as "refugees" but had opted for Pakistan when every civil servant was asked by the British to decide whether he would like to serve with Pakistan or India. When Yahya became the strongman in 1969, he retired 303 people. The figure reverberated throughout Pakistan and was easy to remember because of the way it was pronounced — three nought three, this being the bore of the Enfield rifle introduced into the subcontinent by the British. When Bhutto became the chief, he retired 1,400 people. The "screening" acquired new dimensions under the corrupt Zia regime (1977-88) when thousands were sacked, arrested or harassed on mere suspicion of being of PPP supporters or being "against Islam". The most unfortunate part of the tragedy was that many bureaucrats served as willing tools in Zia's witch-hunting programme, spied upon their colleagues, rejoiced in their humiliations and considered it a step toward the Islamisation of Pakistan. Following Zia's death in the air crash in August 1988, the political period (1988-1999) saw a continuation of the "screening" with great vigour. Bhutto and Zia were both dead, but their followers in the bureaucracy continued to be victims and perpetrators of injustice each time there was a change of regime. Benazir Bhutto and Nawaz Sharif became prime minister twice, and each time they were sacked there was a caretaker regime that organised elections. So this way there were seven governments between 1988 and 1999, and each change of regime meant misery or a golden opportunity for the bureaucrats depending upon which side one was. This is not to say there were no honest and efficient bureaucrats. There were many who indeed served the state and not the politician or general in power. But the amazing point was that instead of being considered an example worth emulating such men were denounced. One of my classmates at the university became a CSP officer, rose to a high position because his efficiency was considered legendary, and he enjoyed the confidence of a president, Ziaul Haq, and three prime ministers — Mohammd Khan Junejo, Benazir Bhutto and Nawaz Sharif. However, he was denounced as a time-server, was hounded out of the government and lived in exile for years before returning during the Musharraf regime. My parents, of course, suffered a disappointment when the call-up notice did not come to me, but I say their grief would have been ten times greater if I had joined the bureaucracy and later been thrown out in disgrace. I thank God for sparing me and my family this agony.

The most memorable event in 1962 was my engagement to Razia, who turned out to be an exceptionally wonderful wife and has been with me through thick and thin. I cannot say whether it was a coincident, because that is how happens when a woman enters a man's life, my salary going up by leaps and bounds. The Dawn salary was inadequate for me, but there was just one other paper, and that was Morning News I have talked about earlier. It was, however, a Dawn reporter who came with some good news. He was a reporter, Shamim Ahmad, who later would be my editor in two newspapers. Cynical to the core and voluble, Shamim had a most original way of expressing himself. It combined humour with irony laced with the choicest of quotes from poetry, English, Persian and Urdu, which his interlocutor might not necessarily have been prepared for. A thorough professional, Shamim annoyed people by his idiosyncrasies and bluntness. With his white hair swept back, Shamim always wore white trousers and bush shirts. Even the strap of his wrist watch was white. He asked me whether I was interested in another job on a higher salary. When I sought details he refused to oblige, but I gathered that a new newspaper was on the way. Was the party launching the paper sound? "Sounder than you think", he replied. He asked me to meet him the next morning at Grand Hotel, which was anything but grand. I presented there myself only to find three other Dawn colleagues there — Salman Meenai, Ibtisam Ahmad, mentioned earlier, and Zamir Niazi, who would grow to become a legend in his lifetime because of his work on the state of press freedom in Pakistan. His books would include the celebrated Press in Chains, which contained a history of anti-press laws made since the East India Company days. To be called Daily News, the new venture was to be an evening daily launched by the Jang group. I quit Dawn.

The mast-head of the new paper, Daily News, was in green, and this caught the reader's attention. Soon Daily News became the leading evening newspaper, and Shamim had ambitions to turn it into a morning daily to compete with Dawn. That was not to be. The management said the paper contained nothing that could push up sales, and that it was the green masthead that sold. A fiercely independent-minded person like Shamim could hardly take it. I resigned only four months after joining the paper because I had received a job offer from Morning News. Shamim followed a few weeks later.

A GENTLEMAN'S MARTIAL LAW

JOURNALISM DOESN'T TIRE ME. It hasn't yet. Today, at 70, a by-line in Dawn excites me as much as it did when I first got it as a young man. Lucky are those whose profession is their hobby. I believe I am one of them. Whenever I am on long leave, which has been rare, I pick up paper and pencil and start writing a story, or catching mistakes in the printed stuff or re-making a page. That's perhaps one reason why I suffer from the misunderstanding that as a journalist I have been a success. Mercifully, I am not the only one suffering from this delusion; many newspersons harbour this false pride and reciprocate mutual disdain. What brought me to journalism is a good question, and perhaps the best answer comes from Walter Lippmann: "Our life is managed from behind the scenes; we are actors in dramas we cannot interpret. Of almost no decisive event can we say: this was of our own choosing". Can we find logic in the "dramas" Lippmann speaks of in the chaos of daily life, in births and deaths, in war and pace? A little after the devastating earthquake that killed nearly 100,000 people in Azad Kashmir and parts of Pakistan on October 8, 2005, I wrote a piece in Dawn that for some mysterious reason appealed to many readers, and I got a very a favourable feedback. Experience tells me, if you fail to write on the spur of the moment, no matter how hard you try later, you can never catch that zing that produces effective writing. I wrote that piece in a hurry and was not sure how it would be received, and whether M. A. Majeed, editor of the leader page, would at all print it. But it seemed to touch a chord with most readers' hearts because, like me, the entire nation was wondering why it had to be Pakistan and us and no other country and no other people that must have a visitation of that horrendous proportion — a mountain tsunami. Faisal, my son, protested when I wrote that "science itself is unscientific" when I conveyed the feeling of a Pakistani wondering why another bout of bad luck should have enveloped his country.

Entitled "Where reason and religion clash", the article (Dawn, October 20, 2005) raised questions about phenomena beyond our control and comprehension. It asked: "Why is a soldier killed in the opening few minutes of a war that lasts six years, while the man next to him is maimed half way through the war and passes all his life in a wheelchair? Why was not he killed during the first few moments when the enemy artillery opened up? Lots of others returned home as victors and lived fuller lives. Why? What was so special about them? They believed no less in the 'kill or get killed' principle, shot and wounded enemy civilians, burnt homes and hospitals, sowed their wild oats and did not take prisoners. Remember, Paul Baumer, the hero through whose eyes the reader sees the horrors of trench warfare in Erich Maria Remarque's masterpiece All Quiet on the Western Front? He was killed on the last day of the war when the headquarters issued the laconic communiqué, 'All quiet on the western front'. A Japanese chooses to come to Pakistan to keep away from his country's frequent earthquakes but is killed by that very phenomenon in Pakistan in 2005. An Israeli woman leaves her country because she fears she would get killed in a suicide bombing but is injured in the London blasts in what came to be known as 7/7. Is there a logic? Or perhaps there is. Why was a tyrant and mass murderer like Saddam Hussein overthrown and hanged while Ariel Sharon will in all probability die a natural death? What is the difference? Is there a relationship between Saddam's deeds and fate and that between Sharon's diabolical crimes and the 'normal' end he is likely to have? One English king had to abdicate because he wouldn't like to give up the woman he loved, while a prince who has lived in adultery with a married woman for 30 years now waits to be crowned king one day. Why? The truth is that this is a law beyond human comprehension. If the Universe is a mechanism run according to the laws of science, then we must have a new definition of science. The universe does not have a scientific basis, it did not originate scientifically and its end is not going to be scientific. Science may try to explain the universe in scientific terms, but science itself is unscientific. Is there a thing called a straight line? You may draw a straight line on paper or on a road, but can you draw a straight line on planet earth or in the universe, both of which are global and spherical? Parallel lines, we are told, never meet. But the longitudes drawn in the shape of parallel lines on maps in our school atlases meet at the two Poles. The nearest distance between two places, science tells us, is a straight line. But when a plane flies from Russia to Canada over the North Pole, it makes a curve and not a straight line, because a straight line does not exist in the universe. The universe is not a mechanical contraption. The more science studies it the more it appears to be one big gel where its components behave irrationally. But irrationality here is subjective, because what appears irrational to us may not really be so. Ultimately, one tends to fall back on religion. There must be the Biblical equivalent of Moses' story contained in the Quran's chapter Al-Kahf (The Cave). Moses is astonished by the behaviour of his pious companion who sinks a boat, kills a young man and repairs free of charge a dilapidated wall in a village whose people were unkind to them. The pious man later explains how he did all that because God commanded him to do so, and ultimately good was to come out of it all."

Yes, accidents and incidents shape our lives. A given incident may appear a non-event to you at that time, but as you grow old and are able to reflect on the past, you see a certain order in what often appeared to you then as an inexplicable and painful chaos. Things happened that way, because they constituted "the dramas" that Lippmann said "we cannot interpret". In the end you are the gainer. Often, you wondered whether things would have been better if they had not happened the way they did. But a deeper analysis of your own self and an awareness of the mistakes you made and the opportunities you lost or made use of will gradually give way to a more agreeable assessment of the drama of life as it carried you, as if on the cusp. What would life have been like for me if I had passed that bulletin board on the University of Karachi campus a minute earlier, or if that official had posted the notice on the board a minute or two late or earlier? The year was 1957, and the KU was then housed in what once were homes on Princess Street. Most Karachiites today wouldn't know where this street is. The nearest I can say is that it is between Lawrence Road (now called Nishtar Rd) and M. A. Jinnah Road and is close to what today is an indescribably chaotic Sindh government-run Civil Hospital. There were some two-storey buildings in which post-graduation classes were held, but the offices of the Vice Chancellor and the Registrar were in a rather impressive building which the education authorities had managed to get hold of to start a university in the post-partition chaos. I had done my B. A. from Urdu College, located in the same area, and I wanted to do my masters in economics. But all seats were filled up. Besides, I did not know how I would combine a university education with a full-time job as PA to a Superintendent of Police. Either I would have to give up my job or look for an evening course in economics. As I walked down a corridor among throngs of students like me seeking admission to various faculties, I saw a KU official sticking a notice on the board. I read the information: it was about admissions to the Department of Journalism, which had been created a year earlier and held classes in the evening. How about it? I said to myself. I would be doing a full-time 9 to 5 job, and get to know journalism in the evening. People I talked to discouraged me, but I applied for admission. There was an interview. Those who appraised me were Dr Mahmood Hussain Khan, who later became Vice Chancellor, some Golarski, an American, who was then Asia Foundation's Representative in Pakistan and later became the NBC's White House correspondent, and Sharif Al Mujahid, head of the journalism department. Half a century has passed since then, but Mujahid has continued to remain my teacher, guide and might I say friend.

There were three teachers for us: Mujahid, Qayyum Malik and Naushaba Hussain. Naushaba would later marry I. H. Burney, a great journalist, whose weekly magazine Outlook was closed by the Ayub regime for its outspokenness. It was, to quote Burney, "the only voice of non-conformism" during the Ayub era. Qayyum Malik edited a weekly called Enterprise, and taught us typography, editing and headline writing. Naushaba's focus was on assignments. But the "assignments" were confined to the classroom. Looking back at that one-year course, which in actual terms came to perhaps 10 months, I am astonished at the high quality of teaching. Both Mujahid and Naushaba had been to the US, and we had the benefit of reading American books on journalism — there were hardly any British books in the department's library — and many things about American newspapers appeared new to us because they were different from the British -style layout and headlining which was followed by Pakistan's English dailies — Dawn, Morning News (published simultaneously in Karachi and Dhaka, then the capital of East Pakistan) and The Pakistan Times, Lahore. For instance, stepped headlines were something new to us, and the New York Times followed this style. (NYT did not have an attractive layout then and it does not have it now.) We learnt the fundamentals of what we called "make-up". We were taught that the front page of a newspaper must be "the same but different" every day. Today's Morning News, we were told, must look like yesterday's Morning News, but it must be different. How the page must be balanced, how the top must not become too heavy and there must always be an "anchor" or "a bottom" to balance the page. A box, set up in bold type, was meaningless unless there was a half-em indent on both sides, and the box must never be in column one or eight, but in the middle of the page, that a person's picture, if it is a profile and not a portrait, must face the matter about him and not away from it, that it is ridiculous for a picture to touch an advertisement, that a page should not be divided into two by a horizontal or vertical rule, that a page should be so made that a story either ends or is carried over to the inside page at the fold, that grey matter must be broken with crossheads, and there must be plenty of white space to give "air" to the page. Besides, there were intro writing exercises, and we were asked to write stories on facts given in chronological order and told to write the intro and the story to conform to the "inverted pyramid" style

These primary lessons in journalism fascinated me. No one had heard of the word computer, the good old blackboard and chalk did the job, the quality of furniture was poor, but the job which the teachers did of us in that dilapidated building on Princess Street was superb. There were three girls also, but none of them — like most boys, except two — took to journalism. The quality of teaching was such that a year later on my very first day as a subeditor in The Times of Karachi, I worked alone, because a deluge had kept most staff members away from the office. ToK was then a six-page rag, — having had its great days — yet I was able to bring out the edition alone on the basis of what I had learnt during those 10 months. The journalism class in the KU had about 20 students, and included some trouble makers, including my friend Fatehyab Ali Khan, who later became a politician, Afaq Ahmad, who would later join a religious party and become a minister in the Sindh Government, and Abdul Rab Shajie, the only student besides me who entered the world of journalism and worked for Radio Pakistan and is now based in Japan. A most unusual student was Afzal Shervani. He failed to have a career in journalism because of his devotion to the communist movement, went underground and was arrested. He was my colleague in ToK during those horrible days when the paper was fighting for its survival and there was a tug of war between the journalists and the new management, headed by Ameen Tareen. Afzal's face always exhibited hardship, dedication and struggle. Decades later he worked as a freelance journalist and wrote for Dawn in the eighties as Afzal Ahmad. By that time his days of hardships were relatively speaking over. One sticking point between the students and the KU authorities related to typing and shorthand. I knew both, but the majority did not even know typing, agitated against their inclusion in the course and even threatened a boycott and strike. A solution was found: shorthand was done away with, and those like me who knew typing and shorthand were given extra marks. I do not know whether I had by then made up my mind that I would have a career in journalism. Friends and elders always discouraged me, saying a journalist's was not a paying job. At the journalism department, after classes were over, I used to work as a voluntary typist for Mujahid for his countless articles on the history of the freedom movement in Dawn and other newspapers. With the benefit of hindsight I realise how true that old adage is — you cannot receive unless you first give. Typing his articles taught me how an author puts his thoughts across logically, how a point must be proved and not just dished out to the reader as a statement, and how it is controlled argument and understatement which have a greater effect on the reader than an adjective-laden, emotion-charged piece of writing.

It was then that a most profound event in the history of Pakistan occurred — an event that would shape the future of Pakistan and blight for decades what till then was a free press — martial law. On Oct 7, 1958, President Iskander Mirza abrogated the constitution, dissolved the national and provincial legislatures, dismissed the government of Sir Malik Firoze Khan Noon and appointed Gen Mohammad Ayub Khan the Chief Martial Law Administrator. Martial law would from now on become a household word in Pakistan. Since there cannot be — as the saying in Urdu goes — two swords in one scabbard, Ayub acted in concert with other Generals to get rid of Mirza. I remember the headline in an American magazine, most probably Time, which said "And then there was one". I was still a student of journalism, but I didn't know that when I would be in Pakistan's mainstream journalism, martial law and all that it stood for would haunt me and fellow-journalists for decades: martial law with its press censorship, arbitrary arrests, denial of fundamental rights, closure of newspapers, brainwashing, fiddling with noble constitutional concepts, short cuts to political stability, the unending search for "a system suited to our genius" and, during Ziaul Haq's rule, flogging of journalists and political workers. I grew as a professional journalist in these dark times — from a trainee in a news agency to Dawn's editorial writer, but not before the consequences of the dictatorship had gnawed at my soul and left their imprints on me and on the Pakistani people's psyche. During these decades Pakistan would suffer many tragedies, the biggest being the loss of East Pakistan and the surrender to India at Dhaka in December 1971, widespread ethnic riots, the murder of three prime ministers, the gradual but subtle erosion of the ideals that Jinnah stood for, and Pakistan's slow but definite descent from a normal country into a state where barbarism would rule under cover of religion as interpreted by semi-literates. The tragedy was that the attack on the noble concepts which led to the creation of Pakistan and which Jinnah's career and personality epitomised would be made under the cover of a shibboleth called "the ideology of Pakistan". Later, when "the ideology of Pakistan" stood discredited, the northern mountains would reverberate to the sounds of guns, and the enchanting valley of Swat would see a colossal bloodbath and a humanitarian disaster as untermenschen would launch a well-organised, well-funded and well-armed fitna — the Quranic term for public mischief — to try to impose on the people of Pakistan values that were diametrically opposite to what Islam stands for. As I have explained elsewhere in this book, by their myopic vision, those claiming to stand for Islam did the greatest harm they could possibly do to the nation by undermining the very concept of Pakistan. It is difficult to give a date when the press became free and the draconian law, especially the notorious Press and Publications Ordinance, enacted during the Ayub regime in 1963, ended. But if at all there is a man who can be credited with liberalising the press, it was Mohammad Khan Junejo, prime minister from 1985 to 1988.

Going to the KU in the evening meant that I could work full-time 9 to 5 at the police head office on McLeod Road as PA to the SP, whose name I rather not mention. His honesty was legendary, and he passed a Spartan life. He milked his buffalo early in the morning, pressed his uniform, polished his shoes and had an athletic built. Before partition he had served in the British Indian Army, joined the police force I think after he came to Pakistan and exhibited several habits and traits that he had picked up from his British colleagues in the army. I had respect for his character, but I regret to say that his outbursts and the chew-outs he gave to other police officers were unbecoming of a civilised human being. I am quite aware of the tantrums characteristic of bosses, especially those in uniform, the world over. Eisenhower, Supreme Commander of the Allied Forces, once vented his anger at George Patton in a way that made the old-timers in the infantry come to attention. Patton cried. This was in the post-Normandy period, and the German offensive in the Bulge had caught the Allies by surprise. While emulating the British, Pakistani officers fail to realise that the British did not behave that way in their own country or with fellow Britons in the subcontinent, except in rare cases. The truth is that a Pakistani in a position of authority — whether a civilian or a man in uniform — has a psyche that is a contemptible mixture of British arrogance as seen in the subcontinent and the Mughal officials' air of royal superiority. Thus when a Pakistani deputy commissioner, or income-tax officer, or a deputy inspector general of police sits in his sceptred office, he feels he is king receiving supplicants. He does not meet citizens who are equal to him in status; he grants audience to his subjects in his durbar. A slight provocation and he hits the ceiling; he may even carry out his duty and sign a given paper because the citizen who approached him deserved to get that order. But the way in which the officer would sign it would be anything but a normal discharge of duty; it would be more like the bestowal of a grant upon a subject — a favour granted to the humble citizen by His Majesty. Travelling downwards, this attitude has seeped down from the inspector general of police and the deputy commissioner to the bank manager and the reservation clerk at five-star hotels.

I remember one particular incident on a Friday concerning a traffic accident. Someone was not satisfied with the way the investigation into the case was progressing, and the investigating officer, a Sub-Inspector of Police (SIP), was asked to report to the "orderly room" i.e. report to the SP. The SIP came at about 11.30, and the SP called me over as he always did over the intercom by a one-word command in English: "Dictation!" Since it was a Friday, I thought it would be over well in time. The SP then grilled the SIP in a way I had never seen before. He seemed to be surpassing his own record. He asked the officer when the accident had taken place. The accident had occurred five minutes past midnight, when the date changes, and the officer mentioned the correct date (I could see that in the papers with me), but in his fury the SP said, "Do you know that the date changes after midnight?" The officer should have maintained his cool, should have replied "yes" and should have pointed out to him that he had taken into account the date change at midnight while writing his report. Under pressure now, he fumbled and gave the wrong date. The SP — with the veins of his neck swelling — bawled at the officer and mourned that he had been saddled with officers who did not know that the date changed after midnight and that what choice he had except to tell the civilian authority interested in the accident case that such incompetents manned the police force. By 12.30pm the senior PA came to relieve me and I left for the mosque. To my astonishment, when I returned from the prayer by about 1:45pm, the officer still stood there and listened to the SP's shouts and what to me appeared a display of anger that was by no means justified in proportion to the purported mistakes the SIP had made. Then he dismissed him for the day and asked him to report to him the next morning. The next day, the officer was standing in front of the SP's room when the Emperor came. Without looking at him but addressing a clerk the SP said, "Bring his service book!" The SIP — I have not forgotten those looks — repeated the SP's order to the clerk in English, "Bring the service book!" It was like a condemned prisoner asking the hangman to prepare the gallows. The SP was an honest man, but his weakness was that he considered others dishonest. All that honesty, and the efficiency and discipline for which he was famous did not in my opinion justify that kind of barbaric behaviour.

My course was proceeding well, and I had begun enjoying every moment of it. As I look back at it all half a century later I feel amazed that commuting in Karachi should have been so easy. On a given day, I would reach my office at 9 in the morning, leaving at 5pm to reach home, and after a rest of an hour or so proceed to the KU. Classes would end by 9, and I would be back by 9.20pm or so. Those days Razi, my elder brother, was posted at the Brigade police station as Sub-Inspector of Police, and our family lived in one of the apartments meant for officers in what today is known as the "Lines Area". The "Lines Area" was once a pivotal part of life in Karachi. Located centrally, it derived its name from the barracks built hastily for Allied soldiers during World War II when Karachi was a major supply and fuel base. The names given to the lines of barracks — Jutland Lines, Tunisia Lines, Jacob Lines and Abyssinia Lines — continued to survive till the early sixties, when all of them were combined into one generic name: the Lines Area. Jacob Lines, however, is still a neighbourhood and runs roughly parallel to M. A. Jinnah Road. Given the scarcity of housing in the wake of the sudden increase in Karachi's population following partition, the barracks with roofs of red tiles were much sought after because they were in the centre of the city and close to most government departments, located then in Saddar. Several of my relations lived in those barracks, which were quite comfortable and roomy with high ceilings. Invariably, they were cool, for they were literally battered by the sea breeze — nature's greatest gift to Karachi. Today, this gift has been denied to the people or drastically reduced by the unplanned and ugly high-rises. Karachi had four- to five-storey apartment buildings even then, built in the British era, along Frere Road (now Shahrah-i-Liquat), and in what would become "old town" — Kharadar, Mithadar and Pakistan Chowk, besides those in Saddar and Empress Market, especially in what was the Christian or Goan district. There were no power breakdowns in the late fifties that I am talking about, and the tall apartment buildings received plenty of fresh air. Today, life in apartment buildings in Karachi is hell even when power is on. But when power goes off, as it does now frequently, apartments become hellholes, because the high-rises exist not only side by side but even behind each other. The Lines Area gradually became a slum; it is still a sprawling slum, and all efforts to reclaim it by making it part of Karachi's urban renewal scheme have failed. By the time we moved into the Brigade police lines in 1956, it had come to be surrounded by unplanned shanty towns that had turned the once well-planned barracks area into one sprawling slum. No bus was available near the Brigade police station, so to get a bus or tram, one had to go to Saddar by tonga — the subcontinent's ubiquitous horse-drawn vehicle around which so much romance exists, especially because of the rhythmic sound of the horse's hoofs. Tongas now do not exist in Karachi, but whenever I go to other cities in Pakistan, the rhythmic beat of the horse's hoofs has a very soothing effect on me, basically because I had heard it so much in my childhood in Aurangabad and Parbhani.

For reaching Saddar, I would pay one anna to the tonga driver, for I would be one of the four passengers on board. At Saddar, I would catch a tram, and pay one and a half anna for a ticket which would take me to Bolton Market. Very few Karachiites are today aware of this name, because the focus of business activity has shifted. Among others, currency dealers had their business in Bolton Market and mostly changed Pakistani and Indian currencies. I am not aware if there were any dollars and pounds in demand. They must have been, but in a very limited quantity, because the immigration craze and the Green Card mania were still decades away. Currency dealers kept the bills in boxes with glass tops, and placed them on the sidewalks, for there were hardly any currency shops in the proper sense of the term. Today currency exchange is big business.

Even though the Karachi I am talking about (late fifties) had expanded, the trams still provided cheap transport to hundreds of thousands of people in the centre of the city. Its working terminus was Saddar, from where the tram lines branched off. One went to the Cantonment Station, another went to the harbour via Bunder Road — then and still Karachi's spine —; another turned from Bunder Road near

Denso Hall toward Napier Road and went on to Rexer Lines (very few Karachiites today would know this name, for it has been lost in what has come to be called the greater Lyari area); another line went from Saddar via Garden Road to Soldier Bazaar. Thus, the system covered central Karachi and connected it to what then were suburbs. The maintenance section and the terminal was the Tram Depot, which also served as a landmark. It was on the junction of Bunder Road and Garden Road, where an unfinished building has been chiding the civic agencies now for the last three decades. The tram system was laid by the British at a time when electricity was not available, and horses used to pull the trams. Later diesel provided the fuel. Gradually, the tramways fell into disuse for lack of maintenance and government interest as buses appeared on the roads in large numbers and provided faster service between the city centre and the newly developed housing societies on the outskirts. Today Karachi has expanded so far and so much that those suburbs are in the heart of the city.

I remember there was a lively debate in the press in the seventies about what to do with the tracks when the trams ceased to operate. The tracks were a nuisance and used to cut into tyres, and they were not without their worth as scrap. I do not know whether the tracks were extracted and sold as iron scrap or they are still buried in those roads, but the disappearance of the tramways is a reflection on the quality of planning for Karachi. Today — 2014 — with a population estimated at over 15 million, the city is still without a mass transit system. As far back as 1973, the Bhutto government decided to have an underground railway system for Karachi in phases. The first phase provided for an underground railway "spine" running between Liaquatabad and Merewether Tower — a distance of five and a half miles. A mass transit cell was set up in the Karachi Development Authority's Master Plan Department, and the cost was estimated at $1,300 million. When Ziaul Haq took over on July 5, 1977, the plan was scrapped and the mass transit cell wound up. Those who blame the "Punjabi bureaucracy" — the small provinces' whipping boy — ought to know that Lahore and

Islamabad too do not have any mass transit systems. Lahore, too, has expanded, and unlike Karachi its expansion is not without grace. But one is appalled at the neglect of transport for the common man in Lahore, whose Mughal character, I regret to say, is fast disappearing as a Karachi-like construction frenzy seems to have gripped it.

As a citizen and as a journalist I was interested in a mass transit system for Karachi and kept tabs on it. However, as time passed, and the project never saw the light of day, I noted how governments in some other Third World countries were able to give their cities modern, comfortable and fast means of travel. It was Hong Kong, if I remember correctly, which was the first to have an underground railway in the time-frame I am talking about. Then Singapore had it, followed by — in geographical order — Kuala Lumpur, Calcutta, New Delhi, Tehran, Cairo, Ankara, many other Turkish cities and Tehran. Once I could rattle off the commissioning of these systems in chronological order from memory while writing an editorial or an article about transport in Karachi and other Pakistani cities. Such was my obsession with an underground railway that on my first visit to Cairo in 1988 my priority was its French-built metro rather than the pyramids. In fact, my editor chided me when I expressed this sense of priority and proportions in an article I wrote for Dawn Magazine when I returned from Egypt.

But back to the days as a student of journalism in the KU. As part of our course I and two other boys were sent to different newspaper and news agency offices to do some practical work and learn journalism in actual working conditions. I was sent to a news agency called Pakistan Press Association (PPA), which later became Pakistan Press International, with its offices at Mohammedi House in McLeod. PPA was a private news agency, formed by those who had broken with the government-owned Associated Press of Pakistan (APP). The founder was Muazzam Ali, who was assisted by a brilliant journalist, Ahmad Hassan, who was News Editor with PPA when I joined it in the summer of 1958 as a trainee. There were three other journalists, Tayyab Bokhari, Fazal Qureshi and Absar Rizvi. Javed Bokhari, Tayyab's nephew, and Ghazanfar, one of

Muazzam's nephews, joined a few months later. Ahmad Hassan had previously worked with Dawn and was arrested during the crackdown on all leftists and communists in the fifties. Old-timers in Dawn told me a story that I have had no way of checking. It concerned Ahmad's arrest. When the police came to the Dawn office to arrest him while he was on night duty, he rang up the Editor. Altaf Husain, as I have narrated elsewhere, was a fanatic Pakistani, the way I suppose I have always been. He hated communists and leftists, and Pakistan was then America's most "allied ally", and did not tolerate any trade union activity in Dawn. When Ahmad told him that the police had come to arrest him, Altaf reportedly said, "I see" and put the receiver down. In PPA, Ahmad was kind to me and I learnt many things from him. Three months later, when our training came to an end, Ahmad surprised me by asking me whether I would like to become a full-time PPA man. Would I? I just jumped at it, resigned from my job as PA to the SP and joined the news agency. I have the appointment letter with me. Dated April 30, 1958, and signed by Muazzam Ali, it appointed me as a reporter-cum-subeditor for Rs 250. My career in journalism had begun, and what a career! It has been a swing through a technological revolution — typewriter, telegram, teleprinter, hot metal, offset, fax, email, modem, computer, cellphone, and photos via satellite, all in a lifetime. The ultimate— ultimate being a relative term — came in Dawn when an entire page would be sent from Karachi to Lahore and Islamabad via satellite by just pressing a key.

A few weeks after I got PPA job my journalism exam results came. For South Asian students and their parents a "position" in the exam results has a special meaning, even though in the longer run these "positions" mean nothing, except perhaps an occasional scholarship. The point to note about the "second position" I got was that I and perhaps no student could possibly do better than Mohammad Afaq, who had done his M A. in the year in which I was born, 1937! I then enrolled for a master's degree in political science. Because the university was then located on Princess Street, I could combine my education in the morning with the PPA job in late afternoon and evening. A reporting stint with PPP taught me many things, including the importance of filing a story immediately after getting it. This is something that newspaper reporters do not follow, because they do not have that sense of urgency which agency reporters have. No matter whether a newspaper reporter gets a story at 9 in the morning or at 3 in the afternoon, he would file his report with the paper at the usual time, which in most cases is evening. This lethargy just does not work in a news agency. Even though Pakistan in 1958 was not what it is now, it still had some evening newspapers in English, Urdu and Gujrati, besides Radio Pakistan. (There was then no private radio station.) So agency reporters like me had to file a story as it came — to catch an evening paper's deadline or to make it in time for one of Radio Pakistan's afternoon or evening bulletins or for its broadcasts in foreign languages. It was in 1959 that I quit the news agency. But that habit is still with me. When I became Dawn's News Editor in 1991, I issued an advisory warning against the compulsive filing of all stories late in the evening. My idea was to avoid pressure at the composing room, but to no avail, because old habits — especially when colleagues gang up — are hard to die. I still feel that a stint with a news agency is essential for all newspaper reporters and desk hands to acquire a sense of urgency.

A fact that needs to be recorded for history was the "presence" of America in PPA and in fact in all news organisations in Pakistan in the form of the press releases sent by what then was called the United States Information Service (USIS) —later USI Agency. The frenzy which gripped America during the Cold War was a phenomenon that has never been seen again. What the world saw following 9/11 does not represent half the madness that we as journalists witnessed in terms of the anti-communist propaganda stuff we received from the American Embassy in Karachi. Daily without fail there was an envelope for every journalist by name. It contained press releases that could be divided broadly into three categories: one belonged to "positive" news from the US and included speeches and policy moves by American leaders and its allies worldwide, especially in international fora like the United Nations, UNESCO, NATO, the Congress for Cultural Freedom and scores of US-backed organisations across the globe; the second belonged to the "good Samaritan category", giving details of American aid to its allies and even to neutral countries throughout the world to set up industries, to increase literacy, fight disease. and raise per-acre yield. This included details about the quality of a given chemical fertiliser which America was supplying free, the best way to spray farms with insecticides, and how to grow more fish in the same pond. There were features and pictures about the work being done by the Peace Corps boys and girls who had fanned out to the backward and "uncivilised" Third World countries. (The term Third World is a latter-day phenomenon. Initially, Europe and America did not know how precisely to describe the countries which had gained independence from European colonialism, or were struggling to gain freedom, and had huge populations living in poverty. Initially they were called "retarded countries". The problem with this term was that there was a close relationship between "retarded" and "mentally". So this embarrassing term was abandoned, and the next term that remained popular for a long time was "less developed countries". This gave way later to "developing countries", since there was no awkwardness attached to it. However, the Third World finally won acceptance worldwide). Some press releases and pictures showed Peace Corps volunteers, brooms in hands, cleaning an Indian village, or carrying a sick baby to a hospital in Lima, Peru. This was designed to show that the Cuban and Chinese methods as demonstrated by Fidel Castro and Mao Zedong were not exactly the best way for Afro-Asians and Latin Americans to improve their people's material conditions and give them bread and butter. The third category of press releases contained unabashed anti-communist propaganda. Words and phrases which were repeated ad nauseam included the Berlin Wall, "the iron curtain", "the bamboo curtain", communist subversion, communist propaganda,

KGB, brainwashing, totalitarianism, thought control, purges, torture, physical elimination, rectification centres, defections, apparatchiks, Mao-think, doublespeak and many such words which were abandoned but were reactivated partly after 9/11. As the détente between the West and "white communists" began and the Cold War seemed to lose its heat, the propaganda against the USSR and its eastern European satellites was softened and it was "yellow communism" that became the focus of USIS press release. We in PPA used these press release, one of whose side was blank, to type our stories.

As a reporter, and like all cub reporters, I began with crime news. This was disastrous, for I am very choosy about people and —if it is in my power — with circumstances, because I just lacked the kind of temperament needed for crime reporting. More than three decades later I had no problem with my job as a Dawn's diplomatic correspondent in Washington D.C. — in fact I enjoyed it — because I was dealing with diplomats and Congressmen. But having a crime beat in Karachi meant I had to go to police stations and talk to cops and all sorts of characters. I never did that, and for that reason was a bad reporter. Ahmad Hasan realised this and agreed that I should confine the reporting part of my job to morning, and work on the desk in the afternoon. Crime "reporting" for me then meant going every morning to the police head office, where there was a press room, where the police department was kind enough to give us "morning reports". These were carbon copies of the reports which all police stations sent regularly to their bosses at the head office. I made no attempt to exploit my contacts at the police head office and instead was content with making news items out of those "morning reports" and sending them on the teleprinter to PPA's clients, though the beneficiaries mostly were evening dailies, three of which were in English —Evening Star, belonging to the Dawn group, The Leader belonging to the Matris and The Sentinel, owned by PPA. The Sentinel's editor was Huzoor Ahmad Shah, who would later become my colleague in Dawn.

The desk job at PPA was more suited to my temperament. It is true that a news agency is basically a reporters' affair, but it is wrong that it is only in newspaper offices that subeditors have a worthwhile role to play. The PPA and Pakistan I am talking about belonged to the late fifties. The principal mode of transmission of news from the news agencies to their clients — newspaper offices, Radio Pakistan (later PTV also), companies, diplomatic missions, luxury hotels and selected government offices — was the teleprinter. Lines had to be laid with the cooperation of the Post and Telegraph Department and worked quite well. The degeneration of the lines in the eighties before the computer took over had disastrous consequences for all. The mode of reception of news in the PPA head office by reporters from outside Karachi was basically of three kinds: telegrams, telephone calls and — in case of news that could wait — mail. The reports by mail came from the rural areas by stringers, most of whom wrote horrible English. My job was to re-write them. Sometimes, reporters in the remote areas rang up to give news that was urgent, say, about some accident, on the telephone and gave me facts in Urdu. I later made a news story out of them. One important news item that I still remember — and whose clippings I have kept with me till this day — concerned Ayub Khuhro's decision to quit the mainstream Muslim League as a protest against the One Unit (the single West Pakistan province created after merging four provinces) and create a new party, the Sindh Muslim League. The report of the proceedings was given to me at the PPA head office by our Sukkur correspondent on the telephone. Khuhro was an important leader, and the report was by any standards an important one. I gave it shape, and had it creeded to our clients. Morning News carried it as its lead story in its issue of April 28, 1958, and Dawn missed it. Dawn began subscribing to PPA a few months later after I had quit the agency, but the Khuhro story miss was one of the factors in Dawn's decision to subscribe to PPA.

To save money on telegrams, the reporters were asked to send stories to the PPA head office in cryptic language, avoiding definite and indefinite articles and using such Latin words as "pro", "ex" and "et" to stand for "for", "from" and "and". Designations and full names were avoided, and verbs were used only when necessary to avoid confusion. For instance a telegram that would say, "Qizilbash said Monday government determined eliminate waterlogging et-salinity with help ex-friends, including US et-Seato allies. Before leaving pro-Lahore, Qizilbash said…. " In this report, the T&T Department would treat "et-salinity" as one word, so would it the words "pro-Lahore" and "ex-friends". The story as released to PPA clients would read like this: "West Pakistan Chief Minister Muzaffar Ali Qizilbash said on Monday the government was determined to eliminate the menace of waterlogging and salinity with help from friends, including America and its SEATO allies. Before leaving for Lahore, the Chief Minister said…"

As the 1958 general election approached — an election that would never be held — my duties as a reporter were extended to include political rallies, whose number was now increasing in frequency. "Political reporting" was, of course, Tayyab Bokhari's beat. I was too young and untrained to venture into that. Bokhari was on a first-name relationship with all politicians, in government and opposition, since Karachi was the federal capital, and he used to talk to them on the phone or visit them at odd hours. I envied him when a phone rang and someone said, "Mr Bokhari, (former prime minister) Suhrawardy is on the line", or Qayyum Khan, the "iron man" from NWFP, who was the chief of the Pakistan Muslim League, or Chaudhry Mohammad Ali, also a former prime minister. How I felt dazed and amazed! Would I ever reach that stage? I used to ask myself. Nevertheless, covering political rallies typical of South Asia was a self-fulfilling exercise. Slogans, processions, flower petals, the decorated dais, party flags and bunting, the loudspeakers, the fiery speeches: so much has changed in Pakistan since the fifties, but this part — mercifully — has not. The only difference between then and now is that there were then no guns and bombs. It was all very peaceful. A few policemen with their steel-tipped staffs stood nearby, and the rallies ended peacefully. The meetings began usually in the evening and the keynote speaker spoke last at about midnight. By the time I had returned to the PPA offices at Mohammadi House, most of which was completely dark and abandoned save for a night watchman or two, it would be 12.30am or so. Ammi felt terribly unhappy, because by the time I returned home it would be 1.30am. Another part of my reporting job was a source of great pleasure for me — cricket! Whenever there was an important match in Karachi, I would go to the National Stadium, watch it ball by ball and report for PPA. Here duty and hobby combined to make me a very happy young man earning a salary of Rs 250 a month.

It was also at PPA that I made a discovery about us Pakistanis' eating habits. While reading encyclopaedias and tourist accounts I used to wonder why they called us wheat eaters. After all, did not Pakistanis eat beef, mutton, fish, chicken, rice, egg and vegetables? One afternoon I found the answer. BOAC had developed a new jetliner — Comet 4-A — and was undertaking a PR exercise in Pakistan by organising a brief pleasure trip for journalists. Ahmad Hasan gave me the welcome assignment, which included a pre-flight lunch at Midway House near the Karachi airport, where BOAC pilots, airhostesses and stewards stayed during their Karachi stopovers. The PPA bosses were hard task masters, and I had a tough day ahead of me. I had not had a proper breakfast, had attended my M.A. classes at the university and, after covering the flight assignment, was to go to a political rally, with my working day coming to end again at about one in the morning. So I was determined to have a mighty lunch. However, as I sat down, I found only one slice of bread on the saucer. On the main table there were plenty of eats, but how would I fill my stomach, because no roti was in sight? Determined to eat my fill and ignoring the awkwardness involved I stacked my plate with chicken legs, fish fried, kebabs and salad and later had a bowl of fruit-ice cream. As I had a cup of tea and then headed toward the plane I had a wonderful feeling. So that's why the world called us wheat eaters. People in other countries — at least in countries which wrote encyclopaedias and travel accounts in English — ate the real thing: beef, mutton, fish and vegetables, while we Pakistanis dipped roti in curry and filled our stomachs. That is one reason why Pakistanis — at least the city bred — are physically unfit with low haemoglobin contents in our blood. Curry is basically slow poison. It consists of a heavy dose of spices and cooking oil or ghee, besides red meat, which itself contains a lot of cholesterol. Since then I have developed a strategic doctrine for eating, for I have strategic doctrines to meet every situation. My culinary strategic doctrine for the Pakistani people is: the stomach can and must be filled without roti. Warning: the Holy Prophet had cautioned against eating too much meat. Medical science tells us eating too much meat causes cancer, and if there is any known prevention it is fasting.

Comet 4-A flew us for about an hour over Karachi, and the most prominent and newly built attraction was the National Stadium. No one pointed it out with greater excitement than Mohammad Ashir, Dawn's News Editor. He remained a cricket enthusiast till his death, and it was because of him that Dawn's cricket coverage was lively and in depth. Each year, he would hire a noted English or Australian cricket writer to cover the Ashes for Dawn. Once Keith Miller, the Australian all-rounder, reported for Dawn when Pakistan visited Australia. By then, Pakistan's win over England in the fourth test at the Oval in 1954, had signalled its meteoric rise in world cricket. I remember one of the headlines to Miller's story: "Watch out this lad from Karachi". From memory it is difficult for me to say who it was about.

From what was believed to be the world's first jetliner, I saw Karachi below. Comparing the Karachi as it then looked through the window of Comet 4-A nearly half a century ago with the city as it is today, I feel heart broken. Discarding all other considerations, this one sentence encapsulates my feeling: Karachi was then a normal human habitat. Period. It was as normal as Lima, Baku and Tananarive today are. Nothing spectacular about it, just normality. The National Stadium was at the end of the city, the land further north being nothing but a wide expanse of brown-green mix of semi-desert, dotted with clusters of Sindhi huts — "goths", as they call them. Through this landscape one road — then called Country Club Road and now University Road — ran all the way to the KU's new campus. (One end of the National Stadium wicket was then called the Country Club Road end). The road went further up to Malir Cantonment. The last workplace on this road was a bulb factory, opposite to where the Civic Centre stands today. I did not know then that in this very vast, empty expanse two decades later I would build a home and another two decades later I would become Grandpa. My single-storey house would be just one of the hundreds of thousands of bungalows, apartments, townhouses and mansions: fort-like mansions whose very size seemed to threaten you — with watch towers, armed guards, ferocious dogs and steel doors so wide that when they opened three Pajeros could drive in and out abreast. This area now goes by the name of Gulshan-i-Iqbal. Malir Cantonment was then away from the city; today it is part of Karachi which has grown to a population estimated today at 15 million. Its population in 1958 was 1.5 million. To the left of the road leading to the university was the aero club. Razi once used to have his training there as a pilot. The aero club and its landing strip have given way to a thickly populated area, with choked gutters, noisy bazaars, pushcarts, a bewildering variety of vehicles competing for space; and monstrous high-rises built in violation of some of the fundamental norms of town planning, accompanied by a kind of vulgar commercialisation the brains behind which ought to face a firing squad.

Below the jetliner the traffic ran at a civilised pace, and it never must have occurred to the motorists down below that they would be caught in a traffic jam or be stranded by some sudden outbreak of violence — a bomb blast in a mosque, a political or religious leader's murder or a shootout between gangsters calling themselves students. Decades later, precisely on this road I suffered a trauma I do not think I would forget. It was May 30, 2005. Tired after a day's work and having driven through a traffic for which chaotic is hardly the suitable adjective, I wished nothing more than to reach home. Suddenly, I found my Suzuki Khyber caught in a situation that was more than a "normal" traffic jam — arson was in the air.

Imagine getting caught in a traffic jam with a mob out burning cars! "There were all sorts of people in all sorts of vehicles", I wrote (Dawn, June 1, 2005). "Suzuki vans carrying soft drinks and chickens; huge trucks taking sugar and wheat to Kabul and beyond; affluent families, children eating ice-cream, going to weddings; village folks returning to Gadap or some sleepy village on the outskirts; inter-city buses, whose very size makes you scary, honking and flashing headlights; and, of course, the ubiquitous minibuses...." Suddenly the motorists "froze as they heard pedestrians shout, 'Don't go that way! They are burning cars'!" A Shia mosque had been bombed by a fanatic Sunni suicide-bomber, and an angry mob was in action. Instead of going up the bridge, I drove along the left track of the road that crosses the now abandoned railway tracks and meets Rashid Minhas Road. This turned out to be a disaster, for this lane led exactly to the restaurant which the mob had reduced to cinders, its only fault being its American name, Pizza Hut. Six people were killed, their ages ranging between 24 and 36. Like the innocents murdered in the mosque, they had committed no crime. I wrote: "With both the bridge and the service lane closed, there was a mad rush for the lanes and by-lanes to the left. Now this part of University Road [opposite Baitul Mukarram] too started closing. There was no pressure on the shopkeepers and restaurateurs, but they were doing so on their own — scared of the unknown... Some eateries switched off their front lights and pulled their shutters half way down but served their customers inside ..." Darkness now descended on an area that otherwise sparkled with light and life well beyond 2am. It is a food street in its own right. Working women and girls in ones and twos headed home. Their parents and families must have expected them home much earlier. With no sight of the jam melting, I thought I must as well utilise the time, managed to park my car in a lane and decided to have my dinner at a restaurant with its shutters half pulled down.

"Is there an emergency exit?" I asked the waiter as I ordered food, for an uncanny feeling bothered me: what would happen if this restaurant too was attacked, we were trapped and the diners inside roasted? Fortunately, there was a way out.

By 10.30pm, most vehicles had found their way out somehow. I drove on the service lane in the hope that all was clear. But a policeman on Rashid Minhas Road blocked the turn to the left. "Go that way!"

he said while pointing to the now virtually deserted University Road. I turned right, cleared the roundabout under the bridge and drove toward Time Square on University Road only to be halted by the sight of the remnants of a bus that had been burnt, and boys — one hooded — had blocked the road. "Kindly turn back!" one of them said with a surprising degree of politeness, as another one hit my car with a stick. The six Pizza Hut killed were not roasted. To avoid the flames, they had taken refuge in the restaurant's cold storage, were unable to come out because the fire had jammed the door, and were frozen. Read their names: waiter Faraz Ahmad, A-C technician Mohammad Saleem, cleaner John Peter, security officer Ghulam Hassan, chief technician Ilyas and accountant Asif. They were not even remotely connected to those who had bombed the mosque. Yet they fell victim to a phenomenon that has over the decades become an accepted part of our collective psyche — the target of one's anger may not necessarily have anything to do with the cause of one's anger. Yes, you, kill and burn for the sake of it, because you must have a target, even if that target shares your anger.

Today, as I recapture in my mind the scene from that jetliner five decades ago and compare it with Karachi today, I feel as if I have crossed the time-space barrier to move in one hop from paradise to hell. That Karachi is lost forever. It belongs in our memory or perhaps to history, for it can never be recreated. Karachi is growing and will continue to grow at a fantastic pace: there will be more monstrous buildings, more shopping malls, more traffic and, yes, more people. But that growth will merely provide indices and indicators for the World Bank and think-tanks; for its citizens that indices-based growth will have no meaning. Karachi has become soulless. It epitomises Hobbes's state of nature in which everyone is at war with everyone, "and the life of man nasty, brutish and short". Perhaps a visionary of some future generation, armed with extraordinary tools and technology, will make Karachi a normal human habitat.

The jetliner landed safely. This needs to be asserted, because later Comet 4-A was grounded after a number of accidents. But I have often wondered how many of those who landed with me safely perished six years later when PIA's inaugural flight to Cairo crashed on May 20, 1965, killing 128 people, including 21 journalists. I was then in Morning News, and my News Editor, Sibte Farooq Faridi, was among the dead when the Boeing 20B crashed as it prepared for landing at Cairo. Also killed in the crash was Dawn Subeditor Saghiruddin Ahmad. He was on board the unfortunate PIA flight by lot, because there were only 21 seats for journalists and many aspirants at a time when air travel for Pakistani journalists was a rarity. Originally, Dawn had nominated Zubair to go on the ill-fated flight. However, the decision to draw lots saved Zubair. He told me how Saghiruddin, who had five children, came to him for tips on what to purchase in Cairo. Going through Dawn's issue of May 21, 1965, I came across this touching paragraph: "Some of them had planned to go for Umra after their visit to Cairo before returning home. Mr Jaffer Mansoor of Hurriyet had taken with him his kaffun (shroud in which the Muslim dead are wrapped) to dip into Aab-e-Zamzam." Also killed in the crash was Major General Hayauddin, a Sandhurst-trained General, who saw action in Iraq, Burma and Indo-China during the Second World War, was mentioned in dispatches and won MC and MBE. The French government gave him Legion de Honour. He was associated with the newspaper industry in his capacity as Chairman of the National Press Trust, the mechanism created by the Information Ministry to take over a large number of English, Urdu and Bengali newspapers to serve as the Ayub regime's mouthpiece. The crash plunged the nation and the journalists into grief, and there was no dearth of conspiracy theories. Many people saw the CIA's hand in it, because Ayub had stunned Pakistan's Western, especially American, friends when PIA became the first airlines from the "free world" to fly to "Red" China. The Soviet-American détente had begun, and it was communism's yellow variety that America thought was fatal to mankind.

Meanwhile, I was getting disturbing reports about a very awkward development. The university was abandoning its Princess Street premises and was moving to a new sprawling campus on the city's outskirts. We knew that a new campus, planned by French architects, was being built, but none of us thought it would be built so quickly as to force a change of location half way through an academic year. I prayed that this never happened while I was doing my masters. Should this happen, I often asked myself, what option did I have? The Princess Street "campus" suited me ideally, because I could attend classes up to 2pm and then be at the PPA office in 15 minutes by tram. But were the university to move to a campus that then appeared to us located far and away, I wondered how I would combine earning with learning. There was no question of giving up my M. A. classes. So if it all such a change was forced on me, I would look for some evening job. Well, the Greater Decider came to my rescue in a way that was initially painful. Does not He say in Al-Quran Ala la-hul khalqo vel amr (Hearken! It is He who creates and it is He who decides). Muazzam Ali was fed up with my incompetence. One afternoon, when I reached the PPA office from the KU, I found a letter waiting for me: I had been sacked. A politely worded letter said that the company was having some financial difficulty and so it had been decided to dispense with my services. The company, it said, would be glad to take me back when its finances improved. Razi had already lost his job in the police department; now I too had been sacked. This means both sons were jobless.

Even though I was with PPA for less than a year, it continues to fascinate me. One reason is obvious: first love is last love. PPP was the first news organisation I worked for, and for that reason I have not forgotten that brief experience half a century ago. Men like Muazzam and Ahmad Hussain were pioneers. In the fifties there were few newspapers, industrialisation had just begun, the middle class was small, newspaper readership was shockingly low — it is low even now — and it took ingenuity and a spirit of enterprise to launch a new wire agency in those circumstances. Muazzam was Editor of the government-owned agency APP and Ahmad News Editor. Both of them gave up these coveted positions to ventures into the unknown. Born in Ferozepur in East Punjab, Muazzam graduated from the Government College,

Lahore, and after completing his education worked as public and press relations officers for the Chamber of Princes in Delhi. After partition he came over to Pakistan and joined APP in 1950 and also was for some time its Cairo correspondent. It was in 1956 that he launched PPA, with the Board of Governors consisting of Sardar Amir Azam Khan, then a federal minister, Z. A. Suleri, Editor of The Times of Karachi, Mr Inqilab Matri, founder-editor of Millat, and some family members, including his Muazzam's brothers Aslam Ali and Muhatram.

At PPA it was also my good fortune to have worked with Fazal and Javed, both of whom would grow to become great journalists. Fazal joined the agency in 1956, and he is still there as Chief Editor (2009). A remarkably hard working man, Fazal, a KU product in journalism and Persian, had several scoops to his credit. These included the news about the historic agreement Pakistan and India had reached to share the waters of the Indus and its tributaries. Fazal doesn't remember that Muazzam gave him a silver cigarette case as a gift on this scoop. Fazal also became PPA's Middle East correspondent (1960-65), based in Baghdad, Cairo and Beirut, and on return home was appointed Managing Director. He also worked side by side for The Times, London, and Newsweek from 1966 to 2002.

One sordid aspect of the PPA drama was the bad blood between Bhutto and Muazzam. During his 1970 election campaign, Bhutto alleged that PPA had come into being through CENTO's anti-subversion funds. He should know because he was an insider and was onetime federal information minister in the Ayub cabinet. It was a charge denied by Muazzam. More unfortunately, Bhutto publicly threatened to "fix up" Muazzam when he came to power. During the first PPP government (1971-77), Ghulam Mustafa Jatoi, (later Sindh's chief minister and interim prime minister in 1990) arranged what obviously was a forced sale, for Lateef Ebrahim Jamal, a tycoon and philanthropist, purchased PPA. Lateef, who helped found the H. E. J. Institute of Chemistry with a donation of Rs 5 million, a huge amount then, was one of Javed's friends. He came to his Gulshan home and asked him to head the agency's editorial department. Javed says he himself played no role in the deal. After Bhutto was overthrown by Ziaul Haq in the July 1977 coup, the agency returned to its owners and Fazal was appointed Managing Director and Chief Editor. Javed left PPA (which by then had become PPI — Pakistan Press International —) to become Director of the Jamal-owned Pakistan Management Corporation, which was in housing and shipping business. Javed left PMC to return to the profession and worked as Executive Director of The Muslim, Islamabad, for 17 years. It was a pleasure for me to work with him again when he returned to Dawn some times in the mid-nineties and worked as economic correspondent. Today (2009) he is editor of Dawn's weekly Economic and Business Review.

Muazzam passed most of his latter life in London, handing over his agency to his brother, Aslam Ali. Over the decades, the world of Pakistani journalism has what can be called a PPA fraternity, for the agency has served as a training ground for hundreds of journalists now spread all over Pakistan and occupying key positions in newspapers and the electronic media. Aslam died in 1978, and his son, Owais Aslam Ali, was appointed PPI Chairman in December 1999. Muazzam died on March 10, 2005.

Having lost my PPA job, I found it extremely difficult to get another one, because I wanted a job that would not stand in the way of my university classes in the morning. There were few opportunities for journalists then, for there were in Karachi then only two English morning dailies (besides The Times of Karachi, which was dying), and a job with any of the evening papers was out of the question because that required working in the morning. Nevertheless, I thought I should try some morning papers and see if they could give me an evening job. I first approached Mohsin Ali, Editor of Morning News. He said there were no vacancies. Eleven years later, Mohsin would invite me to be his paper's

News Editor after the journalists' failed 1970 strike. I think I approached Dawn as well, but failed to get a job. Then somebody suggested that I try The Times of Karachi (ToK), which was going through a difficult period, a new management headed by Ameen Tareen had taken over, and there was union trouble. The staff had some well-known communists, leftists and trade union activists. They included Afzal Shervani, who has been mentioned earlier, Shaukat Siddiqi, the celebrated novelist and author of Khuda ki Basti, and Saleem Alvi, a prominent leader of the Pakistan Federal Union of Journalists (PFUJ). During its heyday, ToK editors included cricket legend Omar Kureshi and Z. A. Suleri. But the paper later fell on bad times, and when Tareen took over it was a six-page rag. Tareen wanted to improve the paper but ran into trouble with the union because he was cutting down on the staff. Tareen was a handsome man, a six-foot tall Pathan with rosy cheeks. He appointed me as a subeditor-cum-reporter at Rs 200. This was Rs 50 less than what I was getting at PPA. Nevertheless, the job suited me because there were just two shifts — late afternoon and night. Both suited me. I was terribly unpopular with the ToK staff, because they thought I was Tareen's man and had been appointed after a number of people had been sacked. My only friend at ToK was Haseen Ahmad, a fellow student at the Karachi University, who was doing his Honours in English. Haseen later joined the American Embassy (later consulate) at Karachi and retired in 1995. We would again become colleagues, this time in Dawn, when Haseen joined it in 1997, first on the staff of the supplements section and later as sports editor.

 Minhaj Barna was a regular visitor to the ToK offices. I had heard of him but had never met him till then. Barna was a confirmed communist and was the Party's card-carrying member. Barna graduated from Jamea Millia Islamia, Delhi, but was expelled from the institution because he clashed with Akhtar Hameed Khan, known to us in Pakistan for his pioneering work the Orangi Pilot Project. There was a literary club, called Bazme Adab, and it had both Muslim and non-Muslim students, but the latter category did not have a vote in the club. Barna launched a campaign for the Sikh and Hindu students to be given the voting right in the Urdu literary club. The Jamea expelled him, and Barna started living at the headquarters of the Communist Party of India which was close to the Jamea Millia. The man instrumental in getting Barna into the CPI was Muqeemuddin Farooqi, Secretary of Delhi CPI. Born in Qaim Ganj in U.P. in 1925, Barna had inherited rebellion from his father, Hakim Taj Mohammad Khan, who was a political activist and was in Quetta at the time of partition. During the anti-British non-cooperation movement (1922-23), Hakim Taj made a highly "seditious" speech at Karachi's Khaliqdina Hall – among the listeners was Haji Sir Abdullah Haroon, one of Jinnah's lieutenants and later owner of Dawn. Hakim Taj was expelled from Karachi. Two years after independence, Barna came over to Pakistan from Delhi and worked as a translator for the Soviet news agency Tass's correspondent Balshakov. His activities could not remain hidden from the government, and he was among those arrested in the 1951 crackdown launched by the government in the aftermath of Pakistan's membership of the US-led military alliances. He remained in jail for six months.

Meanwhile, to embarrass the Western powers, the Soviet Union launched a worldwide peace movement, encouraging communists throughout the world to set up peace committees. Barna, who was then in Lahore, working for the Urdu daily Imoroze, came to Karachi to set up a peace committee. He was its secretary, while Pir Ilahi Bux, a former Sindhi chief minister, was chairman. On Stalin's death in March 1953 the Karachi peace committee passed a resolution, mourning Stalin's death and hailing him as a man of peace. Dawn, in keeping with its support for Pakistan's pro-Western foreign policy, wrote an editorial denouncing the committee's resolution. However, the irony was that Pir Ilahi Bux later denied that he ever acted as chair of the committee that passed the resolution eulogising Stalin. The Secretary General of the Pakistan Peace Committee was Prof. Shamsul Hye while Pir of Manki Sharif was president. Barna began his career in journalism in 1951 with Urdu daily Imroze, which later became part of the chain of newspapers controlled by the National Press Trust, whose formation during the Ayub era and other details I have discussed in a later chapter. Barna became Secretary General of the Karachi Union of Journalist in 1962 and was later transferred to Dhaka as a punishment by NPT Chairman A. K. Soomar following the failure of the strike in Anjam. He remained at Dhaka from 1966 to 1969, but returned to Karachi the next year to play a leading role in the journalists' countrywide strike. I have discussed the strike and its consequences in detail in Chapter 5, because its repercussions have continued till this day, especially in the form of the controversial decision taken to form a vertical union embracing all press industry workers. This led to a significant decline in the journalists' role in press industry trade unionism.

Even though the PFUJ has played a major role in organising Pakistani journalists on trade union lines and struggling for higher wages and better working conditions for all press industry workers, it has often been accused of ignoring the professional side of journalism and concentrating solely on the journalists' economic conditions. The criticism is perhaps valid. Nevertheless, improving the standards of journalism was one of its aims when it came into being on August 2, 1950. Grounds for creating a trade union for Pakistani journalists were laid three months earlier when a convention held at Karachi decided that the PFUJ would come into being after at least two of the provincial unions adopted its constitution. The convention, held in Karachi on April 28-30, 1952, was attended by delegates representing the Sind Union of Journalists (SUJ) and the Punjab Union of Journalists (PUJ), though the journalists from the Frontier sent their best wishes and promised to join it. Those who represented SUJ were M. A. Shakoor (president), Asrar Ahmad (General Secretary), Tufail Ahmad Jamali (Junior Vice President) and Akhtar Hussain Khawja. Shakoor, who was in Dawn before I joined it, chose to pass all his life in exile in London after he came out of prison where he was one of the many left-oriented journalists arrested for being communist. I met him only once when he came to Karachi decades later (1997) and served as one of the chief guests at a Karachi Press Club function and handed me a shield. Tufail Ahmad Jamali, the JVP, was well known for his famous column Gar Tu Bura Namaanay in Imroze. The PUJ was represented by S. Lewis (president), Mohammad Shafi (General Secretary) and Ghayurul Islam. The latter became my colleague in Dawn in the late '80s. After the SUJ and PUJ ratified the constitution, the PFUJ came into being on August 2, 1950.

The PFUJ had following "aims and objects": (i) to raise the status and improve the qualification [professional quality?] of all members of the journalistic profession; (ii) to promote generally the interests of journalists [and] journalism in English, Urdu, Punjabi, Pashtu, Kashmiri, Sindhi, Gujrati and any other language current in Pakistan; (iii) to act for its members for the purpose of protecting their legitimate rights pertaining to wages; (iv) to provide for the protection of its members in the event of a trade dispute; (v) (a) to help unity of all workers of the press industry in Pakistan by all means, including affiliation with trade unions of press industry workers, except rival trade unions formed to disrupt the unity of the working journalists; (b) to promote the cause of the working class in general and to enter into affiliation, provided they are not with a political party; (vi) to assist members, where necessary, in securing employment; (vii) to ascertain the law and practice relating to journalism and to promote where necessary new or amending legislation designed to assist journalists in their professional duties; (viii) to protect the interests of members when in the opinion of the Federal Executive Council (FEC) they are being wrongly dealt for any act in the discharge of their professional duties; (ix) to exercise supervision over its members when engaged in professional duties and to deal with the questions effecting their professional conduct; (x) to maintain and administer unemployment, benevolent, superannuation, death benefit and other funds; (xi) to publish, when conditions permit, an official journal, and (xii) to defend, maintain and struggle for freedom of the press."

(Because of the non-availability of the original document or an authentic copy, I have reproduced the PFUJ's aims and objects from an article written by Abdul Hamid Chhapra, published in Victoria Plus, Karachi, (now closed) in its issue of July 3, 2008, with his permission. Chhapra, a former president of the PFUJ and former chairman of the All Pakistan Newspaper Employees' Confederation, is a legendary figure in Pakistani journalists' trade union movement. A former President of the Karachi Press Club, Chhapra is a tireless worker, known as much for firebrand speeches as for the long distances he covers on foot during his election campaigns. Like many other journalists living in Gulshan-i-Iqbal's Block 4-A, he too is my neighbour. One of Chhapra's acts of sacrifice is to donate a kidney to his younger brother. As for his ability to be voluble, Sultan Ahmad, the doyen of Pakistani journalists, one said: "You talk so much when you have only one kidney. What would you have done if you had both!?"

Reproducing the code of conduct was less of a problem, for any visitor to the Karachi Press Club can find the Code written on a big wooden panel opposite to the reception desk:

"Like other trade unions, formed for mutual protection and economic betterment, the Pakistan Federal Union of Journalists desires and encourages its members to maintain [a] good quality of workmanship and a high standard of conduct. A member of the union has two claims on his loyalty: one by his Union and the other by his employer. These need not clash so long as the employer complies with the agreed union conditions and makes no demand for forms of service incompatible with the honour of the profession or with the principles of trade unionism. Hence, the code of conduct that was made part of the Constitution was: (1) a member should do nothing that would bring discredit on himself, his Union, his newspaper, or his profession. He should study the rules of his Union and should not by commission or omission act against the interest of the Union; (2) whether for publication or suppression, the acceptance of a bribe by a journalist is one of the gravest professional offences; (3) every journalist should treat subordinates as considerately as he would desire to be treated by his superiors; (4) freedom in honest collection and publication of news facts and the rights of fair comment and criticism are principles which every journalist should defend; (5) unless the employee consents to a variation, a member who wishes to terminate his employment must give notice according to agreement; (6) no member should seek promotion or seek to obtain the position of another journalist by unfair methods. A members should not directly or indirectly attempt to obtain for himself or anyone else any commission regularly held by a freelance member of the Union; (7) it is unprofessional conduct to exploit the labour of another journalist by plagiarism or by using his copy for linage purposes without permission, (8) staff men who do linage work should be prepared to give up such work to conform with the pooling scheme approved by the FEC or any Union plan to provide a freelance member with a means of earning a living; (9) a member holding staff appointment shall serve first the paper that employs him. In his own time a member is free to engage in other creative work, but he should not undertake any extra work in his rest time or holidays if by so doing he is depriving an out-of-work member of a chance to obtain employment. Any misuse of rest days won by the trade union on the sound argument that periods of recuperation are needed after strenuous hours of labour is damaging to trade union aims and a shorter working week. (10) While a spirit of willingness to help other members should be encouraged at all times, members are under a special obligation of honour to help an unemployed member to obtain work. (11) A journalist should fully realize his personal responsibility for everything he sends to his paper or agency. He should keep the union and professional secrets, and respect all necessary confidences regarding sources of information and private documents. He should not falsify information or documents, or distort or misrepresent facts. (12) In obtaining news and pictures, reporters and press photographers should do nothing that will cause pain or humiliation to innocent, bereaved and otherwise distressed persons. News pictures and documents should be acquired by honest methods only. (13) Every journalist should keep in mind the danger in the laws of libel, contempt of court and copyright. In reports of law court proceedings it is necessary to observe and practice the rule of fair play to all parties".

～～～～～～～

The drive from the KU to the ToK in the Burns Road maze of lanes took about half an hour (today, on a normal day, it should take 90 minutes.), and I began wondering what use to make of it. Then a very unfortunate idea took hold of me, and I regret to say has remained with me till this day — I must not let even a minute of time go waste. This unfortunate thought has been a source both of torture and many benefits for me. If I had confined the maximisation of the use of time to my political science exams in that 1959-60 academic year, that could have been understandable. While we studied Hobbes, Locke and Rousseau as part of the paper called Political Theory, there was a paper devoted to only these three social contract philosophers. To make use of the time available to me on the bus ride, I began memorising long portions of the commentaries on these thinkers, and sometimes from the texts themselves. The result was that when my M. A. final results were finally announced I got 67 out of 100 marks in this paper. Normally, such high marks are possible in science subjects. But my regret is that the maximisation of time habit did not end with the drive from the KU to the ToK offices; it has remained with me till this day and been a source of anxiety and social awkwardness. For instance, a meeting that lasts beyond the stipulated time gets on my nerves, and often I feel guilty that I have been curt — if not rude — to people who in my opinion had crossed the time which I thought I had allotted to them. Once a colleague resumed his duty after three days because he was down with flu, and I thought I should say hello and ask him how he was feeling. I thought he would understand the formal nature of my social obligation and be equally formal in his reply. Unfortunately, the man went on to inflict his medical history on me and the results of the blood test. Frankly, this was not what I had bargained for. I thought I was performing my duty as a human being and as a Pakistani, but in return he was taxing my patience. While the doctor must have valid reasons for prescribing a blood test, I felt like protesting to my colleague and asking him why —in heaven's name, why — while I was being kind to him he had wasted my eight and a half to 10 minutes on his medical history. Frankly, I pity a man like me who does not have time to waste. A person who does not have time to waste sooner or later becomes a slave of his routine and loses all freedom. Razi is a tremendous time waster. That is the reason why he enjoys the company of people and has an army of admirers among men and women. Ahmad Ali Khan, who was my editor at Dawn for 28 years, was aware of my time consciousness, felt angry inside and sometimes teased me by holding me unnecessarily only to enjoy my predicament. It is besides the point, though, that he himself was a tremendous time waster. But of this remarkable man later.

HAWAI ADDA

'Hawai Adda' is a vulgar Urdu translation for 'airport'. The other translation, "Hawai Mustaqar', never caught on, because it was pedantic and unintelligible to the majority. Radio Pakistan and most television stations use Hawai Adda, because one of the basic principles of journalism is that language must be simple and easy to understand. However, I do not believe that simplicity should mean vulgarisation of language, least of all Urdu, which combines the finest traditions of Persian poetry and Arabic idiom. The people of Pakistan have shown a preference for the English word 'airport' because it is easy to pronounce and is – like 'cigarette', 'ticket' and 'taxi' – is understood the world over. In my own little world, and in the misfortunes that befell me and my family, Hawai Adda was a name we chose to give to a "house" in which we lived for about 10 or so months. Giving that "house" this name was our way of mitigating our suffering. The ground floor and the first floor were normal and housed a school. The building was owned by one of our distant relations, and we moved to that place in Nazimabad Block One in a hurry from the Brigade lines after Razi lost his police job and we did not know where to go. Besides, as narrated earlier, both of us were jobless, Abboo being the only earning member of the family. So we accepted the offer to live in that house free. The second floor on which we lived had no doors and windows, just the bare walls, and no running water. If it had no roof, things could have been less dangerous. Unfortunately, the roof was a mix of cement and thatch resting on beams. The idea was to provide shelter from rain. This was a highly dangerous combination, for the thatch became heavy and solid, and before we moved in, parts of it had fallen on a lady who had lived there before we came in. She was seriously injured. As a safety measure, all of us slept right under the beams, so that if part of the roof fell we would be relatively speaking safe. The most prominent feature of this house was the way the wind howled and seemed to carry everything with it. Since there were no doors and windows everything had to be kept well in place, otherwise, it would simply get blown away by the wind. Saucers, dishes, clothes, books and copies, pencils and paper, and even rotis would fly away unless we kept them well secured. Hawai Adda was thus the apt name for it. It has stuck till this day, and many of our close relations and friends still remember that house in Nazimabad with that name.

Humour and irony that the words Hawai Adda epitomised was our way of putting up with poverty. Later in my more comfortable moments — like when I was the guest of His Royal Highness Hassan bin Talal in Amman or one of the guests of His Majesty King Fahd at Jeddah or in my present home in Karachi, — I have often wondered what kept us going, or why we did not go down and dwell forever at that level of existence, and the only conclusion to which I came and on which my brother and sisters agreed with me was —Ammi! Never even in the darkest hours of our family life did she make us forget education. No matter what happened, we must struggle ceaselessly to pursue higher education at all costs. When we fled Hyderabad we were not children; we were boys and girls at school and had a taste of the kind of refined life we were passing there before the enemy moved in. It is not that we were just aware of our comfortable lives there; we were conscious of the continuity in our beings of the Mughal Empire through the entity called the State of Hyderabad and the Mughal culture and sophistication which the Nizam State and the Hyderabadi Muslims came to symbolise as the north decayed and disintegrated. Those were our precious possessions and Ammi never allowed us to forget them. In spite of being handicapped by asthma, which occurred with extraordinary severity when the weather changed, she remained a tower of strength for us. Whatever our financial condition, she made it clear, if a choice had to be made between education and a job, it was the job that could be sacrificed; education, never! That is one reason, why I changed jobs so often and had — though mercifully short — periods of joblessness. Abboo had his own grief. In a sense it was deeper, because he seldom spoke of Hyderabad and of his days as an officer in the Nizam's bureaucracy. If at all he referred to Hyderabad it was in the context of his days as a student and as captain of Osmania University's hockey team. The place where his grief found a place was his poetry. Our relatives and his admirers often chided us for not getting his divan published. He himself made it clear he would prefer the collection of his poetry to be published after his death. This turned out to be true.

During the 1959-60 academic year my life had three abodes — Hawaii Adda, the new university campus and the ToK offices, where I often slept for the night because no bus was available at 1.30am to take me home. Strictly speaking there was no day shift at ToK; the evening shift — which I called the day shift — began at 4pm. On a given day, I would travel by bus from Nazimabad to Guru Mandir, where the university bus took us boys and girls to the campus. My classes would be over by 2pm, and then I would proceed direct to the ToK offices. The journey took about 30 minutes, and I have already mentioned above what use I made of this ride. I would be at ToK till 10pm and then take the bus home to reach Hawai Adda at 10.30pm. Fellow students at the university laughed when I referred to it as "day duty". The night duty was a totally different affair. After the classes were over in the afternoon, I returned to Hawai Adda in the afternoon, rested and slept to prepare for the night duty and reached the ToK offices at 8pm. Then the night shift would end at 1am, all journalists would go home, but I would sleep right there in the room next to the news room. The next morning, after a reasonably good breakfast — an egg, four slices of bread and a cup of tea — at a Malabari restaurant on Frere Road (today Shahrah-i-Liaquat) — I would proceed direct to the campus by the university bus. In the afternoon, back to Hawai Adda. It was hard life.

Looking back at that period, two things strike me: one, when you are young rigours of life do not really matter. In old age even minor inconveniences look formidable, like an uncomfortable bed, a sudden change in temperature, remaining in the same posture — say, poring over a book — for long, or climbing stairs only to realise you are panting. Two, inflation was unknown and I — like most students — carried in our pockets the precise amount of money we needed on a given day. Eight annas for breakfast — a fried egg for four annas, four slices of bread in two annas, and a cup of tea in one and a half anna (half an anna to spare). For the present generation of Pakistanis who do not know what an anna is: a rupee used to consist of 16 annas. So in today's monetary terms, the breakfast at the Malabari restaurant cost me slightly less than half a rupee. In about the same amount of money I would have dinner at a nearby restaurant, where a plate of curry, with a fair quantity of meat, cost four annas, two naans in one anna, plus the mandatory tea for one and a half anna. Today you make a rough calculation and carry perhaps twice the money.

I have till this day kept some of the clippings of the news I reported for ToK, and I enjoy reading them because they give an indication of the kind of the country Pakistan then was. There were reports about the rise in vegetable prices, about a lawyer writing a novel on Akhtari

Begum, the woman at the centre of a sex-murder scandal that rocked the police department; the eternal question of "refugee rehabilitation", and the difference that martial law had begun making to our lives. Here is one news item in ToK's issue of Sept 29, 1959:

By Our City Reporter

"KARACHI, Sept 28: Over 8,000 refugee families have so far been shifted by the Rehabilitation Ministry from the slum of Quaidabad to the well-built Korangi Colony.

"Very little now remains in (sic) Quaidabad, the slum which once contained over 10,000 refugee families living in hovels and unhygienic — almost sub-human — conditions near the Mazar of the Quaid-i-Azam. There now remain slightly over 2,000 families to be moved to Korangi. The clearing operation had been started on August 1 last when President Ayub Khan inaugurated the colony." There were two more paragraphs.

A decade later Karachi, like the rest of the country, would explode in anger against Ayub Khan and play a leading part in overthrowing a man who was by any standards a thorough gentleman and one of Pakistan's finest rulers. Ayub's system was no doubt authoritarian, but he was not a tyrant, like Zia, nor a drunkard and debauch like Yahya He was a gentleman in the British mould, and he never stooped to the depths to which Pakistan's latter-day rulers would while hounding their political enemies. If Ayub wanted someone arrested, a small posse of policemen would do the job. Under the other dictators, intelligence hounds would scale walls and enter homes like burglars at midnight to arrest the regimes' opponents and drag them, kicking and beating, out of their bedrooms. Ayub committed many mistakes, but his achievements are a matter of historical record. The removal of the refugee slums and the building of a new settlement only for the refugees' benefit were achievements for which the people of Karachi never expressed their gratitude to him.

The following news item, however, gives a fairly good indication of the kind of system Ayub had. It appeared in ToK's issue of Sept 21, 1959:

SECTION CASE AGAINST SECURITY DETENUS

Gazdar, Muzaffarul Haq, Burhani And Murad

By Our City Reporter

KARACHI, Sept 20: The Karachi CID (Political) have registered a case under

Section 121-A PPC and under Martial Law Regulations 24 and 55 against four persons who had earlier been detained under the Security Act.

The four persons — Khwaja Muzaffarul Haq Usmani, Ismail Burhani, Aslam Murad and Hashim Gazdar — have been charged with "conspiring to wage war against the state" and trying to create "alarm and despondency" in the public.

All of them had been arrested about 10 days ago under the Security of Pakistan Act and lodged in Central Jail. Two of the above four — Khawja Muzaffarul Haq and Ismail Burhani — were Minister and Deputy Minister respectively in the dismissed West Pakistan Ministry of Republican Chief Minister, Nawab Muzzafar Ali Qizilbash.

Aslam Murad was an employee of the Pakistan Shell, while Hashim Gazdar had been the Deputy Speaker of former Constituent Assembly and an important figure in the political arena of former Sind Province.

After two paragraphs my story reproduces Martial Law Regulations 24 and 55. MLR 24 said: "No one by word of mouth or in writing or signals, or otherwise, will spread reports calculated to create alarm or despondency amongst the public or calculated to create dissatisfaction towards the armed forces and police or any member therefore".

MLR 55 said: "No person shall organise, convene or attend any meeting or procession of a political nature".

On the educational front, it was nice to be at the new campus — away from the chaos of Princess Street. The campus was still being built and would continue to expand to become what it is today. But we had the honour of being the first batch at the new campus in the academic year 1959-60. We shifted to the new campus after the winter vacation and enjoyed every minute of education and the totally new atmosphere we found there, even though the gardening and landscaping were in their initial stages. There was a cricket match that I would never forget. It was not really serious, but both boys and girls played at what then was a hockey field in front of the political science department. It is a measure of the degradation of Pakistan's society that today such a match would be considered "obscene" and the Taliban among the students would go after our skins. The match was supervised by our teachers, and nobody thought there was something objectionable about it. The teacher most dear to us was Barkat Warsi. He began teaching us at the old campus when we were in the first year of our masters classes — M.A. Previous, as it was called. He was then a Fellow at the university and taught us "European medieval institutions". He was a brilliant man but had a chequered career later. After we were out of the university, Barkat joined the Sindh University at Hyderabad, fell victim to political persecution and lost his job. Later he joined the Public Relations Department of the National Bank of Pakistan. He died in the mid-nineties. The head of the political science department was Prof Ilyas Ahmad, whose monumental work was "Sovereignty: Islamic and Modern". Prof Ilyas's son, Haleem Ahmad, worked for Dawn's sports sections for nearly four decades. Besides cricket reporting, he specialised in horse racing and often betted. The most fascinating character among the teachers was C. A. Salahuddin, who taught us international affairs, and was obsessed with the Nazi era — a bug he passed on to me. After retirement from the university, he migrated to America and died there in the nineties.

I had some wonderful classmates, and some of them rose to great heights in different fields. They included Fatehayab Ali Khan, who led the left-leaning Kissan Mazdoor (Peasants' and Workers') Party and for some time was head of the Pakistan Institute of International Affairs. He caught the nation's attention when he appeared as amicus curie in the farce that was Bhutto's trial. In the Police Science department, romance also blossomed. Fatehyab married Masooma Hassan, who was one year my junior and later joined the diplomatic service; Salman Faruqi, who was one year my senior, married one from my batch, Shahtaj, who was a sister of one of my colleagues at Dawn, Osman Haider. Salman had a brilliant career in government, was universally liked for his efficiency, suffered a lot when he fell victim to intrigues and went into exile. I was happy see to him back when he returned in the post-Musharraf period and was rehabilitated; Yusuf Jamal, who, too, became a CSP officer. As a student he was an excellent orator and had secured the top position in the competitive examination for the civil service when Pakistan then included today's Bangladesh; Syed Mohammad Sibtain, who too became a CSP officer, and retired as Commissioner of Income Tax. Besides Abdul Sattar Pingar, Baughty and Dadabhoy I have mentioned earlier, there was one unforgettable character — Hamdan Amjad Ali. He finally settled for Naushaba, who was herself a journalist with Akhbar-i-Jahan, the Jang group's weekly magazine. Amjad, too, became a journalist and began his career with PPA in 1958. Later he joined Dawn as a reporter and quit it after about a quarter century. His decision to leave the paper was a tragedy for him. He had acted in haste, because he was terrified by staff changes and thought he couldn't work with some of his colleagues. After leaving Dawn he had a tough time. He became editor of a weekly launched by Jam Sadiq Ali when he was Sindh's Chief Minister. The weekly later closed. He also worked for the Pakistan and Gulf Economist, a prestigious Karachi weekly, and also had stints as a public relations officer with Hamdard University and other organisations. But there were often long periods of joblessness. Like many other journalists who had built their homes in Block 4-A of Gulshan, he became my neighbour, too. In October 2007 it was my sad duty to serve as one of his pall-bearers.

3

REVANCHE!

THE MONTH WAS SEPTEMBER, the year 1965. Standing on the Keamari beach, rifle in hand, I looked across the Arabian Sea and roared to myself, "India, here I come! You are going to get it for Hyderabad!" My condition was laughable, for my uniform consisted of a pair of khaki trousers and a shirt which Razi wore when he was in the police. Other soldiers, including the company commander himself, did not even have that. I stood at the Keamari beach as part of a Mujahid Force company whose boys had no uniform, no salary, and no official recognition as part of the Pakistani armed forces. Only patriotism had brought us together. In my case, patriotism was fuelled by a burning desire — Revanche! Unfulfilled till this day, it was a passion more intense and burning than that of France after 1871. Others may view Indo-Pakistan rivalry as an issue between two countries and two governments; for me it has been a personal matter, a revanche unrealisable, chimerical, tragicomic. In September 1965 Pakistan and India went to war, and I found myself on a peaceful battlefield where only Radio Pakistan and the black-out told us that two armies were fighting a war. Seventeen years earlier I had been roused from bed early in the morning and made to say goodbye to my home, which I would never see again. "The Indian Army is near", said one of Father's friends who had come to our home to prepare us for the flight. He had come with two tongas. The year was 1948, the month was September, and the place was Parbhani, a small town in the Aurangabad governorate of the Hyderabad State. Jinnah had died on September 11, and India launched its attack on the Nizam's state two days later.

Hyderabad was the largest of the princely states in British India. In area – we were taught at school – it was larger than any European state, save Russia. Nizam means the governor of governors. Founded in 1730s in the aftermath of Iranian Nadir Shah's invasion of India, Hyderabad was a continuation of the Mughal Empire, though in a limited way. Nadir Shah had looted Dilli (Delhi), massacred its population, and went back home after leaving the Mughal Empire in tatters. One of the nobles who helped stop the slaughter by Nadir Shah was Qamruddin Qilich Khan, a Seljuk Turk in Mughal service, later known as Asif Jah. In fact, it was Asif Jah who wrote in Turkish the peace treaty between Nadir Shah and the so-called Mughal Emperor Muhammad Shah, to whose name people added the word Rangeelay (playboy). However, disappointed by the state of affairs in Delhi, Asif Jah headed south and then established the state of Hyderabad. The Mughals recognized the state and gave him the title of Nizam. (Nizam was the title first given to Abu Ali Hassan Ibn Ali by Seljuk Emperor Alp Arsalan [1030-1073]. Because of his extraordinary success as a vizier, his full title was Nizamul Mulk. Known for his book Siyasatnama, Nizamul Mulk thought of establishing institutions to train bureaucrats for the Seljuk Empire. Those institutions were called madressahs. Nizamul Mulk prepared a tough course of study that was most modern of its times – language, administration, law, logic, history and mathematics.) Centuries later in Hyderabad, this title was held by six of Asif Jah's descendents until the state of Hyderabad came to an end in 1948, the last and seventh Nizam being Mir Osman Ali Khan.

The continuation of the state of Hyderabad for a quarter and two centuries and the kind of cultural flowering it witnessed go to negate the two theories advanced by British publicists. One was that the entire subcontinent was in a state of anarchy and the British gave

India peace; two, that it is the British who gave India an administrative system. Both are the figments of British imagination. In the first place, entire India was not in a state of anarchy when the East India Company started consolidating its rule. As Andrew Ward, an American author, points out in his book on the Cawnpore massacre – Our Bones are Scattered – but for the Mughals the British would have found India a desert, for it was the Mughals who gave India not only roads, bridges, canals, gardens, forts, tombs and architectural wonders but also an administrative system. The administrative system given by Akbar the Great was so sound that the British adopted it virtually unchanged as far as land management and revenue systems were concerned. Even the terminology remained Mughal – zila, taluka, taccavi, challan, and such military terms as subedar, naik, havildar, sepoy, etc. Pakistan and India till today run their administrative systems on the Mughal pattern as modified by the British.

As for anarchy, north India was, of course, in turmoil because of the corruption and decadence at the Mughal court, but the rest of India was peaceful. The state of Hyderabad gave peace and prosperity to its population, which was predominantly Hindu.

As Encyclopaedia Britannica remarks, it was a tribute to the Nizams' rule and the spirit of tolerance which governed Hyderabad that the Hindus preferred to live under a Muslim monarch rather than make common cause with Maratha warlords. One of Hyderabad's most brilliant prime ministers was a Hindu – Maharajah Sir Krishna Prashad. Under the Nizams, there was a flowering of Muslim culture. Among the institutes of learning the Nizams set up were the Osmania University and Darut Tarjuma or Translation Bureau, which began translating scientific books from English into Urdu. It also opened its coffers to men of learning and wisdom who began trekking to Hyderabad from the post-'mutiny' north India, which had been devastated by the 1857 war of independence. The liberal education and cultural atmosphere produced great scholars and attracted talents from other lands. These men included Raziuddin Siddiqi, who was recommended to the Noble prize committee for a prize in physics by Werner Heisenberg, the German quantum physicist; Prof Hamidullah, the noted Islamic scholar who translated the Quran into French, Marmaduke Pickthall, whose Glorious Koran is considered to be the holy book's most authentic translation and is widely quoted by the Orientalists, Maulvi Abdul Haq, who shifted the headquarters of the Anjuman-e-Tarrqi-e-Urdu to Aurangabad, Akhtar Hussain Raipuri, Josh Malihabadi, and scores of others, especially poets, educationists and scholars who moved to Hyderabad from Delhi, U.P. and Bihar. Hyderabad was also a mini-Islamic world: farmers came from the Punjab; soldiers from the NWFP, intellectuals, scholars and .poets from north India, and Arabs from Yemen – employed as treasury guards. Bureaucrats and judges came from Iran. The glory was snuffed out in September 1948 when Nehru ordered the invasion. If he wished he could have taken Hyderabad without war, because the Nizam state hardly had any armed forces.

That many Pakistanis did not then, and do not now, consider India the way I thought of that country has been a source of great anguish and sorrow for me. As time passed I realised – much later, when the damage had been done to my personality – that I considered Pakistan's enemies my personal enemies. This turned out to be a source of considerable social embarrassment for me and added to my discomfiture at gatherings where people who were more articulate than I seemed to prevail. The loss of Hyderabad, Junagadh and Kashmir were not issues that concerned the Pakistan Foreign Office or politicians or editorial writers; to me these were personal losses, and my life revolved round the unshakable belief that one day Pakistan would settle the score. For that single reason, I have loved Pakistan the way no other human being does. My family and friends double up with laughter when I tell them only two people loved Pakistan as much as I do – Jinnah and Bhutto. A third has not yet been born. For me Pakistan essentially existed for the benefit of my personal revanche against India, and I expected all Pakistanis to share my belief. I pity those Pakistanis who do not share my passion for the revanche. The flight from Parbhani took us to the railway station, from there to Balda, the colloquial term for the city of Hyderabad, the state's capital, and after a brief stay of a couple of months there to Aurangabad, my birthplace. While Father left for the Promised Land, we – Mother, brother Razi and three sisters, Qamar, Meher and Qaiser, and I – moved to Aurangabad to live with Ammi's brother, Zaheer. Zaheer had a daughter, Razia. In spite of the topsy-turvy way in which I have written this book and, in that process, played havoc with chronology, the reader must already know Razia.

We joined Father in Karachi in June 1949. I had come home. Two years ago I had heard over the radio the British government's historic June 3 plan which finally announced the partition of India and the birth of Pakistan. I could not follow the speeches and could catch a word or two. But two words I distinctly remember having heard – Jinnah coming on the radio and raising in his Anglicised accent the slogan Pakistan Zindabad! That was the defining moment of life. I have never ever wavered from the path that slogan laid down for me. I would never suffer – as pseudo-intellectuals and liberals have pretended to suffer – from an identity crisis. My identity had been established. I was a Pakistani and would remain so till my death. How wonderful it was that June in 1949 to be in Pakistan! All around me were Pakistanis. Could there be a more fortunate man than me? I have looked at Pakistan that way since that June afternoon, and the passing decades have only tended to reinforce my child's love for Pakistan. For me everything belonging to Pakistan is sacred: its rivers and mountains, its deserts and glaciers, and its fields and forests, and all its people. Those who do not regard Pakistan sacred – would they kindly leave Pakistan? That is the reason why, with the sole exception of Ziaul Haq, I have never really hated any Pakistani leader or government. Fools have often asked me whether I was a Muslim first or a Pakistani first. My obvious answer – that I am Pakistani first and Pakistani last – shocked them. While they – mostly people with a religious bent of mind but low in education and intellect – were shocked they didn't know I considered them imbeciles for asking a question whose obvious answer could be the same for all

– Pakistani first, Pakistani last. (If decades later Musharraf coined the slogan "Pakistan comes first" I assure you he stole the idea from me.) Today, when I look back at that arrival at the Keamari harbour on the June afternoon, my first sight of a camel, the powerful Karachi sea breeze, the wide streets, the magnificence of Bunder Road (now M. A. Jinnah Road), the KMC building, which is a stunningly beautiful example of Anglo-Mughal architecture, the well-ordered traffic, and a mass transit system in the form of the tramways, I still feel an extraordinary sense of peace and exhilaration. I have maintained and cherished that euphoria in spite of all that has happened. Nothing has shaken my belief in Pakistan or eroded my boundless love – even fascination – for this country. No wonder I have seldom welcomed strikes, marches, violence and revolution. In fact I hate them. The only time I wished there was widespread anti-government violence, even revolution, was during the Zia rule. But the revolution never came. Violence and massacres, in plenty, but no revolution. Ultimately, the mangoes exploded.

I got a full-time 9 to 5 job very early in life, and have since then wondered whether it is good to enter the world at such a young age. I remember that when I first appeared for a viva voce at an army recruitment centre in Kohat the officer asked me why I had got employed at such an early age and why the family could not support me. The army, of course, wants boys who are supposed to be officers by birth – officers to whom giving orders comes naturally. They don't want boys who lost a bit of the officer material in them by developing "a clerical mentality". From the benefit of hindsight I think there is considerable truth in this philosophy, for I have realised I have a tendency to be a younger brother, for I never was able to get the confidence of the elder brother. Friends and relatives have often been struck by the difference between me and Razi, my elder brother. Razi is outgoing, gregarious, warm-hearted, a spendthrift, and invariably a focus of everybody's attention because of the repertoire of jokes and repartees at his disposal. I am introvert, self-conscious and absolutely choosy about friends. I'd rather be alone than be in wrong company. Razi wants company and is perfectly at home in the company of men ranging from waiters and vendors to scholars and ministers. He is a born public relations man. I lack these qualities. The profession I have chosen for myself – journalism – does not consist of orders that come in the form of barks, though quite a few of my editors have barked at me. I have seldom barked, because I consider this inhuman and utterly repugnant to my religious beliefs. That's why the Pakistani ulema have disappointed me.

Whether exposure to the world at an early age becomes an asset or a liability depends upon how you enter the world. An industrial tycoon's son may be initiated into the system as an elevator boy. But that does not inhibit his hereditary cruelty toward workers. In my case, I entered the world as a typist-clerk in 1954, two years after completing my high school education from Bahadur Yar Jang High School in 1952. The school is still there on Jamshed Road in the midst of indescribably dirty surroundings. The boys were mostly from Hyderabad, and the school was created and built hurriedly to cater to them. It is amazing how in 1949, when the post-partition chaos was still there, the school got going. There were only five of us in Class VIII – Zaheer, Habib Ali, Shaukat, Lateef Kamal and me. Shaukat joined the army, was injured in the Rann of Cutch clashes in 1965 and retired as Major. Zaheer grew up to become a banker, while Habib Ali became a librarian by profession, working, among others, for the British Council library which was then located in what is now Pakistan Chowk. He was in PIA when he died in the '90s. while Zaheer died in 2007. By the time I reached the 10th Class, the number of students had swelled. Extraordinary as it sounds four of them, besides me, would take to journalism. One of them was Raza Ali Abidi, whose voice would be heard by millions of people over the BBC's Urdu service. Another fellow student, Ghazi Salahuddin, became my colleague in Dawn in 1973. But he had begun his career in an evening English daily, The Leader. Of him more later. Two others who entered the world of journalism were Sanaullah and Shareef Kamal Usmani, Yasser's elder brother. Sanaullah and Yusuf both worked for several Urdu dailies, including Hurriyet, which was once owned by the Haroons.

That brought Yusuf and Sanaullah to the same building where I worked. Both have passed away. Another student who joined me in the 10th class was Ahmad Ali. He went to England for higher studies, became a psychiatrist, and was once head of a group of London hospitals. He now practices at Harley Street. The teachers included Jamil Jalbi. He would later become the Vice Chancellor of the University of Karachi, Head of Muqtadera (Language Authority) and Chairman of the Urdu Lughat (Dictionary) Board. One of his monumental works has included a five-volume history of Urdu literature. In his eighties, he is still going strong. Another teacher I would remain personally grateful to forever is Ishaq, who too fortunately is with us. When I passed my high school exam – "matric" exam, as South Asians say – I had no money to enrol in a college. The fee was something in the neighbourhood of Rs 125, which those days was a fortune. Ishaq gave it to me. Till this day I wonder whether I would have been able to enter college if Ishaq had not helped me.

What characterised boys and girls those days was an extraordinary spirit of defiance of circumstances – an irresistible zeal to forge ahead and not let the partition trauma dampen their spirits. It was normal for all boys if not girls to acquire education while having a job. If moral values are immutable, then some aspect of how they set out to make their lives can be censured. Normally, it is impossible to have a full-time 9 to 5 job while at the same time acquiring a college education. Undoubtedly, the elders helped – elders who ran colleges and government departments. Often boys would attend classes early in the morning and reach their places of work several hours late. Normally, the boss would show understanding, because of the post-partition circumstances and because of the way the young men were struggling to help their parents and themselves. If the boss was of the "wrong" type, the boy would choose an evening college, or perhaps choose an evening job while going to college in the morning. But in most cases, most boys were able – with help from, I say, society – to combine both a fulltime job with education. My own office – the Karachi Joint Water Board, which can be called the forerunner of today's Karachi Water and Sewerage Board – was located at what was then called Ninth Mile – that being the distance between the Karachi Central Post Office and the building which housed the Civil Circle of the KJWB, which I joined perhaps in May when summer vacations had begun.. Today Ninth Mile is in the middle of the city, somewhat next to Awami Markaz. My college – Urdu College – was then located off Princess Street. It is still there but has acquired the status of a university. I could not possibly be at college in the morning and be at the KJWB at the same time. Fortunately, before the vacation ended, I managed to get myself transferred to the KJWB head office located in Napier Barracks, right in Karachi's heart. It was now relatively easy for me to combine education with a job. Often I came late, and the bosses looked the other way. Till this day I am grateful to them for helping me. I made up for the classes missed in college by pouring over books in the evening. The most painful part of the situation was that now I had no time for cricket.

As usual politics was discussed at the KJWB office, as we do now, but there was one difference: today, when Pakistanis talk politics they talk about domestic politics, and that is how it should be. But those days I noticed my office colleagues – my seniors especially – talked mostly about the partition holocaust and about Indo-Pakistan affairs. Today, our heroes and villains are Pakistani politicians, depending upon your political loyalties; those days Pakistani leaders were the heroes, and the villains invariably were Indian leaders, especially Mountbatten, Nehru, Patel and Krishna Menon, the first two especially because of their Kashmir grab. Most of my senior colleagues were from northern India – especially Delhi, the United Province and Bihar – and they exchanged countless stories about the Hindu-Muslim riots, trains being attacked, the butchery, of relatives lost, of the arrival in the Promised Land and the early struggle to settle down and get going. For me, partition essentially meant the Indian attack on Hyderabad and the flight from Parbhani. But then suddenly one domestic development seemed to be the talk of the town: Governor General Ghulam Mohammad dissolved the Constituent Assembly on October 24. 1954. Even though I was then a college student, regrettably I was unable understand the implications of GM's action – GM, for that's how Dawn identified him in its headlines. Eighteen months earlier – on April 17, 1953, – he had dismissed Prime Minister Nazimuddin's government. The assembly GM dissolved served both as parliament and as a constitution-making body, because Pakistan till then did not have a constitution. GM's actions had two grave consequences: first, the process of constitution-making was disrupted; second, a prime minister was dismissed even though he enjoyed the assembly's confidence. The dissolution of the Constituent Assembly by the Governor General was challenged in the Chief Court of Sindh by Maulvi Tamizuddin Khan, the Assembly's President, and the court declared GM's action unconstitutional. However, the Governor General went in appeal, and on March 21, 1955, the Federal Court upheld the assembly's dissolution.

GM had won, but he had not only struck a crippling blow at democracy, he had set a precedent which would be followed later by several heads of state. While dismissing the Nazimuddin ministry and dissolving the assembly he had raised arguments which would be used by latter-day dictators to interfere in the working of constitutional government. Decades later, General Ziaul Haq would arrogate to himself powers to dismiss a government even if the prime minister enjoyed the assembly's confidence and dissolving the assembly itself, and for this had changed the basic law through a series of decrees. The Constitution framed under Bhutto's guidance and passed unanimously by the National Assembly in 1973 was a parliamentary one, in which all executive powers rested with the prime minister, the president being a titular head of state. However, Ziaul Haq through a decree amended the 1973 Constitution and inserted inter alia article 58-2b, which gave him the power to sack the prime minister and dissolve the assembly. Later, two civilian presidents, Ghulam Ishaq Khan and Farooq Leghari, would invoke this law to sack three prime ministers. Ishaq dismissed Benazir Bhutto in 1990 and Nawaz Sharif in 1993. Leghari sacked Benazir in

1996. Nawaz Sharif, when he returned to power a second time with a heavy majority in early 1997, repealed article 58-2b. President Pervez Musharraf re-inserted the article back into the Constitution.

While GM was being criticised in drawing rooms and offices, the national scene was one of peace, for the man in the street seemed utterly indifferent to the assembly's dissolution and went about his business as usual. To find a new prime minister GM – his health failing – could find no one in Pakistan to be the prime minister and chose to recall Pakistan's ambassador in Washington, Mohamed Ali Bogra, to replace Nazimuddin. He was made a member of the ruling Muslim League and sworn in as prime minister. GM and the man who replaced him as GG, Iskander Mirza, would, between them, make five prime ministers go – Bogra, Chaudhry Mohamed Ali, Husseyn Shaheed Suhrawardy, a brilliant lawyer from East Pakistan, and Sir Malik Firoz Khan Noon. Even though Mirza, who became acting Governor General on August 7, 1955, did not have the constitutional powers to dismiss the prime ministers, he manipulated the situation to his advantage and found ready supporters among the politicians. His most unfortunate choice as Chief Minister of West Pakistan was Dr Khan. Along with his more famous brother, Abdul Ghaffar Khan, he was Jinnah and Pakistan's most rabid opponent. Known as Frontier Gandhi, Ghaffar Khan was more loyal to Congress than perhaps Nehru and Gandhi, and copied Gandhi in lifestyle. To quote Philip Talbot from his book An American Eyewitness to India's Partition, Ghaffar Khan's "burning resentment against everything British... is matched only by his devotion to Gandhi... probably the central Gandhian ideal has few more devoted supporters than the man who himself came to be called the Frontier Gandhi". Even though the NWFP had a 99.9 per cent Muslim majority, the two brothers wanted it to join Hindu India rather than Muslim Pakistan. On the eve of partition, Dr Khan was the Chief Minister of the North-Western Frontier Province because the Congress Party to which he belonged had a majority in the provincial assembly. For this sole reason, the British government's June 3 Plan partitioning India had called for a plebiscite in the NWFP to decide whether it would join Pakistan or India. However, because they knew what the results of the plebiscite would be the Khan brothers announced a boycott of the plebiscite, saying that there should have been a third option – Pakistan, India or an independent Pakhtoonistan. When Pakistan won the plebiscite, held in July 1947, Dr Khan, who had promised to resign if the people voted for Pakistan, went back on his words and continued to remain chief minister till his government was dismissed.

A lot of nonsense has been written about the Congress ministry's dismissal after Pakistan came into being, and it was alleged that Jinnah had taken an unconstitutional step by dismissing the Khan ministry. The truth is entirely different. Jinnah throughout his struggle for Pakistan never took an unconstitutional step. As Talbot quotes him as saying, "I am constitutionally and by long habit a very cold-blooded logician". In Talbot's view "no one could have analysed him better". The truth is that the Khan ministry had lost its majority in the provincial assembly. As partition neared, non-Muslim members of the assembly left for India, while the independents started joining the Muslim League, thus making it the majority party. Meanwhile the partition riots had begun. By losing the referendum the Congress ministry had also lost credibility with the people of the NWFP, and the euphoric Muslim League supporters were parading in the streets because the vote had gone in their favour. Pakistan was a reality, and Dr Khan's minority government, bankrupt politically and morally, was unable to maintain law and order. The Governor reported the situation to the Viceroy at New Delhi, Lord Mountbatten, who agreed with the Governor's assessment of the situation and said the ministry must be dismissed. In the meantime, Mountbatten appointed a new Governor, who found the same anarchic situation in the NWFP, with the minority Khan government unable to maintain peace. Pakistan had now come into being, and the new Governor wrote to the Governor-General, who was now Jinnah, and Jinnah ordered that the Governor should perform his constitutional duty under the 1935 Act and dismiss the minority government. When the Pakistan flag was unfurled, Dr Khan did not turn up at the oath-taking ceremony. A decade later Iskander Mirza made this character the chief minister of the newly constituted West Pakistan province, and it goes without saying that he lent full help to Mirza in the making unmaking of the ministries and had a hand in the dismissal of some popular prime ministers, including Suhrawardy. During this era there was at least one prime minister who did not give his political enemies the chance to manoeuvre his dismissal. Ismail Ibrahim Chundrigar, who belonged to the Muslim League, chose to resign on a matter of principle. He had joined a coalition government that included the Republican Party on the condition that One Unit and the system of separate electorates (separate voting lists for Muslim and non-Muslim voters) would be maintained. When the RP reneged on its promise, Chundrigar resigned. Dawn welcomed his appointment. In an editorial entitled The New Cabinet, the paper said in its editorial of October 19, 1957, "Out of evil cometh good...It was not a case of the Muslim League running after power but rather of power running after (the Muslim League)." The most significant part of the comment was: "When a week ago, Mr Suhrawardy resigned at the President's request and a new political crisis confronted the country, even our best friends were assailed by fresh doubts about Pakistan ever attaining real stability". The editorial writer would not have believed that half a century later "our best friends" would still be "assailed by fresh doubts about (a nuclear-armed) Pakistan ever attaining real stability"

The impact of these political developments on the people was negative, though subtle. Nobody came on the streets to burn and kill the way Pakistani mobs do now. But cynicism was in the air, for everybody accused the politicians of indifference to national interests and pursuing what appeared to be partisan and personal interests. I think the reaction showed the political immaturity of the Pakistani middle class. Considering the quality of politicians who would come later, the politicians of this era were angels. What must be acknowledged to their credit is the fact that they observed the rules of the game. Whether in power or in the opposition, they behaved with dignity. There was usual criticism of each other's policies, and coalition governments — full of compromises and having incompatible allies — were formed and broken, but seldom did one find the politicians calling for their opponents' blood. Most of them had quite high education, and they meticulously observed the British parliamentary norms which the Raj had bequeathed to them. If in the opposition, they did not go into self-exile, and if in power they did not believe in throwing political opponents into dungeons, issuing white papers against their misdeeds, unleashing intelligence hounds against them and their families, and torturing and even executing them.

Meanwhile, a second 80-member Constituent Assembly, elected by the provincial assemblies, enacted the country's first constitution, which was scheduled to be enforced on March 23, 1956. On March 5 Mirza was elected the country's first President. His last act as Governor General was to sign the proclamation of the Islamic Republic of Pakistan that signalled the end of what used to be "dominion status" under the British Commonwealth, with the head of state being the Governor General technically appointed by the British monarch.

Looking at Dawn's old issues, especially the one reporting the Republic Day celebrations, you are hit by the shocking difference between what society and politics in Pakistan were then and what they are now. To wit, Pakistan then was a normal country. Today, living in Hobbes's state of nature — a war of all against all, and "the life of man nasty, brutish and short" — we of the 21st century Pakistan would think the people in our country then lived in a state of bliss. They were normal the way the people of Mozambique and Bulgaria today are. There were no fire-brand clerics making war on women and music and art and all finer things of life, nor were individuals and groups thirsting for each other's blood the way we do now. On March 23, a Friday, there was a public rally at Jahangir Park, Karachi, then the federal capital. Reading the proceedings of the rally in Dawn would make you wonder why those pre-Ayub politicians were later so demonized by the martial law regime that overthrew Sir Malik Feroz Khan's civilian government in October

1958. By a modest estimate 100,000 people turned up at Jahangir Park to hear their leaders. Also to speak at the rally were some of the 41 foreign delegates who had come to Karachi to greet the Pakistani people and government on that historic occasion. These leaders included Turkish prime minister Adnan Menderes (alas, hanged later by a general), Prince Fahd of Saudi Arabia, Chinese Vice-Premier Marshal Ho Lung, and a certain Colonel Anwar Saadat, representing Egypt, who prefaced his speech with the first verse of Sura Fathh: "Verily, We have granted thee a manifest victory". Also present was Russian Deputy Prime Minister Anastas Mikoyan. (The same evening at a Pakistan Embassy reception in Moscow, according to a Reuter-AFP report, Soviet Foreign Minister V. M. Molotov offered a steel mill to Pakistan.) Mr Jefferson Caffery, America's Special Envoy, said he had been asked by President Eisenhower personally to convey his congratulations and good wishes to the people of Pakistan, while Commander Allan Noble, MP, said he felt honoured that Sir Anthony Eden should have named him as Britain's special envoy for Pakistan's republic day celebrations. Can any Pakistani city today host a public meeting which would be attended by 41 foreign VIPs without the greater part of the city being turned into a no-go area and transformed into a festung?

That day on March 23, 1956, there were policemen carrying only batons, unlike today's police with AK-47s and the most modern communication equipment. Those baton-carrying policemen managed a crowd of 100,000.

There was a parliamentary opposition then, too, but the respect with which all political leaders treated each other is inconceivable today, and Suhrawardy addressed the meeting at Prime Minister Chaudhri Mohammad Ali's request. There was an incident, though. Guess what? — a bomb blast, an act of arson, a machine-gun spewing fire? No, when the Indian representative, Meher Chand Khanna, rose to speak, the crowd refused to hear him. "No, no, we don't want to listen to you," the crowd said, according to the Dawn report, and it was left to the prime minister to rise and tell the crowd to calm down and let their

Indian guest speak. Anti-Indian chauvinism, no doubt, but there the Dawn report also makes it clear that the government and the people were united in a wave of euphoria that swept the nation on Pakistan becoming a republic.

Earlier in the morning, as Iskander Mirza reviewed the armed forces' parade at the Polo Ground, Nara-i-Takbir replaced Three Cheers for the Governor-General! The parade comprised army, naval and air force units, while the fly-past consisted of old Furies and the newly-acquired jets. Three formations of Furies were led by Sq. Ldr Ahmad, a formation of Attackers by Fl. Lt. Inam and a formation of T-33s by Air Cdr Asghar Khan. Jahangir Park was linked to Radio Pakistan's national hook-up, but, without electricity in most villages and small towns, the public meeting must have been a non-event for the vast majority of the people. Today, cable networks would bring such a meeting to millions of Pakistani homes, but absent would be the Pakistan nationalism that was in evidence at that rally on that historic Friday. But then we should show an understanding of today's chaotic Pakistan. The sense of triumph and achievement generated by the establishment of Pakistan — then the world's biggest Muslim country in terms of population — could not and did not last long. Today, the people of Pakistan are focussed on themselves and demand a solution to their problems. Pakistan is a fact, and the people would like to know what Pakistan has given them. In their cynicism they may appear to talk treason. In 1956, there was little political consciousness, and the dissolution of the constituent assembly by the Governor-General in 1954 had evoked no response from the people. Today even a minor affair like the appointment of a controversial judge to a provincial High Court becomes a national issue overnight, with people ready to shed blood. Today individuals and groups and sub-groups are not only conscious of their rights, they are prepared to resort to violence to achieve them. The Pakistan of 1956 was a Mohajir-urban-Punjabi affair. Sindhi and Pathan middle-classes hardly existed, and people with Sindhi names appeared only in newspaper reports — Khuhro, Pirzada, Rashdi, Talpur. One name that was to rock Pakistan and shake the people into becoming conscious of their rights was yet unknown to the nation — Bhutto.

Politics was then confined to palaces and more than a decade was to pass before Zulfiqar Ali Bhutto was to take it to the streets. The middle class was small. Industrialisation had not yet begun; nobody knew where and what Dubai was, and the green card perhaps referred to annual school results. Cities were still run on the pre-independence British pattern, and the bus was the principal mode of transport for the urban middle class. Now we live in dread of traffic jams. Industrialization, Dubai money, the Green Card and the great trek from villages to cities were to give diabolical dimensions to urban life, making crime and violence a fact of daily life. The biggest difference between 1956 and 2009 when these lines are being written lies in the weaponization of our politics and society now. To this harsh reality must be added religious and ethnic militancy. Pakistan then presented a scene of placidity, tranquillity and normality inconceivable today. The biggest weapon in the hand of a goon was a knife; students went to college to study and not to have gun battles; bus-burning had still not caught on as a hobby, and the leadership that was to forbid male doctors from treating women patients was still in hibernation.

Earlier in the morning, at 7.05 precisely, Iskander Mirza signed the resolution proclaiming Pakistan as a republic. This was his last act as Governor-General. Minutes later, Mr Justice Mohammad Munir — remember this name that has become an unforgettable and notorious part of our constitutional history? — administered the oath of office to Mirza as Pakistan's first President. Mirza then drove to the Polo Ground for the armed forces' parade and uttered these words (heavens must surely have laughed): "This is a democratic country and, as your Commander-in-Chief, I have sworn to ensure that in accordance with the constitution the will of the people will prevail". Thirty-one months later he struck. If only he had been true to his words, Pakistan's history would have been less traumatic. In its issue of March 23, 1956, Dawn published a long poem by Else Qazi and Parwaiz Shami, whose last stanza said:

> Swear by the tear-stained flowers on
> Quaid's tomb
> That through thick and thin, through ebb
> and tide
> In deepest sorrow and in highest glee
> Shall e'er abide with our hope and pride
> With thee Islamic Republic ... with thee!

The constitution was parliamentary in character, the president was a titular head of state, and all powers lay with the prime minister, who would obviously command the assembly's confidence. The 1956 Constitution's biggest achievement – and this goes to the politicians' credit – was a novel formula that laid down the principle of "parity" to solve a demographic anomaly: East Pakistan, situated 1,000 miles from West Pakistan, but constituting less than one fourth of the country's area, contained 56 per cent of the population. This meant that, in a given situation, MPs from East Pakistan would always carry the day. Given the differences between East and West Pakistan in terms of languages spoken and the wide physical and cultural disparities, this was cause for concern. So it was decided that, in spite of having a majority, East Pakistan would send the same number of deputies to the federal parliament as West Pakistan – in other words both "wings" of the country agreed to a 50% share of parliamentary seats. This showed a commendable spirit of accommodation and tolerance among those who were later sought to be discredited and demonised. The frequent changes in the cabinet, the appointment of new ministers and prime ministers, the redistribution of portfolios and mutual mudslinging were made fun of by the people, and newspaper editorials, columnists and poets wrote pieces full of sarcasm and humour. But still the democratic game went on. I remember listening to Prime Minister Suhrawardy when he was the chief guest at a Karachi University students' function. In his speech he referred to the criticism in the press about the power game, but said it would continue till a general election was held. The election, scheduled for early 1959, was never held and the country experienced its first bout of military dictatorship in October 1958 when Iskander Mirza and General (later Field Marshal) Ayub Khan overthrew Malik Feroz Noon's civilian government, abrogated the 1956 Constitution and promulgated martial law.

The letter Mirza wrote to Noon has largely remained unknown to the people of Pakistan. Noon, however, reproduced the letter in full in his book From Memory:

"President's House, Karachi, 7th October 1958

"My dear Sir Feroz:

"After very careful searching of the heart I have come to the conclusion that the country cannot be sound unless I take full responsibility and take over the administration. The constitution of the 3rd March (sic), 1956, is not only unworkable but dangerous to the integrity – and solidarity – of Pakistan. If we go on trying to work it we will have to say goodbye to Pakistan.

"As head of the state, therefore, I have decided to abrogate the constitution, take over all powers, dissolve the assemblies, the parliament and the central and provincial cabinets. My only regret is that this drastic, revolutionary action I have to take while you were Prime Minister. By the time you get this letter Martial Law will come into operation, and General Ayub, whom I have appointed as the Chief Martial Law Administrator, will be in position.

"For you personally, I have great regard and will do all that is necessary for your personal happiness and well-being.

"Yours sincerely

"Iskander Mirza."

After receiving the envelope, the prime minister asked the messenger, who was Mirza's A.D.C., to wait for his reply. The A.D.C. said, "Sir, there won't be a reply" (p 298).

A few days later the two met at a reception given by Sir William Cawthorn, the Australian High Commissioner. The former prime minister and the reigning president, who himself would be ousted a few weeks later, did not come to blows. There were some foreign pressmen present, who later quoted Mirza as saying, "My only regret is that all this happened during the time when the greatest gentleman in the county was my Prime Minister". Noon wrote in his book that this was "small satisfaction when the fate of a country was at stake". Noon did not know that the subsequent coup makers and their victims would never have the decency to be together at a reception. One of Noon's greatest acts of service to Pakistan was to add 2,400 square miles to its territory, for he managed to purchase Gwadar from Muscat in 1958. He got interested in Gwadar as foreign minister in Suhrawardy's cabinet, but felt frustrated because success was hard to come. Noon felt that without Gwadar "we were living in a house in which the backdoor was occupied by a stranger who could, at any time, sell us out to a power inimical to Pakistan and who would also be willing to pay any price for the sale". It was, however, as prime minister that he succeeded in his mission when Pakistan's High Commissioner in London, M. Ikramullah, handed the sale deed to him. Britain helped, and in his book Noon thanks Prime Minister Harold Macmillan, Foreign Secretary Selwyn Lloyd and Commonwealth Secretary Lord Home. India was naturally unhappy over a deal that was in Pakistan's interest. This is typical of the zero-sum game between the two. When Noon met Nehru some time later in New Delhi the Indian prime minister said "I see, you have taken Gwadar". He was worried about "our people", by which he meant Gwadar's Hindu population. Noon put him at ease by saying he would give Gwadar's 300 Hindus Pakistani nationality. He kept his word. This Noon became one of the "discredited" politicians. Gwadar would remain a neglected fishing port for the next four decades, and it would not be until the 21st century that Pakistan would turn its attention to this valuable port that is so close to its sources of oil supply.

Balochistan has seen many political storms, including army action, and there is no doubt its people have many grievances, but for the life of me I cannot understand why Baloch "nationalists" claiming to fight for their people's rights should have objected to building and modernisation of the Gwadar port when the task was undertaken by the Musharraf government. The Karachi port is over-worked. Port Bin Qasim, situated on Karachi's periphery, basically looks after things connected with the steel mill there, but all the country's imports and exports are done through Karachi, which also is a major naval base. Karachi's successful blockade by a hostile power could mean Pakistan grinding to a halt. The building of a second port close to the Gulf was, thus, long over due. Finally, thanks to China, Gwadar is now developing rapidly. If it continues to grow this way, there is no doubt it has the potential to become a major port of trade not only for Pakistan but also, Afghanistan, Central Asia and western China. For the Pakistan Navy it will be a strategic asset and serve as a major base away from India.

Another of Noon's sagacious acts was to appoint Prince Aly Khan as Pakistan's ambassador to the United Nations. The move was initially opposed within the government, but Noon turned out to be right, for Aly became a diplomatic asset for Pakistan. Given his family background and the glamorous personality he had, Aly was the most sought-after diplomat in America, and it became a matter of prestige from New York to Hollywood who got invited to the Pakistan Day receptions. Aga Khan III – as many a grandfather has done in history – ignored his sons and appointed Aly's son, Karim, his successor. The Aga Khan family was devoted to Pakistan, and Aga Khan the Great can be considered one of Pakistan's founders. Decades later Prince Karim registered himself as a Pakistani when he took part in a Swiss ski contest. It is most unfortunate that Pakistan has now lost the goodwill of many minority communities because of the wave of bigotry and narrow-mindedness that has gripped the county. The Aga Khan's advice to his followers had been to live in peace in whatever country they had chosen to be their home. In Pakistan, the Ismailis have had a constructive attitude toward the country and contributed to its economic development, especially in the health sector. Yet, regretfully, that's not how everybody looks at them. (See chapter 10).

※※※※※※※

I was still the KWJB's typist-clerk when I first made an attempt to get into the army. Before candidates were called for tests and interview at Kohat, where the Inter-Services Selection Board was located, they were to take written tests in English and general knowledge. It goes without saying that I passed them, headed for Kohat, cleared all the tests and interviews but was rejected medically. The finding was "substandard weight and chest".

"Why are you in a hurry, boy?" said a medical officer. "You still have many years ahead of you. Come later, well fed".

I returned to Kohat four years later, when I was a journalism student at the University of Karachi, went through the routine tests and interview and was rejected medically – finally. The reason for the medical rejection sent a chill down my spine: "pulmonary tuberculosis quiescent". Half a century has passed, and I should have been in my grave now, but seldom has anyone caught me coughing. As we will presently see, I was to appear before army medical boards twice more, and they declared me physically fit! Rejection twice by the ISSB meant the end of my hopes for wearing a Pakistan Army uniform. But my hopes were revived in 1964, when I was a subeditor at Morning News, and the army invited applications from journalists for recruitment to its public relations department. This time I passed even the medical test – no trace of the "quiescent" pulmonary TB. I waited and waited but the call never came. In the meantime, in May, as I have mentioned elsewhere, I made a dash to India to get Razia to Pakistan. On return to Pakistan, I made discreet inquiries as to why I had not been called. An uncle of mine was Deputy Defence Secretary. He told me the truth, "A man gets selected by the Pakistan Army, and he dashes off to India. Do you think the army is crazy to hire him? If I had known I would have stopped you from going to India."

A few months later, there were reports that the army wanted to raise a semi-military militia by the name of Mujahid Force as a reserve force, and those interested in joining were asked to contact the army. Needless to say I turned up at the Army Selection Centre on Sharea Faisal and was given the philosophy behind the decision. From the benefit of hindsight I can say that the government expected a war with India, because the plans for sending large-scale commandos into Indian occupied Kashmir were obviously in advanced stages. The Mujahid Force was meant to give military training to young men, who could then go back to civilian life, called back for refresher courses and if necessary deployed during war. The army officer – if I remember correctly his name was Sabzvari – asked me whether I could raise a company in the area where I lived. Once I raised such a company the army would then make arrangements for training. I lived in Nazimabad, a middle class locality with 99 per cent literary rate, highly unconscious politically, with the young population consisting of boys who were either indifferent to the Ayub government or were supporters of the Islami Jamiat-i-Taleba, the student wing of the Jamaat-i-Islam. Their priorities lay elsewhere.

"If you raise the militia in Nazimabad, you would be company commander, and we will provide you military training, call you periodically for refresher courses, and put your company in the reserves".

To me, the whole idea appeared bizarre, and I gave him the reason why it was not possible for a force to be raised in that area. Could I be sent to some other company in the city?

There was a Keamari Company ready for training, and if I wished, he said, he would post me to that company.

"Yes" I replied.

"But", he said, "you cannot be the company commander. The Keamari Company consists of tough dock workers, and you must be one of them and speak their language to be able to command them."

As I later learnt, those in the KC were mostly Pathans and Punjabis, besides a small number of Urdu-speaking toughs from the lower classes.

"I can send you to KC but not as Company Commander."

I readily agreed. Our training began I think in March when the Rann of Cutch clashes were going on. The training consisted of rifle shooting, bayonet fighting, grenade use, drills and elementary infantry tactics. The Company Commander, though, was Urdu speaking, lived in the area and spoke fluent Punjabi. Our trainers were from the army, and they deferred to me. What angered me was that I was spared manual work. For instance we were given the size of a given ditch and told to dig. But the moment I picked up the pick-axe they would say, "Tusi na karo janab!" (Not you, sir.) Or if ammunition boxes or blocks of cement were to be moved I would be told to take rest. This made me very angry, but I had to curb my anger because they thought they were being kind to me. A greater problem was my social isolation, for when we rested and the boys talked among themselves I just did not know who to interact with. I tried to talk to them but such was the cultural disparity it was difficult to strike a conversation at the same wave length. Sometimes the trainers came to me and talked to me about the work I did as a journalist and about my family life. When I look back at those six weeks, I am wonderstruck by the fact that I could summon that much energy, for I did not take any leave from Morning News. All I demanded was that I should be put on the mid-shift beginning 2pm. So, while I would be doing left and right at a Keamari sports stadium that served as our training ground and learning bayonet charge till 1pm I would be in my newspaper office for the mid-shift ending at 8 pm. Crawling with a rifle hurt my elbows and knees, and the sores at the elbow became a source of a wide variety of comments of all sorts. Some journalists colleagues tried to suppress their smiles; someone said "You surely will go down in history as Conqueror of Kashmir", but some seniors showed a lot of sympathy. One of them, now dead, said, "If there are more people like you, Pakistan will be a different country." After six weeks the course came to an end, and we were taken to an army firing range to give to "big officers" a practical demonstration of our ability to shoot. If I remember correctly the "biggest" officer was a Major. I emptied my magazine and showed it to him. I still have with me the certificate the army gave me for completing the course.

On September 6, a date my generation is not going to forget, the Indian Army attacked across the international border, some five days after Pakistan had launched an offensive in the Chhamb-Jaurian area in Indian-occupied Kashmir. Like most Pakistanis, I was moved by Ayub's speech. He was the man of the hour. Till then he was my hero, and even though Bhutto later monopolised my loyalty and devotion, especially after the ceasefire and the Tashkent Declaration, I sill retain my admiration for Ayub Khan. There is no doubt he has been Pakistan's best ruler. The Johnson administration was hostile to Pakistan because of the close relationship Islamabad and Beijing had developed, especially after the 1962 India-China clash in the Himalayas. Far from supporting what was supposed to be America's "most allied ally", the Democratic administration cut off the supplies of military spares to Pakistan. British Prime Minister Harold Wilson was sympathetic, summoned the Indian High Commissioner to his office and demanded that India halt all military action across the international border. He repeated the Pakistani version of the attack – "the entire Indian Army less four divisions" was attacking in the Punjab. What mattered to me, however, was the "mobilisation" of the Keamari Company. A more mighty fighting machine the world hadn't seen.

The KC was headquartered in a naval establishment. I think it was PNS Dilawar. We were deployed along the oil pipeline in the Keamari area near the beach, and that's where I had roared. All was quiet, and the darkness all enveloping. Only the stars shone in the brilliant September sky without clouds. There wasn't even an air raid. "Will the Indian Navy attack?" I asked myself. "How wonderful that will be!" I patrolled the beach and felt very important and very Mujahid. I didn't know that decades later the concept and the very word Mujahid would be debased, and the self-proclaimed mujahids would kill more fellow

Muslims than they would kill infidels. They would kill Benazir and exchange congratulations on the cellphone. I did not stay awake the whole night. I was given relief, a charpoy was provided by someone living in a hut close to my "area of operation" and I slept off. But that night has been unforgettable for me. The greatest moment was the Isha prayer, with full boots on, the rifle lying beside me. I felt myself to be at Gallipoli. (I learnt later that the Turkish name for the peninsula was less romantic – Galibolu.) For the next night I was given rest. I slept on the floor on mattresses along with other KC men and was told there would be an inspection in the morning. After breakfast, as we stood in line, a Colonel came to inspect us. He asked every KC man his name, assessed him and moved on as the Navy men watched our rag-tag contingent with amusement. The officer came in front of me, stared at me and asked me my name – in English! I wondered why he spoke English.

As I gave him my name, he asked, "Education?"

"M. A. Political Science", I said. This was a tactical blunder. I should have replied in Urdu, "5 classes".

"M. A. Political Science?" He halted. "Amazing! What are you doing here? Step out!" He gestured with his hand.

Half an hour later I was at the Station Headquarters on Sharea Faisal, banging on a typewriter. I pleaded that I should be allowed to go to "the front" to do my duty to Pakistan. He replied that everybody must do that bit of duty to which he was most suited. KC wasn't exactly the best place for me, and I could better serve the cause of Pakistan's defence by typing those sheets. He asked me to go home for the night and return to the

Station Headquarters in the morning. Meanwhile, the war seemed to be moving toward a stalemate. At the United Nations, Bhutto made one of his most emotional speeches and reminded the Security Council on September 22 of what he had said a year ago: "We will wage a war for 1,000 years, a war of defence". A year ago, when he had raised the subject of Kashmir a Western diplomat had told him that he had brought "a dead horse" to the Council for the benefit of internal propaganda. "But the world must know that the 100 million people of Pakistan will never abandon their pledges and promises – we shall never abandon ours. Irrespective of our size and of our resources we shall fight to the end. But we shall fight in self-defence, we shall fight for honour. We are not aggressors, we are the victims of aggression." It was the duty of the Security Council, he said, "to pronounce itself on who is the aggressor and who is the aggressee. It was Pakistan that was the victim of aggression". Bhutto then read out the message he had received "from the President of Pakistan, which I received from Rawalpindi at 2 o'clock (which is 11 o'clock W.P.S.T.) today (September 22, 1965): 'Pakistan considers Security Council Resolution 211 of 20 September as unsatisfactory. However, in the interest of international peace and in order to enable the Security Council to evolve a self-executing procedure, which will lead to an honourable settlement of the root cause of the present conflict" (Bhutto halted and added the words on his own "namely, the Jammu and Kashmir dispute") I have issued the following order to the Pakistan armed forces. They will stop fighting as from 12.05 hours West Pakistan Time today. As from that time they will not fire on enemy forces unless fired upon, provided the Indian Government issues similar orders to its armed forces. Please accept, Excellencies, the assurances of my highest consideration".

I reported back to Morning News. My war was over – but not the spirit of revanche. In 1966, the army advertised for PASRO – Pakistan Army Supplementary Reserve of Officers. It goes without saying that I went again through the same process of vetting, and was finally selected – even medically. But the call never came. The dream would continue – till I had the satisfaction of seeing Faisal in uniform at Petaro Cadet College 12 years later. From 1954 to 1978 – nearly a quarter century, deserving a mention in the Guinness Book of World Records, if it has a Pakistani version.

Until he agreed to the ceasefire, Ayub had been my hero. Looking back at all that has happened to Pakistan since his resignation in March 1969 following countrywide disturbances, one cannot but come to the conclusion that he has been Pakistan's best ruler. The country has not known peace the way it did under his 11-year rule. He was a benign ruler, though his system appeared authoritarian. The methods he adopted to give himself legitimacy were later followed by other generals. He introduced the concept of "basic democracy" which provided for indirect elections to the federal and provincial assemblies. He was much criticised for this, but given Pakistan's political instability, especially in the formative years, he had a point. But he was not the first to think of it, for Mirza had several times spoken of "controlled democracy". Ayub's system depended upon 80,000 Basic Democrats, who were elected by direct adult franchise. In February 1960 Ayub sought legitimacy to his rule by organising a referendum in which the Basic Democrats were asked to decide whether they had confidence in Ayub as their ruler. Razi had been elected as a Basic Democrat from a Nazimabad, Karachi, constituency on the Jamaat-i-Islami's ticket. Till then a complete mullah, Razi would undergo a radical transformation in thinking and personality in two decades and would be lurking on the fringes of agnosticism. What caused the transformation was the interest he had developed in philosophy and political thought. He became a voracious reader, kept studying Marxist literature till late into night and went to his office the next morning with a load of un-slept hours. No wonder his eyes seemed to be sinking in. Within no time some of Pakistan's leading comrades were his friends, and it became difficult to argue with him on any subject because his analysis revolved round "the Party". In the sixties, however, nothing mattered to him but al-Jamaat, Arabic for "the Party". Razi's wife is a military scientist, who recently retired after working on Pakistan's secret defence projects. She has no interest in Razi's philosophical musings and his other interest, music. However, they have been very cooperative biologically and have produced four sons, three of them doctors.

A few days before the referendum, a policeman came to our house, not to arrest Razi but to request him to come to the police station for "briefing". Government emissaries came to him and argued with him that it was his duty as a Muslim to vote for Ayub, because the Quran says: "Obey God, obey the Prophet and those in authority from amongst you." For more than a millennium, Muslim scholars have argued who falls in the category of "those in authority from amongst you". The Jamaat, then in the opposition, believed only an elected leader fell in that category and deserved obedience from the faithful. Others thought even a tyrant must be obeyed because disobedience could result in social and political chaos leading to mutiny and bloodshed. A decade and a half later, the Jamaat itself would stage a somersault and shamelessly support to the hilt the only tyrant to have ruled Pakistan, Ziaul Haq. As a loyal Jamaati, Razi didn't vote for Ayub.

The result of the referendum, held on February 14, showed that 57,283 BDs constituting 95.6 per cent of the total voted yes. The number of BDs was later doubled – 80,000 for each of the two "wings". The BDs not only elected the two provincial assemblies and the National Assembly, they also formed the electoral college for the presidential election. Ayub's opponent was Fatima Jinnah, the sister of the founder of Pakistan, who was the candidate of the Combined Opposition Parties (COP). The brains behind the COP were some of the old veterans who had been demonised by the military regime. Surprisingly, the campaign generated considerable hate and denied Ayub what many thought would be a walkover. Ayub, of course, won, and there is no doubt pressure was exerted on the Basic Democrats to vote for Ayub. But I still insist that by and large the vote was fair and the majority voted for Ayub.

I remember the disappointment in the opposition camp when the result finally became available. There were emotional scenes, with people ready to burn and kill. But the COP leadership consisted of old hands, some of whom like Khawja Nazimuddin, had taken part in the freedom movement and upheld the highest principles of democracy and rule of law. They refused to countenance any of the "movements" and "marches" that would later become a routine affair in Pakistan. The presidential election had aroused the people the way nothing else earlier had. By the mid-sixties, a middle class had begun to emerge, the people were developing political consciousness, and the parties and the media were yearning for political freedoms. The COP's decision to nominate Fatima as its candidate caught Ayub by surprise, and many thought he would lose. Karachi was now to become for the first time an Opposition city. Traditionally, Karachi had been pro-Muslim League and thus pro-government. Ayub's decision to build a new capital on the Potohar plateau and shift it from Karachi made the Karachiites – a majority of whom till then consisted of Urdu- speaking people – very unhappy. Suddenly Karachi became a COP city. This was also the first time that in my own little world I found myself on the wrong side of my community, for I was a fervent Ayub supporter and often found myself isolated in drawing room talk and social gatherings. The heat the election generated seemed to polarise society in Karachi. I remember what a Pathan watchman told me. He had been in our neighbourhood for a decade, but he had never seen such a condition. He told me, "Everyone seems to have gone mad. Either someone has a flower (Ayub's election symbol) on his shirt or (the drawing) of a candle (Fatima's symbol)". He was right. Karachi had started getting mad. Ayub's election saw a riot when Ayub supporters, with one of his sons, Gauhar Ayub at the helm, led a procession through predominantly Urdu-speaking localities. This was a foolish thing to do, considering the level of emotions on all sides. The resulting clash in Liaquatabad and Gujro Nullah acquired an ethnic colour. The Pathan watchman was right: Karachi had started getting mad.

Even though he believed and perhaps practised "basic democracy" and the system smacked of authoritarianism Ayub did not display any of the tyrannical streaks that later dictators and even civilian leaders would exhibit. He was essentially a gentleman, and if he failed then he was not the only Pakistani leader to have failed. On the whole his achievements are far greater than the mistakes he made. Pakistan's industrialisation began under him, and the country was considered a model of economic development. There is a factoid about a delegation of economic experts from South Korea – now way ahead of Pakistan – coming to this country and wanting to know the secret of its amazing economic progress. Abroad Ayub enjoyed high prestige, though there is no doubt his remarkably handsome face and robust physical appearance added glamour to the fact that he was supposed to be anti-communist at a time when this was the West's, especially America's, sole criterion for judging a leader.

Ayub did not divide the world into "non-communist us" and the "communist them", though there is no doubt he played the role of an anti-communist strongman to America's entire satisfaction to advance Pakistan's geopolitical interests. The 1965 debacle apart, it was Ayub who truly turned the Pakistan Army into a modern fighting force. Ayub had a clear grasp of geopolitics and was lucky to have two brilliant foreign ministers in Manzur Qadir and Bhutto. It is true that Pakistan and China discovered a commonality of interests much earlier when their prime ministers, Mohammad Ali Bogra and Zhou En-lai, met on the sidelines of the Afro-Asian conference at Bandung, Indonesia, in 1955. But the friendship and the military understanding to the extent of being allies developed during the Ayub-Bhutto era. His success in having the Pakistan-China border delineated and the agreement signed despite initial reluctance by Beijing showed his skill at diplomatic manoeuvring. China was, of course, keen to have its borders with both Pakistan and India demarcated and the issue sorted out. But since India was the bigger country – and did not have the stigma being of a member of the Western military alliances – Communist China was keen to have the border issue settled with India first. Luckily for Pakistan, Nehru showed no such keenness. In fact, the big-power chauvinism that characterised his approach toward India's neighbours made him dither.

In Ayub Khan: Pakistan's First Military Ruler, Altaf Gauhar gives an excellent summary of what went on between Beijing and Islamabad before the agreement was finally clinched. On a visit to the United

States, Ayub called for China's admission to the United Nations. This was noted by the Chinese leadership, and when Ayub returned home the Chinese ambassador called on him to thank him for a statement he had chosen to make on American soil. Ayub then pressed the ambassador for taking up the border issue and signing an agreement. But when the ambassador said the issue was "complex" Ayub retorted that China's entry into the United Nation was an even more complex issue. Eventually the agreement was signed much to India's chagrin. The anti-communist world was shocked when PIA, the national carrier of America's "most allied ally", started a service to Shanghai. Other steps included the re-building of the ancient Silk Route and turning it into all-weather road linking Pakistan and China. Monuments along the Karakoram Highway commemorate the sacrifices of those Pakistani and Chinese military engineers who died while building what indeed is a feat of engineering through hard granite.

For an eternal junior like me, defending my criticism of Ayub's decision to agree to a ceasefire was difficult. I remember a remark made by Dr Abdul Qayyum Beg, our family physician. Ammi was having her asthma attack, and I took her to the good doctor, who had his clinic in PIB Colony. The conversation invariably turned to the war, and Ammi told the doctor that I was opposed to the ceasefire. His comment was based on common sense: "Do you think Ayub would have agreed to a ceasefire if Pakistan were winning? Wouldn't he have liked to go down in history as a victor?" A junior like me could not possibly reply to what obviously was a comment based on common sense. Many other elders in family and colleagues in Morning News took the same line. I wish I had had the courage to ask, "Would India have agreed to a ceasefire if India were winning?" Since partition, India had never worried about the UN and its resolutions. It had defied all UN resolutions calling for a plebiscite and gone back on the commitment which Indian leaders, including Governor General Lord Mountbatten and Nehru himself, had made, pledging a plebiscite once hostilities ended. Its intransigence on the Kashmir issue became even more evident after its disastrous war with China in the Himalayas in 1962. The Indian Army's morale lay devastated, and there were hopes this could make Nehru see reason with a view to finding a solution of the Kashmir issue. Among those who shuttled back and forth between Islamabad and New Delhi were Averell Harriman and Duncan Sandys. But even in that condition of defeat and despair Nehru did not agree to a Kashmir solution. If India were winning, I was positive New Delhi would have never agreed to a ceasefire – the Security Council's ceasefire resolution notwithstanding. I have seldom quoted Clemenceau unthinkingly, but I think the 1965 war, its outcome and Ayub's narrow vision as a military man proved to the hilt the truth of his dictum. It is now established from the accounts now available from both sides that there was a stalemate, and neither side was in a position to mount a major offensive and achieve its objective. That being the condition, Pakistan should have allowed the state of war to continue, even if it meant firing one bullet a day. By agreeing to the ceasefire and later by signing the Tashkent Declaration Ayub froze the Kashmir issue. With the narrow vision of a general who calculates war in terms of firepower Ayub called off the war, without realising the consequences it had not only for the Kashmir issue but on the nation's morale.

My stay in Morning News – early 1963 to mid-1966 – saw two major events: the presidential election and the 1965 war. I was one of the editions-in-charge at Morning News, which had no editor, though News Editor, Azhar Ali Khan, was for all practical purposes the boss. Azhar, who now lives in Canada, belongs to one of Bhopal's Pathan families. Under his stewardship, MN gained in circulation and advertisement. MN, as I have said elsewhere, was never much of a competitor for Dawn, but in Azhar's stewardship (1963-64) it had started gaining attentions. There was some dispute between Dawn and cinema hall owners, and they directed their ads to MN. Within no time the number of its pages and circulation had gone up. I remember MN for some very painful moments, though I also discovered two friends whom I miss till this day – S. M. Ishteyaque and Abdul Quddoos Sheikh. The pain arose from the kind of situation that existed in the paper because of the tension between Azhar and some senior colleagues. Newspapers the world over differ from other organisations in the sense that a person senior in position must be there not because of the number of years he has put in service but because of his professional competence, academic background and command over language. In the army, a Lt. Col must obey the colonel, and show respect to him, even if the Colonel is not necessarily a better officer. In journalism, a person in a senior position must be able to justify his position by his professional competence and by his intellectual superiority over his subordinates. This is not always so, and who is competent and not is often a matter of opinion. Azhar was a young man, then in his late thirties, and it goes without saying that there were some very competent senior journalists, too, like S. R. Ghauri, Zawwar Hassan, Hassan Akhtar and Sibte Farooq Fareedi (who was killed in the PIA air crash in Cairo in June 1965). But many other seniors resented Azhar, even though I doubt if they had the required competence. Resentful of Azhar's position, most of them adopted a highly negative attitude. Azhar recruited a number of young men, including me, Ishteyaque and Quddoos. Some of my senior colleagues from Dawn also joined MN, and they included Ibtisam, mentioned earlier, Sami Ahmad and Mahdi Jaffar. Also amongst the seniors was Amanullah Khan. A quiet and diligent worker, Amanullah worked in the commerce section and decades later would become its editor toward the fag-end of the paper.

A most unforgettable character in MN was Hameed Zaman, an art critic. What distinguished him from others was the sophistication of his personality, humility and dry humour. During the decades that I had known him, I never found him angry. To me, this is the greatest virtue that a human being can possibly possess. Regretfully, "religious" people in Pakistan seldom display this quality that was so dear to the Holy Prophet. He had previously worked in Radio Pakistan, and that was where he met Rasheeda. Hameed and I got even closer when we both built homes in the same block (4-A) in Gulshan-i-Iqbal in 1979.

His wife, Rasheeda, was one of Qamar's friends, and Razia and I used to look forward to their occasional visits to our home. Sometimes they invited us over to their home to see "art movies". Like me he was a movie buff, but undeniably he had higher tastes. His death on November 20, 1999, deprived me of a very dear friend. Marjorie Hussain, one of Pakistan's major art critics, recalled how Zaman and she "were among the few to sit through an entire three-hour performance of an Ibsen play performed by an amateur group; I as a mother of a performer, Mr Zaman as an interested spectator". Zaman, she wrote in Dawn, was "a twinkled eye, modest individual" whom the "artists genuinely revered". Zaman once confided to her that he had painted in his younger years and that experience had given him an understanding of creative people's aesthetic problems. She added: "A life devoted to art journalism rewarded him with little material gains. To the end he moved around in public transport. But as he once said his thoughts were so absorbing he hardly noticed his surroundings. Living a life in art, he transcended mundane affairs... In my mind I used to liken Hameed Zaman to a water lily, a flower that retains its purity while growing through murky waters. I never told him that. I wish I had."

Given the onslaught by the seniors, Quddoos, Ishteyaque and I drew closer. Many other points were common to us. Ishteyaque claimed to have discovered Bhutto. I maintained that the discovery was done jointly by us, but he insisted on his monopoly. The discovery lay in a speech Bhutto had made at a law of the sea conference. It was a brilliant speech, and Ishteyaque brought it to my notice. We both agreed it was a wonderful speech, and we wondered why such men were not Pakistan's rulers. Bhutto was then already in Ayub's martial law cabinet, most probably as Minister for Natural Resources, but was by and large unknown to the people. We first saw him when he had just come out of the pink-coloured building of the Pakistan Institute of International Affairs, Karachi, after making a speech. There was no denying the charisma in the man. After Bhutto resigned as foreign minister in the wake of the Tashkent Declaration, the word Bhutto became taboo in

Morning News, unless it was mentioned by way of criticism. As I have mentioned elsewhere in this book, a subeditor can do a lot of mischief while staying within the bonds of policy guidelines. Ishteyaque and I then made a major decision – we will play up anti-Bhutto news. This was the only way we could serve his cause. The editor would not object because after all we were giving due prominence to an anti-Bhutto statement. But we were right in believing that publishing anti-Bhutto news was worth it, because that kept Bhutto in the news. Ishteyaque, I and many others were among those who went to the Cantonment Station to see Bhutto when he arrived at Karachi in the wake of his resignation as foreign minister. Even though he did not at that stage wish to undertake an exercise in mass contact, I have no doubt that the spontaneous ovations he received during that train journey and the crowds that gathered to greet him at the railway stations must have made him think of his future line of action. Quddoos and Ishteyaque remained Bhutto loyalists till their death.

Meanwhile, the seniors felt elated when MN was forced to join the National Press Trust. Unlike the general impression, the NPT was not government owned, though undoubtedly it enjoyed Ayub's blessings. With a trust fund of Rs 5.5 million, the NPT was established on April 8, 1964, with the aim of "helping and encouraging the promotion of sound and healthy journalism" and publishing newspapers and periodicals "with truly objective outlook and devoted to the cause of national progress and solidarity" with no room for "parochial, partisan or sectarian inclinations". Thirty-nine leading businessmen and bankers – the minimum contribution being Rs100,000 by each – executed the trust deed, and – besides such names in Pakistan's corporate sector as the Adamjees, Bawanys, Cowasjees, Dadabhoys, Dawoods, Fancys, Habibs, Ispahanis, Rangoonwalas and the Saigols – the trustees included Agha Hasan Abidi (the leading light of the now defunct Bank of Credit and Commerce International), Kasim Dada, Nasir A. Shaikh, K. M. Muneer, Wajid Ali, Najmuddin Valibhai, A. K. Sumar, Mohammad Bashir, Siddik Adam, Shah Nawaz, Abdul Jalil, E. A. Dinshaw, Mumtaz Hasan, Ataur

Rahman Alvi and Pir Mahfooz Ali. The NPT then acquired or bought over majority shares to become the owner of 10 newspapers and periodicals. They were English daily The Pakistan Times (both editions i. e. Lahore and Islamabad), its English weekly The Pakistan Times Overseas Weekly, Urdu daily Mashriq (Lahore, Karachi, Peshawar and Quetta editions), and its Urdu weekly Akhbar-i-Khawateen, and Urdu daily Imroz (Lahore and Multan editions). Morning News belonged to the National News Publications (Pvt) Ltd, owned by the Adamjee and Khawja Nooruddin. The NPT bought 78 per cent of the shares from them and thus controlled the paper.

Nooruddin had full confidence in Azhar. However, the day the paper joined the NPT Azhar chose to resign and was replaced by Mohsin Ali. He had been the paper's editor previously, but this time he returned as Managing Editor. Even though I was an Azhar appointee I never found Mohsin hostile to me. Ishteyaque, however, remained quite uncomfortable. One immediate decision taken by Mohsin after Azhar's exit was to remove Ishteyaque and me as night editors. We were replaced by two seniors. MN then acquired a brand new printing machine from Germany, and there were high hopes. But editions were constantly getting late, and I remember S. R. Ghauri, a senior who was otherwise quite anti-Azhar, remark, "How long will we be guided by Azhar's ghost?" Within two months, Mohsin had reversed his decision, and Ishteyaque and I were back as night editors. Mohsin had become MN's Managing Editor because of the support he received from Ghulam Faruque, a key figure in Ayub's government. Mohsin was, no doubt, a thorough professional, but being the editor of an NPT-owned paper made its own demands on him, and the paper had to toe a pro-government line. One unfortunate demonstration of this policy was the treatment given to the extracts published from Ayub's book Friends, Not Masters. The paper made the extracts from the book its lead story daily for weeks, and the headline invariably was in red. During the Bhutto years, Sultan Ahmad became its editor. Other editors included Rafiq Jabir and Amanullah Khan, who turned out to be paper's last editor, for MN closed down in May 1991. It is interesting to note that all opposition leaders and parties demanded the abolition of the NPT and attacked its existence as a symbol of authoritarianism. However, when they came to power themselves, they realised the advantage of having 10 newspapers at their beck and call, and the NPT continued to exist. It was finally wound up during the second Benazir government. I left MN in late 1966 to rejoin Dawn, and Quddoos followed me to Dawn a couple of years later. Ishteyaque left MN in 1970 to join The Sun, a new venture launched by the Laris, with Shamim Ahmad as editor.

4

MOBS ARE BORN

THE TASHKENT DECLARATION, SIGNED on January 10, 1966, between Ayub and Indian Prime Minister Lal Bahadur Shastri, consisted of 691 words, with "Jammu and Kashmir" finding a mention just once. The Declaration shell-shocked the Pakistani nation, which had been given an overdose of jingoistic patriotism during the September 1965 war and whose emotions were raised to heights from which a headlong fall into the abyss of disappointment was inevitable when it saw nothing but what it thought was a sell-out at Tashkent. However, before we analyse the Declaration to know why it invoked the Pakistani nation's wrath, it is essential to note the gradual erosion over the decades of Pakistan's basic minimum concept of a Kashmir solution. In 1948, when the hostilities ceased in Kashmir, Pakistan's demand was that a plebiscite be held to decide the state's future. Both Pakistan and India accepted the two resolutions passed by the United Nations Commission for India and Pakistan (UNCIP), which called for ending the hostilities, demilitarising the state and holding a plebiscite to know the people's wishes. In fact, as Bhutto, then foreign minister, told the General Assembly in a speech on September 28, 1965, the two governments had agreed to end the hostilities after they accepted the two UNCIP resolutions of August 13, 1948, and January 5, 1949. The UNCIP resolutions acquired a non-controversial and binding character when Indian leaders, including Governor-General Lord Mountbatten, Prime Minister Nehru, Defence Minister Krishna Menon and India's representatives at the UN declared repeatedly in categorical terms that the only solution to the Kashmir dispute was through a plebiscite. Since those commitments are in danger of being lost and forgotten, it is essential to reproduce them here so that the reader knows that India's position on the Kashmir issue has been morally bankrupt and shall continue to be so until circumstances force it to concede to the people of Kashmir their right to freedom.

I have often found many foreigners, and even the ill-informed among Pakistanis, asking a seemingly very profound but in fact a rather silly question: if the people of Kashmir must have freedom in what way is that Pakistan's business? To remove any misunderstandings on this score it is essential to know the chronology of the dispute of Kashmir and realise that Pakistan is the original and legitimate party to the Kashmir issue – a party which was requested by the reigning monarch, a monarch de jure and de facto, to become party to the state's affairs and partly take over the running of the princely state which had an overwhelmingly Muslim majority. On August 15, 1947, a day after Pakistan had emerged on the world map as a sovereign state and the world's biggest Muslim state, the Maharaja of Kashmir signed a 'stand still' agreement with Pakistan. This agreement was binding on both parties, and under it the Maharaja pledged not to take any unilateral action on the state's status and future without reference to Pakistan. More important, the maharaja asked Pakistan to take charge of the running of Kashmir's railways and post and telegraph services. Kashmir had no rail link with India or any other state, and the only railway line it had linked Jammu with Sialkot in Pakistan's Punjab province. (It would take 61 years for India to build a rail a link with the occupied territory. The railway service between India and occupied Kashmir was inaugurated on October 11, 2008, by Indian Prime Minister Manmohan Singh on a day that saw the occupied territory completely shut down by the people of Kashmir protesting against his visit. Sixty-one years had passed, but India had not been able to win over the Kashmiri people.) The moment the Stand Still Agreement was signed, Pakistan's flags started flying all over Kashmir. There was no Indian flag, and there would be none, till the Indian army planted it in on Kashmir's soil. Thus, when freedom dawned and British paramountcy lapsed, there were only two parties to the Kashmir issue – Pakistan and the maharaja. No third party existed.

A subcontinent was aflame, everyone was not a Jinnah – a block of ice – who could control his emotions as freedom dawned in the midst of massacres and the beginning of what would become history's biggest migration. In Poonch, home to soldiers, the maharajah's army massacred the civilian population, forcing the people to rise in rebellion. Pakistan was still in the process of organizing a state structure. The army existed in terms of units but not as an integrated fighting machine that could move to the rescue of the people of Poonch – its first duty was to guard passenger trains coming to Pakistan and being massacred by Hindu and Sikh mobs. On October 22, 1947, Pakhthoon tribesmen crossed into the state to the rescue of the Poonch people and put the maharaja's army to flight. On the night between 25 and 26 a panicky maharaja fled his capital and took refuge in Jammu. He was still the de jure ruler but by no means the de facto ruler. On the 26th, this fugitive then signed an Instrument of Accession to India, and the Indian government, headed less by Nehru and more by one of Pakistan's sworn enemies, Lord Mountbatten, independent India's first Governor General, ordered an invasion. There was no worthwhile road connection between India and Kashmir, so the Indian army high command had to airlift troops, who landed at the Srinagar airport just about the time when the tribesmen were near it.

Immediately after the fugitive potentate signed the instrument of accession, Mountbatten declared on October 27, 1947: "In consistence with their policy that, in the case of any state where the issue of accession has been the subject of dispute, the question of accession should be decided in accordance with the wishes of the people of the State, it is my Government's wish that as soon as law and order have been restored in

Kashmir and her soil cleared of the invader, the question of the State's accession should be settled by a reference to the people." This was followed by a telegram from Nehru to the Prime Minister of Pakistan, Khan Liaquat Ali Khan, in which he said categorically: "Our view, which we have repeatedly made public, is that the question of accession in any disputed territory or State must be decided in accordance with the wishes of the people, and we adhere to this view." On November 2 Nehru repeated, "Let me make it clear that it has been our policy all along that if there is a dispute about the accession of a state to either Dominion, the accession must be made by the people of that state. It is in accordance with this policy that we have added a proviso to the Instrument of Accession of Kashmir." On November 8, Nehru said in another telegram to Liaquat: "The governments of India and Pakistan should make a joint request to the United Nations to undertake a plebiscite in Kashmir at the earliest possible date." Again Nehru stated in the Constituent Assembly of India on November 25, 1947: "In order to establish our bona fides, we have suggested that when the people are given the chance to decide their future, this should be done under the supervision of an impartial tribunal such as the United Nations. The issue in Kashmir is whether violence and naked force should decide the future or the will of the people." Since the Labour government in Britain was watching the Kashmir drama, in whose tragic enactment it had played a major role, Nehru sent a telegram to Prime Minister Clement Attlee assuring him that the future of Kashmir would be decided by the people of the state. Nehru's telegram to the British prime minister said: "I would like to make it clear that question of aiding Kashmir in this emergency is not designed in any way to influence the State to accede to India. Our view which we have repeatedly made public is that the question of accession in any disputed territory or state must be decided in accordance with the wishes of the people and we adhere to this view." In another telegram, this time to Liaquat Ali Khan, Nehru said: "I wish to assure you that the action Government of India has taken has been forced upon them by circumstances and imminent grave danger to Srinagar. They have no desire to intervene in affairs of Kashmir State after raiders have been driven away and law and order established. In regard to accession also it has been made clear that this is subject to reference to the people of State and their decision. Government of India have no desire to impose any decision and will abide by people's wishes but those cannot be ascertained till peace and law and order prevail."

On October 31, 1947, on the Maharaja's request, Nehru sent a telegram to the Prime Minister of Pakistan declaring inter alia: "Our assurance that we shall withdraw our troops from Kashmir as soon as peace and order are restored and leave the future of this State to the people of the State is not merely a pledge to your government but also to the people of Kashmir and to the world." On November 2, in a radio broadcast, Nehru declared: "We have declared that the fate of Kashmir is ultimately to be decided by the people. That pledge we have given and the maharaja has supported it not only to the people of Kashmir but to the world. We will not and cannot back out of it."

On January 1, 1948, India took the Kashmir issue to the United Nations, calling itself the aggrieved party. Five months later, in May 1948, the Pakistan Army entered the liberated part of Kashmir, since after capturing the Kashmir valley and holding off the tribesmen, the Indian army was moving threateningly toward the Punjab, and Pakistan had to act to save its flanks. According to the complaint lodged by India with the UN, the Kashmir issue stemmed from "Pakistani aggression". The world didn't subscribe to this theory. Philip Noel Baker, then Secretary of State for Commonwealth Relations, who won the Nobel Prize for Peace in 1959, and Lord Ismay, Chief of Staff to Mountbatten, believed "… the one indispensable condition of peace in Kashmir is to guarantee the security of the Moslems. The whole affair … started with the massacre of Moslems instigated by the Prince. When threatened by reprisals … he (the Maharaja) took political refuge by requesting the accession of Kashmir to India" (Gowher Rizvi, South Asia in a Changing World, OUP, p 50, citing Moore, Making the New Commonwealth).

On January 28, 1948, the President of the Security Council said: "... the documents at our disposal show agreement between the parties on the three following points:

"(1) The question as to whether the State of Jammu and Kashmir will accede to India or to Pakistan shall be decided by plebiscite;

"(2) This plebiscite must be conducted under conditions which will ensure complete impartiality;

"(3) The plebiscite will therefore be held under the aegis of the United Nations."

On April 21, 1948, with two abstentions (Russia and Ukraine), the Security Council passed a resolution calling for a plebiscite to decide Kashmir's future. It was then the Security Council appointed the United Nations Commission for India and Pakistan after noting "with satisfaction that both India and Pakistan desire that the question of accession ... should be decided through the democratic way of a free and impartial plebiscite." The UNCIP's resolution of August 13, 1948, said (Part III): "The governments of India and Pakistan reaffirm their wish that the future status of the State of Jammu and Kashmir shall be determined in accordance with the wishes of the people and, to that end, upon acceptance of the truce agreement, both governments agree to enter into consultations with the Commission to determine fair and equitable conditions whereby such expression will be assured."

This resolution (47 of 1948) is a most significant part of the UN's voluminous record on Kashmir, for it would make clear to any impartial observer which state the world body held responsible for the Kashmiri people's plight, which government was obstructing a Kashmir solution and which one needed most to cooperate with the UN so as to give peace to the subcontinent and end the Kashmir conflict by organizing a plebiscite. The resolution made two common demands on Pakistan and India, two demands exclusively on Pakistan and 25 on India. (See Annexure I)

India's representative to the UN, Gopal Swamy Ayengar, told the Security Council: "The government of India have bound themselves that the people (of the state) would be given an opportunity to decide whether they wished to continue to live with India or secede from it." Similarly Mrs Vijay Lakshmi Pandit told the 608th meeting of the Security Council: "We do not seek to go behind the UNCIP resolutions or to ignore the vital elements of principle contained in them..... We have always adhered to the UNCIP resolutions... We cannot be a party to the reversal of previous decisions taken by the United Nations Commission with the agreement of the parties." Years would pass, but Nehru would continue to stand by his commitment to have the Kashmir issue settled through a plebiscite. On June 4, 1951, he repeated this pledge at a public rally in Kashmir and said: "I want to repeat that the government of India will stand by the pledge. Whatever happens that pledge itself stated that it is for the people to decide their fate." Amrit Bazar Patrika, a prestigious Calcutta newspaper, quoted Nehru as saying on June 2, 1952, "Kashmir is not the property of India or Pakistan. It belongs to the Kashmiri people. When Kashmir acceded to India, we made it clear to the leaders of the Kashmiri people that we would ultimately abide by the verdict of their plebiscite. If they tell us to walk out we would have no hesitation in quitting Kashmir. We have taken the issue to the United Nations and given our word of honour for a peaceful solution. As a great nation we cannot go back on it. We have left the question of a final solution to the people of Kashmir and we are determined to abide by their decision." Again in a statement in Indian parliament Nehru said on June 26, 1952: "if after a proper plebiscite the people of Kashmir say 'No we do not wish to be with India' we are committed to accept it though it might pain us." Four years later – on August 7, 1956, Nehru told Indian parliament again: "If, however, the people of Kashmir do not wish to remain with us, let them go by all means. We will not keep them against their will however painful it may [be] for us." On August 7, 1952, in a major speech in Indian parliament Nehru said: "... With all deference to this Parliament, I would like to say that the ultimate decision will be made in the minds and hearts of the men and women of Kashmir and not in this Parliament or at the United Nations...

First of all, let me say clearly that we accept the basic proposition that the future of Kashmir is going to be decided finally by the goodwill and pleasure of her people. The goodwill and pleasure of this Parliament is of no importance in this matter, not because this Parliament does not have the strength to decide the question of Kashmir but because any kind of imposition would be against the principle that this Parliament upholds...The question of Kashmir, as this House well knows, certainly has not been for us a question of territory . . . . Kashmir is very close to our minds and heart, and if by some decree or adverse fortune Kashmir ceases to be a part of India, it will be a wrench and a pain and torment for us. If however, the people of Kashmir do not wish to remain with us, let them go by all means; we will not keep them against their will, however painful it may be to us. That is the policy that we will pursue... So, while the accession was complete in law and in fact, the other fact which has nothing to do with law also remains, namely, our pledge to the people of Kashmir –- if you like, to the people of the world –- that this matter can be affirmed again or cancelled by the people of Kashmir according to their wishes. We do not want to win people against their will and with the help of armed forces; and if the people of Jammu and Kashmir State wish to part company with us, they can go their way and we shall go ours. We want no forced marriages, no forced unions...." Even the Pakistan-hating firebrand Krishna Menon told the 773rd session of the Security Council: "We have accepted (the resolutions of the United Nations Commission for India and Pakistan), we are parties to them, whether we like them or not".

Those commitments were later repudiated by the Indian government on pretexts that are perverse, self-serving and immoral. Nehru used the ridiculous pretext of Pakistan's membership of the US-led military pacts to wriggle out of the plebiscite commitment. Other arguments have included the plea that those resolutions have become obsolete. In the first place, all parties to a given declaration or agreement must agree that it has become obsolete, and no one can unilaterally declare it obsolete and irrelevant. Secondly, freedom cannot become obsolete. By insisting that the UN resolutions and India's own declarations for a plebiscite have become obsolete, India would have the world believe that freedom itself has become obsolete. This is untenable and repudiates the immutability of freedom as an essential condition of human existence. Just as human rights cannot become obsolete, so also freedom cannot become obsolete.

Sweden's Gunnar V. Jarring, who acted as the UN's man on Kashmir, made it clear who he thought was obstructing the world body's peace efforts. In a report to the Security Council on April 28, 1957, the Swedish diplomat dwelt on the "impediments" to the holding of a plebiscite and said "the Government of India, which had brought the case before the Security Council on 1 January 1948, felt aggrieved that the Council had so far not expressed itself on the question of what in their view was aggression committed by Pakistan on India. In their view, it was incumbent on the Council to express itself on this question and equally incumbent on Pakistan 'to vacate the aggression'. It was argued that prior to the fulfilment of these requirements on the part of the Security Council and on the part of Pakistan the commitments of India under the resolution [of January 5, 1949] could not reach the operative stage.

" ... I explained to the Government. of India that the Security Council had properly taken cognizance of their original complaint, and that it was not for me to express myself on the question whether its resolutions had been adequate or not. I pointed out that regardless of the merits of the present position taken by their Government, it could not be overlooked that they had accepted the two UNCIP resolutions.

"... The Government of Pakistan, on their part, in conversations with me, maintained that para I of the first resolution had been implemented in good faith and in full by them, and that the time had come to proceed to the implementation of part II" [the holding of the plebiscite] (Reports on Kashmir by United Nations Representatives, Government of Pakistan, 1962, p 280)

Of the four Representatives appointed by the UN for Kashmir – Gen. A. G. L. McNoughton of Canada, Sir Owen Dixon of Australia,

Gunnar V. Jarring of Sweden and Frank P. Graham of the United States – the last one served the longest, from 1951 to 1967. On the whole Graham gave three "statements" and five "reports" to the Security Council, and they make it clear who the American diplomat held responsible for going back on its words and reneging on the promise to hold a plebiscite in Kashmir.

In "a personal summary statement" given to the Security Council on October 10, 1952, Graham said: "A settlement of this dispute would mean that the status of the people of the State would be finally determined not by the sovereignty of princes but by the sovereignty of the people, not by the might of armies but by the will of the people, not by bullets but by ballots, through self-determination of people by the democratic method of an impartial plebiscite conducted with due regard for the security of the State and freedom of the plebiscite under the auspices of the United Nations (ibid, p 201)

In another report to the UN Council, presented on March 27, 1953, Graham said: "The people of the State of Jammu and Kashmir have waited over four years for the fulfilment of the promise of a plebiscite under the two agreed UNCIP resolutions. The people in the East and the West look for an example from the top of the sub-continent in Jammu and Kashmir, that an agreement for a plebiscite will soon be fulfilled for and by the people of this most ancient, beautiful and historic state. Renewed physical and spiritual energies would be released by an agreed settlement of this dispute" (ibid, p 259).

On March 30, 1951, the Security Council passed a resolution which not only reaffirmed the principle of a plebiscite for Kashmir but noted that "the Governments of India and Pakistan have accepted the provisions of the United Nations Commission for India and Pakistan resolutions of 13 August 1948 and 5 January 1949; and have re-affirmed their desire that the future of the State of Jammu and Kashmir shall be decided through the democratic method of a free and impartial plebiscite conducted under the auspices of the United Nations ... "(Reports on Kashmir by United Nations Representative, Government of Pakistan, page 112)

It is pertinent to note how touching were the sentiments expressed by Graham when he emphasized the need for keeping the promise made to the people of Kashmir for holding a plebiscite. Lawyer, professor of history, educationist and Senator, Graham was the UN's Representative for India and Pakistan for 16 years (1951-67). In a report presented to the Security Council at its 570th meeting in Paris on January 17, 1952, the American diplomat from North Carolina, said: "The plebiscite would keep the promise made to the people of Jammu and Kashmir, who are worthy of the right of their own self-determination through a free, secure, and impartial plebiscite. They are a people of legend, song and story, associated with snow-capped mountains, beautiful valleys and life-giving waters. The valleys are set like gems in the midst of mountains which surround the land and the people and which look down upon them from untold ages of history and from the highest majesty of this earth. These people, Moslems, Hindus, Sikhs, and Christian, as farmers, craftsmen and artists, small shopkeepers, boatmen, bearers and other workers in areas now on both sides of the cease-fire line have, through the centuries, been the victims of exploitation and conflict. The recognition of the rights and dignity, the security and the self-determination of these historic people, under the auspices of the United Nations, might well become a challenging example of the progressive values of self-determination to the dependent peoples of the earth. The people of Jammu and Kashmir through a free and impartial plebiscite would signal through the darkness of these times a ray of hope that not by bullets but by ballots, not through conflict of armies but through co-operation of peoples, is the enduring way for people to determine their own destiny and way of life." (Reports on Kashmir by United Nations Representatives, Government of Pakistan, page 147)

In his speech to the General Assembly on September 28, 1965, Bhutto dealt at length upon the subterfuge colonial powers' employ to deny freedom to the enslaved people. He said: "But despite the universal recognition of this principle, there are always some Powers that try, albeit vainly, to turn back the whole current of history. Human greed being what it is, we find colonial Powers – in Angola and Mozambique, in Southern Rhodesia and in South West Africa denying a people their right to choose their own destiny as India denies it to the people of Jammu and Kashmir. The technique employed by this small but assorted company is one and the same. It is not to question the principle as such, but to assert that it does not apply to the case involved. The excuse is always available to them that the colony is an integral part of their metropolitan territory, or that they are building multiracial or multi-religious societies and, if they permit the self-determination of one group or area, their whole state may disintegrate. In pleading this excuse, they try to exploit the fear of dismemberment among many sovereign states. That this plea is specious and is meant only to delude the world is apparent to anyone who is acquainted with the history of modern colonialism and the struggle for emancipation of subjugated peoples.

"Indian leaders argue that self-determination is a disruptive principle which will lead to the dismemberment of States in Africa and Asia. They assert that the survival of India as a democracy, as a secular State, indeed as a united country would be at stake if a plebiscite were to be held in Jammu and Kashmir, the very same plebiscite which India pledged to the people of Jammu and Kashmir eighteen years ago. This argument has been answered by a well-known Indian leader. Allow me to quote Mr. Jayprakash Narayan '....if we are so sure of the verdict of the people of Kashmir, why are we so opposed to giving them another opportunity to reiterate it? The answer given is that this would start the process of disintegration of India. Few things have been said in the course of this controversy more silly than this one. The assumption behind the argument is that the States of India are held together by force and not by the sentiment of a common nationality.'

"I do not consider it appropriate to go into the question of the nature of Indian secularism and democracy, although much can be said on that subject. I will only say that it would not be rational for Pakistan to wish the destruction or weakening of the Indian Union. Pakistan's own progress and stability cannot be served by chaos and disruption across its border.

Quite the contrary .Whether Indian fears in this respect are the nightmare of a feverish imagination, or just another stratagem by which India has for eighteen years prevented the implementation of its own international agreement Kashmir is a question which needs to be dispassionately considered and answered."

His September 22 speech was highly emotional. He said: "We will wage a war for 1,000 years, a war of defence. I told that to the Security Council a year ago when that body, in all its wisdom and in all its power, was not prepared to give us a resolution. Even last year the Security Council felt that we had brought a dead horse to this Council – that we were trying to make internal propaganda. But the world must know that the 100 million people of Pakistan will never abandon their pledges and promises. The Indians may abandon their pledges and promises – we shall never abandon ours. Irrespective of our size and of our resources, we shall fight to the end. But we shall fight in self-defence; we shall fight for honour. We are not aggressors; we are the victims of aggression. It was the duty of the Security Council to pronounce itself on who is the aggressor and who is the aggressee. It was Pakistan that was the victim of aggression."

When after the ceasefire went into effect and the Security Council took up the Kashmir issue again, since the hostilities had ceased only six days ago, the foreign minister referred to the Indian publicists' claim that the retention of Kashmir by India – even by forceful means – was essential in the interest of Indian secularism and democracy. In his September 28 speech Bhutto said: "The forcible annexation of Jammu and Kashmir by India is not a guarantee of Indian secularism, democracy or territorial integrity. On the contrary, it keeps alive those very fears and suspicions which made it impossible for the Muslim minority to accept a united India State. If the Nagas, the Sikhs and other communities have grievances against the Government of India, then the fate of Jammu and Kashmir can only act as a spur to their fears and suspicions. The Nagas and the Sikhs can be pacified, not by the example of forcible occupation of Jammu and Kashmir, but by redress of their grievances.

"India has long used the argument that the fabric of Indian secularism is too weak to withstand a decision by the people of Jammu and Kashmir to opt for Pakistan. Indian propaganda has raised the spectre of the majority community falling upon the 50 million Muslims of India if Kashmir opted for Pakistan. I will not try to answer the question whether such a mediaeval and reactionary and undemocratic argument is worthy of the country which claims to be a great secular and modern democracy. The fact is, however, that nothing of the kind will happen, unless the Indian Government permits it to happen. This is pure and simple blackmail to prevent the people of Jammu and Kashmir from exercising their right of free choice.

"India asserts that the dispute between Pakistan and India is not concerned with the rights of the people of Jammu and Kashmir but is a struggle between democracy and secularism, between democracy and dictatorship, between nationalism and fanaticism. I shall not go into the history which made inevitable the creation of the two independent and sovereign States in the subcontinent. For 800 years Muslims ruled the subcontinent. It is for historians to ponder the question why in the long period of intermingling, followed by two centuries of unitary administration under the British, it was not possible for a sense of common nationality to emerge in the subcontinent. It is sufficient to say that history cannot be undone.

"The struggle which led to the creation of Pakistan was not a struggle between secularism and religion but between two nationalisms —the Muslim nationalism which led to the creation of Pakistan and which is heir to the 800 years of Muslim rule, and the Hindu nationalism, which harkened back for its inspiration to the epoch of Hindu greatness before the Muslims came to the subcontinent. The creation of Pakistan, where Muslims would be free to develop in accordance with their culture and way of life, was the result of the democratic process of self-determination in which each of the provinces which today form part of Pakistan freely and formally expressed its desire to do so. Kashmir alone of those States, provinces and territories of pre-partitioned India has been deprived of the right to participate in this process of self-determination. This is exactly what we have said all those years, and we say today: let India establish its bona fides, let the people of Kashmir be given the chance.

"This is the basic issue involved in Jammu and Kashmir. Of equal importance is the issue of honouring of obligations under taken through international agreements? This agreement was concluded between India and Pakistan when a plan of settlement of the Jammu and Kashmir dispute was negotiated by the United Nations Commission, submitted to the two Governments, and accepted by both Governments. The plan embodied in the United Nations Commission for India and Pakistan (UNCIP) resolutions of 13 August 1948 and 5 January 1949 provided for: a cease-fire and the demarcation of a cease-fire line; the demilitarization of the State of Jammu and Kashmir; and free and impartial plebiscite under the auspices of the United Nations to determine the question of the accession of the State to India or Pakistan. It was upon acceptance of both resolutions by India and Pakistan that hostilities ceased on 1 January 1949. Then, as now, the cease-fire was meant to be a prelude to a permanent settlement which was to be achieved through a plebiscite under United Nations auspices after a synchronized withdrawal of forces. The whole history of the Jammu and Kashmir dispute is India's exploitation of the cease-fire, the first part of the agreement, for the purpose of evading the implementation of the other two parts, rather than of facilitating them.

"But the non-performance of an agreement by one party cannot render it invalid or obsolete. If it did, there would be no order in international life and the entire basis of the United Nations Charter would be undermined. Even though the agreement embodied in the two United Nations resolutions was not implemented by India, the Security Council repeatedly made clear its binding nature as an agreement and affirmed that its provisions were recognized and accepted by both India and Pakistan. As the distinguished representative in the Security Council, Justice Sunde of Norway said at the 46th meeting of the Council: '....It is for the plebiscite to determine the ultimate fate of the State.' ....I would like to add that this principle, this keystone of the whole structure, has an importance which transcends the obligatory force it derives from the consent of the parties. The principle has its intrinsic value because it embodies the only criterion for the determination of Kashmir's fate which is compatible with modern democratic ideals.

"That the UNCIP resolutions represent the engagement of the parties to the process and method by which the final settlement of the Kashmir dispute is to be reached has been reaffirmed not only by the Security Council. It has also been repeatedly admitted by India itself." Quoting the statements made by various Indian leaders, Bhutto added: "The agreement with regard to plebiscite binds not only India and Pakistan, it also binds the United Nation. Because of its binding nature and because of the principle of the stipulations pour autrui it involves third party beneficiaries —namely, the people of Jammu and Kashmir –it cannot, I submit, be changed or modified even by the Security Council, far less repudiated by one of the parties.

"This is the position of Pakistan. In surrendering it, Pakistan would surrender not only a basic principle of its national policy but the very principle of its allegiance to the United Nations. I can pledge from this rostrum that my Government intends no such surrender."

I have quoted at length from Bhutto's two speeches because they constitute one of the finest expositions of Pakistan's stand on Kashmir, especially with regard to the commitment by all sides – Pakistan, the United Nations and India – to decide the issue of Kashmir through a reference to the people. My idea here is to highlight the difference between what Pakistan's position on Kashmir from 1947 to 1965 was and how the Tashkent Declaration not only made no mention of a plebiscite, the Declaration merely spoke of the issue of Jammu and Kashmir having been "discussed, and each of the sides set forth its respective position".

The first two paragraphs of the Tashkent Declaration said: "The Prime Minister of India and the President of Pakistan, having met at Tashkent and having discussed the existing relations between India and Pakistan, hereby declare their firm resolve to restore normal and peaceful relations between their countries and to promote understanding and friendly relations between their peoples. They consider the attainment of these objectives of vital importance for the welfare of the 600 million people of India and Pakistan.

"(i) The Prime Minister of India and the President of Pakistan agree that both sides will exert all efforts to create good neighbourly relations between India and Pakistan in accordance with the United Nations Charter. They reaffirm their obligation under the Charter not to have recourse to force and to settle their disputes through peaceful means. They considered that the interests of peace in their region and particularly in the Indo-Pakistan subcontinent and indeed, the interests of the peoples of India and Pakistan were not served by the continuance of tension between the two countries. It was against this background that Jammu and Kashmir was discussed, and each of the sides set forth its respective position."

The rest of the nine paragraphs dealt with troop withdrawal, trade relations, the return of the diplomats to the two capitals, besides diplomatic rhetoric like non-interference in each other's internal affairs, ceasing hostile propaganda, the return of the property confiscated during the war, and thanks to the Soviet leaders for hosting the conference. Thus for the Pakistani people, who had been aroused to a new pitch of fervour and patriotism for the cause of Kashmir and made to believe that the liberation of Kashmir was just around the corner, the end-result of the Tashkent summit conference was a Declaration which neither called for a plebiscite, nor did it even reaffirm the Kashmiri people's right to self-determination, nor, more shockingly did it even secure from the two sides a harmless pledge to seek a solution of the Kashmir issue for which they had gone to war. All it did was to say that "Jammu and Kashmir was discussed, and each of the sides set forth its respective position". No wonder, the people took to the streets. The age of the mobs had arrived.

Altaf Gauhar, Ayub's powerful Information Secretary, who later became Dawn's Editor (January 1, 1972-February 15, 1973), was, like Bhutto, a hawk. However, he turned against Bhutto when the later came to power and was arrested. He criticises Ayub for giving Bhutto an opportunity "to appear as a hero in Lahore." His biography of Ayub Khan makes fascinating reading. The "opportunity" came when Chairman of the Chinese Communist Party, Liu Shao-chi, visited Pakistan in the aftermath of the Tashkent Declaration. He visited East Pakistan, came to Islamabad and was scheduled to go to Lahore. Gauhar pleaded with the Field Marshal that he should himself go to Lahore instead of letting Bhutto accompany the Chinese leader. According, to Gauhar, Ayub by then had already decided to sack Bhutto. Says Gauhar: "By giving Bhutto the opportunity to appear as a hero in Lahore in the company of the Chinese chairman Ayub had handed over the political initiative to Bhutto. It was a tumultuous reception. There was not an inch of empty space from the airport to government house. Bhutto was beaming with joy and frantically waving to a hysterical mass of humanity. The people lifted the car in which Bhutto was travelling and carried it on their shoulders. Bhutto had won their hearts. In retrospect, it would appear as if Ayub had himself launched Bhutto on his political career" (Altaf Gauhar, Ayub Khan: Pakistan's First Military Ruler, p 405).

As Pakistan's domestic situation deteriorated, India's attitude hardened. Under international pressure India would hold talks with Pakistan but would talk on every subject under the sun except Kashmir. Now the pressure on India was weakening, because in the wake of the 1965 war Pakistan's status as America's "most allied ally" came to an end, and whatever advantage Islamabad enjoyed from this relationship vis-à-vis its case in Kashmir evaporated. Pakistan now spoke of "self-determination" for the people of Kashmir instead of a plebiscite. Its position was further diluted when Pakistan began speaking of "an honourable solution" acceptable to all three sides – Pakistan, India and the people of Kashmir. To counter Pakistan's allegations that India was not willing to talk about Kashmir, New Delhi did indeed talk about Kashmir, but when the two delegations met — a process that involved several regimes in Islamabad – Indian diplomats "talked" about Kashmir only to say that Kashmir was India's integral part. Now India was positively having fun. Pakistani diplomacy then revolved around getting India to talk "meaningfully" because the two countries could not live in peace unless the Kashmir issue was solved, because it was the "core issue" in their relationship. Thus, a visiting diplomat in Pakistan or a given international conference in any part of the world would appear to do a great favour to Islamabad if the diplomat or the conference called for "meaningful talks" on the "core issue". This was a far cry from what Pakistan's stand on the issue was between 1947 and 1965 – a plebiscite.

Our story about the calvary that is Kashmir will not be complete without a reference to Sheikh Abdullah and the criminal role he played in collaborating with India to deny freedom to his own people. One could understand Sheikh Abdullah taking a stand against Kashmir's accession to Pakistan if his state were situated, say, where Hyderabad was — surrounded on all sides by India. Even though it had a Muslim majority, the sheikh could say, it would be inadvisable to accede to Pakistan for reasons of geography and economy. He could also stick to that view if Kashmir – even if situated where it is, surrounded on three sides by Pakistan and on the north and north-east by China – had a Hindu majority. He could have come up with the argument that, given the religious basis of the partition of India and the choice which the rulers of the princely state had to make in keeping with their peoples' aspirations, there was no choice but that a Hindu-majority state had to join India. The situation, however, was that not only did Kashmir have an overwhelmingly Muslim majority, it was adjacent to Pakistan, with all roads and the only rail link leading south to Pakistan. That in spite of this Abdullah stood in the way of his people's longings for unity with Pakistan defies common sense and can only be attributed to his ego, which expected a man like Jinnah to bow down to it. Nehru the democrat made

Abdullah rot in jail for 15 years. When he was released on April 8, 1964, and went to New Delhi for talks with Nehru, he took with him for his friend and his daughter "honey, almonds, saffron and lilies of the valley" (ibid 258). Instead, while the talks were going on, Indira Gandhi went to America to declare that there would be no change in India's Kashmir policy. It is not confirmed that the sheikh visited Pakistan armed with a new plan for a Kashmir solution having Nehru's blessings. Nehru, who was perhaps more responsible for Kashmir's tragedy than any other human being, had a closed mind on Kashmir, and it is doubtful he would have come up with a plan that provided for freedom for the Kashmiri people. Abdullah met Ayub on May 25 and 26, and it became very clear in the round of talks he had with him that what the sheikh was telling Ayub was less about Kashmir and more about how he felt frustrated by Jinnah's policies during the Pakistan movement. A summary of his talks with Ayub, as narrated by Gauhar, makes it clear he thought he was denied the position which he believed he deserved in the freedom struggle of the subcontinent's Muslims. Once he talked so much about the background to the Kashmir dispute and the different plans he had for its solution that Ayub "suddenly got up and said that he was getting a little fed up with the variety of solutions that were on offer and told Sheikh Abdullah to forget about Pakistan and come to any settlement with India he wanted" (ibid 266).

The mobs that took to the streets in the wake of the Tashkent Declaration were just an indication of what was in store for Pakistan for decades to come. The phenomenon has continued till this day (2009). The second major bout of mob frenzy came in 1968 when the Ayub regime decided to celebrate the Great Decade of Development and Reform. I have no doubt that Ayub's decade in power was indeed a decade of all-round development. I am aware of all the familiar arguments that were made against that era of development – that the rich had become richer and the poor poorer, that it was a development guided and approved by the World Bank and based on American loans and grants, and that this had benefited not the masses but "22 families" – a term that became part of Pakistan's economic and political jargon. The critics forget that it was the era of the Cold War, and Ayub was ruling a country that for security reasons had thrown in its lot with the "free world". Pakistan under Ayub could not possibly follow the socialist road to development while remaining an American ally. He accepted the World Bank wisdom – that economic development based on an unqualified commitment to free enterprise would sooner or later lead to the seeping-down effect, and the people's living standards would go up. Many Third World countries – South Korea was the classic example – had followed that course of development and had made rapid progress. Ayub had no other choice, and I have no doubt if that pace of development had continued Pakistan would be better off economically today.

Following the countrywide agitation Ayub resigned in March 1969 and handed over power to the Army Commander-in-Chief, General Agha Mohammad Yahya Khan. The havoc wrought by the mobs was a victory for anti-Ayub forces, but the common man had tasted violence. Gradually, street violence and arson would become a hobby with them. More regretfully, as the decades that followed showed, many politicians and parties, some of them in the mainstream, would regard resort to force as a practical option for achieving political goals. In a radio and television address to the nation on March 25, Ayub summed up the situation the mobs had created thus: "The situation is now no longer under the control of the government. All government institutions have become victims of coercion, fear and intimidation. Every problem of the country is being decided in the streets. Except for the armed forces there is no constitutional and effective way to meet the situation". Again, in a letter asking Gen Yahya Khan to take over, Ayub said "....all social and ethical norms have been destroyed and instruments of government have become inoperative and ineffective. The economic life of the country has all but collapsed .Workers and labourers are being incited to commit acts of lawlessness and brutality."

In handing over power to the army chief Ayub busted the Constitution, for under the 1962 Constitution, which he himself had got enacted, he should have handed over power to the Speaker of the National Assembly. (Qudratullah Shahab in Shahabnama and Roedad Khan in his A Dream Gone Sour and some other writers say that Ayub had not intended to resign and that he wanted to go on leave. However, the fact that he had decided to quit became clear when he began his speech to the nation with the words: "People of Pakistan. This is for the last time that I address as your President.") Immediately on taking over, Yahya abrogated the 1962 Constitution – the second to be scrapped, the first having been done by Iskander Mirza and Ayub in 1958. A feeling of extraordinary emptiness overwhelmed me as I heard the news of Ayub's resignation. Life without Ayub was unthinkable. He had become part of our existence. Exactly two years after Ayub stepped down, Yahya Khan ordered a military crackdown on mobs in East Pakistan. On December 16, 1971, the country was cut into two, Pakistan suffered a humiliating military defeat, and East Pakistan turned into Bangladesh. Ayub stood vindicated.

Six weeks before Ayub's resignation, Bhutto had given his own view of the anti-Ayub agitation and said the popular agitation constituted a rejection of Ayub's policy by the people. In his affidavit, filed on February 5, 1969, before a special bench of the West Pakistan High Court, Lahore, to challenge his detention under the Defence of Pakistan Rules, Bhutto said: "The popular agitation in the country is an expression of protest against a derelict system, a reflection of the resentment against the general state of affairs. The voices raised in the streets are a spontaneous verdict of the people against the excess of the regime, its dependence on an oppressive bureaucracy, its institutions, its failure to serve the common weal, its pedantic approach to culture, its insulation from the people and its insatiable appetite for family fortunes.

"I should say misrule and oppression — which have alienated the masses, the wave of unrest sweeping the country — is an expression of the general discontent, which had found ways of coming to the surface in spite of innumerable repressive acts of the authorities. The people have come out in open to protest against the years of oppression and all the evils that afflict our society on account of the regime's method of ruling the country.

"Our people are not different from those of other countries. There is a limit to their endurance. They feel the pain of privation and yearn for the happiness of their children. Their poverty is unimaginable but yet they hope for a better future.

"They are entitled to a decent livelihood, to shelter and clothing. Starvation has dried many a father's tears. It's not a law of God that our people must live eternally in despair and that their children should die of disease and want.

"Our people demanded a better life for themselves and for their children. They want food and clothing, employment and protection .These are not wild dreams but the expectations arising out of the marvellous age of science.

"Deny them their rights and they will find a redeemer and if none is available they redeem themselves. No plan for change is needed when the people seek it .The mood of the people is the plan. But arrogant functionaries, oblivious of the current of history, strike out want only to find final solutions for the regime's perpetuation.

"Nothing that I might say or do can possibly stir the masses in any way unless the objective situation was there. The objective situation is that the masses have been around and are protesting on their own initiative. There has been no conspiracy or plot whatever – unless on the government's side — affecting the economic and social well-being of the nation "

Two other landmark agreements on Kashmir deserve to be noted to finish the unfinished diplomatic history of the Himalayan valley that has been soaked in blood since 1988-1989: the Simla agreement (July 2, 1972) and the composite dialogue (January 2004). Bhutto had met Indira Gandhi as leader of a defeated nation. His daughter, Benazir, till then unknown, accompanied her father to have her initiation in the world of summit diplomacy. Under the circumstances obtaining — half of the country under Indian occupation, 90,000 Pakistanis, including over 72,000 soldiers, in Indian captivity, and voices in India calling for "finishing the job", Bhutto clinched an agreement that was not humiliating. He said later in an interview that he had planned his strategy hoping that India would make certain tactical errors. India did that. Bhutto had earlier surprised the world by releasing all prisoners of war unilaterally, but kept such Indian territory as had been taken by Pakistan on the western front. Bhutto said Mrs Gandhi made a mistake by keeping both the territory and the prisoners. This had deprived India of world sympathy. Even though signed by Pakistan in the wake of the military defeat, the Simla agreement pledged the two sides to "a final settlement of Jammu and Kashmir" (paragraph 6), unlike the Tashkent Declaration, which spoke of Jammu and Kashmir having been "discussed, and each of the sides set forth its respective position".

The other major landmark document was the Indo-Pakistan agreement to begin "a composite dialogue" after Indian Prime Minister A. B. Vajpayee visited Islamabad to attend the 12th summit conference of the South Asian Association for Regional Cooperation in Islamabad (January 4-6, 2004). The signing of the agreement was a commentary on the mercurial nature of the foreign policy followed by the Hindu extremist Bharatiya Janata Party, then in power in New Delhi. Vajpayee, who agreed to the composite dialogue, was exactly the man who had rushed troops to Pakistan's border after a terrorist attack on the Indian parliament building on December 13, 2001. The subcontinent once again escaped war by hair's breadth as nearly one million men were involved in an eyeball-to-eyeball confrontation that continued even during summer in South Asia's burning plains and deserts. Even though a bloody war between the two nuclear armed nations was averted thanks to intense behind-the-scenes diplomatic activity by America, Britain and China, the normalisation of the ties did not begin until Vajpayee reached Islamabad for the SAARC conference and signed the joint statement with President Pervez Musharraf on January 6. The actual dialogue began in February. The six-paragraph statement, read out by Indian Minister for External Affairs Yashwant Sinha and Pakistan's Foreign Minister Khurshid Mehmud Kasuri, at separate conferences said: "To carry the process of normalisation forward, the President of Pakistan and the Prime Minister of India agreed to commence the process of the composite dialogue in February 2004." The paragraph about Kashmir said: "The two leaders are confident that the resumption of the composite dialogue will lead to [a] peaceful settlement of all bilateral issues, including Jammu and Kashmir, to the satisfaction of both sides."

There was amazing progress toward a normalisation of relations between the two countries. Diplomatic relations were resorted to the normal level and train service was resumed. More important, in an unprecedented development a bus service was started between Azad Kashmir and the India-held valley. India also allowed Kashmiri leaders to visit Pakistan, and delegations of parliamentarians, writers, journalists and showbiz personalities started visiting across the border. This process was rudely broken when terrorists attacked Bombay, targeting Taj Mahal Hotel, on November 26, 2008. India broke off the composite dialogue. Things have remained there till this day (December 2009).

Nehru was responsible for Kashmir's tragedy more than any other person. His obsession with Kashmir that made him repudiate his international commitments has been, and will continue to be, a source of misery for the people of Kashmir and South Asia. Balraj Puri, a noted political and social worker in occupied Kashmir, had this to say about Nehru in his article for Peace Initiatives, a journal published by the International Centre for Peace Initiatives, New Delhi. Some time "after August 1953", Puri met Nehru to apprise him of the situation in Kashmir and suggested ways to overcome the crisis then sweeping the valley in the wake of Abdullah's arrest. He says: "Nehru warned me against being too idealistic and asserted that national interest was more important than democracy." He deplored Chief Minister Bakhshi Ghulam Mohammad's "unscrupulous methods" but added: "We have gambled at the international stage on Kashmir, we cannot afford to lose it. At the moment, we are there at the point of a bayonet. Till things improve, democracy and morality can wait." (Balraj Puri, Kashmir's Exclusion from Indian Democracy, article in Peace Initiatives, Vol III, No I, February 1997, p 4).

5

A NUCLEAR SUB

PAKISTAN WAS BORN WITH and into dangers and crises. It has stayed that way. Jinnah's correspondence with world leaders during the 13 months that he lived after he created Pakistan gives us an idea of what he had to put up with to save Pakistan from extinction during the weeks and months following independence (Jinnah on World Affairs, compiled by Mehrunnisa Ali and edited by Dr Syed Jaffer Ahmed, makes fascinating reading.) Visualise this scenario: the Maharajah of Kashmir is conspiring with New Delhi with a view to managing the Muslim-majority state's accession to India; Afghanistan votes against Pakistan for a UN membership and expresses reservations about the NWFP becoming part of the new state; Radcliffe and Mountbatten steal Ferozpur from Pakistan; the Indian leadership refuses to abide by the terms of the transfer of power agreement and declines to hand over to Pakistan its share of assets and ordnance; India masses troops on Junagadh's borders and prepares for military action in Kashmir; the Khan of Kalat dithers over accession to Pakistan; Burma expresses concern to Pakistan over its possible claim to a piece of territory adjacent to East Pakistan, while millions of refugees pour into the country as religious frenzy engulfs the subcontinent. It was then that Jinnah, his health failing, proved himself to be a man of indomitable courage and energy, for without the presence of what Beverly Nichols in his Verdict on India calls a 'giant', it is doubtful Pakistan would have survived the conspiracies launched by its enemies to destroy it in its infancy. There is no doubt that saving Pakistan from collapse during the 13 months that he lived after August 1947, building the new state's administrative infrastructure and placing Pakistan on the world's diplomatic map constitute as great an achievement on his part as that of creating Pakistan. This aspect of Jinnah's life has not received the attention it deserves. Going by the amount of work, correspondence and state business Jinnah had to attend to one is overwhelmed by the fact that this task should have been undertaken by a man who was so close to death. No one in that state of health could perhaps have undertaken the task he did without having the kind of will-power he possessed.

Long after those formative months and years were over, political crises continued to haunt Pakistan. But there was a difference: before Ayub and Mirza staged their coup d'état in October 1958 and made the politicians redundant, the crises were "purely" political — in the sense that the politicians jockeyed for power, and governments fell and were formed, but the lives of the people remained unaffected. More significantly, there was no law and order problem, and the country continued to remain peaceful. Under Ayub, too, peace reigned until riots in the wake of the celebrations marking the Great Decade of Development and Reform rocked Pakistan and led to Ayub's resignation on March 25. Since then, political crises, often involving foreign powers, have become endemic. In fact, I have often wondered whether Herbert Feldman would like to re-name his classic, From Crisis to Crisis, to something sounding funny but appropriate – From 'From Crisis to Crisis' to Perpetual Crisis. I may be accused of indulging in a bit of patriotism, but I think that living perpetually in a state of crisis has not necessarily had negative consequences, for the Pakistanis have learnt to live with it. No crisis seems to bother them, especially their leaders.

The difference between the beginning and the end of my second stint with Dawn (1966 to 1971) couldn't have been more striking in terms of the nation's mood. In 1966, peace reigned, and Ayub appeared firmly in control of the levers of power, the agitation in the aftermath of the Tashkent Declaration having fizzled out. However, the developments two years later radically altered the political picture, for Pakistan — state and society — would never be the same again. In 1968, as the government celebrated the Great Decade, one of my special assignments as a subeditor was to edit supplement after supplement which the Ayub regime got published to highlight its achievements in different sectors – education, industry, agriculture, aviation, and the mighty hydro-electric and irrigation projects like dams and "link canals" built in the wake of the 1960 Indus waters treaty, which gave India the exclusive use of three eastern rivers – Beas, Sutlej and Ravi. (As a Pakistani I feel mighty proud that Pakistan has one of the world's biggest irrigation systems: it has three big reservoirs, including Tarbela Dam, the world's biggest earth-filled dam, 19 barrages, 12 'link canals', and 59,200 kilometres of water courses. (Article by Bilal Hassan, Dr Rashid Ahmad and Khawar Jabbar, Economic and Business Review, Dawn, Oct 17, 2007).

Toward the end of 1968 disturbances broke out, leading to Ayub's resignation in March next year, the assumption of power by Yahya Khan and the abrogation of the 1962 constitution. The next year, 1970, saw an election campaign that dragged on for a full year, because the polls had to be postponed after a devastating cyclone hit East Pakistan in November. The principle of parity – that East and West Pakistan should have an equal number of deputies in parliament – was discarded, and Yahya Khan's Legal Framework Order provided for parliamentary representation in proportion to the population ratio. This meant East Pakistan would get 56 per cent of the seats in the federal assembly. The elections in December 1970 – Pakistan's first general election held on the basis of adult franchise – saw Bhutto's PPP sweeping polls in West Pakistan and Mujibur Rahman's Awami League capturing all seats in East Pakistan except two – those of Nurul Amin and Raja Tridev Roy. Even before Yahya ordered a crackdown in March 1971 rioters led by Awami League workers were attacking West Pakistanis and depriving the Awami

Leaguers of considerable sympathy which anti-PPP elements in West Pakistan had for it. The army's crackdown on the pro-independence demonstrators led to a mass exodus of refugees to India, which attacked Pakistan on November 3. The Pakistan Army surrendered on December 16, 1971. An independent Bangladesh became a reality. My revanche received a blow.

The man who brought me to Dawn a second time was Shamim Ahmad, an extraordinary character. In 1962 he had me lured away from Dawn and to Daily News, the English venture of the Jang group. In 1966 he re-joined Dawn as City Editor and asked me if I would leave Morning News to come back to the 'mother paper' a second time. I readily obliged, because the pay was Rs 1,000, which, given the price structure then, was a wonderful amount. Shamim was a talented man, wrote excellent copy, had command over language, but his jokes and jibes earned him many enemies. Shamim was dreaded because no one was sure when he would fall victim to his biting wit and satire. If someone dared reply, Shamim's retort would be even more devastating. That was the reason why his stay in newspapers was generally short, and he couldn't rise to the positions he deserved. A reporter, he hated subeditors to the point of disgust and believed that newspapers could be published without them. In this he was decades ahead of his times. He liked me tremendously and later in 1971 dragged me to The Sun. But he and I clashed quite often on the subeditor's role. His second stay in Dawn was again short, because he fell out with the editor, Jamil Ansari, who had replaced Altaf Husain as editor when the latter joined Ayub Khan's government as a minister in 1965.

Those days the world was hearing of nuclear submarines, and in keeping with that era Ansari, who liked me, used to call me 'a nuclear sub'. One of his greatest acts of favour to me was to put me on permanent duty with Evening Star. Akhtar Adil Razwy then was its editor. According to tradition, Dawn's senior most assistant editor was ex-officio editor of Evening Star. Razwy wrote editorials in a style that was all his own, and it goes without saying that I learnt a lot from him, even though as

Star editor he seldom had time to write editorials for Dawn. Razwy, now living in retirement, has a sophistication that I admired. Well versed in Urdu and Persian literatures, Razwy quotes profusely from Urdu and Persian classics to make a point. He ate Paan with panache and carried a pouch which opened and closed as he pulled a string. Initially I was put on the Star duty as a stop-gap arrangement after the regular Star staffer went on a month's leave. When he returned I told Razwy that I liked morning duty and was sorry to go back to Dawn with its rotating shifts. He asked me if I would like to stay on with Star. On my yes, he spoke to Ansari, and he agreed to let me stay on with the Star.

Being an evening paper, Evening Star obviously concentrated on local news, but there were many problems involved. Our competitors were two other dailies — The Leader and Daily News — and their spirit of competition centred not on what news they carried but on who hit the streets first. The idea was that the evening papers must be on sale by 1pm. This meant that printing should begin at 12.30pm. This had disastrous consequences on news contents, for if the pages had to be handed over to the printers at 12 noon, copy should close at 11.30 am. The crime reporters were poor stuff, their salaries were shockingly low, and even lower were their educational standards. News reports basically meant crime stories, which were badly written. To fill the pages I had to rely on the 'leftovers' of foreign and national news that Dawn could not accommodate the night before. Sometimes there was no local news at all that could be made a lead story. So I had to rely on foreign news, which was available in plenty, because Dawn subscribed virtually to all wire agencies of repute — Reuters, AFP, UPI, AP and German news agency DPA. Two foreign news items that I still remember had to be lead stories anyway and were world shaking — the Vietcong's Tet offensive on January 31, 1968, and the burning of the Al Aqsa mosque by a Jewish fanatic, Michael Dennis Rohan, on August 21, 1969. Later it was claimed that Rohan, an Australian, was not a Jew but a Protestant. While the first shook the Johnson administration and led his successor, Richard Nixon, to seek a negotiated settlement with Hanoi, the second led a month later to the formation of an organization of the world's Muslim nations and the holding of the first Islamic summit on September 22-25 at Rabat, Morocco.

On November 7, 1968, there was a clash between the police and some students of the Rawalpindi Polytechnic, and one student – Abdul Hameed – was killed. Bhutto, never the one to lose an opportunity like this to create trouble for Ayub in his citadel, led a big procession from Rawalpindi to Pindi Gheb where the boy was laid to rest. On November 11, a young man – Hashim – fired two shots at Ayub as he spoke at a public meeting. November 13, 1968, as the agitation against Ayub grew in intensity countrywide, Bhutto was arrested. Now other parties and personalities also joined the stir and formed the Pakistan Democratc Front. Bhutto was later shifted from the Rawalpindi jail to Larkana and confined to his home, Al Murtaza. On February 13, I still do not know what came on me, I suddenly decided I must go to Larkana and meet Bhutto to get an interview for Evening Star. I remember this date because the next day – February 14 – there was a general strike called by the Democratic Action Committee, of which Bhutto's PPP was not a part. Within minutes I had packed up, dashed off to Cantonment Station, caught Khyber Mail that left Karachi at about 10pm, changed trains at Kotri and reached Larkana early in the morning. I stayed at what then possibly was the only liveable hotel in Larkana, and after breakfast reached Al Murtaza, Bhutto's home. The police told me I had to have the Deputy Commissioner's permission to meet him. The DC was one Mohammad Khalid. Years later he would join Bhutto's PPP and would be known to the public as Mohammad Khalid Kharal. The DC told me no one was allowed to see Bhutto, even if he was a journalist, but said if I saw him in the evening he might reconsider my request. When I went to him in the evening he told me Bhutto had been freed. I reached Al Murtaza to find scenes of jubilation. Bhutto had been garlanded by his supporters, the ground inside Al Murtaza was full of people who were chanting slogans, and Bhutto was addressing them. A few days earlier I had written a piece for Evening Star on the political situation, and I was surprised when Bhutto, a voracious reader, shook hands with me and said he had read my article. Asghar Khan, a former air force chief who had joined politics, was present there, and evidently they had talked politics when Bhutto was possibly still under arrest technically. The antipathy that later developed between these two leaders would later be a source of misfortune for Pakistan.

Bhutto spoke to the crowd in Sindhi, and I took notes with the help of a translator. I remember the pause which Bhutto maintained each time the man standing next to me translated a sentence from his speech into Urdu for my benefit. After the speech Bhutto asked me whether I would like to be his guest for the night, but since I had a train to catch I left. I regret this decision till this day. The train arrived in Karachi early in the morning and I reached Dawn's new offices at Haroon House direct from Cantonment Station and barged into Razwy's room. I was anything but mannerly. I had come flushed with success and felt as if I had with me a mighty scoop. The way I entered the room, dumped my luggage on the floor and told him very excitedly about what I had "achieved" and started banging on the typewriter seemed to have annoyed Razwy. Nevertheless, in spite of my impudence, Razwy maintained his cool, and I wrote the story and made it Star's lead. I then gave the story to Ansari, who published it in Dawn the next day. (The make-up man made a blunder in placing matter, the order of paragraphs was destroyed, and even lines were mixed up.) A few days later Bhutto came to Karachi, and I interviewed him in detail at his Clifton home about his future plans, his manifesto for the coming general election, the PPP's "founding principles" and his concept of a mixed economy.

People — ignorant as well as well-informed — have accused Bhutto of using his manifesto and campaign promises as a stunt, because he allegedly forgot all about them once he came to power. This goes against historical truths. Whether the nationalization of heavy industry, banks and insurance was a mistake is a separate issue. Undertaking such a large-scale nationalization without well-trained party cadres was indeed a mistake, and retarded the industrial growth that was the chief characteristic of the Ayub era. Nevertheless, Bhutto was true to the promises he made, and his government placed under state control heavy industry and a significant portion of the financial sector when he came to power twenty-two months later. It was a lengthy interview, published in Dawn's issue of March 2, 1969, and Bhutto outlined his future nationalisation policy clearly. He said: "We have already made clear which sectors of economy we want to nationalize. The (PPP's) Foundation Meeting Document No.4 lays down in an unambiguous manner what we intend to do. Briefly, our nationalization must cover banking and insurance, all key industries such as iron and steel, nonferrous metal, heavy engineering, machine tool, ship-building, armaments, motor car assembly and essential electrical equipment meant for power production: all sources of supply of energy like electricity gas, oil, etc, all major means of public transport, and mining".

The PPP's Document 4 had spelled this out clearly: "The private sector will play its own useful role in the kind of mixed economy envisaged, but will not be able to create monopolistic preserves. It must flourish under conditions proper to private enterprise, namely, those of competition, and not under the shelter of State protection such as is the case at present. ... Nationalization will not destroy individual initiative: it should, on the contrary, act as a stimulus by releasing the suppressed energies of the working class and other wage-earners. Public ownership will not be allowed to degenerate into capitalism."

Bhutto fulfilled the promises and then paid with his life. He was hanged not for the murder he was charged with but for striking a mortal blow at Pakistan's comprador capitalist class, which could not accept the loss of its business empires and the consequent decline in its political power. "A man forgets his father but not his patrimony", said Machiavelli. The beauty of the quote can be appreciated in Latin in which the words patrimonium and pater highlight the irony.

The year 1970 saw a colourful election campaign. Even though Pakistanis are politically an emotional people, the campaign was largely violence-free despite the high pitch to which the emotions were taken by the religious lobby led by the Jamaat-i-Islami. I attended Bhutto's first public meeting of the campaign at Karachi's Nishtar Park. It was a sizable crowd, but not of the kind that would come later. Bhutto played the Tashkent card again and said he was going to finally let the people know what the secret he had been talking about for so long was. He took off his coat, saying he was doing this because the mention of the word Kashmir had warmed him, and he was going to talk about the way the cause of Kashmir was betrayed at Tashkent. He then dragged on his speech, till the muezzin called for Maghreb prayers and the crowd dispersed. This was deliberate, for Bhutto would continue to talk about the Tashkent secret throughout the year but would never reveal it. In fact there wasn't much to reveal. I remember a cartoon in a Karachi daily, with Bhutto shedding his coat and the caption saying: Political striptease. One day at a private gathering at his Clifton home where I was present, Bhutto revealed what the "secret" was. He said Ayub had offered to sign a no-war pact with India without a Kashmir settlement.

By now Bhutto's shibboleth — Islamic socialism — was not only attracting the people's attention but also worrying the industrialist class that had fast emerged during the Ayub regime. As the election campaign gained momentum, one started hearing of Islamic "ideology". Since socialism was an ideology, the religious right thought there was no better way of countering the Bhutto phenomenon than by discovering an ideology of its own. For the first time, thus, our religion, Islam, was reduced to an ideology. An ideology is intolerant, exclusive, fearful, revengeful and dogmatic — the very opposite of what Islam stands for. The leading proponent of the newly discovered Islamic ideology was Gen Sher Ali Khan, Information Minister in Yahya's cabinet, and he kept no secret of his personal distaste for Bhutto. However, the party that espoused the ideology cause with great zeal was the Jamaat-i-Islami. Its election campaign was emotional and couched in a powerful Islamic idiom but without an intellectual base. The JI propaganda jargon, which was picked up by other parties and groups also, then began dividing all Pakistanis into two categories — "Islam loving" and those outside this category. This marked the beginning of the polarization of Pakistani politics and society, for it had continued in various forms till this day. There is no doubt sooner or later all industrial tycoons and feudal politicians would have united against the PPP, and personally against Bhutto, anyway. But the anti-Bhutto campaign would not have acquired the pseudo-religious character it did had not the JI given it that direction.

The JI's opposition to the PPP was not based on the latter's actual programme that was available in black and white; instead, the JI gave an impression that it was engaged in a jihad against "atheistic communism" and that once Bhutto came to power all mosques would be locked and Pakistan turned into a Soviet republic. To buttress its anti-PPP stance, the JI reproduced in Urdu cheap anti-communist USIS propaganda literature that was available in plenty those days. One such article which the JI's powerful propaganda machinery distributed and which I remember reading told its readers that in communist countries all old people were shot, because they did not contribute to production, and so that was going to happen to Pakistan, too, if the PPP won the election. The JI's behaviour was remarkably close to what Bernard Lewis wrote in one of his books about the Catholic Church. I cannot say which book it was, but I read it decades ago, and the remark he made about "ideology" was part of his narrtive about the destruction of the Arab civilisation by the Mongol hordes in the 13th century. Lewis said there was a lot common between the Christian world and the Muslims than between Mongols and either of them. But the Catholic Church, blinded by its hatred of Muslims in the wake of the disastrous Crusades and guided by its "ideology", had sent emissaries to Halagu's court and egged him on to attack the Muslim heartland. Even though the JI leaders' speeches, statements and party literature paid lip service to the concept of social justice and economic equality, in practice it allied itself closely with the capitalist and feudal classes and made it clear it considered a change in the socio-economic status quo a heresy. To the capitalist class that had emerged during the Ayub era, the JI's propaganda machinery and the party's religious credentials came in handy.

The JI always got a good coverage in the newspapers, because it had the support of some powerful media barons, especially in the Urdu press. While the English newspapers, too, were not very sympathetic to Bhutto, they by and large tried successfully to maintain professional standards in news and comment. Dawn did not toe a rabidly anti-Bhutto policy, but in news coverage and comments it tended to give an impression that it supported a combination of three parties — a faction of the Muslim League, called the Council Muslim League headed by Mian Mumtaz Daultana, the National Awami Party, headed in West Pakistan by Abdul Wali Khan, and Sheikh Mujibur Rahman's Awami League in East Pakistan. Truly speaking, Pakistan had no communist party, but if there was a party that came close to being one it was Wali Khan's NAP (headed in East Pakistan by Maulana Bhashani, some time referred to as Red Mullah). Yet, the JI seemed happy with the NAP, in spite of the latter's close identification with the USSR and the funding and propaganda support it received from India in its Pakthoonistan stunt. The more the election campaign advanced and it became clear that Bhutto rallies were drawing larger crowds, the more the JI's anti-Bhutto frenzy increased. In 1965-66 there was a massacre in Indonesia, but it had no relevance to Pakistan. Indonesia had the non-communist world's biggest Communist Party, and Ahmad Soekarno, father of Indonesia's freedom and an anti-imperialist crusader, had patronized it. The massacre that killed hundreds of thousands of people was Indonesia's internal affairs, and no political parties, except the JI, tried to drag this issue into the election campaign. In fact, if it had some sense of responsibility and political common sense and if the larger national interests were dear to us, the JI should have ignored it instead of repeatedly referring to the massacre to arouse passions. Instead, amazing as it sounds, the JI literature was cautioning people against a planned massacre by the "socialists" in Pakistan. More unfortunately, the JI party literature focused on Bhutto's personality and made the most vicious kind of attacks even on his mother.

In 1968 I was closely involved with some JI journalist-friends in an informal association we had formed during the anti-Ayub movement, because hostility to the Field Marshal's regime was common to journalists supportive of both the PPP and the JI. However, after Ayub was overthrown I noticed that to my JI friends Islam essentially boiled down to a jihad against the PPP, and this helped the party get massive doses of money from the industrialist class, which suddenly discovered its Islamic roots and became God-fearing and pious overnight. There were two indications of the obsession the JI had developed with Bhutto. One was a disclosure by a JI friend to me that "socialists are preparing lists". He appeared serious and said the lists contained names of "Islam-loving people" whom the "socialists" would one day suddenly massacre. I found it hard to suppress my smile. The second came in the form of a decision by the JI leadership to order its cadres to take precautionary measures against a possible swoop by the "socialists" at an unearthly hour, and the least they could do was to move upstairs. Originally I thought this was a big joke, but one day I was stunned when I found that a major JI leader in the Nazimabad block where I lived had moved to a new house and rented the upper storey. The JI's obsession was now turning into neurosis. Evil words, especially those directed at others, have a way of recoiling on those who utter them. The PPP would never ever — till this day (2009) — have the strength, arms, organization or the inclination needed for a massacre, but decades later some other party would emerge as the JI's scourge — the Mohajir (later Muttahida) Qaumi Movement, MQM for short. The year 1970 would also be remembered by Pakistani journalists for a countrywide strike that shook the newspaper world and led to repercussions, including vast retrenchments in newspaper offices and a controversial structural change in the press industry's trade union movement. The strike did not exactly turn out to be the unmitigated disaster the opponents of the leadership of the Pakistan Federal Union of Journalists made it out to be. Nevertheless, nearly 150 journalists lost their jobs as the managements attempted to crush the journalists' trade union activity. Unfortunately, the response to the strike by the politicians and the press got mixed with the polarization discussed above and served to embitter relations between the journalists and managements for a long time. In keeping with its "socialist" phobia, the JI propaganda would have the world believe that the journalists' strike was actually a cover for a communist revolution which Bhutto and Bhashani were planning. The truth was that the strike was decided as a weapon of last resort on what came to be known as "interim relief". This needs to be explained.

In March 1959, the Pakistan Press Commission, formed in 1954 and reconstituted in 1958, recommended — on the journalists' persistent demands — the formation of a Wage Board to fix wages for the newsmen and lay down rules for service conditions. To give legal cover to the Wage Board's recommendations, the Ayub government enacted by decree the Working Journalists' (Condition of Service) Ordinance in April 1960. Headed by Justice Sajjad of the West Pakistan High Court, the first Wage Board gave its award on December 31, 1960. It revised the journalists' salaries, laid down a pay structure, and specified healthcare benefits. It also classified the newspapers into various categories and related their obligations to revenue and circulation. The award made it clear that it would be reviewed after five years. The second Wage Board, however, was set up four years late, in 1969, headed this time by Justice A.S Faruqui of the West Pakistan High Court. Since the Board's deliberations would have taken a lot of time, the Board announced that, pending the final announcement of a comprehensive award, the managements should give all journalists a small amount of money (Rs 35) as an interim relief. Some managements, including those of Dawn, were willing to pay the "interim relief", but the consensus among the press barons was against giving any relief to the journalists. This paved the way for the countrywide strike.

Given the nature of the strike and the fact that it was to cover the entire country, the PFUJ, headed then by K. G. Mustafa, an East Pakistani journalist from, decided to hold a referendum among its members to say Yes or No to the strike. As a PFUJ member I cast my Yes vote at the Karachi Press Club. The final results of the referendum held in all major newspaper centres in East and West Pakistan showed 90 per cent voted Yes for the strike. The strike began on April 15, 1970, and lasted till the 24th. Initially, it was a stunning success. In Karachi, Pakistan's major newspaper centre, no paper was published, though in Lahore Nawa-i-Waqt, the Urdu daily, managed to publish a restricted paper. By the sixth day, however, the strike was showing signs of fizzling out in Karachi, as some papers began to publish rags with the help of "new journalists". These "new journalists" were actually men drawn from the managements, and they managed to produce some sort of papers, with full help from print workers and proof-readers. The strike was called off after 10 days. The PFUJ leadership claimed that it called it off after 90 per cent of the managements had agreed to pay the "interim relief". Unfortunately, the PFUJ either did not bother to seek the cooperation of the non-journalist staff, or if it did, the cooperation wasn't forthcoming. Barna's detractors insisted that the strike was a failure and that the PFUJ had no choice but to call it off because the strike had either already failed or was about to. However, 150 journalists lost their jobs, the worst sufferers being those who worked for the newspapers controlled by the National Press Trust. Among the news agencies, the PPI was the harshest on its staff. In Dawn, no one was fired. I was back on Evening Star duty.

The aftermath of the strike led to intense debate among the journalists on the future strategy and on the very structure of trade unionism in the newspaper industry. Many thought that the strike failed to achieve results because the non-journalist staff was not on board. This gave birth to the idea that what the newspapers needed was a trade union that would represent all the workers in the newspaper industry, journalists as well as non-journalists. The problem was that the non-journalists included not only white collar workers like managers, clerks, typists, accountants and telephone operators but also blue collar workers like foremen, lino-machine operators, make-up men, proof boys, electricians, drivers, security guards and cleaners. Uniting them under the umbrella of one organisation meant creating a multi-class structure that ran counter to the basic principles of trade unionism. Nevertheless, the majority stood for a new trade union that would include all those working in newspaper offices. So that is how the All Pakistan Newspaper Employees' Ad Hoc Committee came into being in 1973. Three years later, after elections, it turned into the All Pakistan Newspaper Employees' Confederation (APNEC) with Barna as chairman. He remained APNEC chief for 13 years, till he went to Britain as APP's London correspondent. The late Abdul Quddoos Sheikh, my closest friend among journalists, became associate chairman and was later elected chairman in 1991. A driving force behind the journalists' trade union movement has been Abdul Hamid Chhapra, who became APNEC chairman in 2003. Earlier he had been Secretary General of the Pakistan Federal Union of Journalists (1989-92) and its president in 1996 and suffered imprisonment for journalists' cause.

APNEC represented all employees of the press industry and not the journalists alone, and since the non-journalists were in a majority the newsmen's interests got mixed up with the rest, with consequences not wholly to their advantage. To begin with, the PFUJ, even though it existed, was reduced to a debating forum, because it was no more in a position to enforce a strike or to break it, because the power to do so rested with the non-journalists. With the coming into being of Apnec, the Wage Board's scope, too, widened, for it had to make recommendations for service conditions and pay structures not only for the newsmen but also for the non-journalists ranging from managers to drivers and cleaners. The managements reacted angrily. They were already unhappy with what was a Wage Board meant only for the journalists. If the Wage Board award stipulated higher wages for the journalists, the managements could put up with it, because journalists in a newspaper office are always a small minority, compared to the clerical and printing staff. But an award for Apnec members meant a bloated salary bill and a heavier financial burden on the managements. The managements dithered and often delayed the awards' implementation for years.

Apnec's formation and the Wage Board's new responsibility served to obscure the fundamental difference between a journalist and a non-journalist, for a journalist could work only in a newspaper office (TV had not till then made its appearance in Pakistan), while a clerk or typist or a driver could get a job in a bank or airline office. Besides, the journalists had rights and privileges peculiar to their profession; that was not the case with the non-journalist staff. The managements conceded this point, but they could not raise the journalists' wages because the union would accuse them of discrimination, and the journalists would themselves be exposed to the charge of betraying the non-journalists' interests.. Many senior journalists, among them Ahmad Ali Khan, opposed the formation of a multi-class trade union and, instead, stood for closer coordination with print workers' unions and the managerial associations instead of forming a vertical trade union in which the journalists would be a minority and the members' interests clashed.

There were several advantages in being at the Star. First there was no night duty, and I passed a 'normal' life. Second, this meant I had a lot of time to indulge in my favourite activities – afternoons in the libraries and movies in the evening. Sattar had by then returned from Lincoln's Inn after his law studies, and our gang of four – Sattar, Baughty, Bogra and I – had evenings to ourselves. Evenings basically meant movies, dinners and prolonged political discussions at Old Clifton. Young Karachiites hardly knows what Old Clifton is. It is a sort of promenade at a height overlooking the Arabian Sea. The beach is about a mile from there, and one has to descend rough ground to reach the beach. We never bothered to do that. Those who came to take a walk were mostly old people, especially Parsis. There was a cathedral, some old British era bungalows, a car park, mostly vacant then, a snack bar, and some benches. A mosque was built later. The area was dimly lit, and that added to the ambiance. We would walk there mostly after movie and dinner, and then had endless discussions on every political topic under the sun. A song which was very popular then was Duma dum must Qalandar. This Sindhi song was later to enchant entire Pakistan. The few young men who came there played this song quite loud on their car tape-recorders. Sometimes minstrels played this music on sitars, and the listeners gave them generously. The Dubai phenomenon (chapter 13) was more than a decade away, and the semi-literate rich had not till then destroyed the decency of public places. Our gang of four was a mixed lot. Sattar was a lawyer, so was Bogra. This was the name we had given to Mohammed Ali Karimjee, who had passed his youth in South Africa. He was I think the most well-read man in our group. To avoid a name mix-up, we began calling Karimjee as Bogra – after the name of Pakistan's third prime minister, Mohammad Ali Bogra – while the gang referred to me simply as Journalist. Baughty spoke refined English and copied Walter Pidgeon and Clifton Webb in language and gestures. He has remained undecided about his profession till this day now that he is 70 plus. He was initially with the Pakistan National Oil, then left it to try to run a recruiting agency – sending Pakistani workers to oil-rich sheikdoms – and then gave it up to become a farmer. As a farmer he failed magnificently, for it was a costly hobby that seldom gave him much money. Extraordinary as it sounds, the refinement that was characteristic of his personality faded as he took to farming seriously. Even though he did not become completely rustic, there was a marked deterioration in the way he dressed, and most regretfully he gave up workouts, because he thought driving a jeep from Karachi to his farm in Chohor Jamali was itself an exercise. This was wrong, for his health declined rapidly, he has become diabetic and finds reading difficult. Bogra gave up legal practice to become legal adviser and later chief administrative officer of a sugar company, and remained there till his death in 1998. Sattar is our prima donna. In 1967, he married Rafat, a girl from the Tabani family, one of Pakistan's leading industrialists, and it goes without saying that our group got jealous of her and vice versa, both accusing each other of monopolising Sattar. Our wives did not meet with the same frequency. Nevertheless, there were grand picnics at Sandspit and Hawks Bay off and on. Baughty's choice for a wife was one of his Multan-based cousins, while Bogra was the last of us to get married.

There are two remarkable features about Sattar: one, people – in fact total strangers – behave toward him with friendly sentiments. Two, food has a special place in his scheme of things. One day he sought an adjournment, and when the High Court judge asked him why, he told the astonished judge that he wanted to have lunch with his wife on time. The judge remarked that he had never in the past come across a lawyer who had sought an adjournment because he wanted to have lunch with his wife on time. He granted the adjournment. Now an old man like me Sattar spends money on books and foreign travels. Even though he is a millionaire there is no trace of snobbery in him, and I have found him utterly indifferent to things ostentatious. Abdul Qadir Dadabhoy too was with us at the Karachi University in the Political Science Department, but he joined our gang later, because during the sixties and seventies he was mostly in East Pakistan. An industrialist, he and his wife are American nationals, though they have maintained their Karachi home.

~~~~~~~~

For a short period in the 1960s, in a departure from the Dawn tradition of having a professional journalist serve as editor, Yusuf Haroon, then chairman of the publishing company, served as chief editor (April 13, 1966, to April 5, 1967). But there was a political background to it. Soon we subeditors began to see the difference in Dawn's style if not contents. Headlines became smaller, and for some reasons we were told to avoid verbs in headlines. For instance, "five killed in accident" would appear as "death of five in accident" or "criminals rounded up in Rawalpindi" as "round-up of criminals in Rawalpindi". The "downsizing" of headline points had the undesirable effect of hiding or underplaying news items. This ran counter to the well-established principle of daily journalism that headlines should catch the reader's attention, instead of making him search for a news item. The readers were complaining that it was becoming increasingly difficult to find news in Dawn.

However, from the benefit of the hindsight I can see what the motive behind this policy guideline was: the news concerning Ayub and his economic achievements, of which he was so proud, was now virtually hidden from the reader, and no one was quicker to note this than the government itself. The chief editor's most audacious decision was to instruct us not to put Ayub's pictures on the front page – in violation of the tradition which made us print Ayub's picture even with such routine news items as his arrival and departure notices. As was bound to happen, the government's fury fell on the house of the Haroons, and Yusuf had to make a dash out of the country. With his departure, the editor, Jamil Ansari, who had been sidelined during this period, resumed his duty and saw Dawn through the turmoil of the revolt against Ayub Khan (1968-69) and the beginning of Yahya's disastrous rule.

One lesson learnt during the great revolt against Ayub Khan was that press freedom is not something that can exist independent of freedom of the political platform. As a young journalist, I often felt embarrassed, and, in fact, found myself unable to defend myself in drawing rooms dominated by elders, when they accused the press of being servile. A perusal of Dawn of 1969 and 1970 would show a surprising degree of freedom in news and views in the aftermath of Ayub's ouster, so long as the legitimacy of Yahya Khan's rule and the Legal Framework Order were not questioned. In fact, the press and politicians seldom doubted Yahya's pledge to hold a free and fair election (which, in fact, he did) and were thus occupied principally with the "ideological" issue.

The whiff of fresh air was short-lived, for the military crackdown in East Pakistan in March, 1971, and the consequent "security" considerations brought us back to square one. However, even before the crackdown, the freedom the press supposedly enjoyed was not used to present East Pakistan's point of view to the people of West Pakistan. By and large, the press here was opposed to Sheikh Mujib's Six Points. This prevented the press from playing a part in opposing the drift towards civil war and catastrophe. The official press notes were now the media's primary source of news about the civil strife and the war with India that broke out in December, 1971. At the UN Security Council an angry Bhutto tore up the papers on which he had written his speech. For years the religious right and the press it controlled told the nation that Bhutto had torn up the Polish resolution. In the first place it is doubtful that, if Bhutto had not purportedly torn up the copy of the Polish resolution, India would have halted its military operations and made its army return home without cutting Pakistan into two. That it was Bhutto's own speech which he tore up was confirmed to me in an interview (published in Dawn Magazine of January 18, 1985) by the man who was sitting next to him at the Security Council – Iqbal Akhund, Pakistan's Permanent Representative at the UN

The gloomiest days of my professional career were those passed in the darkness –literal and figurative – of 1971: a premonition of things to come. The military crackdown in March 1971 in East Pakistan and the denial of newsprint from the country's only newsprint plant at Khulna meant a drastic reduction in the size of all newspapers. With Dawn reduced to six or eight pages, very little space was left for news after advertisements consumed a big chunk. The staff was at the usual strength, but had little to do. The management asked all those who had accumulated months of leave to avail themselves of it. There was no fun in having the usual three shifts in the newsroom – 8am to 2pm; 2pm to 8pm and again 8pm to 2am – since the morning and evening shifts which worked on inside pages had nothing to do. Only the night shift turned up in the evening. The atmosphere in Haroon House was such as would turn even the most optimistic into a manic depressive. All its corridors, which normally hummed and bustled with activity, were dark, the management having decided to switch off all lights to save on electricity. It was also a rare and gloomy sight to find the newsroom closed, for the newsroom is the one place in any morning newspaper which never really closes.

As I handed Evening Star pages each day at noon and walked towards the exit, the sight was ghostly. All corridors were enveloped in a darkness that was not only haunting, but seemed like foretelling the disaster that was in store for the nation. Not a soul was in sight. Little did we know that the darkness would continue until it reached the ultimate on December 16 that year. After a two-year interlude spent at The Sun (1971-73) I was happy to return to the "mother newspaper" when Haroon House was more or less back to normal, though Dawn itself would take several more years to come into its own under the leadership of a most remarkable editor — Ahmad Ali Khan.

6

'MR RAMAY'S BILL OF INDICTMENT'

THE PRESS INDUSTRY'S WORST DAYS in terms of its financial health were those in the aftermath of the secession of East Pakistan in December 1971. Terrible days in terms of repression, censorship, unabashed persecution and whipping were to come later during Ziaul Haq's barbaric dictatorship (1977-1988), but from the point of view of the newspapers' solvency the early seventies were bleak. The newsprint factory at Khulna was lost to Bangladesh, and the newspapers had to import it according to the meagre quota allotted by the left-leaning Bhutto government, which itself was fighting for survival. When Ahmad Ali Khan took over as acting editor in February 1973, Dawn was a six-page affair, there were hardly any advertisements because of the post-war depression, and the company's fortunes had sunk so low that it had to get money on overdraft to pay its staff. To quit a job under such circumstances was a crime against one's own self, and I committed it. "You must trust me", he said, as I saw Khan sitting in the editor's seat for the first time. He was reacting to the disappointment he had seen in my face over the terms and conditions of the job he was offering me. I was wrong, for I was not in a position to bargain. I had resigned my job in The Sun in a huff and become jobless, with a wife, three kids, and two old and perpetually ill parents to look after. My assets then were Rs 250 in the bank — after 12 years in journalism — and a rickety Volkswagen that I realise from the benefit of hindsight gave me excellent service in spite of the virtual absence of maintenance on the part of its bankrupt owner. I had approached Ahmad Ali Khan — whom the staff invariably called as Khan Saab — for a job. He already knew me, because we were colleagues before I left Dawn in 1971 to join The Sun. But I was a newsroom man, while AAK was then on the writing side. So there was little interaction between us, and he knew little about me as a journalist. Caution, perhaps over caution, characterised all his actions.

When I approached him for a job after leaving The Sun I discovered in him — in spite of his refusal to appoint me — a deep sympathy for me, and I believe it continued till his death. While he did not offer me a job, he asked me to write for Dawn and suggested a topic — Pakistan's party system. I had a typewriter at home. I had purchased it on instalments, and it served me as well as and longer than the German-built 1962 model car which I had bought in 1968 for Rs3, 000. While I was quite capable of writing on the topic, I thought I should seek someone's guidance. Barkat Warsi was my teacher at the Political Science Department at the Karachi University, and I approached him one evening at his Muslim League Quarters home to brief me on the subject. I must say he did an excellent job. I wrote three pieces and AAK liked it, so did Salman Meenai, then Assistant Editor and, until then, quite close to AAK. The articles on the party system appeared in the Dawn Magazine, edited then by Ahsan Yahya. However, in spite of this, AAK made no offer to me. Much later I came to know why: he never made a promise if he thought he was not capable of fulfilling it or if there was even one per cent of doubt that something may go wrong at the eleventh hour. In fact, as I drew closer to him, I realised that even if an appointment letter were ready in his drawer and he intended to hand it over to the job seeker the next morning, he would hate to tell him that his appointment letter was ready and he should get it the next day. All he would say is, "See me, tomorrow, and let me see what I can do for you."

A few days after my last instalment appeared in the magazine, a neighbourhood boy came to me, saying there was a phone call for me. I had no phone at my Nazimabad home then. AAK was on the line, and he wanted me to see him at the earliest. It was July 1973. I think I saw him that very day, and he asked me to report for duty immediately. My appointment letter, he said, would come in due course, but I must start working. I thanked him and he ordered tea. This was the beginning of a friendship that would last until his death 34 years later. There were many ups and downs in our relationship, there were many mistakes on my part, and quite often AAK never hesitated to apologise to me where he thought he was wrong. On many occasions, when I thought I was being unfairly treated, I protested, and many times I perhaps crossed the limits and quarrelled. But he was magnanimous enough to show understanding. However, politically we were often on the wrong side, and it was during political discussions that we argued with raised voices. And at least once I just walked out of his room and found myself, of all places, in Afghanistan and wondered what I was doing in Dawood's post-Zahir Kabul. Nevertheless, the sincerity and warmth in our relations not only survived all crises, the passage of time consolidated our relations to a level that I could not have perceived as I sat in his office sipping tea in July 1973. He liked tea as most Pakistanis do, but in the mid-nineties he switched over to green tea and had endless cups of it. One of his younger brothers had died of prostrate cancer, and he borrowed the wisdom that green tea was anti-cancerous.

When the appointment letter came I was greatly disappointed. I had been Assistant Editor in The Sun, and the pay that I was getting there was quite high compared to what he was offering. I wanted to be appointed Assistant Editor with a higher pay. He said he was offering me the pay I was drawing when I left Dawn two years ago, plus the increments I would have earned. This was quite generous of him, but he refused to accept my other demand. He said promotion would come in due course and I must trust him. Trust him, with the situation so fluid? Dawn had recently seen three editors go in quick succession:

Jameel Ansari had resigned on his own, while Mazhar Ali Khan and Altaf Gauhar had quit under government pressure, and I was not sure whether AAK would himself survive. He read me correctly and said there was not even one per cent of a chance that he would quit or be made to quit. "You must trust me", he repeated. Well, I trusted him. Five years passed he was there; 10 years passed he was still around, 20 years, he was still there, a quarter century, he was still reigning as Chief Editor. I was myself now an old man, and trusting him had indeed paid off, for there was no post that a newspaper office has which AAK did not place me on.

Thirty-four years later — March 2007 — I would be asked to do the painful job of writing his obituary. It was a heart-rending job, because AAK was alive, though in an intensive care unit. "In the death of Ahmad Ali Khan ... " I began, and then froze. How could I write this, knowing that he was alive? What if by some miracle he were to enter my room — as he did quite often during the nearly three decades that I worked with him? Wouldn't that be embarrassing for me? But then I was sure he would have reacted the way a thorough professional does. All obituaries in such cases are written in advance, for no newspaper wants to get caught unprepared, especially when death appears imminent. I was positive if he were to enter my room and read those words he would have said, "Go ahead, sir! Yes, the obituary should be ready in advance". In fact, his sense of humour would have come up with some apt remark. I remember once my mouth was full with some eat, and he entered my room and saw my bloated cheeks. I found it difficult to talk and merely mumbled something. He replied, "Go ahead, sir, you look wonderful!" One of his jokes has remained stuck in my memory: there was a mistake in a headline on page one, and the night editor explained it by saying that he was in a hurry and had consulted a number of colleagues at the eleventh hour, and he let the word go that way because the majority thought that was correct. AAK said that while he was greatly impressed by his attachment to democracy he wished, when it came to English, he prefer dictionary to democracy.

On July 28, 1973, I reported for work, and I must record my gratitude to a colleague now dead — Mahdi Jafar, who had known me since our days at Morning News. He had intended to migrate to the United States, and told AAK that I could handle the leader page, which Jafar then edited. What was Dawn like then, especially its leader page? Before me now is the leader page of Dawn's issue of September 1, 1973, and the page, like the entire paper itself, testifies to the paper's poor financial conditions and the consequent, shockingly low production quality. The top article, by a foreign journalist about the non-aligned summit that was due in Algiers on September 5, is the only article on the page, and most probably is taken from some syndicated service to which Dawn still subscribes in spite of the financial straitjacket it is in. There is no middle article, nor one at the bottom; instead, news items fill the remaining space on the page. The first two columns carry two editorials: the first one is about the Arab world entitled "Arab unity in stages" — with the "stages" in double quotes, while the second is about the floods then ravaging Pakistan, especially Sindh. The letters to the editor do not have even two columns (7 and 8) for them, for at the end there is a double-column astrology box, "This Day for You", by Sophie Roline. So there is room only for three letters, plus four Points from Letters. AAK insisted that since many letters could not be accommodated for reasons of space the least we could do to satisfy the letter writers was to accommodate points from them. The top letter that day is by M. A. Bari, who complains against high prices, and criticises Dr Mubashshar Hassan, Federal Finance Minister, for his policies. Two of the Points from the letters say: "Mr Mohsin Ehsan Mufti from Lahore wonders why the Federal Finance Ministry's notification regarding National Pay Scales does not apply to the Education Department...", while another Point says "Miss Shigufta, an Islamabad student, now stranded in a relief camp in Larkana, appeals to the Federal Education Minister, Abdul Hafeez Pirzada, to extend college vacations by a month so that the floods subside and students return to their colleges..." Column 3, next to the editorials, contains news items. The top has a three-line headline in 24 point C.H. It is a machine type, unlike the standard Century Bold, which is hand composed. Subeditors prefer the CH type because that gives them more letters, hence more words, per column. The second item is longer than the top — something anomalous — and has a three-line headline in12 point CB, followed by a small two-paragraph story headlined "Boycott by newsmen". The second paragraph of the story says: "The decision has been taken by the union because of the reported misbehaviour of the Minister with the Lahore Correspondent of Karachi daily Hurriyet, Mr Tawseef Ali Khan". At the end is a single column item with an appropriate 10 point headline in capital letters: "Bank holiday". The front page carries a photograph showing Prime Minister Z. A. Bhutto with UNESCO's visiting Director General Rene Maheu. A single story informs the readers that Bhutto is leaving on a six-day visit of the United States, and a single column news item below the fold tells us that "Nixon has hay fever". There were some advertisements, but very surprisingly there were no cinema ads, even though cinema halls were the only source of entertainment for the people of Pakistan and had aficionados who cut across all social, age and gender groups. Tragedy would strike the film industry a decade later, and it has not recovered till this day. There was also an eight-page supplement on Housing and Construction, with the leading article by I. H. Burney, then City Editor. This was AAK's way of restoring the paper's health. As time passed, the frequency of commercial supplements would increase, and that served to make Dawn a little less dependent on government ads, because revenue from state ads then constituted 70 per cent of the paper's total income. The price of the newspaper was 35 paisas, "by air 40 paisas". Within a year the situation had improved. Even though Dawn had many more years to go before its financial health would be fully restored, AAK had pulled the paper out of the jaws of imminent death. I have before me now the leader page of Dawn's issue of September 1, 1974. The advertisement-news ratio has increased, there are government ads, too — for instance two by PIA, one by State Life and another by the Pakistan Machine Tools Factory, there is a quantum jump in classified ads, and two full pages go to cinema advertising. My page, the leader page, looks like "emerging". The letters still do not have two full columns for themselves, for at the end are the crossword and a word game, but the article display has improved, for in columns 4-6 are two articles: one on top entitled "Middle East disengagement" by Major General (Rtd) Sarfaraz Khan and one at the bottom entitled "Libya's guiding philosophy", timed to coincide with the fifth anniversary of the officers' coup, led by Moammar Qadafi, that overthrew the monarchy in 1969. The article is by Akhtar Jamal. I do not remember now what say I had in the publication of this article, because Jamal is a friend, and we have many things in common, including a common fascination for Turkey. Much younger than me, he operates globally and is seldom in Pakistan. Column three still has news, and the editorial, entitled "Mr Ramay's bill of indictment", is a solo and consumes columns 1-2. Re-reading it today astonishes me. I do not know who wrote it, because I was still not part of the writing side, but its style leaves me in no doubt that AAK himself wrote it. It highlights two important facts: one Dawn, in spite of being in serious financial trouble, is still asserting its right to dissent; two, it shows, contrary to the propaganda, the extent to which the Bhutto government accommodates criticism, even though Ramay, the Punjab Chief Minister, is, like Ghulam Mustafa Khar, still Bhutto's right hand man. The cause for Dawn's ire is a controversial speech by Ramay. The Punjab chief minister is being self-righteous, and his criticism of the journalists is cheap — of the kind I heard during Ayub's time when the people expected the journalists to rise against dictatorship while other "enlightened" sections — politicians and the judiciary — refused to get up. The editorial says in parts:

"THE Punjab Chief Minister, Mr Hanif Ramay, chose the occasion of a ceremony for handing over the transfer deed of a piece of land for the Lahore Press Club to reprimand the journalistic profession publicly for its alleged faults and inadequacies. His carping criticism extended to several aspects of the working of the profession – its integrity, its level of ability and understanding, its awareness of its professional responsibility and so on. If all of what he said were true, there would be a good case for asking all the journalists to pack up and go home, after delivering the keys of their offices to an official public relations outfit. For surely the country deserves a better Press than the one Mr Ramay has found to be in existence. The bill of indictment Mr Ramay has framed is a lengthy and elaborate one, and it goes before the grand jury of the people for a verdict. The charges range from the violation by the journalists of their code of ethics, lack of proper education, inability to comprehend the problems facing the country and failure to report events 'honestly and fearlessly'. Speaking in reproof of the journalists' indifference to their professional responsibilities, Mr Ramay mentioned the case of the Tarbela tragedy. In any other country, he pointed out, such a major development would have brought the whole range of the reporting and investigative talents of the Press corps into full play. But the Pakistan Press, he bemoaned, did not care to report in depth the many likely causative factors and ramifications of the Tarbela affair. We must confess that we think the reproof is in a way well deserved. But we do not know if Mr Ramay knows how inhibited the reporters' fraternity has become over a long period of time and why.

"The Punjab Chief Minister has been an insider. This gives him a special privilege to speak on the state of the Press. But precisely because he has been an insider, he has an obligation to look to the other side of the coin while evaluating the performance of newspapers in reporting events or in commenting 'honestly and fearlessly' on the issues and problems facing the country. He surely knows enough to discourage an impulse to condemn the Press incontinently. He is certainly aware that the injunction against candour has throughout been in force and that the limitations of information that have been in existence could not produce an inquiring Press. Surely it can be said that the Pakistan Press generally has ample reason to do a great deal of heart-searching. As far as the development of some of its weaknesses is concerned, its own role has been autonomous rather than reactive. Nevertheless the basic fact remains that the primary responsibility for the inability of the Press on occasions to report and comment without fear or favour rests squarely upon the failure of public opinion and of the social and political elites to realize that the defence of Press freedom is actually the defence of the people's right to know how the Government they put into power and its administrative machinery are discharging their duties. Walter Lippmann once said that most people lived in 'an invisible environment', a state of ignorance about how decisions affecting their individual and collective lives were made – generally in their name.

"Coming to the question of ability and understanding, journalists certainly need more of both. But so do most politicians, whether in or out of power. If the journalists have lost some of their natural aptitude and drive for in-depth and objective reporting, can the Press be held entirely responsible for it? The major obstacle in the way of the national Press attaining a higher standard of performance in relation to its legitimate functions is not so much a deficiency in the professional training and qualifications of pressmen as the non-recognition of the need for a free and inquiring Press. As a group, the journalists do not suffer by comparison with those in any other profession, including the country's political fraternity. Their main disadvantage stems from a long legacy of arbitrary controls and restrictions that have been sedulously evolved, perfected and maintained to curtail the effective functioning of the Press.

"... The Punjab Chief Minister has also questioned the willingness of journalists, writers and intellectuals to make sacrifices in upholding popular causes, forgetting that over the past quarter century or so many journalists and writers have suffered imprisonment and various other forms of punitive action, and quite a few newspapers and periodicals have gone out of existence or endured suppression of one kind or another. And they have gone through these rigours not out of any expectations of reword or public credit, but out of a genuine conviction and belief that they have a role to play in the struggle for the people's democratic rights and socio-economic aspirations...

"One more word on the Tarbela issue. The point is that since in such matters the traditional practice has been for the Government to decide what facts to pass on for public information, the performance of the Press has necessarily been as good or as bad as the official briefings themselves. It is plain enough that because of the involvement of foreign firms and consultants in the Tarbela projects, newspapers are generally apt to be cautious, for, on a number of similar occasions in the past, even a mild deviation from the established practice invited angry accusations of having caused embarrassment to the Government or putting stains on the country's external relations. The question is that, in the present instance, if there was no such apprehension this has not been clearly conveyed to the Press... This emerges as the basic contradiction in Mr Ramay's angry outburst and his self-righteous sermonizing on the role and responsibilities of the newspapers....

"In the end we are unable to resist the temptation to quote the following couplet from a 'ghazal' by Mir Taqi Mir.

"Na haq ham majbooron pay tuhmat hai mukhtari ki /chahein so aap karein hein ham ko abas badnam kiya. (What irony that captives of a course ordained are, alas, for all deeds done, blamed)."

~~~~~~~~

The year 1974 also saw a momentous event in Pakistan's history — the holding of the second Islamic summit at Lahore on February 22-24. Thirty-seven countries, 21 of them represented by heads of state and government, attended the summit that was inaugurated by President Fazal Ilahi Chaudhri. Never again in the lifetime of my generation would a galaxy of such great Muslim leaders again be seen together: King Faisal, Anwar Saadat, Hafez al-Assad, Moammar Qadafi, Houari Boumedienne and Yasser Arafat. Others included the founder of the United Arab Emirates, Sheikh Zayed bin Sultan al-Nayhan, the founder of the United Arab Emirates. Missing was the Shah of Iran. Gaddafi had perhaps said that the gathering at Lahore would be of "brothers", and the shah did not like it. After all he was sitting on the Peacock Throne and was no ordinary mortal. He was His Imperial Majesty Mohammad Raza Shah Pahlavi, King of Kings, the Light (or some say Lamp or Sun) of the Aryans. He did not wish to stand with Gaddafi and other "brothers". The poor king did not know that Ayatollah Khomeini was waiting in the wings, and the days of the Peacock Throne, which he said was 2,500 years old but which his father, Corporal Raza, had founded only half a century ago, were numbered. (Frankly, as a Pakistani I often miss the King of Kings, for he was consistent in his friendship with Pakistan, unlike Islamic Iran, whose foreign policy has been characterised by unpredictability. Pakistan stood by revolutionary Iran during the Iran-Iraq war, despite tremendous pressure from the Arab world and from the US. In fact Pakistan supplied non-military aid, like food and medicines, to Iran. However, few people have registered the fact that, to show their displeasure over Islamabad's pro-Iran tilt, not a single Arab head of government or state attended Ziaul Haq's funeral. But the post-Shah Iran has seldom displayed any warmth toward Pakistan.)

The largest delegation of 19 members was from Saudi Arabia, which was a co-sponsor of the summit. Many Islamic summit conferences have been held since then, but none of them had such an impact on the Islamic world and such electrifying effect on the people of Pakistan as the one that began in the Punjab Assembly chamber on February 22. I would say this was Bhutto's finest hour. Millions still remember the TV images conveyed live to the nation, with the cream of the Muslim leadership praying together at Badshahi Mosque. Mahdi Zaheer mesmerised the nation when he and his choir sang what became the Summit Anthem, written by Jameeluddin Aali, with its refrain of Allaho Akbar. Decades have passed but the tune still enchants the people, whenever PTV replays it on some national occasions. Sung no doubt by Zaheer and his choir, the song is inextricably entwined with Bhutto's memory. To ensure adequate coverage AAK set up a Dawn Summit Bureau, and much to the reporters' annoyance the stories did not carry their names, except in rare cases. Dawn also published a 36-page supplement, edited by Mahdi Jafar, who had returned from the United States. My own contribution to this supplement was a book review of The Zionist State by Syed M. Suleman. I do not know how it got there. The supplement contained profiles of all Muslim countries, besides articles by names either forgotten or on the verge of being forgotten — S. Hashim Raza, Dr Abdul Salam Khurshid, Latif Ahmad Sherwani, S. Rahmatullah, who was life-member of the Iqbal Academy, Inamullah Khan of Motamar al-Alam al-Islami, Maulana Asadul Qadri, S. M. Ovais and K. Murad Bay. The lead article was by Sharif Al Mujahid, while Maulana Maudoodi wrote a long piece, which contained his ideas about how to promote and consolidate Muslim unity. His proposals were in the form of point by point recommendations some of them characterised by their impracticality. There were some sensible suggestions, as for instance about the need for "balanced education" in Muslim countries and for the Muslim countries to pool their resources for arms manufacturing. However, one suggestion called for "dual nationality", saying "any Muslim wanting to settle in another Muslim country for trade or service should be allowed to hold dual nationality". Another recommendation to the summit conference called for relaxing travel conditions among Muslim countries and "rather there should be no restrictions at all". There was harsh criticism of the United States for its unqualified support for Israel, and the article asked the summit leaders to declare that, by continuing its pro-Israel policy, America would forfeit the friendship of the world of Islam. Maulana Maudoodi died on September 22, 1979, and three months later, and five years and 10 months after the Lahore summit, the Soviet Union invaded Afghanistan, and Ziaul Haq's "Islamic government", supported to the hilt by Maulana Maudoodi's party, the Jamaat-i-Islami, turned Pakistan into one of America's most faithful allies.

The Dawn editorial on the summit was spread over three columns, had four crossheads (something very unusual for the paper) and was entitled "The caravan is again on the move" — inspired no doubt by

Iqbal's Hotha hay jada paymaan phir karravan hamara. Above the Dawn logo on the front page was the Quranic verse Wa' tasemu be-hablillah-e jameeiyon wa la tafarrqu in Sadquain's calligraphy in green. The English translation said: "And hold you fast to God's bond, together, and do not scatter". The name of the translator was not there. Other translations of the same verse are: "And hold fast, all of you, to the cable of Allah and do not separate"(by Marmaduke Pickthall); "And hold fast, all together, unto the bond with God and do not draw apart from one another" (by Muhammad Assad, formerly Leopold Weiss); "And hold ye fast, all of you, to the cord of Allah, and separate not" (by Abdul Majid Daryabadi); "Hold on firmly together to the rope of God and be not divided among yourselves" (by Prof Ahmad Ali); "And hold fast, all together, by the Rope which Allah (stretcheth out for you) and be not divided" (by Allama Yusuf Ali, who explains the word Rope thus: "The simile is that of people struggling in deep water, to whom a benevolent Providence stretches out a strong and unbreakable rope". Even though I do not consider myself qualified to give my opinion about the various translations of the holy book into English, I feel they do not at all convey even a small fraction of the beauty and meaning of the Quran to English readers. It is not that something is wanting among scholars of such repute as Pickthall and Yusuf Ali, but there is something in the Quran itself that defies translation. In fact several translators have themselves made it clear that the Quran is beyond translation. For instance "a big reward" appears a big joke as a translation of ajran azeema, the last two words of the last verse of Sura Fathh. Similarly, I have yet to see an apt translation of fabay ayye aalaye Rabbekuma tukazziban, which appears repeatedly in Sura Rahman, which indeed is one of the Holy Quran's most captivating chapters. Allama Yusuf Ali translates it thus: "then which of the favours of your Lord will ye deny?" Other translations are: "Which is it, of the favours of your Lord, that ye deny" (Pickthall); "And which, then, of the benefits of your Lord will ye twain belie?" (Daryabadi), and "How many favours of your Lord will then both of you deny?" (Ahmad Ali); "Which, then, of your Sustainer's powers can you disavow?" (Allama Assad).

With full respect to the great scholars, none of the translations captures even a small fraction of the beauty and majesty of Sura Rahman. As for verse 103 of Aale Imran about holding on to the "Rope of Allah", frankly I have been reading it and hearing about it in sermons since my boyhood, but I do not think the Muslims have ever bothered, at least in my lifetime, to pay heed to this Quranic injunction.

The very fact that such a summit was held — and held in Pakistan — showed how Bhutto was able to read the Arab mind correctly in the aftermath of the Ramazan war. Since independence Pakistan had tried — often childishly — to bring all Muslim countries together and was unsuccessful, even rebuffed. India's approach, on the other hand, was far more intelligent and developed a base in the Arab intelligentsia. Surprising as it may sound, the biggest opposition to Muslim unity has continued to come from the Arabs for reasons which I have discussed elsewhere in Chapter 17. Opposition here does not mean a rejection of the idea of Islamic unity; opposition stemmed from the Arab world's geopolitical compulsions, the role which Christians played in the Arab people's anti-colonial struggle, and the demographic realities of some leading Arab countries. The Yom Kippur war in October 1973 had stunned Israel and trounced the theory that the Arabs were incapable of fighting and winning a modern war. The Egyptian armies crossed the Suez Canal on October 6 after Friday afternoon prayers with surprising ease, taking prisoners Israeli soldiers some of whom were pressing their trousers. However, by the second week the Israelis had blunted the Egyptian assault in the Sinai and gone over to the offensive, crossed the canal and were threatening Cairo when the ceasefire went into effect. On the Golan Heights the Israelis later wrested the initiative, which initially was with the Syrians. The end of the war saw the Arab world's disappointment accompanied by the euphoria over stunning successes in the early stages of the war. At one stage, Moshe Dayan appeared so depressed he thought there was no option other than the use of nuclear weapons. In his book Story of My Life, Dayan does not speak of the nuclear option, even though he is widely quoted as saying that he thought the end of Israel was near. Howard M Sachar in A History of Israel: from the Rise of Zionism to Our Time quotes the Israeli Defence Minister as telling air force commander Benyamin Peled, "The fate of the Third Temple is at stake". Martin Van Creveld in his Moshe Dayan says: "During the night of 8/9 October Dayan, casting about wildly for anything that might prevent the Syrians from reaching the Jordan Valley and the Israeli settlements there, put Israel's nuclear force on alert. Having done so, he contacted Kissinger and asked him to pass a suitable warning to Damascus" (p 167).

This means Saadat and Hafez had after all succeeded in unfreezing the issue and focussing the world's attention on the need for Israel's withdrawal from the occupied territories. (The 'the' should be noted, for Israel has accepted the French version of the Security Council's Resolution 242 and not the English version because of the definite article.) The Arabs also used the oil weapon with great skill, and it must be recorded for history that the Shah of Iran, in spite of being demonised for being a Western agent, played an invaluable role in rationalising oil prices and tackling the multinationals, often considered more powerful than many Western governments put together. The Arabs needed support for forcing an Israeli withdrawal and for more equitable oil prices. Bhutto seized the moment: the summit would be held to mobilise the Muslim world's support for the Arab cause. Which Arab leader wouldn't welcome it? This was a departure from most Pakistanis' ridiculous quid pro quo nostrum — we support you on Palestine, you support us on Kashmir. That never cut much ice with the Arabs.

On the eve of the summit, Bhutto issued a statement saying the conference marked the "rebirth of Muslim unity". The statement was poorly drafted and was written perhaps by some junior Foreign Office official, for it lacked Bhutto's flair. Never before in modern times, he said, had "the World of Islam been presented with such opportunity to acquire economic strength and political influence as it is today. The people of Pakistan, who rejoice in the Muslim renaissance, are particularly proud to be hosts to the great leaders of the Muslim countries who are participating in this conference." In his presidential address to the summit on the first day of the conference, Bhutto gave one simple reason why Muslims alone could be Jerusalem's "loving and impartial custodians". The city, he said, held "a special place in Muslim hearts" and was "inscribed on our souls" because it was "a unique symbol of the confluence of Islam with the sacred traditions of Abraham, Moses and Jesus, all of them prophets whom Muslims hold in highest reverence." More important the city was "tied to our innermost spiritual fibre" associated as it was with the ascension of the Last Prophet. He called Jerusalem a Muslim city. "Except for an interval during the Crusades it has been a Muslim city — I repeat a Muslim city — from the year 637 A.D. For more than 1,300 years Muslims have held Jerusalem as a trust for all who venerated it. Muslims alone could be its loving and impartial custodians for the simple reason that Muslims alone believe in all the three prophetic traditions rooted in Jerusalem. We gladly recognize that Jerusalem affects the cherished sensibilities of men and women of three world faiths. But there are 2000 million Muslims and Christians, and 15 million Jews in the world. Out of these less then three million owe their allegiance to Israel. What principle of justice would confer on this minority the right to hold dominion over the holy city? What except a kind of cynicism can allow the city of peace to be treated by Israel as the spoils of war?

"I must make it clear that it is not our position on Jerusalem but Israel's which is contrary to the objective criteria by which the status of territories is determined. It is Israel which cites the name of a religion and a culture and invokes its memories or emotions in order to lend justification to acts that are wholly illegal. Such attempts can only make a conflict implacable and bring in its train a religious war. Viewed in a non-religious perspective, the question of Jerusalem's status cannot be unrelated to the sovereign rights of the people of Jerusalem itself, the majority of whom were Arabs, violently expelled and uprooted from the western part in 1948. Nor can the special attachment of Jewish people to Jerusalem override the principle of the inadmissibility of territorial acquisition by force. The Jewish right to Jerusalem certainly connotes the right of access and worship. We cannot recognize any additional right.

"On the basis of all these considerations, the issue of the Holy City of Jerusalem admits of no doubts or division in our ranks. Let me make it clear from this platform that any agreement, any protocol, any understanding which postulates the continuance of Israeli occupation of the Holy City or the transfer of the Holy City to any non-Muslim or non-Arab sovereignty will not be worth the paper it is written on."

Bhutto concluded his speech with a prayer that ends the Holy Quran's second chapter, Al Baqra:

"Allah tasketh not a soul beyond its scope."

"For it (is only) that which it hath earned, and against it (only) that which it hath deserved."

"Our Lord! Condemn us not if we forget, or fall into error!

"Our Lord! Lay not on us such a burden as Thou didst lay on those before us!

"Our Lord! Impose not on us a burden greater than we have the strength to bear!

"Pardon us, absolve us and forgive us and have mercy on us,

"Thou, our Protector, grant us succour against those who reject Thee".

On Anwar Saadat's recommendations, the conference unanimously adopted a motion inviting Sheikh Mujibur Rahman to the summit. The Bangladeshi prime minister and founder of the country came to Lahore in an Air Algeria plane and was greeted at the airport by President

Fazal Ilahi and Bhutto. Pakistan recognised the breakaway part of its country as a sovereign nation, with Mujib telling the world that the "new chapter" in Pakistan's relations with Bangladesh would contribute to peace in the subcontinent. Fifteen months later Mujib was assassinated by his own people. How ironic that, besides Mujib, three of the summit's leading personalities should have been assassinated — Bhutto, Saadat and Faisal! The king's assassination had little or no political fallout, but Bhutto and Saadat were murdered by men and parties claiming to be the harbingers of Islamic revolution. However, their murder did not result in an Islamic revolution in Egypt or Pakistan. While Pakistan was to suffer Ziaul Haq's tyranny for 11 years, Saadat's murder by the fundamentalists led to Mobarak's secular dictatorship, which has continued till this day (2009).

7

TERROR COMES TO DAWN

MANY SENIOR MEMBERS OF the staff on desk, reporting and writing didn't give Ahmad Ali Khan the cooperation he deserved. One assistant editor resigned, and many others made no secret of their unhappiness. One group of sub-editors was opposed to him, because Jamil Ansari's departure had made them uncomfortable and deprived them of a sense of involvement in Dawn's affairs. Since Altaf's days, Dawn had editors who were allergic to the Left and were ardent supporters of Pakistan's American alliance. As I have said elsewhere, Altaf was himself a rightist to the core, but once Pakistan's relations with the US started deteriorating in the wake of the India-China clash in 1962 and the 1965 Indo-Pakistan war, Altaf became a fanatic China supporter. Mazhar Ali Khan, who was acting editor (Feb 7, 1972, to December 20, 1972), was a confirmed Marxist, but he was not a Dawn man and had come from the outside. Ahmad Ali Khan, on the contrary, was from among the staff and was a confirmed leftist. He was once a member of the Communist Party and had been arrested for communist activity when he was with The Pakistan Times, Lahore. He told me once, referring to the group mentioned above, "These people think an atheist has become Dawn's editor". Unfortunately Dawn's weekly column on religion had fallen victim to the shrinkage of Dawn's pages owing to newsprint shortage, and AAK was keen that it should be revived. I managed to develop some new writers, and the religious column was resumed. AAK wanted us to have a name for it and I suggested "Friday Feature". He liked it, and I am happy that the Feature has continued till this day, though its name was dropped when Zaffar Abbas gave *Dawn* a new layout in December 2013. I continued to edit it until October 1980 when AAK asked me to take over Dawn Magazine, till then the paper's only weekly magazine. Meenai then took over the Friday Feature and continued to edit it uninterrupted till his retirement in August 2008 — quite an achievement. Meenai also used to edit the full page devoted to 12th Rabiul Avvel, the Holy Prophet's birthday, and the 10th of Moharram, marking the tragedy of Karbala. In the first decade of the 21st century, however, the full page was discontinued, replaced by a single article. This evoked protests from several quarters.

When he became editor in February 1973 AAK made no radical changes in the paper's policy, though he gave it a liberal direction in conformity with his social democratic views. Indeed the circumstances were such that he could not afford to be radical. The issue before him was to keep the paper going, and in the wake of the 1971 trauma, and given the paper's financial problems, he could not afford to go against the broad spectrum of the urban middle class from which the Dawn readership came. Under his editorship, Dawn provided the classic example of how the editor's personality and his relationship with the management go to determine a paper's policy. Every management wants the paper to be a commercial success, even if the owners happen to be a political family, as Dawn's owners are. Where a management's policy stands in the way of higher sales, it has to think whether the cause it is espousing can be dispensed with for the sake of commercial success. Where no cause exists, except in a restricted sense, and all that a management wants is more money, it has to choose the right editor — someone who would have no other aim save that of increasing the circulation and ensuring higher revenues, irrespective of all other considerations, including the sanctity of the printed word. AAK was not that kind of editor, nor did the

Haroons ever want Dawn to be turned into a minting machine, given the role the family and the paper had played in the freedom struggle and the Pakistan movement. AAK was clear in his aim. Dawn must survive in what was a difficult economic situation with a hostile government. While it would not kowtow to the government, Dawn would not get involved in a fruitless confrontation with the Bhutto government. Such a confrontation would advance the cause neither of the paper nor of the freedom of the press. Closing a paper down and rendering hundreds of journalists and workers jobless was not, in his opinion, the best way of advancing the cause of press freedom.

Akhtar Adil Razwy, decades after he had retired, paid handsome tributes to AAK and lauded how he had been "steering Dawn's course, navigating through difficult channels for more than two decades". On the question of an editor's responsibility to keep the paper going Razwy's opinion may not be universally valid, but given the Pakistani context and the curbs on the press, he tended to side with AAK. In an article, titled "Looking back", in Dawn's fiftieth anniversary supplement (July 29, 1997), Razwy referred to a statement made by AAK during the course of a hearing before the National Press Commission. Wrote Razwy: "Queried by a member how in the deadening pattern of conformity he pursued his commitment to the freedom of the press and value of freewheeling debate and the right of dissent, etc. Ahmad Ali Khan tersely remarked it is also the function of the editor not to allow his paper to go under. That I think is the quintessential wisdom". The previous two editors — Mazhar Ali Khan and Altaf Gauhar — were great in their own way. Mazhar had been The Pakistan Times after Faiz Ahmad Faiz quit. Even though he belonged to one of Punjab's feudal families, Mazhar was a confirmed Marxist. He was Dawn's acting editor when Altaf Gauhar was in jail. Gauhar became editor on January 1, 1972, an appointment that roughly coincided with Bhutto's assumption of power and earned his wrath because of the confrontationist policy he pursued.

In 1975 AAK launched Dawn Overseas Weekly, which was intended to serve Pakistani expatriates the world over. Even though some journalists, among them Zubeida Mustafa and Sami Ahmad, were hired specifically for DOW, most of the paper was manned by regular staffers. The weekly, whose first edition appeared on August 31, 1975, contained fewer mistakes for one obvious reason — DOW consisted of news, editorials, columns and articles which had already been published in daily Dawn. Editing a published piece was easy and mistakes were quickly spotted and corrections carried out. However, DOW had very few ads and never had much chance of success, for the majority of Pakistani expatriates were in the Middle East, and most of them were semi-skilled or manual workers, who were either illiterate or who at best could read Urdu. DOW thus had a limited circulation among educated Pakistanis in Europe and America. Besides, the government bought I think 3,000 copies for free distribution among parliamentarians, diplomats and the media in foreign countries. Going back to the time when DOW was launched I cannot but recall the turmoil it created in the staff. The issue was once again money. Since work for DOW entailed extra hours besides those devoted to the daily paper, the staff members, rightly, wanted more money. Besides, not all staff members were engaged with the DOW job, so there was heart-burning among those left out. It is easy from the benefit of the hindsight to wonder why some people were so sore, but then our lives in the seventies were in the grip of inflation. The oil crisis following the 1973 war had led to what to my mind was the Pakistani people's first experience with inflation, and the Bhutto government found it difficult to control prices. It looks now incredible that the Western governments, egged on no doubt by the oil multinationals, should have considered the slight rise in oil prices from the pre-war $2.48 per barrel to $3 pb an untenable increase. (From 1960 to the early seventies, the average oil price was one and a half dollars pb). Compared to the whopping bouts of inflation which came later — especially the one raging now (April 2009), — the inflation of the seventies was a minor discomfort. I used to get an allowance of Rs 350 per month for my DOW work, and after two years I caught AAK in one of his relaxed, post-lunch moods while we both sipped tea: "Look,

Khan Saab", I told him, "I have been getting Rs 350 for the DOW duty for the last two years now, and ..." and he interjected "you will continue to get it!". — Then, suddenly terrorism came to Dawn.

The word "terrorism" had not till then caught on – not at least in the national context. The Afghan war was four years away, and even far more into the future was religious militancy that was to change our entire political and social landscape. For us at Dawn, terrorism and terrorists were bad words. We detested them, because the terms were used indiscriminately by Western wire agencies for all liberation movements and freedom fighters, whether it was Mozambique or Palestine. As good Afro-Asians, we took it all very seriously, and did our duty to the world people's anti-colonial struggle by dutifully changing "terrorists" into "freedom fighters" or to a non controversial "guerillas". That bomb explosions, killings and kidnappings would become a Pakistani social and political phenomenon in less than a decade did not occur even to the most pessimistic among us. All until then was normal. Karachi was peaceful, Pakistan was tranquil and 'usual', and so were our lives. Western climbers and tourists could visit Swat Gilgit, Hunza and Baltistan – Roof of the Earth – without being abducted and slaughtered. You could park your car without worrying that it could be stolen; you could walk the streets well into small hours without fear, and when someone was late from college you knew he must have gone to a playground or, perhaps, to a movie. Educational institutions were meant for education and not for hoarding arms and ammunition, and hostels were occupied by students and not armed hoodlums masquerading as students.

But on March 31, 1975, terrorism hit us with a bang — literally. Dusk had fallen as I headed towards my room from the washroom on the northern side of the first floor that houses Dawn's editorial offices in Haroon House. I had hardly walked a few paces when a deafening blast rocked the building flattening three of the cubicles in the lavatory. I had been there half a minute ago, three of the walls of concrete with wainscot never seemed to have existed as a plastic device went off. Lucky was M.J Zahedi, Assistant Editor, who had left for home

10 minutes ago and on whose desk an entire adjoining wall had fallen. If they had timed the device to explode earlier in the day, or later in the evening, when the night staff worked, it is impossible to see how deaths and serious injuries could have been avoided. Still, two staff members were hurt. One of then was Shafi Mansoori, then editor of Dawn Gujrati. He came out of the lavatory possibly 10 seconds after me, but was hardly out of the main door of the washroom when the device went off. He escaped injuries, but the blast turned out to be ear-splitting for him and he suffered damage to one of his ears. Also injured was stenographer Mohammad Mushtaq, who was hit by shards of glass in the face, neck and arms. The blast, which was heard up to five miles, tore away several doors, shattered glass-panes in the corridor, ripped open water pipelines and felled several staff members to the ground. No one claimed the responsibility for the deed, though the federal government blamed it on "anti-state people".

The Editor thought the site of the bomb blast had been carefully chosen. By planting it in the Dawn offices, the perpetrators of the deed had hoped to extract the maximum publicity inside and outside the country for their "cause". We were, of course, shocked beyond belief .How could "they" — how could anyone — target Dawn, the paper founded by Jinnah and associated with the Pakistan Movement? To me and many others in Dawn it was obvious that the explosion was the work of the National Awami Party. Headed then by Abdul Wali Khan this party was part of coalition governments in Balochistan and the NWFP, and Prime Minister Bhutto had dismissed both. NAP had also carried out several bombing attacks elsewhere, including the bombing of a post office in Karachi, and was suspected of involvement in the murder of Hayat Sherpao, one of Bhutto's lieutenants and then the senior minister in the Frontier government, on February 16. However, AAK thought the Bhutto government had planted the bomb. It was difficult to argue with AAK when it came to Bhutto. He admired several aspects of Bhutto's personality and policies, especially his left-leaning programme, his populist idiom, and the contribution he had made to Pakistani politics by pulling it out of the confines of palaces and drawing-rooms and taking it to the masses. But he detested the authoritarian streak in Bhutto's character and was harshly critical of the PPP government's curbs on the press, and I have reasons to believe that some of their meetings did not go well. I have no details about the meetings, but whatever AAK told me during our countless gossip sessions, I gathered he had personally felt hurt by Bhutto's attitude. They had first met in Lahore when Bhutto was information minister in Ayub's cabinet in the late fifties, and AAK was editor of The Pakistan Times. He asked AAK about his assessment of the political situation in the country, and he said he thought the youth in East Pakistan were getting alienated, and that if this trend continued, the gap between East and West Pakistan could widen, leading to disaster. Bhutto's reported reply was: "Well, the president knows best". I do not know how a man of Bhutto's political calibre could utter this nonsense, nor was AAK misquoting him. Obviously, there must be more to the dialogue. After Bhutto came to power, AAK met him in Islamabad — this time for an exclusive interview for Dawn. The paper was fighting for its financial survival, and common wisdom suggested that we carry an exclusive interview of the prime minister as an indication of cordiality if not surrender. AAK, it need be repeated, was the editor of a paper whose owners had been hurt by the PPP's nationalisation policies. Bhutto's man, Abdul Sattar Gabol, had defeated Saeed Haroon in the 1970 general election in Karachi's Lyari district, which had always been the Haroons' stronghold. Yet that had not led AAK into adopting a hard-line anti-PPP policy or into being vitriolic editorially. Bhutto had by then carried out his sweeping nationalisation programmes, and AAK wanted to know what his government intended to do to make a dent in the huge land holdings and launch a land reform. Bhutto, according to AAK, spoke in a vein that made AAK feel he had come to meet the prime minister as a representative of the industrial class. The interview did not go well, and the result was a very small story appearing as Dawn's lead.

The year 1975, saw some positive developments personally for me toward the end. I do not believe in astrology and palm reading now, but then — like most young people — when life appeared full of possibilities I occasionally consulted palmists and astrologers and took them seriously. Friends dabbling in astrology and the occult did it free of charge, but some astrologers charged money and fooled me. In October, a man whose name I only remember as Raja, came to me. Iqbal Manjal, Managing Director of the Pakistan Herald Publications Ltd., the company which owns the Dawn group of newspapers, had sent him to me. He had come with certain political predictions and wondered whether I could publish them. I told him this was not Dawn's policy, but he turned out to be a good conversationalist, appeared to be on my side politically and said he would come after a few days after drawing my horoscope. I had unloaded all my frustrations on him: told him I had still not been promoted, was 38 years old but hadn't seen a foreign country, and all three of my sisters were unmarried. He kept his promise, returned a few days later and told me I would be promoted "next year". He also told me that, from then on, I would hear some good news on the 21st of every month. I found this rather amusing and forgot all about it. In October, AAK called me over and asked me whether I would like to write editorials for Dawn. Even though, as I have narrated earlier, AAK never made a promise and was over cautious in such matters, the decision to ask me to start writing editorials meant I had been promoted. When Raja met me I told him he had predicted that I would be promoted "next year" but I had been promoted "next month". Raja said, "Any astrologer will tell you the year begins toward the end of November." But in my case it seemed to have begun toward the end of October. I joined the writing side, and AAK made it clear that he was not promising promotion, that he was merely giving me an opportunity to prove myself, and that I must write editorials in addition to the job I was doing. He perhaps repeated, "You have to trust me". My first editorial, thus, appeared in Dawn on October 30, 1975. Entitled "Coal and minerals" it was a second, because Dawn then used to carry only two editorials, with a total wordage of

1,200 plus. For all practical purposes I had been promoted. On the 21st of November the family heard the good news that Qaiser's marriage proposal had made definite progress. On another 21st, the date of her engagement was finalised — or perhaps the betrothal took place —, and on another 21st the date of her wedding was fixed; on February 21 I received a telegram from the Cardiff-based Thomson Foundation (TF), saying I had been granted a scholarship for the wonderful spring course, and I must be in London on April 22. The TF people had expected me to buy the air ticket myself, and I was obviously in no position to do so. So it goes without saying that AAK asked the management to give me the return ticket. On March 23, 1976, Qaiser was married off at a ceremony at the KMC park in Nazimabad No 1. By any standards it was a happy occasion for me, for both our parents were alive and had the satisfaction of seeing their youngest daughter become a bride. Society was still normal, and food was served promptly at about 9pm. (Two decades later, wedding dinners would be served at midnight or even later.). Relieved of the burden that brothers in Pakistan carry on their shoulders till their sisters get married, I boarded a Pan-Am flight for London on the morning of April 22. Raja was after all right.

8

A HOT COUNTRY

THE 1976 VISIT TO BRITAIN was a disaster. There were many disappointments, including the discovery that Britain wasn't after all a cold country. Or so I, a migraine patient, thought. Who were those people who had made me believe since my childhood that Olde England was a cold country? As a migraine patient, I loathed sunlight and longed for shade everywhere. But Britain was full of sunshine — no fog, no snow, little rain. In Karachi, all my movements had this cardinal principle before me: I must not expose my head to the sun before 1pm. The migraine attack took place every Monday and Friday, and with surprising accuracy the first wave of pain above the left eyebrow struck me at 1.20pm. It would then gradually spread in arrow-like fashion to take the entire left side of the head in its grip, reaching the neck. One of my friends took away my wrist watch from me, saying I developed the pain by looking at the watch. No, when the first wave struck I could predict it was 1.20pm. One colleague — Mohsin Askari, a complete agonistic and cynic — said I got it on Monday because I did not wish to work, and I got it on Friday because I did not want to go to the mosque. That simple! Actually, besides the sun in the ante meridian period, other factors also triggered migraine — air-conditioned rooms, a stuffy atmosphere, as in a cinema hall even if it was cold, an empty stomach, gases and tension.

The last one was rare. I then got used to it and kept working even if it was a stabbing pain above the left eyebrow. Once home I would close the door of my bedroom, switch off lights and go to sleep. Within 40 or so minutes, the pain would subside and then disappear and I would have dinner. It was very rare that I threw up.

On the evening of April 22 I landed at the Heathrow airport without a visa, because that was not required, even though Pakistan had still not re-joined the Commonwealth, having quit it because of Britain's perceived pro-India tilt during the Bangladesh crisis. Pakistan had also quit the pound sterling area and joined the dollar area. At the airport, the Immigration official asked me in a routine why I was there, and asked me to show proof when I said I was on a scholarship. I produced the papers, and he stamped my green book. After checking in at the hotel as arranged by the Thomson Foundation, I went out of my hotel for a walk and dinner, and found nothing new or unusual. In fact, it appeared to me I had been there before. That I suppose is true of most Pakistanis and other South Asians with an English education. The next morning we drove in a TF bus for the journey to Penarth, near Cardiff. Until that drive to and through South Wales, my idea of a "developed country" was distorted. To me a developed country was one that had more factories, built aircraft carriers, had an educated, prosperous population, and carted off all the gold medals at the Olympic Games. I never thought being a "developed country" meant not only that technology was at the service of the people, this also meant that every footpath, every culvert, every green, every bit of fencing, every road sign, and every bus shelter had been taken care of. In fact it often appeared to me as if someone personally stood there and saw it from the point of view of a citizen and had it fixed. Until mobile phones came to Pakistan in the first decade of the 21st century, I don't think one could say that technology was at the service of the people. Sometimes, the simplicity of the British ways of doing things was amazing, and care and common sense rather than technology helped people. One day in Penarth I was standing under a tree to take shelter from rain, and a sign on it read: "In case of a heavy downpour, go to the tree to your left" — some such words.

In Penarth, we were lodged at the International House of South Wales. My room number was 55, and the view from my window was spectacular. Opposite to the hostel was a miniature golf course, and to the left Bristol Channel. At night the lights of Weston Super-Mare across the channel shone, and on the right the houses along Plymouth Road looked like toy houses. The entire scene was one of a picture postcard, because the work of nature and man seemed to coalesce into one magnificent enterprise. I remembered Iqbal's verse — *bay zauq naheen agarchay fitrat/ jo ussay naho saka vo tu kerr*. (Nature is not without a sense of aesthetics; where it is missing, do your bid.) The beauty of Pakistan's north is not to be found anywhere else in the world, for three mighty mountains — the Himalayas, Hindukush and the Karakoram — meet, with a perpetual snowline on dozens of peaks. But what is missing is man's work that could supplement nature's work as urged by Iqbal. While we lived in the Penarth hostel, our classes were held in the offices of the TF's Editorial Study Centre at Cardiff in a building that also housed the offices of Western Mail and evening daily Echo. The 12 students were not necessarily all from the Commonwealth: there was one from Indonesia, another from South Korea. There were two Indians, and I was the only one from Pakistan. Our teachers were thorough professionals, but they underestimated us. All of us belonged to the same age group and had about the same experience in journalism. Within a week, the team of teachers headed by Don Rowlands realised they had to re-draw the course and raise its standard if it was to have any meaning for us. The name of the course was "layout and copy flow", and they tested us and found nothing lacking in us. For me layout lessons were useful, because Dawn's layout was horribly unprofessional, and I discovered that the African students, and those from South-East Asia — Philip Khou of Straits Times of Singapore, and Sebi ben Abu Bakr of Straits Times's Kuala Lumpur edition — were far ahead of their South Asian colleagues and had higher make-up standards with appropriate emphasis on white space calculated in ems and ens. We visited various newspaper offices, but the computer had not yet made its full impact on the newspaper industry in South Wales. Western Mail and Echo were still a hot metal affair, and by merely looking at those working in the lino room I could tell who did what. As I watched the zinc plate being chipped, Khou said the system had been discarded by his paper and Straits Times had gone computer. The Sinic world was coming into its own.

The International House of South Wales was run by a church organisation, most probably the Methodist. Impeccably clean, it operated on a shoe-string budget. Its frugality was seen especially in food, for the quality and quantity of food were disappointing. Dinner was taken at 6, and for a Pakistani this was hardly dinner time. On weekends, husbands wanted their wives working for us to reach home early, so the women served us dinner on Saturdays at 5.30pm. Sometimes dinner consisted of one boiled fish with scales intact, plus some cucumber slices so thin they were transparent. Sometimes I either did not eat at all, or if I nibbled at something I became hungry late in the evening, because like most other students I went walking. The evening never seemed to end. The sunlight went yellow by 6.30pm and, unlike what we in the tropics are used to, the South Wales sun never appeared very keen to set, the twilight lasting for hours. The sunset in Penarth was then at 9.40pm, and the time for Isha prayers at the Cardiff mosque was sometimes after 11. But the sky never went pitch dark. The mosque had been built by Yemeni sailors who had settled in Cardiff after serving with the British merchant navy, and both Shias and Sunnis prayed together. The solution to the food problem was easy: every now and then I would go out and have my dinner at a Pakistani or Bangladeshi restaurant, and even though the Thomson Foundation was not very generous with money, they paid enough for me to indulge in this luxury. I did not smoke, much less drink, but some of the other students were always short of money because they did all three things.

The summer of 1976 was one of England and South-Wales's hottest, the temperature at Wimbledon shot to 109F, and passengers in the

London underground smashed windowpanes to cool. Our classroom faced the sun and became unbearably hot, and my migraine worsened. Our class began at 9am, and there was a tea break at 10.30. The first session ended at 12. After lunch we assembled again at 2 and there was a tea break at 3.30. I was till then a compulsive tea drinker, and each time an old lady wheeled her trolley to me, I followed Oscar Wilde's advice — the best way to overcome a temptation is to succumb to it. I quaffed the tea, thus worsening my headache. I missed Pakistan, because our homes and buildings are so built as to let fresh air in. In Britain, homes and building are designed to keep the cold wind out. Also, the British have no concept of fans, except as soccer hooligans. In hot climates, when we enter a building from the outside the first thing we do is to switch on the fan. In British homes and offices I looked at the ceiling time and again only to find there was no fan, much less an air-conditioner. One day in the post-lunch session I felt miserable and sought the teacher's permission to leave for my hostel. Half way on the bus ride to Penarth I got down because I felt like throwing up. As I sprawled myself on the grassy patch next to the footpath, every now and then a car would pull up and someone would prop up his or her head and ask, "You, orright?"

I have often wondered whether we Pakistanis hate or love the British. My answer is: both. Britain's political role in Afro-Asia, especially the Middle East, is despicable. But for Britain, the Palestinians would not be what they are today, homeless and "terrorists". But for Mountbatten, there would have been no Kashmir problem. Pakistan and India would eventually have become nuclear powers but without the hatred created by the wars they have fought – 1947-48, 1965, 1971 and 1999. In the nineteenth century the British replaced Muslims as the ruling power in India, destroyed the Mughal Empire, and hanged Mughal princes and countless others for their part in the 1857 war of independence – the "sepoy mutiny". In the Middle East they began the process of nibbling at Ottoman territories by first taking over Egypt's financial control and then formally occupying it. British diplomats double-crossed Hussein bin Ali, the Sharif of Mecca, by promising to make him the head of an (eastern) Arab empire if he revolted against the Turks, and have till this day insisted that the Balfour Declaration did not violate the assurances made to the Hashemites in the Hussein-McMahon correspondence. Unknown to the Sharif, the Sykes-Picot pact had already divided the Ottoman empire's Arab provinces between Britain and France under the garb of the League of Nations' "mandate", and but for Ataturk, Constantinople and the Straits of Dardanelles would today be either part of Greece or perhaps be under a UN trusteeship. Towering over all these tragedies is Allenby's proclamation when he entered Jerusalem in December 1917: "Crusades have ended today." The discussion above leaves out British role in Iran, Afghanistan, Malaya and the Gulf. (Zanzibar was under Oman's control, and the British used the slave trade pretext to wrest Zanzibar from Oman and eventually occupied the latter, too) In the first decade of the 21st century, Britain has been the Bush administration's faithful ally, and Tony Blair had no qualms of conscience about putting up with a doctored intelligence dossier and taking part in the WMD hoax to attack Iraq. But all this has not served to stop South Asian Muslims from taking a more balanced view of the British. In fact, a South Asian, whether Muslim or Hindu, is a big hypocrite if he does not confess to a sense of deep and abiding admiration for the British people and their culture. I found the British humane and their sophistication worth admiring. During one of my weekend visits to London, my cousin Adeel, with home I stayed at his St John's Wood apartment, remarked to me that in practice the British were close to Islam. "They only have to utter the kalema", he said, and I agreed with him.

My stay in South Wales coincided with one of Britain's worst patches in race relations, especially in Blackburn, where the activities of the National Front had led to violence, and the local yellow press added to the climate of hate. The situation started getting out of hand when the National Party, a breakaway group of the National Front, won two seats in council elections. The polls coincided with the blaze of publicity given to the National Party Chairman, Kingsley Read, even though he was warned by a court not to make inflammatory speeches against the coloured community. Alarmed, the Pakistani and Indian groups got in touch with trade union, church, community relations, Labour, Tory and Communist Party leaders to form an Action Against Racism Group. When this Group marched through the streets of Blackburn, it was subjected to insults and abuses by National Party supporters. Richard Varrall, one of the National Front leaders, defined the party' race relations policy thus: "The National Front is opposed to a multi-racial society and it is our intention to worsen the racial situation as much as we can. The multi-racial society is collapsing and we are helping it collapse". The Front organised provocative anti-immigration marches through predominantly coloured localities. Yet Varrall proclaimed his Front's peaceful intentions: "We don't hate these people, only the politicians responsible for bringing them here" and he added: "we condemn any kind of violence against these people who are not to blame." Who was to blame — the National Front, the now forgotten Enoch Powell, illegal immigration, police "bias" or the politician with an eye on the vote? Maybe, none of them singly, or perhaps all of them put together seen against the background of soaring unemployment, union militancy, the shrinking pound and shooting prices. To the police, however, the violence had no racial overtones; it invariably blamed the "vandals" and "teenage gangsters" for assaults and damage to coloured property — like the attack on two London mosques in which prayer carpets were cut open with knives.

The Blackburn Asians lived in a state of fear because the police had failed to give them protection. The immigrants then started organizing vigilante patrols and were closing their ranks. Said Sibghatullah Qadri, leader of the Standing Conference of Pakistani Organizations in the United Kingdom: "For ten years we had thought racialism to be a problem for immigrants from West Indies and Africa, but now it clearly concerns the Asian people." Qadri, who was my senior at the University of Karachi, said "Our prime purpose is to crush the National Front. They will not come in our streets." He was supported by Jimmy Bazy of the

Afro-Caribbean Association, who said, "West Indian and Asian unity is inseparable and must involve the working class as a whole." The most unfortunate aspect of the situation was that the Conservative Party, which was then in the opposition, looked askance at the activities of the National Front, and indeed in one case a Tory Mayor said he would retain his party membership even after joining the National Front. To this, all that the Tory spokesman, Ivor Freeman, could say was: "There is no rule, as far as I know, against it. Local associations have tremendous latitudes." Apart from the immigrants, the most genuine opposition to the National Front came from Britain's Leftist organizations, which repeatedly clashed with National Front marchers, shouting: "Fascist pigs!" This was in response to the National Front's slogan: "If they are black, send them back; if they are Red, send them dead." Said Tom Bell, General Secretary of the Young Communists: "We are now facing a major effort by reaction using the media to mount a diversionary campaign of hysteria against black people, especially Asians." Wrote the Marxist daily Morning Star: "In the pre-war period, it was the Jews whom the fascists sought to blame for the economic difficulties of the people arising from the crisis of the capitalist system. Now it is the black people, but the aim is the same: to divide the working class movement and to divert its attention away from the real culprits — the big business monopolies. These are ones who are forcing down the value of the pound on the money markets...and not the black people. If there is a housing shortage, it is because there are not enough houses being built, not because of black people. We can all understand the anxiety and resentment felt by young people unable to find a job. Only a few days ago, thousands were poured on to the labour market from the schools with practically no prospect of a job."

Personally, however, I never found anyone slapping a racist slur on me or behaving in anyway that was offensive to me. The attitude that I came across was one of cold aloofness. They said nothing, but their eyes seemed to tell, "So, you are a foreigner! You are different." Did their eyes also say "I am afraid you are not wanted here"? Frankly I did not get this feeling. I am certain that a white foreigner, too, would come across the same attitude, and I believe — though I have no evidence — that a Polish or Czech immigrant would have as much problems with his neighbours as Pakistanis and other South Asians. Niraj C. Chaudhri, the Indian writer, insisted that racism was alien to British culture. Nevertheless, the truth is that wherever the British have gone they have created a race problem — South Africa, America and until recently "whites only" Australia, and the signs "Chinese and dogs not allowed" or "Indians and dogs not allowed" would forever remain etched on Asian memory. I do not know if there is a book called "The Ugly Briton", but most certainly the British aren't at home what they were abroad. In their colonies they were imperialists in the classical mould, and came in all types — military, diplomat, legal, bureaucrat — Kitchener, Cromer, Dyer, Napier, Mountbatten, Radcliff and many more. But back home, looking at them it became difficult for me to believe that the British nation was able to produce such scoundrels. To quote John Rose, "the scale of British genocide is breathtaking. In Bengal alone up to 20 million people were slaughtered at the end of the 18th century", (John Rose, *Myths of Zionism*, p 140, Pluto Press, London, 2004).

Our course ended in mid-July. There was a group photo, and obviously the majority in the photograph consisted of Africans and West Indian. I sent it home. Abbu, ever an admirer of beauty, female specially, was horrified. But there was nothing unusual about it. South Asia is the world's most race-conscious area, and Pakistanis, Indians and Bangladeshis worship fair skin. In fact, in black company the South Asians consider themselves white. Being in South Wales was not exactly a disaster. In the beginning I was quite race conscious, all the time aware of my 'native' identity, but by June I had begun enjoying my stay in spite of social isolation. This was, I still believe, less due to the fact that I was coloured and more because, as I have explained earlier, that is how the British are. From Penarth I went to live for a week with a pen-friend in Glasgow. He had a strange surname — Uddin. He later told me that Uddin was a hybridisation of the suffix "din" often found at the end of many Muslim names. After a night-long journey by coach, I reached Glasgow early in the morning and went about looking for my friend's house, but talking to people in the streets I realised the people of Scotland spoke an entirely different language. "Go lay, en ray" meant "go left then right". Some youngsters in my friend's home were either born in Scotland or had migrated with their parents very young. So I heard plenty of Scottish accent at home. Scotland's relative poverty was shocking, for in no other city, besides Bangkok, did I see so many women of easy virtue. When evening fell it appeared the people of Glasgow did nothing but drink beer. Urine ran on footpaths and the goings-on in backstreets and under staircases in abandoned buildings were stupefying. Central Glasgow truly epitomised the decaying inner city. The year was 1976, and Europe perhaps was still reeling from the effect of the oil crisis in the wake of the 1973 Yom Kippur war. I hope the intervening decades have done away with all this, and the Scots have less cause to grumble against the English. During the visit to the Edinburgh museum I saw the Kohinoor diamond, which was in news those days because Bhutto had said he would demand the legendary diamond's return to Pakistan. Again, I saw the word "slain" at the legend to Tipu Sultan's blood-stained shirt. In history books as well, the English never use the word "killed" for "Tippu sahib" and invariably say "slain". "Killed" in battle gives dignity to a soldier, while "slain" could perhaps mean he was murdered, perhaps in bed.

On return to London I realised I had some unfinished business — to make a sentimental pilgrimage to Lord's cricket ground, which was near Adeel's home in St John's Wood. Even though it was summer no match was in progress, and the groundsmen let me in. I went to the pitch and had a close look at it. The groundsmen must have thought some great ex-cricketer was having a bout of nostalgia. For me as a school boy the Pakistani team's 1954 visit to England was an unforgettable event. Kardar, Fazal and Hanif have remained my heroes till this day, and the greater achievements later by men like Imran Khan, Wasim Akram, Javed Miandad and Inzimam have not served to diminish my school-boy fascination for the Oval heroes even in this old age. The rain-hit Lord's test was drawn, the second at the Trent Bridge was lost by an innings, the third test at Old Trafford was washed out, but Pakistan became the first side to defeat England in a test on their very first tour when they won the fourth test at the Oval and drew the series. Fazal was the hero, and Kardar the architect of victory, for he had put Pakistan on the world's cricket map. At Lord's Khan Mohammad bowled England opener and captain Len Hutton for zero with a new ball. More than half a century has passed, but I still remember seeing a picture in a newspaper: Hutton going forward, beaten by a swinger that shattered his stumps as the bails flew. The caption to the picture said: "The master mastered". Hutton till then held the world record — an unbeaten 364 in test cricket. Pakistan was the only team that never suffered Hutton's mastery with the willow. At the Oval, Fazal dismissed him twice quite cheaply — for 14 and five. Khan Mohammad died in London on July 5, 2009 at age 81. His best figures were against New Zealand in the 1955-56 test series when he captured six wickets for 21

Adeel's father and Abbu were first cousins. Besides, he was related to Razia also. He then worked at the National Bank of Pakistan's London branch. About 30 years later Adeel would do something great. He would re-do our family history. The first book about our clan — the Makhdooms — was written before World War II by Masood Ali Mahvi, a family legend. Father and many of my elders used to call him B.A. Chacha — (or B.A. Uncle) because he had the honour of belonging to the first batch of graduates from the Aligarh University. After the partition holocaust and the Indian occupation of Hyderabad State it was doubtful if the family history would ever be re-written. Since our ancestors had come to Hyderabad from Fatehpur in U.P. we referred to ourselves as Makhdoomzadgan-e-Fatehpur — the brood of Makhdoom from Fatehpur. By the end of the 20th century, the Makhdooms were all over the world, the young ones were hardly aware of family history, and one often wondered whether someone would be able to do an update. Adeel did this in 2005. His work involved serious labour, and it was a commendable job. To make things easier, he asked all those capable of writing their biographies to give it to him. He consolidated them, gave shape to the book and finally it became an up-to-date family history.

On the way back to Pakistan, I had planned to visit Turkey. But Pan-Am had by then changed its route and touched Teheran instead of Istanbul. I had a very dear friend in Tehran, Sajid Rizvi, who then worked at Teheran Journal. Later he became the UPI Bureau Chief for Iran but was forced to flee during the revolution. He was later posted with the UPI in Turkey. We were colleagues at Morning News, and Sajid told me to forget Turkey and drop in. What happened to me at the Tehran airport is a measure not only of my stupidity but of the Pakistani people's romantic, even infantile, notions of such concepts as Islamic brotherhood or Islamic ummah or the fraud that the RCD was. RCD was a short form for the Regional Cooperation for Development, which grouped three pro-Western Muslim governments — those of Turkey, Iran and Pakistan. In America's military jargon this group of states was known as the "upper tier" — the undefined lower tier being the Arab states. The RCD, in whose formation Ayub and Bhutto had played a major part, was wound up 30 years later unsung without having accomplished any of the fabulous economic and cultural projects it had before it. As a journalist I do not know how many write-ups and editorials I did on what turned out to be a propaganda exercise for the benefit of no one. We were supposed to be brothers, though I would not like to deny the genuine sentiments of love and friendship that have existed among the Turkish, Iranian and Pakistani peoples. But as a political and economic entity the RCD existed only on government files and in newspapers. Taking the RCD brotherhood as a reality which I thought every taxi driver and pushcart owner in Tehran were imbued with I boarded a Pan-Am flight without a visa for the oil-rich country. At the Mehrabad airport, the immigration officer wanted to know why I did not have a visa. I told him about the RCD, showed him my ticket for Karachi and made a blunder by telling him I was a journalist. His radar screen beeped. Within no time an English-speaking officer came, asking me to collect my luggage and re-board the flight.

"This flight does not go to Karachi," I said. "It goes to Bangkok".

"Doesn't matter", he replied. "You go to Bangkok and then return to Karachi. Collect your luggage!"

Experience tells me every journalist is regarded a spy in all dictatorships. Six years later I would have an even worse experience at the Jakarta airport where I had landed in October 1982 to attend a conference on environment, organised by a London-based NGO, Earthscan, but hosted by the Indonesian government. At the Karachi consulate they told me point blank "We do not issue visas to journalists". The Earthscan people had expected this and had warned me in advance to let them know if there were any problems in getting a visa. I wrote back to them, and evidently their intercession with the consulate mattered, for I received a phone call asking me to come over. I was asked to fill three massive forms — without the benefit of a carbon paper — and was told to collect my passport the next day. It so happened that a school friend worked for the Indonesian consulate and that helped me somewhat. I was even entertained with a glass of cold drink — something I have never in my life relished. The next day I collected my passport, thanked the Indonesian official and was about to leave when he said, "Wait!" He took my passport, made what looked like a star or a cross on it and handed it to me.

Curious I asked, "What is this?"

He replied, "This will help you at the airport".

There couldn't be a greater act of villainy. At the Jakarta airport, the immigration officer cleared one passenger after another, stamping passport after passport, and the queue before me shortened. He stamped my passport, too, and was about to hand it over to me when the star caught his attention.

"Why you kome to Indonesia?" the immigration officer, who must have known Dutch quite well, asked.

"To attend the conference at Denpasar".

"We do not give visa to zhournalists".

203

"But I already have it. Your people at Karachi gave it to me. Your education minister is going to inaugurate the conference".

He was flummoxed, called two other immigration officials over and had a chat with them. Evidently, the others asked him to let me go. The official returned and told me brusquely, "This visa for 12 days. OK? If you overstay you go to jail! Understand?"

"Yes, I understand", I told him, because I had no intention of going to prison. Under Suharto, you only had to tell a police officer that a man was a communist and he would disappear and rot in prison for years. In contrast to the immigration officials, the Indonesian people were a different lot. I found them very friendly toward Pakistan and, unlike us Pakistanis and other South Asians, very peaceable by nature. In fact, ignoring Turkey, I found people in no other countries friendlier toward Pakistan than those of Indonesia and Malaysia. But to continue the story at the Tehran airport: as I waited for my luggage and cursed my star, another Iranian official appeared. He spoke better English and asked me what my problem was. I showed him the ticket to Karachi, made an unintelligent reference once again to my shady profession and showed him the Thomson Foundation papers. He returned a few minutes later with my passport.

"This is a visa for 24 hours", he said politely. "You must get it extended". He did not visualise a jail term for me.

Sajid had my visa extended, and I passed six delightful days in Tehran, and it goes without saying that I fell in love with Iran. Sajid's wife was in the family way and had gone to Karachi. So we had not one but several boys' nights out. Being in Iran was an extraordinary experience. The sophistication of the Iranian way of life, the order and cleanliness that characterised Tehran, the stunning beauty of Iranian women, the low tones in which the Iranian people conversed, the respect which they showed for each other, Agha being the common form of address that cut across class — all this overwhelmed me. There is no other country in the world with which we Pakistanis share so much of culture, including and especially the bonds that tie Urdu to Persian. In the generations preceding mine a person was considered uncouth if he did not know Persian. The shame attached to me was the greater because Abbu — then alive — was well versed in Persian and wrote poetry in it as well. I never bothered to read Persian beyond school, but because of my family background and the reference which Abbu made to Hafiz and Saadi and the frequency with which he quoted from Ghalib and Iqbal's Persian verses Persian has remained part of my being. I have continued to read and memorise Iqbal's Urdu works, but as Abbu once pointed out Iqbal's Urdu poetry is basically in Persian, because if you drop prepositions and conjunctions what remains is Persian. Amir Khushro was also Abbo's favourite poet, and I remember by heart his Persian na'at — Nami danam chay manzil bood — with its superb maqta steeped in the mysteries of time-space quantum. The first verse of Hafiz's divan — "ala ya ayyohus-Saaqi..." gained in popularity in the early 20th century because of the parody by Akbar Allahabadi in the wake of the Gallipoli misadventure — a Churchill brainchild. Said Akbar:

Ala ya ayoohach-Churchill nazar kun sooay saahil ra

Ke jang aasan namood avval walay uftad mushkil ha.

(Hearken, O Churchill! Look toward the coast; war looks easy in the beginning; disasters come later.)

As was bound to happen, the Indic Muslims' isolation from the Middle East and Central Asia after the British conquest of South Asia had an effect upon their understanding of Persian, too: it has remained mired where it was possibly in the 18th century, and the change in usage in Iran altering the meaning of many words has remained unknown to them. Pronunciation, too, has undergone transformation. At times the change was shocking to me. Taigh, which in Urdu means sword, is pronounced teegh and means a razor blade. Bachkana in Urdu means childish; in modern Persian it means anything concerning children. One sign on the entrance to what looked like a gymnasium showed two boxing gloves, beneath which was written musht-zani (u as in 'push'). Obviously it was a place for learning and practising boxing, but in Urdu *musht-zani* has a more smutty meaning! A visit to the older parts of Tehran gave me an extraordinary sense of peace and déjà vu with, as if, Noor Jahan singing in the background — *'Ye tho vohi jaga hay guzray thhay hum jahan se'* (this is the place where we had once sojourned). Tales heard in childhood appeared not only real but as if they happened yesterday and just here — of Ali Baba and forty thieves, of mosques and taverns, the pious and the impious, of Omar Khayyam with his cup and Nizamul Mulk with his madressah, the poets and the storytellers, the hakims with their potions, the hammams with fair ladies and their attendants, of the shahs with their palaces and white steeds, of princes and princesses and their romance, the Laila-Majnoon and Sheereen-Farhad legends, camels loaded with carpets and spices and Chinese silk, the chivalrous bandits who responded to the muezzin's call in the morning and robbed caravans at night, of caravanserais where beggars and the rich mixed, and finally the Mongol hordes, putting everything to the sword and destroying a civilisation; out of the ashes rising like phoenix the Safavids – with their Turkic cousins: the Mughals in the east and the Ottomans in the west; Humayun, a fugitive from a kingdom usurped by Sher Shah, returning after 10 years with soldiers provided by Shah Tahmasp and regaining his throne at Delhi; the unending battles between Ottomans and Safavids for the control of Iraq, especially Baghdad, the collapse of the Safavids, Nadir Shah's rise and the flash of his word seen from Delhi to Tiblisi: suddenly you seem to lose all track of time and space.

The Iran that I saw was Pahlavi Iran; its days were numbered. Superficially it was all calm. There was complete freedom — cultural. Black chador was in evidence, but I did not see the hijab that would later become Islamic Iran's hallmark. Pairs walked in parks or sat on benches, the pubs did roaring business, and even pork was sold. What was missing was the real freedom — to vote and be voted and to criticise the government, much less the shah. The dynasty the shah belonged to was only two generations old. His father, a one-time private in an Iranian army brigade officered by Russians, ousted Ahmad Shah, the last Qajar king, from power with the help of the Allied powers because of his pro-German leanings. But Raza, whom history, or to be more specific his son, would call Kabir (Great) did one thing most clever: he named his dynasty Pahlavi. There are two interpretations why he chose that name. One, he belonged to the Pahlevan tribe; the other, more accepted theory is that, to give respectability to his dynasty and fabricate ancient roots, Raza chose the name Pahlavi because it was the name of the pre-Islamic, classical Persian. Raza also changed the Hijri calendar and switched over to the Pahlavi calendar but later rescinded his decision after the ulema protested. (His son reversed the decision in 1976.)

Things would have been different if his son, who became king in 1941, were truly secularist, for a person who believes in secularism gives everyone the right to pursue his religion and abhors persecution. But the shah wanted to cast Iran in his own image. To take his father's pre-Islamic notions to ridiculous extremes, the shah spent a staggering amount — $100 million — on a festival held at Persopolis (Takht-i-Jamshid) in 1971 to celebrate the 2,500 years of Iran's monarchy. An educated man, he should have known that there was no historical continuity in Iranian monarchy and that there was a gap of at least 900 years beginning with the destruction of the Sassanid Empire at the hands of the Arab Caliphate in the seventh century. After being restored to the throne by a CIA-engineered coup against Ahmad Mossadegh, the shah established in 1953 the dreaded secret police Savak (Sazman-i-Amniyet va Ittilaat-i-Kishver). Headed first by Taymour Bakhtiar, it was expanded and made "efficient" by its third chief, Nematollah Nasiri, later ambassador to Pakistan. By the time the shah left Iran for good on Jan 16, 1979, Savak's personnel numbered 100,000, and the number of political prisoners was about the same. I remember I was standing in front of a royal palace and was talking politics, when Sajid told me in Urdu, "Don't speak English! We are being watched." Savak agents were standing nearby and obviously wanted to know who was standing near a royal palace and why. This represented one bitter truth about Pahlavi Iran: freedom was confined to culture; in politics, freedom was taboo.

The most horrible of Savak's crimes was the burning of Rex Cinema in Abadan on Aug 19, 1978. A fire broke out, and when people ran to the gates, they were found bolted from the outside. A minimum of 480 people were burnt to death. Savak's aim was to blame the ulema for the crime. In an extraordinary display of cynicism, some opposition leaders began calling it "the Kebab House of the Sun of Aryans". The stage had been set for Iran's Islamic revolution, and the shah's days in powers were numbered. As I headed home on July 30 I did not know Bhutto had even fewer days left.

9

FLOGGING AND HANGING

SHUBBKHOON CAN BE TRANSLATED into English as night attack. However, a night attack is an objective term, denoting an attack at night by an army or a company of soldiers. Shubbkhoon contains the word "khoon", which means blood. Thus a shubkhoon is more than a night attack: it smacks of treachery. On July 5, 1977, Pakistan's army chief, Gen. Ziaul Haq, carried out a shubkhoon on the country. Since then, Pakistan has not been a normal country, and the people of Pakistan have lost the ability to think straight in collective matters. Every Pakistani crowd is a mob or a potential mob. Zia also followed policies that served to plant in the minds of the people of Pakistan the pernicious idea that Islamic punishments — like flogging for adultery, drinking, etc. — can be used as a form of entertainment. This profoundly repulsive idea spread rapidly and has been a source of great misfortune for the people of Pakistan. This marked the beginning of the brutalisation of society in Pakistan. The less educated a person was the more he subscribed to the cave-man's concept of entertainment propounded by Zia and the coterie around him. Zia promised to hold elections within 90 days, but went on to rule for 11 years without holding a single election in the real sense of the term. The only election he held was in 1985, and since — in spite of Bhutto's murder and the unabashed persecution of the PPP

— his intelligence hounds had estimated that the PPP would again gain a landslide victory, Zia made it a non-party election. While all dictators wish to rule until overthrown or murdered, Zia too wanted to rule for life. However, the most unfortunate aspect of the Zia phenomenon was that some leading religious parties lent full support to his tyranny to prolong his regime so as to avoid an election which they knew they were not going to win. This marked from a moral point of view a steep decline in the political conduct of Pakistan's religious parties and elements. The first indication of the fact that, in spite of being overthrown, Bhutto had not lost his popularity came when, after being released from detention a few weeks after the July 5 coup, Bhutto undertook a train journey. All along he received tumultuous receptions which Zia and his "religious" supporters had not expected.

I was present at the Karachi Cantonment station when the train carrying Bhutto pulled in on August 1. I placed myself on the steps of a wooden bridge and hoped to catch a glimpse of him. There was so much crowd on the platform I wondered if I would be able to take a look at him. Well, the train came to a halt in a way that the compartment in which Bhutto was travelling was in front of my perch. I was perhaps 10 feet from him. Bhutto stood at the door. He was wearing a cream-coloured shalwar-qamees and he had a white handkerchief in his hand and was most probably having a running nose. Otherwise, he looked hale and hearty. As the crowd milled around and Bhutto stood smiling and in triumph, I suddenly had this uncanny feeling: this was the last time I was looking at him. I would never see him again. Ramazan was approaching, and I knew Bhutto would be going to Larkana for the holy month, so I made my final bid to see him on the evening of August 2. I went to his 70 Clifton home, but realised it was impossible to meet him. Stakes were high, Bhutto was in session with party colleagues, a large crowd was waiting outside to catch a glimpse of him, but it was impossible even for newsmen to see him. He was arrested that very night and hanged 18 months later after a trial that Dorab Patel, one of Pakistan's most eminent judges, called "judicial murder".

The train journey and the Bhutto-mad crowds convinced the Generals and pro-army parties and newspapers that, in spite of being overthrown, Bhutto was going to sweep the elections which Ziaul Haq had promised to hold within 90 days after assuming power. If elections were held, and if Bhutto won, what would become of the claim by the parties belonging to the Pakistan National Alliance that the elections held earlier in the year (March 1977) had been manipulated? They had carried on a nationwide campaign that had paralysed the state machinery, brought the country to a halt, caused many deaths and did incalculable harm to the economy. All along their movement, the PNA leaders — who included retired Air Marshal Asghar Khan, Wali Khan, Mufti Mahmood, Shah Ahmad Noorani, Nasrullah Khan, Mian Tufail Mohammad and Professor Abdul Ghafoor Ahmad — had declared repeatedly that their idea was a free and fair electoral exercise, because the March elections had been rigged. However, euphoric over the Bhutto overthrow, the PNA leaders had not taken one fact into account — the silent majority. A small minority can overthrow a government by terror, or even by a lesser form of violence of the kind that has now become Pakistan's trade mark — bus burning, stone throwing and 'wheel jam' — but that does not mean that the majority is with the agitators. The big issue before the PNA leadership was how to put off or possibly cancel the elections. A ruse had to be found to call off the elections, even though the election campaign had already begun and the PPP rallies were drawing 10 times more crowds than they were when Bhutto was in power. Then a shibboleth was found — accountability. Suddenly the PNA leaders, and the media supportive of them, came up with a catchy Urdu slogan: pahlay ehtisab, phir intikhab (accountability first, elections later).

In the ultimate analysis, it is the PNA leadership that must be held responsible for the postponement of the elections, for it is they who provided Zia with a subterfuge for postponing and then calling off the elections. All PNA leaders subsequently denied that they ever pleaded with Ziaul Haq to postpone the elections. But the truth is that all of them went public with the demands for the postponement, and the subsequent denials constitute a blatant lie. In fact, it is doubtful if Ziaul Haq, in spite of his lust for power, could ever think of postponing the elections if both PPP and PNA were opposed to a postponement of the general election. He called off the polls because the PNA leaders assured him of their full backing in violation of the pledge he had made in his first TV address to the Pakistani people to hold a fair and free election within 90 days. Asghar Khan denies that he ever demanded a postponement of the general election and asks us to read what he wrote in his books. What he wrote subsequently is of no consequence. I would recommend to the readers a most revealing correspondence between Asghar and that icon of Pakistani journalism, Irshad Ahmad Haqqani. The latter held Asghar and other PNA leaders responsible for postponing the election. Decades later, in his column in Jang of January 17, 2002, Haqqani says Asghar was the first of the PNA politicians to propose to Zia the cancellation of the election. Asghar replied to this charge and Haqqani produced Asghar's denial in full in his column of Jan 27, 2002, but the columnist stuck to his guns.

The most controversial of Asghar's decisions concerns the incitement to the armed forces to overthrow Bhutto. Asghar denies this charge vehemently, and to prove that he never incited the officers and men of Pakistani armed forces to sedition he has reproduced the text of that letter in the latest of his books, My Political Struggle. It is a most self-incriminating document, for any impartial reader would get no other impression save that, between the lines, Asghar was encouraging the army to revolt at the height of the PNA movement. The army coming to the aid of the civilian authority and acting 'unlawfully' was not a phenomenon confined to the PNA movement, when any government worth its salt would have sought the army's help to quell the disturbances, given the scale of the agitation. Bhutto was not the first or last ruler to use troops to tackle an agitation. The army was used to control the anti-Qadiani agitation in the Punjab in the '50s, the Ayub government deployed the troops during the anti-government agitation in the winter of 1968-69, Yahya unleashed the power of the army to crack down on demonstrators in East Pakistan in 1971, Bhutto used the army in Balochistan years before the PNA movement, but I do not think Asghar thought that occasion fit for a similar letter to the armed forces to "do your duty". During the Musharraf years, too, the soldiers' behaviour had been no less "unlawful". However, the adjectives used by Asghar against Bhutto in that letter, the reference in highly emotional tones to "mothers and sisters", the possibility of the Pakistani armed forces turning into "a degenerate police force fit only for killing unarmed civilians", and finally telling them that '"time has come. Answer this call honestly and save Pakistan" would make it clear even to a less discerning reader what the motive behind the letter was.

After postponing the election, Zia needed "a hang Bhutto cabinet", and many PNA parties were only too willing to help. It was also during the rule by the PNA cabinet that journalists were flogged. The information ministry was then headed by Mahmood Azam Faruqi, belonging to the Jamaat-i-Islami. Those whipped on May 13, 1978, were: one of my former colleagues at The Sun Masudullah Khan (then working at The Pakistan Times), Iqbal Ahmad Jafri, Khawar Naeem Hashmi and Nisar Zaidi. That day the Headquarters of Martial Law Administrator, Zone A, (Punjab), issued the following press release: "Various summary military courts in Lahore today sentenced eleven journalists, [and] press workers to various terms of imprisonment and released five newsmen and press workers after giving warning. They were tried under MLRs [martial law regulations] 5 and 33 for organizing meetings at an open public place, raising slogans, displaying banners and starting [a] hunger strike. The punishments awarded are as follows: Mohammad Ilyas (The Pakistan Times, Rawalpindi) nine months' R.I. (rigorous imprisonment), Rs. 5,000 fine (in case of default will further undergo three months' R. I.), Nisar Zaidi (Nawa-i-Waqt) and Iqbal Ahmad Jafri (The Sun) nine months' R.I., five stripes and fine Rs. 3,000 each (in case of default will further undergo three months' R.I.), Khawar Naeem Hashmi (Musawat, Lahore) nine months' R.I., three stripes, fine Rs. 2,000 (in case of default will further undergo three months' R.I.), Abdul Hamid Chhapra (Jang, Karachi) six months' R.I., fine Rs.2,000 (in case of default will further undergo three months' R.I.), Masudullah Khan (The Pakistan Times, Rawalpindi) six months' R.I., five stripes and fine Rs. 2,000 (in case of default will undergo three months' R.I,), Fateh Mohammad. (Dawn, Karachi) six months' R.I., Syed Mohammad Soofi (Musawat, Karachi) and Khawaja Nisar Ahmad (Jang, Karachi) six months' R.I. and fine Rs.1, 000 each (in case of default will further undergo three months' R.I.), Rana Nayyar Iqbal (Musawat, Lahore) and Mohammad Ashraf Ali (Sadaqat, Karachi) three months' R.I."

The news, published in Dawn of May 14, was carried by government agency APP and the privately-owned PPI. According to the All Pakistan Newspaper Employees' Confederation — the journalists and press workers' umbrella organisation — the journalists were flogged within 70 minutes of the pronouncement of the military court's verdict. The Apnec press release said: "Four out of 11 newsmen, who were awarded sentences of lashes in addition to rigorous imprisonment and fine, were flogged tonight (May 13) i.e., the sentences of lashes were executed within 70 minutes after the judgment awarded by the summary courts. Those who were flogged are: Masudullah Khan, Iqbal Ahmad Jafri, Khawar Naeem Hashmi and Nisar Zaidi."

Those in power and participating in acts of tyranny weren't merely the Generals; they included "religious" leaders and parties. During the Ayub and Bhutto regimes the JI stood for democracy and freedom of the press, and there is no doubt it suffered persecution that included the closure of its newspapers and periodicals and arrest of its leaders and workers. However, once it became part of Ziaul Haq's cabinet, the JI followed polices whose effects have persisted till this day, for the party staged a political somersault that was stunning for a party that claimed that not only was its aim the establishment of an Islamic state, it upheld Islamic values in its political conduct. Nevertheless, as a party one of whose ministers headed Zia's information ministry, the JI suddenly discovered the virtues of thought control, declared openly that press freedom could not be a licence, that an "Islamic state" had to save society from such a dangerous concept as press freedom, and that only "communists and enemies of the Islamic ideology" believed in such concepts. The JI, which in the first decade of the 21st century spearheaded a campaign against Musharraf for being Head of State as well as army chief, went on to support Ziaul Haq as President and Chief of the Army Staff for full 11 years till his death. Here I would like to quote the prophetic words written in an editorial by Dawn's legendary editor, Altaf Husain, as far back as 1964. Titled "Ayub and COP" (Combined Opposition Parties, of which the JI was a component), the editorial, which appeared in two parts in the issues of November 22 and 23, 1964, said: "In order to achieve its objective the Jamaat will not hesitate to resort to far graver tyranny and repression than it now lays at the door of the Ayub regime. Tyranny will then be justified in the name of Islam." His words turned out to be true, as recorded by history.

I travelled with Ziaul Haq on several foreign trips and observed the courtesy and manners which the pro-Zia, rightwing papers never tired of publicising. Actually, Zia's manners were a deception that appealed only to men with low intellect and to those politically motivated journalists who tried to turn him into a god. For instance, one day on a foreign trip he asked a TV camera man to lead the prayers. This was a superficial demonstration of social equality on the part of a man who was wedded to the Pakistani middle class's decadent social values and had — like most of his religious admirers — no concept of human dignity as is understood in the civilized world. Once a journalist known to be his admirer asked him at a press conference why he was wearing such a costly uniform, while the poor in Pakistan had nothing to wear. This was superb flattery. Every Muslim child knows that Umar, the second Caliph, was once questioned by a common Muslim as to why his robe was longer than his. The legendary caliph — whose armies had humbled the Roman and Sassanid empires — replied that his son had given him his share of the spoils of war. The questioner must have gladdened Ziaul Haq because the man was comparing a usurper and tyrant to Umar the

Great. Gestures like asking the camera man to lead the prayer would be a glorious sight for the Ziaists, who would write column after column to emphasise his "Islamic character" and the simplicity of his nature. In truth, Zia displayed the traits which were the very opposite of what Islam expects of a believer: he lied brazen-facedly and was essentially dishonest and a flatterer. Once he wiped cigarette ash off Bhuttto's shoes, and once put hurriedly into his pocket his hand containing a burning cigarette when he saw Bhutto approaching. On one occasion in Garhi Khuda Bux, he swept the grave of Bhutto's father and kept telling people around to let Prime Minister Bhutto know of his deed. Once a military court condemned two young boys to death by hanging. Pakistan's law forbids the execution of a person under 18. Zia let the two live in jail. When they turned 18 he had them both hanged.

While returning from Turkey on an official tour in 1987, Ziaul Haq decided to stop over in Saudi Arabia for Umra –- off-season Hajj. This was not on the schedule and enabled me, like the rest of the entourage which included a number of journalists, to perform Umra. I naturally felt grateful to him. We stayed at one of the royal palaces in Jeddah and then proceeded in the evening by car to Mecca. After I had completed the circumambulation of the Kaaba I found Ziaul Haq standing close to me. Perhaps overcome by the sanctity of the Grand Mosque, whose foundations were laid by Patriarch Abraham and his son Ishmael, I felt myself utterly clean, a kind of feeling I never had before, devoid of all negative sentiments toward humanity at large — as if I had been born just there and then and known nothing of whatever had happened to me or to the world outside before that first visit to Kaaba. I found Ziaul Haq was standing a few paces from me. I said Janab-e-Sadr! (Mr President!). He turned and I shook hands with him. This was the only time when I did not have negative feelings toward him. The next handshake at Islamabad at a lunch at the President House in March 1988 turned out to be the last.

The circumstances leading to the Islamabad luncheon need to be told, because it was a reflection of the tension that had developed between him and Prime Minister Mohammad Khan Junejo — Zia's own protégé. Unlike his image, Junejo turned out to be far more intelligent and politically astute than Zia or the people expected him to be. His biggest clash with Zia came over the Afghan war as it seemed to draw to a close. The Soviets had agreed to withdraw, and the Geneva agreement was due to be signed. If the agreement were signed Zia would lose his position as a key American ally, and all US aid would come to a halt because it was obvious that the certificate which Presidents Ronald Reagan and George Bush Sr. had been issuing regularly every year as required by the Pressler amendment would not be forthcoming. Junejo was keen to go ahead with the Geneva accords because he wanted the war to be over. He had seen the disastrous consequences of Zia and America's backing of religious militancy and the role which the militant organisations had started playing in Pakistan's domestic politics. So long as Zia was at the helm, the Islamist militias behaved themselves, and even though the Inter Services Intelligence served as the link between the militia leaders and the CIA, the American agency often bypassed the ISI and supplied arms and money directly to the anti-Soviet resistance groups based in Pakistan. When Zia was gone, these militant organisations would become a state within a state. The full impact of their power, organisation and indoctrinated cadres would be felt during the political period between Zia's death (August 1988) and the takeover by Gen Musharraf in October 1999.

On August 12, 1983, Ziaul Haq addressed the unelected Majlis-i-Shoora (consultative assembly) consisting of hand-picked politicians, "safe" industrialists, feudal lords and tycoons, and "Islam-loving" journalists, and announced to the nation a plan for the restoration of democracy. He announced that elections to the provincial assemblies, the National Assembly and the Senate would be completed by March 23, 1985. However, on December 1, 1984, contrary to the pledges he had made previously that he had no intention of holding a referendum, Zia repudiated the pledge and suddenly announced a referendum for December 19. Since parliamentary elections were to be held in 1985,

Zia had two motives behind holding the referendum: one, to have himself "elected" to ensure the continuity of his absolute power before, during and after the general election; two, to let the state machinery know that they should not take the proposed election seriously and must cooperate with him fully for ensuring "positive results" — a term he and his supporters frequently employed to mean results in which the PPP would lose; three, his very presence at the helm as head of state and army chief would not unnerve his political supporters while facing the PPP at the hustings. Called the Referendum Order, 1984, (President's Order 11 of 1984), it spelled out the question that was to be put to the voter: "Whether the people of Pakistan endorse the process initiated by Gen Muhammad Ziaul Haq, the President of Pakistan, for bringing the laws of Pakistan in conformity with the injunctions of Islam as laid down in the Holy Qur'an and Sunnah of the Holy Prophet (be peace upon him) and for the preservation of the ideology of Pakistan, for the continuation and consolidation of that process and for the smooth and orderly transfer of power to the elected representatives of the people." If the majority cast a Yes vote Zia would stand elected President for five years. The irony of a Muslim being asked to say Yes or No to an Islamisation process, was highlighted by a British newspaper, The Guardian, thus: "It is like asking Midwesterners to vote against motherhood or apple pie".

What would be the consequences if the majority voted Yes? The Referendum Order's Section 7, entitled "Consequences of the declaration of the result" said "if [the] majority of the votes cast is in favour of the answer Yes, the people of Pakistan shall be deemed to have endorsed all steps [emphasis added] taken by the President of Pakistan for bringing the laws of Pakistan in conformity with the injunctions of Islam as laid down in the Holy Qur'an and the Sunnah of the Holy Prophet (may peacebe upon him) and for the preservation of the ideology of Pakistan, for the continuation and consolidation of that process and for the smooth and orderly transfer of power to the elected representatives of the people; and Gen Muhammad Ziaul Haq shall be deemed to have been duly elected President of Pakistan for five years…" beginning with the first joint session of parliament.

A day before the referendum, to make sure of his victory, Zia withdrew the requirement of a national identity card for the voter. A news item released by the government news agency APP and published on Dawn's page one said: "The President's order provides that, when a voter presents himself to vote at the referendum, the Presiding Officer shall issue a ballot paper to him after satisfying himself about his identity on [the] production of such documents, material or evidence as the Presiding Officer may deem fit and that he need not insist on the production of the identity card issued under the National Registration Act, 1973". This precaution to ensure a massive Yes vote was taken in spite of the fact that all political activity was banned, no rallies or processions were allowed, and a number of leading opposition leaders, including Tikka Khan, a former army chief and Secretary-General of the PPP, were in jail. Sole candidate Zia went on a campaign and sought votes because he said it was the Islamic system that was the aim of his rule. The headline to Dawn's lead story on December 13 said: "Zia says Yes would be for Islam not for himself".

Most, though not all, religious parties lent full support to Zia's referendum fraud. The way they mobilised their workers and party machinery for helping Zia win the thoroughly bogus referendum in December 1984 was a clear indication of the consolidation of a phenomenon that had begun much earlier and has persisted till this day: the religious parties and elements would not mind ditching all moral values if this helped them advance or achieve their political goals. Discarding all norms of propriety, state officials loyal to the religious parties and working in government departments and state-controlled corporations had no qualms of conscience about misusing their official positions and using state vehicles and fuel for organising bogus voting.

As the referendum began, most polling stations wore a deserted look except for the Election Commission officials, who were taken aback by the sudden reversal of the identity card condition a day before voting. There were hardly any voters to be seen except those taken to the polling stations on government vehicles or by parties supporting Ziaul Haq. The opposition claimed that the voter turnout was five per cent, the government said it was over 60 per cent, though neutral observers put it at 15 per cent. Qaiser, my sister who was a school teacher, was on duty at a polling station in Karachi's Sabzi Mandi area on University Road. She told me the story of that fraud: very few people came to cast their vote, except for those bussed to the polling stations and some who indeed came on their own. She remained idle most of the time. But, when the polling time was over, policemen entered the polling station and asked her and her boss to start putting the Yes stamp on the ballot papers. No wonder, the General received a 97.1% Yes vote. Holding a referendum was a violation of the pledges he had made several times to the press and the people that he had no intention of getting himself elected through a referendum. Pervez Musharraf would perpetrate the same fraud on the nation 18 years later. But there were two vital differences between the referenda in 1984 and in 2002: one, Musharraf did not inflict that fraud on Pakistan in the name of Islam; two, Musharraf later had the decency to go public with his confession that the referendum was anything but fair. Zia never had the moral courage to acknowledge his guilt.

Dawn's editorial on the results of the referendum was a masterpiece of editorial sophistication. The country was under martial law, much of the press was frightened into submission or consisted of zealous Zia supporters, and there was no sign of courage on the part of the political parties to challenge his dictatorship in a religious garb. Benazir's return was still one and a half years away, the Afghan war was at its peak, President Reagan had purged America's foreign policy of human rights, which was an important plank in Carter's foreign policy, the level of America's commitment to the anti-Soviet resistance and personally to Zia was never higher, and Ziaul Haq seemed destined to rule like a Franco or perhaps go down in history as the Conqueror of Afghanistan. While other papers congratulated Zia on the "victory" in the referendum, Dawn avoided the issue by focussing on other matters.

Saying that "opinion may differ on the question of voter turnout, which is generally regarded to be crucial, especially when a positive verdict is to have the status of a national mandate", Dawn editorial of December 24, entitled Referendum and after, questioned "the wisdom of some last-minute decisions and changes, especially the one waiving the requirement of producing the Identity Card by each voter. Some critics have also voiced dissatisfaction over instances of bureaucratic interference and prodding to influence the voter's choice... Having this as a long-delayed watershed, the national focus must now shift to the next phase of the promised transition – elections to the federal and provincial assemblies and the Senate which are to be completed by March 23 next. With presidential continuity now assured, the government is now normally bound to address itself in all seriousness to its commitment to begin re-democratisation." The main question before the nation was, it said, "whether the forthcoming elections are to be held on party or a non-party basis. Given today's complexities of life, it is impossible to build and work a governmental system without organized opinion – and that means parties of different political persuasions. Can organized opinion be counted upon, in a non-party arrangement, to feel any significant sense of allegiance to the system that comes up next?" Referring to the need for combating "regional, ethnic and linguistic exclusivity and assimilating these into the still forming matrix of nationhood, of providing participatory channels of convergence and interaction which are capable of reconciling diverse ideas..." the paper said "needless to say, political parties alone in their role as moulders and reflectors of public opinion can answer these problems ... Indeed, taking a broader view of the overriding national interests and imperatives, it will be advisable for the Government, even at this late stage, to try to reach some understanding and accommodation with the oppositions leaders on the basic political, electoral and constitutional issues that are now at stake, secure their participation in the coming polls and thus pave the way for a wider base of support for the next governmental set-up. Thus prospect for such a development will be greatly facilitated if, before the elections, [the] government announces its plan for all the constitutional amendments it wants. A caution must be sounded here against any drastic change affecting the basic character and provisions 1973 Constitution which, in spite some modifications in the past, still remains the nation's agreed Basic Law and, in our particular circumstances, one that is irreplaceable. Some of the consequential amendments, specifically related to the December 19 authorization, may be in order but bringing structural changes in the 1973 document, especially its provisions relating to the parliamentary form of government, the distributions of powers between the Centre and the provinces, the status of the Prime Minister as the principal focus of authority in day-to-day working, and so on, would be ill-advised and, therefore, must be avoided. The government must also take care not to do anything politically, constitutionally or even administratively, that might create an impression that the constitutionally provided parliamentary system of government has been virtually replaced by a presidential one..."

Zia had chosen Junejo as prime minister because he wanted nothing more than a docile prime minister from Sindh, since it was a Sindhi prime minister whom he had hanged. Even though the general election that brought Junejo to parliament was fought without the political parties being allowed to take part in it, Junejo soon discovered his strength vis-à-vis an unelected ruler. Junejo was sworn in as prime minister on March 23, 1985, and there is no doubt Zia expected him to be grateful and loyal to him. However, once in office Junejo seemed to have become aware of two realities: one, the awkwardness for an elected government to work under the shadow of martial law; two, his own power. Zia, no doubt, had the army behind him, besides the support base he had created for himself in Pakistan's powerful religious lobby, but Junejo was an elected prime minister, and the religious parties — in spite of all their street power — had largely been rejected by the people in the 1985 election. Even though the election was party-less the loyalty of every candidate was known to the voters. Besides, the state-controlled media and the government machinery had worked over time for the benefit of the religious parties. The press too was largely anti-PPP, and the most influential of Urdu newspapers were all for a continuation of the Zia dictatorship. Of the three English newspapers that mattered, two —The Pakistan Times and Morning News — were owned by the government-controlled National Press Trust, but Dawn maintained its independence, even though Mahmoud Haroon, Dawn's owner, was Zia's interior minister.

The outcome of the election must have shocked Zia and the religious parties and must have confirmed Junejo in his belief that Zia lacked a political base. Junejo himself did not support or belong to any party, but, as always in Pakistan, the dictator helps his loyalists hijack the name of the Muslim League, the party which created Pakistan. Obviously, a government cannot function without legislative support. So Junejo joined the Muslim League, so did a large number of time-servers, and that is how the Muslim League once again became the ruling party. There is no doubt Junejo annoyed Zia by making repeated promises to the people — without Zia's permission — that martial law would be lifted "soon" and by advising Zia privately to give up the post of army chief and become a civilian president. In fact, in his very first speech to parliament, Junejo declared that martial law and democracy could not co-exist. This was the beginning of the split between the two, and Zia felt surprised that the affront should have come from his protégé, who until his nomination as prime minister was largely an unknown figure. Martial law was finally lifted on January 1, 1986, making it the country's longest period of rule by decree — eight and a half years. A few months later, Benazir Bhutto returned to Pakistan, and the Junejo administration did nothing that should have annoyed Zia. What Junejo did was to order the administration not to interfere with Benazir's arrival in Lahore and the subsequent programme in the other cities. This was enough to annoy Zia, for he — like most other people — had never expected Benazir to get the kind of reception she did in Lahore and later in other cities. One visible impact of Benazir's return was to be seen in Zia's decision to appear in uniform with greater frequency. After martial law was lifted on January 1, 1986, Zia chose to appear in public wearing a sherwani to emphasise the civilian character of his rule. However, after Benazir's triumphal return he switched back to uniform.

Tensions had been developing between Zia and Junejo on a number of points, and Zia felt angry about issues where he was vulnerable, like the continued pampering of the armed forces' officer class, especially the Generals. Thus came into being the "Generals in Suzuki" controversy. The prime minister could not understand why the Generals should have costly cars, and announced that he would put the Generals in 800cc Suzukis. Junejo took two more steps that offended Zia greatly. Sahibzada Yaqub Khan was Pakistan's Foreign Minister and was greatly admired abroad, especially in the US, which found it easy to deal with a General who was at the helm of Pakistan's foreign ministry. With the Geneva accords approaching, Junejo wanted a civilian minister and a person he could trust. He relieved Yaqub Khan as foreign minister and appointed Zain Noorani in his place. Zia was not only president, he was also Chief of the Army Staff, and expected Junejo to remember this and keep his hands off the army. Junejo, however, seemed determined to assert his role as elected prime minister and shocked Zia by refusing an extension to Gen. Rahimuddin, Chairman of the Joint Chiefs of Staff Committee; retiring Zia's deputy, Gen. K. M. Arif, and appointing commander of the Peshawar-based 12th corps, Mirza Aslam Beg, as Vice Chief of the Army Staff with the rank of a full General.

As a prelude to the signing of the Geneva accords, Junejo decided to call a meeting of all opposition leaders, including Benazir Bhutto. There could be no greater provocation to Zia, for he saw in the meeting with the opposition leaders a conspiracy on Junejo's part to isolate him politically. The prime minister also decided to give an off-the-record briefing to the media on the Afghan war and the peace accords to be signed at Geneva and invited editors over to a dinner in Islamabad.

I was then acting editor of The Star. AAK came to my Gulshan home early at dawn to pick me up for the flight to Islamabad. The Prime Minister House -– now one of Islamabad's landmarks –- was still being built. So Junejo held his dinner for us at a building that later became Musharraf's camp office. All of Pakistan's editors and top journalists were present as Junejo spoke to us and emphasised the need for bringing the Afghan war to an end and signing the Geneva accords. We were scheduled to leave for Karachi the next day, but word came from the President's Office: could the journalists from outside Islamabad extend their stay by a day and have lunch with the president? Wasn't it bad manners that we were leaving without hearing Zia's side of the story?

Another day in Islamabad wasn't a bad idea. Each time I visited the city its locale fascinated me and I felt proud over the way the pride of Pakistan's urban planning was coming up. Ayub had angered the people of Karachi by taking the capital away from them to the green Potohar plateau dominated by the Margalla Hills. But Ayub had reasons. As was his policy he appointed a commission to go into the question of a new capital. The commission gave many reasons why the port city should not be the capital, and one of it was that Karachi was prone to mob violence, which could pressure any government into taking a wrong decision. I think I was in a minority of one in my family and friends, but the decision was correct, even though Karachi had not till then experienced the kind of mob frenzy that would rock not only the city but Pakistan itself decades later. Today (2009) I feel terribly concerned over the fact that Pakistan's capital is so close to the centre of Taliban military activity. Critics also said that East Pakistan was shocked over the transfer of the capital from Karachi to Punjab and that this was one of the reasons behind East Pakistan's secession. While it is true that the Bengali people did not react favourably to the change, the causes of the secession were far deeper than the mere change of the capital. I had first visited Islamabad in 1964 when it was still being built. As a journalist I was amused by the fact that all government news was datelined Islamabad, because Ayub wanted to give the impression that the state machinery had shifted to the new capital. Actually most government departments were functioning in Rawalpindi, and Islamabad existed as a capital city only in newspapers. In 1964, when I first visited Islamabad, the quiet, little town, most of whose population worked for the government, was green and pollution-free. Nature had still not been destroyed, and brooks and streams, now dry, were running. By 1988 Islamabad had acquired the appearance of a city, and the President House, where we had our lunch, had been completed, and it goes without saying that it is a magnificent building. I do not know how true this story is, but members of an American delegation that visited Islamabad and the President House reportedly remarked, "After visiting your capital and the President House we feel it is Pakistan that should give us aid". Whether it is a joke or fact, the irony of it was not lost.

After lunch in the dining hall we moved to another room where we sat around a U-shaped table, as Zia came and shook hands with each one of us. Then he spoke on the Afghan war, and it appeared obvious to everybody that he was in no hurry for peace. He was terribly afraid of a sudden aid freeze by America and other Western powers if the war ended. He gave two reasons why he thought Pakistan should not rush into signing the Geneva accords. First, there were still four million Afghan refugees in Pakistan, and he wondered who would take care of them if the war ended and all aid dried up. Second, if the Soviets pulled out without a prior agreement on the political set-up in the post-Soviet Afghanistan there would be a terrible massacre in Afghanistan, for there would be a civil war which no one would be able to control. (He turned out to be right.) During his last visit to Britain, he said, Mrs Margaret Thatcher had asked him if she could do anything for Pakistan, and Zia had replied, "Yes, tell the British press to keep Afghanistan on their front pages". On the plane back to Karachi I had an uneasy feeling: while Pakistan was not at war but was certainly living in war conditions, the president and the prime minister seemed to be working at cross-purposes. While this may have consequence less in the realm of foreign affairs – because it was the CIA that was conducting the war in Afghanistan with the help of its beloved mujahideen – a split between Zia and Junejo could have disastrous consequences for democracy. Even though what existed then could hardly be called democracy, at least Junejo was struggling against all odds to assert civilian leadership in the face of Zia's iron grip over the civilian administration. More important Junejo had made one vital contribution to the democratic process – he had made the press free.

In 1987 Junejo visited the US. All one can say about the visit was that it was not a failure. Even though Junejo lacked charisma and was anything but a brilliant politician, much less a statesman, Washington dealt with him the way the prime minister of a 'front-line state' should have been. There was no cause for Zia to feel uneasy, but when Junejo began liberalising the press — with an eye on the 1990 general election — and opened out to opposition politicians, especially Benazir, Zia's fears worsened. He remarked, "I hope the visit doesn't go to his head". To add to the tension between the two, there was a clash in at Chauhar Harpal in Rawalpindi between some soldiers and a group of men led by a member of the Punjab Provincial Assembly, and Junejo made it clear he wanted to take action against the army men involved in the brawl. Then a calamity rocked Islamabad and Pakistan: an ammunition dump located between Islamabad and Rawalpindi blew up on April 10, 1988, killing and injuring hundreds of people. The depot at Ojhri had arms and ammunition, including thousands of Stinger missiles, meant for the mujahideen, funded and armed by the United States for the liberation of Afghanistan. Because of the causes still not determined, there was an explosion, with hundreds of rockets with their fuses lit or getting heated flying in all directions with their deadly payload. By accident, a majority of them went in the direction of Islamabad. The projectiles destroyed homes, shops and government buildings, killing men, women and children. Since the Stinger is a heat-seeking missile, many cars and other vehicles were blown to bits. One of the victims was Khaqan Abbasi, Minister for Production in Zia's cabinet, as he proceeded in his car toward his Murree home. The actual number of the dead and injured has not till this day been determined, but it came close to 1,000. The calamity became one of the major causes of tension between Zia and Junejo and finally cost the prime minister his job.

Pakistanis are good rumour mongers and adept at levelling allegations. It was rumoured that someone had sabotaged the dump to conceal the illegal sale of Stingers to unwanted customers, like the mujahideen on the wrong side. One name cropped up repeatedly – Major General Akhtar Abdul Rahman, ISI chief and one of Zia's closest lieutenants. However, there was no proof that such was the case. (Gen. Rahman was among those killed along with Zia in the plane crash on August 17 later that year). In the meantime Junejo proceeded on a tour of China, South Korea and the Philippines. It was during this visit that he made up his mind to take action against the Generals he thought were responsible for the Ojhri disaster. AAK was among the editors who had accompanied the prime minister on the tour. A day before he was due to return home, Junejo told the editors that he had decided to act against those responsible for the blast at the ammunition dump. According to AAK, who narrated the incident to the Dawn staff, Junejo made a call to Islamabad to ask his office to get the file on Ojhri ready. This was a blunder, for the ISI, which was monitoring the prime minister's conversation, tipped off Zia. When the plane landed in Islamabad on the evening of May 29, he was told he had been sacked and the National Assembly dissolved. In fact, the prime minister was taken in "protective custody" on the night between May 29 and 30.

Even though Junejo enjoyed the confidence of the House, Zia acted under clause 58 (2-b) which he had arbitrarily inserted into the Constitution. But even this clause authorised him to sack the government provided "a situation has arisen in which the government of the federation cannot be carried on in accordance with the provisions of the Constitution and an appeal to the electorate is necessary". This was not the case at all, because the Junejo government was functioning normally. Zia acted because he wanted to pre-empt Junejo's move to fix responsibility for the Ojhri blast and go ahead with the Geneva accords.

Junejo was an honest man but a weak one. He could have gone to court to challenge Zia's action, and even though it is obvious that a judiciary which was in the president's pocket could not have overturned his action, Junejo could at least have made a point. The court declared Zia's action illegal after the dictator had died in the air crash on August 17, 1988. Junejo was not a corrupt man, but he had to go along Zia on many issues. For instance Zia developed a most ingenious method of bribing the legislators, for he had decided that all development money for a given area should be given to the legislator of that area. This served to ensure that the lawmaker would be on the right side of the military regime. After Zia's death, Junejo failed to capitalise on his own 'political martyrdom' and never tried to make a serious bid for power. In any case, in the aftermath of the Zia crash, no one could occupy centre stage because a most remarkable woman was already there. Few could match her charisma. Zia died on August 17. On December 2 Bhutto's daughter became the Islamic world's first woman prime minister. For Pakistan, the Ziaist nightmare was over -– but not quite.

Zia's mode of governance and witch-hunting was like the Stalinist system which divided humanity, and the USSR's own citizens, into people and anti-people forces. The latter were out to destroy the Soviet state of peasants and workers, and it was the state's duty to protect the people and destroy the anti-people forces, because they were agents of world imperialism. Anyone who criticised government policies and disagreed with the Stalinist system fell in the category of anti-people and anti-party forces. Hence rectification camps, Siberia, the gulags, people's courts, and mass murders. In Pakistan, Ziaul Haq's regime divided the Pakistani people into two categories — "Islam loving" (or believers in the "Ideology of Pakistan") and the enemies of Islam and of Pakistan's ideology. This was a convenient tool for unabashed persecution of the regime's critics. With Zia's full approval, the ISI, its chiefs and operatives — estimated at 98,000 around the time Zia died — arrogated to themselves the task of saving Pakistan from the enemies of the "ideology of Pakistan". In effect this meant persecution of the regime's critics, "disappearances", torture and death. While the following pages will see the involvement of the army chief and two ISI heads in distributing money to the regime's political favourites and forming a pro-Zia political alliance, even after he had died, a character that deserves a mention is Brigadier Imtiaz Ahmad, billed Billa (tomcat).

In August 2009, two decades after the Zia era had passed into history, Billa made a comeback in the media when he made disclosures which were supposed to be startling. While, as we shall see later in this chapter, ISI chief Hameed Gul made some confessions and offered to be hanged, Billa said nothing about his criminal record as Zia's spy chief. As Zaffar Abbas put it in his front-page piece for Dawn: "As these revelations jog one's memory, one is propelled back in time to the period when Imtiaz Billa's name had become synonymous with dirty, horrible, tactics in dealing with Zia's political opponents. During this period, arrests, torture and even death in custody of political opponents dubbed Indian or Soviet agents had become the order of the day... It was during these days in August 1980 that a group of left-wing activists approached a few journalists at the press club in Karachi to seek their help in highlighting the news of death in custody of communist student leader Nazir Abbasi.

"Abbasi had died during torture as attempts were made to extract information from eight prominent members of the defunct Communist Party of Pakistan (CPP). The news had come out once his body was handed over to his relatives for burial, but the newspapers were unable to publish the reason for his death because of strict censorship.

As Professor Jamal Naqvi, one of the arrested communist leaders, later mentioned in his testimony during the famous Jam Saqi trial, it was Nazir Abbasi's death that saved the rest of the detainees from further torture, as they were soon shifted from a military interrogation cell to a Karachi prison. The ISI's political cell under Gen Zia had acquired a much bigger role with the hijacking of a PIA plane by the so-called Al Zulfiqar in 1981. This incident gave a new lease of life to Gen Zia, as he used it to his advantage to allow the intelligence to round up thousands of political activists in the country – perhaps the biggest crackdown since the mass arrest of political activists to coincide with Mr Bhutto's hanging. ...The role of the military intelligence services in former East Pakistan is often described as the worst as ... hundreds disappeared and popular opinion was suppressed by arresting and trying Awami League leaders as foreign agents. But a close study of Gen Zia's days, and the powers that were given to people like Billa, or the entire ISI under first Generals Ghulam Jilani and then Akhtar Abdur Rehman and finally Lt-Gen Hameed Gul, may show how blatantly they violated the law and human rights." (Dawn, September 1, 2009).

In the post-Zia period, some leading political and military personalities, including Generals claiming to be fighting for Islamic causes, remained true to their Ziaist creed and played a most dirty role in violation of law and Constitution to manipulate the election due on November 16. They included Senate Chairman Ghulam Ishaq Khan, who became President following the air crash, Chief of the Army Staff Gen Mirza Aslam Beg and ISI chief Lt.-Gen. Hameed Gul. The last two, plus Gen Assad Durrani, another ISI chief, confessed to their crimes but have till this day not been given justice. According to the Constitution, the dismissal of a government under article 58 (2-b) must be followed by an election within 90 days. This way, the election should have been held before the end of August. Ziaul Haq busted the Constitution, violated the 90-day stipulation and fixed elections for November 16 so as to create physical problems for Benazir, who was pregnant. (Benazir proved smarter: she kept Zia guessing. As prime minister for the second time, she told Larry King during his April 1995 visit to the US that this was the "biggest spy game" she had played, and the baby came two months earlier than what the Zia-led opposition had expected.) Since Zia had chosen not to have a caretaker prime minister (in violation of article 48 (5-b), Ishaq Khan followed suit and, this way, enjoyed the powers of both head of state and prime minister. More shockingly, the Zia loyalists ordered the state machinery and the government-owned press and electronic media to queer the pitch for Benazir. The PPP's election symbol was a sword, but Zia had so amended the political parties' act that the PPP was refused the sword symbol and it had to settle for a new one – an arrow. As the election neared, state-controlled PTV telecast a play about a plane being hijacked, and the close-up showed a small sword which one of the hijackers had on his shirt.

The most criminal of the acts by this gang was to float a new political alliance by means whose disclosure later shocked the nation. Ordered by Ishaq Khan to create a new political alliance to defeat Benazir, General Beg by his own admission withdrew Rs 140 million from Mehran Bank and gave it to Gen. Durrani for distribution among parties and individuals loyal to Zia to shore up their electoral chances. The man who actually intrigued hard to create an anti-PPP alliance – the Islami Jamhoori Ittehad (Islamic Democratic Alliance) – was Hameed Gul. Two decades later Gul suddenly responded to the call of his conscience and offered to be hanged because he was so ashamed of his role. Gul, of course, knew that his 'offer' had no chance of being accepted, because in Pakistan it is not Generals but prime ministers who are murdered and hanged –Liaquat (October 16, 1951), Bhutto (April 4, 1979), and Benazir (December 27, 2007). The occasion for Gul to confess to his crime was a meeting of Pakistan Ex-servicemen's Association in Islamabad toward the end of January 2008 during the anti-Musharraf stir. Attended by retired Generals who had violated the Constitution and sabotaged democracy without a qualm of conscience in the heyday of their power, the meeting considered a proposal by Gul that all of them jointly apologise to the nation for their crimes. As reported by Umar Cheema for The News (February 2, 2008) the meeting rejected the proposal because Asghar Khan argued that the time was not ripe for an apology. But what Gul told reporter Cheema deserves to be recorded for history. Weeks before the 1988 election, Gul went to see Benazir on the directives of Ishaq Khan and Gen. Beg and told the would-be prime minister, "Look before you get to know from elsewhere, let me frankly admit that IJI has been made by the ISI." Gul said Benazir was shocked to learn this and said: "Alas, General I wish you had not done this. They (IJI) are creating troubles for me." He told Benazir, "I was obliged to obey an unlawful command." As reported by The News the former spy chief told Benazir he could not disobey "this illegal command" since he could expect no "relief from a pliant judiciary" if he were sacked. He was ready for a trial over his role. "My trial, if it sets a good precedent and can bring the country out of further disasters would not be a big sacrifice. I am ready to be hanged". He said he was demanding his trial so that others involved in similar acts would face such trials along with him. We can perhaps only quote the Urdu verse: hai us zood pasehmaan ka pashemaan hona!"

Long before Gul confessed to his crime to The News, it was Benazir's Interior Minister Naseerullah Babar who, speaking in the National Assembly, on June 11, 1990, informed the people about the Mehran Bank scandal and the role played by Ishaq Khan and the three Generals in subverting the electoral process. Gen. Beg confessed to his crime, saying he had indeed taken Rs 140 million from Yunus Habib of Mehran Bank and given it to Gen. Assad Durrani, then ISI chief, for distribution among the IJI parties and others. Yet it is a measure of the military's hold over Pakistan's fortunes that the Generals have till this day not been tried for this crime. The Supreme Court finally registered a case under Article 184(3) of the Constitution after Asghar Khan moved the apex court on a human rights petition which mentioned Beg, Durrani and Younus Habib as respondents. Asghar's petition (HRC 19/96) carried an affidavit by Durrani, who gave details about the money distribution.

The organisations receiving money in several instalments included FRIENDS (Foundation for Research on National Development and Security, a think-tank founded by Gen Beg). The list of the politicians given money by the ISI is long, but those who benefited from Gen Beg's charity at the expense of the Mehran Bank included Ghulam Mustafa Khar (Rs two million), Abdul Hafeez Pirzada (three million), Nawaz Sharif (3.5 million), Lt General Rafaqat, who ran the election cell set up by Ishaq Khan to manipulate the polls, (5.6 million), two former prime ministers –Ghulam Mustafa Jatoi (five million) and Mohammed Khan Junejo (2.5 million) – Pir Pagaro (two million), Yusuf Haroon (on behalf of the MQM: five million), former ambassador to the United States Abida Hussain (one million), Humayun Marri (5.4 million), the Jamaat-i-Islami (five million), the JI's Liaquat Baloch (1.5 million), MQM chief Altaf Hussain (20 million), and Yousaf Memon for distribution among several politicians (50 million), with the lion's share going to PPP-baiter Jam Sadiq Ali, then Sindh's Chief Minister (70 million). (The total exceeds Rs 140 million, because the figures include payments made subsequently.) Beg later declared under oath that, while he was aware of the existence of a political cell and knew of money distribution, he was not personally involved. Nawaz Sharif was grateful to Gen Beg not for the 3.5 million rupees he received from him – that was peanuts for a billionaire like Sharif –; he was beholden to the army chief for destabilising the Benazir government and paving for its dismissal. Nevertheless, this did not stop the former prime minister from maligning Gen. Beg and the ISI when he told the Washington Post in an interview in September 1994 that, when he was prime minister, Gen Beg and the ISI had come to him with a plan for heroin smuggling on a big scale (Details in Chapter 12). Lawrence of Arabia was right: politics is a low occupation.

Surprisingly, Dawn's editorial on the Mehran Bank scandal, entitled Our secret godfathers (April 25, 1994), was quite muted, though the paper took issue with Beg's claim that there was nothing unusual about it. "... [I]t is no secret", the editorial said, "that our intelligence agencies, especially since General Zia's martial law, have dabbled in politics. While they have felt no qualms about doing this, what is equally reprehensible many of our politicians have not hesitated to have links with them. It is because of this sinister nexus that in Pakistani politics events taking place behind the scenes have often been more important than anything taking place on the surface. It is this factor that is also responsible for fostering an atmosphere of intrigue and conspiracy in Islamabad. During the many political upheavals and changes of government in the country since 1988, the intelligence agencies have had an important if not decisive role to play. Sadly, the press, too, for all its self-righteousness has not been immune to these currents, with many of its members keeping in touch with, and often getting their cues from, the shady operatives of Pakistan's intelligence underworld...And now, of course, comes General Beg's rather brazen admission that he did receive a huge sum of money from Mr Yunus Habib some of which was spent by the ISI during the 1990 elections. For good measure he has also said that different people had been making similar donations in the past and that, therefore, there was nothing unusual in this. Coming from a person who held such a senior and sensitive position in the past, this is indeed a strange assertion. Political parties receiving donations is one thing but intelligence agencies receiving donations and then spending them on elections — that is, if his version of events is to be taken at face value — is not only different but utterly impermissible..."

The case was pending with the Supreme Court when Nawaz Sharif became prime minister for a second time in 1997. The ISI wanted the case to be tried in-camera because of the purported sensitive nature of the case, though so much had already appeared in the press that a secret trial made no sense. To add to Sharif's nightmare, the court was also hearing a case of defamation against him. Armed with what the press called a "heavy mandate" which the general election had given him, Sharif made up his mind to get rid of the Chief Justice, Sajjad Ali Shah. To quote Ardeshir Cowasjee, one of Dawn's most popular columnists, "Asghar's lawyer, Habib Wahabul Khairi, countered by saying that as the entire matter had been aired in the press, with all the names involved fully listed, there was little left to warrant in-camera proceedings, and, besides, the people had every right to know how their money had been used and whether the use in question was permitted by law. The court, however, allowed the recording of Babar's and Durrani's statements and their cross examination to be held in camera on November 19 and 20. Seven days later, on November 27, 1997, the Supreme Court was stormed by Nawaz's goons and shortly thereafter Chief Justice Sajjad Ali shah was sent home." Twelve years later, this Sharif would lead a march on the President House on Islamabad for upholding the independence of judiciary!

In 2001, Lt.-General Khalid Maqbool, later Governor of Punjab and then chief of the National Accountability Bureau, called some journalists over for tea in Karachi. I asked him why the Mehran Bank scandal had not been taken up by his organisation even though Gen Beg had confessed to the crime and a case was pending with the Supreme Court in which Gen Durrani had filed an affidavit giving details of money distribution. Gen Maqbool said NAB handled a bank case only when the State Bank of Pakistan forwarded it to him. Period. The case has remained frozen till this day.

~~~~~~~~~

The 1988 election had given the PPP a plurality in the lower house, but the Ishaq-led Generals made it clear to Benazir that she would not be allowed to become prime minister unless she accepted certain conditions, which included (a) she would have nothing to do with the nuclear question, and the uranium enrichment plant at Kahuta, would remain off limits to her; (b) she would have to accept Gen Mirza Aslam Beg as army chief; (c) Sahibzada Yaqub would be the foreign minister; (d) she would not change the ISI Director General, Gen Gul; (e) and it would be advisable if she kept out of the Afghan issue, because they thought the mujahideen leaders would find it awkward to deal with a woman prime minister. The fact was that the Zia loyalists and the religious parties had hoped for a massive electoral win, because they controlled all levers of power and propaganda, and never thought the PPP would be able to make a comeback after 11 years of unabashed persecution. However, when the PPP finally formed government, the Jamaat-i-Islami was calling for a 'mid-term election' within months of the election that had brought Benazir to power. There is no such thing as a mid-term election in a parliamentary democracy. In America the term is used for elections to the House of Representatives and to one-third of Senate seats two years after the presidential election when, to use

MacArthur's words, "the temporary resident ... of the White House" is half way through his four-year term. In a parliamentary system there can be a snap election if needed, but there was no need for it within months of the 1988 general election in which the Zia loyalists were roundly defeated. However, Ishaq and the coterie had made up their mind to manipulate her removal. On August 6, Ishaq invoked the 58-2b article to sack the Benazir government and dissolve an assembly elected only 20 months ago. I remember seeing a cartoon in a newspaper in 1996 when President Farooq Laghari dismissed the second Benazir government. The cartoon showed Ishaq Khan, then in retirement, watching Laghari on TV and telling his grandchildren, "Children, I made this speech twice". This way he was reminding his grandchildren that he had not only dismissed the Benazir government in 1990, he also had the dubious distinction of getting rid of another prime minister, Nawaz Sharif, in 1993 under article 58-2b. When Nawaz Sharif returned to power a second time with "a heavy mandate" in 1997, he used his brute majority in parliament to make changes in the Constitution and have this clause abolished. When Musharraf seized power in October 1999 he tampered with the Constitution and reintroduced this clause into the basic law. It is still there (2009), even though the two major parties, the PPP and PML-N, agree that the clause should be done away with.

10

FIREWORKS AND A WEDDING

AHMAD ALI KHAN BECAME the Dawn editor in February 1973 and quit more than a quarter-century later. He retired on his own in March 2000, was recalled in February2003 and finally called it a day in 2004. He died three years later on March 13. He belonged to that "partition generation" which had to migrate from India to Pakistan to start a new life. This meant, like millions of others, he had to re-build his life from scratch in what then population-wise was the Islamic world's biggest country. Lahore and Karachi were the two cities where he passed most of the 83 years of his life, as against the 23 years he spent in Bhopal, where he was born in 1924; Aligarh, where he acquired his education, and Bombay, where he worked as a journalist. The stay in these cities and the profession he chose also meant interacting with a bewildering variety of men and women.

As Dawn's editor alone he dealt with governments headed by Z. A. Bhutto, Ziaul Haq, Benazir Bhutto, Nawaz Sharif, Benazir again, Nawaz Sharif a second time and Musharraf, besides the half a dozen caretaker governments in between. If to this we add his years with Dawn before he became Editor and his jobs with other newspapers, including The Pakistan Times, whose editor he was for three years, his career as a journalist spanned 60 years. No wonder he worked under circumstances ranging from secret underground activity to editorship during war, civil war and dictatorships. As a student at Aligarh University and later as a journalist in an Urdu daily of Bombay, he saw the freedom movement against colonial rule, was marginally involved in political and trade union activity in Bhopal, lived through the partition holocaust, and then witnessed as a citizen and journalist the tragedy upon tragedy that befell Pakistan. The personalities he was associated with varied in profession and political philosophy, while the nature of the regimes he dealt with ranged from Bhutto's populist despotism and Ziaul Haq's rule by lashes and hanging to the incompetent democratic regimes that ruled Pakistan from December 1988 to October 1999, besides that indefinable phenomenon that Pakistan was under Musharraf ("neither a democracy nor a dictatorship", to quote a British journalist). His stay in Lahore first as a staff member and later as editor of The Pakistan Times brought him into contact with some of Pakistan's leading communists, including Faiz Ahmad Faiz, the paper's editor, Mazhar Ali Khan, who succeeded Faiz as editor, and Mian Iftikharuddin, the paper's owner; and with the left-leaning Progressive Writers, one of whom he eventually married and lived on to become a great grandfather.

Outside his family, perhaps no one knew him better than I, because he remained my editor for a continuous 27 years, followed by another year when he returned. Two other journalists who were with him for these 28 years were M. A. Majid and Zubeida Mustafa. I both enjoyed and suffered. He seemed to enjoy company, held conferences that dragged on over endless cups of tea, talked, discussed, reminisced, philosophised, advised, harangued, shouted, suffered counterattacks from colleagues like me with dignity, was convivial, sometimes indecisive for uncomfortably long periods, but nevertheless knew when to finally act. Quite often he kept others guessing. He had his own methodology for solving problems. Sometimes he talked for no apparent purposes, telling old stories and repeating himself ad nauseam. But I gathered much later that this way he gave himself time to think, to know his colleagues' views and to finally arrive at a decision.

He had weak nerves. Yet that never led to surrender. Often he showed impatience, restlessness and undue haste, and that wrecked the nerves of those around him like me. But astonishing as it sounds the cumulative effect of all this never resulted in impetuous action. In fact, all his decisions were based on pragmatism. The reason for his success as a social being and as editor, I think, was an uncanny insight into the psyche of the person or group he was dealing with. In moments of crisis he fought both his nerves and the challenge before him with courage and wisdom and was more often than not successful. A remarkably intelligent man, AAK was quick to assess a man and detect his motives. That was the reason why he survived personal and professional crises that could normally have made other men give up. Many times when I entered his room, I realised he had detected why I had come. If I had come with a set of demands which he did not wish to accept or grievances he wasn't willing to remove he would go over to the offensive even before I uttered a word. Sometimes I went to him to break some good news, and he would welcome me with warmth, friendship and humour even before I had spoken. More important, as an editor he knew the stuff around him and was careful about what assignment to give whom. He sometimes made mistakes, as all of us do, but as a rule he was astonishingly successful in his choice of men and women for key posts: for instance, Majid, who remained the editor of the leader page for two decades; Ghazi Salahuddin, whose Karachi Diary during the stifling atmosphere of Zia's dictatorship was like a breath of fresh air, and Zubeida Mustafa. As a leader writer who specialised in international affairs and foreign policy, Zubeida later diversified her interests. Her most outstanding contribution to Dawn is *Books and Authors*, which is one of Dawn's most well-read weekly; Mohammad Ziauddin, who later became the first editor of Dawn's Islamabad edition, and is now (2008) Dawn's London correspondent; Shaheen Sehbai, who replaced me as the paper's Washington correspondent in 1995, and Akhtar Payami, who worked as news editor and city editor.

Among the freelance writers he encouraged, four became outstanding columnists — Ayaz Amir, Ardeshir Cowasjee, Irfan Husain and Kunwar Idrees. The first three began writing when Ziaul Haq was in power. But AAK believed — as I have said elsewhere — that closing a paper down wasn't his concept of fighting for press freedom, and the challenge was to make use of the opportunities available within the system. Ayaz began writing a column for Dawn Magazine in the eighties when I was its editor. Obviously he focussed on social issues, and politics was on the periphery. Nevertheless he had amply demonstrated his power as a wordsmith with a display of witticism, irony, sarcasm and humour that is all his own. Later, with the coming of democracy, Ayaz came into his own and became perhaps the most well-read and talked about columnist in Pakistan's English journalism, though with no dearth of denigrators. As an editor and as a reader I felt often irritated by Ayaz's fixation with a given leader at a given time. There was endless repetition in his columns and he often relied on lampooning rather than on objective criticism to convey a point. AAK thought the moment a columnist wrote for entertainment he undermined himself. Nevertheless, even in repetition, Ayaz maintained a remarkable originality in style. AAK discontinued his column when he joined the Muslim League (Nawaz group) and was elected to the Punjab Assembly. A former army officer and a well-read man, Ayaz felt uncomfortable among the kind of uncouth politicians he had to deal with. He quit politics and returned to writing. Prior to the 2008 elections, he rejoined the Muslim League and later won a seat to the National Assembly from Chakwal, his home constituency. His column disappeared from Dawn again, and now (2009) he writes for The News. Cowasjee, too, began writing in the eighties. He focuses on exposing corruption in government, especially on the decline, and might I say fall, of Pakistan's judiciary, the persecution of the dissidents by the governments by 'judicial' means by stuffing the judiciary with sycophants — one judge was willing to oblige the government if he were given a diplomatic passport. Besides exposing financial shenanigans, he has campaigned for a cleaner environment and against illegal constructions. He has shown courage by taking on powerful personalities and fascist groups. After the death of Ziaul Haq and the coming of democracy, cursing a government was no big deal. You curse Benazir and Nawaz, hit them below the belt and level every kind of allegations against them, even if it is based on hearsay, and get away with it. In fact you become a hero because both, in spite of being elected prime ministers, presided over weak and corrupt governments at a time when the opposition and the militias were stronger than the state. Cowasjee's courage lies in standing up to the militias and the 'religious' and ethic fascists. He is especially popular with those who share his pathological hatred of the Bhuttos. Irfan Hussain began writing for Dawn in the eighties as Afzal Hussain. Later he adopted the penname Mazdak. Now he writes under his name and is widely read. Idrees's effort is all the more remarkable because he was a bureaucrat. When he began writing, we in Dawn detected several problems with his writing; however he later honed his writing skills and developed as an analyst of government functioning. He enjoyed an advantage in this because he himself was once part of it. During Ziaul Haq's days he took a very courageous step. He saved Benazir from languishing in solitary confinement in jail by turning her residence into a sub-jail. This spared Benazir and family a lot of hardships.

In November 1980, AAK changed my assignment and asked me to take over our weekly magazine, Dawn Magazine, published on Friday, because those days Friday was Pakistan's weekly holiday. I didn't like the assignment, for I had been writing editorials for long and expected to be promoted Assistant Editor. AAK had expected me to react negatively. As a I can recall, his sessions with me over a period that stretched to a quarter century plus three years usually fell into three categories — he called me over just for gossip; he asked me to see him for professional reasons, and sometimes he wanted me in his room to let off his frustration and took it out on me, even if someone else had hurt him and caused a problem. He repeatedly pointed out to me what he thought was a weakness in me: he told me that I developed a feeling of insecurity each time my assignment was changed. He asked me to go into the past and discover why I had developed this weakness and how I could overcome it. I had assets, he said, and that must give me confidence. I accepted the new assignment as magazine chief very grudgingly. However, from the benefit of hindsight I realise this was the finest thing to happen to me professionally. The beginning couldn't be worse, for on November 21 Ammi died. I did not really cry, because I had cried when she was alive, cried over her moans and shrieks when she had asthmatic attacks sometimes the whole night, the degree of pain and shrieks varying. She suffered mild attacks year round, but when the season changed — as in October and March — asthma attacked with a severity that was difficult for her children to stand. Today I can spot an asthmatic patient in a crowd by simply looking at him or her. She died only 25 days after Abboo breathed his last at Abbasi Shaheed Hospital. I remember an uncle of mine telling me, "It is true the man-wife relationship begins with body, but it ends in spirit". Abboo and Ammi had always lived with me. This is an honour which God seems to have reserved for the youngest son in every family. In the beginning of October, Abboo moved to Razi's home, because the areas where I had built my home in Gulshan was still not 'developed'. There was no doctor around, and no medical attendant was available. As he was leaving my home I could see the despair on his face. A sportsman – captain of Osmania University's hockey team – he seemed acutely aware of his infirmity. Even though he was by no means a stretcher case, he had difficulty in walking. From Razi's home he went a few days later to Abbasi Shaheed Hospital.

The Eid commemorating the act of sacrifice by Patriarch Abraham sacrifice fell in mid-October and I greeted him in his hospital bed and told him it was Eid day. Often quite original in his response, Abbo replied, "So?" He was right. Eid and festivities are meant for people who can enjoy and who hope to live. He knew his end was near. It was still dark on the dawn of October 25 when the bell rang at my Gulshan home. As I opened the door I saw Razi. I knew instantly why he had come. As

I reached the hospital the muezzin called for prayer. What do I do first? I asked myself. Do I go to the hospital and collect the body or first offer the Fajr prayer? One of Iqbal's verses, and Abbo's favourite, came to my mind like a flash:

Ye naghma fasl-e gulo laala ka naheen pabund; bahar ho kay khizan la ilaha ill-Allah. (This song is independent of season: whether it is spring or autumn [one must always sing in ecstasy] there are no gods but one God.)

Twenty seven days later, I received the news of Ammi's death on the telephone in my office. She had been having a terrible asthmatic attack for nearly 10 days, and a nurse had told me she doubted if she would be able to live through the Moharram holidays. Again there was no hospital in my locality, so I had planned to visit the Holy Family Hospital at Soldier Bazaar to enquire about her chances of admission. Then a neighbour rang me up to say there was no need for doing that. No one in the family was more devoted to her than I was. I was my mother's son. The way she cared about me and loved me she cared about no one. Suddenly, it appeared time and space had ceased to exist. I remember hailing a taxi, and the next moment I was standing beside her. I did not remember how the taxi covered the distance. Surely, it must have gone through the route I took daily from Haroon House to Gulshan and must have driven past Karachi's familiar landmarks, including Governor House, Jinnah's mausoleum in white marble, the Islamia College building, which hadn't seen a whitewash for three decades, and Central Jail, but to me it appeared I had covered the distance in the blink of an eye. Among the saddest moments of my life was the scene on Mother's grave the next day. Rose petals had been placed on her grave and a strong wind scattered the rose petals. That's the truth about life. I returned home as all mourners do to resume life, since life must go on, but I knew that that would happen also when I am lowered into my grave.

Dawn Magazine was a dull and dreary affair when I took over its editing. My predecessor was Ahsan Yahya, a dedicated journalist whom I would rather call a soldier because of the way in which he continued to work for the paper despite his failing health and struggling with gout well into his mid-seventies. The magazine wasn't in one forme; it was spread over the regular edition, with continuations on several pages. My job was to make it a separate four-page magazine. It grew to six and later to eight pages. Ghazi told me "You will have to fight several battles." He was referring to the fact that I had to get rid of some columnists, do what AAK often called "talent scouting" and discover new writers. Getting rid of old writers wasn't that difficult; the problem was to change the display for some veteran columnists used to pampering. Gradually, I overcame the crisis, recruited new writers and the magazine began to click. Azim Kidwai was already writing a science column and was quite prolific. In fact, he won a Unesco prize for science journalism. Others who continued to write included Anwar Enayatullah, who reviewed TV programmes, and my namesake, who wrote a literary round-up under the penname of Ariel. Among the new ones I recruited was Omar Kureishi, the cricket commentator and a legend in his lifetime. I had been listening to his cricket commentaries as a school boy, and it was a great honour for me decades later to get to know him personally and edit his articles. Another columnist was Afzal Iqbal. A former diplomat and an official in the information ministry, he wrote his memoirs — A Chapter from Memory — and penned highly readable pieces about the personalities he met and the diplomatic incidents he was witness to.

There was a shortage of staff, because I had only part-time help for the Women and Children's page, the helper being Rukhsana Mashshadi. When she quit, Najma Sadiq and later Maisoon Hussein started editing the page. Throughout her life, she carried the scars left on her soul by the execution of her father in Iraq. In 1991, when I was back writing editorials, Dawn launched its third weekly magazine, Young World, catering to the younger readership. Very appropriately, Maisoon became its first editor. Maisoon was a dark horse. I first saw her in Yahya's room when she was still a freelance journalist, and I found her strikingly beautiful — the word 'maisoon' I suppose means some flower in Armenian. Strictly speaking, she was not of Middle Eastern descent, but nothing about her was South Asian. Belonging to the Gokal shipping family, Maisoon had her early life in Iraq and education in Britain. Holding a master's degree in Sociology, Maisoon devoted her life to human rights causes. Abul Hasan Gokal, her father, was tortured before being hanged in Iraq. She never could overcome the trauma and developed some personality problems herself. For instance, she never appreciated a phone call at home, and she hated working in small rooms. One day I rang her up at her home on a holiday – I think it was Eid – for some official purpose. She protested to me the next day, "Mr Siddiqi, you spoiled my holiday". I never phoned her again at her home. Similarly she preferred sitting in the Dawn library with its natural light. Most probably, she received the news of her father's execution on the telephone, and a small room reminded her of his death cell. In her spare time I found her reading Quran, her head covered with dupatta, or offering the obligatory prayers. She aged, as all humans do, and I remember once telling her in a corridor: "Maisoon, we have grown old walking these corridors". She agreed with me and smiled with a certain sadness, for I seldom found Maisoon really happy. Yet, inside she was granite and often gave me tough time when we differed. In 2002 she gave up her fulltime job, because she was now battling with cancer. She continued to write for human rights causes, and died in March 2003. A very badly edited collection of her articles appeared in book form, For Life, Peace and Justice, posthumously in 2005. Another new hand hired was Lalarukh Hussain. She had joined The Sun after I had quit it in 1973. A trade union activist and potentially a good journalist, she had been arrested during the Zia regime and joined *Dawn* after resigning her job with Daily News in November 1981. She helped me with the editing and layout of the other pages and wrote features herself. She quit the paper in 1983, took up the editorship of a woman's monthly magazine, taught journalism at the Karachi University for a while, worked for the government-owned news agency APP and left it. Finally she was caught by the Dianetics bug. She left for the US in 1997 and remained associated with the Church of Scientology in Hollywood up to her death from brain tumour in Los Angeles in March 2013.

While I had occasionally written for my paper, it was as editor of the magazine that I began writing regularly. In February 1982 I began writing a column titled Of People. Those were Ziaul Haq's days, all newspapers were censored heavily, and AAK was keen to make the magazine a little less dreary. My original aim, on AAK's prodding, was to focus on non-celebrities, but as my column progressed it became impossible to find a non-celebrity every fortnight. Later I turned it into a weekly column and contained the interviews of a variety of people, Pakistani and foreign. They ranged from Sohbat Khan, a timekeeper on a bus terminal near my home, whose discipline and punctuality I said could be the envy of a Lufthansa manager, to Pakistani and foreign scholars and writers. Since politics were banned and the regime's criticism constituted a violation of martial law, I circumvented the ban by asking my interviewees to say things that apparently had nothing to do with Pakistan but which constituted the government's indirect criticism. Among the foreign scholars I interviewed were Asghar Ali Engineer, John Esposito, Lawrence Ziring, Nikki Kiddie, Abdo Elkholy and Alvin Z. Rubenstein. Read, for instance, this quote which I produced from Lawrence Ziring's book Pakistan: The Enigma of Political Development: "Political stability may be paramount, but it is not a substitute for innovative political organization. All governments are stable until overthrown, all leaders are all powerful up until the time they fall."

It was also while in the magazine that I got foreign reporting assignments. The visit to Indonesia was as boring an assignment as reporting the proceedings of a seminar could be. It was a seminar organized by a British NGO, Earthscan, at Denpasar, Bali, and concerned the world's bio-resources. I had heard much about Bali's legendary beauty, but frankly for a Pakistani it had nothing to offer. The Dutch liked it for its sunny beaches, the tranquillity of the sea and the topless girls of yore. It was a tourist paradise, and I suppose it still is, but terrorism would rock Bali two decades later when bomb blasts in nightclubs frequented by tourists, especially those from Australia, led to heavy casualties. The visit to Indonesia, and on the way home to Kuala Lumpur, Singapore and Bangkok was revealing, for it appeared to me that, while Pakistan was more advance than these countries in science and technology and some other fields, on the whole these nations had their priorities right and had paid special attention to education and the development of human resources. Pakistan has been much criticised by the UN's special agencies and by the liberal opinion in Pakistan itself for neglecting the social sector, and there is no doubt the criticism is valid, but the critics fail to notice the country's security concerns and the circumstances which forced all governments to spend heavily on defence. India did the same, and the result has been equally disastrous. As Arundhati Roy pointed out in one of her articles India lagged behind Somalia and Sudan in the hunger index (article in The Guardian, December 12, 2008).

In the eighties there was no dearth of American scholars visiting Pakistan because of the US-funded anti-Soviet jihad in Afghanistan. The USIS kept me well informed of such visits, and this way I interviewed Americans regularly, exposing myself to the charge from friends and non-friends alike that I wanted to be on the Americans' right side. This was absurd, of course. But the critics claimed victory when the USIS included me in what was called the visitors' exchange programme, organised by the USIS and Delphi, an NGO, and included journalists from many countries. I was the only one from Pakistan. AAK approved of the visit, and I landed in New York in June 1984. The year was 1984 and President Ronald Reagan looked set for a second term. The runners for the Democratic ticket were Walter Mondale, Jesse Jackson and Gary Hart, the last one falling victim to sex scandals. For me, it turned out to be a superb coast-to-coast programme, ending at San Francisco for the Democratic Party convention. The Americans insisted that I break journey in London and had provided for a layover. However, I chose to stay with Dr A. A. Khan, psychiatrist to a group of London hospitals, who was also on Mrs Thatcher's committee on mental health for immigrants. He was with me at Bahadur Yar Jang High School at Karachi and later married one of my cousins.

The way the Americans organised the programme, including a night's stay in London, showed the difference between a developed country and one that is not. I had a similar experience with the British, and saw the details that went into organising a conference or a seminar. The result of the night's stay in London and the way the rest of the schedule ending at San Francisco was organised spared the participants the torture which foreign tours some time become when they are mismanaged and the hosts look at the itinerary and the tight schedule from their point of view, forgetting how the guests will take it. At JFK, as I was going down the escalator, I found a black lady displaying my name. "Hurry up!" she said. "Your flight to Washington is about to leave". She helped me clear the Customs, had the passport stamped, gave me the boarding card for the Washington flight, and I was airborne.

The convention at San Francisco must be remembered for Gary Hart's candid comment, after his denigrators and political rivals had discovered a mistress for him on the eve of the convention. Asked what he thought of it, Hart replied "I will not be the first adulterer in the White House" — and "not the last" he should have added, for less than a decade later the world would hear of Paula Jones and Monica Lewinsky. The winner, who would be decisively beaten by Reagan, was Mondale. He was already trailing 15 to 19 points behind Reagan before the convention at the Mascone Centre began, and his choice of a woman, Geraldine Ferraro, a lawyer from New York, as his running mate sealed his fate. Opinion polls had reacted negatively to Ferraro's choice, for the Democratic ticket had become a north-north affair, Mondale being from Minnesota. Yet, in spite of the glittering show that the convention at Mascone Centre was, — ticker-tape, fireworks and balloons — I could not help recall the following dialogue between Lawrence and Prince Ali in Lawrence of Arabia, with Peter O'Toole as the British army officer and Omar Sharif as the Hashemite prince as they relaxed under the open sky in the Arabian desert:

Lawrence: What do you intend to do after the war?

Ali: I want to enter politics.

Lawrence: Why? Politics is a low occupation.

It is low indeed, not just in Third World countries without democracy but everywhere, including the US, where money and sex scandals seem to have become an essential part of electioneering from county councils and city governments to state congresses, US Congress and the White House. Ethnic, professional and other lobbies make sense in a country that is a mosaic of cultural diversity and a bastion of free enterprise, but the cartels and the media (in turn controlled by the cartels) have acquired a position where, as in the communist system, the people have to choose between candidates already selected by the Party. As the cliché goes, they sell the president the way they sell a product. The role of the Zionist lobby in American politics, media, academia and think-tanks is a subject unto itself. But a candidate who is not more Israeli than an Israeli is unlikely to be elected if he deviates from the "brief". As Jimmy Carter said after he was denounced as anti-Semitic for his book Peace not Apartheid, "It is impossible for any candidate for Congress to make a statement like 'I favour balanced support of Israel and Palestine'". This, he said, had made White House and Congress "submissive" (to Israel) on the Palestinian question.

I was not on a reporting assignment, but I chose to report for Dawn, using the local telegraphic company's telex facility, for email and modem were still far away. I also sent a curtain-raiser on the Los Angeles Olympic Games where Pakistan won the only gold — in hockey. There was a demonstration of Pakistanism when, as I waited at the LA airport for the New York-bound flight, a total stranger came to me and said, "Hockey gold mobarak ho". I do not know who he was and how he came to know I was a Pakistani, but he guessed correctly and we embraced each other. As I landed in New York for a brief stay before heading for Pakistan via Turkey a realisation dawned on me — all along the tour

I had never been colour conscious. Unlike Britain, where in 1976 I was acutely aware of my status as a foreigner, I felt quite at home in the US. This was surprising because the subcontinentals have more in common with "Olde England" than with America. While prejudice is a human condition and the Americans are not above it, I did not find race to be the basis of American prejudices. Instead, what the Americans seemed to take pride in was their country's economic, political and technological power. Besides, unless he is psychopathic, an American cannot pass normal life if he does not adjust to the reality of America's multiracial character. The Americans recognised the reality of a multicultural, multiracial milieu much before Europe started coming to terms with the immigrant phenomenon toward the end of the twentieth century. All along the six-week journey in which geographical and demographic features ranged from Charlottesville in Virginia to Berkley in California, I did not feel self-conscious and had no difficulty in interacting with the American people. This helped me a great deal when I returned to the US in November 1992 to take up my assignment as Dawn's Washington correspondent.

By the mid-eighties Dawn had overcome its financial crisis and had begun to expand because newsprint was now relatively speaking easy to get. But, given the Zia dictatorship, there was little scope for free political debate in newspapers. If there had to be a new weekly, it would obviously not be political in contents. As AAK used to say, one must do "intensive thinking" before making major decisions, and — he often quoted Mao Zedong — one should not make mistakes in the fundamentals. While mistakes in details could be rectified, a mistake in the fundamentals could prove disastrous. He finally decided that, given the condition of the press in the country, it was safe to have a weekly devoted exclusively to economics and business. That's how the Economic and Business Review, printed on pink pages, was launched in 1982 and became a weekly magazine delivered with the paper's Monday issue. EBR thus not only turned out to be a pioneer in economic journalism in Pakistan's daily press, it raised the level of economic debate to a high level, with contributions coming from some of Pakistan's leading writers on economy and business. While politics were taboo, a review of the government's economic policies and the exposure of the corruption and mismanagement in state-owned corporations gave a political touch to EBR and helped subtly start political debate on the overall conduct of the military government. Initially AAK made S. G. M. Badruddin EBR's editor; later Ghayurul Islam edited the weekly. He remained in that position for a decade, till bad health made him bow out in December 2004. At present, EBR is being edited by Jawaid Bokhari, my colleague in the PPA news agency way back in the late fifties. A more hard working man I haven't seen. He has increased the number of articles in the EBR by cutting down on wordage.

Less than two years later, on January 1, 1984, Dawn launched its Lahore edition. The "real" Lahore edition would come later in 1996 when technical advance made this easy and worthwhile, but the edition launched in 1984 merely meant printing an early edition at Karachi and sending it to Lahore by air to be delivered to the subscribers early in the morning. Putting the bundles of Dawn's copies on board PIA's 'night coach' to Lahore meant that printing should end at 11pm and that pages should be handed over to the printers by 10.30 pm. This meant copy should close at 9.30 pm or so. This way the Lahore edition missed many important news items. Yet the response in Lahore was beyond our belief. On October 13, 1990, the Lahore office began printing what came to be called Section 2. It consisted of Lahore city news besides 'district news' in and around Lahore not covered in the main section sent from Karachi. Twelve years later, when AAK was still the boss, Lahore would have a full-fledged 'normal' edition of its own because technology made our job easy. Now pages of regular Karachi edition were sent to Lahore at the flick of a button over a dedicated telephone line and the facsimile of the pages received at the Lahore office were turned into plates for printing at the local rotary machine. Thus Lahore really had a Dawn edition of its own from June 19, 1996 onward. Some time later, because we did not trust the government and feared that they could tinker with the telephone line or cut the line altogether, we decided on a safer mode – the satellite. Now pages made in Karachi are sent by satellite not only to Lahore but also to Islamabad, which started having its own Dawn edition in March 2001, when Saleem Asmi was the editor. Both Lahore and Islamabad offices have their Metro sections, the op-ed pages are the same in all the three editions, but the two editors do make changes on front and back pages if they think this is necessary for local readers.

In the winter of 1984, I got an opportunity to visit the Roof of the World, Pakistan's majestic, snowy north "where the mountains meet". Known then as Northern Areas, its name was changed in August 2009 to Gilgit-Baltistan, which includes the legendary Hunza, whose water is supposed to be the secret behind the Hunza people's longevity. G-B has three of the world's mightiest mountains – the Himalayas, the Hindukush and Karakoram — and it has the world's longest glaciers outside the polar region. Politically the area is sensitive. On the north-east is China, to the east and south-east Indian occupied Kashmir, due south Azad Kashmir, in the south-west the North-Western Frontier Province, and to the north and north-west the Wakhan corridor — that bit of territory which was given to Afghanistan in 1896 during the Great Game so that the borders of Tsarist and British Empires should not meet. Some 200 miles long with an area of nearly 13,000 square kilometres, Wakhan, part of Afghanistan's Badakhshan province, is now nearly empty. The people were mostly Kyrghiz, who migrated to Turkey after the Soviet invasion. The visit to G-B was arranged by the Aga Khan Foundation, which wanted Dawn to publish a supplement on its Rural Support Programme. We flew from Islamabad to Gilgit in an AKF helicopter and had the opportunity on the way to see Pakistan's breathtaking beauty as the machine flew over green valleys, with rivers and rivulets, topped with snow. With Anwar Rammal, AKF's man in Karachi, also on board, the pilots navigated in squally weather through narrow gaps in barren, almost vertical cliffs whose heights and dimensions appeared threatening. The month was December, so no wonder it was minus 10 degrees Fahrenheit when we landed at the Gilgit airport. In the past, because of heavy snow, G-B used to remain cut off from the rest of Pakistan for six months, and the people had to wait for air drops to get food and medicines. The construction of the Karakoram Highway with Chinese help has improved the transport situation dramatically, for the KKH is now open around the year, except when rock-falls block this extraordinary feat of engineering. Cut, dug and paved through hard granite, the KKH hugs the Indus all along as it winds its way up through some of the world's most enchanting scenery.

Poverty in G-B lacks that subhuman wretchedness that is the hallmark of poverty in South Asia's urban slums, for I could see even through the window of the helicopter that the people were better placed in terms of their economic future. The visit, which took me close to what then was the border of the Soviet Union — now it belongs to Tajikistan—, astonished me, because of the way the people were struggling hard in a harsh climate to improve the quality of life, acquire education and have greater access to healthcare. Even though fertile, G-B 'bowl' is a tableland short of water. The river Gilgit flows several hundred feet down, and it is difficult to get water, except through electrically operated water machines, and electricity was then in short supply. The Aga Khan Rural Support Programme has done wonders to G-B. It has cut channels on mountain slopes to bring water to the villages in the valleys, and it has established schools and set up clinics to bring modern healthcare to far-flung villages, some of them close to the Chinese border. This extraordinary effort has led to a fall in infant morality, a dramatic rise in literacy and a general improvement in the quality of life. Between 1991 and 2005 the per capita real income tripled from Rs 3,000 to Rs 9,000. During the same period poverty fell form 67 per cent to 25 per cent, while the number of what can be called 'dirt poor' fell from 33 to five per cent. The area is often referred to as the Crescent of Hope because G-B has immense natural resources and a low population (now estimated at one million). The harshness of climate and terrain finds a match in the people. The men are hardy, so are women, indifferent to cold and suffering. The children are roses. You hardly find a beggar, and the people, even in the remotest of valleys, appear well-clothed. One reason for this lack of abject poverty is that landless peasants aren't so numerous. Often, newly claimed land is jointly owned by a village. On average, each household owns at least two kanals of land. The bird's eye-view from the helicopter gives you a clear idea of the average cultivator's advantage, and a clear-cut socio-economic pattern seems to emerge.

The pattern consists of a river (call it Hunza, Gilgit, Shimshal, Yasin, Gupis or whatever); a valley, made fertile and wide by the changing course of the river; houses, not hovels, sometimes grouped together, sometimes separate; a plot of land opposite each house or for each house (something inconceivable for tenant-peasants in the plains of Sindh and Punjab); and in every house cows, sheep and chickens — they ran wild as our helicopter flew low ever them — besides cash-generating fruit trees: apricot, pomegranate, apple, pear, fig, berries of all sorts and grapevines. The peasants I talked to invariably said they cultivated for themselves. No one shared their crops with them, at least after the 1972 land reforms by the PPP government. Most lands have only one yearly crop — mostly maize; some have two, the other being wheat. But the yield despite the primitive methods employed is at some places higher than the per-acre yield in Punjab and Sindh. The concomitant of poverty — squalor — is mercifully missing, because, unfortunately, the people do not have environmental consciousness and throw garbage into rivulets. But despite so many rivers, rivulets and waterfalls, the area is short of water both for cultivation and for daily use. Most rivers have gone deeper, while the fields had turned into dry table-lands at least when I was there. A house or a field may be perched on the bank of a river, but is unable to make use of its water, because there are no means by which water could be pumped up. One way to get water for farms and homes is to trap water when the snow in the mountains melts. It is here that the people have shown an extraordinary spirit of hard work and self-help by digging channels on the edges of mountains for miles and miles. Some channels that I saw were more than 30 miles long and had been cut through granite by manual work. This way water is available in plenty in summer, but in winter it gets frozen. Electricity shortage is a national problem, but the AKRSP launched some of its own power production plans.

A most inspiring extraordinary feature of community life in G-B is the direct Swiss-style democracy, for the Aga Khan's money flows not into an individual but into cooperatives that come into being after "dialogues." Usually there are three "dialogues". In the first, people come out with their priorities and reach a consensus; in the second, they elect leaders; in the third the cheque is given to him in the presence of the 'electors' after they reaffirm their confidence in them. Schools are there even in the most inaccessible of villages. This is a clear lead over the rest of Pakistan. In the valleys of Yasin and Gupis, links with the outside world by jeep are tenuous, yet every village has a school. People I talked to in Hanuchal, which is on the way to Skardu not far from the Indus gorge, said all children went to school. I checked this claim elsewhere and found it more or less correct. Even if this were only partly true, this means G-B's one million plus people will have a very high literacy rate when today's children become adults. Records and minutes of village coops' meetings are kept in Urdu, which is understood everywhere. Several factors — the Army, the KKH and the consequent increase in the volume of business, transport and domestic tourism — have contributed a great deal to Urdu's spread.

Until the coming of the Afghan refugees in the eighties, there were hardly any sectarian feelings, and three communities — Shia, Sunni and Ismaili — lived in peace and constituted one closely knit family through intermarriages and the common stakes in developing their land. In the eighties a top official of the Aga Khan National Council for Pakistan came to me to seek my advice on how to deal with a Karachi Urdu weekly that was spreading poisonous propaganda against the Ismaili community. The weekly had started a malicious campaign against the Ismaili community and Aga Khan officials, accusing them of planning to create an independent Shia state in a geographically sensitive area. There could not have been a greater fabrication of lies. Aga Khan III, the grandfather of Prince Karim, now the Ismaili imam, was one of the founders of Pakistan, and the Ismaili community has contributed a great deal to Pakistan's development because of the high quality of its entrepreneurs. Its contribution has been significant in the field of education and healthcare. The Aga Khan National Council was worried and wanted my advice. I told him to see a certain foreign diplomat, who would speak to Ziaul Haq and the latter would sort the weekly's editor out. I have reasons to believe my advice was followed and the weekly stopped its campaign. In the November 2009 elections to the G-B Legislative Assembly, the PPP got a majority, and that should surprise no one, because Bhutto had effected land reforms in the area, given lands to the tillers, and done so much to bring G-B into the mainstream.

～～～～～～～

Two brilliant newswomen – Zeenat Hisam and Anjum Niaz. – headed Dawn Magazine after I moved to political reporting. Zeenat has a master's degree in psychology from the University of Karachi and later did Master's on development studies from Holland. She quit Dawn in 1990 and developed into an author and development research scholar. During 1989 and 2004 she co-edited an Urdu monthly Aaj. It was here that she made a major contribution to the history of Karachi by co-editing along with Ajmal Kamal a two-volume book that traces the history of Karachi from the time it was a small fishing village called Mai Kolachi in the 18th century to what it is today. Besides translating Urdu short stories into English and vice versa, Zeenat has authored a number of research reports on labour and women and co-authored a book on community development in Mingora, the capital of Swat, which the Taliban occupied in 2008, forcing over 300,000 people to flee their homes in the cool heights of what was once a tourist paradise to the burning southern plains. At present Zeenat is working with Pakistan Institute of Labour Education and Research as Senior Research Associate. Anjum and husband Javed are our family friends, and Razia and I find it hard to believe that it is not Cupid but their parents who brought them together. Both had illustrious fathers, both cricket buffs. Niaz Ahmad, Javed's father, was an ICS officer and opted for Pakistan after partition. As Commissioner of Hyderabad he built a cricket stadium which he named Hyderabad Stadium. However, after his tragic death in an accident near Wah in 1964 at age 49, the Hyderabad municipality named it Niaz Stadium. Fida Hussain, Anjum's father, held a key post in the Ayub government. Today's Pakistan with four provinces was then one province. As the province's Chief Secretary, Fida was West Pakistan's uncrowned king and later served as Cabinet Secretary, Defence Secretary, Principal Secretary and then Advisor to Ayub. In July 1976, Bhutto appointed him envoy to India, and he re-opened the Pakistan mission, closed since the 1971 war. Before partition as a youth he had played for a cricket team called North India and, after Pakistan came into being, was the manager of the Pakistan team that won the historic test at Oval in 1954.

With two Master's in English and journalism, Anjum has a powerful pen, and I have been urging her for a long time to venture into novel writing, because she has shown she is capable of combining the magic of words with her power of imagination. Another Pakistani newswoman who I believe can be a great success as a fiction writer is Farida Said. Educated in America, with a Master's in English from the University of Wisconsin, Farida, a voracious reader, is a walking encyclopaedia of English literature. You name a book in English — fiction, poetry, drama, art, history, literary criticism, adventure, biographies — and in all probability she has read it. Often to avoid going into Google I would just ring up Farida to ask her about a book and she would give me the A to Z of it. However, she is very selective about writing. A Booker is not her pocket because she could be quite cynical about these matters. She even seems to hide her female identity by writing her articles as F. Said. Few would believe this is a woman's name. Let me unveil a secret: her full name is Farida Munaver Jahan Said. She is from the former Hyderabad State, where girls' names usually end at Jahan. (Two of my own sisters have this ending, Qamar Jahan and Qaisar Jahan.) Farida has edited two monumental books — The Holy Sinner, an illustrated coffee-table hard cover book on art paper with four CDs on the art and poetry of Pakistan's most well-known artist, Sadequain, and Requiem for an Unsung Messiah, which contains her English translations of Faiz Ahmad Faiz's Urdu poetry. Another book she has edited is under publication – As Dawn Saw It, an illustrated history of Pakistan as reported in Dawn. The other two books she wrote concern artist Tapu Javery and photographer Arif Mahmood. It is my firm belief that Anjum and Farida have the potential to be among the august company of many Pakistani and South Asian writers who have won recognition as fiction writers in America, Britain and other Commonwealth countries: Bapsi Sidhwa (The Pakistani Bride, An American Brat), Mohammed Hanif (A Case of Exploding Mangoes), Kamila Shamsie (Salt and Saffron, In the City by the Sea), Musharraf Farooqi (The Story of a Widow, The Cobbler's Holiday or Why Ants Don't Wear Shoes), Uzma Khan (The Geometry of God, The Story of Noble Rot), Mohsin Hamid (Moth Smoke, The Reluctant Fundamentalist), Sahba Sarwar (Black Wings), Sara Suleri (Meatless Days, Boys Will Be Boys), Reginald Massey (The Splintered Mirror — poems), Maniza Naqvi (Sarajevo Saturdays, A Matter of Detail), and Shaila Abdullah (Beyond the Cayenne Wall, Saffron Dreams), to name only a few, besides many Indians like Anita Desai, Arundhati Roy and that Satanic writer, Salman Rushdie. Anjum edited Dawn Magazine from 1987 to 1993 and later became Dawn's diplomatic correspondent based in Islamabad after Javed was posted to the capital by the Pakistan Tobacco Company. A tripos in economics from King's College, Cambridge, Javed retired in 1999 as PTC's corporate manager. Both Anjum and Javed had a long stay in America, where as Managing Editor of The Earth Times, New York, she was responsible for the daily website and the bi-monthly print edition. It was, however, as a columnist that she came into her own, for she has been writing a column for Dawn and freelancing for other papers since the nineties.

On January 1, 1987, AAK put me on political reporting. There was now a lot to report, because martial law had been lifted, the press was relatively free, and the Junejo government was trying hard to distance itself from the army and reassert civilian authority. The Afghan war was at its peak, but peace moves had been initiated, and it was a question of time before the Soviets would be gone from Afghanistan. But the criminalisation of Pakistan's politics with its inevitable impact on society had begun. Ethnicity was also on the rise. Because Zia feared a PPP victory all political parties had been barred from taking part in the 1985 election which had brought Junejo to power. The inevitable consequence of the ban on politics was the rise of parochial tendencies, for the politicians appealed to the voters' ethnic, regional and sectarian loyalties to become popular and secure votes. The religious parties were now well armed, because Zia had given full freedom to them to turn Pakistan into a recruiting and training ground for the war against the Soviet Union in Afghanistan. Zia also patronised Sindhi nationalist parties so as to erode the PPP's home base. This unthinking move had disastrous consequences in the long run. The PPP's founder may have been a Sindhi, but the party had won the previous two elections (and would win again in 1988, 1993 and 2008) because Punjab voted for it. However the encouragement to nationalist parties among Sindhi politicians had its impact on Sindh's Urdu-speaking population, where a student party – APMSO (All Pakistan Mohajir Students Organisation) – began gaining attentions. Till then, the Urdu-speaking community had traditionally voted for the Jamaat-i-Islami. The founder of the Jamaat-i-Islami, Maulana Abul Ala Maudoodi, was himself an Urdu speaker, had opposed the creation of Pakistan, was personally hostile to Jinnah, but chose to come to Pakistan after partition to resume his mission. Amin Ahsan Islahi, a leading JI ideologue, was a Mohajir, so were some other major JI members – like Professor Abdul Ghafoor Ahmad, Mahmood Azam Faruqi and Munawwar Hassan, who would become the JI chief in April 2009. The last three had played a leading role in the 1977 PNA movement that resulted in Bhutto's overthrow and the military takeover. During the Ayub and Bhutto periods, the JI had emerged as a well-established opposition party that preached its creed peacefully and – discarding its previous opposition to 'Western', especially parliamentary, democracy – struggled democratically for a place in the sun. Ayub's ban on the party was unnecessary. The ban only helped the JI, and when the court set the government decision aside the party grew in strength, especially in the Urdu- and Punjabi-speaking middle class. In fact, the JI provided the manpower and party machinery for Fatima Jinnah when she challenged Ayub in the presidential election. Its opposition to Bhutto was rooted in its distaste for the very word 'socialism', but surprising as it sounds the JI's party structure and its attitude toward cultural freedom bore a surprising resemblance to communist theory and practice. The JI is perhaps Pakistan's only party which has internal democracy, for it regularly holds party elections. But no one is allowed to stand for office himself or put forward his own case for a party office, because this is considered un-Islamic. A person who himself covets a position in party or government, so goes the JI philosophy, believes in self-aggrandisement and must be shunned. What the party does is to name three to four candidates for a given post, and the members of the JI Shoora (consultative body) are asked to vote for one of the candidates. It is through this process that the Amir (chief) of the JI is elected for a period of five years. This bears a remarkable resemblance to the communist mode of election. Once he is elected, he must be obeyed, for itaat-i-Amir (obedience to the chief) is the fundamental discipline for all JI workers. It smacks of fuhrerprinzip, for believers in an ideology world over forfeit the right to original thinking and question the fundamentals. The continuation of this kind of authoritarian philosophy and party discipline has done enormous harm to the JI, for the party has failed to get a substantial position in parliament and democratic politics despite decades of political experience behind it. No wonder, from the time of Qazi Hussain, who was party chief for four terms (1987 to 2009) the JI has often acted in a way that makes one feel as if it considers non-democratic methods of mobilisation of public opinion and change of government as a political option. This is truly a tragedy for a party whose cadres and voters come from the educated middle class and is in direct opposition to Maudoodi's policies.

It was during Ziaul Haq's dictatorship that one could detect subtle changes in the attitude of the JI leadership and rank and file. The JI claimed, and rightly, that it was the spirit behind the PNA movement, and that Bhutto's ouster and the coup d'etat by Ziaul Haq would not have been possible without its efforts. For the JI, thus, Zia's rule basically meant Jamaat rule, and the party became the dominant force in the military-run administration. One could see a JI touch in the way the state-run radio and television ran their programmes, with PTV ending its night transmission showing scales – which has always been the JI's symbol. The greater tragedy was the coming to the fore of the fascism latent in the party's philosophy. The word Taliban was not yet known to Pakistan, much less to the world, but it was the JI's student wing – Islami Jamiat-i-Talaba – that adopted the role of moral police and gave the campuses a taste of student militancy. Using the Zia shibboleth – the 'ideology of Pakistan' – as a pretext, it waged its own war on fahhashi (obscene or lewd behaviour), on the campuses. As is true of all parties and men with religious inclinations, girls were the focus of the IJT attention, for the prime condition for an Islamic 'system' was that girls must conform to the criteria laid down by the IJT. In practice this meant keeping a watch on boys and girls talking or having meals together in campus canteens. A wide variety of cultural activity fell within the IJT's concept of fahhashi, including the annual send-off parties and get-togethers, which included skits, songs, mimicry, etc. Since 'normal' students did not accept these restrictions, the IJT used force to break up such functions, often resulting in violence. Once the Karachi University's annual convocation fell victim to violence unleashed by the IJT. It also pressured the teaching community and the campus's administration to follow its direction, and at least one Vice Chancellor had a heart attack and died following an altercation with the IJT workers. Whether the heart attack resulted from the IJT's behaviour is not clear, but there is no doubt that the IJT had misbehaved with one of Pakistan's leading educationists, Dr Mahmood Hussain. Gradually the level of violence increased and fatalities went up as arms became freely available, thanks to the Afghan war.

In Karachi buying a gun was like buying a match box. You only had to go to an Afghan peddler or his local contact and it would be made available to you at the lowest possible rate. The variety of arms ranged from hand guns and the automatic Kalashnikov submachine guns to grenades. The arms were those produced in the tribal factories in Darra Adamkhel or captured by the Mujahideen from the Soviets. Now other student groups also began arming and organising themselves on ethnic lines, and soon the Karachi University campus was seeing gun battles between half a dozen armed student groups – the Pakhtoon Students Federation, the Baloch Students Organisation, the Punjabi Students Organisation and the most ruthless of them: APMSO, guided, controlled and headed by a man whose very name would send a chill down the spines of all its enemies – Altaf Hussain. In due course Altaf would become a Mohajir fuehrer.

I met Altaf in Karachi's Dastagir area where he was staying with a family friend after being released from prison in 1987. I was shocked to see him. He had in his hand a kutta of betel leaves, and the way he was smoking the cigarette and flicking the ash made it clear to me that I was going to interview a politician who was nowhere near the giants whom South Asia's Urdu-speaking community had chosen as their leaders. Till then the Urdu-speaking people's representatives since before partition were a class by themselves – Sir Syed Ahmad Khan, Hakim Ajmal Khan, Mohammad Ali Jauhar, Dr Mohammad Iqbal, Bahadur Yar Jang,

Liaquat Ali Khan, Abdul Rab Nashtar, I. I. Chundrigar and Mohammad Ali Jinnah. Now, thanks to Ziaul Haq's de-politicisation of Pakistan, the vagaries of politics and the rise of ethnicity, Pakistan's most educated and politically conscious community had chosen a lout as their leader. Adept at appealing to raw emotions, and by any standards a remarkable organiser, Altaf made full use of the ethnic clashes in Karachi to turn his MQM into a mass organisation in southern Sindh. The ethnic riots began in Karachi in April 1985 when a girl student, Bushra Zaidi, was killed in a traffic accident involving a minibus. Even though the driver wasn't a Pakhtoon, the riot acquired an ethnic colour. Subsequently, there were several riots, including one that saw firing at Sohrab Goth on a procession which Altaf was taking to Hyderabad, causing many fatalities. The most terrible of massacres took place in December 1986 in Aligarh and Qasbah Colonies in mixed localities, and had repercussions elsewhere in the city and in Hyderabad. The massacre at Aligarh-Qasbah districts continued for several hours, but neither the army nor the police intervened to stop what by any standards was one of the worst acts of communal frenzy in Pakistan. Altaf was quick to seize the opportunity to become the Mohajirs' leader.

I went one evening to his Azizabad residence and listened to his recorded speech in which he asked the Mohajirs to sell "useless things" and buy "useful things". He said in Urdu: "Sell your TV sets, your carpets, your sofas, your VCRs. Buy things that could be of use to you". He repeatedly said that the government had failed to protect them and that the Mohajirs must defend themselves. There is no doubt by "useful things" he meant guns. Altaf then set out to organise a well-armed, well-funded, well-trained and highly indoctrinated militia that would terrorise Karachi for decades and be a source of instability to the four democratic governments that ruled Pakistan between 1988, when Benazir Bhutto first came to power, and 1999 when the generals overthrew the Nawaz Sharif government. The ethnic clashes were the JI's undoing in Sindh, for in all subsequent elections, it was Altaf Hussain's Mohajir Qaumi Movement that would cart off all votes in southern Sindh. The PPP, however, has so far managed to retain its hold over some Karachi localities which have traditionally voted for it. The APMSO outdid all other student militias when it came to kidnapping, torture and murder, but it must be recorded for history's sake that it was the JI's student wing that first began hooliganism and violence on the campuses when, flushed with success over Bhutto's overthrow and execution, the JI thought it had conquered Pakistan for itself and would cast Jinnah's country in its own image. One of the IJT's worst acts of violence was an attack on the offices of Pakistan's leading Urdu daily, Jang. Provoked by a news item that had claimed that the IJT chief was arrested at the Karachi airport while carrying a gun an IJT mob ransacked and burnt the Jang building. However, instead of the IJT or its mother party, Jamaat, offering apology the two saw to it that it was the newspaper which apologised for the publication of the news item.

Zafar Samdani had something very original to say about the Jamaat-Zia war on fahhashi. A loveable man, Samdani shifted to Karachi in the mid-eighties and began writing a column on showbiz for the magazine. He had previously worked with AAK in Lahore at The Pakistan Times, joined electronic journalism and became PTV's general manager for news. He developed differences with General Mujib, Zia's spin doctor at the federal information ministry, and resigned. It was then that he began writing for Dawn Magazine, and we became friends. A fascinating character, Samdani had a repertoire of jokes which he inflicted on me, and there was no stopping him. Once he barged into my room while I was engrossed in work. "I am hungry," he said, "but I want tea first. I will have my second cup of tea after lunch. And I will make several calls from your phone and will keep talking to you, and if that disturbs you that's your problem, not mine". He was true to his word. A cricketer, poet, journalist, socialite, and admirer of female beauty, Samdani had a large circle of friends and acquaintances in the world of politics, journalism, showbiz, sport, and the military and civilian bureaucracy. As a TV man he had seen the absurdity of the moral guidelines which the military government had laid down for the state-controlled radio and

TV to follow, and once explained to me how the war on 'obscenity' had backfired and exposed Pakistani homes to greater obscenity from India. By terming all showbiz activity as un-Islamic, he said, the Zia government had destroyed the Pakistani film industry and open floodgates of Indian movies.

The VCR came to Pakistan in the mid-eighties, and with the Pakistani film industry having virtually ceased to exist, Indian films became the only source of family entertainment in our homes. In the eighties, the VCR prices were high, and very few lower middleclass homes could purchase it. So people hired VCRs from video shops for a night and saw as many Indian films as was possible in one night. It was during this era that I first heard the name Amitabh Bachhan. An Indian film icon, he became an idol for Pakistanis, too. India's classical dances are among the best in the world and have a beauty of their own, but the kind of dances shown in Indian movies are indescribably vulgar and suggestive and truly fall within the definition of obscenity. Thanks to Ziaul Haq's perverted vision, three generations of Pakistani females – daughter, mother and grandma – watched these shows the whole night under one roof, because Zia's 'Islamic' regime had outlawed the Pakistani film industry. While Pakistani actresses Zeba, Shabnam, Shameem Ara and others had been turned into whores and moral lepers who must be shunned by the God-fearing Pakistani people, Rekha, Perveen Bobby and Zeenat Aman became their idols. It is amazing that when after Ziaul Haq's death Benazir Bhutto came to power, some religious parties launched a campaign in newspapers against fahhashi, and their workers would go from home to home to ask people to stand up to the fahhashi which was being purportedly dished out by the PPP government. The truth was that if there is any government which truly spread fahhashi in Pakistan it was the Zia government.

Toward the end of 1987, the management thought Star needed a new editor and wanted me to head it. AAK agreed to this only as a stop-gap arrangement and insisted that I should return to Dawn and a new editor be found within three months. However, once there I found myself stuck up. There was a world of difference between Evening Star, as it was called when I was its shift-in-charge between 1967 and 1971, with Akhtar Adil Razwy as editor, and Star that I was called upon to edit in 1987. As mentioned earlier, Evening Star did not have a staff of its own, and it was Dawn's morning shift that used to bring out the paper. In 1971, the paper was de-linked from Dawn administratively and started having its own staff, with a newsroom of its own. The first editor was G. M. Mansuri, who had almost snatched the editorship from his friend, Razwy. When I took over as acting editor in November 1987 I was appalled by the complete lack of professionalism among the staff. The paper no more subscribed to either of Pakistan's two leading news agencies – the government-controlled APP and the private PPI – and when I asked why I was told that my predecessor had decided to do away with the agencies as a measure of economy and that the reporters would fill the pages. While there were, no doubt, some good reporters, the ambiance was not professional, and often the reporters recycled old stories. Editorials had also been dispensed with, and inside pages on weekends consisted of matter lifted from foreign showbiz magazines. I told Hameed Haroon Star needed money, because it must have agency service and I must pay Dawn staff members who would write editorials for me. Hameed agreed, and when I wanted to know how much, he replied, "Unlimited". I asked Zubeida and Safdar Barlas to write editorials for me, and Star began getting agency services. Mahmoud Haroon, no more a minister in Ziaul Haq's cabinet, was keen to have the mess in Star cleared up and often called me up to brief me and commend me for my work. He was upset over Star policy on Benazir's impending wedding and wanted a change.

The issue was a column that a Lahore journalist used to write for Star Weekend, the paper's Saturday magazine, and it attacked Benazir in a way as if getting married was a crime. Mahmoud said he couldn't understand why anyone should object to Benazir, or any girl, getting married, and that while the columnist had every right to air his views on all subjects and criticise Benazir for her policies there was no justification for criticising her for getting married. I told the editor of Star Weekend to inform the columnist of our policy and asked her not to publish anything of that nature till the wedding was over. One Sunday, I was home when Amber rang me up.

"Have you read the column in today's Star Weekend?" she asked. The magazine was not delivered to me on Sunday, and I used to read it the next day in the office.

"No" I replied.

"There is that usual column on the wedding, and Mahmoud saab is very angry".

I told her that I had specifically asked the magazine editor not to publish anything of that nature and she had assured me the next column contained nothing about the Benazir wedding. A few minutes later, Amber rang me up again. She said, "Mahmoud saab says that not only has policy been violated but the editor been lied to. She must be sacked". The girl lost her job. I felt very sorry for her. She was otherwise a nice person. My guess is that she didn't reconcile to the change in editorship, for she used to edit the magazine quite independently and did not accept what she thought was interference by me. She later joined a wildlife magazine and died rather young in the '90s. She was replaced by Sherry Rahman. Once Sherry was in place, Star Weekend ceased to be my headache, for we developed an excellent working relationship.

I remember my stint with Star for one recurring phenomenon and one calamity: the recurring phenomenon was student violence on the Karachi University campus and other universities and colleges in the city in which people of my generation had their education in peace. Now, in the late eighties I am writing about, gun battles between different student groups leading to fatalities were virtually a daily affair, and often the educational institutions had to be closed for weeks. Discipline in the universities had disappeared, student activists were armed to the teeth, the teaching staff was itself divided on 'ideological' and ethnic lines, teachers were often roughed up, and administration had all but collapsed. Often the police were called in to restore order, though the arrests had often nothing to do with the guilt. The press was critical of the entry of the police on campuses, though personally I thought the criticism was based on the theory that the precincts of educational institutions were sacred and the police had no business to be there. The criticism was hollow, because the situation had reached a point where the teachers, students and the political parties operating behind the scenes and the partisan role which the Zia bureaucracy played had destroyed the sanctity of the very concept of education. To the IJT, the educational institutions were not meant for acquiring education; they were meant for 'enforcing' the Islamic 'system'. For the APMSO hoodlums, the aim was less to equip themselves with knowledge and learning and more to advance the party's ethnic interests. Other ethnic groups thought and organised themselves on similar lines, and the hostels meant for students from outside Karachi turned into cells where student groups plotted and armed. The overall result was virtual destruction of Karachi's educational atmosphere, with engineering and medical degrees that normally required four or five years for a degree taking as much as seven to eight years.

The situation continued this way till it would take a courageous Sindh Governor to stop the rot. On April 19, 1989, a year after my assignment in Star had ended, Fakhruddin G. Ebrahim, one of Pakistan's leading jurists, was appointed Governor of Sindh. By that time the student groups had become a law unto themselves, especially because their 'mother parties' were taking no steps to control them. On the contrary, the Jamaat-i-Islami and MQM were both hostile to the press, and strange as it appeared to us both accused the newspapers of favouring the other side in news and comments. By any standards the attitude of these two parties toward violence on the campuses was symptomatic of the gross irresponsibility and indifference to national interests that have characterised our politicians in general. Till then most newspaper offices did not have the kind of modern security system that would later became inevitable when terrorism came to Pakistan. 'Security' was till then the responsibility of the traditional chowkidars, mostly semi-literate, to control student activists and party leaders, who bullied them and barged in to vandalise newspaper offices. Only drastic measures could change the situation, and this came in the form of Governor Ebrahim's decision to deploy Rangers outside the university's perimeter. The Rangers were asked to search students for arms before they were allowed to enter the campus. The frisking and the Rangers' deployment were harshly criticised by the press and sections of the politicians, but there is no denying the fact that there was no other choice for the government if sanity were to be restored to the university. The move had a dramatic effect, violence ceased and classes were resumed. Ebrahim was among those three Supreme Court judges who had refused to take the oath under the Provisional Constitution Order promulgated by Ziaul Haq by decree in 1981.

The calamity I referred to earlier was a devastating blast at the Ojhri ammunition depot at Faizabad, a densely populated locality located between Rawalpindi and Pakistan's capital, Islamabad, on April 10, 1988. Its impact on Pakistan's politics has been discussed by me in an earlier chapter. Briefly, the Ojhri blast became one of the major causes of tension between Ziaul Haq and Junejo and cost the prime minister his job. As a journalist and citizen I was so shocked by the Ojhri blast that, violating all traditions, I put my editorial on Star's front page in the issue of April 11.

Entitled "A holocaust is not an accident", the editorial said: "... A holocaust is not a train accident; a rain of death and destruction is not a minibus overturned; and a gigantic fireball over two cities not a kitchen stove burst. ...[I]t was a deafening and visible – in fact blinding – demonstration of the way the Defence establishment runs this country, and itself. Over a greater part of the last four decades, the Defence establishment has arrogated to itself the sole monopoly of wisdom – from constitutional expertise to dairy farm production. However, before it set out to do these things it should have paused to ponder whether it could do its own job properly...True, as said by the Prime Minister, the arsenal had been there since the pre-Independence days. But a great deal of change had occurred, and areas previously uninhabited or scantily populated had been overtaken by urban growth. In fact, Rawalpindi's growth and the springing up of Islamabad had brought the Faizabad area dangerously close to the population centres, and it should have occurred to those who manage ordnance to remove the lethal dump from its locations. That no one bothered to give a thought to this potential source of mass death and destruction points, as we have said earlier, to the way the establishment runs this country, and itself. We also know for sure no one would be great enough to take the responsibility and resign. The nation indeed will wait anxiously for the results of the enquiry ordered by the Prime Minister. Whether the tragedy stemmed from sabotage or from a careless spark the responsibility must not only be fixed but made public."

I wrote this editorial over 20 years ago, and till this day (2009) the reports of the two inquiry committees – one set up by Junejo and the other by the army – have not been made public. In 2004, when Musharraf was in power, someone raised a question about the Ojhri blast inquiry in the Senate, but the question was disallowed.

An unforgettable event during my stint with Star was Benazir's wedding, and the celebrations included an awami – people's – reception at Kikri Ground, located in that part of old Karachi which till this day is a PPP constituency. I parked my car far away and walked to Kikri Ground along with thousands of others. Luckily, the government had the common sense not to deploy the police, and left the management of the reception and security to PPP workers. The height of the boundary wall had been raised and barbed wire placed to prevent unauthorised entry. When I reached the place, all gates had been closed, and many people including me were refused entry even though we showed the invitation cards. Standing beside me in an elegant lounge suite and looking equally forlorn was a man who had come all the way from Canada to attend the reception. He was a Canadian of Pakistan origin and was a professor at some Canadian university. The entire scene symbolised the PPP's appeal for the people of Pakistan, for the thousands present there – whether invited or waiting for gate-crashing – cut across social classes and ethnic groups. Young and old, rich and poor, educated and uneducated, all came in droves to testify to the charisma that the Bhuttos were. Unable to get into the ground through a gate, I looked up at one of the party's Makrani workers perched on the boundary wall. As he looked at me, I waved the invitation card to him. He talked to someone and then perhaps took pity on my plight. I stretched my hand, and he pulled me up. The next moment I was on the boundary wall and having a breath-taking view of the reception and the stage where the bride and bridegroom and their families were seated. Then the Makrani worker did a similar favour to the Canadian professor. I then got down and wove my way to the media enclosure, which was close to the stage. Lucky were the families having a grandstand view from their balconies in the apartment buildings that surrounded the ground. The sea breeze was missing – typical of Karachi's winter – but there was a nip in the air. The sky was star-lit, the audience sat enraptured and a group from Lahore lit up the sky with a brilliant display of fireworks as Mohammad Ali Shehki began singing nazar nazar tayray hi jelvay hayn.

Not being a woman, I do not remember what dress Benazir wore that evening. Nevertheless she was all that goes into the making of a Pakistani bride. Together she and Zardari made a stunning pair. Anyone next to Benazir was always dwarfed. A few days later, Aftab Shahban Mirani, a senior PPP leader and later Sindh Chief Minister and federal minister, held a reception at his Defence home. I remarked to Wajid Shamsul Hasan, now (2009) Pakistan's High Commissioner in London, "Zardari hasn't come to the dinner". He replied, "Asif is standing next to Benazir". He indeed was. Eight years later I would be at the White House covering a joint press conference by Benazir and Bill Clinton. The American president, too, had a sparkling personality, but there was no doubt that in the Grand Foyer where the press conference was held, with millions watching on TV, he was overshadowed by the dazzling personality of Pakistan's prime minister. I wonder what my reaction would have been at the Kikri Ground reception that December evening if I had known that precisely two decades later in about the same kind of weather, in the same month and surrounded by cheering crowds in a city where Pakistan's first prime minister was assassinated, Benazir, the Islamic world's first woman prime minister, the idol of millions not only in Pakistan but in all parts of the world, would be murdered, as her father was, by religious fanatics, who would congratulate each other on their cellphones on their achievement (See chapter 16).

༺༻༺༻༺༻༺༻

Meanwhile, I was getting desperate and wanted to get out of Star. The management had assured AAK that my assignment would at best last three months and they would find an editor. However, five months had passed but somehow they had failed to find one, and I suspected they wanted me to stay on. The lack of professionalism in the paper was disgusting and making my job difficult, and at least once it got me into serious trouble, because one subeditor, a girl, let the four-letter word pass several times in a showbiz article. The four-letter word no more shocks newspaper readers and movie-goers in the West, but in a conservative society like Pakistan, the publication of the four-letter word was and still is taboo. In what to me was utter violation of the copyrights law besides sheer stupidity the girl used to fill two full pages with matter lifted from foreign magazines, and the previous editor had no objection. In fact, she never bothered to read the matter she selected, confining herself to headlines. She used scissors, handed the clippings to the composing room for setting and shoved the matter in on the page when it was composed. The article concerned an interview in which Katherine Hepburn talked about her lovers, especially Spencer Tracy. She was candid and used the four-letter word generously, and the entire piece appeared unedited in a paper that carried my name in the print line. When I asked the girl to see me she hid her face in shame. I told her I was angry less about the word and more about the gross neglect of fundamental principles of journalism and copyrights. We published an apology and luckily there was no fall-out. While I was able to improve the quality and quantity of news coverage and editorial comments, I found myself unable to chip away at the old attitudes. I, thus, felt greatly relieved when Zafar Samdani finally replaced me as editor in mid-April. It is a tribute to Samdani's personality that perhaps half a dozen people claimed credit for getting him in Star. Majid was one of them, though I think it was I who finally prevailed upon Samdani to accept the editorship.

Samdani stayed at Star, I think, for a little more than a year, and left for Lahore to join a new venture, Frontier Post, launched by Rahmat Afridi. Following differences with Afridi, Samdani quit the paper. That turned out to be his last newspaper. He continued to freelance for Dawn and several foreign magazines and newspapers, but would never again work for a daily paper. He would come to Karachi every now and then after a month or two and make my room his headquarters. As he used to say there was no other person in the world whose office he could misuse the way he did mine. A spendthrift, Samdani had a sense of humour all his own. Once he told me, "I have proved by practical example how a man can live beyond his means". By this he meant the way he took loans to keep going. He repaid them all. He was often quite forgetful. Once he took a friend's car, a blue Suzuki FX, to go to the airport and returned to inform him he had come back. But when his friend went there to go home, he found that Samdani had returned with someone else's blue Suzuki FX. Fourteen years later, in the summer of 2004, I stayed in Lahore for three days on my way to the cool heights of Murree to be with my cousin, Farrukh Saeed, then a Colonel (later Brigadier) in the artillery. For May, Lahore was surprisingly cool, because it rained the day I landed in the Mughal city. Whenever I am in Lahore I try to hide my emotions. It is impossible not to be happy and sad at the same time. There is no other city in Pakistan where history speaks to you. You only have to listen. While Punjab is now Pakistan's most important province in every sense of the word, people forget that it enjoyed virtually the same position in the mighty Mughal Empire that included today's Afghanistan, Pakistan, India and Bangladesh. Even in that sprawling empire, the sultan at Delhi gave Punjab's gubernatorial assignment to his most trusted lieutenant, for he knew that if an invader took Punjab, Delhi would be his next stop. The last two invaders to do so were soldiers of fortune, Iranian Nadir Shah and Afghan Ahmad Shah Abdali. Wiser after the disaster of the first Afghan war, the British secured the trans-Indus passes, drew and legitimised the Durand Line and made Punjab safe. Luckily, Pakistan controls those passes today.

Even though I had stayed at a hotel, I was for all practical purposes Samdani's guest. I had dinner with Samdani the day I arrived and the next day we had a delightful day together, driving round Lahore, and ending the evening with a hi-tea with him and his wife, a teacher by profession, at their Muslim Town home. I did not know I would never see him again. Never very religious, Samdani went on Hajj in 2005 along with his wife. I wanted to talk to him about his Hajj experiences, but never could meet him again. He occasionally phoned me up from Lahore but it was difficult to hear him, because he had developed cancer of the throat. He died in June 2006.

In his obituary note on Samdani, Tahir Mirza, then Dawn editor, gave us a glimpse of the kind of crowd there was at The Pakistan Times where he and Samdani were colleagues in the sixties: "There was the late Maqbul Sharif, known as 'judge sahib' because he covered the higher courts, and Nasim, who went into public relations and died young. Khalid Hasan joined the team a little later and brought a touch of wit and humour with him. The whole team gelled well, and despite the fact that the paper was owned by the government's National Press Trust, there was a good deal of independent reporting. Samdani was not very tall, but he had the loose-limbed gait of a tall man. He never had any inhibitions about reporting on anything or writing about anyone. Where he picked up his penchant for economic reporting is unclear. But he was part of a catholic group of students who had studied at the Government College, Lahore, and was well-connected. He wasn't with The Pakistan Times for long, leaving to head the PTV news team when television began from Lahore in 1964. He held various positions with the organisation, and those who worked with him remember him as always ready with appreciation where it was merited. PTV, after its earlier, creative days soon slid into political infighting and Samdani perhaps fell somewhere on the wayside. As a free-lancer, he was absolutely versatile, including an informed insight into the cinema industry, and was saved from hack writing only because of his innate good taste. Whenever someone in Dawn wanted a piece from Lahore on short notice, the call went out: Ask Zafar Samdani. Our paths didn't cross often enough after the PT crowd dispersed, except in Lahore, when he would regularly drop in at the Dawn offices for a cup of tea, a smoke and to fax or email his articles to the head office in Karachi. Samdani once came to Dubai [where Tahir was editor of Khaleej Times] and spent most of his time in shopping for his family, for whom he cared so much. One day he had landed up in Washington [Tahir had replaced Sehbai as Dawn's Washington correspondent in July 2001] and there was a small reunion at a bay-front restaurant with Khalid Hasan [then correspondent for The Nation, Lahore] and Akmal Aleemi of Imroze, the PT's sister paper...[then with the Voice of America]. Not many of us knew till later that Samdani was also a poet, and was part of Lahore's literary circle and the Tea House crowd before he wandered into journalism. He was a civilised, gentlemanly journalist, but will also be remembered as the quintessential Lahori". Tahir wrote these words in June 2006; a year later he himself fell victim to cancer.

In April 1988, with Samdani firmly in place as Star editor, I returned to the mother paper and resumed editorial writing. On July 27, 1989, Dawn Overseas Weekly closed down, its last edition covering the "Week ending August 2, 1989." A notice on page one, addressed To Our

Readers, said: "Effective from next week, Dawn Overseas Weekly will suspend publication for an indefinite period. As a sequel to this step, our subscribers will soon hear from Business Manager (Circulation) about the mode of settlement of the unutilised amount of their subscription. — Management, Pakistan Herald Publications (Private) Ltd". Even though AAK was DOW's editor, Majid, Senior Assistant Editor, headed the team. He wrote a weekly "National Diary". Today Dawn's internet edition has rendered the concept of such a weekly obsolete. In November 1991 I moved to the newsroom. This period between – April 1988 and 1991 November, when I took over as news editor – was marked by dramatic changes in Pakistan's history. To wit, from a military-led semi-democracy, the country returned to what by any standards was a truly democratic dispensation. The events moved with rapidity. On April 29, 1988, Zia ruled in full majesty, his dismissal of the Junejo government and the dissolution of the National Assembly evoking no popular protests. On August 17 he was killed in the air crash, and on December 2 Benazir became the Muslim world's first woman prime minister. Twenty months later, shortly after Saddam Hussein invaded Kuwait in August, Benazir was dismissed as prime minister. I am not amongst conspiracy theorists. If Nawaz had been sacked you could hear to no end claims that America had got Nawaz dismissed because Washington wanted a more pliant government at a time when Bush Senior was preparing for an attack on Iraq to liberate Kuwait. I believe that both Benazir and Nawaz Sharif, dismissed twice, fell victim to political jealousies, intrigue and vendetta, and neither America nor any foreign power had anything to do with this. As Henry Kissinger said in an article published in the Washington Post, (extracts in Dawn, March 11, 2008), the former secretary of state asked America to concede that "the internal structure of Pakistani politics is essentially out of the control of American political decision-making".

11

ON THE POTOMAC

MY FIRST THOUGH RATHER limited exposure to the American way of life and to a practical demonstration of the concept of social equality came through the US Embassy, which was then in my city, because Karachi was still Pakistan's capital. I had resigned my job with the Karachi Joint Water Board in August 1955 because a common friend said the US Embassy needed people and was a good paymaster. The KJWB gave me Rs 120 each month. Normally, a clerk in government offices those days received a "basic" salary of Rs 60, plus allowances — like the house rent (Rs 15), a special "Karachi allowance" of Rs 15 because Karachi those days was supposed to be the nation's costliest city, and a conveyance allowance (Rs 10), plus some other allowances. The total came to Rs 110. I was getting an extra 10 rupees because my office, Construction Circle, was located at Ninth Mile, so-called because it was supposed to be at a distance of nine miles from the city centre. Going there entailed more expenses on transport. The Construction Circle was on the junction of Sharea Faisal (then called Drigh Road) and H. I. Rahimtoola Road a.k.a Karsaz Road. It was then a narrow and bumpy road, where a bus or a car passed perhaps in 10 minutes, unlike the thoroughfare it is today with a naval establishment on one side and the posh Mohammad Ali Society on the other. However, the job with the embassy fetched me Rs350, nearly three times more, though many friends said it was still lower than what I deserved.

Many things about the embassy and the Americans there looked strange, disgusting and fascinating to me. The mode of payment of salary was itself great. In the KJWB, I had to stand in line to get the salary, find a two-anna revenue stamp and sign on the register. At the embassy, a white envelope containing crisp currency notes was given to me each week. Getting it every week was a thrill, and was in sharp contrast to the 30- or 31-day wait at the KJWB. If the first of the month fell on a Sunday, the wait could stretch to 32 days. More important, Pakistanis at the embassy, who included my elder sister, Qamar, informed me that there were 52 weeks in a year, and so that way I would get one extra month's salary. My first "upset" came when the American accent bewildered me. Prior to joining the embassy, I was assailed by doubts whether I would be able to speak English fluently. However, what turned out to be the problem was the American accent. When Maggie — I do not now remember what her full name was — started dictating to me and after finishing a sentence said "Pirriyo" I wondered what "pirriyo" was. As I drew a blank she took my dictation notebook and made a cross, which in Pitman's shorthand stood for a full-stop. Then I realised that she was saying "period", and that "period" stood for a full-stop. My exposure to foreign English accent was then confined to the BBC's cricket commentaries, and I had not till then fallen victim to what was to become a dominating feature of my life well into old age — Hollywood films.

The section I worked for was the Military Assistance Advisory Group, pronounced Mag for short. All American staff consisted of armed forces personnel, but they were seldom in uniform. Gen Brown, the Mag chief, was a friendly type and came in uniform regularly. My boss was Captain Magnus P. Studer, Mag adjutant. I am a meticulous keeper of record, and I still have the character certificate he gave me more than half a century ago when I quit the embassy in 1956. Typed on the letterhead of Headquarters, Military Assistance Advisory Group, Pakistan, APO

616, Box 1, New York, it read: "To whom it may concern. This is to certify that during the period 8 August 1955 to 13 April 1956, Mr Muhammad Ali Siddiqi was assigned to the Military Assistance Advisory Group to Pakistan, Adjutant Section, as Clerk-Typist under supervision of the undersigned. Mr Siddiqi was a very willing employee. He worked during the above period to our satisfaction. He left our service due to his B. A. Examination. Sincerely, Magnus P. Studer, Captain, AGC, Adjutant." Punctuation, style and the big E of "examination" were typical of the Pakistani bureaucratic English, because the certificate was drafted by a Pakistani friend, and Studer signed it .However, my slave driver was Sergeant George F. Ausdreau. Sergeants constituted the bulk of the staff and handled most of the desk work. Each sat behind a desk, on the one side of which was a typewriter. The desks were in rows, and there were three rows, one each along the walls of the big hall, and one in the middle.

I then noticed the level of efficiency in Mag. A letter would come from a Pakistan army, air force or naval office, would land at my desk, and I would hand it over to the relevant sergeant. The sarge would go through the relevant file, discuss it with the officer concerned, type a reply and show it to the officer, who would either sign it or make changes. In any case, the reply would be ready in half an hour, and it would be gone. In the KJWB, the process was slow, cumbersome, passed many hands and required acknowledgment of receipt at every stage. I was in what is called in Pakistan the R&I (receipt and issue) section, and letters addressed to the Superintending Engineer (SE), my boss, would come to me. When a sufficient number of letters had been accumulated, I would enter them in a register, stamp the letters, write the serial number within the space provided for in the stamp and then ask the peon (read about the institution of "peon" later in this chapter) to give it to the head clerk (HC), who sat in the same hall opposite to me. The HC would examine the letters and send them to clerks concerned. Day one was over. The next day, the clerks would go through the files and write notes for the benefit of the HC to indicate the lines on which the reply should go. The clerk would write a DFA (draft for approval), and it would go to the SE, who may perhaps have gone to the "site", and DFAs would keep piling up on his desk. When he returned, he would examine the DFAs, make changes and a final draft would be ready. This would now go to the typing pool. When it came from the typing pool, it would await the SE's signature. If he signed it that very day, it would go to the dispatch clerk. Again the process of entry into the register began, followed by an entry into "peon book". The peon would then take the letters to the addressees. This would take anything from three to six days. From the benefit of the hindsight I say there was nothing wrong with the quality of the staff, and the problem was with the system, especially with the rule that the letter must have a receipt at every stage. In sharp contrast, the Americans seldom wanted a receipt and the system worked on trust. Sometimes, Sgt Ausdreau asked me to deliver an important letter personally, and Transport Officer Hafizullah would place a jeep at my disposal.

The place where I drove to in the jeep most frequently was the office of Pakistan Military Accounts, opposite to where the Karachi Press Club today is. The road was then called Ingle Road, its name now being M. R. Kayani Road. Hafizullah was quite popular with the Americans, but invariably they dropped the H in his name and turned Z into soft C. So the embassy often resonated with the sound of "Feesculah!" He was not a very educated man, and one day I asked a friend why Hafizullah was so popular with the Americans. He replied that Hafizullah had been with the embassy for a long time, and understood the American accent and mind well. He did not worry about the rules of grammar, conveyed his ideas adequately and did not irritate the Americans the way other Pakistanis did by saying "pardon" too many times. The Americans had also by then learnt the word Achchha both as an equivalent of Yes and as an exclamatory query Achchha!? (They had not yet learnt to say theek hai or bilkul theek, because I think it is a later development, and we Pakistanis had not yet begun using these two words with the frequency with which we use them today. This dawned on me in Dawood Shah's

Kabul in 1977 when Afghans quite often confirmed and reconfirmed a given price or a wake-up call by asking theek hai? or bilkul theek? The 'th' was, of course, soft and appeared amusing to me.)

The sergeants were of all sorts, mostly polite and likeable. But some were positively piggish. One such was Sgt Lawrence, who could be quite nasty with the Pakistani staff as well as with fellow Americans. He used to suffer from cold — that could perhaps be one reason for his irritability. One day I approached his desk and stood while he worked. I, too, was then having a running nose, and perhaps pulled on my nose a little too hard. He got up and without asking why I had come to him took out a couple of tissue papers and thrust them into my hand. He was annoyed that I was sneezing and coughing and did not have a handkerchief with me. One day he did not mean to annoy me when he gave me a document and asked me to give it to Sanneback.

"Who is Mr Sanneback?" I asked.

"The guy who hired you", he replied.

N. H. Sanneback was the personnel officer and worked one storey below.

"The man down, there" he said gesturing to the floor below."

"Oh, that is Mr Sanneback?"

"Yes, that is Mr Sanneback!" He was now positively nasty.

"Why did you say 'hire'?" I asked, because I had felt hurt, since I thought one usually hired a taxi. "Nobody hired me. I was given a job here", I said.

He was now furious, and failed to realise that I had raised that question because the usage of "hire" in that sense was not known to me or to perhaps entire Pakistan because Americanism was still decades away. The letter Z was still referred to as zed and not zee, and nearly five decades were to pass before I would hear my granddaughter Maleeha call it Zee!

"Look, everybody gets hired", he said. Then pointing to the picture of President Eisenhower he said "That guy hired me!" So, I came to know, not only taxis but even human beings got hired.

The Americans' ignorance of other peoples and world geography was shocking. One day, a sergeant asked me what the difference was between a Hindu and a Muslim. I could understand someone asking me about the difference between a Christian and a Muslim, or a Muslim or a Jew, but someone wanting me to tell him the difference between Hindus and Muslims was indeed stupefying. On another occasion I remember an envelope was going to Dacca, and a sergeant — his name was possibly Hughes —brought it to me for dispatch. I added the words "East Pakistan" after Decca.

"Oh, it is in East Pakistan?" he asked innocently.

"Yes", I replied".

"Where are we?" he asked.

"We are in West Pakistan".

So living in Karachi, he did not know the city was located in West Pakistan. One day Sergeant Lawrence came to me and wanted to know the spelling of what to me appeared "Barraat".

"What Barraat?" I asked

"Barraat", he repeated offensively, and then added, "near Pabbi." He pronounced it as Paybi.

Pabbi was where the American air base was being built. It later came to be known as Barabed. But Pabbi was in the NWFP, and for the life of me I did not know what "Barraat close to Pabbi" Sgt Lawrence was referring to. Then someone cleared the issue. He was referring to India, which those days was referred to in Pakistan's English press as Bharat. So Barraat was Bharat.

Reminiscing about the embassy half a century later, I wonder why there were no blacks in Mag or in the embassy. The entire staff was what I would call Nordic, with some Hispanics here and there. But one thing became obvious to me: I was getting exposed to a higher culture. The biggest proof of this reality was the total absence of that obscene phenomenon called peons in South Asia. Most people in the English-speaking world would find it difficult to understand who or what a peon is, though the word is found in the English dictionary. According to the

Oxford Advanced Learner's Dictionary, a peon is "a worker on a farm in Latin America". In American English it is, humorously, "a person with a hard or boring job that is not well paid and not considered important". According to the Chambers Dictionary, a peon is "a day labourer, esp in formerly Spanish-speaking America, one working off a debt by bondage; in India a foot soldier, a policeman or a messenger; in SE Asia a minor office worker". Actually, none of these definitions truly reflects the institution that the peon in the subcontinent is. He cannot be called an errand boy because in New Zealand or Canada, a high school dropout can be an errand boy without losing his dignity. One problem with Pakistani society then and now is lack of dignity of labour. Muslims they may be, but the Muslims of South Asia have imbibed many despicable local traits, including contempt for manual work. This is evident from the contempt attached to professions and those who practise them. Hajjam (barber), Mochi (cobbler), Chamar (tanner), Teli (one who sells or extracts oil), Julaha (weaver), Lohar (iron smith), Lakar-hara (wood cutter), Qassab (butcher), Gowali (milk seller), Bhangi (toilet cleaner), Bhishti (water carrier), Barhaey (carpenter), Naanbaey (bread baker),— all have acquired a connotation that is full of contempt. In sharp contrast, no humiliation is attached to such professions in the Middle East, Europe and America, and I suppose that must be the case in China and Japan and South-East Asian societies as well, because the contempt for manual labour stems directly from Hindu society's division into castes. Thus it is quite normal in the English speaking world to have names like Barber, Carpenter, Shepherd, Baker, Mason, Gardener, Taylor, Forest, Wood, Smith, Cooper, Carter, Shoemaker, Butcher, Hide, Hair, Bell, etc.

The peon had a lot of contempt attached to him because he mostly did manual work, if at all he did any work. Lowly paid, and usually in dirty clothes (unless the company gave him a uniform), he sat on a stool and obeyed the white collar worker to get a pack of cigarettes or deliver an envelope or letter to the man in the next room. The absence of the peon would create quite a problem for the sahibs, because in that case they would themselves be forced to take a file or a paper from one room to another. He was seldom given any tip, and — except for the toilet cleaners — he belonged to the lowest stratum of society. In the US Embassy there were no peons, as they are unlikely to be in any civilised society, and this created quite a problem for the Pakistani staff, as we shall see. Normally, the entire Mag staff moved papers themselves, and they helped each other in the sense that a sergeant going to another section — say, to the Attaché's office, which was on the same floor but at a distance — would carry papers for that department himself. I was in the R&I section, though the Americans called my desk "Message Centre". Anyone who passed my desk would take a look at the pigeon holes, pick up some documents and deliver them to other sections. Gen. Brown, too, did the same. The full realisation of the absence of peons in Mag came to me when a few days after joining the embassy I saw Gen Brown coming up the stairs carrying with him lots of personal belongings and official papers. "Does not he have a peon?" I said to myself. Then I realised this institution did not exist in the US Embassy.

The most painful part of the system for the Pakistani staff came at around 4.30pm when it was time to go home. The issue revolved round dignity of labour and confidentiality, because all correspondence in Mag concerned military matters, and draft-letters and other secret memos and minutes of meetings re-typed and discarded were torn up and consigned to the waste paper basket. However, the discarded stuff could not be treated like normal garbage; it had to be burnt, and for that there was an incinerator on the roof of the embassy. For that purpose, precisely at 4.30pm, two people would go from desk to desk. While one person, usually an American, would hold a large bag, the other, usually a Pakistani, but sometimes an American as well, would empty the waste paper basket's contents into the pouch. Once this was done, the pouch would go to the incinerator. This process was a source of both agony and fun for the Pakistani staff. While embarrassment was writ large on the face of the Pakistani whose duty that particular day was to do the "dirty work", the other Pakistanis covered their mouths with handkerchiefs as they thoroughly enjoyed their colleague's agony. The next day, of course, one of them would himself be picking up waste paper baskets and emptying the contents into the pouch. There were other misunderstandings, too. One day, as I was going to the canteen below, Sgt Hubbard gave me some money and said, "Siddick, get a coke for me!" I gave no response. He realised my embarrassment and said, "Next time I go to canteen, you can ask me to get anything for you". Another occasion that involved a lot of physical hard work was the day the APO pouches landed in the Mag office. The Army Post Office was instituted in Pakistan much later and was copied from the Americans because of the security it provided for armed forces personnel's personal correspondence. But the APO gave me an idea of the amount of correspondence and gifting the Americans did. All concerned Americans and Pakistanis gathered as the pouches were opened. Breaking their seals open, pulling boxes and other stuff out of the pouches, putting them back into pouches after mail had been sorted and then distributing them in the Mag office required a lot of physical effort, and that was one of the reasons for my the decision to quit the job. Stationery has fascinated me since childhood, and in the embassy, even though I was then a young man, I was struck by the variety in American office stationery and also realised there was a thing called standardisation. The eraser came in the form of a pencil, at the end of which was a brush meant for wiping specks of rubber on paper after the error had been erased, and instead of the traditional pencil sharpeners, there were sharpening machines fixed to tables. I do not know why but whenever I entered a Pakistan government office and worked there, which I did twice, and saw tables and almirahs and stationery, it all appeared to belong to the East India Company days. Everything was moth-eaten and worn-out, and office work revolved round old-style registers and heaps of files.

The mainstay of paper work was the foolscap which the overhead fan made difficult to manage, and often it was quite thin, because the typist had to make several copies of a given order or letter. So instead of typing it twice, he used as many carbon sheets as was possible to get the maximum number of copies. Sometimes, the last two copies were hardly readable. The embassy, too, had files, but they were kept in modern-style cabinets, and the Americans used the A-4 size paper, which was easy to handle, and for the first time I noticed that carbon paper was built into pro forma forms. This was something that was to come to Pakistan decades later. I am not implying that the government offices where I worked were inefficient. On the other hand, contrary to what was to come later, the KJWB and the police office where I once worked as a stenographer were quite efficient. The staff was punctual, and discipline was strict. It was the system that required modernisation. Standardisation at Mag also reflected itself in the format of correspondence, and every letter had to conform to it. A violation of the indent rules meant re-typing the letter. To begin a paragraph one had to press the space bar on the typewriter five times, and there were similar rules about the beginning and the end. In Pakistani offices, spacing for paragraphs was left to the sweet will of the typist, and sometimes the indent covered half of the first line of the paragraph. I am writing about indenting and spacing because I was a professional typist, and these things mattered to me. They still do, because for a journalist white space and correct spacing are an essential part of newspaper layout.

I was a good typist, and my American colleagues often asked me where I had learnt it. I took typing lessons at an institute which was run by the Hyderabad Trust, formed after the fall of Hyderabad, for the benefit of Hyderabadis in Pakistan. If I remember correctly, the Trust also ran a match factory in Landhi. The institute charged five rupees per month, but for Hyderabadi boys and girls it charged one rupee less. So I paid four rupees and began learning typing. When the next month began, I could come up with only two rupees, but the institute's manager still let me work on the rickety Remington. After 15 days, I realised that while other boys had moved over to brand, new Olivettis I was still banging at the old Remington. When I asked the manager why, he said this was because I had not paid the full month's fee. I quit, but by then I had mastered the keyboard. Today, more than half a century later, I can say without exaggeration that no other skill which has proved more lucrative to me than typing. Thanks to typing, I had no difficulty in switching over to the computer which I first began using in Washington D.C. in the early nineties. While I am grateful to my parents for giving me the six rupees for the one and a half months of training and induction into the world of typing, I remember the manager with gratitude for letting me learn for 15 days of the following month. Because of typing, I have always felt confident that I would not be jobless in and any English-speaking or Commonwealth country. God alone knows how many millions of words I have typed as a journalist, especially for Dawn. My son Nasir once counted the number of editorials I have written for Dawn, and by March 31, 2013, they numbered 2,800. The figure does not include those which I did not bother to save or which I threw away in disgust when I found language and argument distorted when they appeared in the paper the next day. The editorials are in addition to the millions of words I wrote in articles, news stories and features and book reviews. How many foreign newspapers quoted my editorials I do not know. But when the Lal Masjid stand-off in Islamabad was at its peak in the summer of 2007 and when I wrote one editorial a day as the situation moved toward the military crackdown in the first week of July 2007, Dawn editorials were extensively quoted by the international media. While my articles have appeared in foreign newspapers, I could never land a well-paid job as a foreign correspondent. The nearest I came to was a brief stint with the Los Angeles Times when the Afghan resistance to the Soviet occupation was at its peak. It published my articles and paid me handsomely. The only lead story I got in a foreign newspaper was Arab News of Jeddah. It so happened that the day Ziaul Haq died in the plane crash in August 1988, I was not well and was at home. A friend in Arab News rang me up and asked me whether I could report for them. I agreed to do a desk job. I monitored TV and radio and wrote what I later found to be an excellent piece of reporting because I had the benefit of facts from radio and TV which reporters on the spot did not have. This is of course a major dilemma for all correspondents, who, like soldiers in trenches, often feel isolated and have no idea of the larger picture. Today, I do not remember how I sent the story to Arab News. While I can remember minor events half a century ago I am unable to guess what the mode of transmission of the story to Arab News was in August 1998. Fax had not till then come to Pakistan in a big way, and I could not possibly have gone to the post office for sending the story by telex because I was ill. My guess is that perhaps I dictated the story to the Arab News staff over the phone.

At the embassy, I also noticed that the Americans were very helpful to each other and cared. In Pakistan, then as now, help is confined to those whom you know, and courtesy is seldom extended to strangers. Quite a few Americans did not bother to hide their arrogance and were colour conscious, but toward each other they were respectful and caring. Besides, there was hardly any difference in the way they dressed — all wore the same kind of trousers and bush shirts. As a lad still uninitiated into the ways of people other than South Asians, I was often surprised to see a sergeant sitting on his officer's table and drinking and eating while discussing official matters with his boss, who could be a colonel. This was, and is, inconceivable in the Pakistani armed forces, where officers and men come from different classes and where this kind of behaviour on the part of a jawan would drive the officer mad. Political thought and philosophy were still years away from me, but it was a kind of classless society that I saw in action at the embassy. The Americans, it did not appear to me then, were a "normal" people — like the Turkish, Malaysian, Iranian and Chinese peoples I had occasion to interact with later — while the Pakistani middle class appeared to live in Mughal times. I think it still does. There were, of course, negative aspects of American behaviour. For instance, I found most Americans an extremely suspicious lot. Often it was not unusual for an American to suddenly stop if he found Pakistanis talking somewhere, just stand there and look at us, saying with their eyes, "May I know what exactly are you people doing?". Those were mad, mad anti-commie days, and nothing like this was to grip America again till Osama bin Laden crashed those planes into the World Trade Centre and the Pentagon in September 2001. Many

Americans felt irritated if some Pakistani failed to understand a word, slang or a command. But I suppose that was inevitable. Everybody on planet Earth knows what status his language occupies in the world. Notice how Urdu speakers expect people from all over Pakistan — even from areas close to the Chinese border in Gilgit and Hunza — or Afghan refugees, who sometimes could be ethnic Uzbeks or Tajiks, to speak flawless Urdu, and how they make efforts to hide their disappointment or even anger when they hear faulty pronunciation or a wrong idiom.

My stay with the embassy lasted less than a year, because I was keen to finish my B.A. Even though I had a full-time 9 to 5 job with the embassy, I was a student at Urdu College. But attendance rules those days were lax, because most colleges knew that, in the aftermath of partition and the unsettled conditions in Karachi, most boys earned while in college. I wanted at least three months' leave to attend college and prepare for the examination. However, a three-month leave was not possible, and Sgt Ausdreau tried his best to dissuade me from going ahead with it.

"Siddick", he said, "Pakistan produces 20,000 BAs each year (Sanneback had given him these figures). What will you do with a BA?"

I said this would give me a better job and more money. He could not digest this philosophy and asked, "What has your school got to do with more money?" He was looking at it from the point of view of a developed, industrial society where it is skill and not academic education that gives you money. Steeped in the South Asian concept of education and aware of the importance of a B.A. degree in Pakistan for a middle class lad, I failed to convince Sgt Ausdreau that "school" was important for me. I resigned. Twenty-eight years would pass before I would renew my contact with America, and another eight years would lapse before I would have a home in Washington, D.C.

The year was 1984 and President Ronald Reagan looked set for a second term. The runners for the Democratic ticket were Walter Mondale, Jesse Jackson and Gary Hart, the last one falling victim to sex scandals. For me, it turned out to be a superb coast-to-coast programme, ending at San Francisco for the Democratic Party convention. The visit to the US was organised by the USIS and Delphi, an NGO, and included journalists from many countries. I was the only one from Pakistan, because I had caught the USIS's attention because of a column called "Of People" I used to write for Dawn Magazine, which I then edited. Those were Ziaul Haq days, all newspapers were censored heavily, and AAK was keen to make it a little less dreary. My original aim, on the editor's prodding, was to focus on non-celebrities, but as my column progressed it became impossible to find non-celebrities every fortnight. Later I turned it into a weekly column and contained the interviews of a variety of people, Pakistani and foreign. They ranged from Sohbat Khan, a timekeeper on a bus terminal near my home and whose discipline and punctuality I said could be the envy of a Lufthansa manager, to foreign politicians and scholars like Asghar Ali Engineer, John Esposito, Lawrence Ziring and Nikki Kiddie. The last three were some of the Americans I interviewed during a time when, because of the anti-Soviet resistance funded by the CIA, there was no dearth of American scholars visiting Pakistan regularly. The USIS kept me well informed of such visits, and this way I interviewed many Americans, making friends and non-friends ask why Americans were my favourites. This was not the case, and those I interviewed for my column included people from many countries, including Arab and communist. But the critics seemed to have won when the USIS included me in what was called the visitors' exchange programme. AAK approved of it, and I landed in New York in June 1984. The Americans insisted that I break journey in London and had provided for a layover. However, I chose to stay with Dr A. A. Khan, psychiatrist to a group of London hospitals, who was also on Mrs Thatcher's committee on mental health for immigrants. He was with me at Bahadur Yar Jang High School at Karachi and later married one of my cousins. The way the Americans organised the programme, including a night's stay in London, and the way the rest of the schedule ending at San Francisco was planned spared the participants the torture which foreign tours some time become when hosts look at the itinerary and the tight schedule from their point of view, forgetting how the guests will take it.

The convention at San Francisco must be remembered for Gary Hart's very candid comment, after his denigrators and political rivals had discovered a mistress for him on the eve of the convention. Asked what he thought of it, Hart replied "I will not be the first adulterer in the White House" — and "not the last" he should have added, for less than a decade later the world would hear of Paula Jones and Monica Lewinsky. The winner, who would be decisively beaten by Reagan, was Mondale. He was already trailing 15 to 19 points behind Reagan before the convention at the Mascone Centre began, and his choice of a woman, Geraldine Ferraro, a lawyer from New York, as his running mate sealed his fate. Opinion polls had reacted negatively to Ferraro's choice, for the Democratic ticket had become a north-north affair, Mondale being from Minnesota. Yet, in spite of the glittering show that the convention at Mascone Centre was, — ticker-tape, fireworks and balloons — I could not help recall the following dialogue between Lawrence and Prince Ali in Lawrence of Arabia, with Peter O'Toole as the British army officer and Omar Sharif as the Hashemite prince as they lay relaxed under the open sky in the Arabian desert:

Lawrence: What do you intend to do after the war?

Ali: I want to enter politics.

Lawrence: Why? Politics is a low occupation.

It low indeed is, not just in Third World countries without democracy but everywhere, including the US, where money and sex scandals seem to have become an essential part of electioneering from county councils and city governments to state congresses, US Congress and the White House. Ethnic, professional and other lobbies make sense in a country that is a mosaic of cultural diversity and a bastion of free enterprise, but the cartels and the media (in turn controlled by the cartels) have acquired a position where, as in the communist system, the people have to choose between candidates already selected by the Party. As the cliché goes, they sell the president the way they sell a product. The role of the Zionist lobby in American politics, media, academia and think-tanks is a subject unto itself. But a candidate who is not more Israeli than an Israeli is unlikely to be elected if he deviates from the "brief". As Jimmy Carter said after he was denounced as anti-Semitic for his book Peace not Apartheid, "It is impossible for any candidate for Congress to make a statement like 'I favour balanced support of Israel and Palestine'". This, he said, had made White House and Congress "submissive" (to Israel) on the Palestinian question.

I was not on a reporting assignment, but I chose to report for Dawn, using the local telegraphic company's telex facility, for email and modem were still far away. There was a demonstration of Pakistanism when, as I waited at the LA airport for the New York-bound flight a total, stranger came to me, "Hockey gold mobarak ho," he said. I do not know who he was and how he came to know I was a Pakistani, but he guessed correctly and we embraced each other.

As I landed in New York for a brief stay before heading for Pakistan via Turkey a realisation dawned on me — all along the tour I had never been colour conscious. Unlike Britain, where I was acutely aware of my status as a foreigner, I felt quite at home in the US. This was surprising because the subcontinentals have more in common with Britain than with America. While prejudice is a human condition and the Americans are not above it, I did not find race to be the basis of American prejudices. Instead, what the Americans seemed to take pride in was their country's economic, political and technological power. Besides, unless he is psychopathic, an American cannot pass normal life if he does not adjust to the reality of America's multiracial character. Anti-Americanism has never been an article of faith with me. In fact my attitude is similar to what Bhutto once said about himself vis-à-vis the British — "I am reasonably anti-British". I may be more Arab than an Arab when it comes to America's Palestine policy, but that has nothing to do with accepting the fact that the Americans recognised the reality of a multicultural, multiracial milieu much before Europe started to come to terms with the immigrant phenomenon toward the end of the twentieth century. All along the six-week journey in which geographical and demographic features ranged from Charlottesville in Virginia to Berkley in California, I did not feel self-conscious and had no difficulty in interacting with people. This helped me a great deal when I returned to the US in November 1992 to take up my assignment as Dawn's Washington correspondent.

I was assailed by doubts whether I would be able to do justice to the job. It is true I began my career in journalism as a reporter first in PPA (now PPI) and later in The Times of Karachi, but in Dawn I have all along been on the desk, the reporting assignments being mostly a welcome diversion from writing editorials or editing a magazine. Besides, reporting on summit conferences or presidential visits is entirely different from what one is supposed to do as a foreign correspondent — and in Washington D.C! How can you get exclusive reports for your paper if you do not have friends and "moles" inside government departments that matter, and what chance did I ever have of having contacts in the Pakistan Embassy, the State Department, Congress and the White House? Yet, America is easy to report, if you learn to make use of the Freedom of Information Act and the sunshine laws, and be selective. The last point is important, because plenty of information is available to you, and you are in serious danger of getting lost in information and tons of fliers on issues which are of no interest to you or may, at best, are of marginal interest. I experienced this phenomenon several times whenever there were Asia-Pacific rim summits or high-level conferences involving America and Mexico (surprisingly, Canada is seldom in the America media) and states further south in Latin America. The Foreign Press Centre, run by the State Department for the benefit of the hordes of non-American journalists in the D.C., would flood us with information that was often tempting but was of little use to me. But the first problem was that of finding a home.

Initially, I lived with Yameen Zubairi, one of my classmates at the B.Y.J. High School and my volleyball team captain, at his Potomac,

Maryland, home, a virtual ranch. The weather was harsh, snow had not yet fallen, and in spite of autumn the trees still had leaves. Having never practised the "early to bed and early to rise" principle in my life, I thought I had a chance to live up to this adage. Dinner was taken at 6 and I did hours of reading to find that it was still 10pm. When I woke up at 6 it was still dark. "Here is a chance", I said to myself. "I could discard decades of habit which newspaper work had given me and be really a good boy by going to bed and rising early. It was late November, and Yameen suggested, and rightly, that I should have a home in Washington D. C. so that I could be closer to my sources of news — the White House, the State Department, Congress, the Foreign Press Centre and the Pakistan Embassy. Looking at Yameen and his career I have often wondered how astonishing it was that a school set up in a hurry in the aftermath and chaos of partition should have produced some brilliant scholars. Yameen has two masters and a PhD and has taught and done research work in biology, toxicology, biochemistry and human physiology at some of America's leading universities, including the University of California, Berkley, University of Wisconsin, Madison, University of Minnesota, Minneapolis, University of Maryland, Baltimore; US National Cancer Institute and National Institute of Child Health.

The unseen hand was at work when Yameen took me one day by metro to the Voice of America office on Independence Avenue, to meet Nazakat Ali Khan, a common friend who worked for the VOA's Urdu service. I had known Nazakat since days he worked for the government-run news agency APP in Karachi. The two took me to a nearby apartment building, whose manager, a friendly black, studied some charts and said, "Do you want an apartment here or in that building?" pointing to a high-rise opposite. I said that made no difference to me, and I left it to him. My main worry was how I would manage my food. There were no doubt some restaurants nearby, but you cannot live on restaurant food. Then he said, "I am giving you apartment 130 in this building". Unknown to me Safia Kazim lived in apartment 230, which was right above 130.

My food problem was solved. I have since then often wondered what it would have been like if the manager had given me an apartment in the other building.

When I first visited the VOA office in Yameen's company, a very impressive-looking, bespectacled woman in a sari seemed engrossed in work. I approached her only to convey the good wishes which Hameed Zaman and Badar Rizwan, her former colleagues at Radio Pakistan, wanted me to convey to her. Badar is a relation of mine, and is still working for Radio Pakistan now when he is in his eighties.

Safia had come to the US earlier in the year (1992) and, instead of living alone, invited a friend, Nuzaira Azam to live with her. Nuzaira then used to work in the Pakistan Embassy's Press Section and from the point of view of a newspaper man her position was priceless for me. When Razia joined me in 1993, we became a family that also included our common friend, Mrs Khan, who was with me and Qamar at the American Embassy. Later Arshad and his wife Sue were trapped by Safia into friendship. Arshad never recalled Safia ever being her university colleagues, but he had no choice but to admit what in any case wasn't much of an embarrassment. Sue and Arshad are a lovable couple and epitomise the success of marriage between two people belonging to totally different cultural backgrounds. Soon Mona, Safia's daughter, who was a medical student at Karachi, came on her first visit to her mother. Naughty and mischievous to the core Mona added colour to our family. Like all mothers, Safia was keen to become mother-in-law, and people from other cities came to "see" Mona in the Pakistani style. Often, they stayed with me. For Mona, entertaining guests who had come on probing missions was a source of fun, and she told us countless jokes about boys and their families who had come to "see" her in Karachi. Safia, Mona, Nuzaira, Arshad, Sue, Mrs Khan, Razia and I felt ourselves to be part of a family and it goes without saying that we enjoyed every moment of our lives in the US because 9/11 was nine years away. Shopping was Safia's hobby, and as Mrs Khan once put it, "Safia goes to the mall one day to shop and the next day to return things".

Sue and Arshad had met as students. Arshad had a Masters in Sociology and taught at the University of Karachi before going to the U.S. in 1970 for his doctorate. He acquired another Masters and Ph.D. in Sociology from Michigan and taught at different universities before settling in the Washington DC area. He met Sue in Michigan, where Sue was getting her Masters in Library Science. They married in Kalamazoo, Michigan, in 1977 and eventually moved to Silver Spring, Maryland, to take teaching positions. Sue became a media specialist with the Montgomery County educational system and Arshad became Associate Professor of Sociology/Criminal Justice with the University System of Maryland. Our visits to their Maryland home – if not every week then at least once a month – were something Razia and I looked forward to.

With the exception of Mrs Khan, whom I had known since 1955, none of this group was known to me till I came to Washington, but with the benefit of the hindsight I can say that what brought us together was, by chance, a common political philosophy, for none of us tormented each other by airing political views that someone would consider obnoxious. For an understanding of the Pakistani mind, it is essential to know that every Pakistani is a born politician, he takes politics seriously, and he finds it difficult to have a harmonious relationship with a person who is not on his side of the political divide. There is always a divide. For me, especially, the membership of this group was a joy, because one of my greatest weaknesses is an unfortunate inability to have normal social intercourse with Pakistan's perceived enemies. This attitude has done me enormous harm and deprived me of the friendship of many nice people, though I have continued to wonder till this day if an enemy of Pakistan can really be a nice person. If he is Pakistan's enemy he must be a scoundrel.

What I have often failed to realise is that hypocrisy is an essential part of political articulation. If you blurt out what you actually believe to be your genuine political views then you are acting contrary to Dale Carnegie's advice on how "to win friends and influence people". Elsewhere in the world I have found supreme hypocrisy reigning in the airing of one's political views, and how despicable ideas — views that run counter to all accepted human values — are dished out in the garb of noble phrases that would seem more appropriate for inclusion in the United Nations Declaration of Human Rights. For instance, Dr. A. Q. Khan, Pakistan's atomic genius, has been denounced by the Western propaganda machine as an evil man, a thief and a spy who invented a lethal death machine. But Shalhevet Freier, who was also an active member of the Pugwash Council, was also the father of the Israeli nuclear bomb. This Pugwash Council had the blessings of two of the world's greatest anti-war crusaders — Albert Einstein and Bertrand Russell — and was set up in 1955 following the release of correspondence between the two and was known as Russell-Einstein Manifesto. But one has to be a supreme hypocrite to combine in himself the contradictory roles of a crusader for world peace and a builder of nuclear weapons. Evidently, the Pakistani mind is incapable of such hypocrisy. But back to my job — reporting for Dawn.

AAK had briefed me thoroughly on my reporting priorities. First, the US-Pakistan relations; second, the US-India ties, because they had an impact on Islamabad's relations with Washington in what has always been a zero-sum game between Pakistan and India; third, American policy toward the Arab and Islamic world (the slaughter of the Muslims of Bosnia was then going on), fourth, America's relations with China, and fifth anything that made news. In the beginning I was panicky, because there was no office, no stationery, and no contacts, and my only assets for setting up an office were a fax machine and a TV set which Tariq Zaheen, who reported for Dawn before I reached Washington, had given me, besides Yameen's electric typewriter. My apartment was unfurnished, and I had to rent some furniture: a sofa that could be turned into a bed, a small, round dining table with three chairs, and a small working table that could hardly accommodate Yameen's typewriter and a chair. The money that Dawn gave me was limited, but I had to make use of it to purchase some blankets, two pillows and a kettle. Yameen also gave me some pots and pans. A greater problem was electricity. In Pakistan homes, the electrification scheme provides for wall lights, but in most apartments in America electrical fixtures are provided in bathrooms and kitchens, and you have to purchase lamps to light up your rooms. I did not have money to buy lamps, so initially I used to work mostly in the well-lit kitchen. One day, while closing my day's work, I brought the top of the electric typewriter down in such a manner that it cut the electric wire, there was a small flash as negative and positive met, and the entire apartment went dark. It was a Friday evening, and when I went to the leasing office to complain the only man working there told me that an electrician would not be available till Monday morning! Earlier in the day, a more fearsome incident had occurred. I had gone to the Foreign Press Centre for some work, but when I returned I found my money belt slightly away from where I had left it. I checked it to find $60 missing. I had no intention of lodging a complaint with the leasing office, but the mere thought that a burglar could enter my apartment was scary. The scene outside was such as to discourage going out, for Fourth Street South-West was as deserted and desolate at 2pm as it was at 2am. One hardly saw any people; only cars. The following three nights were full of agony. Here I was without a proper office, lying in my convertible sofa in total darkness, my apartment having been burgled, the money I had come with was running out, there was no indication when the next cheque would come from Karachi, and I was supposed to report for my newspaper! With a sinking heart I pictured myself returning to Karachi as a failure who had wasted the company's money on the air ticket.

Finally came Monday, and an electrician restored power by a flick of the knob of the circuit-breaker. I could have done this on the Friday evening myself, but I didn't know where it was. (I am a good detective, and I was determined to find out who stole my money, and thanks to Sherlock Holmes I know that a criminal usually re-visits the scene of crime. I suspected one worker, but I had no evidence. Three months later, the bulb at the entrance to my apartment blew out, and I complained to the leasing office. They said rules required that I pay for it. I agreed. Then the man I suspected came and put a bulb in the holder.

As I went for my pocket to pay for the bulb, he winked at me and said he had managed to get the bulb from somewhere. I instantly knew he was the burglar.)

The biggest problem in settling down and starting work was money. The money I had brought with me was now dwindling, and the man whose duty it was in Karachi to transmit the money to me did not seem aware of my predicament. Personally I believe there is nothing more terrible in a foreign country than to be without money. I had landed in November, and the apartment company had asked me to deposit two months' rent because I did not have a credit history. That made my financial position critical. The cheques came late — sometimes after an interval of two months — and they were in the form of bank drafts payable at the National Bank of Pakistan's New York branch. It was from March 1993 onwards, when Tanvir Ahmad became Assistant News Editor and took charge of all money matters concerning foreign correspondents, that I started getting the cheques regularly. Instead of sending me a bank draft each month, Tanvir would deposit the money in the National Bank of Pakistan's branch in the Haroon House, where the offices of Dawn are located, and I would get the money in a day or two. It was thus in April that I received several thousand dollars extra for "capital expenditure" and set up what can be called a proper office with a computerised word processor, a modern fax machine, plenty of stationery (how I have loved it!), a state of the art TV set with a built-in video recorder, and a personal telephone so as to avoid using the official phone for my personal calls to Pakistan. They say a man should not disclose his pay. But let me do it: my salary initially was $2,500 a month. I do not smoke, much less drink, I have never in my life gone for fancy clothes or shoes, and, when I built a home, I never worried about tile and mosaic — I left these things to Razia. The salary was more than enough for me. America was, or perhaps still, is a cheap country. Food is especially cheap, and grocery worth 100 dollars was more than enough for Razia and me for a week, and even when Nasir, our youngest son, joined us in Washington there was no appreciable increase in the food bill. The apartment's rent was $550, and this included gas and power charges, and the price of The Washington Post on week days was 25 cents. The only luxury I indulged in was the money spent on lunches and dinners which Razia and I often gave for our gang in Pakistani restaurants Our favourite was Food Factory, a Pak-Afghan eatery at Ballston, Virginia, where the Americans sometimes outnumbered Pakistanis. Thus we were able to save $1,000 a month. Soon I became rich — in the land of Bill Gates. I did not own a car because three metro stations — Federal Centre, L'Enfant Plaza and Waterfront — were nearby. Of the four news sources for me — the State Department, Congress, Pakistan Embassy and the White House — the first two were within a walking distance. Besides, Safia's car was as good as mine, and it was a pleasant surprise for me that the speed limit within the District of Columbia was 25 mph.

Establishing a contact with the Pakistan Embassy was a bit awkward initially, because, before my arrival in the D.C., Dawn had published a couple of news items which were unfair to the ambassador, Abida Hussain. AAK had given me a formal letter to the embassy about my posting as Dawn correspondent, but he was quite aware of the awkwardness created by the two unconfirmed news items. His advice to me was: "you have to have a working relationship with the ambassador and the embassy staff. Do not keep yourself so away from the ambassador and the embassy that you miss news; at the same time, do not get too close because that could be counterproductive". While the Foreign Press Centre (FPC) was aware of my arrival in advance and was asking Yameen about my date of arrival, I was wondering when to contact the embassy when the ambassador herself rang up at Yameen's place. The occasion was a TV interview by Benazir Bhutto, who was then in the opposition, and concerned some remarks about Pakistan's nuclear programme in a two-part NBC programme. Abida had been sent to Washington as ambassador by Nawaz Sharif and she wanted me to cover her reaction to Benazir's interview. Her reaction surprised me, because it had nothing to do with Pakistan's recognised position on the nuclear question and made no attempt at damage control if at all Benazir's interview had created a problem for the Pakistan Foreign Office; instead, her reaction seemed to have come not from a Pakistani ambassador but from a Muslim Leaguer, with an eye on Pakistan's domestic politics. The NBC programme and the Benazir interview served to focus the media's attention again on Pakistan's nuclear question. The media claimed that Pakistan had seven nuclear weapons, though White House spokesman Richard Boucher, who later became Assistant Secretary of State for South Asia in the junior Bush administration, said the United States remained "unable to certify that Pakistan does not possess a nuclear explosive device." The implication for Pakistan's domestic politics became obvious when the NBC showed Benazir claiming that during her tenure as prime minister she was not taken into confidence on the nuclear question. This prompted Abida to allege that the PPP Co-Chairperson had chosen to "distance herself from Pakistan's security considerations." The NBC programme, in which Senator Larry Pressler and John Glenn also appeared, said Benazir's fall from power stemmed form the nuclear issue. In a programme watched by millions of Americans, Benazir said: "I think it is criminal that the Prime Minister who is ultimately responsible in the eyes of the people and in the eyes of history should not be taken into confidence on such a major issue." The programme alleged that the former prime minister learnt more from CIA than "from her own military." From Washington I rang up Bilawal House, Karachi, but Benazir was not available for comment. Abida's response to the NBC story was: "it was unfortunate that a claimant to Pakistani leadership should choose to distance herself from Pakistan's security considerations and opt to place such massive reliance on foreign agencies." On the issue whether Pakistan possessed any nuclear weapons, the ambassador reiterated Pakistan's known position — that its nuclear programme was "for peaceful purposes and not weapons-oriented." Boucher's comment was: "we have certainly had serious concerns about their nuclear activities ... We have addressed those concerns repeatedly to the Pakistan government. We've also been actively engaged, both with Pakistan and India, in efforts to prevent nuclear proliferation in South Asia. We've urged both countries to join nuclear non-proliferation regimes, to begin confidence building steps, and to participate in multilateral discussions aimed at averting a regional nuclear arms race." The aid to Pakistan was suspended in October 1990, and Boucher said "the status is still the same. We are unable to certify that Pakistan does not possess a nuclear explosive device."

While I faxed the story from a private post office — because I was still in Yameen's home — Abida invited me over to a lunch which she had thrown the next day for the Pakistani community leaders. The lunch did not turn out to be newsy, but I was astonished by Abida's hostility to Benazir. She told the gathering that Benazir's lobby was the Jewish lobby. She repeated it several times. She resigned as ambassador when Nawaz Sharif lost power in 1993. A decade and a half later, Abida would join the PPP and was in that Benazir procession which was bombed in Karachi on October 18, 2007. Abida's geopolitical idiom was excellent, and she acquitted herself quite well at a time when, at the beginning of the Clinton presidency, the murder of two CIA employees by a Pakistani, Mir Aimal Kansi, had put a strain on US-Pakistan relations.1 (1 On January 25, 1993, Mir Aimal Kansi, using his AK-47, shot dead two CIA officials, Frank Darling, 28, and Lansing Bennett, 66, at the CIA headquarters in Langley, Virginia. He fled to Pakistan, was captured in June 1997, tried and executed by means of a lethal injection on November 14, 2002, in Virginia).   The Charge d'Affaires at this time was Sarwar Naqvi, who would run the embassy during the long interregnum between Abida's departure and Maleeha Lodhi's posting as ambassador when Benazir became prime minister a second time.

During Abida's tenure there was a hilarious faux pas by a ranking Senator, and I must share it with the reader. The Senator belonged to the Senate Foreign Relations Committee, and Abida accompanied by Sarwar called on him as part of her duty to give the ranking Senator Pakistan's views on the relations between the two countries. Abida, quite articulate, spoke in detail about the Kashmir issue and problems of interest to Pakistan while the old Senator, who had been in the upper house for perhaps more than a quarter century, listened to her with rapt attention and offered coffee. When the interview was over, the Senator came up to the door and said to Sarwar, "I must say Mr Ambassador your wife is very talkative. She could be a better ambassador than you are!" There is no doubt about the authenticity of this joke because both Abida and Sarwar told it to me on two different occasions.

Perhaps because of the two news items or whatever the reason I could not establish a relationship of trust with Abida. Consequently this part of my stay in Washington is completely devoid of any worthwhile reporting. She granted me a long interview, which Dawn published, but I never got a tip-off from her for some story. If there was some hard news, she would ring up the APP correspondent, then based in New York, and I would miss the news. It was Maleeha who was instrumental in having an APP man in Washington, D.C. Perhaps because she was not a career diplomat and was like Maleeha a political appointee, Abida did not receive the cooperation she deserved from the embassy's diplomatic staff. For that reason, most people who should have been a source of news to me were indifferent if not hostile to me. The situation would change for the better for me as a result of the political crisis back home, when Prime Minister Nawaz Sharif was sacked by President Ghulam Khan under article 58-2b of the Constitution. Even though the Supreme Court declared the presidential action unconstitutional and Sharif became prime minister again a month later, Abida resigned as ambassador. She had resigned, she said, because the President's action was "extremely unfortunate". The dissolution of the National Assembly in an (American) election year, she said, was "unseemly and incorrect" and was "neither in the interest of Pakistan nor that of the democratic process."

Ghulam Ishaq Khan had dismissed Benazir's government 27 months earlier on charges of corruption, but later inducted some of the "corrupt" ministers into his caretaker government which was to supervise the impending general election. Said Abida

"It is very chaotic and very aberrant behaviour that you accuse people of crime and guilt with public authority 27 months ago and

27 months later you induct them in your cabinet." During his meeting with President Ishaq in Islamabad in March she said she had pleaded within him to "smoothen out" the differences with Nawaz Sharif instead of once again resorting to action under 58-2b. But she did not find Ishaq the same man she had known all these years. She alleged that President Khan "violated the constitution" first in 1988 when as acting president he failed to appoint a caretaker prime minister as required by the constitution. (Abida was wrong: Ziaul Haq himself had chosen not to have a prime minister when he dismissed Junejo's government, and President Khan merely continued with that.) Abida said Ishaq was guilty of "a second violation" when acting as president he nominated "a prime minister (Benazir) even though the Constitution stipulated that a president be elected before a prime minister was chosen." It is interesting to note that, even while criticising Ishaq for using article 58-2b to dismiss Sharif, Abida did not fail to have a dig at Benazir, saying Ishaq's decision to use the same article against Benazir was "not uncalled for" because "Benazir ran the government very incompetently". She said she had always believed President Khan to be among those who put national interests above personal interests. But when she met him last time in Islamabad she was "distressed to find that he was not thinking of Pakistan but of himself. First he thought there was something wrong with Benazir, and Mian Nawaz Sharif was the solution. Then he decided within two years that there was something wrong with Nawaz Sharif, and Benazir was the solution...that shows very faulty judgment". She said she suggested to the president to study Nawaz's proposals for re-amending the Eighth Amendment, since parliamentary sovereignty had to be restored because the circumstances in which the eighth amendment was enacted had changed. But she alleged the president seemed to take a more "literal view of the constitution" and the decision that he ultimately took had more to do with "his vanity" than with national interests. She had been an admirer of the president and had often defended him, but at the end of the conversation she said she "felt horrified". After her meeting with the president she told Nawaz

that the president was close to dissolving the National Assembly and dismissing his government.

Abida had come to Washington 15 months ago, but found the going tough with an administration that had changed from Republican to Democratic, which seemed in no mood to resume economic and military aid cut off in October 1990 because of the Pressler amendment. It was also during her stay in Washington that Pakistan was put on America's "watch list" of countries supporting terrorism, much before Aimal Kansi was to add to Pakistan's misfortunes. But it was also during these 15 months that, in spite of the Pressler amendment, the ban on Islamabad from purchasing military spares was lifted, and commodity aid and population welfare programmes were resumed. On a more poignant note: Nuzaira and I went to the embassy for a farewell call on Abida. Nuzaira was especially close to Abida, and cried, and Abida instructed the embassy staff to look after her. For me Abida had one brief sentence to say, "I am glad I got to know you." Aristocratic by birth, extremely articulate and a lively conversationalist, Abida, nevertheless, had a bluntness that annoyed sections of the Pakistani community and some US-based Pakistani journalists.

The state of US-Pakistan relations about this time was "normal". Pakistan was neither an American ally, as it was in the fifties and sixties, and again after 9/11, nor was Islamabad in a state of confrontation with Washington. In fact, as a review of their relationship shows, the United States and Pakistan have never truly been locked in a hostile relationship. Periods of difficulties — as those in the aftermath of the 1965 war, when the Johnson administration cut off all military supplies to Pakistan — were many, but there is something in Pakistan's geographical location and something in America's own perception of its geopolitical interests in the region in which Pakistan is situated that keep bringing the two countries together periodically. After the 1965 war, Pakistan continued to remain a member of the Central Treaty Organisation and the South-East Asia Treaty Organization, but for all practical purposes America's military relationship with Pakistan came to an end, and the US air base near Peshawar was closed down in January 1970, when Gen Yahya Khan was Pakistan's strongman. During his visit to the US, Bhutto, who assumed power on December 20, 1971, tried to secure American arms for Pakistan but failed, even though, from Pakistan's point of view, the man in the White House was once Eisenhower's Vice President, Richard Nixon, known for his friendly sentiments for Pakistan. His book, In the Arena, begins with friendly references to Pakistan and dwells at length on the role Islamabad played in effecting a rapprochement between the United States and China and the secret visit which Secretary of State Henry Kissinger made from Nathiagali to Beijing.

In his book, Nixon describes the drama attached to the invitation he finally received from Prime Minister Chou En-lai, and how Kissinger ran all the way from his residence to bring him "the most important communication to an American President since the end of World War II". Wrote Nixon: "It was here (the White House) that I received what Henry Kissinger described as the most important communication to an American President since end of World War II. I had been sitting in this same chair catching on some of my reading material after a state dinner that evening. It was almost eleven o'clock. Henry burst into my room. He was breathless. He must have run all the way over to the residence from his West Wing Office. He handed me a message. It was Chou Enl-lai's invitation to visit China, which he had sent through President Yahya Khan of Pakistan. As Chou put it later it was a message from a head, through a head to a head. Neither Henry nor I generally had a drink after dinner but on this occasion we toasted this historic event with a very old brandy".

Even though Nixon would visit China much later after he became America's 37th president, Ayub Khan had suggested to him as far back as 1964 when the two met at Karachi to undertake such a visit. The idea must have sounded bizarre to Nixon, a Republican, at a time when Lyndon B. Johnson, a Democrat, was the man in the White House and the Vietnam war was at its peak. Ayub had just returned from a visit to China, and when Nixon asked him why he wanted him to visit the People's Republic Ayub replied: "People, millions of people in the street clapping cheering, waving Pakistani and Chinese flags". Nixon did visit China in February 1972, becoming the first American president to set his foot on the soil of Communist China, but the reception he was accorded was anything but of the kind the Pakistani president had received. It was, in his words, "eerie". As Nixon notes in In the Arena the streets were deserted. "The curtains on the Chinese government limousine were drawn. But as I looked through the tiny openings, I could see that except for a lonely sentry stationed every few hundreds yards, the streets were totally deserted". Nixon also quoted what he called one of Ayub's "haunting remark(s)" in 1964. President Diem of South Vietnam had been murdered, and many saw an American hand in his assassination. According to Ayub "it is dangerous to be a friend of the United States; that it pays to be neutral; and that sometimes helps to be an enemy".

More than a decade later, when I was in China, my interpreter told me that "every child" in China knew that it was Pakistan which had brought his country and America together. Yet, in spite of this, there was no substantial change in the Nixon administration's attitude toward Pakistan, and military aid was not revived. All that history speaks is America's "tilt" to Pakistan's side during the 1971 Indo-Pakistan war over Bangladesh, Nixon's goodwill toward Pakistan notwithstanding. Kissinger in his book mentions Nixon's angry phone calls every now and then, asking him what Kissinger was doing about the war. Frankly, there was nothing America or China or any power in the world could do anything to help Pakistan, in such a suicidal situation had we Pakistanis placed ourselves.

When Bhutto visited Washington, the Nixon administration was paralysed because of the Watergate scandal, and no major foreign policy initiative was possible. In his speech at the National Press Club in Washington, D.C., Bhutto was asked to speak on the Watergate scandal, and Bhutto said he could not possibly speak on America's domestic problems, "because I do not want a protest note" from Kissinger, who was sitting there. But as a student of American history he said, to a burst of laughter, "You make those gadgets!" Then he asked the Americans to get over with the crisis because it had begun to affect America's foreign relations. A more profound event during the Nixon era was India's nuclear test in May 1974 and Bhutto's decision to launch what the Western media would later call the "Islamic bomb". The Nixon administration disapproved of it, with Kissinger telling Bhutto in Lahore that if he went ahead with the nuclear plans for military purposes, America would make "a horrible example" of Pakistan — remarks which Kissinger later denied. Nevertheless, America was determined not to let Pakistan develop nuclear capability, even though it was clear to all that Pakistan had been left with no choice but to go for the nuclear option because of what obviously was India's challenge to it. Nixon's ouster from the White House, the brief Ford presidency, the Democratic victory in the American presidential election in 1976, and Bhutto's murder by Ziaul Haq were followed by the Soviet invasion of Afghanistan on Christmas Eve in 1979 and the burning of the American Embassy in Islamabad following the seizure of the Grand Mosque in Mecca by anti-Saudi radicals.

The Soviet invasion of Afghanistan on Christmas Eve in 1979 would again turn Pakistan into a front-line state, and Pakistan would once again receive massive doses of America's economic and military aid, besides the CIA's covert aid to the mujahideen, but not before Jimmy Carter would fail to gain a second term. Carter had a strong human rights agenda, and his stature as a world statesman soared when he brought Anwar Saadat and Menachem Begin together at Camp David to do Israel a favour by normalising its relations with the Arab world's most important country in exchange for its withdrawal from the Sinai. The Soviet invasion came as a shock to America, and the administration was under tremendous pressure to respond adequately to the Soviet provocation. But Carter hated Ziaul Haq's barbaric dictatorship and proceeded to place sanctions on Pakistan for its nuclear agenda. Nevertheless, under congressional and media pressure Carter reluctantly agreed to offer

Pakistan a quantum of aid which Zia termed "peanuts" — perhaps the only original bit of geopolitical expression by this country bumpkin. The wholehearted support to anti-Soviet resistance and the big doses of aid would come when Ronald Reagan would capture the White House and herald a Republican era that would last 12 years. Nevertheless, the CIA had begun arming and funding the mujahideen during the Democratic administration, though Carter did not wish to be embarrassed by the Soviet Union, which could display captured American arms used by the mujahideen. Thus began a most bizarre era in a clandestine relationship between Ziaul Haq's Pakistan and Israel when the Soviet-made arms captured by Israel during Arab-Israeli wars were funnelled to the anti-Soviet resistance groups by the CIA. George Crile's book Charlie Wilson's War gives a most interesting and revealing account of the scheming, intriguing and the bypassing of the normal American and Pakistani channels that went into the CIA's aid to the mujahideen — mujahideen who two decades later would turn into the hated terrorists. Such was the love for the anti-Soviet mujahideen in the CIA that several American officials started wearing shalwar-qamees and converted to Islam. Zia was, of course, handsomely rewarded by the Reagan administration in September 1981 in the shape of a five-year $3.2 billion aid package, half of which was for military purposes. The most prized part of the aid package, however, was not the deal over F-16s but America's decision to look the other way while Dr A. Q. Khan worked on the "Islamic" bomb.

I have dwelt at length somewhere else in this book on the price state and society in Pakistan had to pay for its involvement with the resistance to the Soviet occupation of Afghanistan and for the CIA's covert and overt aid to the mujahideen. But it should be understood that the issue is far more complex than is generally considered. A difference should be made between what Pakistan had to do in the face of the Soviet invasion of Afghanistan and how Pakistan did it. If the Soviet invasion posed a threat to Pakistan's security — just as the invasion of its neighbour by a superpower would do any state in the world — Islamabad's response should not have taken the form it did. An analogy should not be drawn between Pakistan's role in the US-led war on terror during the Musharraf era and the way the Ziaul Haq government acted when the brains in the Reagan administration thought time had come for the US to settle scores and turn Afghanistan into Russia's Vietnam. As time passed and the resistance to the Soviet occupation grew, America developed a partnership with a military regime that was headed by a strongman whose mental horizons were those of a traffic cop. But a traffic cop can be honest; Zia used the Islamic bogey merely to consolidate his power and persecute the Pakistan People's Party in a manner that he thought would render it impossible for Bhutto's party to regain power again. The exact number of people jailed and publicly whipped by Zia's military courts ran into thousands, but — with Carter and his human rights agenda gone and Reagan in the White House — Zia enjoyed unqualified American backing, and aid continued to pour in. Islamabad's real gain, however, was Congress's indifference to its nuclear plans. It was not until October 1990 that George Bush Sr. would decide not to issue the certification required under the Pressler law.

Unlike the general impression, Larry Pressler's move initially helped Pakistan by skirting the Symington amendment. The Symington amendment, made in 1976 to the Foreign Assistance Act, 1961, forbade American aid to any country suspected of a nuclear programme geared to military purposes. Pakistan, thus, was not entitled to America's economic and military aid because its nuclear plans had started gaining Western attention. France had reneged under American pressure on its agreement with the Bhutto government to supply a reprocessing plant to Pakistan, but that had not deterred Bhutto from making Pakistan a nuclear power. As he had said on one occasion, "I want to bring Islamic civilisation on a par with Christian, Buddhist and Hindu civilisations". Dr. A. Q. Khan had come to Bhutto voluntarily from Holland and, even though a metallurgist, he had come armed with the uranium enrichment technology he had acquired at the Dutch nuclear plant he worked for. American intelligence knew this, and as a rule all American aid should have been cut off under the Symington amendment. But in 1985

Larry Pressler, a Republican Senator from South Dakota, came up with amendment, named after him (Section 620E[e] of the Foreign Assistance Act) that the aid to Islamabad could continue if the American president issued a certificate which assured Congress that he was satisfied that Pakistan was not engaged in a secret plan for manufacturing nuclear weapons. Since American aid packages are voted upon each year by Congress, Presidents Reagan and Bush continued to issue the certificate every year. However, once the Soviets pulled out of Afghanistan, Pakistan seemed to have lost its utility to the US, for George Bush stopped issuing the certificate, and the aid to Pakistan came to a halt in October 1990.

Pakistan being on the "watch list" of terrorism and the freeze on the sale of the F-16s were the two major issues between Pakistan and the United States when Bill Clinton began his presidency. I watched the inauguration parade on Pennsylvania Avenue, which was about 10 minutes walk from my home. On the way I asked a cop for help for catching a glimpse of the parade and the cop told me I would not be able to be anywhere near the parade. Obviously he did not know what a crowd means for an American and what it means for a Pakistani. Like any other Pakistani I have watched and taken parts in mammoth rallies where sometimes people would stand for hours in rows perhaps 20 deep to catch a glimpse of their leader. Nevertheless I still expected a large crowd to watch the inauguration parade about which I had heard so much. However, as I reached Pennsylvania Avenue I was at the front row and watched the parade. Because of the extreme cold, I had on a Mongol cap made of fur, with forehead, ears and the back of the neck fully covered. "Excuse me, sir" said a man in the crowd. "Are you from Russia?" I replied that I was from Pakistan, but questions like the oft repeated — "Oh, you speak excellent English. Where did you learn it?" — give a fairly good indication of the basic simplicity of the common American and his appalling lack of knowledge of the world outside. Yet this simplicity is grounded in his soil, for an average American's knowledge about his country is simply amazing. You ask him about the civil war and the national parks and the details he will give you would make you think he is a Ph.D. He may in fact be a high school dropout, but his educators had their priorities right.

For me the State Department was the main source of news, followed by Congress and the White House. Anyone can attend the committee hearings because they are open to the public. For the White House, you needed a pass. But even in those pre-9/11 days, the moment you applied for a pass you were put under surveillance, which may last up to six months. I did not want that. Not that I was not being watched. All foreign journalists are watched everywhere in the world. Democratic countries do this as much as dictatorships. In America, even though 9/11 was nine years away, acts of terrorism involving Muslims had already occurred. Besides the bombing of the World Trade Centre on Feb 26, 1993, involving a blind Egyptian cleric, Sheikh Omar Abdul Rahman (though the master mind was Ramzi Yousuf, who was later arrested in Pakistan in February 1995), Aimal Kansi had brought shame to Pakistan. The motive behind Kansi's criminal deed is not yet clear, more than a decade after his execution. But he had only added to Pakistan's misfortunes, because Pakistan was already on America's "watch list" of countries supporting terrorism. So if foreign journalists, especially Muslim, were being watched that did not surprise many. Maybe I was wrong, but often I had a feeling that my movements were being watched and my fax messages were intercepted. One clear proof of this came one day. Razia was to join me in Washington, and I had to go to New York to receive her at JFK. However, one day while I was talking to an official of the Foreign Press Centre, I told him I would not be available on a certain date, and he said "Yes, you are going to New York to receive your wife." He suddenly froze, realising perhaps too late that he had given himself away. Till then I had no friends at the FPC whom I could have told about my visit to New York. I pretended not to have noticed his faux pas. Sometimes, on entering my apartment, I had a feeling that someone had visited my home in my absence. But I did not care. I had nothing to hide, and if some agents were doing their duty to their country that was fine with me. Besides I did not care about a White

House pass was because the briefings at the White House are mostly devoted to America's domestic issue, unless the president himself turns up to say something about a foreign policy issue. That was rare, but as the Clinton presidency progressed, Pakistan figured at his press conferences quite often, and invariably he sounded friendly to me. The one foreign policy issue that consistently came up at the White House briefings was Somalia. Pakistan had sent troops to Somalia and suffered casualties and that invariably received very sympathetic comments from Clinton. For me, as for most foreign journalists, however, it was the State Department that mattered, and I never bothered to obtain a permanent pass because my FPC identity card was enough for entry into the daily briefings which began at noon daily.

Unlike what it appears on the television screen, the State Department briefing room is rather small, and dimly lit. The spokesman for the greater part of my stay in Washington was Mike McCurry. The briefing seldom began at noon, because Mike used to obtain briefings from his bosses till the last minute before coming to face the media. In the first row sat the correspondents of the Washington Post, the New York Times and AP, "the Israel lobby", and Mike took questions from them first. However, sometimes issues concerning Pakistan were of vital interests to the Clinton administration, and the briefing began with the State Department's view of a given development in South Asia. Then he would take questions from South Asian correspondents. Nevertheless, going to the State Department daily was a waste of time, for there were days in a row when there was absolutely nothing worth reporting for Dawn. Then I went to the State Department only when I was alerted by the Pakistan Embassy or by someone in the State Department. The best place from every point of view, and if something came up unexpectedly at the State Department, was the FPC.

A visit to the FPC was never a waste time. From my home on 3-G Street, South-West, I would be at the FPC in 15 minutes — five minutes' walk to the metro station, four minutes of metro ride and another five minutes into the FPC. Once there one had the benefit of watching all the three briefings — by the State Department, White House and the Pentagon — on the big screen. Besides, other foreign journalists — Indians, Arabs, Europeans, Latin Americans and Americans reporting for foreign newspapers – were there and this helped. The time difference between Pakistan and America's east coast — nine hours in summer and 10 in winter — was both an advantage and a disadvantage. That meant it would be 10pm in Pakistan when I returned home from the FPC or State Department at say 1 pm local time. By the time I had finished my story or stories, depending upon how long they were, it would be 2pm Washington time and the Dawn newsroom would be closing most copy at 11pm, except the front page stuff. After 2pm, with the deadline in all Pakistani newspapers over, I had lunch, did some reading and relaxed. Then I would go to the FPC for a second visit in the evening, for by then the transcripts of all the three press briefings held earlier would be available and I could go through them and sometimes get material for more investigation for news items to be sent early next morning. On TV there may not necessarily be a development of interest to Pakistan, but there may be other purely American developments that would interest Dawn readers — like the president's state of the union messages, the ever-green Middle Eastern question, any American initiative on Bosnia (then a crisis spot), the US-China relations, the perennial congressional hearings, and local developments like the Paula Jones case and Monicagate that rocked the Clinton presidency. While I would watch TV, take notes and prepare draft stories, the next day's newspapers would add to my perspective. This would constitute my first batch of the stories of the day. I must add that this was utterly unprofessional.

A foreign correspondent is not supposed to file a story daily like a metro reporter. A story may come his way, but it is doubtful that this would happen every week, much less every day. The job of a foreign correspondent is to investigate, gather facts and then send exclusive stories to his paper. I did send many exclusive stories, which Dawn carried as leads, but getting exclusive stories in America for a Third World correspondent is not that easy. Cultural barriers stand in the way. FPC officials admitted that it was easy to arrange interviews for European, Japanese and Arab correspondents and that their job became difficult when it came to Third World journalists. Until Warren Christopher became the Secretary of State in the Clinton administration, the Assistant Secretary of State for the Middle East also used to handle South Asia. Christopher created a new post, that of Assistant Secretary for South Asia, the first to head it being Robin Raphel. She was widowed when her husband, Arnold Raphel, American Ambassador to Pakistan, was asked by Ziaul Haq to accompany him on the fateful C130 flight. He died in the mysterious crash in Bahawalpur in August 1988.

I remember one of her press briefings for Pakistani and Indian journalists for three reasons. First, we were told that Secretary Raphel was not to be identified, and that our reports should quote "a senior American official". I conformed to this understanding, but the problem was that all down the story it was nauseating to repeat "the senior American official". If to break monotony I used "he" then it would be factually incorrect; if I wrote "she" Mrs Raphel would be identified. Nevertheless, my story published in Dawn of October 30, 1993, contained "the senior American official" or "the senior US official" all along. The press conference was held on the eve of her visit to Pakistan and India and turned out to be very uncomfortable for the Indians, for Robin emphasised the need for a Kashmir settlement several times and pleaded for an end to rights abuses by the Indian army in occupied Kashmir. A few days earlier, Clinton had addressed the UN General Assembly and called for a Kashmir settlement. I think Clinton should be given full marks for what was an act of audacity from the Indian point of view. The Indians were piqued. A Sri Lankan journalist, who worked for an Indian newspaper, asked Robin whether Clinton's assertion that Kashmir was a disputed territory was an attempt to internationalise the issue. She replied that Kashmir was a disputed territory, and it was the American government's policy that Pakistan and India must have a dialogue to resolve the dispute. When the Sri Lankan requested a follow-up question and said there was a storm in New Delhi over the Clinton speech, she replied that it was "easy to create a storm in Delhi". Then an Indian newswoman said that if President Clinton's speech was seen in the context of the US attitude on human rights in Kashmir and the bid to re-emphasise the international character of the Kashmir dispute, then it appeared that the Indians were being made to "accept the unthinkable" and write off Kashmir. Robin — "the senior American official"— said the US had no desire to make India accept the unthinkable. The US position was that a solution must be found to the Kashmir dispute. While Washington had not offered to mediate, it was willing to help in a Kashmir settlement if the parties asked for it. Three, at least one Indian journalist broke the understanding and named her in his story. The man was penalised and was kept out of several subsequent briefings.

WITHIN months of assuming presidency, Clinton ran into problems with Congress because the Senate rejected some of his nominees to important cabinet posts. Even though Congress still had a Democratic majority, the issues centred round the powers which the three organs of the state — the executive, the legislature and the judiciary — have to check each other and which are often a source of tension if not conflict between Congress and President. Unlike other parliaments, Congress is perhaps the only legislature which has a meaningful say in foreign affairs, unlike parliamentary democracies, where the legislature, whether unicameral or bicameral, is a debating forum. The opposition may tear the ruling party or coalition's foreign policy apart, but there is nothing it can do to block the executive's foreign policy initiatives, and it is left to the government to get wisdom from the opposition's criticism, which is often politically motivated and is exaggerated. In the United States, there is, in the first place, no such thing as an opposition party in the strict sense of the term. The President may be a Republican while the Congress may have a

Democratic majority (as is the case today, 2007). This may serve to create hurdles in the way of the administration's handling of foreign policy and may even frustrate the president's vital diplomatic initiatives. The American constitution gives Congress two major instruments of control over foreign policy. One is the Senate's role in money bills. Throughout the world, it is the lower house where the money bills originate; in America, however, the Senate must approve every piece of budgetary legislation, which obviously includes all foreign aid appropriations, and gives the administration the powers to — to use a cliché — advance America's global interests. However, in this harsh world of geopolitics, foreign aid constitutes both carrot and stick, for the administration can reward or punish a recipient government by continuing with the aid, curtailing it, denying it altogether or attaching conditionalities to it, as has been in the case with several countries, especially Pakistan, where at least two punitive pieces of legislation — the Pressler amendment and the aid bill assented to by President George Bush in mid-2007 — were Pakistan-specific. While the Symington amendment, referred to above, was of a general nature and prohibited American aid to any country that pursued a nuclear programme geared to military purposes, the Pressler amendment, as discussed above, was Pakistan specific. Similarly, the aid bill for Pakistan passed by a Congress that had a Democratic majority in the summer of 2007 linked aid to Islamabad to a certificate from the President that Pakistan was doing all it could in the war on terror. Among the law-makers who showed extraordinary zeal for attaching conditions to Pakistan was House Speaker Nancy Pelosi. It is disputable that Nancy was guided solely by some anti-Pakistan bias; she was guided more by the anti-war wave and the rising American casualties in Iraq and, like other Democrats who were feeling euphoric over their triumph in the mid-term elections in November of 2006, wanted to frustrate the Republican administration. That President Bush could have vetoed the Pakistan-specific bill goes without saying. Even though he and other Republican officials had expressed serious reservations over the bill, which was spearheaded by some Democratic Congressmen belonging to the India caucus and known for their anti-Pakistan views, a presidential veto might not have served its purpose, for there was no guarantee that the bill would not be tossed back to the White House by a two-thirds majority, in which case the President has to sign it. The other, even more effective lever in the Senate's hand in the realm of foreign policy concerns the treaties which the federal government may sign with foreign powers. The American reaction to the questions of war and peace in the "old world" has varied between two extremes — complete isolationism and over involvement. Its true involvement in world affairs came in the aftermath of World War II following the end of the British and French empires, the perceived "communist threat" to the "free world", and the emergence of the Soviet Union as the other superpower. Otherwise as late as the outbreak of World War I, some organisations were recruiting Americans in the German army.

In January 1993, President Clinton nominated Zoë Baird for attorney general, and the Senate, which must approve all presidential nominations, began hearings. The press reported that Baird had hired two illegal immigrants from Peru for her children as a babysitter and a driver and had not made social security payments. The Senate could have rebuffed the president by rejecting the appointment. Instead, it conveyed to the White House unofficially that it would not accept her appointment. To spare the president the embarrassment of having to withdraw her nomination, Ms Baird herself requested Mr Clinton that her nomination be withdrawn. As her replacement, Mr Clinton chose Kimba Wood, a black. Again, unbelievable as it may sound, during Senate hearings it transpired that Wood, too, had employed illegal immigrants for her children. This nomination also went up in smoke. Fed up, President Clinton then chose a woman who was unmarried - Janet Reno. The issue for the Senate and the US public was simple: how could a woman who had violated a law - howsoever minor - be trusted with the office of attorney-general? Those fond of West-bashing must ask themselves: are we anywhere near these standards of morality, our Islamic pretensions notwithstanding?

There was another case of corruption in America. A Clinton aide used a government helicopter to go to his golf course. The press reported the matter, and the man lost his job. The White House staff offered to pay collectively for the petrol consumed in the short flight to the golf course. But that was not accepted. The issue was: he had used a government facility for personal use. Janet Reno was the woman who presided over a massacre at Waco, Texas, on April 19, 1993, to end the 51-day stand-off when she had a go at David Koresh's ranch headquarters where he and his followers — some of them believed to be hostages — had barricaded themselves. The crackdown led to the death of 79 people, including Koresh himself, 51 adults, including two pregnant women, and 21 children. Fourteen years later I could not help draw an analogy between what happened at Waco and at Islamabad's Lal Masjid in July 2007. In both places, pseudo-religionists had brainwashed their followers into unquestioning loyalty. When some parents complained to the American government that their sons and daughters had been held hostage by Koresh, the head of the Branch Dravidians denied the charge and said the boys and girls were there on their own. Koresh's aims were as vague as those of the Ghazi-Aziz brothers, leaders of the rebellion at Islamabad. Koresh came from a broken home, and never in his life was he able to have a stable relationship with females who ranged in age from 11 to those in their sixties. He slept with an astounding number of girls and women, claimed he had the right to have 140 wives and 200 concubines and fathered at least 15 children. He claimed to be the Messiah and was reportedly murdered by his deputy when the crackdown began. But apart from the charges of hostage taking, which have remained unproved, Koresh violated no law, he harassed no one outside his ranch headquarters, he did not send out commandos to raid shops and massage parlours and kidnap law-abiding citizens like the Ghazi-Aziz brothers did in Islamabad.

Clinton's frustrations with Congress did not end with the Kimba Wood rejection by the Senate. Even though Clinton always appeared calm, cool and confident, at least once he lost temper, snubbed a TV reporter and walked away, turning what would have been a long press conference into a one-question session. The occasion once again was a woman he had named for the US Supreme Court —Ruth Bader Ginsburg. A few days earlier he had second thoughts on Lani Guinier, whom he had chosen for the post of Assistant Attorney General to head the Civil Rights Division in the Justice Department. However, he withdrew her nomination after her "racist" views on civil rights became known. Lani Guinier, a law professor and a black, thus, became the third woman to have suffered that fate after Zoë E Baird and Kimba Wood fell victim to "nannygate". The Lani affair had especially hurt the President because some White House aides had thoroughly bungled the job, giving the president the go-ahead for her nomination without having read the law professor's controversial views. This time Clinton was cautious and took 87 days to make a decision —the first nomination of a Supreme Court judge by a Democratic President in 26 years. Clinton seemed moved and was in tears when Ginsburg finished her speech. Then ABC's Brit Hume asked a rather long-winded question which was less a query and more an indictment. He said: "The withdrawal of the Guinier nomination, sir, and your apparent focus on Judge Breyer, and your turn, later it seems, to Judge Ginsburg, may have created an impression, perhaps unfair, of a certain zigzag quality in the decision-making process here. I wonder, sir, if you could kind of walk us through it, perhaps disabuse us of any notion we might have along those lines." An angry Clinton abruptly ended the press conference and walked away after replying, "I have long since given up the thought that I could disabuse some of you of turning any substantive decision into anything but a political process. How you could ask a question like that after the statement she just made is beyond me." White House press Secretary Dee Dee Myers said President Clinton could not take further questions because many, including the First Lady, had started applauding and moving away.

Clinton's foreign policy, too, was coming under attack in Congress, especially in the Senate whose Foreign Relations Committee seemed to be on the warpath. Personally I feel America's committee system is the finest example of democracy in action. I attended quite a few of committee sessions, especially when foreign relations committees of the Senate or the House of Representatives grilled the Clinton administration officials on issues relating to Pakistan and India. Such was the power and prestige of the committees that when they appeared before the committee, the administration officials often looked like errant school boys before a teachers' committee. The Senate Foreign Relations Committee was then headed by Senator Claiborne Pell (D-R.I), but its most feared member was Jesse Helms, Senator from North Carolina, because he could be quite nasty and was responsible for the rejection of more presidential nominees for top posts than any other senator. On one occasion, he had Warren Christopher in his iron grip at the Dirksen Building, which houses the Senate Foreign Relations Committee. Other Senators also grilled Christopher, but none of them was half as malicious as Sen. Helms, who seemed determined that day to skin the U.S. Secretary of State alive on foreign policy, which in his opinion resembled "the streets and highways" of Washington D.C. – all "torn up." Christopher, who like Cassius "seldom smiles", kept his cool, and it is a matter of opinion who was more convincing. But the exchanges that November day in 1993 in the Senate Foreign Relations Committee served to testify the power which constitutional institutions wield in a democracy. Of late, Senator Helms had been very unhappy with the way the Clinton administration had been conducting its foreign policy, especially its handling of Somalia and Haiti, if not Bosnia, which by then was on the backburner. To add to his discomfiture, old Carter hand Christopher found himself under attack from Congressmen on both sides of the aisles, not only for perceived foreign policy blunders but also for why he had been allegedly avoiding an appearance before the Senate Foreign Relations Committee, and why he cancelled a scheduled appearance before it in October. The duel with Senator Helms began after Christopher finished reading his opening statement that covered in his words "the strategic priorities of American foreign policy" in the post-Cold War world in which stability would be based not upon old-style confrontations but on "common interests and shared values."

Senator Helms, who had ten minutes to speak, began on a very emotional tone, referred to the moving sight of young Americans singing Navy Hymn, which has verses from the Bible, said those who died in Mogadishu "were sent on a useless mission", and then fired a broadside on the Secretary himself by adding that what was "equally disturbing" was that in high places "there are some who did not even yet appear to have learned a lesson from Mogadishu." Then, he added, "I challenge anybody to demonstrate that restoring Aristide to power in Haiti is worth one American life." He criticised the multilateralism that seemed to be the cornerstone of American foreign policy and asked, "Are we so bereft of vision that we must defer to an international community before every foreign policy decision?" Even when "bad decisions are made", he said, – like "chasing Aideed, trying to land in Haiti" – "we're scared off by a few two-bit Third World gangsters." He said he once asked "your assistant secretary" for inter-American affairs whether Aristide believed in "necklacing" he replied, "rather sarcastically", saying, "I remember reading something in the Press that Aristide had made a speech in which it could certainly be interpreted by some people to be condoning necklacing at the very least." This was, Helms said, "double talk, double talk, Mr Secretary." He said he had put a similar question to "your human rights assistant secretary, Mr Shattuck," who confirmed that while in power Aristide incited riots, and Haiti's freedom of the press was abridged by violence and intimidation. "And yet we talk about restoring democracy in Haiti. When in the hell, Mr Secretary, did democracy prevail in Haiti?" Calling Haitian President Jean-Bertrand Aristide a murderer who had committed many human rights violations, Senator Helms quoted a press report to say that President Clinton wanted to instal Aristide back to power to please the black community. He was reported to have said, "I just don't have the money, but I can give them back Haiti." He asked Christopher whether it was true that the decision to send ships to Haiti was made by the

Deputy National Security Adviser, and the President said it was made without his knowledge. If that was true, he asked Secretary Christopher "who's in charge?" ..."I regret to say," said Helms "that many Americans can't answer those questions, and when there's a policy nobody seems to explain it; it changes the next day." Senator Pell, Committee Chairman, provided an interlude by asking Christopher to react to reports that Russia had modified its nuclear doctrine. After Christopher had explained the U.S. administration's position on it, Senator Helms was back with his offensive, pinning Christopher down on his purported unwillingness to consult with Congress.

Christopher: "I've been on Capitol Hill for meetings like this with Senators 31 time since I've been in office. Twelve of them have been in formal hearings; 19 of them have been in briefings..... In addition to that I've always tried to be available to Senators. I have a rule that I return all calls from Congress within the day.... I did that with Senator Helms on a matter where he was quite right to call me ... But I want you all to know that I realise that I serve the American people and I serve Congress.... My 31 appearances here, I think, in the time since I've been in office, considering the amount of travel that a Secretary of State has to do, has been a good record, one I don't apologise for.

Helms: When was the last time you were before this committee? I'm not going to argue with you about the 31. I don't know how many times you went to a closed session in the House, and so forth, but when was the last time you were before this committee in this room?

Christopher: Senator, I don't have the date, I'm sure.

Helms: I'll tell you. It was May the 11th. It doesn't matter how many times you've been up here, what does matter you cancelled out on October 15 and October the 19, when all of us needed to know things.

Helms then referred to the State Department's 1992 report on human rights and read out a paragraph which said one Haitian army office was murdered on the order of President Aristide. Then he asked, "It is fair, Mr Secretary, to assume that you do not dispute this part of that report?"

Christopher: I don't dispute the report, but I do know that President Aristide has denied that.

Helms: I said this part of the report.

Christopher: I do not dispute that part of the report.

Helms: Okay.

Christopher: But I do know that President Aristide has denied it himself.

Helms: Well, would you confess to it if the charge was made to it and you had done it? Of course, he denied it! But your own – the own – State Department…. you were not a part of it then, but nobody has disputed this thing. They're just saying, well, we've got to restore democracy in Haiti. And they haven't had democracy, and you sure as hell ain't going to get it, with Aristide back in power. But you don't dispute that part of it, but you don't confirm it either. Is that what you're saying?

Christopher: That's right. President Aristide has denied that, Senator Helms. I might also point out to you that the administration of [senior] President Bush, that filed that report, supported the return of President Aristide, just as we do…….

Helms: Well, you're not going to make any point with me about criticising George Bush's State Department, because I criticised that State Department, too. So, now, do you believe in your heart of hearts that Aristide did order the assassination of his chief political rival, Roger Lafontant? Do you believe that he did or didn't?

Christopher: Senator, I don't know. The allegation was made and he has denied it.

Helm: Well, do you have any credible evidence that anyone other than Aristide ordered that murder?

Christopher: Senator, I have not investigated that particular murder.

Helms: Have you tried to?

Christopher: Pardon me?

Helms: Have you tried to? I think it's significant to know about this man. Just because he denies some thing doesn't give him sainthood.

Christopher: Yes, sir.

Helms: Now, he's been no friend of the Catholic Church. (Helms then quoted a Catholic priest who said Aristide supporters had gutted and destroyed the Vatican Embassy in Port-au-Prince.)

Christopher: I think that the quote you read, Senator, referred to Aristide's supporters. I would say to you once again, Senator, that our support for President Aristide is based upon the fact that he won a democratic election in Haiti which was certified to be an open and free election.

Helms: So did Hitler.

Christopher: Senator, we have to base our judgments on the basis of what the democratic processes were in an adjacent country. And as I say, based upon that and our own contact with him, we think he's worthy of our support.

Helms: Churchill didn't … Well, there's an on-going dispute within the administration as to whether the CIA has its fact straight. Are you among those who are critical…. of the CIA?

Christopher: Senator, I don't discuss intelligence matters in open session. If you'd like to talk to me about that privately, I'd be glad to do so. But I will not talk about intelligence matters in an open session.

Senator Pell then informed the committee that a CIA briefing was scheduled for that afternoon.

Helms: Well, I think ….. the Secretary….he can at least say, "No, I think the CIA did a pretty good job," or "Yes, I have been criticising it." But, you know, to hide behind this classified stuff, when the CIA has made public all of this stuff – and verified it, as far as I'm concerned – well….is it fair to assume that you have received a CIA briefing about human rights abuses during Aristide's rule?

Christopher: Senator, I'm not going to talk about intelligence briefings that I may have received. I've indicated to you that I'll be glad to discuss that with you in private. Senator, I've lived quite a while, and a few people have sometimes misunderstood my courtesy for a lack of resolve. But I think they've been sorry when they've made that mistake. I want you to know I don't intend to discuss these intelligence matters in a public session.

Helms: That's your choice. My time is up.

It was then the turn of Senator Sarbanes (D-Md), who said intelligence matters could not be discussed in public for the purposes of "haranguing the Secretary."

Helms: Mr Chairman, I dislike, and I take offence at that, particularly from Senator Sarbanes, who has beleaguered witness after witness when the president – the previous administration – sent people up here. But you can have your opinion as to when I'm abusing him....

Sarbanes: Well, I didn't say abuse, I said harangue."

Helms: Well, "harangue", what's the difference?

Sarbanes: "Abuses" may be an accurate description of it as well. I'm not going to quarrel over that.

Helms: Well, quarrel if you wish. It suites me fine.

~~~~~~~~~

A MAJOR international event of 1993 and of the Clinton era was the signing of the Declaration of Principles on the lawns of the White House and the famous handshake between Yasser Arafat and Yitzhak Rabin on September 13. Clinton called it "a peace of the brave" that reconciled the security of Israel "with the hopes of the Palestinian people." Mahmoud Abbas, then number three in the Palestine Liberation Organisation hierarchy, and Israeli Foreign Minister Shimon Peres signed the autonomy treaty on the same 124-year-old table that was used nearly one and a half decades ago by Anwar Saadat and Menachem Begin to sign the historic Camp David accord brokered by Jimmy Carter. A day prior to the signing of the agreement, I had my first glimpse of Arafat. He happened to visit the National Press building located at 14-F North-West .I did not know what brought him there. I was going down in an elevator, and as it stopped at a floor and the door opened I saw Arafat walking with his aides down the corridor. He came to the same building a day after the accords were signed to speak at a Washington National Press Club luncheon. The question and answer session was lively, and Arafat gave the audience a full dose of his humour. Men, women and children from all nationalities and ethnic groups proffered their hands to Arafat for a handshake and Arafat obliged them and posed for cameras. The Arabs have no hang-ups about their language. At the White House ceremony, I noted, everybody spoke English except the Palestinian leaders —Arafat and Abbas. Speeches were made by President Clinton, Secretary of State Warren Christopher, Israeli Prime Minister Rabin, Foreign Minister Shimon Peres and the Russian and Norwegian foreign ministers. Clinton, who spoke twice, in the beginning and toward the end, made a brilliant speech, captured the spirit of the moment, referred to Arab and Jewish histories, spoke of Prophet Abraham and Middle East as the common source of eternal values for the world's Muslims, Christians and Jews and pointed to the history of Spain where Muslims and Jews worked together "to write a brilliant chapter" in culture and literature. He said the Arabs and Israelis had pledged "to put sorrows and antagonisms behind them and to work for a shared future, shared by the values of the Torah, the Bible and the Holy Quran." He ended his speech by saying, "Shalom, Salaam and peace". Arafat, the last but one to speak, began his speech with *Bismillah-ir Rahman-ir Rahim* (with the name of God, Merciful and Almighty) in a way that appeared to come naturally to him. So was the case with Abbas. In both cases, there was a world of difference between, on the one hand, our leaders and TV news readers say *Bismillah* and, on the other, the way the two Palestinian leaders said. Both were saying *Bismillah* to themselves, utterly indifferent to what the people of thought, the word *Bismillah* coming to them as naturally as they do to us Pakistanis at home while eating or drinking. In public I have seen our TV news readers say *Bismillah* less to themselves and more to reassure the viewers as to their Islamic credentials. I have also seen how TV news readers in the Arab world utter *Bismillah* and how it comes so natural and normal to them.

Arafat wore a military uniform, his head and part of forehead covered with the traditional black and white kaffiyeh, with a white patch in the middle. Strange as it may sound, Zionist publicists and leaders considered that white patch a sign of hostility because they said it resembled the map of undivided Palestine. Addressing the people of Israel and turning toward where Rabin, Peres and Russian Foreign Minister Andrei Kozyrev were standing, Arafat said the right of self-determination of a people did not mean violating others' rights and said peace and coexistence would be possible only if both Israelis and Palestinians showed mutual determination and courage. "We want to give peace a chance," he added. The signing of the declaration of principles, he said, marked the end of a chapter of suffering for a century and the ushering in of a new era of peaceful coexistence and cooperation, and added that peace in the world was unthinkable without peace in the Middle East. "In moving toward peace", he said, it was the Palestinian and Israeli responsibility to settle the question of Jerusalem, the Israeli settlements and the question of refugees at the negotiations which were scheduled to begin in two years. Rabin, however, reiterated the Zionist belief in Jerusalem being Israel's "eternal capital". In his opening speech President Clinton said the day's agreement had set the stage for what he called "an extraordinary act in one of history's defining dramas" and warned that there were difficulties because "every peace has enemies." Yet, he said, what the Israeli and Palestinian leaders had done "by their tenacity and vision" must be done by others, because "a peace of the brave is within our grasp." In a speech before the signing, Peres said the Israelis did not wish to shape the destiny or lives of the Palestinians because a new era had begun in which the two peoples were moving from "bullets to ballots". He looked forward to an era of good neighbourliness and comprehensive peace that would make "Gaza prosper and Jericho blossom." Rabin, who spoke after the deed had been signed, was most emotional and repeatedly referred to the Jewish and Israeli dead in the Holocaust and in battles with Arabs. Like Peres he ended his speech with a Hebrew prayer and asked the audience to say Amen.

Like millions of people the world over, I took the agreement seriously. The time-table given for the implementation of the DoP and the Interim Agreement on the West Bank and the Gaza (also called Oslo II signed again between Arafat and Rabin) was precise in detail to the point of being arcane and a "final settlement" was to come into being in less than six years. The timetable was:

October 13, 1993 (i.e. within a month of the signing ceremony on the White House lawns), the "Declaration becomes effective. Israeli military administration begins to transfer authority in West Bank and Gaza to 'authorised Palestinians'.

December 13, 1993, Israel and Palestinians to have agreed protocol on withdrawal of Israeli forces from Gaza Strip and Jericho area. Military withdrawal to begin upon signing.

April 13, 1994. Israel to have completed military withdrawal from Gaza and Jericho area. Israel to transfer power to nominated Palestinian authority. Beginning of the first five-year period of interim self-government to a permanent settlement begins.

July 13, 1994. Elections to a Palestinian Council to have been held. Elections to be followed by inauguration of Council and the dissolution of Israeli military-run civil administration in the occupied territories.

April 13, 1996. Israel and the Palestinians to have begun negotiations on a permanent settlement. April 13, 1999. Permanent settlement to be in force."

The DoP is now on the dustbin of history, and Arafat's critics — among them such personalities as Edward Said and Hanan Ashrawi — turned out to be right, not because the agreement itself was a sell-out, as Arafat's enemies made it out to be, but because Israel's post-Rabin governments torpedoed it. Besides, his critics never pointed out what choice Arafat had. They criticised him severely but never came up with a practical alterative. Edward Said's suggestion was Utopian:

let there be one state, with equal rights for the Palestinians, too. Did this theory ever have a chance of being accepted by the Israelis? From day one, the Zionists' aim was to found a Jews-only state in which the Palestinians would not exist or exist perhaps as serfs. The Law of Return, passed by the Knesset on August 23, 1954, said any Jew anywhere in the world had the right to "return" to Israel. No such provision was made for the nearly 700,000 Palestinians who had fled their country during the first Arab-Israeli war (1948-49). Besides, if ever a one-state solution materialised, the Jews would be in a minority because of the higher Arab population growth. The aim before Arafat was clear — has the principle of a Palestinian nationhood and a sovereign Palestinian state been recognised? And he achieved this objective in the face of the odds that were nine to one against him, for those who had denied the very existence of the Palestinian people and regarded Arafat little better than a "terrorist" finally shook hands with him at the White House lawns.

Would the Oslo process have succeeded in its aim and given peace to the holy land if Rabin had not been murdered? Personally I feel even if Rabin had not been assassinated by a Jewish fanatic on November 4, 1995, the peace process had to collapse. It is not that only the religious right on the lunatic fringe was opposed to the DoP; subsequent behaviour by three successive Israeli prime ministers — Benjamin Netanyahu, Ehud Bark and Ariel Sharon — showed very clearly that the Israeli establishment never was sincere in implementing the DoP and found one pretext after another to sabotage it. Netanyahu fought his election campaign on an anti-peace platform; his successor, Barak, promised to revive the peace process but, instead, sabotaged it at Camp David. At a series of summit conferences, including those at the Wye River plantation and attended by Clinton himself, the DoP was virtually renegotiated and altered, throwing out of kilter the entire withdrawal programme and the schedule for the final settlement. The final nail in the coffin of the peace process was driven at Camp David in July 2000, and it seems Clinton had the hammer in his hand.

There is no doubt in his last term in office Clinton wanted to go down in history as a peacemaker; another Democrat, Jimmy Carter, had made a remarkable effort at peace and succeeded in bringing Israel and Egypt to the peace table. The result was Israel's withdrawal from the Sinai in return for Cairo's recognition of the Zionist state. Could he succeed the way Carter did? It goes without saying that Clinton was well armed with the tools of statesmanship, and had the might of the United States behind him; the problem was he was too much of a Zionist to be neutral. When the summit failed, Arafat mad a blunder by leaving for home without giving the world his side of the version; this was a godsend for Israel and America, for the world was made to believe that Barak had made concessions after concessions and that it was Arafat who stood between peace and holy land because he was afraid of peace. Nothing that could be more absurd.

Fortunately, over the decades, a lot of literature has appeared, and some remarkable books have been published which give us a true picture of what happened at Camp David. A most revealing book in my view is The Truth About Camp David: the Untold Story About the Collapse of the Middle East Peace Process by Clayton E. Swisher. From the very beginning, the talks appeared one big scam to the Palestinians because Clinton acted not as a mediator but as a committed Zionist. The American delegation had done no serious homework, and it appeared to the Arafat team as if the Israelis and Americans constituted one delegation. The US side also did not stick to the terms of reference used in previous negotiations, namely UN Resolution 242 (('land for peace'). On two key questions — Palestinian sovereignty over Jerusalem and the right of the Palestinian refugees to return home — the American-Israeli side came up with no meaningful offers. As for the "concessions" Barak offered to Arafat, it is pertinent to examine the Israeli concept of this word. Israel proper today consists of 78 per cent of Palestine; the rest of it, i.e. 22 per cent, has been under its occupation since June 1967. It has established Jewish settlements there, built highways that plough their Palestinian lands and orchards and has completed the Wall whose alignment has enabled Israel to annex more Palestinian land. Israel does not like the word Wall, because it reminds the world of the Berlin Wall, so it calls it "separation barrier". Jimmy Carter calls it the "imprisonment wall". However, when Israeli leaders speak of "concessions" they mean something over and above the 78 per cent of Palestine they already possess. Swisher quotes Israeli and American officials to point out that Barak's concessions were a big hoax, and that the Americans had all their proposals and plans vetted by the Israelis before they were presented to Arafat. Two-thirds of the American delegation consisted of such ardent Zionists as Dennis Ross, Martin Indyk and Madeleine Albright.

Basically, Clinton had only two aims: one, he wanted to go down in history as someone who finally ended the Arab-Israeli conflict; two, he should do nothing that would compromise Hillary's chances in her bid for a Senate seat. Apparently, he found the two aims incompatible, for he could accomplish only the latter. In fact, the second factor was so important that, in the midst of the summit talks, Clinton had to intervene with the press to clarify Hillary's use of profanities against a certain campaign manager who was Jewish. Swisher's findings are based on extensive interviews he did of American, Israeli and Palestinian delegates involved in the marathon discussions, the records of personal conversations available to him, and the truth he was able to establish because of the obvious contradictions that any intelligent observer can detect in a web of lies. According to Swisher, Clinton made "a conscious decision" to break his pledge to the Palestinians and blame Arafat for the summit's failure (p 335).The most unfortunate aspect of the talks was the insulting way in which the Americans and Israelis treated Arafat. When they first met at Camp David, Barak did not even look at Arafat, much less exchange pleasantries. Clinton once shouted at Arafat and said, "It is impossible ... to ignore ... the rights of Jews on the Temple Mount." At one stage, Clinton grasped Arafat's forearm, brought his forehead close to his' and looked like assuming the role of an interrogator — tactics which, according to Swisher, Barak "precisely" wanted (p 299). Clinton also shouted at Ahmad Korei, later Palestinian prime minister, and said, "This isn't the Security Council here. This isn't the UN General Assembly. If you want to give a lecture, go over there and don't make me waste my time. I am the president of the United States..." His shouts could be heard far away.

There was also what Swisher called "an absurd debate" between Clinton and Arafat, with the former giving Judeo-Christian perspective to Jerusalem against the latter's Islamic dimensions. According to the author, Barak and Clinton adopted a "colonial approach to diplomacy: bring in the natives, use ... psychological pressure, and hope they succumb." The man of steel that Arafat was, he refused. He was categorical, "The Palestinian who will give up Jerusalem has not yet been born. I will not betray my people... Don't look to me to legitimize the occupation!"

The peace process died finally when Sharon came to power. Ignoring the warning that he should not visit the Islamic holy sites in Jerusalem, Sharon visited the Sacred Sanctuary (Haram Sharif), thus touching off the second (Al Quds) intifada. He won the elections early next year and became prime minister in 2001. In 2002 he reoccupied the areas which Israel had vacated, destroyed Arafat's headquarters and living quarters in Ramallah brick by brick, and carried out another massacre — in Jenin this time — but failed to break Arafat's nerve. TV viewers the world over saw the Palestinian icon, gun in hand, peering through the window, in a gesture of defiance, while Sharon's tanks stood yards away. But the Oslo process was dead. Two years later Arafat died. Sharon did not allow his burial in his birth place, but he willed that his grave be filled with earth from Jerusalem.

Contrary to the popular belief, the Camp David accords (1978-79) brokered by Carter were not confined to bilateral Egyptian-Israeli matters; they also concerned the Palestinian question and reaffirmed the commitment to UN Resolution 242. Begin also promised to Carter a freeze on the settlements. He broke it. Nobody was shocked more than Carter. His book Palestine: Peace not Apartheid, gives us an insight into the Israeli psyche and points a particular incident where Carter — no more a president — was treated by Begin in a humiliating way. On an unofficial visit to Jerusalem, Carter wanted to remind Begin, then still prime minister, that he had not been faithful to the assurances he had given him about a settlement freeze. But Begin showed no interest in the conversation, responded laconically — "just a few words spoken in a surprisingly perfunctory manner" — and made it plain that he wanted a quick end to the conversation. He snubbed the former US president by holding negotiations with him in a small dimly-lit room. As Carter notes in his book, "We had been sitting in a small, sparsely adorned room ... The exchanges had been cool, distant, and non-productive. As I left, I noticed that the adjacent room was large, brightly lighted, attractive and vacant" (p 107). Carter quotes Sharon as saying what news reports had confirmed him as saying much earlier: "Everybody has to move, run and grab as many hilltops as they can to enlarge the settlements because everything we take now will stay ours...Everything we don't grab will go to them" (p 147). Carter's view of Israel's intentions and the prospects of peace are summarised in these two sentences: Israel believes in "imposing a system of partial withdrawal, encapsulation, and apartheid on the Muslim and Christian citizens of the occupied territories"; and "Israel's continued control and colonisation of Palestinian land have been the primary obstacles to a comprehensive peace agreement in the Holy Land".

Perhaps the most exhaustive study of the Israel lobby's hold over the policymaking apparatus in America has been made by John J. Mearsheimer and Stephen M. Walt in their book, The Israel Lobby and US Foreign Policy. Both Mearsheimer and Walt came under attack and had the usual 'anti-Semitic' epithet slapped on them when they pointed out in the book how the powerful Israel lobby in the US worked against America's interests; how it was patently absurd to say that a strategic alliance with Israel was in America's interest, and how successive US administrations have ignored or even abetted in Israeli crimes to stay on the lobby's right side. The book rocked the Bush administration and upset its neocons and an academia not used to hearing, seeing or researching on anything that may constitute Israel's criticism. The foreword explains how the two scholars — one at the Chicago University, the other at Harvard — found it difficult to get their book published and how publisher after publisher and even prestigious universities and academic institutions refused to print what originally was an essay.

The story began in 2002 when The Atlantic monthly asked the two to write an article on the Israel lobby in the US. The two professors kept the Atlantic editors informed of their research and the central theme, but when the essay was finally in their hand the editors refused to oblige. Disappointed, Mearsheimer and Walt thought of writing a book but were discouraged because none of the publishing companies they contacted was willing to touch a manuscript of the kind. However, somebody gave a copy of the rejected manuscript to London Review of Books, and it agreed to publish a revised version in 2006. This proved to be a turning point for the article which was subsequently posted on some prestigious websites, and despite the initially negative reaction from sections of the media, things began to change and there was a lively debate on the issue. The book was finally published in 2007. The writers' thesis is that America's economic and military aid to Israel cannot be "fully explained on either strategic or moral grounds", and that the Israel lobby which seeks to manipulate American foreign policy consists of "a loose coalition of individuals and groups" who do not even fully reflect the views of the majority of American Jews. This group, according to the authors, has played "key roles" in shaping US foreign policy on Palestine and encouraging the Bush administration to launch the "ill-fated invasion of Iraq", and engage in the "on-going confrontation with Syria and Iran". The book quotes Steven Rosen, a former official of the American-Israeli Public Affairs Committee, as telling Jeffrey Goldberg, a New Yorker journalist, after putting a napkin before him, "In 24 hours, we could have the signatures of 70 Senators". The authors add, "These are not empty boasts"(p 12). Ant-Semitism, the authors say, is a charge that "is a widely used weapon for dealing with critics of Israel".

Some observations by the authors deserve attention: "As of 2005, direct US economic and military assistance to Israel amounted to nearly $154 billion dollars (in 2005 dollars), the bulk of it comprising direct grants rather than loans" (p 24). The generally believed $3 billion figure for annual American aid to Israel is misleading. As pointed out by Congressman Lee Hamilton, because of the other benefits that Israel enjoys, the annual per year figure comes to $4.3 billion (p 27). Most aid recipients get American loans in quarterly instalments, but since 1982, "the annual foreign aid bill has included a special clause specifying that Israel is to receive its entire annual appropriation in the first thirty days of the fiscal year. This is akin to receiving your entire salary on January 1 and thus being able to earn interest on the unspent portion until you used it." (p 27). Similarly American law requires that all defence loans must be utilized in America to keep the US defence industry going. But a special clause allows one fourth of the money to be spent in Israel, thus enabling that country to develop its own arms industry. By 2004, say the authors, "Israel, a comparatively small country, had become the world's eighth largest arms supplier." (p 27)

The Israel lobby persecutes and hounds those daring to criticise Israel. Robert Fisk once went to a missile-manufacturing company in California and showed to one of the top executives the shrapnel of the missile that was used against Palestinian civilians. The company executive begged Fisk not to mention his name in whatever he was going to write. In 2002, Israeli Prime Minister Ariel Sharon sent troops and tanks into areas Israel had vacated, including Ramallah, and had Yasser Arafat virtually under arrest. The book gives us an excellent quote: "Mr Sharon has Mr Yasser Arafat under house arrest in ... Ramallah, and he's had George Bush under house arrest in the Oval Office. Mr Sharon has Mr Arafat surrounded by tanks, and ... Bush surrounded by Jewish and Christian pro-Israel lobbyists, by a vice president, Dick Cheney, who's ready to do whatever Mr Sharon dictates, and by political hardliners telling the president not to put any pressure on Israel in an election year — all conspiring to make sure the president does nothing". The quotation is from a piece in the New York Times by Thomas L. Friedman.

~·~·~·~·~

SETTLING down was quite a problem, and it was not until the middle of 1993 that I could be said to be ready for concentrating on work. I had been to America before, but there was a world difference now, for the things to which a tourist would be utterly indifferent acquired a different perspective when one had a home and tried to pass a "normal" life. While I was on what could be called an extended short-stay, Americans I came across behaved as if I was in for good and demanded proof. Embarrassment was always around the corner. I did not know the street idiom, I was not familiar with some of the fundamental norms of life in America ("Your driving licence, please!", "may I have your social security number?", "Do you have a credit card, sir?"), and I was not used to a five-day week in which a disappointment at a government office on a Friday evening would mean a patient wait till Monday morning. (Pakistan has a six-day week, and I pray to God it stays that way.) Above all, I was not attuned to a system of de-personalised services which serve you well but in which the human touch is lacking. From purchasing a metro ticket to withdrawing money from the bank, it was electronic gadgetry that was at my disposal. How I missed the personalised inefficiency of my native system in which the clerk chatted on the telephone or looked the other way, while you stood at the counter expecting to be served! The absence of people in the streets served to create gloom, for I often felt while taking long walks along the south-west's empty streets, especially during intense cold, that I was in Moscow (I have never been to Russia!) in which the KGB shadowed every pedestrian and all terrified citizens stayed indoors while outside the Siberian winds howled. Sometimes I went out on probing missions for miles, but never once did I come across what could by any standards be called a street crowd. All I saw were cars and dimly-lit homes. Unlike Pakistanis, the Americans do not appreciate well-lit exteriors, and if a dog barked a chill went down my spine, for I am morbidly afraid of dogs and snakes. However, unlike the British, the Americans are not exactly crazy about dogs.

Unlike the 1984 visit to Washington, when the USIS and Delphi took care of me, I was this time closer to life and had to take care of such things as the weekend business hours of the nearby grocery store which sold low-fat milk at a discount, or how her substitute would behave when Nicky is off — Nicky, the beautiful, black post office girl, who made it a point to leave a message in my answering machine that an air registry (that hopefully contained my cheque) had after all arrived from Pakistan. Blacks were then still called blacks, unlike now when they are referred to as Afro-Americans, and for the first time I became conscious of the acute tensions that run through America's social life. The population of the District of Columbia is overwhelmingly black, with whites and the immigrants, mostly Koreans and Japanese ("Asians", as the Americans would say), constituting a minority. But the way the blacks ran America's capital deserved kudos. Unlike the image they had in the past, the blacks were now producing professionals at an astonishing speed, and it was they who manned the District's offices and commercial centres. One of their major achievements was the cleaning of the Potomac river, along which I used to take my daily walk. The promenade by the river that winds its way through the District of Columbia was about 10 minutes of walk from my apartment, and I used to value this exercise. In fact, from the point of its location, my apartment building was a valuable piece of real estate, even though the whites did not consider the southwest worthy of their attention. The Potomac's water is crystal clear and reminded me of Pakistan's fast-flowing rivers and rivulets in Dir, Swat and Chitral where rivers give an impression as if some glacier has just melted, unlike the muddy rivers in the plains of Sindh and Punjab.

I had no idea till I began settling down that you could not deal with the corporate sector or any part of the huge government machinery unless you carried in your pocket legal proof of your existence, for wherever you went for a purpose other than buying the cheapest of things for which you paid in cash you were required to have two IDs. Whether it was a question of opening a bank account, or writing a "check" at shopping malls after some heavy shopping or renting a car you had to have your driving licence, besides a workplace ID. For the workplace, I had the Foreign Press Centre card, but obtaining a driving licence took four months. So, until then, my passport served as the second ID, though not without moments of embarrassment. Those were Kansi days. If the murder of the two CIA workers had occurred in some other American town my predicament would have perhaps been a little less unmitigated. But the CIA headquarters was in Langley, Virginia, which is part of the Greater Washington Metropolitan Area, and no newspapers covered the Kansi affair more fully and thoroughly than Washington papers and TV channels. Most of the times salesgirls accepted my passport as a second ID. Sometimes, however, she would take a look at my passport and disappear inside to show it to her manager. As minutes ticked I waited as if, instead of the manager, agents of the unseen but ubiquitous CIA and FBI would turn up. National guilt? Possibly. But as any psychologist would tell you, the innocent are more nervous than the guilty. Invariably, the manager obliged, but I had a feeling that the manager was doing me a favour. Until I obtained my driving licence to serve as the second ID, I had to rely on Arshad's goodwill. Invariably Arshad wrote the cheque and later I paid him back. The office that I finally set up in my apartment was paid for by Arshad and later I reimbursed him. The same feeling of national guilt haunted me each time I went to my bank to deposit my salary cheque drawn on the National Bank of Pakistan — given the BCCI racket and the "no questions asked" ad in the Wall Street Journal. (The ad in the WSJ was a disaster and showed how our government leaders — whether in uniform or without it — expect the world to accept their skewed concepts of justice. Every regime change in Pakistan brings with it a quota of reforms and a resolve to clean up the Augean stables. Actually the reforms are shallow and do not correct the structural imbalances in the economy.

The WSJ ad concerned the money stashed away in foreign banks, especially the millions of dollars amassed through money laundering. Those involved in trade in narcotics were, and are, powerful people, some of them well-entrenched in the establishment. No government can crack down on them for fear of consequences. The WSJ ad appealed to their patriotism and good sense and promised "no questions will be asked" if they transferred their dollars to Pakistan. American officials and banking circles were horrified. Not that American banks are not involved in money laundering. Given the crime syndicates in the United States and the drug empires in Latin America, money laundering is big business in the US and involves some of America's major banks. In 1994, The Washington Times, which launched a smear campaign against Clinton, alleged that drug barons had financed his election campaign for Arkansas Governor. The charge remained unproved. All this notwithstanding, money laundering remains what it is — a criminal activity —and no American government ever announces amnesty for sleazebags. The Pakistani ad in WSJ was, however, shocking for the American media and public because here was a government which, instead of prosecuting and jailing the criminals, promised not to ask any questions.) Sometimes — not always — the bank girl would take a look at the NBP cheque and disappear to talk to the manager. I could see the manager telling her to accept it. While she talked to her boss, the queue behind me lengthened, adding to my embarrassment. How I envied those natives whom the bank girl disposed of quickly!

And finally the Internal Revenue Service. Till I arrived in Washington, the IRS was a distant phenomenon, a butt of Art Buchwald jokes. Now the IRS was a reality. Opinion was divided on whether I should file the IRS return. No foreign correspondent fell in the category I did. Most were either American nationals working for foreign newspapers or were green card holders and had to file the returns in any case, even if they received their cheques from abroad. In my case, I was neither an American national (and would never be anything but Pakistani until my dying day) nor a green card holder, and I did not earn any money in the United States. I received my cheques from Pakistan. No opinion was final. But one day I met two IRS officials at a party, and when I asked them the question and gave them the details about me, one of them said, "Why do you want make Uncle Sam rich?" The other one kept quiet. I chose not to file the returns but always lived in fear. One day I received a legal notice, and I held my breath. It turned out to be innocuous, for the court asked me to sit on the jury in a given case. This was optional, and for the life of me I do not know why I declined. I still feel if I had accepted the offer I would have had some fun and taken part about an aspect of American life which I had seen so many times in Hollywood films and TV serials.

All along my stay, America's gun control laws were a source of major controversy in Congress and the media and proved how strong the gun lobby was, headed then I think by Charlton Heston. In his highly readable The Deserter's Tale Joshua Key, who deserted the American army after a stint with it in Iraq, gives an account of gun culture in Guthrie, a town of 10,000 near Oklahoma City. He says "J.R. (his third stepfather) was obsessed with guns, but everybody else in the family had them, too. My mother kept one by the side of her bed, and to this day my 80 years old grandfather packs a pistol in his pocket...I shot a .375 Magnum on my ninth birthday, brought down my first deer by the age of twelve, and could clean, load, and shoot any of dozens of firearms my stepfather kept in our trailer. I was an excellent shot before I was old enough to shave". Clinton had a strong anti-crime agenda, and among his achievements was the increase in the number of policemen throughout the country. But he ran into stiff opposition each time he made policy moves designed to rid America of crime. An indication of how the public was keen to get rid of crime and guns was available in the ingenuity shown by some stores to fight the guns in their own way. In December 1993 a New York carpet store offered toys plus $100 to people in exchange for guns, while a store offered a shoe-gun swap in Washington DC, which then had one of the cities' highest crime rates. In 1993, which was truly speaking my first full year in the District, 2,000 people were killed or injured by firearms. The decision by firms and private individuals to devise newer ways of discouraging the use of guns constituted a slap in the face of Congressmen and politicians who, despite a frightening crime picture and decades of pressure from the populace, had failed to enact a worthwhile gun control law.

In his Making of the President, Theodore S. White wrote of the election campaign that brought Lyndon B. Johnson to power, "Violence scarred and lacerated American politics through 1968...Crime and killing, robbery and looting, perversion .... Riot, sniping, assassination all pounded on Americans." As he signed a crime bill in 1968, President Johnson said, "My overriding concern...is for safe streets in America." A quarter-century later, most analysts agreed, the situation had remained the same. Purchasing a gun was like going to a grocery store and buying vegetables, because all efforts to introduce even moderate checks had failed to break the resistance by strong gun lobbies in Congress and state legislatures. (Today things aren't any better in Pakistan, except that it is far easier to get a gun by means other than obtaining a government licence for a gun.) The state of Virginia, which borders Washington, D.C., had in the beginning of the year 1993 a lively debate on gun control, with citizens' associations, parents, teachers and church groups joining hands to press for a revision of the state's gun laws. But the result after months of heated discussions and press commentaries was a ridiculous compromise law that "limited" a citizen's right to purchase a hand gun to once a month. Said William P. Robinson, Delegate to Virginia's House of Delegates, "Do you know anyone who needs more than one handgun a month?" There were exceptions, too, and a person could purchase more guns if he justified it to the police he needed them. Yet, odd as it may a appear, Governor Wilder, who signed the bill into law, felt ecstatic about it, called it "the triumph of the public good over the special interest," and hoped this would end Virginia's reputation as "the gun-running capital of the United States." In the District of Columbia, carrying a gun is a crime. But still, 1993 saw 467 people killed, and over 1,600 wounded by firearms.

In his campaign to tighten gun control, President Clinton poignantly referred to the crime situation when he said Americans were missing an element of their civilization if children had to pass through metal detectors to enter schools, and apartments were to turn into prisons. First Lady Hillary Rodham Clinton called Washington "a city under siege." Yet, in spite of his vigorous efforts to push an effective gun control law through Congress, all that the federal legislature did was to pass a bill that would require a gun purchaser to wait for five days before he would get it. In those five days, the police were supposed to carry out checks on the would-be purchaser. Yet many Americans said that even if a law that totally banned gun purchases was passed, it would have little effect on the crime situation because the number of guns already in citizens' hands was colossal. A knowledgeable FPC official, who was once posted with the U.S. Consulate in Lahore, told me there were an estimated 200 million guns in the country. "My own father," he said, "kept fifteen guns." The one sacrosanct law behind which the gun lobby was taking cover was the Second Amendment, which grants every citizen "the right to bear arms." But this right was given in a context where the country's freedom could have been endangered by colonial armies, and where the people themselves constituted the militia that would defend the country. The repeated failures by the legislators to halt gun proliferation — coupled with periodic reports of some psychopath opening up with his gun in a crowded store or restaurant — have created an atmosphere of national cynicism in which Americans seemed to have resigned themselves to the existing crime situation. When Clinton moved into the White House, the National Rifle Association became openly alarmed and began a campaign to "awaken" gun manufacturers and sellers to what the new president would do, unlike his predecessor, George Bush Sr., who was an NRA member. In an advertising campaign – that cynics said turned Clinton into an NRA ally —the Association launched a vigorous membership drive, telling its supporters that Clinton was a "gun owner's worst nightmare." Claiming that "for the first time in this century we have an anti-gun president," the NRA said in a four-page brochure, "There has never been a more important time for gun owners like you to join the NRA. Your government is moving closer and closer to banning your rifles, your shot guns, your ammo and your hunting." Among the examples it gave of Clinton's anti-gun views were Hillary's plan for a tax on guns and ammunition to pay for healthcare, Clinton's appointment of Janet Reno, "the notorious anti-gun zealot," as Attorney-General, and how he "kissed Sarah Brady at rallies." Sarah's husband, James Brady, was the White House spokesman when Ronald Reagan was President and was injured in a 1981 assassination attempt on Reagan. Subsequently, Sarah and Brady — the former in a wheel chair — campaigned for tougher gun laws. President Clinton chided the NRA for obstructing gun control legislation and said he did not think attempts at gun control "affect the right to keep and bear arms." He added, "I don't believe that everybody in America needs to be able to buy a semi-automatic or an automatic weapon, built only for the purpose of killing people, in order to protect the right of Americans to hunt and practice marks and to be secure."

There was no doubt Clinton was serious about enacting a tough anti-gun law. But the way it was finally passed, the Brady bill, as it came to be called, did little more than lay down a five-day waiting period for a gun purchaser. The bill also laid down that the waiting period would be abolished after five years even if, by that time, a fully computerized, nation-wide "instant check" system did not come into being. The Brady bill was in addition to Clinton's $22 billion crime package, which put another 100,000 policemen on the streets, provided for stricter punishments for sex crimes against women, and prescribed the death penalty for some 50 offences, including drive-by shootings and some drug-related crimes. In Washington D.C. murders continued almost till the very end of 1993 when a 37-year-old woman was shot dead in the final minutes of the year. Moments later, when the New Year was only 60 seconds old, a police officer shot dead a man after he pointed a gun at him. The year's second murder occurred two hours later when a woman was stabbed to death in her apartment. The 467 deaths for 1993 were 16 more than those for 1992, though less than the 489 for 1991.

Police and community officials considered drugs to be the single biggest source of crime, as was evident from the phenomenal rise in murders since the mid-1980s. From 1980 to 1987, murders averaged 200 a year. However, when drugs, especially cocaine, hit the District's streets, the crime rate soared, murders going up dramatically – 345 in 1988; 438 in 1989, 483 in 1990; 489 in 1991; 451 in 1992 and 467 in 1993. However, a research conducted by the Columbia University showed that nationwide alcohol was responsible for 95 per cent of violent crimes, including nine out of ten rapes, on American campuses. The study blamed drinking for forty per cent of all academic problems and twenty-eight per cent of dropouts and found that heavy drinking among students occurred on average five times a week, sometimes daily. Thirty-five per cent girls "drink to get drunk," and sixty per cent of female students who acquired sexually-transmitted diseases were drunk at the time.

~·~·~·~·~

Clinton has been much criticised for his five-hour visit to Islamabad in March 2000, and this has often been cited as proof of his hostility toward Pakistan. Personally I feel George W. Bush Jr. would have behaved no differently if he were to visit the subcontinent in the pre-9/11 period. Conversely, Clinton would have behaved no differently if he were President on September 11, 2001 and would have been an equally gracious host to Musharraf at the White House or Camp David. As I have said earlier, during the period Clinton was at the White House (1992-2000), Pakistan and America had no military relationship of the kind that had existed earlier (in the fifties and sixties and again after the Soviets invaded Afghanistan in 1979), but Clinton seemed fully conscious of Pakistan's importance in a region where America had economic and geopolitical interests and seemed to make an effort to maintain a warm relationship with Pakistan and convey friendly sentiments to Islamabad. My feeling that he had a soft corner for Pakistan was vindicated when Indian Prime Minister Narasimha Rao visited the United States in May 1994. Each time a Pakistani or Indian VIP visited Washington, the District's South Asians — born politicians — became active. There were pro and anti rallies, preceded by highly partisan reporting and comments in the ethnic media. But there was one difference: the Indians made a clear difference between leader and country, and said or did nothing that could harm India itself; the Pakistani, regrettably, made no such difference. To them the visiting leader must be hurt, maligned, humiliated, character assassinated and, if necessary destroyed, and if in that process Pakistan itself got hurt they could not care less. When Rao came to Washington there were anti-Rao rallies by ethnic Indians opposed to Rao's Congress-led government; the rallies that could be called anti-Indian were those held by Kashmiris, Sikh separatists and Sri Lankans. I mingled with the protesters outside the White House, and the Sikhs became especially warm when I told them that I was from Pakistan and represented Dawn.

Inside the White House, things were going nasty for Rao, for Clinton raised the Kashmir issue on his own — a fact that became clear when the two addressed a joint press conference. Asked whether Clinton had twisted his arm, Rao said to a burst of laughter, "My arm is absolutely intact. The president didn't even touch it." There were differences between the two sides not only on Kashmir but also on India's human rights record and on the question of non-proliferation, and the joint statement issued later said the two sides had "agreed" on the need for a Kashmir solution, hoping it would be resolved according to the Simla agreement. Indian diplomatic sources felt happy that the reference to Kashmir did not mention the people of Kashmir. The paragraph on Kashmir said: "The two leaders agreed on the need for bilateral negotiations between India and Pakistan to resolve outstanding issues, including Jammu and Kashmir, as envisaged in the Simla agreement."

Indian diplomats felt elated that the key paragraph on non-proliferation also accommodated New Delhi's point of view by referring to the issue not within a South Asian framework alone but within "the global and regional contexts."

The sentence said: "President Clinton and Prime Minister Rao offered their strong support for efforts toward the non-proliferation of weapons of mass destruction and their means of delivery and towards their progressive reduction with the goal of elimination of such weapons, which are among the most pressing challenges to the security of states in the post-cold War era. They discussed these challenges in both the global and regional contexts." No less than a dozen drafts were made, altered and rejected. At one stage, the Indians were not keen on a joint statement at all if it failed to accommodate the Indian point of view on such key issues as Kashmir and non-proliferation. As it finally appeared the statement showed a touch of Deputy Secretary of State Strobe Talbot's moderating influence.

The nine-point joint statement said:

1. President Clinton and Prime Minister Rao today (Nov. 19, 1994) called for a new partnership between India and the United States.
2. The two leaders agreed that democracy, respect for human rights, and economic liberalisation provide the best foundation for global stability and prosperity in the post-Cold War era. They promised to cooperate in the search for [a] solution to global challenges posed by weapons of mass destruction, AIDS, environmental degradation, population growth, poverty, international terrorism and narcotics trafficking.
3. The President and the Prime Minister agreed to expand the pace and scope of high-level exchanges on the full range of political, economic, commercial, scientific, technological and social issues.
4. Both leaders noted with satisfaction their cooperation in support of UN peacekeeping operations, in particular in countries where

forces of both countries have served. The leaders agreed to seek ways to expand their cooperation at the UN. They welcomed the progress in the Middle East peace process and hailed the recent elections in South Africa.

5. The two leaders agreed on the need for bilateral negotiations between India and Pakistan to resolve outstanding issues, including Jammu and Kashmir, as envisaged in the Simla agreement.

6. President Clinton and Prime Minister Rao offered their strong support for efforts towards the non-proliferation of weapons of mass destruction and their means of delivery and towards their progressive reduction, with the goal of elimination of such weapons, which are among the most pressing challenges to the security of states in the post-Cold War era. They discussed these challenges in both the global and regional contexts.

7. They pledged that their two governments would intensify their cooperative efforts to achieve a comprehensive test ban treaty and a verifiable ban treaty and a verifiable ban on the production of fissile materials for nuclear weapons.

8. The two leaders welcomed the successful conclusion of the Uruguay Round and pledged their governments would work to help the new World Trade Organization continue the process of expanding trade. President Clinton praised Prime Minister Rao's courageous economic reforms and noted that the enthusiastic response of the business communities in both countries has produced record levels of bilateral trade and investment. Prime Minister Rao welcomed the investor response to India's new policies. Recognizing the potential to build a strong and positive economic relationship, both leaders agreed to work to remove impediments that exist to remove bilateral commerce. Commerce Secretary Brown will lead a presidential trade and investment mission to India in November 1994 and Energy Secretary O'Leary is to visit India in July 1994.

9. President Clinton and Prime Minister Rao expressed satisfaction with the accomplishments of thirty-five years of exchanges between scientists and researchers in the United States and India. They noted the discussions that have taken place with respect to a new [for] framework Science and Technology Agreement that will carry the world's most extensive bilateral science and technology collaborative programme into the 21st century. They welcomed the signing of two other agreements on cooperation in the areas of narcotics awareness and preservation of cultural heritage sites. They further noted that the United States and India have begun negotiations on a new extradition treaty and on an agreement on renewable energy resources, which they hope to complete in the near future. They are also exploring a treaty on protecting bilateral investment.

The question answer session was lovely, and there were bursts of laughter, and the newsmen questioned both Clinton and Rao not only on Indo-American relations but also India-Pakistan problems, including Kashmir.

Q: Mr President, would you say after your talks with the prime minister that some of the problems which have dogged Indo-American relations have now been overcome, but in other words, the areas of agreement are so large that you can afford to play down the areas of disagreement or leave them aside for future reference? And also, you mentioned the global partnership, and in that connection, I'd like to ask you about the statement made by the new ambassador – ambassador-designate — that if India is included in the Security Council it will undermine cohesion? And if the largest democracy in the world cannot be a member of the Security Council, then who can be?

I also have a question for the prime minister .The question is that in India people said that President Clinton is going to twist your arm. I want to ask you: what is the state of your arm after your talks today.

Clinton: Well, I can answer the three questions very quickly — or the two, and then you have one for the prime minister. First of all, when two nations are friends, it doesn't mean that they agree on everything or that they should. But in the context of their friendly relationships, they are then able to discuss differences, problems or issues between them. We discussed, in a very, I think, open way all the things that you might imagine we discussed today. But I have been disturbed by the apparent either strain, or perhaps the better word is limitation, on the relationships between the US and India as reported in the press, not only here but in your country. We have a very great stake, it seems to me, in the end of the Cold War, in having not only a friendly relationship, but a constructive and operating relationship. We, the – two great democracies with a great future together, and I – we – emphasise that positive today, not in any way not dealing with the other issues of difficulty , but knowing that it all has to be put in a proper context in the interests of the American people and in the interests of the Indian people.

Secondly, with regard to the Security Council issue, that is an issue that I think the United States should keep an open mind on. We have been on record — I have been personally and our administration has — for some considerable amount of time favouring permanent membership for Germany and for Japan, who were our two principal opponents in World War II and who since then have built enormous economic superpowers in the context of peaceful countries, not on the backs of military domination, not even with the development of nuclear weapons, but basically because of their enormous ability to develop the capacities of their people. That does not mean that I think we should have a definitive position prohibiting anybody else from participating in that way. I think that's something we should keep an open mind on.

After Rao's answer that "my arm is absolutely intact" and "the president didn't even touch it", a questioner asked him about "widespread allegations of Indian human rights violations in Kashmir. Are they true?"

Rao: No. They are not true.

Clinton: No. (Laughter, applause).

Q: My question is to Mr President, to you, regarding Kashmir, and it is in two parts. Recently, a report was released by the State Department in which it said, and I quote, "there were credible reports in 1993 of official Pakistani support to Kashmiri militants who under took attacks of terrorism in Indian controlled Kashmir."

Clinton: Yes, in the back.

Q: Israelis are known to possess nuclear arms but the US doesn't seem to be doing anything about it while there is a lot of pressure on countries like India. Why this double standard?

Clinton: Well, first of all, sir , we are trying to deal with the international nuclear problems .We also believe very strongly that the fewer countries who become nuclear powers, the better off we're all going to be and if there is a system in which the security of nations who think they many have to develop nuclear weapons to protect themselves can have their security guaranteed in other ways, we think that that's our job to try to put that system out there, to put those alternatives out there so that people will see that it's not in their long-term security interests to develop such weapons. That's our position. What we're trying to do is to keep the number of people in the nuclear club as small as possible and then reduce the nuclear arsenals that they have, including our own. As you know, we've worked hard to reduce our own with the Russians. So, that is our position. But our position further is that no one should be asked to put their own security at risk to achieve that. So any dialogue that we have with India on this will be in the context of what is pivotal for India's security, how we can enhance your security, not diminish it. It would be wrong for the United States to tell your great nation or the smallest nation on the face of the earth that we recommend a course of action for them that would reduce security. We should be in the business of increasing security. But I believe that you can increase your security and avoid becoming a nuclear power. Japan did it, Germany did, a lot of other countries have done it; we can do it together.

Q: Last year, the House Republican Task Force on Terrorism branded Pakistan as a terrorist state. My question is: will U.S. now put Pakistan back on the list of states that sponsor terrorism? With all the radical statement – statements, rather, made by the State Department, what is your stand, Mr President, on Kashmir now?

(Evidently, Clinton had expected such a question and was ready with a piece of paper from which he quoted to spell out his position on the issue.)

Clinton: Well, since the spring of last year, based on our best evidence, official Pakistani material support to the Kashmiri militants has dropped. The Secretary of State concluded last July and again this past January that the available evidence did not warrant a finding that Pakistan – and I've got the exact language here –"has repeatedly provided support for acts of international terrorism." Plainly there is still assistance to the militants by private parties in Pakistan, and all I can tell you is we will have to continue to monitor that situation and deal with it based on the facts as we see them. The ultimate answer there is for these two great nations to get together and resolve that.

Q: How far advance do you think India's nuclear programme is? And how many bombs do your think India possesses?

There was again a burst of laughter when Clinton replied: "I think you asked the wrong person that (question). I don't think I should – I don't think I can or should comment on that.

Q: Yes, after this summit, have the differences between India and the US ...NPT and human rights ...have been narrowed down, or does it stand where it is?

Clinton: I wouldn't say they have narrowed down, but I think – they should be seen in the context of the whole relationship. We both support a comprehensive test ban treaty. We both support an end to the production of fissile materials for nuclear weapons. If we did both those things that would dramatically reduce the prospect of nuclear development anywhere in the world if in fact those treaties were adhered to by everyone and enforced. We have some things that we have agreed to continue to discuss with regard to the human rights issue and the proliferation issue, and we will continue to discuss them.

But I think that what you should say is that the differences remain but in the context of our common interests and our common values we believe they can be managed in a very constructive way and still allow this relationship to grow and strengthen.

As he prepared for departure, two scandals seemed to have spoiled the Indian prime minister's visit. They weren't really scandals, but the media had a field day because of a "whites only" order at the Boston hotel where Rao and his delegations were staying. This was followed by the detention of two Indian security guards for carrying a pistol at Washington's Dulles International Airport. One of them was in fact handcuffed. The first incident showed the ludicrous level to which VIP security is taken. The management of the hotel where they were lodged — Four Seasons — was not so much to blame, because it was Rao's security staff which had made a "whites only" request, since it suspected a wide variety of people to be security risks. To begin with, the management was told that Sikhs and Kashmiris and South Asians in general could pose a threat to the prime minister. But the destruction of the Babri mosque had angered Muslims throughout the world, and no one knew how "an Islamic terrorist" would make an attempt on Rao's life. So, the hotel bar was asked not to service Arabs, Turks, Iranians and Muslims during Rao's stay. To make matters worse for the Indian security staff, lots of Afro-Americans also happen to be Muslim. In fact, a study showed that Afro-Americans then constituted 42 per cent of America's Muslim community. To make Rao's security foolproof, the Four Season management was requested that the prime minister be served only by "white Americans or Europeans." The instructions were in the form of a written request. The hotel management not only agreed, it admitted to the press that it had ordered that the prime minister be not served by coloured staff. The state authorities then investigated the matter after the hotel's coloured staff, which constitutes 60 per cent of the 500 workers, complained to the Massachusetts Commission Against Discrimination. MCAD chief Michael T. Duffy said it was "fantastic" that Four Seasons would "indulge the prejudices of a guest," while a spokesman for the hotel said: "I personally, as the employees know, can truthfully say this (whites only) decision was made on short notice without the involvement of the most senior management." A spokesman for the US secret service said it had nothing to do with the episode and added: "The US secret service does not make requests like this." The Boston Globe quoted a black worker as saying: "I don't know whether to cry or to quit. This should have never happened." The paper said the Indian security staff complained when a black worker came to pick up laundry, while another was told he could not participate in the prime minister's check-in". The management later apologised when the news leaked out and said "the whole issue here is that the hotel has made a gross error in their zeal to continue to service their clients." The hotel management later paid $700,000 to the MCAD to end the controversy.

The security incident was even more bizarre: S.N. Tiwari, Director of the Special Protection Group (SPG), was detained by the US secret service for carrying a gun, even though he had been told he and his men could not carry guns at civilian airports. The SPG Director had earlier annoyed the Americans by insisting that he wanted to do a round of the White House to see the security arrangements himself. Later, at the Andrews air base he feared the tarmac would sink. He gave up when US authorities told him that the plane carrying the President landed sometimes twice or thrice a day. At the Dulles airport, Director Tiwari and another SPG official were apprehended when the metal detector they were passing through beeped. While Director Tiwari handed over his gun correctly — butt first — the other official went for his holster and tried to surrender his gun the wrong way, barrel first. Then, in what could have been a scene from a Hollywood thriller, US security men grabbed him by his arm, threw him to the ground and handcuffed him in the back. The two were freed after Indian Embassy and State Department officials intervened.

12

BENAZIR IN WASHINGTON

DURING MY STAY IN WASHINGTON as Dawn's correspondent, Benazir Bhutto visited America twice, first as leader of the opposition in the summer of 1993 and later as prime minister in March-April 1995. The last time she had visited America was in June 1989, when she took the country by storm, for she had come to America after years of jail, five of them in solitary confinement, where Zia's agents tried to plant in her mind the idea of suicide (Benazir Bhutto, Daughter of the East, p 194). More important, she had made history by becoming the first woman to be the prime minister of a Muslim country. Her struggle was titanic, for she had stood up against a military dictator who, and against parties which believed in physically eliminating the Bhutto family — a process that ended ultimately with her own assassination on December 27, 2007. Between June 5 and June 10, 1989, Benazir made on the American leaders, people and media an impression few non-Western leaders had made. Here was a Muslim woman, charismatic, Western-educated and endowed with courage and brilliance demolishing the Muslim woman's stereotype image painted by the American media. Even though the Soviets were winding up in Afghanistan, the Pressler amendment was still on, and aid to Pakistan still continued. On June 6, President George Bush Senior and Benazir watched as Pakistani and

American officials signed a series of agreements worth nearly half a billion dollars, including $465m for economic development and $1.5m for eradicating drug trafficking. On June 7 she met Defence Secretary Dick Cheney because she was herself then Pakistan's defence minister, but the climax to the visit came later in the day when she addressed US Congress where she received a standing ovation. The Senators and Representatives repeatedly applauded her as she told of the horror of the 11 years of Ziaul Haq's tyranny and the hopes which her election had aroused in Pakistan. In a speech watched by millions of Americans on TV, Benazir gave Congress the background to her triumph as the Pakistani people's elected leader and told her audience what is still true of Pakistan: "Our democratic institutions are still new and need careful tending. Democracy's doubters have never believed that it could successfully address the problems of developing countries. But democracy in Pakistan must succeed to signal nations in political transition all over the world that freedom is on the rise". She added: "For me and the people of Pakistan, the last 11 years have encompassed a painful odyssey. My countrymen and I did not see our loved ones die, or tortured, or lashed, or languished in solitary confinement, deprived of basic human rights in order that others might again suffer such indignities. We sacrificed a part of our life, we bore the pain of confronting tyranny to build a just society. We believed in ourselves, in our cause, in our people and in our country. And when you believe, when you have faith, there is no mountain too high to scale. This is my message to the youth of America, to its women and to its people". After her speech she shook hands with some Senators and came under intense criticism back home from the bigoted for this "shocking" behaviour on the part of a Muslim woman. A day later she visited Harvard University, where she was a student between 1969 and 1973, and recalled in her commencement address that events two centuries ago had earned "Cambridge, Boston and the surrounding region the sobriquet of 'the cradle of liberty'…. Cambridge and Harvard were my cradle of liberty, too" she said and told her cheering audience that her first act as prime minister was to free all political prisoners and commute the death sentences. Pakistan, she said, was "heir to an intellectual tradition" of which the most "illustrious exponent" was Iqbal, who saw the future course for Islamic societies in a synthesis between adherence to the faith and adjustment to the modern age. The hallmark of this tradition was "tolerance, open-mindedness, pursuit of social justice, emphasis on the values of equality and social concord, and encouragement of scientific inquiry". This tradition drew strength from the fact that "Islam admits no priesthood and that Muslim culture, in its most vital and creative periods, accommodated and advanced what was best in other cultures. Intensely devoted as the pioneers of this tradition were to the Islamic spirit, they were also strongly opposed to bigotry and obscurantism in all their forms. Xenophobia, or prejudice against other civilizations, Western or non-Western, was repugnant to their outlook. I am indeed proud of this heritage. It is this heritage that has enabled me to take on the awesome responsibilities of the prime ministership of my country".

Seven years later, her visit was under circumstances that were anything but favourable to her country, for the US-Pakistan relations were going through one of their periodic lows, and the media, especially The New York Times and The Washington Post, never missed an opportunity to spew venom. The State Department had put Pakistan on its "watch list" of terrorism in January 1993, and no one helped it more than a Pakistani, Aimal Kansi, who had murdered two CIA officials in Langley, Virginia, on January 25 and fled to Pakistan. Also about that time, Pakistani peacekeepers, along with American troops, were doing a useful peacekeeping job in Somalia, often suffering casualties. Yet the WP and NYT continued their Pakistan bashing instead of lauding the peacekeepers' efforts to fight off warlord Mohammad Farah Aideed's guerillas. Yet, in contrast to the media's attitude, I found Clinton favourably inclined toward Pakistan, and even in situations where Islamabad seemed to have thoroughly bungled, Clinton appeared keen to show a surprising understanding of Pakistan's position. The death of 23 Pakistani soldiers in Somalia evoked completely different reactions from NYT and WP on the one hand and from Clinton on the other. While the president sent a message of sympathy to Nawaz Sharif, then prime minister, the Washington Post demanded that the Pakistani soldiers be disciplined. In an editorial entitled "Killed by UN peacekeepers;" the influential daily said when the Pakistani troops opened fire "an image of UN peacekeepers mowing down innocent civilians sped around the world." The editorial admitted that the Pakistani soldiers fired because they suspected "another human shield operation" by Farah Aideed, whom it called "a thug," who was "trying to come on as a nationalist hero." If investigation warranted, the paper said, "the offending [Pakistani] unit must be disciplined and UN rules of engagement revised. A force sent in to rescue a country from criminal warlords can hardly itself claim immunity from standards of military competence and decent conduct." The Washington Times was a little more balanced in its comment and said no one could fault the Pakistanis, because "they saw their friends murdered" by Aideed's men "hiding behind a crowd of women and children." It opined that the Pakistani response was "awful and unprincipled," and claimed that "the Pakistanis are simply not up to the job they have been handed." Whatever reservations one might have about their effectiveness, the paper said, "these troops, be they Pakistani or Scandinavian or American, are putting their lives on the line to help others in more places than ever before in the history of the United Nations. They are being killed in Yugoslavia and Cambodia as well as Somalia. To let General Aideed's wanton act of provocation go unpunished would be immoral and embolden him further." At a Rose Garden press conference Clinton said that the issue was "whether the Pakistani soldiers erred, and that's for the UN [to] resolve and I'm sure that it will", adding that "you can't have these kinds of conflicts and expect that there will be nothing controversial about that... that is not to exonerate or condemn." The Americans had also bombed the guerillas, and Clinton said the action was "I think appropriate in response to what happened, which is that Pakistani peacekeepers were ambushed and murdered. There's no question about that. The action that we took was designed to minimise, as much as we possibly could, any damage or any injury or any death to civilians. Now, what happened with the Pakistanis is in some doubt in sense that they're saying the first time they were ambushed, they were ambushed by people who stood behind women and children and used them as a defence, and as I understand it, the UN is trying to get to the bottom of that. I expect them to do it and to take appropriate action and to take a very appropriate step to make sure that UN peacekeepers do not, do not cause injury or death to innocent people in Somalia. That is the United Nations' job and the United States expects them to do it."

In May, Clinton annoyed India by calling for a dialogue between Islamabad and New Delhi "focussing on achievable near-term steps such as demilitarisation of the Siachen glacier". In a report to Congress on "Progress toward Regional Proliferation in South Asia", Clinton asked Pakistan and India to take confidence-building measures so as to reduce "a nuclear exchange with devastating consequences". The report, sent to Congress in the same month in which Benazir was in America, showed Clinton's grasp of the complexity of the Indo-Pakistan relationship, the nature of rivalry between the two, the ambitions of the nuclear capable rivals, and the compulsion for Pakistan to have nuclear weapons. While he claimed that China was helping Pakistan in developing weapons of mass destruction, he made it clear to Congress that Islamabad was "driven primarily by specific security concerns vis-à-vis India". He perhaps read the Pakistani mind correctly when he said Pakistan also sought "equality of status and rights with India, although it has no aspirations to global equality of status with the nuclear weapons states. Many Pakistanis argue that Pakistan needs nuclear weapons and ballistic missiles capability as a deterrent against a more powerful India which, they believe, has never fully accepted Pakistan's existence as an independent nation state". He said New Delhi "has long been concerned about China's military relationship with Pakistan" and believed that "China, therefore, does not approach Indo-Pakistan regional security and proliferation issues as a disinterested party".

The powerful Indian lobby must have raised its eyebrow when the Clinton report said India's "latent security concerns about China are a major obstacle to gaining New Delhi's support for any regional discussion in view of Indian belief that Chinese nuclear and missile progress also must be taken into consideration". Pakistan, President Clinton said, had not raised any "non-discrimination" issue directly, but had insisted that it would not sign the NPT unless India did. The President said in both Pakistan and India there was domestic consensus on the nuclear question. In India, eighty-five per cent of the people believed in keeping the nuclear option open while in Pakistan there was "a widespread belief" that no government could survive for long "if it were to dismantle unilaterally the nuclear programme", for such a move "would be seen as capitulating to Western pressure." Pakistanis believed that the United States tackled the missile proliferation issue by focusing on "import/ export behaviour" while leaving "unaddressed indigenous ballistic missile development programmes, such as India's Pirthvi and Agni missiles." Consequently, he said, dealing with the proliferation issue required that the "US and others take into account both Indian and Pakistani domestic political concerns and regional security threat perceptions, including those extending beyond the two countries themselves. It cannot be addressed on the basis of external pressure by the United States alone." He noted that while Pakistan, China and Russia had accepted the United States' five-party proposal on non-proliferation, India had not because in its opinion the scope of five-party talks left the question of Chinese strategic forces unaddressed. "We believe that proliferation in South Asia is primarily a regional problem and, in the end, will require a direct high-level dialogue between India and Pakistan and a regional solution." The "over-arching" obstacle to a regional agreement on the nuclear and WMD issues was "the persistent level of tension and consequent distrust between India and Pakistan, arising from domestic political constraints, popular emotions fed by the memories of partition and three wars, and the unresolved dispute over Kashmir."

As an example he referred to the demolition of the Babri mosque "by Hindu militants" which made New Delhi and Islamabad, pressured by domestic opinion, defer actions "aimed at improving bilateral relations." The US chief executive outlined American objectives thus: "The US seeks to prevent nuclear and ballistic missile proliferation in South Asia. Our objective is first to cap, then over time reduce, and finally eliminate the possession of weapons of mass destruction and their means of delivery. We seek also to help reduce tensions and avoid conflicts which could escalate to the use of WMD. Therefore, we seek to help create a climate in which each country's sense of security is enhanced through tension reduction and confidence-building measures and where both India and Pakistan perceive distinct advantages in rejecting WMD and ballistic missile delivery systems, and recognize the disadvantages inherent in their possession. In addition, the US seeks to inhibit the export of WMD, the missiles that carry them, and related technology from the region to other countries. We also actively discourage the export of WMD-related equipment and technology from other countries to India and Pakistan." In America's discussions with Pakistan and India, he said, his administration was urging the two countries to reach agreement on near-term tension-reducing and confidence-building measures, and added, "We strongly encourage dialogue between India and Pakistan to address and resolve the issues dividing them, including Kashmir as well as nuclear and missile proliferation. Our role is that of a catalyst, seeking to promote a serious dialogue between the two countries and with others." The near-term and confidence-building measures suggested by Clinton included "a regional cut-off of fissile material production," a regional agreement not to conduct nuclear tests and extending the nuclear no-attack pledge to cover population centres.

"Sikh rights" also drew Clinton's attention and evoked an official Indian protest when he wrote a letter to Congressman Gary Condit on the human rights situation in Indian Punjab. In a meeting with Assistant Secretary Raphel, Indian Ambassador Siddharta Shankar Ray conveyed his country's "great concern" over the letter and expressed his dissatisfaction with the State Department's "guidance" on the issue. Clinton's letter had not mentioned Khalistan but had spoken of "Sikh rights." India had two objections: one," Sikh rights" are not "minority rights" in the sense the black minority in the United States has, because the Sikhs are a majority in Indian Punjab. Two, Congressman Condit's letter to Clinton did not mention "Punjab" but spoke all along of "Khalistan", where there were human rights abuses. When Raphel replied that the State Department had subsequently issued a guidance on the Clinton letter and that the President's letter spoke of improvements in the human rights situation in Punjab, Ambassador Ray said the press guidance had not spoken of "Punjab." What the Indians wanted was that the State Department's guidance, issued on January 24, 1994, should have clearly used the word "Punjab" to make it clear that it was clarifying a situation with regard to "Punjab" and not with regard to "Khalistan", which Congressman Condit had mentioned in his letter. Another Indian objection was to Clinton's reference to the need for "a solution that protects Sikh rights." India (according to an official statement issued in New Delhi) claimed that "a solution has indeed been attained in Punjab by the people of Punjab by democratic means, where rights of all Indians, including Sikhs, are protected under the law, regardless of their religion." Secretary Raphel replied that the United States did not believe that Khalistan held much sway over the Sikh people, and that Washington believed in India's territorial integrity. It was significant; however, that the Indian envoy used the Clinton letter on "Sikh rights" to register India's protest over "such issues as Kashmir," and said they created problems in relations between the two countries. He said: "Negative. pronouncements and communications by the US government on such issues as Kashmir, human rights and Punjab could not but create difficulties and complicate India's sincere endeavour to develop a multi-faceted and positive relationship with the United States." President Clinton's letter to Congressman Condit came on the heels of his letter to Dr Ghulam Nabi Fai, Executive Director of the Kashmiri American Council, in which the US Chief Executive hoped to "help bring peace to Kashmir" and "shared" his concerns over human rights.

~~~~~~~~~

As leader of opposition, Benazir arrived in America in May 1993, some four months after the State Department had put Pakistan on its "watch list" of terrorism, and there was no indication when the "watch" would be over and Pakistan would be taken off the list. In fact, things were scary, for a few days before she came, CIA chief James Woolsey said Pakistan (along with Sudan) was "on the brink" of being declared a terrorist state — i.e. a state which sponsors terrorism. The charge, of course, was absurd, but Aimal Kansi's crime had strengthened the hands of what I call the New York Times-Washington Post lobby. Testifying before the Senate's Judiciary Committee, chaired by Senator Joe Biden, the CIA chief said Pakistan continued to support "Kashmir and Sikh groups" and give them "safe haven and other support." Bracketing Pakistan with Sudan, Woolsey said the United States had "warned each of these countries that it could soon be listed." In spite of the warning, he said, Sudan had welcomed "a growing number of well-known terrorists and violent religious extremist groups, groups like Lebanese Hezbollah, the Abu-Nidal Organization, Hamas, and the Palestine Islamic Jihad." As for Pakistan, the CIA chief said: "It has supported the Kashmiri and Sikh groups, which have been waging long-running insurgencies against India's central government. The Kashmiris and Sikhs have found safe haven and other support in Pakistan, while forcefully redressing grievances against New Delhi."

Of the six countries then on the American list of state-sponsors of terrorism, four were Muslim – Iran, Iraq, Syria and Libya. The other two were Cuba and North Korea. Very surprisingly, even though Syria was on the list, Woolsey said "we have not linked Damascus to any international terrorist act since 1986." Yet he alleged that Syria continued to grant "safe haven in Syria and Syrian-controlled Lebanon to several terrorist groups." In keeping with America's traditionally pro-Israel policies, Woolsey called as "terrorist groups" those fighting for the liberation of territories occupied by Israel. While Libya, Syria, Cuba and North Korea, Woolsey said, were not "now directly involved in international terrorist attacks, none has irrevocably abandoned the terrorist option." Woolsey's real ire seemed to have been directed at Iran, which he labelled "the most active and dangerous state sponsor" (of terrorism). Noting that Iran has not reversed the edict (fatwa) on death for Salman Rushdie, the CIA chief said Tehran had instead "increased the bounty for killing Rushdie". Denying that the country was "a moderate or a pragmatic post-Khomeini Iran," Woolsey held Tehran responsible for "35 terrorist acts since Rafsanjani was elected President in July 1989." Among other acts he accused Iran or Tehran-supported groups of blowing up the Israeli Embassy in Buenos Aires, killing an Iranian opposition leader in Rome, helping violent religious groups in North Africa, allegedly applauding the assassination of Algerian President Boudiaf and strengthening "ties to radical Palestinian terrorist who share Iran's long-term goal of destroying Israel." He alleged that Iran's "media organizations are funnelling propaganda to the rest of the Islamic world that the United States is a great Satan whose policy is to oppress Muslims."

Later the same Woolsey reminded Aimal Kansi, then on the run and hiding somewhere in Pakistan, that "we do not forget, and do not give up." Testifying before the Senate's Intelligence Committee Woolsey referred to the arrest, finally, of Mohammad Ali Razaee, who was allegedly responsible for hijacking a plane and killing three Americans. Woolsey said: "We are using our resources to provide whatever information we can to help locate and bring to justice Mir Aimal Kansi... On this particular, I would like Mr Kansi to know that as Mohammad Razaee discovered eight years after his crime, we do not forget, and we do not give up". Senator Howard Metzenbaum (D-Oh) asked him what he thought of Islam because "many Americans really don't understand much about militant Islam, but every so often it seems to rear its head, and what it does it seems to create problems for America's security interest". Woolsey replied that "Islam itself is a magnificent religion" and in much of its tradition "Islam is peaceful and humanistic". But, he said, there were several things going on "under the rubric of what is sometimes called Islamic extremism or militant Islam". He mentioned Sudan and Iran as examples of countries which were trying to achieve "political objectives and even terrorist objectives" under cover of Islam.

Benazir arrived in Washington on May 5, 1993, and I and other Pakistani journalists went to Washington's National Airport to see her. Also to receive her was Pakistan Charge d'Affaires Sarwar Naqvi, besides the embassy's security officials. There must be American security men, too, but in keeping with traditions in recognised democracies that the less you see of the cops the better no American security personnel were visible. Also present was Mark Siegel, the PPP's American PR man. As we waited in the arrival lounge for her to emerge from the aviobridge, Hanan Ashrawi, Arafat's choice as leader of the Palestinian team for the Madrid negotiations, came first, looked at us and said: "She is coming". The former prime minister, accompanied by her husband, had flown in from Georgia, where she and Ashrawi were the CNN's guests. A caretaker government was ruling Pakistan, Nawaz Sharif and Ghulam Ishaq Khan having both resigned, and a general election was due in October, while an American decision on the "watch list" one way or the other, was expected in June. Benazir had a point when she told us that the Clinton administration should not make a decision before an elected government took power in Islamabad. She said: "I believe a decision on this issue is expected in June, and that's why as former prime minister, Leader of the Opposition and head of the PPP, which is Pakistan's biggest party, I thought I should take up this issue (with administration officials) now that I am here". About the home situation, she said it was wrong to compare her government's dismissal in 1990 by Ishaq with the sack of the Sharif government. She had come to power through an election that was fair, and Nawaz Sharif had accepted it. But the election that brought him to power had been manipulated. This was something that became known much later, for the IJI coalition government that came to power in 1990 election had been helped financially by the intelligence. In fact, after his retirement, Army Chief Mirza Aslam Beg admitted that he had distributed Rs 140 million, taken from the now defunct Mehran Bank, to other parties for creating an "Islamic alliance" (Details in Chapter 9). Accompanying Benazir was, of course, the much-maligned Asif Zardari. He remained in jail for two and a half years on corruption charges, yet Ghulam Ishaq Khan had no qualms of conscience about making him a minister in the interim government and administering the oath of office to him. Complaining that he would "sue them", because "they kept me in jail for two and a half years without a charge", Asif said it was "wonderful to be free", and it did not really matter whether it was Pakistan or America, though "home is the best" place.

Later that evening at a reception given by Maryland Senator Barbara A. Mikulski Indian journalists tried to pin Benazir down on the terrorism issue and asked her whether her government would support " Kashmiri terrorists" if she returned to power. Benazir said when she was prime minister a freedom movement was going on in Kashmir, but Pakistan was then not being accused of supporting terrorism. The reason was, she said, that "the spotlight was on Indian violations of human rights in Kashmir". India had to realise, she said, that Kashmir was a disputed territory and that the people of Kashmir had the right to decide which country they wanted to join. She had offered to India induction of foreign observes to monitor the alleged infiltration across the ceasefire line. But the offer was rejected by New Delhi. "This offer stands today", she said and added that she would be ready to allow UN, Commonwealth or any other foreign observers to monitor the situation in Kashmir "because I do not believe that the situation in Kashmir is Pakistan-inspired".

I listened to her carefully, because I had noted back home that sometimes her views on delicate foreign policy issues lacked clarity, unless the vagueness was deliberate, and she appeared to talk longer than necessary. But here I could see that she spoke with restraint and showed the wisdom and maturity expected of a statesman. To persistent questions from the Indian newsmen she said: "We don't believe in terrorism, we have never believed in terrorism and we will never support terrorism in any part of the world. But we do believe in political support where the right of self-determination is concerned, whether it is self-determination for the people of Palestine or the question of apartheid or the right of self-determination for the people of Jammu and Kashmir". Since the war in Bosnia was on and the slaughter of Muslims was going on she said "political support must be rendered when people in the heart of Europe — in Bosnia — are dying. And if we are living in a global world, let us draw up a global agenda, where humanity, human rights, democracy ... fighting terrorism, fighting narcotics become not the concern of one country or another but of all of us".

A couple of months after BB left for home, Pakistan was taken off the "watch list". That she had a meeting with President Clinton was not confirmed. PPP sources hinted that a meeting at the White House was on the cards, but it was never confirmed. Nevertheless, in July Pakistan's name was removed, while there was no change in Sudan's position. On the morning of July 14, I received a phone call from Charge d'Affaires Naqvi, telling me that an important announcement was expected from the State Department and that I better be there. I reached there in time. Also present was Khalid Hassan, then US correspondent for The Nation, Lahore, now dead. A brilliant journalist and author, Khalid wrote and edited over 40 books in English and Urdu on a variety of subjects that ranged from literature, politics, diplomacy and journalism to social themes and cricket. Because he was a Kashmiri, born in Jammu, he felt strongly about his native state's freedom and, no wonder, was a confirmed Bhuttoite. He became Bhutto's press secretary for a while, then joined the diplomatic service, and served with Pakistani missions in Paris, Ottawa and London. He resigned when Bhutto fell and lived in exile. His English books included The Crocodiles are Here to Swim , Give Us Back Our Onions, The Return of the Onion (RPT Onion), Question Time, The Fourth Estate, A Mug's Game, and twenty books of short stories translated from Urdu and Punjabi into English, including Saadat

Hasan Manto's Letters to Uncle Sam and other short stories, including those on partition riots, two of Faiz Ahmad Faiz's books of poetry — A City of Lights and The Unicorn and the Dancing Girl —, and three books on his beloved Kashmir — Kashmir Holocaust, Azadi: Kashmir's Freedom Struggle and Memory Lane to Jammu. His edited works included two books on Jinnah and three volumes of Bhutto's writings and speeches; a book on Afghanistan, and several books of memoirs and remembrances. Because he was based in Lahore and later in foreign countries, I never had the opportunity to learn from him. It was when he was The Nation's correspondent in Washington that I got to know him. He had a lively sense of humour and could quote from Urdu, Persian and English poetry aptly to make a point and enliven the gathering. He died at his Virginia home on February 5, 2009 of prostrate cancer. Six months later, President Asif Ali Zardari conferred on him Sitar-i-Imitaz for his "outstanding services to journalism" in Pakistan.

Khalid and I heard Mike McCurry, the State Department spokesman, declare that the United States had decided not to put Pakistan on the list of countries supporting terrorism, though Washington would continue to "monitor the situation". According to "the determination" made by Secretary of State Warren Christopher, McCurry said, circumstances did not warrant a finding that Pakistan "has repeatedly provided support for acts of international terrorism". Said McCurry: "He (Secretary Christopher) made this determination because Pakistan has taken a number of important steps that appear to have responded to our concerns about reports of official support for Kashmiri and other militants who commit terrorist acts against India". The situation "today" (July 14, 1993) was not same as it was prior to 1992, because Pakistan's attitude was "much more cooperative". Asked why Pakistan had not been put on the terrorist list "prior to 1992" McCurry said the requirement of the law had not been met i.e. of Pakistan repeatedly providing, support for acts of international terrorism. On the contrary, he said, Pakistan had taken "a number of important steps" that seemed to have satisfied the United States on that score. Asked whether "monitoring the situation" meant Pakistan continued to be on the "watch list", McCurry said there was no such thing as a "watch list". I asked him whether there would be another "period" — like the 180-day period announced in January — he said there was no fixed period, and that technically the Secretary of State could designate a country a state-sponsor of terrorism any time.

The following was the text of the State Department spokesman's reply to the question, why the Secretary of State had decided not to place Pakistan on terrorism list: "After a review of the facts and the law, Secretary Christopher determined that the available information did not warrant a finding that Pakistan 'has repeatedly provided support for acts of international terrorism'. He reached this determination because Pakistan has taken a number of important steps that appear to have responded to our concerns about reports of official support for Kashmiri and other militants who commit terrorist acts against India". Replying to a question he said there had been "real progress" in talks between Pakistan and the United States and that Islamabad's attitude had been "much more cooperative". The situation today with regard to Pakistan's alleged support for Kashmiri militants was different from what it was "prior to 1992." McCurry said he was not in a position to provide full details about the United States' ongoing dialogue with Pakistan but said Islamabad had addressed Washington's "concerns" on the issue.

A significant change in the July 14 announcement was the decision to monitor "the situation." On April 30, when the State Department released its report on terrorism, former State Department spokesman Richard Boucher had said no new names were being added to the list but that the US administration was watching "Pakistan's behaviour." Now it was "the situation" that was being monitored, and that, too, was said by McCurry in reply to a question. The "Press Guidance" transcript contained only the two paragraphs reproduced above and did not speak of "the situation" being monitored. The Clinton administration's decision came a day after State Department Counsellor Timothy E. Wirth told a House subcommittee on terrorism that "democracy does not sponsor terrorism." There was no doubt in my mind that one major factor behind the American decision was the realisation that placing Pakistan on the list would have meant adding one more Muslim country to a list of "bad boys ". This would have only served to reinforce feelings in the Islamic world that the US policy had acquired a distinctly anti-Muslim hue, given its inaction in Bosnia and the media blitz on "Islamic fundamentalism" in the wake of the 1992 blast at the World Trade Centre in New York — an act of terrorism that would pale into significance when Osama bin Laden would strike the WTC and Pentagon on Sept 11, 2001. "Our position stands vindicated," a beaming Sarwar Naqvi told me. There was no ambassador at the moment, Sarwar himself being the boss. Abida had returned home having resigned, the ambassador-designate Akram Zaki had not arrived, and it would be quite some time before Benazir would win the election and Maleeha Lodhi would come to the US on her first assignment as ambassador to the United States.

My membership of the Foreign Press Centre, which I often treated as my office, also gave me an opportunity to watch the behaviour of Indian journalists and that of the Pakistani. For instance, besides attending press conferences about South Asia, I also attended press briefings on the Middle East and Bosnia. That was understandable, given Dawn readers' involvement in these issues. But I also attended press talk on transatlantic affairs and those concerning America's relations with the Pacific community. However, I never found Indian journalists attending any other press briefings save those concerning South Asia. The fact is that the Indians are focussed on India, and this is their advantage as well as disadvantage. Personally I feel Pakistanis have a tremendous desire — in fact a passion — to operate at a global level, even if the means they adopt are not very flattering and do not cast Pakistan in a good light.

There were two Indian journalists with whom I developed friendship in Washington —Bharat Bhoshan of the Indian Express and Arora of the United News of India. While Bhoshan was on an assignment that turned out to be uncomfortably short, Arora is an American national and reports for the United News of India, which is that country's largest news agency. As I will explain later, this turned out to be a source of mutual professional advantage, and I realised that it pays to have friends among correspondents who do not represent a rival newspaper. I often tipped them off about news of interest to them without jeopardising the exclusivity of my stories for Dawn, and vice versa. The benefit of this understanding came in the form of a scoop during what from my point of view was a lean period, because I had not sent any worthwhile news to Dawn for at least a week. The story the two tipped me about revolved round Senator Pressler and the F-16s Pakistan had paid for. At a press conference in which he invited only the Indian journalists, the Senator from South Dakota said he had heard from several sources that the Clinton administration had decided to release the F-16s to Pakistan, and for this reason it intended to ask Congress for a one-time waiver for the Pressler amendment. While he had known of the move for quite some time, the decision, he said, had been conveyed to him in a letter by Frank Wisner, Under Secretary of Defence. An angry Pressler then gave the Indian correspondents the copies of the letter he had addressed to President Clinton seeking an interview. So desperate was he to block the waiver and the release of the F-16s to Pakistan that Pressler said if it was not possible for Clinton to grant him a five-minute interview in his office then it could be done during the president's morning jog. The decision concerned 71 F-16s, 11 of which were part of America's second six-year $4 billion aid package to Pakistan approved in 1986. The remaining 60 were to be purchased by Pakistan, and Islamabad had already paid $658 million for 28 of them.

Pressler alleged that the Clinton administration was under pressure from Lockheed, which had purchased the fighter-aircraft unit from General Dynamics. If the F-16s were not given to Pakistan, he said, Lockheed feared it would have to pay back $658 million to Islamabad. In November 1993, the Clinton administration had decided not to incorporate the Pressler Amendment in the foreign assistance act (called the Peace, Prosperity and Democracy Act, 1994) but gave up after the Indian lobby in Congress got active, and the Democratic administration did not believe, according to Brian Atwood, chief of the US Agency for

International Development, to get into a confrontation with Congress. Pressler told the Indian journalists that the move was contrary to the assurances he had been given by the administration, because "... Frank Wisner and the Defence Department do not seem to be in line with what the State Department has been saying".

His letter to President Clinton said, "I would like to request five minutes at your earliest convenience to discuss nuclear non-proliferation. Despite repeated assurances from members of your administration, including Deputy Secretary of State Strobe Talbot and Secretary of State Warren Christopher, I have heard from several sources within the administration about an attempt to grant an exemption to the Pressler Amendment. As you may recall, the Pressler Amendment prohibits aid to Pakistan unless the President certifies annually that Pakistan does not possess a nuclear explosive device.

"Mr President, I seek a meeting with you to underscore the importance of retaining the only nuclear non-proliferation law in force currently. I would appreciate having a meeting of no more than five minutes, which can occur at your office, or during a morning run. Should such a meeting prove impossible to schedule, I will raise the issue the next time I am at the White House, or if you should visit the Senate. While I would rather not raise this issue in such a public setting, I think it is critical for the administration to send a consistent signal about the importance of nuclear non-proliferation."

Pressler sent the copies of the letter to Defence Secretary William Perry and Secretary of State Warren Christopher. At about 12.30pm the same day, Bhoshan rang me up and informed me of the development. He also faxed the Pressler letter to me. I sent the story to Dawn, which published it as a lead under the heading, "U.S. to release held-up F-16s". The strap line said, "Pressler angry, protests." No other Pakistani paper carried the news. The administration's move was sabotaged by the powerful pro-India lobby in Congress, which had come to accept the Indian claim, pressed by Indian Ambassador Siddharta Shankar Ray, that Pakistan had modified the F-16's wings to enable the Pakistan Air Force to drop nuclear bombs. The issue dragged on and various solutions were suggested, including the sale of the F-16s to a third party, but there were no buyers. At a White House Press conference, which I attended to cover the joint press conference by Clinton and Benazir Bhutto, when she came to the US as prime minister in April 1995, the former deplored the fact that Pakistan should be denied both the money and the planes. He said he was the first president to have acknowledged this oddity. The issue was resolved finally (without Pakistan getting the F-16s) in the form of the 1996 Brown amendment, named after Senator Hank Brown, who had introduced the bill, which provided for a one-time sale to Pakistan of military items worth $368 million which were in the pipeline before President Bush Senior declined to issue the certificate, and the aid cut-off went into effect. America also paid to Pakistan $324 million from a special litigation settlement fund, besides some commodity aid. The military items included Harpoon missiles and some surveillance planes. For the F-16s to arrive in Pakistan, Islamabad had to wait for the 9/11 holocaust and the Musharraf government's decision to throw in its lot with Washington in the war on terror. But those F-16s would have nothing to do with the Pressler amendment or its one-time waiver; they were part of the $3 billion economic and military package pledged by President George Bush Jr. when he and Musharraf met at Camp David on June 24, 2003. It would be June 2006 when the Pentagon would officially inform Congress that the defence department had finally decided to sell 36 F-16s and other high-tech accessories to Pakistan. But I have jumped in time.

One of the pleasures of working in my apartment was the freshness with which I sat to work on my desk after breakfast without suffering Karachi's rash traffic. Those days, before I left for Washington in November 1992, Karachi did not have the kind of traffic jams that have now become a regular feature of life in this city of over 15 million. The drive between my Gulshan home and the Dawn office in the late morning then took 35 to 40 minutes. In the evening, while returning home, I drove with caution because motorists in Karachi do not bother to dip their beams and this took me 45 to 50 minutes. A decade later, it would take me 50 minutes to reach the Dawn office in the morning, and in the evening anything up to 90 minutes or more, depending upon whether or not I got trapped in a jam. But in Washington it was a pleasure for me to move to my desk immediately after breakfast and start working. However, as weeks and months passed, a question bothered me: if this is my office where is my home? While work has always been a pleasure for me, and a reporter is supposed to be on duty 24 hours, I thought I was entitled to rest and relaxation away from the workplace, and here the very fact that I ate and watched TV and slept in what basically was my office served to create an extraordinary boredom, especially because Razia had not yet joined me. Also contributing to boredom was the location of the apartment building, for there was no street life on 4th Street, South-West. This aspect of the American way of life is something that takes time to adjust to, for elsewhere in the world streets are full of people and you get to know a place basically when you move around. Here all I saw through my balcony was a constant stream of cars. No shops, no people, no noise; just an eerie silence the subcontinentals are not used to. The offices of the US Information Agency were on 4th Street, but whether it was 2pm or 2am, the scene was one of all-enveloping, aggressive silence. Further up the street as you headed toward Independence Avenue, there was a Roy Rogers on your left. It closed punctually at 9pm and contributed to the darkness. A block later on the right were the offices of the Voice of America in which so many Pakistanis worked. Again no people; just cars parked in neat rows.

This often made me wonder whether there was a relationship between development and organised living. In other words, is it necessary for a country to be fully developed before its society can become organised. Here 'organised' means putting some sense into urban activity; it means doing everything the way it should be done; and, to make it even simpler, 'organised' here means being the very opposite of what cities like Karachi and Lahore are. From my apartment, I had a view which was anything but spectacular: a row of trees within the building compound; a two-storey car park; touching it and above it Highway 395, and to the left a tree-line street with ordinary houses. In other words, there was nothing a Pakistani did not have back home. However, in reality, there was more to it than met the eye, for beneath every tree, every parking lot, every street and every apartment building there was that air of organisation that make the difference between chaos and order. Getting organised does not necessary mean that a country should be a member of G-7 (G-8, if Russia's inclusion out of courtesy in the grouping of rich nations is considered), but it does require that a country have a high literacy rate, and that those who run the country — from top to bottom — and those who live in it are educated. In Washington, everything was standardised, and one could see planning going into every bit of activity, so that one legitimate activity did not blot out or interfere with any other, equally legitimate activity. Above all, there was one rule that is alien to us of South Asia — that each and every individual abide by rules and regulations, which were for the good of all. There were no exceptions. The row of trees that ran parallel to my side of the building was not an accident. Parallel to that side of the building which I could not see and which faced the main street there was another row of trees. Along it at a distance was another row close to the wall that marked the building's boundary. The wall itself was not right on the street, for on both sides of it ran green patches the size of a normal Karachi footpath. Thus, between the sidewalk and the main building were a hedge, a green strip, an iron fence, a green strip again, a row of trees, an 'open' area, trees again that rose to touch balconies on the third or fourth floor, and a hedge again. There were no apartments on the ground floor, which was reserved for two more car parks and the apartment company's offices and the waiting lounge. On my side of the building, beyond the trees (in between there was a basketball field) was the double storey car park, where you had to pay a hefty monthly fee. Yes, hefty, because the system ran on the immutable assumption that one must pay for every utility. Those who lived in the building where I lived — called Capital Park Towers — paid a little less, but outsiders like several of my VOA friends who lived in Virginia and Maryland and came to the D.C. for work had to pay more.

This then was one of the major differences between an organised society and a chaotic one like ours where even those rich enough to pay throw money on everything but for services like this. To the left of my balcony, there was a big iron fence. It would open only for the fire brigade and for the garbage van that turned up dutifully each morning, or for some work gang. Under no circumstances would it open for any other vehicle. There were two yellow lines, right under my balcony, and no one but the garbage collectors and firemen were allowed to park their vehicles. If anyone else did, his vehicle would be towed away at the owner's expense, even if Bill Clinton were the owner. On the frontside of the building, there was a place in the waiting lounge marked only for movers. It is away from the place where taxis and cars dropped passengers. If you were moving in, or moving out, the movers would park their truck at that appointed place, and nowhere else, and they would do so only between 9am and 9pm; they would do so only on week days, and under no circumstances would they move the luggage through the main entrance in the lobby. They would move the luggage through the side entrance, and a folding wooden partition would be drawn so as not to disturb residents using the lobby and the elevators.

The most extraordinary feature of this building was its safety, security, hygiene and environmental standards. Mind you, when I — repeat I — could afford to live in this building, it would be anything but luxurious. But its standards of hygiene, security and environment were the same as in other luxury apartments. There were regular environmental checks by government inspectors. One day, when I was busy writing a story as the deadline neared, there was a knock on the door and two men along with the building's security guard entered my apartment. They had come, they said, to examine the paint on doors and windows to check whether they contained lead in excess of safety limits. They had brought meters and scanners with them, and when they left I noticed that they had drawn red circles on the doors. Two days later, those doors were changed, and this happened with all the 280 apartments in the building. A couple of months later, a new set of inspectors barged in. They said they wanted to check the amount of lead on the railings of our balconies, because lead in excess of authorised limits was a health hazard. Unbelievable as it may sound, all the railings were sawn off, and the balcony door sealed off, pending replacements. Fire alarms were regularly tested and the smoke-detectors shrieked at the weakest whiff of smoke. I know some cooking, because I was a good son to Ammi, and one day as I prepared a paratha which let off some smoke the siren, much to my embarrassment, shrieked. I received an immediate phone call from the leasing office to ask if there was a fire. Garbage chutes on every floor were regularly deodorised, and the residents were expected to follow the rules about garbage disposal, for there was a given place for newspapers and books, which must not be shoved into the garbage bag meant for the kitchen stuff. Nowhere was this regard for order and discipline reflected more thoroughly and might I say humanely than in the treatment given to the school bus. You could spot it from a mile from its peculiar shape and yellow colour. There are specific traffic rules governing it. When I went to the D.C. government office for getting a driving licence, I had to go through a multiple choice test on the computer which asked such questions as: if you see a stationary school bus with flashing red lights, will you (a) reduce speed and pass with caution?; (b) stop not less than fifteen feet from the bus? (c) proceed after yielding right of way to children entering the bus? (The correct answer was b). My thoughts went back to Suzuki carriers back home in which children were herded like cattle, and where no motorist, from the 'civilised' middle class sahib to the illiterate bus driver, had the least regard for the school "van" even on dangerous turnings and bridges. In America, order and discipline were reinforced by technology, because every violation was detectable by a wide variety of electronic gadgetry. But the important point to note was that the regard for order and discipline was independent of technology, because it was built into society, beginning with home and school. I have visited at least two countries — Malaysia and Jordan — which are not developed but where urban societies are highly organised and where order, discipline and civic standards compare favourably with developed countries.

There is something in South Asian history that has given us genes which rebel against discipline. We love to operate in chaos, and seem not to realise that whatever we do could produce better results if the same were done in an orderly fashion, even if the parameters were to remain the same. During my stay, Washington Metro celebrated its anniversary, perhaps 50th, and three more stations were added in 1993. A mention of the underground railway system is warranted here, not only because I have a private, unannounced fixation with metro but also because a country's transport system is a fair indication of its level of development and whether or not it has a humane attitude toward its citizens. Both are germane to the issue at hand, namely, the ability to organise. Why Pakistani cities lack a modern transport system is not necessarily an economic issue. Its neglect stems basically from two causes: one, the heartlessness of a ruling bureaucracy that is indifferent to the misery to which millions of people are subjected daily; and, two, the ignorance of the educated city dwellers of the very concept of organised living. In fact, if I were to choose, I would choose the latter more than the former, because we have seen the educated urban class launch so many political movements that wrought havoc with the country and overthrew dictators, but the same middle class does not think modern and comfortable mass transit systems for the millions of city dwellers are worth its attention. These lines were written in 2009, and I am sure by the time this book is published metro systems for Karachi, Lahore and Islamabad will remain a dream. One reason why traffic jams did not torment Washington was the ease with which outward-bound traffic managed to move from side streets into the highways. I seldom found any traffic jam in the streets near my home because motorists bound for the suburbia were able to access the link road that took them to 395, the highway that went to Virginia and Maryland. Thanks to America's acute racial problem and the consequent decay of inner cities, affluent whites lived in Virginia and Maryland and came to the District — as Washington is often referred to — for work and then returned home. But there was hardly any traffic jam of the kind Karachi suffered because the outward-bound traffic had alternative routes to follow.

In April Pakistan lost a valuable friend — America's 37th president. Richard Nixon, who could not till his last moment understand why the world had turned against him, died on April 22, 1994. I think he was America's greatest president since FDR. Intellectually and administratively, he was eminently qualified to be America's president, having been Eisenhower's vice president for eight year. The Watergate scandal ruined him, but history will not forget the role he played — with crucial help from Pakistan — in normalising his country's relations with China. That was the reason why he never forgot Pakistan. These words in italics have been taken from the headline to my story that appeared in Dawn's issue of April 23, 1994. Even though Nixon embarked on his seminal China journey much later when he became President, he was urged to visit China as early as 1964 at the height of the Cold War when the very idea of a visit by an American chief executive to Communist China sounded heresy. The man who made this suggestion was Ayub Khan. One of his popular books, In the Arena, begins with Pakistan and contains a number of anecdotes that speak of his abiding interest in Pakistan and its people. When he finally visited China in February 1972, he called the drive from the airport to the government guest house in Beijing "eerie." In the opening paragraph of the first chapter, entitled Peaks and Valleys, Nixon wrote: "In my years as Vice President, and

President, I had made official visits to the Vatican, the Kremlin, the Imperial Palace in Tokyo, Versailles, and Westminster, but nothing could prepare me for this – the first visit of a President of the United States to the People's Republic of China. President Ayub Khan of Pakistan had urged me to go to China when I saw him in Karachi in 1964. He had just returned from Beijing. I asked him what impressed him most. He replied, 'People, millions of people in the streets clapping, cheering, waving Pakistani and Chinese flags'." What Nixon and, perhaps, Ayub forgot was that the reception reserved for the Pakistani President was not necessarily to be extended to every Head of State, for there were hardly any people as Nixon's motorcade drove through Beijing's empty streets.

Wrote Nixon: "The curtains on the Chinese government limousine were drawn. But as I looked through the tiny openings, I could see that except for a lonely sentry stationed every few hundreds yards, the streets were totally deserted." Nevertheless, a new page was turned in the history of relations between the two countries as Nixon shook hands with Chou En-lai, who had personally selected the men for the honour guard – "tall ramrod straight, and immaculately, dressed."

Of the message that invited him to visit China, Nixon quoted Kissinger as saying it was "the most important communication to an American President since the end of World War II." It was Kissinger who had flown from Nathiagali on a secret trip to China to prepare the ground for his President's epochal visit when Pakistan was under martial law and Gen. Yahya Khan called the shots. Wrote Nixon: "It was here (the White House) that I received what Henry Kissinger described as the most important communication to an American President since the end of World War II. I had been sitting in this same chair catching on some of my reading material after a state dinner that evening. It was almost eleven o'clock. Henry burst into my room. He was breathless. He must have run all the way over to the residence from his West Wing Office. He handed me a message. It was Chou En-lai's invitation to visit China, which he had sent through President Yahya of Pakistan. As Chou put it later, it was a message from a head, through a head, to a head. Neither Henry nor I generally had a drink after dinner, but on this occasion we toasted this historic event with a very old brandy….."

That America ditches its friends when they are of no use to it found an echo in his mind when as ex-President he attended the funeral of the Shah of Iran, who died in exile in Cairo following the Islamic revolution. No one from Washington, he wrote, represented the United States "at a funeral for a leader who had been one of our staunchest and most loyal friends". Then he quoted what he called "a haunting remark" by President Ayub Khan in 1964. In commenting on US complicity in the assassination of President Diem of South Vietnam, Ayub said events proved "that it is dangerous to be a friend of the United States; that it pays to be neutral, and that sometimes it helps to be an enemy." Wrote Nixon very significantly, "It was an observation that again came to mind when I was informed of the mysterious death, in an airplane crash apparently caused by sabotage, of another staunch friend of the United States, President Ziaul-Haq of Pakistan."

In the Arena is replete not so much with the Watergate scandal itself as with human attitudes, the ingratitude of men he had patronised, the refusal of newspapers to publish a retraction when a charge turned out to be false, or when old friends avoided him. The title of the opening chapter, Peaks and Valleys, symbolised his rise to peaks of greatness and the fall to the valleys of degradation when he faced impeachment and jail. As I looked for reactions to his death for my story to Dawn, comments then pouring in were uniformly positive in keeping with the occasion. But those made in the past during the Watergate scandal and after it had blown over are mixed a lot, and testify truly to Nixon's "peaks and valleys."

President Ford, who pardoned him, said, "I've made up my mind to pardon Nixon …. I think it's right for the country … The man is so depressed, and I don't want to see the president go to jail." Adlai Stevenson: "Nixonland — a land of slander and … of sly innuendo, of a poison pen, the anonymous phone call and hustling, pushing shoving

– the land of smash and grab and anything to win." Ronald Reagan: "Richard Nixon is a man who understands the world... I don't think it's an exaggeration to say the world is a better place – a safer place – because of Richard Nixon." George Bush Sr.: "Nixon worked in the most pragmatic of arenas, yet insisted that politics is poetry. He believed in love of country, and in God …. and protecting loved ones."

The general election held on October 6, 1993, led to a hung parliament, with the PPP securing 86 seats (as against Nawaz Sharif-led Muslim League's 73), making the Washington Post remark that that Benazir was "pushed into power with the help of the sizable block of independent and minority parliament members who, in recent days, began joining her ranks in increasing numbers." The result of "the past two weeks of lobbying independent and minority members", the paper said, "was reflected on the faces of the two candidates as they walked into the chamber….Bhutto strode in to cheers from the galleries and smiled broadly as she made her way to her seat. Sharif appeared grim-faced as he slid into his seat". However, The Post called Sharif's speech in the National Assembly, extending cooperation to Benazir "one of the best of his career."

In the paper's opinion if the PPP government failed this time, there would be no new elections and "the army will take over." WP, of course, went wrong. Benazir's government was dismissed in 1996 not by the army but by her own choice for the president, Farooq Ahmad Khan Laghari, and the army was to take over three years later when Brigade 111 (the army's "coup brigade") ousted Sharif, and the world for the first time heard of Pervez Musharraf, who himself was midway between Colombo and Karachi. Saying that the Harvard- and Oxford-educated Benazir "courted the West during her first term," WP said "she entered her first term as one of the youngest and most glamorous heads of government in the world. The aura that surrounded her was magnified because she was the first woman ever elected to head the government of an Islamic state." But now, Benazir had "reclaimed the stewardship of a country ravaged by political and economic turmoil at home and ostracized internationally over questions of nuclear weapons, terrorism and drug trafficking."

The Post carried the Pakistan story on its page one with a four-column heading and a double-column picture of Benazir's with daughter Bakhtawar. The heading said, "Bhutto elected Pakistan's Premier, says she hopes to end isolation." Later, in an interview, Benazir told the paper her first priority on the international scene would be to "improve Pakistan's deteriorating relationship with the United States." However, the paper said Benazir "gave no ground on the (nuclear) issue that has contributed most to souring those relations." Describing Benazir as "politically more hardened and bruised," the paper quoted the prime minister from what she told the nation in her first radio and TV address: "We will protect Pakistan's nuclear programme and will not allow our national interest to be sacrificed." While her "battle — the long harsh fight to regain her post as prime minister of Pakistan" was over ", on Oct 20, "her first full day on the job" she was face to face with a war. This "war", the paper's correspondent said, was "a country that could find itself in a military confrontation any day now " over the Hazrat Bal issue with India ; "a treasury so strapped that it can barely meet its monthly debt payments; and a people so demoralised by political upheaval that most voters did not really care who was elected." Yet, despite the gravity of these issues and the fact that three-fourths of its people are illiterate, Pakistan "has become a critical world player by virtue of its nuclear weapons programme." The paper said if the Indian forces stormed the Hazrat Bal Shrine, "many observers say Pakistan could be pushed to take military action against its long-time enemy." She told the paper: "We don't want any issue to blow up. The situation for us is not just the siege of the shrine. It's the culmination of four years of ....random, ruthless killing." The paper noted that the Benazir government had come to power in the wake of the reformative policies undertaken by caretaker Prime Minister Moeen Qureshi, who "many observers say did more to push Pakistan toward a sound democracy in three months than elected governments have done in years." She told The Post: "We feel that a moral jihad, a moral war, was necessary to clean up Pakistani society. In fact, (Mr Qureshi) did a great service to Pakistan by introducing these reforms, which have been resisted in the past." But, the paper said the prime minister faced a nation "weary of a succession of governments — hers is the fourth in seven months — and suspicious of all politicians." It quoted Mian Habibullah, President of the Federation of Pakistan Chambers of Commerce and Industry, as saying: "We hope Benazir will not repeat past mistakes. The Pakistan People's Party has been telling us, 'We have learned our lessons'. We look forward to seeing if they've really learned lessons." On women's issues, Benazir said she planned to review laws that were discriminatory, like when they are jailed for adultery, while in fact they reported rape.

In August a parliamentary delegation headed by Ghulam Mustafa Jatoi came to Washington to "mobilise" American support for Pakistan's cause and present our case to American lawmakers. For the U.S media, the lawmakers and American television viewers the visit was a non-event. Led by the former prime minister, the 11-man "parliamentary" delegation included a Foreign Office official, a retired ambassador, a newsman and others. But it was strange that those who worked out the itinerary did not know they were choosing a most inopportune time for the visit, for Washington in August is a ghost town in terms of activity, or the lack of it, in congressional corridors. It is a month of vacation in which those who stay on at their desks do so only out of courtesy, or under protest. In fact all Congressmen would have gone home immediately after the U.S House of Representatives rejected the crime bill on August 11, but stayed on only because Clinton rebuked them. In late-night sessions a compromise was worked out between Democrats and the Grand Old Party and the bill was passed on August 25. This was exactly the date on which the Jatoi team landed in Washington and Senators and Representatives went home not to return until Sept 12, by which time the delegation had left America, rounded off the Canadian part of the trip and was home.

To be worth the dollars spent on the costly visit, the programme should have included a meeting with the Chairmen and members of the Senate and House Foreign Relations Committees, both of which, especially the former, are key decision-making bodies when it comes to appropriations for foreign aid. In fact the deal over the F-16s would have been clinched but for unrelenting opposition from Congress which basically meant resistance from these two powerful bodies. While the House Subcommittee on Asia and Pacific was headed by Rep. Gary Ackerman, who was by no means hostile to Pakistan, the HFR Committee's ranking member and one of its former chairman was Lee Hamilton, who had a very open and unbiased mind about South Asia. It was Hamilton who wrote the op-ed piece in the New York Times against the Pressler amendment. It was also the Congressman from Indiana who stunned Indian diplomats and newsman when in an Asia Society speech on US relations with New Delhi, he delivered what the Indians considered a highly pro-Pakistan speech on such vital issues as nuclear proliferation, the missile race in which Pakistan and India were then engaged and then still fresh F-16 proposal.

The Jatoi team would have found no better listener than in Hamilton and some others on the House Foreign Affairs Committee, including Dan Burton (R-Ind), Robert Torricelli (D-NJ), Dana Rohrabacher (R-Cal) and Thomas Sawyer (D-Oh). Like their counterparts in the Senate Foreign Relations Committee they were on a vacation and all that our "parliamentary" delegation was able to do was to meet the committee staff. "Staff" here means not secretaries and clerical help but those who are Congressman's eyes and ears. They write their speeches and letters, advise them on legislative business and do research work for the lawmakers' benefit. They include PhDs. While the meeting could be called useful it was no substitute for the windfall that would have followed if the Jatoi team had met Hamilton or Senator Claiborne Pell, chief of the Senate Foreign Relations committee.

"Speaking at George Washington University, Mr. N.D. Khan said" might sound very impressive, but actually not a single American teacher or student was among the listeners, and save for two Afro-American Muslims, the rest of the audience consisted of Pakistani students. Not that this was a Pakistan-specific boycott; I am positive if Turkey or Indonesia had sent a similar delegation to America the result would have been the same. But I don't think either Ankara or Djakarta would spend money so lavishly on a fruitless visit. The Jatoi delegation also met David Phillips, President of the Congressional Human Rights Foundation. Again it is a very imposing title, but the Foundation has nothing to do with Congress, it is not funded by Congress, does not report to any congressional committee, and no Congressman is on its panel. It is so called because some Congressman founded it, though undeniably Phillips was doing a very useful job for Pakistan by highlighting Indian atrocities in Kashmir. The Washington Post did not devote a single paragraph to the delegation's activities. I remember how unhappy Indians in D. C. were when The Post printed not a word about Prime Minister Narasimha Rao's address to a joint session of Congress three months earlier. Again, this was not an India-specific boycott. Like mature media the word over, American newspapers do not report rhetoric and speeches devoid of substance, no matter who it is. The nearest the Jatoi team came to media coverage was a single-column story in The Washington Times reporting on the Pakistanis' exchange of ideas with its editors and reporters. It was a nice piece, and quoted. N.D. Khan and Khalid Saleem of the Foreign Office at length to give a Pakistani perspective to the Kashmir situation. As for television, nobody in his right senses would expect the America media with all its prejudices and priorities to report on the activities of a delegation that had come to highlight atrocities on Kashmiri Muslims. There were business considerations also. Months before the Jatoi delegation's visit, this aspect of American television was highlighted by Suzan Mazur, a freelance woman journalist, who spoke knowledgeably at a seminar organized by Phillips on Capitol Hill. She said that in some cases television was willing to air programmes on rights abuses in Kashmir, but there were no sponsors. Some 145 companies were approached, but all of them refused because she said they had business interests in India.

The delegation had better luck when it came to officialdom, for it met Robin Raphel, Assistant Secretary of State for South Asian Affairs. If Raphel was cool to the spilling of Kashmiri blood that was to be expected. As Human Rights Watch/Asia remarked so aptly in its report released about this time, the Clinton administration "has abandoned what had been a refreshing new candour about Indian human rights violations, apparently in the hope of promoting better trade and security agreements" (with India). Those who saw human rights endangered globally because China arrested half a dozen dissidents turned a deaf ear to the cries of Kashmiris. That is realpoltik. Also, there was one more awkward truth here: Pakistani politicians are second to none when it comes to demagoguery to arouse passions and launch a popular agitation to overthrow a government. But in matters of foreign policy, one requires if not professional training or a penchant for geopolitics then at least the idiom that is peculiar to modern diplomacy. The Jatoi delegation, except for the Foreign Official and the former ambassador, had no such skill. This truth became obvious at a Pakistan Embassy news conference when the subject switched to domestic politics, and suddenly the former prime minister and fellow MNAs came into their own with cogent arguments and lively repartee. Besides being a non-event for the American media, the visit was a waste of foreign exchange. But was it? For those who organised this visit, the dollars were well spent. All Pakistani governments send potential dissidents and critics on foreign junkets at the nation's expense from time to time to keep them happy and ensure that they are on the right side when it comes to a no-confidence motion against the prime minister or a controversial bill is to be passed.

In September 1994, Nawaz Sharif dropped a bomb-shell that devastated the Pakistan Embassy and the Pakistani community if not the American government and highly embarrassed its supporters at Capitol Hill. Pakistan was not without its friends in Congress. India, of course, had a much larger and more powerful lobby that made every effort to torpedo Pakistan aid legislations and advance New Delhi's case on Kashmir. It was also the powerful India Caucus in Congress which scuttled the Clinton administration's move to grant a one-time waiver to Pakistan and release the F-16s blocked by the Pressler amendment, as discussed in the previous chapter. Congressmen Robert Torricelli was one of Pakistan's friends, and in March 1992 Islamabad conferred Hilal-i-Quaid-i-Azam on him because of his "services toward the consolidation of US-Pakistan ties and his consistent support for just causes of the people of Pakistan". Presenting the award to the Congressman from New Jersey at a ceremony at the Pakistan Chancery on May 18, Ambassador Lodhi called him "a stalwart on the side of human rights and democracy". From "the jungles of Central America to the killing fields of Kashmir", she said, Congressman Torricelli had "consistently and unwaveringly stood by the cause of self-determination, justice and freedom". The citation said, "Congressman Torricelli is a firm and committed friend of Pakistan and has consistently supported aid to Pakistan during the period he was on the (House) Subcommittee on Asia and the Pacific. He has advocated the cause of Pakistan in the House and has supported an even-handed United States' policy in South Asia. He has also been a staunch supporter of the proposal for a five-nation non-proliferation conference of South Asia. He has been extremely consistent in his criticism of human rights violations, especially in India, and is a strong proponent of strengthening United States-Pakistan relations".

The embarrassment to Pakistan's friends came in the form of Sharif's claim that, when he was prime minister in 1991, army chief Gen Beg and ISI head Gen Assad Durrani had come to him to seek his approval for a plan to smuggle heroin on a large scale to raise funds for the anti-Soviet resistance in Afghanistan. In an interview with The Washington Post at Sharif's Lahore residence, the opposition leader said he was "flabbergasted" by the two Generals' alleged suggestion, refused to give what the paper called "operational details" of the purported military plan, and said he had no sources to confirm whether the ISI obeyed him. The alleged plan was presented to him within three months of his assumption of power, but, Sharif said, "I told them categorically not to initiate any such operation , and a few days later I called Beg again to tell I have disapproved the ISI plan to back heroin smuggling." The meeting between him and the two Generals, according to the former prime minister, took place at his official residence, when Beg made a phone call and said he wanted to brief him on a sensitive matter. Said Sharif, "Both Beg and Durrani insisted that Pakistan's name would not be cited at any place because the whole operation would be carried out by trustworthy third parties." Sharif claimed Durrani told him, "We have a blueprint ready for your approval."

Ever since the Afghan war, the involvement of Pakistan's top military leadership in illicit drug trade had been rumoured from time to time. But it was for the first time that a former prime minister and Punjab chief minister and a person who was so close to the late General Ziaul Haq had come out with allegations of this nature. The sensational statement dragging the army into the underworld of global drug operations was carried by The Washington Post as its lead story in its World News section with a single column Sharif picture and a four-column heading — "Heroin plan by top Pakistanis alleged." The second deck of the headline said, "Former prime minister says drug deals were to pay for covert military operations." It was difficult to decipher

Sharif's motives. The 'disclosure' in no way hurt his main political rival, Benazir, then prime minister. More surprisingly the interview sought to portray Army Chief Beg and Gen Durrani as potential drug smugglers, even though he should have been grateful to the two, for it was Beg who as army chief gave Rs 140 million to Durrani for distribution among Benazir's rivals, including Sharif himself, who received Rs 3.5 million for electioneering (Details in Chapter 9). The only motive for Sharif could be to endear himself to the Americans, without realising how much slur he was casting on Pakistan and its army for political reasons. There was "no credible evidence" that there was drug corruption at "senior levels in the Pakistan government or the military," a State Department official told me when I sought his views for a story for my paper.

The Pakistan Embassy, of course, denied Sharif's claim and said the allegations were "unsubstantiated" and "riddled with contradictions." Generals Beg and Durrani both denounced Sharif, calling his claim "irresponsible" and "preposterous." Said Gen Beg, "We have never been so irresponsible at any stage. Our politicians, when they're not in office and in the opposition ... say so many things. There's just no truth to it." The Post quoted Durrani, then Pakistan's Ambassador to Germany, as saying, "This is a preposterous thing for a former prime minister to say. I know nothing about it. We never talked on this subject at all." The paper quoted Brig. S.M.A. Iqbal, whom it called "a spokesman for the armed forces" as declaring, "It is inconceivable and highly derogatory; such a thing could not happen." John Ward Anderson and Kamran Khan, who interviewed Sharif, quoted a Western diplomat as saying: "It's not inconceivable that they could come up with a plan like this. There were constant rumours that ISI was involved in rogue operations with the Afghans — not so much for ISI funding, but to help the Afghans raise money for their operations." Another Western diplomat thought Sharif was "a loose cannon" and said, "I'd have a hard time believing" his allegations against the army. His belief was the opposition leader wanted to keep Prime Minister Benazir Bhutto and Pakistan-India relations off balance. "If anything should bring these two countries together, it is their common war against the drug problem, but this seems to fly in the face of that." In a letter sent to The Post, the Pakistan Embassy said "the baseless allegations" by the former prime minister were "riddled with contradictions" and the whole account was "spun around a hypothetical scenario" for which the story offered no factual evidence.

Sharif's statement found an echo in Congress when three members of the House of Representatives attacked Pakistan and called for a review of US policy toward Islamabad. Representative Robert E. Andrews expressed his "grave concern" about Pakistan waging a proxy war in Indian occupied Kashmir and Islamabad's alleged involvement in "terrorism". The Democratic Congressman from New Jersey based his attack on Pakistan on two reports to which he sought to draw the House's attention "revealing a Pakistani link to fundamentalist groups." The first was a CNN documentary in which Peter Arnett tried to show a link between Pakistan and Gulbadin Hikmatyar's guerrilla groups. The second was Sharif's interview, and Rep. Andrews quoted its first paragraph for the House's benefits and pleaded with the State Department to place Pakistan gain on the watch list of countries supporting international terrorism. He said, "We should address this situation in the interest of preserving security in an increasingly volatile region." Sharif's "confirmation" that Pakistan had the bomb found a mention in a speech by Representative Sherrod Brown, who alleged that Pakistan's Kashmir policy was no more in Islamabad's control. The Democratic Representative from Ohio quoted extensively from an article in The Times, London, to substantiate his theory that there was a rise in "terrorist acts being perpetrated against Indian citizens in the province of Kashmir." Until recently Pakistan's Kashmir policy was being directed "largely by the Pakistani Army." Now, however, he alleged "the military support (for Kashmiris) has given way to foreign Islamic extremists allied with Gulbadin Hikmatyar." First, he claimed, Pakistan had "declared war on India three times" over Kashmir; second, "former Pakistani Prime Minister Nawaz Sharif recently stated publicly that Pakistan has for some time possessed nuclear weapons, despite statements to the contrary to the world community for the past seven years. Former Army Chief of Staff General Mirza Aslam Beg also has said publicly that Pakistan would be prepared to use these weapons against India in any future war between the two nations."

A third Democrat to refer to the former prime minister's bomb disclosure was Representative Maurice D. Hinchey, who linked it to the M-11 missile which Pakistan was acquiring from China. The Congressman from New York quoted from a Washington Times report to say that US intelligence had "found new evidence" that Pakistan was "going forward with a plan to purchase M-11 missiles from China." The M-11, he said, was "capable of delivering a nuclear warhead." Rep. Hinchey alleged, "This disclosure is very ominous, because it comes less than two week after the former Pakistani Prime Minister Nawaz Sharif announced publicly that Pakistan has possessed nuclear for some time." Pakistan's "nuclear ambitions," he said, "are a source of grave concern for the United States and every nation which is opposed to the growth of nuclear weaponry." He sought the House's unanimous consent for placing The Washington Times article on Congressional Record.

A most extraordinary feature of the three speeches was what appeared to be a tutored pro-India line — that Pakistan had forced "three wars on India," and that Pakistan was "exporting terrorism" not only to occupied Kashmir but to India itself. Forgetting the fact that the third and last war with India was on the question of East Pakistan, Rep Brown said Pakistan had declared war on India "three times" over the past four decades and "each of these wars has involved Kashmir." Congressman Andrews quoted press reports that provided "considerable detail on the degree to which Pakistan's military leaders have been involved in their pursuit of a nuclear bomb and export of fundamentalism to India." Rep. Hinchey' allegation seemed to be coming straight from the Lok Sabha when he said, "Nuclear proliferation experts are worried that Pakistan will use these weapons against India in a future war over Kashmir. Pakistan has gone to war with India over Kashmir three times in the last 40 years."

No one seems to have been hurt by Sharif's statement more than Pakistanis in America, especially professional associations and groups. One such group was the Pakistani Physicians' Political Action Committee (Pak Pac), then based in Las Vegas but now in Washington. Without naming Sharif directly it said its efforts to advance Pakistan's cause, especially when it came to discriminatory legislation in Congress, often suffered setbacks because "responsible personalities in Pakistan make irresponsible statements." The group noted "with deep concern" that such statements were used by people like Senator Pressler and Congressman Bill McCollum "to assert and reinforce their respective negative points of view" regarding some of the crucial issues facing Pakistan. In a statement faxed to me Pak Pac perhaps hit the nail on the head when it asked government and opposition leaders in Pakistan "to develop national consensus on key issues," including Kashmir, nuclear proliferation and relations with the United States "in the greater interest of the country". It appealed to all Pakistani leaders to "carefully think out the statements which may be meant for local political consumptions but which may have significant, serious and adverse consequences" abroad. "We hope that rational thinking will prevail." Dr. Ikram U. Khan, chief of Pak Pac's Board of Directors, said while Pak Pac supporters had made "strenuous efforts over the years" to monitor and follow developments in the country of their birth, the organization had been "deeply distressed" by recent utterances, and found its job of creating a positive image for Pakistan in this country "rendered difficult by our own people". Pak Pac, he said, was a neutral body and did not take sides in Pakistan's internal politics, it wished the government and the opposition well, but it expected people on both sides of the political divide "to exercise restraint, keep Pakistan's interests above those of party and be not carried away by partisan considerations." Sharif's spokesman later said in Lahore that the former prime minister had asked the paper to issue a denial and sued it for $100 million. However, when I talked to The Post's legal division they said they had not received Sharif's notice.

Benazir arrived in the United States for the second and last time as prime minister on April 5, 1995, for her first-ever meeting with America's equally if not more charismatic President. It was a nine-day visit preceded by a move that was welcomed by the Clinton administration —the extradition to America of two of Pakistan's most wanted drug barons, Iqbal Baig and Anwar Khattak. State Department acting spokesman David Johnson said the extradition was "the type of action that we like to see in the positive relationship that we're building with the government of Pakistan." One of the Pakistani newsmen shivering at the windswept Andrews Air Force Base in an unusually colder April weather asked whether she would speak to them. Benazir replied "You have to wait". There was some scuffle between PPP supporters and a small group of MQM workers as both wanted to occupy the front row at the barrier beyond which entry was not allowed. The MQM men had mixed themselves with the newsmen and PPP supporters bussed to the airbase. As the plane carrying Benazir and party approached the runway, the MQM supporters raised anti-PPP and anti-Benazir slogans, provoking the other side. Shouting and scuffle continued for about five minutes until American security authorities separated the two groups. The MQM men, carrying their party flag, later moved back and continued their demo. Benazir later boarded a helicopter that took her to the Washington Monument ground, where she walked past an honour guard and later drove to Willard Hotel.

On April 6 she met no less than 25 members of the House of Representatives on the foreign relations committee and its sub-committees to brief them on Pakistan's position on the aid cut-off and its negative impact on relations between the two countries. There was consensus among the Congressmen that the Pressler amendment should be done away with because it was a discriminatory law and had failed to advance America's non-proliferation concerns. Among those who expressed their disillusionment with the results of the Pressler amendment were some leading Congressmen, including Representative Benjamin Gilman, Chairman of the House Foreign Relations Committee, Congressmen Lee Hamilton, its former chairman, and Congressman

Robert Livingston, Chairman of the House Appropriations Committee. Some of the Congressmen agreed with Benazir in her denunciation of the Pressler law and used strong language. Representative Dana Rohrabacher, a member of the HFR Committee, who recently introduced a resolution on Kashmir in the House, called the Pressler amendment "outrageous," while Congressman Doug Bereuter, Chairman of the Subcommittee on Near East and South Asia, said he would like to "wipe it off the statute book." Several members of the subcommittee agreed with their chairman and said they realised that the amendment named after the Senator from South Dakota had failed to promote non-proliferation and had become an impediment in relations with Pakistan.

Briefing newsmen on the outcome of the first phase of the Prime Minister's dialogue on Capitol Hill, Ambassador Maleeha Lodhi said the agreement between the administration and Congress on the futility of the Pressler amendment was a hopeful sign for Pakistan. By visiting Capitol Hill, she said, the Prime Minister had also shown a fuller understanding of the bipartisan nature of America's legislative process and the close relationship between the administration and Congress in the conduct of foreign and aid policies. The Prime Minister told the Congressmen it was now for the administration and Congress to decide how to handle the release of military equipment worth 1.4 billion dollars held up because of the Pressler law. A continued "freeze" on the issue would "give a wrong signal" to the world on how the United States treated "a long-standing friend like Pakistan."

Benazir also touched upon Indo-Pakistan issues and pleaded for a third party intercession if the Kashmir issue were to be resolved. The two major agreements between Pakistan and India – those on the Rann of Kutch and the Indus waters – were the result of third party intercession. Until another party came forward to assist the two, she said, a solution of the Kashmir issue was unlikely. She regretted that India was not willing to have a meaningful dialogue on Kashmir, because New Delhi pedalled the "integral part" line to scuttle talks. Questioned about Pakistan's alleged support for Kashmiri freedom fighters, she said Pakistan had offered the stationing of foreign, neutral observers to verify the truth or otherwise of Indian allegations. But New Delhi had not agreed to such a suggestion because this would expose the hollowness of its allegations against Pakistan. A UN observer force was already there along the Line of Control, and Pakistan had asked for its expansion. But India had refused to go along. On Afghanistan, the Prime Minister said Pakistan had been trying to end the civil war and supporting UN efforts to ensure peace in that country. However, the main hurdle was the warlords' refusal to agree on a power-sharing formula. Ambassador Dr Lodhi described the Congressmen's line of questioning as "very positive from our point of view." Congressman Hamilton, one of Pakistan's solid backers on the Hill, and Congressman Gilman paid tributes to the Prime Minister and the Bhutto family for their sacrifices for the restoration of democracy in Pakistan. Congressman Gilman praised Pakistan's role in peacekeeping and in a tribute to the Prime Minister said she had "a unique ability to deal with issues with courage, wisdom and compassion." As I write these lines in 2009, I am sure Congressman Hamilton would not have had the slightest idea of how courage would cost Benazir her life 12 years later in the same park in Rawalpindi where Pakistan's first prime minister was assassinated. The Congressman recalled his meeting with Benazir's father and said his was one of the "sharpest and most impressive minds" he had ever met.

Benazir raised the F-16 question again at a meeting with a restricted meeting of the US-Pakistan Council at Willard Hotel, where she and the party were staying. The US-Pakistan relations, she said, had been "frozen by the application of discriminatory statures" and she had come to the United States to "raise the fairness question" – either the planes or the money. "That simple, that fair." Pakistan, she said, was "every bit as critical to the world and to the United States today" as it was in "the hottest days of the Afghan war" and added, "We remain a central asset – politically, strategically, culturally and economically – in the post-Cold War period." She had a go at India when she said while Pakistan "did not waver" during the Cold War, India aligned itself with the Soviet Union and the communist regime n Kabul. "Although the enemies have changed,

Pakistan remained a front-line state against international terrorism; we are a front-line state against international narcotics trafficking; we are a front-line state for moderation and pluralism, against the forces of extremism and ignorance." Pakistan, she said, would remain important "in the new millennium." She criticised America's non-proliferation policy and demanded that the United States honour its contractual obligation. The Pressler amendment was "a veto in the hands of India, a tool and a club in the hands of those who stood against America and with the Soviet Union for fifty years." It rewarded "Indian intransigence" and punished "Pakistani loyalty and friendship." This must be changed "so that normal relations between our two great countries can be strengthened." She offered "to go anywhere, at any time" to sign the Nuclear Non-proliferation Treaty if her Indian counterpart did the same. "I will joyfully agree to a treaty to ban nuclear weapons in South Asia, to create a missile-free zone in South Asia, to stop the production of missile material in South Asia, as long as the only proven nuclear power on the subcontinent adheres to the same treaties."

Implying that Pakistan was a model for other Muslim countries of the region, she said the stakes were "terribly high" because the world's one billion Muslims were at a crossroads. They must choose, she said, between "tolerance and bigotry", between "technology and repression," between "xenophobia and internationalism." Ultimately, they must choose "between the past and the future." Pakistan stood ready, she said, "to assist them in their transition to democracy, in their transition to free market economies, in their transition into the modern era." She had come to the US to talk to the President, Congress and the press about "the Pakistan we Pakistanis are building." It was a Pakistan which was "committed to MoUs and not IOUs, to partnership, not dependency, to trade not aid." Listing her government's achievements on the economic front, the prime minister told the Pakistanis present it had built over 7,000 schools in the last seventeen months, with 10,000 more under construction. "It is a Pakistan which has electrified 7,700 villages since our re-election; it is a Pakistan which has increased by about five fold in just one and one-half years the foreign investment in Pakistan in the last quarter century."

On April 10, a day before meeting Clinton at the White House, Benazir spoke to a packed hall at the Paul Nitze School of Advanced International Studies of the Johns Hopkins University. Asked whether she would prefer the money or the F-16s, the prime minister said she would prefer a relationship between "our workers and your workers." The reference to the workers followed a hint in her prepared speech that if Islamabad were denied the F-16s she would turn to other countries. While Pakistan needed modern jet planes, "the issue is whether they will be built by American workers, by French workers or by Russian workers. Obviously we prefer American planes built by American workers."

The same day, appearing in the Larry King programme, Benazir said she aimed at redefining the relationship between Pakistan and the United States in the post-cold war era. She would tell President Clinton that Pakistan was "an important friend and ally" and still had an important role to play in the region, situated as it was close to Central Asia and the Gulf region. She called the Pressler amendment "a strange law" which targeted Pakistan by name and imposed sanctions, even though the administration admitted Islamabad did not possess a nuclear device. She told a caller from London that there were extremists in Pakistan who thought their country was being penalised, in spite of not possessing a nuclear weapon, because it was Muslim, while India, a Soviet ally, had no such sanctions imposed, because it was non-Muslim. Even though the issue was not that simple, she said the "discriminatory treatment" must go. India had detonated a nuclear device, it was building missiles which could carry nuclear and chemical warheads, its missiles could hit every Pakistani city, and the long-range ones that could hit countries beyond Yemen. She said she would tell Clinton that under America's present non-proliferation policies, India had no incentive to respond positively. She referred to the withholding of military equipment worth 1.4 billion dollars by the United States and said Pakistan was turning to other countries for military purchases. While

Pakistan had already contracted to buy submarines from France, and could go for tanks and other purchases from other countries, Islamabad would prefer American military items. She did not agree with Larry King that the Kashmir question was "unsettleable". When issues could be solved in the Middle East, South Africa and North Ireland, there was no reason why the Kashmir issue could not be resolved. However, just as solutions to the issues in the Middle East and South Africa resulted from foreign mediation and the pressure of the international community, so in Kashmir also third party mediation was needed. Pakistan, she said, was happy with offers of outside help and mediation but India was not. Asked by Larry King how she felt about President Clinton, Benazir said she felt empathy, because he was the leader of a new generation educated like her in the 1960s and again like her was an Oxford graduate.

Watched by millions of Americans during the prime time telecast , Benazir replied to questions about her personal life and also dwelt on Pakistan's domestic situation, especially that in Karachi, and said she had a vested interest in seeing peace in Karachi not merely as prime minister but as a Karachiite. The beginning of her second tenure as prime minister had embroiled her government in bigger issues — Pakistan was isolated internationally, the economy was bankrupt, and an army operation was going on in Sindh. The situation in Karachi was the result of the Afghan war, and drug traffickers were battling for the possession of territory. But there was violence only in 20 out of Karachi's 80 police stations. The situation would improve. "Give us some time, and hopefully the problem will be solved." She replied to questions about her childhood, how she felt about being in politics, and whether she enjoyed being prime minister. The birth of her first baby was "the biggest spy game" she had played by keeping her political opponents guessing. The baby came out two months earlier than what her opponents had thought and hoped that she would be stuck in a hospital bed. She said she did not enjoy being prime minister, but it was a "tremendous responsibility". With her father, politics was "romance with the people", while what she wanted was a staid job in the Foreign Office or in a newspaper. Her reply to King's question about the possibility of her assassination turned out to be prophetic. King asked her whether she feared for her life, and she replied it was in "God's hands. I don't worry about it. When it has got to come, it has got to come."

~~~~~~~~

The Benazir-Clinton meeting on April 11 was to begin at 11.30am, but we were told by the White House security staff that all Pakistani journalists must be there at 9am. The embassy advanced it by an hour to my unhappiness — I am a late-riser, I have said several times — by asking us to be at the chancery at 8am. We reached both the places well in time, but once in the White House we were sequestered. No one would be allowed to go out, and we must wait for president and prime minister to end their talks and meet the pressmen. Inside the waiting area, there was no TV set or anything that could keep us busy. So all we did out of boredom was to drink from the slot machines and go to toilet. While security agencies throughout the world are known for what they are, one extremely despicable habit on their part is the waste of time they inflict on others for the sake of VIP security. I can understand their security concerns, and if they do not trust anyone, including newsmen on the presidential entourage, I can fathom even that. But the way they are indifferent to others' inconvenience is shocking. But then I suppose I am talking nonsense. To expect those who "disappear" people and run torture chambers to be kind and considerate is to be naïve. As I have said in an earlier chapter, I cannot stand someone wasting my time. In fact, to me, making me waste time is perhaps the greatest torture I can be subjected to, short perhaps of electric shocks.

I have not forgotten the heartlessness of the security agencies on a December night at Flashman's Hotel in Rawalpindi in December 1985. Ziaul Haq was to go Dhaka to attend a summit of South Asian nations to give shape to the seven-nation South Asian Association for Regional Cooperation — a debating society that after more than two decades of its existence has achieved nothing except made us report their trite rhetoric and write editorials on their non-performance. I had flown from Karachi to be part of the entourage the next morning, and the Information Ministry lodged me along with other journalists at Flashman's. Built in British days, Flashman's has a charm of its own, for instead of being a vertical monstrosity like most of today's five-star hotels, it consists of blocks of rooms spread out, surrounded by a low boundary wall and has some greenery. The flight to Dhaka was scheduled for 8.30 in the morning, and I told the operator to wake me up at 6. After dinner and mandatory tea I kept reading and then slept off at 1am. At 2 the telephone rang. The operator said it was time to be up. I said I had requested a 6am wake-up call, but he said he had orders to wake us all up at 2, because we would go to the airport much before Zia arrived. We had an early breakfast, I did some walking on the lawn and waited for the muezzin to call, which did not happen until 6. Finally we were taken to the airport at 7, boarded the plane at about 7.45, Zia came at 8.15 and the plane took off at 8.30. I just wondered what the fun was in rousing us from bed at 2am. I had a similar experience at Istanbul in 1987. We had a very hard day from morning to evening on the last day of our stay in Istanbul. Irshad Ahmad Haqqani, the doyen of Urdu journalism, and I wanted an interview with Prime Minister Turgut Ozal, but somehow the Turkish hosts could not arrange it. There was a lunch given by the Turkish prime minister for the Pakistani delegation, and there were other engagements, besides a reception followed by dinner at the Pakistan Embassy. Suddenly, I was told that an interview had been arranged with Ozal, and we had to dash to the prime minister's official residence. The interview went well, but from the benefit of the hindsight I think we were rude to the prime minister, for instead of asking questions about Turkey's relations with Pakistan and other countries, we focussed on Turkey's domestic scene. There were some controversial constitutional changes Ozal was planning, and we pinned him down on this. We had also done some homework, and quoted the Turkish constitution's clauses while poor Ozal looked puzzled. As we reached the Pakistan Embassy for the reception, we were told to stay on for the dinner. After the reception ended, the dinner and the postprandial talk dragged on, enlivened by that great conversationalist, Sahibzada Yaqub, then foreign minister and a candidate for Unesco presidency. We reached our hotel at about 1am, and were told to immediately pack up and place our luggage on our doors, for it will be picked up during the night. "Security" was at work. I had done some shopping, too, things were spread all over the room, and I had a couple of stories to do. Tired I began stuffing things in and slept off after placing my bags outside. When we woke up in the morning, we found our luggage exactly where we had left it the night before. "Security!" We buoyed up, however, when we were given the good news that, instead of returning directly to Pakistan, we were going to the holy land for Umra.

Eight years later, and in another continent, I sat bored and sequestered in the White House as anti-Benazir demonstrators gathered outside. The demos were being held by the opposition, especially by the supporters of Mian Nawaz Sharif and the MQM, and because of the hostility between these two groups, they were asked to stand away from each other. Shaheen Sahbai had arrived to replace me, and it was decided that while I would be inside the White House, Shaheen would cover the demos. To watch the demonstrators and to catch a glimpse of the prime minister, Razia, too, was there along with Safia, who was there to report for the VOA's Urdu service. Because the BB-Clinton meeting had taken more time than expected, we were allowed after two hours of sequestration to go out and return before 1230. I saw the demos and the discipline which the American system had imposed on them and also chatted to Razia and Safia. I then returned to the White House, and we were taken to the Grand Foyer, where Benazir and Clinton finally turned up at about 1245

One unusual feature of presidential press conferences is the American newsmen's tendency to put questions to the President on the country's domestic politics, ignoring the foreign guest, who must feel belittled. I often watched on TV American newsmen asking their president questions about domestic issues while the foreign guest felt embarrassed, if not ignored. In this case, however, no American journalist asked a question on America's domestic politics, and all questions by Pakistani and American journalists related to the bilateral relationship. This I think went to Benazir's credit. During my sojourn in Washington, especially when the Bosnian war was at its peak, quite a few European heads of government visited Washington, but — in spite of what often appeared to me a rather muffled voice that resembled the drone in Kissinger's — Clinton overshadowed them all with the brilliance of his personality. However, in that Grand Foyer on April 11, 1995, Benazir eclipsed her host. On the whole Clinton appeared friendly to Pakistan, and there is no doubt that, during their talks before they met the press, she must have made him realise the immorality of withholding the delivery of the F-16s without paying the money back to a Third World country. The Pressler amendment, Clinton said, had put Pakistan "in a no man's land," and that was why "I do not think it is right for us to keep the money and the equipment". He said he had no intention of "dumping Pakistan" when a newsman asked him whether or not the world would get a wrong message if America dumped Pakistan. Instead, he said, said as America's president he had done "everything possible to broaden our ties with Pakistan". He would not abandon Pakistan because "the future of the entire that part of the world where Pakistan is depends in some large measure on Pakistan's success." Clinton quoted Jinnah and said he was glad that Pakistan was trying to uphold the founder's ideals, and he referred to Pakistan repeatedly as a moderate, progressive, Islamic country that was keen to combine the best of its Islamic traditions with democratic ideas.

In her opening statement, Benazir said: "Since 1989, my last visit to Washington, both the world and Pakistan-US relations have undergone far-reaching changes. The post cold war era has brought into sharp focus the positive role that Pakistan, a moderate, democratic, Islamic country of 130 million people, can play from its strategic location at the tri-junction of South Asia, Central Asia and the Gulf, a region of both political volatility and economic opportunity. Globally, Pakistan is active in UN peacekeeping operations. We are in the forefront of the fight against international terrorism, narcotics, illegal immigration and counterfeit currency. We remain committed to the control and elimination of weapons of mass destruction as well as their delivery systems on a regional, equitable and non-discriminatory basis. Since 1993, concerted efforts by Pakistan and the United States to broaden the base of bilateral relations have resulted in steady progress. In September 1994, in a symbolic gesture, the US granted Pakistan about $10 million in NGO support for population planning. This was followed by the ... visit of Energy Secretary Hazel O'Leary, which resulted in agreements worth $ 4.6 billion. During Defence Secretary Perry's visit in January 1995, our countries revived the Pakistan-US Defence Consultative Group. During First lady Hillary Clinton's visit we had an opportunity to discuss issues relating to women and children. I urged an early resolution of the core issue of Kashmir, which poses a grave threat to peace and security in South Asia. It has retarded progress on all other regional issues, including nuclear and missile non-proliferation. A just and durable solution is the need of the hour based on the wishes of the Kashmiri people as envisaged in Security Council resolutions. Pakistan remains prepared to engage in a substantive dialogue with India to resolve this dispute. But not in a charade that can be used by India to mislead the international community.

Pakistan asks for a re-assessment of the Pressler amendment which places discriminatory sanctions on Pakistan. In our view this amendment is a disincentive for a regional solution to the proliferation issue. I am encouraged by my discussion with the President and the understanding he has shown for Pakistan's position. I welcome the Clinton administration's decision to work with Congress to revise the Pressler Amendment."

The next day's newspapers highlighted the Clinton-Bhutto talks and press conference and added remarks by administration officials that the United States was considering "low level" cooperation with Pakistan. The New York Times, The Washington Post, The Washington Times, USA Today and The Los Angeles Times either made it their lead stories or put it on page one. All papers carried their pictures. At a dinner given the same day in her honour, Vice President Al Gore said Pakistan and the United States had "travelled a long road together since the dawn of your nation some 47 years ago." More significantly, he told Benazir: "Your citizens can be proud that Pakistan has emerged as an economic power and a solid bridge between fanaticism and modernity, and between extremism and progress for all of Islam to follow." He said this development "in large measure" was due to her. Recalling Benazir's struggle for democracy, Gore said, "As a young woman at Radcliffe, you came to the United States having left a Pakistan that knew neither democracy nor political freedom. You returned to your homeland as a dedicated and self-less advocate for both. ... Despite several dark years of prison and house arrest you emerged to become the first democratically-elected Muslim woman to serve as head of government, a bright symbol of hope for millions, and living proof that democracy can find enduring roots in Islam's rich soil." Friendship between the US and Pakistan must continue until "peace in South Asia becomes a reality....It must continue until the promise of the ancient Islamic teachings to resist tyranny and to promote justice, tolerance and understanding is fulfilled throughout the world." He translated one of Allama Iqbal's famous verses thus: "Life is reduced to a rivulet under dictatorship. But in freedom it becomes a boundless ocean."

In an interview published in the International Herald Tribune two days after her meeting with Clinton, Benazir appeared bitter when she said a West that was now making so much noise against some of Pakistan's religious laws had kept quiet when they were enacted by a dictatorship. She spoke of the "subterranean culture" at religious madressahs and said she would not allow people "to preach hatred and violence" or let the country be used for "subversion against any other country". The interview was conducted in Singapore where she had gone to seek investment. To the IHT's claim that Islam was turning "increasingly violent in Pakistan", she said, "Islam is not a violent religion. It is a message of brotherhood, peace, tolerance and harmony. However, Pakistan has had a violent past. We had a dictatorship from 1977 under General Zia-ul-Haq. During those years, different groups were patronized to quell and subjugate the rest of the people and keep them in fear. Internally, the dictatorship tried to clothe itself with the legitimacy of Islam, portraying the religion with its own narrow vision rather than what it really is. This led to much fanaticism. A lot of laws were passed which now need constitutional change. They include laws discriminating against women and minorities. The sad part is that the West never spoke up against these laws at the time". Asked why, she replied: "This was the period when the Soviets went into Afghanistan. As a result, Pakistan became the frontline state in the battle against Communism. From 1979, Muslims from all over the world came to Pakistan to help the Afghan resistance. They began schools which gave militant training to students to go and fight in Afghanistan. When the Soviet occupation ended, two million Afghan refugees were left behind in Pakistan along with a series of well-organized and well-financed schools which are called religious but are not imparting religious training. Instead, they promote sectarianism and terrorism by teaching hatred or giving military training. This entire subterranean culture with its secret cells existed in Pakistan until my government was elected in October 1993".

To a question what she intended to do about it, Benazir said: "We have started regulating the schools. We are not going to allow people to preach hatred and violence. We are exposing this culture and creating public awareness about it. We signed an extradition treaty with Egypt in 1994 so that extremists wanted there could be sent back. With the expeditious extradition to the US of Ramzi, we have sent out a clear message that Pakistan will not allow its soil to be used for subversive action against any other country". Pakistan, she said, was not getting "the type of political and moral support" she thought it should get from the West in its fight against sectarianism, militancy and the drug trade. Pakistan was "a frontline state against the forces of extremism and fanaticism. It is a wall of modernity against all those values that undermine global stability. Pakistan has a constitution and a democratic government. It ought to be strengthened and supported". From the United States she wanted Pakistan to get "the type of moral assistance and political support that a country like Egypt gets". The "main support we want from the US is for the Pressler amendment to go. It cut off all military and economic aid to Pakistan because the President said he could not certify that Pakistan did not possess a nuclear explosive device. Pakistanis feel this is a discriminatory law because it does not apply to all countries of the world". Pakistan had paid the US about 1.2 billion dollars for F-16s and other equipment. "We are getting neither delivery nor our money back. Pakistanis can't understand why America is doing this. These are the very things that fuel fanaticism". Asked what she would tell Washington about the status of Pakistan's nuclear plans during her tour, she said: "Pakistan does not possess a nuclear device. Pakistan has developed certain technology; it has enough knowledge to put together a nuclear device, but has deliberately chosen not to do so to support the objectives of regional and global non-proliferation. Even the US now admits that we have not put together a device". America "is a fair country", she said, "yet it continues to penalise Pakistan unfairly. It must re-evaluate its policy".

The prime minister continued her blitz on the Clinton administration on the F-16 question when she reached Los Angeles on the last leg of her tour. Calling for amendments that would make the Pressler law "less discriminatory", she asked America to honour its "contractual obligations." In a speech largely, though not entirely, devoted to foreign policy, she told the Los Angeles World Affairs Council that, while she would very much like to see the sanctions lifted, she wanted the release of the equipment "that sits in Arizona". Because of Pakistan's strategic situation "our air force needs defensive aircraft". As she began speaking a lone MQM worker created a stir when he shouted anti-government slogans and displayed a banner that he had managed to smuggle into the hall by wrapping it round one of his legs. Security men removed him from the hall, and Benazir continued her speech. Pakistanis, she said, were "security conscious" because of the 1971 trauma and the three wars with India, and since New Delhi had detonated a nuclear device, Pakistan had to take every step to ensure its territorial integrity and sovereignty. If America could not fulfil its contractual obligation, Pakistan expected its money back. "Once we are beyond this impasse in our relationship", she said "we hope that the United States would then work with us, as we develop a long-term programme to promote around the world the values and concerns that we share." These values were democracy, human rights and human dignity, constitutional law, free market economics, decentralization and privatization.

However, she dwelled mostly on the domestic situation when she addressed the Pakistani community of the Los Angeles area on April 14. Hamid Nasir Chattha had accompanied her on the tour, and she eulogised his role in giving political stability to Pakistan. Chattha's party, PML-J, was then part of the PPP-led coalition, and the prime minister said all the economic progress that had been achieved since she came to power would not have been possible if the country's biggest province were hostile to the federal government — a reference to the situation during her first government when Mian Nawaz Sharif was Punjab's chief minister. In fact, she said other political alliances could learn from the way the PPP-PML-J alliance was working. Benazir's man in Punjab then was Chief Minister Manzoor Ahmad Wattoo, who belonged to PML-J and headed the coalition government with the PPP. (Four months later, Wattoo was made to go and was replaced by another PML-J man, Mohammad Arif Nakai.) Unlike her previous arguments about the situation in Karachi, Benazir this time gave a historical background to the reasons why Pakistanis in general were so politically conscious and quick to assert their rights. Under Jinnah's leadership, she said, the entire Muslim nation of the subcontinent was involved in a democratic struggle for the creation of a separate homeland for South Asia's Muslims, whom she called "a highly politicised society." In Pakistan, struggling for one's rights was "a legacy of the freedom struggle" compounded by Pakistan's experience with dictatorship. Pakistanis, she said, had made sacrifices for the restoration of democracy and for their constitutional and political rights. When she became prime minister a second time, she said, the situation was precarious both internally and externally.

While internationally Pakistan stood isolated, economically she quoted interim prime minister Moeen Qureshi as saying that the country stood on the verge of bankruptcy. The law and order situation throughout the country was deteriorating, there was ethnic and sectarian violence in major cities, and the preceding government had deployed the army in Sindh. Her government, she said, had restored stability to the country, one proof of which was the flow of foreign investment. As for the memoranda of understanding worth 20 billion dollars signed with foreign investors, she said even in a highly developed county it took 14 months for a project to mature. But in Pakistan four big projects had matured in 12 months' time, which was a record.

The venue of her address to the Pakistani community was originally to be Convention Centre. However, after a minor distraction caused by two MQM supporters, the venue was changed to Regent Beverly Wilshire Hotel, where the Pakistan delegation was staying. The Los Angeles Times printed pictures both of the prime minister addressing the Los Angeles WAC and of the lone MQM worker being hustled out of the hall. A local TV channel also briefly showed anti-government demonstrators, mostly Pakistani Christians, protesting against the blasphemy laws. A most unusual feature of MQM demonstrations in Washington and in Los Angeles was the bracketing of the prime minister with the army, with fierce attacks on both. Outside the hotel, as she spoke on foreign and domestic policies, MQM demonstrators carried placards and raised slogans denouncing Benazir, the army and the generals. Several placards referred to "Corrupt Benazir, corrupt Generals" while another condemned "military dictatorship" and "war crimes". She later had a meeting with the editorial board of The Los Angeles Times, who called on her at the hotel.

At two minutes past nine on the morning of April 19, 1995, in Oklahoma City Timothy McVeigh blew up with remote control his truck containing

5,000 pounds of ammonium nitrate, destroying the Alfred P. Murrah Federal Building, killing 169 people, including19 children, and wounding 480 people. I was then winding up in Washington, and did not know that this would be the forerunner of what would come six years later on the morning of September 11. Then Shaheen rang me up. He said "a certain Siddiqi" was being sought by the police. He was serious, but I laughed it off. My only worry was that perhaps they would question me, and my departure might be delayed. Within 48 hours McVeigh had been arrested and executed exactly three months before Osama bin Laden and his pilots struck the World Trade Centre. I did not like this backdrop to the end of what has been a wonderful experience among a basically nice and cultured people. Professionally I had gained so much. Until the Washington assignment my reporting was basically in the form of welcome diversions from editorial writing and other "staff" duties. But this was for the first time that I had a stint as a diplomatic reporter for a long time. I was especially happy for Razia, for she had a taste of the American way of life and seemed to thoroughly enjoy it. Then began a series of send-off parties that I still remember with fondness. At a dinner that was given by Maleeha as a reception for Shaheen and a send-off for me a Senator shook hands with me and said: "We will miss you, Mr Siddiqi!" Actually we had never met before, but that's how all politicians are. Maleeha had asked me whether I would want someone to be invited to the dinner. I said that Abdul Salam Masseruah should be invited. A Palestinian, he was chief of the Foreign Correspondents' Association in Washington and was a very dear friend of mine. He came with his wife and their child in a carrycot. The last time I had heard of him he had moved back from the US to the West Bank.

13

SOCIETY CHANGES

THERE WAS A WORLD of difference between society in 1958, when I entered the world of journalism, and that when I began writing this book half a century later. In 1995, when I returned from America after completing my assignment as Dawn's Washington correspondent, the world of Pakistani journalism had changed not just in technology but in the quality of manpower and in the lifestyle of a new breed of journalists, especially women. I could see that in my office. The typewriter — my love — had disappeared, and the noisy chatter of the teleprinter had given way to the clinical quiet of the computer world. The stuffy newsroom, where ceiling fans provided the only relief from summer heat, was now sometimes uncomfortably cold with its giant-size air-conditioners. Outside Haroon House, chaos reigned, as all authority appeared on the wane. The lazy native — how the British loved him! — had disappeared. He was replaced by a new Pakistani — quick, rude, ruthless but hard working to a degree that was mind-boggling. He had no time even to say an extra hello or be kind to a fellow citizen needing help, so caught was he in the rat race. More unfortunately, he was prone to violence, and ready to fight and burn at the slightest provocation. Violence, to him, was the only way in which he could defend himself, because the law didn't seem to deliver. The British-era values were now being discarded without being replaced by viable alternatives. The concept that knowing English was a sign of intellectual and cultural superiority was on the wane. The pace of life was maddening, and getting crushed under the wheels of a speeding mini-bus, and its burning by an enraged mob, were considered normal by a society that was fast losing its moral values. The Mohajir was in decline. Having created Pakistan and run the state in its formative years as a joint Punjabi-Mohajir enterprise, the Urdu-speaker now didn't have the courage to face facts and accept the country's demographic reality. Gone was his commitment to books and poetry, for he was now susceptible to ethnic demagoguery. In Karachi, the street scene was dominated by the redoubtable Pakhtoon community, and even the land-bound Sindhi started venturing into Karachi, gradually affecting its demography. This intermingling of the ethnic groups brought both tensions and colour to Karachi, enriching its culture in more ways than one. It truly became mini-Pakistan.

During the Ayub regime (1958-1969) industrialization was consistent and even-paced, even though it wasn't adequately horizontal and was confined to pockets, but it added slowly to the growth of the middle class and created a new class of professionals who would be Pakistan's asset. The urban scene did not change rapidly, but there was that inevitable trek from village to city — a concomitant of industrialisation the world over. Barring exceptions, the impact on the urban scene from this population transfer during the sixties was positive, gradual and largely peaceful. Urban slums started expanding and multiplying, but civic agencies seemed to be coping with them somehow. The seventies saw two phenomena which were to change Pakistan's face in every sense of the term: one was the social consequences of the secession of East Pakistan. People the world over sometimes do have the courage here and there to own mistakes, but few are prepared to plead guilty and hold themselves responsible for disasters, especially when they have national dimensions. The humiliating surrender to India in December 1971 was a trauma no Pakistani political leader or citizen was prepared to accept blame for. In fact, ironic as it sounds, everyone thought his own political philosophy stood vindicated; it was the others who were to blame. Those who stood for unadulterated democracy said if they had been listened to, and Ayub and Mirza had not imposed martial law and introduced 'basic democracy', East Pakistan would have not been lost. There were champions of provincial autonomy and the rights of minorities. If all provinces, including East Pakistan, had been given provincial autonomy, they argued, things would have not come to such a pass. Then there were the leftists of all brands – hardcore communists, social democrats, drawing-room revolutionaries, and believers in Islamic socialism. The issue, they argued, was neither democracy nor provincial rights. If there were economic justice, if poverty had been eliminated, the exploiting classes had been done away, land reforms were undertaken, the capitalist mode of production was abolished and the state monopolized the means of production, poverty would have been wiped out and a prosperous East Pakistan would have no reasons to secede. Then there were the Islamists: "We told you if we had established the Sharia we would not have suffered the ignominy of losing half the population and surrendering to India". Since there was no consensus on exactly what led to the defeat and everyone believed it was the others who deserved to be hanged, Pakistan became a hate society. This reflected itself in politics and human relationships. The anarchist tendencies we find among all sections of Pakistanis today owe their origin to some extent to this lack of agreement on what led to the 1971 disaster. The second phenomenon which would turn Pakistan's social scene into an amalgam of affluence, poverty and chaos stemmed from one word – Dubai.

As oil prices rose in the wake of the 1973 Ramazan war, the Gulf countries required workers of all sorts – from highly qualified technocrats, engineers, doctors and bankers to auto mechanics, welders, plumbers and masons. Pakistan was nearest to the Gulf and was the obvious recruiting ground for the oil economies, but one major hurdle in manpower export for Pakistan was the difficult process of getting a passport. Among other formalities, the passport form asked the applicant to get all his all particulars testified to by "a Gazetted Officer Class One" — an extraordinary and threatening term retained since the British days. This required a visit, or perhaps several visits, to some officer who fell in the category of "a gazetted officer class one", having his signatures on the passport form, and having the clerk stamp it with the officer's seal. While those who had access to such officers and had friends and relatives in government offices could manage that signature and stamp, for the majority, especially those in rural Pakistan, this was not just a hassle but a hurdle that only wasted time and sometimes required pleading with the officer's clerk to get it done. Bhutto abolished the "gazetted" condition, and he gave a simple argument for this. The condition was intended to stop a crook from getting a passport, but he would manage it anyway; the loser will be the law-abiding citizen, who would be put to unnecessary hardship. So why not do away with it? Once this condition was abolished, a citizen only had to go to the passport office and get the green booklet after a given number of weeks. The Dubai age had begun.

Dubai Chalo, a PTV play, with Ali Ejaz as central character, adequately conveyed the social part of the phenomenon that the rush to Dubai became. While the professionals could migrate to America and Canada, for the semi-skilled and the illiterate, Dubai was the nearest destination. Dubai here means not just the city and one of the seven emirates of the miracle called the United Arab Emirates, created, nurtured and developed by that remarkable man – Sheikh Zaid bin Sultan al-Nayhan; Dubai here stands for all those Arab countries which had oil but had small populations or lacked skilled manpower: countries like the UAE, Saudi Arabia, Oman, Bahrain, Qatar, Kuwait and Libya. (For some mysterious reason Iraq, whether under Saddam Hussein or before and after him, never welcomed Pakistani guest workers.) This black-gold rush was not without its quota of illegal activity, exploitation and tragedies. Often the unscrupulous among the recruiting agents fleeced and cheated the village simpletons, many of whom were arrested by host countries for illegal entry. In fact, the recruiting agencies and human traffickers developed ingenious methods to evade the law with results that were sometimes tragic. Often the recruiting agent would ask a Dubai-bound worker to pledge part of his salary for the next six months to him before he would hand him his passport, work permit and air ticket. Sometimes there was outright cheating, and would-be workers would fall victim to fraud. Boats would sail with their loads of illegal workers and then make the job seekers wade through waste-deep water to reach ashore at the dead of night to evade detection. Drowning was not uncommon. In one case, a launch carrying Dubai-bound workers developed engine trouble and was stranded for days in scorching heat as water and food ran out. Those who died were thrown into the sea. All of them would have died had not a US navy ship come to their rescue. Another case involved fraud of a most ingenious kind. A racketeer, who was never seen again, charged fabulous sums for taking job seekers to Dubai, telling them he was merely promising the journey, and it was for them to find refuge and get jobs. Hoping to make big money in Dubai, the fortune-seekers boarded a rickety sail boat one evening at Ibrahim Hyderi, a Karachi suburb. The boat was manned by men who had masked their faces. After a journey of three nights and two days the boat finally reached a deserted beach early at dawn.

"We have reached Dubai", the leader of the boatmen said. "Now get going. I have brought you as close to the land as possible. Now move! Good luck!"

The group dispersed and proceeded inland to go where they thought they would meet their local contacts. However, there was no sign of the landmarks they were told they would see. Finally when they reached a road they saw some cars and jeeps carrying Pakistani licence plates. How come? They wondered, "Why do these vehicles have Pakistani licence plates?" They hid themselves for a while, believing the Pakistani vehicles were there for some official purpose. As they pressed further inward, a skyline familiar to them came in view. "Does Dubai have the same kind of skyline we have back in Karachi?" they asked themselves.

Finally it dawned on them that they had been victims of a colossal hoax, for the boatman had – after four days of voyage – dumped them on Manora, a small island off Karachi, a few miles from where they had begun their journey three days ago. They had come home! Some of them had borrowed money and sold family silver to reach El Dorado.

Barring these tragedies, the oil-rich countries became a source of wealth for Pakistan's under-privileged, especially in the villages. This coincided with the transistor revolution, for the war-ravaged Japan was now on its feet and was in millions of Pakistani homes through its transistors, motorcycles, TV sets, cameras, VCRs and the Suzuki carriers. Until then the preserve of the rich and the educated, these gadgets now found their way into the homes of large sections of the once poor throughout urban and rural Pakistan, transforming the sights and sounds of society in a way unimaginable a decade ago. The cumulative effect of this inflow of petrodollars – estimated at $51 billion between 1972-73 and 2002-03 – was the rise of a new middle class: uneducated and rustic but bubbling with energy and determined to enjoy every bit of its new-found wealth. In some cases, families in this class had more money than the families of white collar workers, most of whom were victims of Pakistan's anachronistic British era wage structure.

The world over, the middle class is educated and is the bastion of all values that a society cherishes. Now Pakistan's 'traditional' middle class, squeezed by inflation, was feeling uncomfortable, faced as it was with what it thought was intrusion by the unwanted yokels into parks and playgrounds, recreation centres, cinema houses and even airports and jetliners. One visible impact of this Dubai phenomenon was society's sartorial degeneration. Till then the Pakistani middle class had worn trousers, and shalwar-qamees was confined to homes. It was inconceivable for an educated person to go to his office or to a party or for a teacher to turn up in class in shalwar-qamees. Bhutto had broken the taboo and popularized shalwar-qamees by appearing at several public rallies wearing this dress. There is no doubt shalwar-qamees is ideally suited to Pakistan's hot climate and is common to all regions of

Pakistan and Kashmir. Now it was no more unusual for an educated middle class gentleman to attend a wedding or a birthday bash in starched and well-pressed shalwar-qamees. By and large, however, the middle class continued to stick to trousers. However, the Dubai phenomenon changed all this. Now all public places presented a sight that to sahibs and begums was disgusting. They wouldn't want their children to interact with them, but they had no choice, for the Dubai hand had more money, enjoyed himself without inhibitions, ate to his heart's delight, coughed and laughed and smoked and spat without restraint, and expected to be treated by the waiters and salesman on a par with the educated.

Not that the 'normal' Pakistani middle class had any higher sense of civic discipline and cleanliness. But it had education, and this gave it an edge, especially because it knew English. Now places of entertainment, shopping malls and classy restaurants were swarming with families with lots of money but little culture. The inevitable result was that even the middle class took to the Dubai ways. Now white collar workers, professionals in higher management and even teachers started going to workplaces in shalwar-qamees. The concept that one must go to a place like a bank or an airline office in clothes which should present a business- and efficiency-oriented atmosphere that inspired a customer's confidence disappeared. Often it appeared as if an official in a tax office or a teacher had come to work in the same clothes in which he had slept the night before. The sartorial degeneration acquired a religious legitimacy when a new breed rose, a breed that combined the Dubai money with religion. Flaunting their religion, men in this category overcame the social disadvantage of not knowing English by their beards. The manager of a five-star restaurant could refuse entry to a Dubai hand if he was not properly dressed, but it was simply impossible for him to do the same to the one who sported a beard and gave the appearance of a pious man. Piety in Pakistan is confused with rituals. A person punctual at his rituals is considered pious, even if he is a great scoundrel and lacks basic honesty. This class acquired a sense of power in the wake of the Afghan war and the defeat which the Soviet Union suffered. While the mujahideen, no doubt, received massive doses of arms and money from America, Saudi Arabia and Egypt, there is no doubt that it was the raw courage of Afghan resistance fighters and Pakistani Pakhtoons which brought the Soviet Union to its knees. This had an impact on Pakistan's social scene, too, because such a noble concept as jihad was being spread in a society where the majority hadn't been to school. Add to this the Pathan people's physical prowess, their fierce tribal pride, their gun culture, their inherent pugnacity, and one can see how all this did not necessarily find a practical expression in higher political and social causes. At street level, this showed itself in lawlessness, defiance of authority, violence and disregard for the law, because all law suddenly became a symbol of the 'Christian' West. Gradually this 'Pathan spirit' took hold of the entire country.

The sartorial change affected Pakistani women, too. Until 9/11, Pakistani women wore a dress that was Pakistani in essence and spirit. It was beautiful, and it represented the liberal spirit of Pakistani Islam. Shalwar-shirt and a dupatta that ran from one shoulder to another across the breasts were modest by any standards and conformed to Islamic standards. A housewife found it as convenient as a lady doctor, an airhostess, a farm hand picking cotton, or a TV announcer. Burqa was still there, but the educated girls and women wore shalwar-shirt, and no one ever thought it was un-Islamic. Following the Islamist wave in the wake of the Iranian revolution and society's gradual slide into bigotry and Taliban-led barbarism, a large number of Pakistani girls started wearing hijab. I have never argued for or against hijab on religious grounds. My complaint is that hijab is not a Pakistani dress. A Pakistani woman should look Pakistani, and for centuries her dress has always been shalwar-shirt and dupatta. If Iranian women or those in South-East Asia and the Levant chose to wear hijab, well, good luck to them. But why should Pakistani women give up their national dress – their identity – and look like Middle Eastern or South-East Asian women? I bet that the vast majority of Pakistani girls and women who wear hijab do so less for religious reasons and more as a fad picked up from TV.

In my city, the MQM had a lot to do with the lawlessness that gripped Karachi in the eighties and nineties. In the wake of the dismissal of Benazir's first government in August 1990, Altaf and Nawaz became quite chummy, flushed as they were with their electoral success and the PPP's rout. Immediately after Nawaz became prime minister, he addressed a mammoth rally at Liaquatabad — an MQM stronghold — in December 1991. Nothing in common between them except hostility to Benazir, the two basically incompatible allies appeared at the balcony, beaming with joy, their faces radiant with success, putting hands round each other's shoulders and waving to a predominantly Mohajir crowd that went into a rhapsody as the prime minister pledged to build a mass transit system for Karachi and announced an immediate grant of seven billion rupees for the city's development. As was expected, the bonhomie between the two proved short-lived. First the MQM split down the middle over the extortion racket and the way Altaf ran the party. Second even Nawaz seemed fed up with him. Even though his party was now part of the Nawaz-led government, in the heart of his heart Altaf was an unhappy and insecure man, because the split in the party acquired a threatening dimension when the dissidents decided to form a new party, calling themselves MQM Haqiqi (Authentic). Now there were regular shootouts between the MQM regular and Haqiqi, causing fatalities. Every MQM worker had to take sides and be ready to pay the price, for whatever his choice his life was in danger, because cadres on both sides knew such party secrets as hideouts, safe houses, torture chambers, arms depots, and all that associated with the underworld – but an underworld which was political in character. In the words of Ahmad Ali Khan, politics had been criminalised and crime had been politicised.

Then Karachi saw a bewildering phenomenon: Altaf ordered walls to be raised to ensure against a possible blitz by the Haqiqi men on his headquarters in Azizabad — known as Nine Zero — and on party offices elsewhere in the city. No matter which MQM strongholds you visited, you found walls blocking your way, except through gates manned by the MQM's gun-toting cadres. I had lived in Nazimabad for seventeen years. Even though the 'slummisation' process had begun when I left it in 1979 June to move to our Gulshan home, it was still a wonderful and reasonably clean middle-class locality, with schools, colleges, libraries, well-planned mosques, shopping centres, cinemas, parks and playgrounds. However, on a visit to Nazimabad one evening when the walls had gone up I was shocked to find a once-peaceful locality turned into a ghetto, with suspicious characters lurking around and staring menacingly at every pedestrian and car. By now the MQM had become a state within a state in the nation's largest city, and not even the Nawaz government would tolerate it.

Concerned over his safety, Altaf chose to enter a hospital. Perhaps he was really ill, given the tensions he had, but many thought that the Abbasi Shaheed Hospital provided an ideal place of safety for him. Egged on by the army, Nawaz made up his mind to launch a crackdown on the MQM, demolish the walls and gates, end the 'no-go' areas which it had established, and arrest leading party cadres. Tipped off by Sindh Chief Minister Jam Ali about what was to happen Altaf boarded a flight for London on January 1, 1992, and has not returned till this day. On June 19, 1992, the army launched its operation, demolishing walls and gates, opening the 'no-go' areas, and arresting a large number of MQM workers. However, the army made one major blunder, for the Haqiqi rode into 'no-go' areas virtually on the army's shoulders. Whosoever comes riding an army tank loses credibility. Babrak Karmal had no credibility with the Afghan people because he had come to Kabul along with the Soviet army. Now here the wave of revulsion against the MQM was offset by the realisation that the Haqiqi was a creation of the army and was therefore not to be trusted. Suddenly, while sinking, Altaf and his party had been given a lifeline to survive and re-emerge once again as a virulent but powerful political force in southern Sindh.

Violence and social chaos were now having their impact on the newspaper world, too. The government wasn't the only side that was pressuring us; non-state actors were a greater threat — physical threat — to us. Gone were the days when political parties, labour unions and student bodies would deposit their Press releases at the reception and go home without so much as a verbal protest against why a certain press release had not been printed. Now, in the changed scenario, with the country awash with guns and bristling with well-armed militias and brainwashed thugs, every political half breed thought it was his right to dictate to newspapers. Now political, trade union and student leaders would come barging into the Dawn newsroom and not only demand that their Press release be published in full, they would expect explanations as to why a certain news item had been underplayed or why a statement by the 'wrong' party had been overplayed.

Two events came as a shock to us. On May 27, 1989, Dawn published a picture which carried a caption that in the opinion of APMSO, the MQM's student wing, was factually wrong. Instead of asking for a correction or a retraction, six hoodlums, one of them armed, barged into the editor's office, locked the door from inside and held him hostage. The whole Haroon House was shocked, and we all worried about AAK's safety. Hameed Haroon managed to break in and tried to argue with the thugs immune to reasoning. I was in Majeed's room as I saw the goons finally coming out of the editor's office, running down the corridor and shouting abuses as if in a frenzy. I thought they had murdered the editor. A greater profanity was in store in March 1991 when the Jam Sadiq Ali coalition was in power. The villain of the piece was Jam's security chief Irfanullah Marwat, whose uniformed and secret police were guilty of either sitting idle or encouraging MQM gangsters in their "boycott" of Dawn for a crime it had not committed. The boycott was a euphemism for unabashed violence that saw attacks on circulation teams, the burning of the paper's copies, and the siege of Haroon House. The offending piece had appeared in a sister publication, but the Jam government and its coalition partners took it out on Dawn. As Star reported in its issue of March 19, 1991, the attackers had come "armed with Kalashnikovs in Sindh government vehicles". For four days, the paper's distribution was possible only partially, finally forcing the management to stop publication. On Friday, the paper could not be distributed at all in southern Sindh — which meant readers in two of the province's biggest cities, Karachi and Hyderabad went without their copies of Dawn. On Saturday, the printing was resumed, and as a press release issued by the management on March 22, 1991, informed its readers: "The management of Pakistan Herald Publications (Private) Ltd. had to suspend the publication of Dawn's edition meant for circulation in Karachi and lower Sindh on Friday because it had become impossible to guarantee the physical safety of our distributors and hawkers. We regret the inconvenience caused to our readers who could not receive their copies on Friday (March 22) .However, now that we feel that our normal functioning will not be disturbed any more, we are resuming publication from today" (Saturday).

Karachi was now growing fast, new housing schemes were coming up, house rents were shooting, and television, introduced during the late sixties by Ayub Khan, had raised the people's expectations, as lifestyles of the affluent societies came into the drawing rooms. What happened if the breadwinner died? Would the family be on the streets? Thus owning a home became the prime object of every urban Pakistani. This required, first and foremost, a piece of land (popularly called "plot"), then a bank loan and then the ability to pay it off. This was difficult within one's monthly wages. So earning extra money — not necessarily by foul means — became a major fixation with this generation. It was during this period that commitment to work, whether as a university teacher, a sanitary engineer, a postman, a clerk, a telephone operator, a bank officer or as a journalist, virtually disappeared. Teachers spent more time on securing higher salary levels and giving tuitions to students at their homes than in trying to do their duty in class. One incident I would never forget. This was in the mid-eighties when I headed Dawn Magazine. A university teacher had written a very mediocre article on the importance of geology, and he wanted me to publish it. There was absolutely nothing in it that could possibly justify its publication and

I ignored it. The lecturer, otherwise a nice man, kept pestering me to no end. He even appealed to my compassion, "Should I look forward to its publication in the next edition? Please, Siddiqi saab, do not disappoint me!" I was outraged and hiding my anger asked him why he was so keen on having this utterly useless article on the importance of geology published. After some hesitation he told me that in matters of promotion the university authorities took into consideration the number of research articles published by a teacher. Research articles? Could an article on the "importance of geology" or any other discipline fall within the category of a research article? Besides, to merit recognition, such articles must appear in reputable research journals in Pakistan and abroad. I did not publish the article, but the episode serves to give an idea of the kind of pressures to which the middle class was exposed. It was not a question of keeping up with the Joneses; it was a question of keeping your head above water. The journalists belonging to this generation were a great disappointment. With some notable exceptions, very few advanced in the profession, and in spite of holding a college or university degree few were ever caught reading a book. No wonder, the quality of journalism and journalists during this era is shockingly low.

I can now broadly classify the journalists I have worked with into four categories from the point of view of professional excellence, their academic backgrounds and lifestyles. To the first category belonged those with whom I had the honour of working in PPA and Dawn, men who had had their education before independence. Most had literary backgrounds in English, Urdu and Persian. To this category belonged, besides Altaf Husain and Ahmad Ali Khan, many others, including Mohammad Ashir, Dawn's news editor from 1947 to 1964, and others I have already written about earlier in the book. With two other greats of Pakistan's English journalism who belonged to this category — Mazhar Ali Khan and Altaf Gauhar — I did not have the opportunity to work, because they were at the helm in Dawn when I was in The Sun (1971-73). Faiz Ahmad Faiz was in a class by himself. Besides being Urdu's greatest living poet of his time, he was editor of The Pakistan Times, and I only heard from AAK about Faiz's greatness, his style of holding editorial meetings and all that associated with the work of an editor. Other legends with him in PT were Zuhair Siddiqi, killed in a traffic accident, I. A. Rahman who later became PT's editor and is now Director of Pakistan Human Rights Commission, and Tahir Mirza, who was my editor at Dawn (2004-2006). Another great journalist of that era was A.T. Chaudhri. He was my colleague at The Sun, even though he was based in Lahore. Later, in the seventies he wrote a column for Dawn when I edited the leader page. There must be many others who do not find a mention in this book for two reasons: one, I did not have the opportunity to work them; two, when I began writing this book most of the journalists of that era were dead, and I regret that I failed to get the maximum information from the seniors I worked with. For instance I know nothing about S.G.M. Badruddin, except that, when AAK launched the weekly Economic and Business Review, he chose him to be its editor, till Ghayurul Islam took over. Badruddin was resident editor of Morning News, Dhaka, and remained in East Pakistan till the 1971 tragedy. It was, however, during his editorship of the Lahore edition of Masawat, the PPP party daily, that the paper recorded the highest circulation for an Urdu paper in the late seventies during Bhutto's trial leading to his execution. Badruddin died in November 2006 at age 88.

To the second category belonged those like me who had most of their education after independence when the British-crafted educational system was still in tact. Those who belonged to this generation must be grateful to their parents for one obvious reason: they had the courage to re-build their lives in the aftermath of the partition holocaust and, in spite of all the odds, give their sons and daughters the best education they could under the circumstances. By the mid-eighties people in my age group were in middle-senior positions. The third generation entered journalism in the mid- or late seventies. While there were exceptions, most of them were the product of an era when the decay in the education system had become all too obvious, and the standard of English teaching had plunged to new depths. This era — mid-seventies to early nineties — is one of low standards of English journalism, compounded by political factors, like the absence of press freedom, unsettled political conditions, impact of the Afghan war on society, rise of violence, lack of commitment to work, and the beginning of ethnic and sectarian tensions. Cumulatively all these factors combined to lower the quality of journalism, especially English. Crime news interests everyone. Even if a paper is not a tabloid, crime news still attracts the reader's attention. However, a review of Dawn's city pages during this period would show shockingly poor English, lack of structured stories, and the absence from the stories of that human element without which crime stories appear stereotypes. Often several crime stories would be lumped together, with the last sentence saying: "A woman was found murdered at her home in New Karachi. The police are investigating". Who that woman was, what was her age, who were the possible suspects, what the motive could be, how she was murdered and such related questions were absent from many such stories. It was quite possible that the news was received late when the deadline was near, but there was no follow-up in the next day's paper, and the story was forgotten. This kind of perfunctory attitude had less to do with the reporters' inability to express themselves in a foreign language and more with a low work ethic. During the large-scale nationalisation of industries, banking and insurance by the Bhutto government in the early seventies, labour laws tended to give extraordinary security to workers. This led to lack of interest in duty on the part of most workers in the belief that their jobs were secure because of a very cumbersome procedure for a management to dismiss a worker. Often, the managements tended to ignore bad workers rather than invite union trouble. Even though the greater part of the era I am talking about — from the mid-seventies to the late eighties — was under Zia's military dictatorship, he and the parties around him chose not to change the Bhutto-era laws for fear of losing the workers' sympathy. This invariably reflected itself in the world of journalism, where punctuality and work suffered because of the sense of security enjoyed by the workers. This generation — in journalism and other professions, including the state bureaucracy — spent most of its energy on bettering their economic status. While those like me who belonged to the earlier generation equally believed in this, we did not sacrifice work ethic and moral values on the altar of legitimate efforts for a better life.

The fourth generation entered the world of Pakistan's English journalism in the mid-nineties, and for lack of a better term I would call it the 'Green Card' generation, though I include in this term those young Pakistani boys and girls who were nationals of European countries as well. Some of them were born in Europe and America, but the majority consisted of those who had gone there with their parents in their early teens and returned when they were in their early thirties. They were at home both in Pakistan and the West, and seemed to adjust to cultural changes with surprising ease. This was an entirely new breed and differed from the previous three generations in many significant ways. First, their exposure to Western society, their education, jobs and training in Europe and North America and the variety of their experience, including teaching, research and social work, were of an astonishing variety. Two, they enjoyed a higher standard of living, and unlike the first two generations for whom the bus was a primary mode of transport, this was a car-borne generation, and they did not live in Nazimabad or Gulshan (no disrespect meant to these localities) but in Defence and Clifton. Three, their attitudes were modern, and this served to have a positive impact on work atmosphere, even though the religiously inclined, especially among non-journalists, raised eyebrows on girls wearing jeans and smoking. I have worked with this generation for at least two decades, and in spite of these superficial symbols of modernism, I found both boys and girls in this category good Pakistanis. Invariably, the girls belonging to this Green Card category worked with Dawn's weekly magazines, and it goes without saying that they improved them in terms of the quality of writing, editing and layout. There were, however, two problems with them. One, many of them turned out to be a passing phenomenon and returned to the West. Sometimes, they cheated Dawn in the sense that they promised to stay on but returned to Europe or America after gaining experience. Two, it was difficult to discipline them, because at the first hint of a confrontation developing with the editor, they would threaten to quit. The threat often worked, because they were of use to the paper and the editor did not wish to lose them. He had to compromise with them, but this led to heart burning among the "natives". However, in spite of a higher and "better" lifestyle, the Green Card generation truly speaking lacked culture, because its modernism, etiquettes and manners were essentially those of an American fast-food crew. While they knew every bit of the slang on Manhattan and the latest fashion on Bond Street, they were truly speaking culturally hollow. Men like AAK or Akhtar Adil Razwy or Jameel Ansari had a sophistication of their own — something I never could achieve. Their repartees, their sense of humour, their courtesy and their mannerism reflected that Persian element in Pakistani culture which now seems to have all but disappeared. They came up with apt verses from Ghalib and Iqbal and from Hafiz and Saadi, they had anecdotes to tell from the Arabian Nights, and they could talk about the impact which Thomas Hardy and Charles Dickens had on them in their youth. When the Karachi water agency once supplied water that contained silt, Dawn ran a story whose heading was "A cup of Indus silt and thou". Only those who had read Fitzgerald's translations of Omar Khayyam's rubaiyat could come up with such a headline. I was then in college, also working as a typist in the Karachi Joint Water Board, and heard my boss, a minor official, enjoying every bit of it and quoting the original "A cup of wine and thou". The partition holocaust was both a tragedy and a triumph for them: tragedy, because they were uprooted and lost all their ancestral property and roots in the India they had left behind; triumph because they had helped create Pakistan. They were proud of this achievement

The lifestyle of the Green Card generation was in sharp contrast to what I would call the 8-A generation. 8-A was the route number of a bus that ran between PIB Colony and Merewether Tower. Since life in Karachi those days revolved round roads that ran north to south, every bus invariably ended at Merewether Tower, whether it originated from Nazimabad or from P.I.B. Colony. However, the utility of 8-A was that it reached Tower via McLeod Road (I. I. Chundrigar Road) and picked up and dropped passengers at the PAF Recruitment Centre (demolished long and ago, and replaced by Shaheen Complex). This area was often referred to by us as 'Fleet Street' since most newspaper offices, including those of Dawn, were located at the tri-junction of I. I. Chundrigar Road, Dr Ziauddin Ahmad Road and M.R. Kayani Road. This way, 8-A was of invaluable use to us journalists. If 8-A were not there, journalists living in P.I.B. Colony or Nazimabad would have no way other than that of walking to their offices from Burns Road. The 8-A route was abolished in 2007, but by that time the transport picture had come completely changed, most journalists had cars, and the enterprising Pakhtoon transporters had put new buses on a variety of routes throughout Karachi to end the journalists' dependence on 8-A. I did not recall having made much use of 8-A, because I had a car 1968 onwards. Nevertheless, I would remember all my life friends and colleagues in various newspapers who used 8-A for decades. Till this day, the image of the 8-A buses with their colours burnt by Karachi's strong, year-round sun, passengers standing in the aisle, and the bus conductor weaving his way through them to collect fares for which no tickets would be given signifies to me the journalists' hardship and the low wages they used to get. In 1968 when I bought my first car — a 1956 model white Austin Cambridge — there was no parking problem at Haroon House. By the mid-eighties, the car park was overflowing with vehicles, with double and triple parking.

The way the Green Card journalists "lived" in their offices was in marked contrast to the working conditions for the earlier generation. The ceiling fan was the maximum we got for relief from the summer heat, and it was not until the late eighties that the Dawn offices would be air-conditioned. The Green Card journalists came in Pajeros, and many women journalists had chauffeurs. AAK used to say it was difficult to discipline "begum sahib journalists", because normal disciplinary tactics and punishments – like holding back the annual increment, transfers to unpleasant jobs or denial of leave for long summer vacations in America or Europe – didn't work with them. They would quit rather than be disciplined. While the 8-A generation would wait for years before a foreign visit came their way, for the Green Card generation, annual vacations in the West was a ritual. Their office rooms betrayed their lifestyle back home. Adorned with potted plants, their rooms had fancy electrical fixtures which they got installed at their own expense because they thought the office stuff was poor and posed a threat to their eyes, they brought their microwave ovens and fridges from their homes, and had their own arrangements for making tea and coffee. For the 8-A generation a cup of tea brought by the canteen waiter was the maximum luxury.

I remember, in 1958, when I joined the PPA news agency, news editor Ahmad Hassan alone had a car, and it was parked right in front of the main entrance to Muhammadi House on what then was McLeod Road. There must have been other cars, but I didn't notice them. It was then an era when you had the luxury of parking your car anywhere anytime you wanted for as long as you wished — a position that more or less remained unchanged till the early '70s. Today, McLeod Road – renamed I. I. Chundrigar Road – is like the rest of Karachi choking with cars and vehicles, and traffic jams and power outages have combined to make life in Karachi a horror you have to live with, especially in summer. The neo-rich in their flashy Japanese cars had contempt for each other. "I bet his father never rode a car", you said. Well, the man in that Pajero had the same opinion about you. He honked ceaselessly, and you honked ceaselessly, even though you had seen that an old woman was getting out of the car with difficulty and was being helped. But you honked, nevertheless, and you honked at 2 in the morning when you returned home, and it didn't matter what the neighbours thought of you, because the neighbours, too, were no different.

There was now a mushroom growth of apartment buildings built in a way that would make any town planner in the world faint. The buildings were often in rows, back to back, sometimes the distance between one apartment building and another being less than 10 feet. When power failed, life in apartments became hell, because the buildings made of concrete emitted heat, instead of absorbing it. This was not the case with the buildings and houses made of stone in the earlier days. Because of the all-round expansion of economic activity and the greater use of air-conditioners, kitchen gadgets and electrical appliances, the demand for power had gone up. But sadly, there was nothing but disaster on this front, because no dams had been built — despite the availability of the Indus waters —, and thermal units had made no significant contribution to power production. This resulted in power outages, which, initially confined to summer months, later occurred year round and tormented the people in winter, too. In Karachi's hot and humid summer nights, boys and girls sweated from head to toe as they pored over books in candle light for taking examinations the next morning. Some were lucky to have UPS — uninterrupted power supply — units. Others just showed courage living in those hellholes.

Yet a drive through the "marriage districts" would make one believe Karachi had surplus energy, for the marriage halls, draped in colour lights, presented a picture of affluence and plenty. The marriage proceedings were painfully slow. Sometimes when you reached the marriage hall at 10.30pm, fearing you were late, you found that even the hosts had not arrived. Cars were parked tight close, as genteel men and women started arriving as late as 11pm for a dinner that would be served at 1.30 in the morning. Everyone cursed everyone for the "dinner at 1.30am" scandal, but nobody bothered to inject some sense into the Pakistani wedding extravaganza and effect a reform. In evidence were both riches and lack of sense of proportions. You returned home to find the neighbourhood enveloped in darkness, the noise from the neighbour's gas-operated generator getting on your nerves and adding to your depression. Boys, unable to bear the heat inside, sat outside their homes, enjoying the cool sea breeze, talking on cellphones and texting. They seldom read any books besides the textbooks, because the craze for TV, DVDs and cellphones had rendered books useless. The posh localities had shopping malls but few book stores, and hardly any libraries. While Musharraf boasted that "even our toilet-cleaners have cellphones", Ghazi was right when he wrote in his Karachi Diary of "the poverty of our affluence".

~~~~~~~~~

"Are there any Norwegian troops in Afghanistan?" I asked.

"Yes, there are. But we are from Sweden, sir". This is how an informal session began with a Swedish delegation that had come to the Dawn office. Diplomats come to the Dawn office from time to time to exchange ideas, and it helps both sides. This was probably in February 2009, and Editor Abbas Nasir had excused himself, asking me to be the host. I had expected colleagues Ayesha Azfar and Reema Abbasi to be there, too. But Ayesha was busy, so we two had a lively session with the Swedes. As any journalist would testify, mix-ups are quite common, and at least one journalist told me that after a long discussion with a Korean delegation — and after the Koreans had left — the staff were wondering whether the guests were from the north of the 38th parallel or from the south.

Another indication of the deteriorating law and order situation is the virtual disappearance of diplomats from our — journalists' — lives. Now diplomats dropping in are a rarity. Receptions on national days are now perhaps the only forum where we get to meet diplomats, but the presence of invitees of all sorts, including government functionaries, merely means small talk. Besides, the embassies have turned into fortresses, after Karachi saw a devastating attack on the American Consulate on June 2002, killing 12 Pakistanis. I had worked at the American mission in Karachi way back in the fifties when it was an embassy. Later, when the embassy shifted to capital Islamabad, the new quake-proof consulate building opposite to the Frere Hall Park was my favourite haunt. I had quite a few friends at the consulate, including

Haseen and Mrs Khan, and I didn't have to bother about any security, because the entire atmosphere was care-free and idyllic. One of my favourite libraries was the USIS library, and Mrs Khan happened to be its librarian. It was also in that library that I found and read Arthur Koestler's Invisible Writings, which provided the format for this book decades later. The library also had a small cinema hall, which often showed Hollywood classics, and there were discussions.

I used to park my rickety Volkswagen right in front of the consulate on the road coming from the Commissioner's office. There were no restrictions, and no security personnel were in sight. Sometimes I would drop in only to have coffee with Haseen and exchange gossip with Mrs Khan. It was also at the consulate that I first met Farida Said at an Iftar party given by the Consul General. From the windows of the USIS offices overlooking Abdullah Haroon Road, the scene was breathtaking and green. I felt proud of my city. The situation would remain more or less unchanged till the early nineties. In 1991 November, when I was posted to Washington and wanted a visa, I just handed in the passport and the visa form to Haseen, and he phoned me three days later that the Consul General wanted me to have tea with him before I flew off to the US. A year later Razia joined me, and she didn't even go to the consulate. She handed her passport to Tanvir, and a few days later she had it back, with the visa duly marked. Today the consulate is a virtual fort. You cannot park a car anywhere near it, and from the outside it appears ghost-ridden. I do not know why the consulate exists, for it performs neither diplomatic nor consular functions. Now visa seekers from all over Pakistan go to Islamabad to get it.

14

PRIESTS

*F*OR DECADES AFTER PAKISTAN *came into being on August 14, 1947, one didn't have to argue in favour of values universally accepted as essential conditions of civilised living — education for all, women as human beings, immunisation of children against polio, smallpox, and TB, and the need for sports, music, drama, poetry, and the arts for the individual's mental health. Murder for whatever cause was considered abhorrent, the citizens' loyalty and commitment to the State of Pakistan was taken for granted, and religion was a positive force — a source of social cohesion, spiritual bliss and comfort in distress. Islam had still not become an ideology. Foreign tourists and sports teams came in droves and returned with praise for the Pakistani people's warmth, friendship and hospitality. The values in which the Neanderthal man believed existed only in the textbooks.*

~~~~~~~~~

MA'KOOS is an Arabic word, meaning 'reverse' or 'negative'. I first came across it as a school boy in Karachi six decades ago. It was part of a slogan written on a wall that I found to my left as I walked to Bahadur

Yar Jang High School on Clayton Road from my home in P.I.B. Colony. The wall constituted the perimeter of the Karachi Central Jail situated in what then were Karachi's suburbs. The Urdu slogan said: Vai afsoos, humnay taraqqieye ma'koos ki ('alas, we have made negative progress'). The year was 1949, and Pakistan was less than two years old. The graffiti were painted all over Karachi — and I presume in other cities — by a religious party. I was curious and angry. Who wrote it and why? Today as an old man of 70 I still say that those who scrawled that slogan in black paint on the wall of the Central Jail when Pakistan was not even two years old were doing no service to the country. The Taliban philosophy had been given birth to — an idea that would ultimately eat into the vitals of Pakistan and be a source of mischief, mass misery and colossal bloodshed. As years turned into decades and decades into half a century and more, the idea epitomised by that graffiti grew in dimension and intensity to turn Pakistani society into an abnormal society whose members lacked a sense of proportions and considered persecution and victimisation of fellow citizens not only justifiable but a sacred duty and divine mission. One could understand if the government of the day were criticised; that is the right of every citizen. But what the men behind those writings were doing was to assume the role of reformers and political activists in one go without having the wisdom and qualification to do so. Slowly but surely, Pakistani clerics were making themselves felt. Even though nobody attached much importance to them in the wake of independence and the euphoria that gripped the people in the wake of the birth of Pakistan, the political clerics were trying to invent a role for themselves.

Broadly speaking I would divide Pakistani clerics into two categories: conventional and political. The first breed was innocuous, less educated and posed no threat to society's equilibrium, for it operated on traditional lines and preached things that no sane mind would oppose. Normally, they avoided politics in their Friday sermons because they knew this could divide their listeners and lead to pandemonium in mosques. Mostly, they concentrated first and foremost on rituals and asked their flock to: offer prayer five times in the mosque, fast during Ramazan, pay alms, marry off their offspring early, and avoid music, theatre and cinema. They gave examples from the life of the Holy Prophet and his companions and the persecution they suffered to inspire Muslims to be ready for hardships in the way of Allah. However, I seldom found an average mosque imam exhorting the people to wage jihad or resort to violence to overthrow the existing government or social order. The mosque imam was seldom controversial, for he retained the traditional wisdom associated with the neighbourhood imam. He seldom had college education and didn't know English – a great drawback, since in Pakistan (as in Bangladesh, India and Sri Lanka) a person is not considered really educated, and cannot get a white collar job, if he doesn't know English. For that reason he was on society's sidelines. His sermons had a low intellectual level but he never said anything that ever made me angry. Where he failed was in the domain of human relationships, for he never laid emphasis on one of Islam's major tenets — mercy, compassion and forgiveness. While he warned of hellfire if the faithful didn't uphold the five pillars of Islam – Kalema (the basic faith upholding the Oneness of God), five obligatory prayers, Ramazan fasts, Zakat (alms) and Hajj (once in life) he placed no emphasis on the need for Muslims to be kind to God's creatures, including animals. To be fair to him, however, he never incited his listeners to rebellion. It was basically the political breed among the clerics who have played a most destructive role in Pakistan's politics and society.

The political mullah was educated, knew English and, thus, didn't suffer from any sense of inadequacy, which was the lot of the first breed. While the mosque imam denounced the traditional sinner, he had no particular grouse against that which was the political cleric's obsession – maghribi tahzeeb (Western culture or civilization). Denouncing the West for what it did to the Muslim world during the colonial times and what the West is doing even now in the Middle East, especially Palestine, is not something confined to the Muslims; liberal opinion even in the West is also aware of the Western powers' role in the Middle East, especially since World War I. However, the politico-religious activist had some other reason for denouncing the West, for his outpourings were in fact an expression of his deep-seated and unspoken jealousy of the Muslim world's successful leaders who had pulled their countries out of colonial subjugation and turned them into independent nations. I refuse to call as secular the giants whose struggle brought freedom to the Muslims, because in the heart of their hearts they were as good or as bad Muslims as the political clerics. This needs some explaining.

The battle against colonialism was spearheaded by men who knew the world in which they lived, were aware of the overwhelming odds against which they were pitted and were guided by pragmatism. The tactics and weapons they adopted against the Western occupiers of Muslim lands depended upon the kind of challenge they faced. Sir Syed Ahmad Khan, the 19th century reformer, thought modern education was the best weapon for the Muslims; Jinnah chose the path of law and constitutionalism to create Pakistan, the mid-twentieth century's biggest Muslim state population-wise; Ataturk used the Turks' martial traditions to save Turkey, Mossadagh used the economic weapon to arouse the Iranians; Nasser used a mixture of diplomacy, disastrous military confrontations and bold tactics, like the nationalization of the Suez Canal, to unleash Arab nationalism; the Algerian leadership resorted to guerilla war to liberate the country, Soekarno used a combination of military and political skills to liberate and unite Indonesia, Arafat resorted to diplomacy and an unsuccessful guerilla war to put the Palestinian issue on the world's front pages; and Anwar Saadat launched a stunning blitz across the Suez Canal to break the image of Israel's invincibility, revive the peace process and win back the Sinai. The political clerics had nothing to their credit, except negativism, for quite often they created hurdles in the way of most leaders of Muslim freedom movements and tried to sabotage their efforts. No wonder when freedom came, the political type felt jealous, for he found no place for himself in the new order – except as a rabble-rouser who railed day and night against the maghribi tahzeeb, even though his real targets were the successful Muslim giants who had led their peoples to freedom.

The political cleric denounced the West without reservations, attributing to it every imaginable evil, without grasping the truth about why nations and civilisations rise and fall, why the West was able to steal a march over the Arab-Islamic Muslim world from the 18th century onward, why Europe was able to unleash the energies and potential of the European peoples and advance technologically and in political organisation, why it was able to complete its domination of Afro-Asia by the middle of the 19th century, and why the West had been able to perpetuate its hold on the globe till this day. The political cleric's concept of the West was an indication of one of the two shocking realities about him: either he was intellectually disadvantaged or he was a victim of brainwashing, for to him the West meant nothing but unwed mothers, nudist beaches and gay marriages. He forgot that the West also meant inter-galactic probes, scientific research, institutes of higher learning, unfettered democracy, rule of law, cultural pluralism, literate and affluent populations, social discipline, honest judges, efficient and conscientious state officials, and human rights bodies which protested irrespective of who the victim was. The West was also host to millions of Muslim migrants with equal citizenships rights who could go to court to challenge discrimination. No Muslim country — except Pakistan, caught in circumstances beyond its control — has opened doors to Muslim migrants and given them citizenship. Extraordinary as it sounds, a large percentage of Muslims who have made the West their home are exactly those who denounce the West in the strongest terms, harbour the Taliban philosophy and yet have no qualms of conscience about enjoying a higher standard of living, besides education, healthcare, pollution-free living, social security and other benefits they drive from their living in Western countries.

The political breed's shocking ignorance of the West was evident from its identification of the state of Pakistan with the West. Everything about Pakistan and all its institutions was evil because Pakistan was being run by maghrib-zada (Westernised) elite. There could be no greater and ludicrous absurdity, because the Pakistani elite, far from being Westernised, was steeped in feudal traditions and rejected some fundamental Western values: it ran the state on authoritarian and sometimes tyrannical lines, it did not believe in press freedom and free speech, it held elections which actually were large-scale exercises in fraud, it persecuted the opposition and often believed in the physical elimination of its political dissidents, it enslaved the judiciary, controlled free thought even in places of learning, and was in most, though in all, cases financially corrupt. This misplaced and palpably false and perverse identification of things Pakistani with the West — the West as perceived by the politico-religious class — had disastrous consequences. Gradually, a perverse idea got hold of the people: since everything about Pakistan was Western — read evil — it deserved to be destroyed, consciously or unconsciously. Whether it was a Pakistani college or a bus, a lady doctor or a PIA air hostess, a tax office or the Governor's House, a hospital or an ambulance, a gas pipeline or a petrol pump: all were stripped of sanctity. This idea didn't remain confined for long to things governmental; gradually, the individual, too, fell victim to this anarchic philosophy. The man next to you in the street, in the bus, in shops, in hospitals, in colleges, in restaurants, in cars, in parks and playgrounds, and in trains and planes lacked a moral basis for his existence, and therefore whatever belonged to him — his freedom, his property, his family, his honour — could be dispensed with at the slightest provocation. This partly explains the reasons why Pakistani mobs today burn and kill without mercy, because they think they have a religious sanction to destroy. In contrast, let us note that during the Iranian revolution the mobs' targets were Shah- and Savak-specific, and private property in most cases remained unharmed. In Pakistan now mobs resort to arson by habit or instinct. Among the targets burnt and bombed (long before the Taliban emerged on the scene) have been homes, hospitals, ambulances, mosques, and religious processions and gatherings. The most shocking part of mob violence was the development of a tendency in which unrelated targets were burnt and destroyed. For instance, during the protests against the sacrilegious cartoons published in a Danish newspaper, furious mobs in Lahore, Peshawar and Rawalpindi burnt hundreds of cars, motorcycles, gas stations and public and private buildings. It was not clear what crime the owners of those cars and motorcycles had committed.

I was caught in quite a few situations where frenzied mobs were killing innocent people and burning and destroying whatever came their way. In Chapter 16, I have described the Karachi part of the violence that rocked Pakistan on the night between December 27 and 28, 2007, following Benazir's assassination. So widespread was violence that the general election had to be postponed and the railway system was partially dislocated because the mobs burnt stations and trains and pulled out the tracks. But the pattern had been set by what happened in earlier years.

Beginning with 1998, Karachi witnessed the murder of several religious scholars respected for their learning and belonging to some of Pakistan's most renowned madressahs, including the Binnori madressah. Those who were assassinated included Maulana Habibullah Mukhtar in 1998, Maulana Yusuf Ludhianvi in 2000 and Mufti Shamzai in 2004. In each case, the assassination touched off widespread violence that included arson, looting and the suspension of all street life. In each case, the religious leadership didn't bother to wait for investigations to begin and for its outcome, it didn't know who the killers were, and it made no attempt to restrain madressah boys when it gave calls for strikes. What happened on May 18, 2000, the day Ludhianvi was assassinated, was symptomatic of Pakistani society's proclivity for descent into chaos and violence at the slightest perceived hurt. Ludhianvi was a religious scholar, and his column in Urdu daily Jang containing answers to questions raised by readers on religious matters was widely read. He came out of his home and was driving to his office at Old Exhibition in his white Corolla 1998 model when two people on a motorcycle intercepted his car and opened up with revolvers, killing him and his driver, Abdul Rahman, and wounding his son, Yahya. Shocking, no doubt, the murder of a scholar of Ludhianvi's stature was, there was no reason why the

Milli Yekjehti Council — an umbrella organisation of several religious parties — should have given a call for what has in Pakistan over the decades became a fad: a "wheel jam" strike, i.e. nothing should move. Such "wheel jams" may or may not lead to the arrest of the guilty, but they have been a source of misery to millions of men, women and children, often leading to tragedies, especially when children returning from schools are stranded. Ludhianvi was assassinated on a Thursday, and the MYC gave a call for the strike for Friday. However, mob violence, looting, forcible closure of shops and restaurants and the burning of buses, cars and gas stations had begun that very evening.

As I drove home from the Dawn office in the evening, I found my way blocked, for all traffic had disappeared from the main roads, because it was the madressah boys who were in command. They were carrying sticks, burning tyres, forcing shops and restaurants to close and torching anything they fancied. They were devoid of mercy and common sense. Soon the entire city was in the grip of lawlessness. Also attacked and burnt were the offices of English daily Business Recorder and two banks, which were looted. The burning of the BR offices led to two deaths, and the staff had to save their lives by jumping into a nearby bungalow. As a press release issued by the BR management said: "Probably, they [the dead] were two of the arsonists who had gone to mezzanine floor while the other mobsters set the ground on fire". Why were the 10 million people of Karachi punished for no faults of theirs? Regrettably not one among the ulema stood up against this mass vandalism and took the MYC to task for ordering a strike whose victims were innocent men, women and children going about their way. One can only guess what must have happened to heart patients and women in pains whose ambulances were not allowed to proceed to hospitals. This last point serves to underscore the point that compassion and mercy have no place in the Pakistani clerics' scheme of things. What matters is a display of temporal power masquerading as commitment to religion.

The lead story in Dawn's Friday edition was to be Ludhianvi's murder. However, by midnight it had to be changed, because the news of the murder was overshadowed by what was happening to the entire city. Saleem Asmi, then news editor, had originally planned to make the murder story Dawn's first lead. By late night the picture had dramatically changed, because the city was hostage to mobs, which roamed unchecked. He correctly gave the murder story a single column headline and made the mob rule the lead, with the headline: "Mob paralyzes Karachi". The strap-line said, "Scholar's murder sparks riots: newspaper offices ransacked, banks looted". The same drama was repeated in Karachi in 2004 when the month of May saw the murder of Mufti Shamzai and a bomb blast in a Shia mosque in Gulshan-i-Iqbal. In the latter case, the furious mob burnt down, besides scores of vehicles, a restaurant because it had an American name, killing six KFC workers who had taken refuge from the flames in the cold storage. Its door was jammed and they were frozen to death. The same heartlessness repeated itself in 2005 when furious mobs protesting against the publication of blasphemous cartoons in the Danish daily Jyllands-Posten burnt down hundreds of cars and motorcycles in Rawalpindi and Peshawar and attacked the Punjab Assembly building, causing structural damage. Like the six KFC workers, the owners of these vehicles and the builders of the Punjab Assembly building had done nothing that deserved the mobs' attention

These incidents serve to point to an astonishing contrast between Pakistani behaviour and that in the Arab world in such matters. We know, for instance, that in the Satanic Verses case, the Arab world maintained that contemptuous silence which the Salman Rushdie book deserved. It is the non-Arab world that got worked up. The police had to open fire in Islamabad, killing five people and wounding 83, there were disturbances in India and Bangladesh, and Iran issued a death fatwa. But no such emotionalism was witnessed in the Arab world. Similarly in the case of the Danish cartoons, no Arab country witnessed the kind of mob violence that Pakistan saw. But, then, we need not be surprised, because the works of South Asian ulema are singularly devoid of liberal thought. Barring the sole exception of Shah Waliullah (1703-1762), whose writings contain some very original ideas on labour, land ownership and social equality, most other religious writers of South Asia have not ventured beyond the traditional fiqh issues and have shown a disappointing lack of interest in issues of economic justice and civil liberty. Even though the Arab world was ravaged by the Mongols and suffered a political and intellectual setback from which it has not yet recovered, the Arab mind retains a liberal outlook and does not suppress the spirit of free inquiry as exemplified by Ibne Rushd – Averroes – considered the world's first free thinker; the highly controversial ideas espoused by the rationalist Mutezlite school of thought, the light of enlightenment that Baitul Hikma emitted, the impact of Greek philosophy on Arab thought, and the encouragement given by the Abbasid caliphs to free debate.

Another incident years later deserves to be noted. On July 13, 2009, part of a village in south Punjab, about 95 kilometres from Multan, was flattened by an explosion, killing 12 people, including nine children. The village – 129/15-L – had a seminary run by a man called Riaz Ahmad Kamboh. His links with militants were known to the villagers, he had gone to Afghanistan for training and been arrested by the police and later released. Unknown – or perhaps known – to the police Riaz ran a seminary next to his home, and he managed surreptitiously to store a huge quantity of arms and ammunition, including rocket launchers. Among the debris the police found after the blast were hate literature, audio and video cassettes and suicide jackets. It was obvious that he was using the madressah as a cover for organizing a terrorist cell and for training young people into becoming terrorists and suicide bombers. A press report said he even had plans to assassinate Prime Minister Syed Yusuf Raza Gilani. While relief work was going on, the people threw stones at the police. One could perhaps understand this, because the simple village folk must have been shocked by the police's inefficiency which led to the tragedy in their village. However, the inevitable resort to irrationality did take place when the people stoned the Shaheen Express and tried to block the railway track. The engine driver was roughed up. Once again, it was not clear what the passengers and the train crew had done to deserve the attack.

I am not at all saying that it is the religious rhetoric alone which encouraged mob violence in Pakistan or that it was only the religiously oriented mobs which burnt and killed. In fact, when it comes to burning and killing, the MQM's detractors allege that it is unbeatable, for they allege it is this party which laid the tradition of burning buses and gas stations as a curtain-raiser for the next day's strike. The idea here is to underline the inevitably negative — in fact horrendous — consequences the impact of the religious demagoguery had on the people. Equally responsible for this violence-oriented psyche were popular religious columns in the Urdu press and the large amount of religious literature in monthly and weekly journals and in free promotional material churned out by thousands of charities and religious organisations throughout Pakistan. In this voluminous literature, positive instructions in the traditional Islamic jargon are juxtaposed with the evil aspects of Western culture, especially those relating to sex, with warnings that Pakistani society, too, could become permissive. An essential feature of this preaching has been its misogynist character. Islam itself doesn't make war on women, nor does it approve of purdah, especially of the kind that exists in South Asia. It was later that, to quote Karen Armstrong, "men would hijack the faith" (Karen Armstrong, Islam, p 16). This profusion of religious literature reproduces selected Quranic verses and traditions of doubtful validity to give Islam a misogynist and intolerant character. Without any intellectual input of its own and in utter disregard of the social conditions obtaining in Pakistan this form of popular writing has a profound effect on the young minds. Now everyone in Pakistan assumes it is his right and mission to "spread good and suppress evil," and that if anyone does not agree with his interpretation of Islam he has the right to burn and kill. In other words, the right which rests with the State has been usurped by citizens often acting as mobs and armed militias led by semi-literates.

Today, Pakistan is an abnormal society. Its chief characteristic is its approval of violence. Throughout history, all religious movements have taken root among the poor, but in Pakistan what one sees is a stupefying marriage of lucre with religion. Religious parties and institutions now operate in a spirit of rivalry and self-projection, and the thing farthest from them is humility. More important, they unleash their power of demagoguery and the armies of well-armed volunteers they command to brow beat the media and threaten their rivals. I was often amazed at the sight of some religious rallies where clerics wearing garlands walked at the head of processions with an air of stupefying smugness. To me the sight was indescribably obscene. I would here like to recall an incident — one of the countless such incidents — that took place in Karachi on July 1, 2009, and it concerned the Sunni Tehrik. I am Sunni myself, but I do not see why Pakistan — a Sunni-majority country — should have a Sunni party to defend Sunni interests. As a Sunni Muslim I have never had problems with society and never felt my interests as a Sunni threatened. This party is now one of Karachi's most well-organised, well-funded and well-armed party, and its volunteers, riding motorcycles and wearing green turbans, are a familiar sight in Karachi and other cities. One of its chiefs, Abbas Qadri, was killed when a suicide bomber blew himself up amongst 15,000 people offering evening prayers at Nishtar Park on April 11, 2006. It killed 50 people and wounded and maimed 70. The blast was an act of villainy, and came as a shock to entire Pakistan because it created havoc at a public rally on the occasion of the birthday of the Holy Prophet (may peace be on him.) The mayhem that followed was symptomatic of the Pakistani people in moments of crises: frenzied mobs went on a burning spree; they attacked fire engines, and they blocked the movement of ambulances carrying those injured in that very blast. There was no one to restrain them, because that's how Pakistani mobs today are, and that's how they have been trained to look at things and act. There is no element of mercy around. Three years later another incident involving the ST workers, though with fewer casualties, deserves to be noted.

The family of the assassinated leader, Qadri, had been living in a rented house, and, according to the house-owner, it had failed to make regular payments, the arrears of the rent accumulating to a considerable sum. The man went to court, and on July 1, 2009, the police reached the place along with the bailiff to serve the court order. What followed was something no religious movement could be proud of, no matter what the provocation. There was not only an exchange of fire between the police and Sunni Tehrik workers, killing two ST activists; there was that usual symptom of mob fury and irrational behaviour — a bus was burnt down. That a party claiming to be religious should arm its workers constitutes a commentary both on the party leadership and on society itself. The ST workers said they didn't open the fire, and it was the police who did. The police denied the charge and accused the ST workers of firing on the police. Let us assume that the police fired first — why it would do that beats me —, but even if the cops were in error, the exchange of fire, the acts of arson and the vandalism that followed symbolised the hauteur that now characterises all religious leaders and their acolytes in Pakistan. The attitude often is: "You, you, challenge us! Us! Don't you know who we are? Islam is with us. We can do no wrong."

In his book Islam and Theocracy, Mazheruddin Siddiqi traces the history of the development of theocracy in Europe and points out how Pope Innocent IV (1243-1254) maintained it "to be the duty of all clerics to obey the Pope, even if he should command what they knew to be wrong." According to Siddiqi "the doctrine that one person or a group of persons constitute[s] the infallible interpreter of the Divine Will," was a claim which "the Holy Quran explicitly and eternally repudiated when it called on the Jews and Christians 'to come together on a creed which may be common to all of us, namely, that we shall serve none but God and associate none with Him and that we shall not take some among us to be the final authority, besides God'." (Islam and Theocracy by Muhammad Mazheruddin Siddiqi, published by the Institute of Islamic Culture, Club Road, Lahore; 1953 edition, p 25).

Mullahism is essentially a non-Arab phenomenon. In Saudi Arabia, the cradle of Islam and now under a puritanical dispensation, the royalty reigns and rules, and the clerics obey the government without demur. The same is true of the Gulf sheikhdoms, where the Friday sermon is approved by the state. No deviation from the approved text is tolerated. In the 'northern' Arabian belt — from Iraq to Morocco but excluding Algeria, which is a case apart — the clerics' ability to claim parallel power and challenge the writ of the state, as in Afghanistan and Pakistan (and until the revolution in Iran), is limited. Part of the clerics' claim to the proprietorship of Islam and issue fatwas stems from their knowledge of Arabic, though with some exceptions their knowledge of Arabic is defective and their comprehension of Islam questionable. More regretfully they confuse religion with culture, for Pakistani (and all South Asian) clerics regard as sacrosanct the subcontinental Muslims' customs and practices which are local in origin and have in some cases entered Muslim society because of interaction with the Hindus over a millennium. The craze for processions, the reverence shown to the pictures of Muslim holy places in Mecca and Medina, the ban on women to visit graveyards, the attachment to the graves of saints, and the 'urs' phenomenon — a subject unto itself — show the impact of Hindu practices on South Asia's Muslim society.

At the same time, contradictory as it sounds, South Asia's Muslims define their religion as something essentially antithetical to Hinduism. For instance, there is no denunciation in Quran of sculpture, music and dance as an art form, but a rejection of these arts is a cardinal principle with the subcontinental Muslims' religious beliefs. Here we can clearly see the contrast with Iran. Because in Iran the majority became Muslim after the Arab conquest, the Iranian people had no reason to disown those aspects of their pre-Islamic culture which were not violative of Islamic beliefs. During my visit to Iran in October 2006 I found pieces of Quranic calligraphy displayed alongside drawings of human figures, including copies of Western masterpieces in watercolour or woven into carpets. In the subcontinent, however, the majority remained Hindu, so the Muslims, especially the conquering and ruling elite, defined themselves in opposition to whatever Hinduism stood for.

Writing about Muslim society of his times i.e. pre-partition India, Marmaduke Pickthall, whose Glorious Koran is considered one of the most authentic English translations of the holy book, says, "The veiling of the face by women was not, originally, an Islamic custom. It was prevalent in many cities of the East before the coming of Islam but not in the cities of Arabia. The purdah system as it now exists in India was quite undreamt of by the Muslims of the early centuries, who had adopted the face-veil and some other fashions for their women when they came into the cities of Syria, Mesopotamia, Persia and Egypt, at once as a concession to prevailing custom and as a protection to their women from misunderstanding by peoples accustomed to associate unveiled faces with loose character" (Marmaduke Pickthall, The Islamic Culture, p 129). He adds, "… [T]he purdah system is neither of Islamic nor of Arabian origin. It is of Zoroastrian Persian and Christian Byzantine origin. It has nothing to do with the religion of Islam, and, for practical reasons, it has never been adopted by the great majority of Muslim women" (ibid p 130). He adds, "The Turkish peasantry are very good Muslims indeed. Nowhere does one see Islamic rules of decency more beautifully observed than in the Turkish villages of Anatolia. Yet women in those villages and in Egyptian villages, and in Syrian villages, and in Circassian villages and in Arabian villages and among the Bedawi and other wandering tribes enjoy a freedom which would stupefy an Indian [and today a Pakistani] Maulvi" (ibid p133). Armstrong supports this view, "There is nothing in the Quran that requires the veiling of all women or their seclusion in a separate part of the house. These customs were adopted some three or four generations after the Prophet's death. Muslims at that time were copying the Greek Christians of Byzantium, who had long veiled and segregated their women." (Karen Armstrong, Islam, p 16)

The South Asian clerics' attitude toward sculpture is even odder. Because the Hindus are pagans and idol-worshippers, the Muslims of South Asia regard statues even as monuments and objets d'art as sinful. In contrast Muslim peoples elsewhere have no problem with statues and busts, for any visitor to Middle Eastern and Central Asian countries would find statues and busts honouring their heroes. There is one extraordinary irony here. One of the Ten Commandants says: "You shall not make for yourself an idol, whether in the form of anything that is in heaven above, or that is on the earth beneath, or that is in the water under the earth." Yet Christians and Jews have no inhibition about sculpture, while it is the Muslims of South Asia who are puritanically biblical about it, even though nowhere does the Quran lay down such a prohibition. The same obsession about everything Hindu surrounds their attitude toward dance as an art form. The problem with the word 'dance' is that it is translated into Urdu as nautch. Ignoring the classical dances, most Indian dances, as seen in films and practised in brothels by singing girls, are positively lewd and repulsive because of an overemphasis on female anatomy. The British were so horrified by this vulgar form of entertainment that they refused to call it dance; instead, they borrowed the word nautch and made it and nautch girls part of the English dictionary. However, for a Pakistani or Indian Muslim, the very word nautch is revolting and symbolises all that is vulgar and is for that reason shunned and abhorred. The correct translation of 'dance' is raqs, not nautch, and the whirling dervishes represent it in a most sublime form in Konya at Mevlana Rumi's mausoleum. The same is true of music, because it is part of Hindu culture and religion, even though there is no verse in Quran denouncing music. Again, the Arabs, Turks, Iranians, Central Asians and Muslims of South-East Asia do not share this view typical of South Asian Muslims' Hindu-centric outlook.

The rigidity in Pakistani clerics' thinking stems from their refusal to look at the works of Islamic scholars of the classical age critically, for they consider it a heresy to challenge, say, Imam Abu Hanifa or Ibn Taimya, even though the imams themselves had claimed no finality about their views and often made it clear that what they were saying was their opinion not binding on others. According to Dr Mohammad Iqbal in spite of "their comprehensiveness" the legal systems evolved by the medieval imams were based on what after all were "individual interpretations and as such cannot claim any finality. I know the Ulema of Islam claim finality for the popular schools of Mohammedan Law... but, since things have changed and the world of Islam is today confronted and affected by new forces set free by the extraordinary development of human thought in all its directions, I see no reason why this attitude should be maintained any longer. Did the founders of our schools ever claim finality for their reasonings RPT reasonings and interpretations? Never. The claim of the present generation of Muslim liberals to re-interpret the foundational legal principles, in the light of their own experience and the altered conditions of modern life is, in my opinion, perfectly justified. The teaching of the Quran that life is a process of progressive creation necessitates that each generation, guided but unhampered by the work of its predecessors, should be permitted to solve its own problems" (Reconstruction of Religious Thought in Islam, p168).

In sharp contrast to the clerics' ossified thinking, the people of Pakistan have on the whole shown maturity of judgment and a remarkable degree of openness of mind and have seldom shown resistance to change. As results of the general elections held in 1970, 1977, 1985, 1988, 1990, 1993, 2002 and 2008 show, the people of Pakistan did not fail to realise that religious parties had nothing but empty rhetoric to offer. Victims of their own rhetoric, the clerics thought the unending denunciation of the West on their part was enough to give a new direction to the Pakistani people. Of the men I have mentioned earlier in this chapter — from Sir Syed to Anwar Saadat — not one relished or basked in, or tried to capitalise on anti-Western rhetoric, even though it was the West which in each case stood between them and their missions. Neither Jinnah nor Soekarno nor Nasser or Arafat ever wasted their time in fruitless West-bashing. This was also true of such non-Muslim greats as Sun Yet-Sen, Mao, Gandhi and Mandela. The tragedy is that the influence the clerics have with the people and the street power they command have never been pressed into the service of the country or its people. In fact, by focusing on inanities – 'there should be no mixed marathons', 'one's religion should be mentioned in passport particulars', 'women TV news readers should have dupatta the right way on their heads, 'there should be no co-education', 'Ramazan and Eid moon sighting should be by eyes and not through astronomical calculations,' etc. – they have failed to give the right priorities to a country which since independence has been fighting for its survival and has an acute security problem. It need not be emphasised that Pakistan can meet the threats to its security by developing internal strength, which can only come from a speedy and all-round economic development, the acquisition of science and technology, universal literacy, land reforms, equal rights for women and minorities, a contented and prosperous population, democratic institutions and internal peace and cohesion. Regretfully, the Pakistani clerics not only have no concept of these essential attributes of a modern state, the religious establishment has mostly pursued polices which have been counterproductive and have led to social chaos, internal strife, instability and economic stagnation.

What the ulema feel frustrated and angry about is that the non-existing Westernized elite of their imagination and society on the whole do not concede to them what they think is their sole right – to interpret Islamic law. To quote Mazheruddin Siddiqi again: "It is also a false idea that Islam has given any special status to divines and theologians in the administration of the state, because Islam is basically opposed to any kind of privileged classes being formed in Muslim society, whether they are of the religious or the secular type. Islam essentially envisaged a classless society. The divines and theologians in an Islamic society are just like specialists in any other field. They are entitled to have their say in the affairs of the state, but on economic, financial or technical matters they cannot claim that their viewpoint should be necessarily taken as final and decisive. Similarly the divines and theologians cannot impose their viewpoint on the whole nation. In the running of an Islamic state, the views of all kinds of experts and specialists will be taken into consideration. But the final decision will rest with the elected representatives of the people. It is they who will have to decide ultimately what is good for the people and the state. Of course, they will have to take into account the opinions of specialists, if the matter under decision requires specialized knowledge of any field. But they are not bound to follow their advice" (Islam and Theocracy, p 45-46). We find the same point of view in Reconstruction, where Iqbal makes it clear that he thought in modern times parliament represented ijma (national consensus) and the right to legislate and interpret Islam in the modern context rested with it. "The transfer of the power of ijtihad from individual representatives of schools to a Muslim legislative assembly, which, in view of the growth of opposing sects, is the only possible form ijma can take in modern times, will secure contributions to legal discussion from laymen who happen to possess a keen insight into affairs. In this way alone we can stir into activity the dormant spirit of life in our legal system, and give it an evolutionary outlook" (Reconstruction, p 174). John L. Esposito sums up Iqbal's views on ijtihad thus: "This right [to ijtihad] belonged to all qualified Muslims and not just the ulema. He believed that the traditional criteria used to designate one as an interpreter was both self-serving and short-sighted. The failure of the ulema to broaden their training left them ill prepared for resolving many new, modern issues" (John L. Esposito, Islam the Straight Path, p 140) . Esposito is being charitable to the clerics when he interprets Iqbal to say that they have failed to "broaden their training".

Pakistani clerics are living in a world of their own, victims as they are of clichés and their rhetoric. In the countless sermons which I have heard since my childhood, I found that the clerics have nothing original to say, have no solutions to offer for the problems Pakistan is facing today and obstruct progress and development because by their very "training" they consider as sacrosanct and inviolable the opinions and fatwas contained in what Iqbal calls "the popular schools of Mohammedan Law".

Character building is a duty Pakistani ulema have abjured. While the politicized lot believes that Islam is nothing but a political doctrine stripped of its spiritual essence, the conventional ulema's obsession is overemphasis on the finer details of the rituals —right foot first while entering the mosque; left foot first while leaving it; reciting Allaho Akbar while going upstairs; and Subhanallah while going down; trousers should not cover ankles – something the Arab and South-East Asian faithful do not follow – etc. While there is nothing wrong with being punctilious about rituals, one is shocked to see the absence of some fundamental human values among Pakistanis when they are outside the mosque. I have repeatedly lamented in this book the absence among Pakistanis of compassion, fellow feelings, basic courtesies, cleanliness, discipline, sanctity of human life, and that which is the essence of Islam – honesty. Honesty doesn't necessarily relate to financial matters; it means honesty in every minute of your life, like doing one's duty diligently, no matter whether you are a school teacher, a state employee, a receptionist at a tourism office, a traffic cop, an engineer at a water distribution agency, a telephone operator at a railway inquiry, an invigilator at an examination centre or a road builder. For those who deliver Friday sermons these are non-issues, for I am a man of 70, and I have yet to hear a mosque imam emphasise the importance of cardinal virtues, of work ethic, of keeping promises, and of being kind to all of God's creatures, including animals. The heartlessness behind traffic anarchy (Pakistan is among countries having the highest rate of traffic accidents) and the selfishness seen at parking lots are symptoms of a disease that at a higher level translates itself into politics without principles, the sale and purchase at the judicial bazaar, and defections by the MPs when it comes to saying Yes or No to a motion of no-confidence against the prime minister. Few people realise that the political crises – actually political traumas – which Pakistan faces from time to time point to the moral depravity of leadership in all spheres of national life.

Like other journalists I have written countless editorials and been mighty proud of profundity of comment by blaming it all on military interventions and on the absence of democratic institutions and a free judiciary. This utterly shallow explanation for the wounds Pakistanis have inflicted upon themselves doesn't tell us why other countries which have had military interventions and do not have democratic institutions have had a smooth sailing. For instance there are no democratic institutions in Arab monarchies and in countries which have authoritarian regimes like those in Iran, Syria, Libya, Tunisia, Morocco; in South East Asia, Myanmar, Thailand, Malaysia, Indonesia; all Central Asian republics, Azerbaijan and Kazakhstan. There are differences, of course, for Pakistan has been a much more open society, and even if it has not been a democracy for the greater part of its history, it has had 'democratic exposures', besides the infrastructure of parliamentary institutions bequeathed by the British. More important, Pakistan has had – and now has – an electronic and print media which by any standards is free. But this exactly is the point to note: that such freedoms as are available to us – like a free media or the right to free association – have been misused by the politicians, the powerful military and civil bureaucracies, the feudal class, the corporate sector, the educated middle class on the whole and the journalists. Instead of using these freedoms to build Pakistan, to consolidate democratic institutions and to focus on the people's welfare, the ruling elite has abused these freedoms to destroy freedom, to overthrow elected governments, to manipulate a malleable judiciary, and take Pakistan to the precipice. All this because of the absence of character in the ruling elite and the bourgeois class that runs Pakistan. The clerics have made no attempt to stem this rot. Secularism is their anathema, but little do they realise that they themselves are the greatest upholders and practitioners of secularism by focusing solely on rituals and totally ignoring what happens outside the mosque. All that the political breed has is a hollow slogan, "Islamic system", which it has been trying to give us since 1977. Instead what it has ended up giving us is a society rife with drugs, guns and colossal bloodshed.

Does the "Islamic church" that we have in Pakistan condemn suicide bombings? Yes, it does, though it was forced to do so under public pressure. On October 14, 2008, ulema attending a four-day conference organized by the Muttehida (United) Ulema Council at Lahore declared suicide bombings as "haram" and also forcefully condemned American drone attacks inside Pakistan territory. The ulema repeated these views in another conference held in Lahore on May 17, 2009. Among those who spoke at the 2009 conference was Mufti Muneebur Rahman. Twice a year in Islam's lunar calendar, Mufti Muneeb becomes the most important Pakistani in the world and has the nation's attention riveted to him, for as head of the moon-sighting committee (this is the best possible translation of Ruet-i-Hialal Committee) he decides whether the Ramazan moon has been sighted; and 28 or 29 days later whether the faithful should end fasting and prepare for the next day's Eid celebrations. He doesn't believe in the modern instruments of astronomy, and takes his clue from "reliable" eyewitnesses – reliable according to Sharia. He is not alone and is assisted by a dozen other ulema representing various schools of fiqh and sect. Sometimes reliable eyewitnesses are not available to the committee till midnight, so 170 million people wait eagerly for Mufti Muneeb to finally appear on TV and give his verdict. At the Lahore conference on May 17, Mufti Muneeb categorically spoke against the Taliban and against suicide bombings. Though he ritualistically did condemn the drone attacks by the US in Pakistan's tribal area, Mufti Muneeb denounced the Taliban in unequivocal terms, backed the army action then in progress against the terrorists in Swat, said the militants were slaughtering even children, and demanded that those who were fighting in the name of Sharia should first uphold Islamic values themselves. A pious man who spoke on the occasion was Maulana Dr Sarfaraz Naeemi. He called for national unity against "conspiracies" by the Taliban, Sufi Mohammad (leader of the Swat rebellion) and by the "enemies of the country". Dr Naeemi was an outspoken critic of the Taliban and had earned their ire. On June 12, 2009, he paid with his life when a Talib suicide bomber blew himself up, killing besides him two others at his mosque-seminary in Lahore. The man who claimed responsibility for his assassination was

Hakeemullah Mehsud, who would don the Taliban's leadership mantle when Baitullah Mehsud, the man who had exchanged greetings with other Taliban 'heroes' for murdering Benazir Bhutto, was himself killed in a US drone attack on a farmhouse along the Afghan border in the first week of (most probably 5) August 2009. The graffiti that I read as a school boy six decades ago turned out to be seminal: Talibanism had been born.

That Pakistanis still retain a high degree of altruism and a laudable spirit of volunteerism is a tribute to the values handed down to them from earlier generations. The people's response to the earthquake that devastated Azad Kashmir and parts of northern Pakistan on October 8, 2005, was overwhelming. Like one man they rose from Karachi to Khyber to donate and rush relief supplies to the survivors of the quake that was truly called a land tsunami, killing 100,000 people and rendering millions homeless. A study by the Canadian aid agency and the Aga Khan foundation showed that Pakistanis donated on average Rs 72 billion in charities every year. (This figure is at least a decade old). The same spirit of selflessness was seen when, in a most morally depraved act of terrorism, the Taliban blew up the International Islamic University at Islamabad on October 20, 2009. Ashfak Bokhari, my colleague at Dawn, had to rush to Islamabad because one of the victims of the blast, Amna Batool, was his niece. Doing a master's, she was struck by a pellet that went into her brain. She went into a coma and died four days later. Ashfak told me he was surprised by the students' response to the tragedy and the help they rendered to the injured and the victims' families. They donated so much blood that the blood bank ran out of space.

Is there any force which can reverse this tide of bigotry and make Pakistan a normal country? Frankly, no. Only an Ataturk can do this, and Pakistan has had no Ataturk because all Pakistani Generals have been Generals in defeat. I am repeating myself when I say that the results of all general elections have proved that the vast majority of Pakistanis do not subscribe to the kind of retrogressive views most ulema hold. The majority is already against Talibanism, but there is no one who could have the courage to openly denounce the clerics and strip them of the halo of self-assumed sanctity they have built around themselves. That's why I say that I am perhaps the last Pakistani who still believes that the Pakistan of Jinnah's vision will once again bounce back into reality. The Pakistan in which I passed my boyhood and youth has disappeared — I wouldn't say forever. Its spiritual foundations are solid. The clerics have tried subtly to undermine Jinnah and have failed, because Jinnah remains truly speaking the only non-controversial figure with the Pakistani people. My hope is that, perhaps, the excesses committed by the Taliban, the blood they are shedding of innocent men, women and children, and the terror they have created among the people by their cold-bloodedness in every nook and cranny of the country will one day produce a spontaneous and awesome backlash from the people of Pakistan and break their image of social invincibility. This perhaps is Pakistan's only hope.

15

9/11 AND PAKISTAN'S DOMESTIC SCENE

'TALIBAN PASS INTO HISTORY': this was the headline to my editorial in Dawn's issue of December 9, 2001, a day after Kandahar fell to the US-led coalition forces in Afghanistan. The Pakistani in me felt greatly relieved, though subsequent events proved me wrong, both because the Taliban did not "pass into history" and because my sense of relief was false and short-lived. As a Pakistani, I had two concerns: one, the war should not drag on; two, protest demonstrations in Pakistan against Islamabad's support for the American war should not get out of hand. I was quite nervous. What happens if the protest demonstrations take an ugly turn, leading to many deaths? In Pakistan, those who organise protests use deaths in police measures as an opportunity to rouse passions against the government of the day and add to the scope of protest rallies. The angrier the protesters become the harsher the law enforcement authorities become, leading to widespread destruction and fatalities. Violence thus snowballs. Would violence then acquire the level of the 1977 PNA movement and lead to the overthrow of the Musharraf government, the imposition of martial law and the subsequent scenario familiar to the world? Would regime change in Pakistan be to our advantage, or would it mean consequences of horrendous proportions?

For the life of me I could not understand what the demonstrations were about and what choice Pakistan had under the hair-raising circumstances that confronted it during the first few days after 9/11. The issue was one of Pakistan's survival, all other matters being of secondary importance. America had been attacked for the first time in a way it had never been before. Pearl Harbour was far and away. The Japanese attack was, no doubt, a tactical surprise, but it was not a strategic surprise, because America had been aware of a Japanese threat since the days when Japan was not even an Axis power. Besides, Japan was one of the Great Powers of its time and had stunned the world by demonstrating its military prowess in the 1904-05 war against Russia. The attack on the twin towers was an altogether different matter. For the first time in history, continental America had been attacked — not by another Power but by men who had become outlaws by hijacking commercial jetliners and killing thousands of innocent men, women and children of all nationalities and belonging to all the world's religions for no fault of theirs. The wave of national anger and revulsion that gripped America was unprecedented. America was edging to go and to vent its anger, on any target, on any country and on any people, guilty or not.

Pakistan was in no way responsible for 9/11. None of the 19 hijackers was a Pakistani and none of them had training as a pilot in Pakistan — most had been trained in America and Europe. But Pakistan's fault was that it was at some stage among the three countries that had diplomatic relations with the Taliban's Afghanistan. But later, when Saudi Arabia and the UAE ended their ties with Afghanistan, Islamabad was the only capital that had a Taliban envoy. The world also knew that it was Pakistan that had trained and armed the Taliban and helped them take Kabul after defeating the other mujahideen militias. But, barring the ignorant, the world also knew what compulsions Pakistan had and what motives it had in training and arming the Taliban and sending them into Afghanistan to 'conquer' it. I have already discussed in previous chapters what had made Ziaul Haq's Pakistan panicky over the Soviet invasion of Afghanistan on Christmas even 1979 and how gauche the

Zia regime was about allowing the CIA to use Pakistan as a funnel for aid to anti-Soviet resistance fighters in Afghanistan. But the Taliban were a post-Zia, post-Soviet phenomenon which began in the mid-nineties, more than half a decade after Zia's death in the plane crash, and it represented Pakistan's — I think justified — belief that it was the only chance it had of burying the Pakhtoonistan stunt forever and having a friendly regime in Kabul.

Since its independence in 1947, Pakistan had to put up with Afghanistan's unremitting hostility, focussed on Kabul's irredentist claims. Headed by King Zahir Shah and later by his murdered cousin Dawood, the Afghan regimes received full support in this anti-Pakistan campaign from India and the Soviet Union. The support for Kabul by India was understandable, given the history of Indo-Pakistan relations, but Moscow became an avowed champion of Pakhtoonistan during the Cold War when Pakistan joined the US-led military pacts and became America's "most allied ally". In his last speech in the National Assembly, Bhutto said he had the "gut feeling" that he could solve the Pakhtoonistan problem, and there is no doubt Dawood, who had overthrown his cousin-king, Zahir Shah, was coming round to the idea of a rapprochement with Pakistan because he seemed to have become conscious of the dangers inherent in relying too heavily on the Soviet Union and depending solely on Moscow for the country's economic survival. Soviet technical and military advisers were already in key positions in Afghanistan, and the two factions of the Afghan Communist Party — Parcham and Khalq — waited in the wings to take over. Dawood visited Pakistan to listen to Bhutto, and the Shah of Iran, equally worried over Afghanistan's drift, appeared keen to help the Dawood regime with large doses of Iranian financial help to wean Dawood from what appeared to be a suicidal course. Dawood visited Pakistan, and Bhutto told J. G. Heitink, Assistant Editor-in-Chief of De Telegraf, Amsterdam, on October 5, 1976, that he had developed "an immense admiration" for the Afghan president because of "his sincerity, vision of history, for his clarity of thought, for his perception …" A British journalist had asked him how long the problem with Afghanistan would last and "I said how can I say, because you have had an Irish problem for 700 years". Dramatic developments in a couple of years would shatter all dreams of a rapprochement between Pakistan and Afghanistan, and the region itself would plunge into strife from which it has not recovered till this day. Bhutto was overthrown, Dawood was murdered, so were those who followed him — Nur Ahmad Taraki and Hafizullah Amin. Iran saw its Islamic revolution, and the shah went into exile, never to return. On Christmas Eve 1979, Babrak Karmal came to Afghanistan virtually riding a Soviet tank.

The Soviet withdrawal after a decade of blood-letting, the fratricide among the victorious mujahideen, the final victory of the Taliban over their erstwhile comrades and their control of 90 per cent of Afghanistan gave Islamabad what it thought was the only opportunity it had to have a friendly regime in Kabul that would not help India create a 'second front' on Pakistan's western borders. Islamabad also cherished the fond hope that a friendly Afghan regime would finally give up its irredentist claim on Pakistani territory and sign a treaty formalising the 1893 Durand Line as an international frontier between the two countries. Pakistan had no other aim. The links between the Taliban and Pakistan's military, especially the ISI, were deep and multifaceted, and there is no doubt investigative journalists and scholars can come up with fantastic details to establish the ISI's links with the hijackers, including the $100,000 cheque purportedly given to Mohammad Atta, one of the hijackers, by ISI Director-General, Major General Mahmood Ahmad, who happened to be in Washington on September 11. One also cannot deny the tribal and blood relationship which the Pakistani Taliban had with fellow tribesmen in Pakistani armed forces. During the night-long airlift before Kunduz fell, when the Americans allowed the ISI to pull out its operatives, the ISI also managed to lift over 1,000 Taliban fighters, as claimed by Ahmed Rashid (Descent into Chaos, p 90-91). According to Rashid, quoting Seymour Hersh, the Bush-Cheney duo had agreed to Musharraf's request to let Pakistan pull ISI operatives out of the Kunduz area, and that the US-led coalition forces delayed their capture of Kunduz to let the ISI complete the job. But such and other details still fail to prove that the ISI was in anyway involved with 9/11. No Western government, too, has ever blamed Pakistan on this score. Yet one had to listen to the first press conference which Colin Powell addressed after 9/11 to realise the extent of pressure on the American government to act against Pakistan. An American woman reporter preceded her question by 'informing' the Secretary of State that Pakistan was the only country which had diplomatic relations with the Taliban Afghanistan and would America then attack that country? An Indian journalist repeated the question. Powell's reply and his performance at the press conference were reassuring for Pakistan and must have disappointed the two journalists.

The question by the American journalist, nevertheless, represented both the wave of anger sweeping the American nation and the obvious answer: a target must be found, on which America should vent its anger, and the target-nation should not only be punished and reduced to rubble, it should be made to evaporate. The issue before Islamabad was: should it allow Pakistan to become a target of American anger? As army chief Musharraf went into a huddle with his corps commanders, and again there is no dearth of 'scoops' of what happened inside what was called a stormy session in which Musharraf pleaded with his General officers that Pakistan had no other option but to cooperate with America in the war on Afghanistan and accept all its seven demands, which virtually constituted an ultimatum. Personally I doubt if a corps commander in his right senses would have failed to grasp the disastrous strategic implication of what it would have meant for Pakistan if it had chosen to defy Washington. But if there were some doubts, a statement from Jaswant Singh, the Indian Foreign Minister, served to clinch the issue. Singh, the least agreeable of Indian foreign ministers and closest to Krishna Menon in spirit and articulation but perhaps more educated and sophisticated than Nehru's defence minister, saw in the situation a chance for him to isolate Pakistan, and offered America bases in India for the US air force. Singh should have waited a little more.

Who threatened to bomb Pakistan into the stone stage has over the years become a topic one could do a PhD on. May be it was uttered by Deputy Secretary of State Richard Armitage. Later it transpired that the ISI Director General said he had conveyed the spirit of Armitage's threat to Musharraf in Urdu — using the phrase einth sey einth baja dayna. What Armitage actually said is not on confirmed record. He added to the confusion by denying and reaffirming all this when he visited Pakistan years later. But whatever he said, and ignoring the actual words he uttered and the purported translation, there is no doubt that Musharraf's rejection of the seven demands would have given Pakistan a foretaste of what Iraq was made to suffer in 2003 when the neocons in the Bush administration chose to attack it despite the Hans Blix commission's report that it had found no 'smoking gun' that could establish the existence of WMDs in that country. Let us, for a moment, visualise what would have been Pakistan's fate if America had focussed on and bombed solely non-military, strategic targets and civilian infrastructure. The country's railroad and highway system and the bridges which are Pakistan's life line have been so built that the impairment of even part of it is enough to dislocate, block and throw into chaos the country's entire transport system and the movement of all cargo. First there is the Kotri bridge, where the main-line railway track and highways cross the Indus about 100 miles north-east of Karachi. Even its partial damage will halt all rail and road traffic to Punjab and cut off all supplies, including oil, from the Karachi harbour. From Kotri onwards, the railway runs on both side of the Indus, the track on the Indus's eastern side crossing the Sutlej over to its right bank and to move further onto Lahore. From Lahore it takes a turn toward the west, with the railway track now running parallel to Grand Trunk Road. To reach the North-West Frontier Province via Islamabad, this road and rail system has to cross four major rivers — the Ravi, Chenab, Jhelum and the mighty Indus at Attock. The destruction of these bridges would bring all civilian and military movement to a halt and cause indescribable chaos in a country where the population had not been trained in the rudimentary concepts of national discipline. Then there are dozens of big and small dams, including the world's biggest earth-filled dam, Tarbela, which produce electricity for domestic and industrial purposes and ensure water for irrigation throughout the year. Their destruction would have literally thrown Pakistan into the stone age, whether or not Armitage said it. Add to this the threat to harbours, airports, oil refineries, steel mills, nuclear installations and the economic and industrial infrastructure Pakistan had built over the decades, and one could understand what a week of concentrated American bombardment of these targets would have meant for Pakistan. I have not touched upon the military aspect of the situation, nor hazarded a guess as to what chance our army, navy and air force had if America had unleashed its firepower on Pakistan through its B-52 bombers, carrier-based aircraft, and cruise missiles. In such a situation, I personally feel, the Indians would have been required merely to send in their cadets to finish the job. It is quite possible that the doomsday scenario I have painted above would not have materialised if Pakistan had not gone along. But should Pakistan have taken a risk of that nature? And if it should have, then for whose benefit — for Afghanistan's?

The domestic opposition to Pakistan's decision to throw in its lot with America in the wake of 9/11 came from two sources — at loggerheads with each other but united for very odd reasons against America: the religious right and the traditional, secular left. While I will take up the reasons for the religious right's opposition to Pakistan's American alliance later, let me briefly deal with the secular left. The traditional left in Pakistan never had its feet on the ground. Its approach to Pakistan's gargantuan problems — the well-entrenched feudal system, the direct or indirect control of the country's policymaking, legislative and bureaucratic apparatus by the feudals, the condition of the landless peasants, the absence of a truly nationalist capitalist class and, instead, the emergence of comprador capitalism, and the grievances of the minority provinces — was theoretical, inspired by Communist romanticism. Beholden to the Communist dogma, the leftists never tried to relate it to Pakistani conditions. One of the reasons for this was the role played by the Urdu-speaking people in the parties of the left. The Urdu-speaking people — or Mohajirs, as they were called or chose to call themselves — had no rural base. This denied them a rapport with the peasants. Their impact on the politics of the left was through their writing prowess, for they used fiction, poetry, drama, political discourse, pamphleteering besides rabble-rousing and political agitation to advance the cause of the left. It was, however, with the urban proletariat and the trade union movement that they had some success, and it goes without saying that they were sincere to the left and suffered persecution like hundreds of fellow leftists all over the country.

A most intricate phenomenon was the position the Awami National Party occupied in Pakistan's left. Ultimately, this turned out to be a tragedy, for NAP had an agenda that had nothing to do with the cause of the left, and despite the word 'National' in its name the party never had a national outlook. Based in the North-Western Frontier Province and headed by Wali Khan, the NAP donned the mantle of a Communist party and managed to acquire national status because of the support it received from large sections of middle class intellectuals in the other provinces, especially Punjab, which had leftist traditions of its own and where Lahore, its capital, had for long been a leftist bastion. The problem with Wali Khan was the political heritage he got from his father, the redoubtable Abdul Ghaffar Khan, whose "burning resentment against everything British" says Phillips Talbot was "matched only by his devotion to Gandhi. It is odd to see this giant of a man, broad-shouldered, long-legged, and physically hard, sitting next to the little, stooped, unhandsome ascetic. Yet probably the central Gandhian ideal has few more devoted supporters than the man who himself came to be called the Frontier Gandhi" (An American Witness to India's Partition, p 197).

Ghaffar Khan was one of Jinnah's most rabid enemies and opposed his mission tooth and nail. He had boycotted the 1947 referendum in the NWFP on the plea that the option for the voters should not have been limited to "Pakistan or India?" There should have been a third option — independence. During his visit to the NWFP Talbot noted that the Afghan support for Ghaffar Khan's demand for Pakhtoonistan had angered the Pathans, who were wondering what Ghaffar was up to by going out of his way to stop the NWFP from becoming part of Pakistan. That the voters gave their verdict in favour of Jinnah and Pakistan did not mean much to him, for he continued to remain hostile to Pakistan till his death, never swore loyalty to the state, and continued to plead for Pakhtoonistan. To him Pakhtoonistan meant either that there should be a state which should incorporate Pakhtoons on both sides of the Durand Line, or the NWFP should be severed from Pakistan and incorporated into Afghanistan.

Ghaffar Khan was not the only Muslim leader to have opposed the creation of Pakistan: there were many secular and religious giants who opposed Jinnah and his Muslim League for many political and religious reasons. Hussain Ahmad Madani, for instance, was a firm believer in a united India and was opposed to the establishment of a separate Muslim state in South Asia. But once Pakistan came into being he admitted his mistake and wished it good luck. Loosely translated, he is reported to have said: "one can oppose the construction of a mosque at a given place for any number of reasons. But once the mosque becomes a reality one has to accept its sanctity and protect it" (op-ed article by Saeed Ahmad Jalalpuri, Jang, June 5, 2009, quoting Maulana Taqi Usmani). Another Muslim opponent of Pakistan, Syed Ataullah Shah Bokhari, the Ahrar leader and a fiery speaker, said: "I am happy. My happiness is unlimited... I lost my argument the day Pakistan came into being. Let's end this controversy here. I cannot be accused of chicanery. (I am happy) because imperialism is gone. I consider imperialism against the spirit of Quran. Now I will defend every nook and cranny of Pakistan with my blood" (ibid). Maulana Syed Abul Aala Maudoodi, founder of the Jamaat-i-Islami, was personally hostile to Jinnah.

In his monumental book on the Jamaat-i-Islami, 'Islamism and Democracy in India', Indian author Irfan Ahmad dwells at length on the changes in the JI's philosophy in post-partition India and points out how it considers secularism as a welcome ideology that serves the party's cause. Ahmad also traces the party's role in pre-independence India, its attitude toward the Muslim League and the Congress and the position the Jamaat adopted on the Pakistan movement and its view of the Muslim League and Jinnah. Ahmad quotes Maudoodi as saying, "It is sad that from the Quaid-i-Azam ['the Great Leader', which Jinnah was called] to the ordinary followers [of the League] there is not even a single person who has an Islamic outlook and feels the affairs [of politics] from an Islamic viewpoint. These people do not know at all the meaning of being Muslim and his special status' ('Islamism and Democracy in India', Princeton and Oxford University Press, p62. According to Saadia Toor, Maudoodi's "preferred epithet for Jinnah was Kaafir-i-Azam" (the Great Infidel): The State of Islam: Culture and Cold War Politics in Pakistan', Pluto Press, p106. However, once Pakistan emerged as an independent state Maudoodi apologised not by words but by action by coming over to Pakistan and pledging to create an Islamic state there. Ghaffar Khan never accepted the reality of Pakistan. Not for him Madani, Bokhari or Maudoodi's realism and change of heart.

Like his father, Wali Khan remained true to his father's creed till his death, and it appeared his policies, political statements and the book he wrote were calculated to justify Ghaffar Khan's failed mission. Because of problems with his eyes, Wali couldn't acquire a college education and wrote his book — Fact are Facts — in Pashto, which his wife translated into Urdu, which was in turn translated into English by someone. The book reflects the frustration and anger of a man vanquished. It pours venom on Jinnah, eulogises Gandhi and the Congress leadership and doesn't hide his deep sorrow and anger over the establishment of Pakistan. Wali Khan visited Kabul regularly, was given VIP treatment by the Afghan regimes, and had no qualms of conscience about accepting financial doles from India. He adopted an anti-American posture less because he was in any sense a committed leftist or was anti-imperialist at heart but because India followed a neutralist foreign policy and welcomed shrill protests from within Pakistan against its membership of the American-led military pacts. When the world Communist movement split, Wali gave his NAP a pro-Moscow orientation, though personally I doubt if Wali Khan had the vaguest idea of what the ideological split between Beijing and Moscow was about. Khrushchev 's denunciation of Stalin's "personality cult" at the 20th Party Congress in February 1956, his "revisionism" when he repudiated Lenin's theory about the "inevitability of war", and his belief in "different roads to socialism" essentially stemmed from and reflected a clash between the national interests of China and those of the USSR. Wali had no love for China for two obvious reasons: one, China and India were rivals and had fought a war in the Himalayas in 1962; two China was not only Pakistan's friend in the bilateral sense of the term; Beijing shared Islamabad's concerns about New Delhi's hegemonic ambitions in the region and was determined to resist it. That settled the issue for Wali. The advantage that he gained from his anti-American rhetoric was the support he got from leftist elements throughout Pakistan, and this conferred on NAP the mantle of a Communist Party, which it was not. That it was an ethnic party became evident when NAP's Baloch wing broke away to form a party of its own, Pakistan National Party.

Led by Mir Ghous Bizenjo, the Baloch wing broke from Wali Khan because in the wake of the secession of East Pakistan, Bizenjo had done some serious thinking and come to the conclusion that a solution to Pakistan's ethnic problems had to be found within the Pakistani federation. He had seen the fate of Bangladesh, and thought India's support for the rights of Pakistan's ethnic minorities was a tactical ploy to create turmoil within the country and destabilise its western neighbour, and Wali Khan was a willing tool. In the mid-eighties, Rasool Bux Palijo, a Sindhi nationalist and by any standards an intellectual giant, joined ANP. This had profound consequences for the left. The two met, of all places, in New Delhi to decide the future course of action, and one of the decisions taken was to virtually expel all Punjabi- and Urdu-speaking leaders and workers from the party. Those expelled included dedicated workers who had languished in jail, gone underground and suffered persecution for decades. This monopolisation of what was supposed to be a 'national' leftist party by two leaders with an ethnic agenda did enormous harm to the socialist movement in Pakistan. Whatever was left of the left vanished when the Soviet system of states collapsed.

It is against this background that we find the remnants of the left trying to find a role for themselves by rallying round the anti-American campaign provoked by the Bush administration's attack on the Taliban Afghanistan in October 7, 2001. The leftists' opposition to the American attack was instant. They didn't bother to examine the consequences of America's attack from the point of view of Pakistan's interests, because their ideology barred loyalty to a bourgeois state, which they were told was an instrument of oppression in the hands of the ruling classes. Add to this ANP's role we have discussed above, and we can clearly see why the leftists — feeble, voiceless, and without a mooring — found in the Afghan situation an opportunity to regale themselves with a new bout of ideological fervour, for the Communist manifesto and the Theory and Practice of Socialism, whose volume upon volume they had devoured, forbade loyalty to Pakistan, or so they thought. The leftists had allies among Pakistan's liberals, most of whom lived in a Utopia of their own. As epitomised by column writers in Pakistan's English press, these liberals unconsciously sabotaged some of Pakistan's most liberal and democratic regimes by aligning themselves with the religious right. During the PNA movement in 1977 following the general election, they exhibited a greater degree of anti-Bhutto passion than some of the religious parties of the nine-party alliance did, despite knowing the fact that it was the religious right, with full American sympathy, which was behind the anti-Bhutto movement. Similarly, during the two bouts of PPP rule under Benazir (1988-90 and 1991-93) the secular liberals outdid the religious right in undermining her government. Democracy had returned after 11 years of Zia's tyranny, and returned to a country that had no traditions of democracy and consistent constitutional government. But our liberals wanted Pakistan under Benazir to reach the standards of Scandinavian democracies in one go. For a large majority of them, anti-Americanism was a fad, and that made them the natural allies of the ideologically bankrupt left and the religious right.

For the religious right, the issue in October 2001 was simple: an "Islamic government" was under attack from infidels, and it was the duty of all Muslim countries, including and especially Pakistan, to join the jihad. It was a formula cut and dried. It brooked no opposition: every Muslim must take part in this anti-American jihad; if a Muslim didn't do so, he would be beyond the pale of Islam. Musharraf, all members of his government, and all offices and soldiers of the Pakistani armed forces fell in that category. Anyone supporting the Musharraf government was himself an infidel. That the Taliban's was an "Islamic government" was news to most Pakistanis. The full impact of the Taliban's barbaric philosophy would be felt by the people of Pakistan half a decade later when they would seize parts of Swat and launch a full-fledged revolt to capture power and blow up schools and CD shops to let the world know of their brand of Islam. But even before the Swat rebellion, the true nature of the Taliban philosophy and the kind of tyranny they had imposed on the Afghan people had filtered through to Pakistan and earned them few friends. Their main supporters were the religious parties which saw in the American blitz an attack on what to them was their fief. They could have, if they so wished, registered their protest against the American war and Islamabad's support for it peacefully. They had a tradition of organising protest rallies, which often turned violent. But this time, the protest had a religious fervour resembling or perhaps exceeding that during the PNA movement.

While the PNA movement, purported to be a stir against the falsification of the electoral results, was also an agitation against "godless socialism" and aimed at Bhutto's physical elimination, this time the protest was against infidels themselves because "Crusaders" had attacked a country run by an Islamic government. Whosoever stood between them (the religious right) and their protest against the Americans deserved to be wiped out. If this meant a direct clash with the Pakistani armed forces so let it be. If this meant Pakistan's destabilisation, then Pakistan could go to hell. If Wali Khan's ANP with its pseudo-leftist policies had little love for China, the clerics showed in ample measure they cared two hoots for Pakistan's China alliance. If the leaders of the Lal Masjid mutiny abducted three Chinese at an Islamabad health parlour, the Taliban did one better by not only kidnapping but also murdering several Chinese engineers working on different projects in the NWFP. Thus, if dialectical materialism and communist dogma stood in the way of the left's loyalty to Pakistan, the religious right assumed it was the Holy Quran that prevented their loyalty to Pakistan. The twain had met, for neither was Pakistani in spirit.

What mattered was the "Islamic government" of Afghanistan. For the clerics, a barren piece of land in Afghanistan, a rock, a hamlet, if it flew the Islamic flag, was worth more than entire Pakistan. Jinnah's Pakistan was after all an infidel state. All its institutions were un-Islamic and deserved to be destroyed and replaced by a truly "Islamic system". There was nothing sacred about Pakistan because it was a replica of a "Western state"; it represented maghribi tahzib (chapter 14). They had not forgotten their humiliation at Jinnah's hands. Jinnah didn't intend to humiliate them; he wanted their cooperation, which most, though not all, of South Asia's clerics denied him. The people followed Jinnah, who triumphed and gave them Pakistan. This Jinnah was hardly a Muslim, not because of his Western life-style and known weaknesses but because he had not bothered to kowtow to the clerics and thus hurt their pride. For this crime, if they could not punish the man whom the people called the Quaid-i-Azam (the Great Leader) they could at least take it out on his country once Jinnah passed away. They were true to their resolve. The practical demonstration of this spirit was their attitude toward Pakistan in the wake of the American attack on Afghanistan, for it showed their utter indifference to Pakistan's very survival.

On October 21, following a rally by the Jamaat-i-Islami and the speeches made at Committee Chowk in Rawalpindi, the government registered a case of high treason against six JI leaders, including its leader, Qazi Hussain Ahmad, but that hardly deterred Qazi and others, for they continued to say things that were outright treason. Also in the forefront of the anti-American crusade was Maulana Fazlur Rahman, chief of his faction of the Jamiat-i-Ulema-i-Islam (JUI-F). Addressing a rally in Lahore on October 28, Qazi asked his following to be ready for a march on Islamabad for a sit-in. He asked them to bring their food with them, because they would not leave Islamabad until Musharraf was overthrown. The JI's deputy leader, Liaquat Baloch, told a rally in Quetta on October 26 that "God-willing, we will remove Musharraf from power and drag him ... to the streets". As quoted by the Reuters, Baloch said, "We ask the Pakistan army, its corps commanders and staff officers to take a decision according to their conscience and rid the nation of Musharraf ..." Uttering these words during the Zia days would have meant death by hanging. The weak and vacillating Musharraf government did register the case but it never had the guts to try them.

Little did the religious leaders realise that, unconsciously, they were acting as tools for the real infidels, for New Delhi was pinning its hopes on them. If the demonstrations had gone out of hand and there were a regime change in Islamabad, the Bush administration — determined to destroy the Taliban government anyway — would have found in India a willing ally. American planes, then, would be using Indian bases to overfly Pakistan, and one can only hazard a guess what attitude the Bush administration would have adopted toward a new regime in Islamabad. In fact I doubt if a new General — once having denied cooperation to America — would have managed to stay neutral. To put it the other way, I doubt if America would have allowed Pakistan to remain neutral. Powell made America's mood clear to Musharraf in his September 12 phone call when he said, "You are either with us or against us." (Pervez Musharraf, In the Line of Fire, p 201). Recalling Armitage's "most undiplomatic statement", Musharraf wrote, "this was a shockingly barefaced threat, but it was obvious that the United States had decided to hit back, and hit back hard" (ibid, p 201) Neutrality, thus, was no option, and Musharraf and his corps commanders had the common sense to grasp this truth.

Meanwhile, India was in a state of shock and grief and boiling with rage. Here was Pakistan, a friend of the Taliban's, and here was America: instead of punishing it to India's delight Uncle Sam was pampering Pakistan with massive doses of aid and promising a long-term relationship — an indirect admission of the mistakes America had made by abandoning Pakistan after the job was done and the Soviets pulled out of Afghanistan and subjecting all aid to the certificate required under the Pressler amendment. More painful for New Delhi, America and Britain publicly acknowledged that Pakistan enjoyed in Afghanistan a position which no other state did — a stance they later abandoned. In December 2001, following an attack on the Indian parliament building, New Delhi moved troops to Pakistan's border, forcing the Musharraf government to respond. The scary eyeball-to-eyeball confrontation lasted nearly six months, until India realised the futility of a gesture that never had a chance. Pakistan never flinched. If India had attacked, I doubt if any country, ally or non-ally, would have come to Pakistan's help. But India also realised Pakistan would fight back and New Delhi would get anything but a walkover. Behind the scenes America, Britain and China worked to defuse tension.

Anti-Americanism is a fad the world over. In Pakistan this has often served to inject bitterness into our bilateral relations, because Pakistanis, if not their governments, view America through the prism of Washington's policy on the Middle East, especially Palestine. I do not think there is any other country in the world where people sacrifice their own country's interests for the sake of others. I am more Palestinian than a Palestinian, and it would be the happiest day of my life when a Palestinian state emerges on the map of the world and the Arab flag flies at Al Aqsa. But I would hate to hurt Pakistan's interests for the sake of any country or people in the world, knowing full well that when Pakistan is in trouble no one would stir. This is not to deny the fund of goodwill that exists among the Arab countries for Pakistan, but given its lack of military and technological impoverishment, there is nothing that the Arab-Islamic world can do anything practical for Pakistan. As for Afghanistan, our interests lie in a truly peaceful and friendly western neighbour. No two countries are so inter-twined geopolitically and economically as Pakistan and Afghanistan. Bhutto once said that if he were asked which country geopolitically was most important for Pakistan he would name Afghanistan. But no regime in Kabul has ever shown willingness to accept the Durand Line as an international frontier. Even the mujahideen were never ready to do so. Once — in the pre-Taliban days — I asked Gulbadin Hikmatyar in Karachi why the mujahideen did not accept the Durand Line as an international frontier, especially because Pakistan had sacrificed so much for the sake of Afghanistan and helped in its liberation. Gulbadin equivocated, sounded melodious, praised Pakistan, said people on both sides were the same, and the Durand Line was an artificial border, etc, etc. I told him I knew all this. But shouldn't the mujahideen as a pro quid pro recognise the Durand Line as the international frontier and thus help Pakistan get rid of a major headache since independence? He talked a lot again but the one thing he didn't say was yes to my question.

Pakistan's decision to join the US-led war on terror was justified by all canons of geopolitics. That the Taliban were replaced by a corrupt and incompetent government led by Hamid Karzai turned out to be one of Pakistan's misfortunes. The Pakhtoonistan stunt has not been buried, and India now has a major economic and intelligence presence in Afghanistan. Notwithstanding its stance that Islamabad should destroy "the infrastructure of terrorism in Pakistan", India's sympathies are with the Taliban, for these champions of Sharia have delighted New Delhi by embroiling Pakistan in a civil war with a heavy cost in terms of men and material. India would like this situation to continue for a century. More important, in Karzai India has found a willing tool. Presiding over a thoroughly corrupt regime, which includes drug barons, he has given the Indian missions in Afghanistan a free hand to foment trouble in Balochistan and help the insurgents with funds and training. This way the Karzai government has outdone the Zahir and Dawood regimes.

16

2007 CRISIS

IGNORING THE EAST PAKISTAN crisis leading to the emergence of Bangladesh, no other domestic crisis in Pakistan lasted as long as that which began with President Pervez Musharraf's sacking of the Chief Justice, Iftikhar Mohammad Chaudhri, on March 9, 2007, and ended with Musharraf's resignation on August 18, 2008. The crisis that toppled Ayub began in November 1968 and ended four months later when the Field Marshal-President resigned in March 1969. The movement launched against Bhutto by the Pakistan National Alliance in the aftermath of the general election held in March 1977 began in April and was over on July 5 when Zia struck. However, the political and constitutional developments flowing from the Chief Justice's sacking by Musharraf were grave, seminal and nerve racking. During the agitation against Ayub there was only one issue – demonstrators wanted Ayub to go. In the case of the PNA movement, the nine-party alliance's purported aim was a re-election, though the real aim was to oust Bhutto from power. However, the crisis that began on March 9, 2007, had many dimensions and involved, besides Musharraf's personality, many constitutional, political and judicial issues, each as important in itself as the other. After every event I thought the denouement had begun, and things would be normal soon. I went wrong time and again.

The biggest event was Benazir Bhutto's assassination in Rawalpindi on December 27, 2007. No event had broken me since Bhutto's hanging the way his daughter's murder at the peak of her glory did. For Bhutto's death I was mentally ready. We knew from the day he was ousted on July 5, 1977, and Ziaul Haq gave up even the pretence of being the impartial referee he once proclaimed he was, that Bhutto's days were numbered. PNA leaders had volunteered themselves obsequiously to be part of his "hang Bhutto cabinet" and had no qualms of conscience about asking for a postponement of the general election due in November. However, Benazir's death was sudden and left the nation, including her bitterest foes, stunned. Her assassination was one of the events that followed in rapid succession the presidential Reference Musharraf sent to the Supreme Judicial Council, headed by Rana Bhagwandas, against Iftikhar. The train of events included the Lal Masjid rebellion in the capital city, its side-effects themselves turning into full blown crises. These "side-effects" included the army crackdown on July 3 on the Lal Masjid mosque, leading to the death of about 93 people, many of them innocent, but most of them rebels and criminals who had committed serious crimes against the state and people of Pakistan; the lawyers' protests against the humiliation of the Chief Justice, who had been made "non-functional" by the Reference; the clashes between the police and the protesting lawyers; the media's coverage of these incidents, including the government's belief that the electronic media showed a lack of responsibility; the collapse of the Lal Masjid rebellion and the retaliation by the Taliban in the form of suicide bombings; the stepped-up Taliban military activity in the Federally Administered Tribal Area; the Supreme Court's judgment of July 20 that went against Musharraf and restored Iftikhar to his position as Chief Justice; Nawaz Sharif's arrival on September 10 from London in Islamabad and his deportation to Saudi Arabia — after the Supreme Court's decision of August 23 that every Pakistani had an "inalienable right" to return to Pakistan; Musharraf's pledge to the Supreme Court on September 18 through a statement filed by his counsel Sharifuddin Pirzada that "if elected" he would quit the army post even before taking the oath of office as president (the actual words were: "if elected for a second term as president, Gen Pervez Musharraf shall relinquish charge of office of chief of army staff soon after elections and before taking oath of office as president"; the Supreme Court judgment of September 28 dismissing on technical grounds the admissibility of the petitions challenging General Musharraf's right to contest the presidential election; the same court's painful decision at the eleventh hour — on October 5 — to give the go-ahead to the presidential election the next day (October 6) but declaring that the results be not notified by the Election Commission; the resignations by legislators belonging to some religious parties to quit the assemblies to deny Musharraf an electoral college; the drama surrounding the vote of no-confidence against the Frontier Chief Minister and the subsequent dissolution of the provincial assembly; the holding of the presidential election, with the unofficial announcement that Musharraf had won; the painful wait for the court to announce a verdict about notifying the result of the October 6 election; Benazir Bhutto's return to Pakistan after an eight-year exile on October 18 and the bombing of her procession in Karachi at midnight killing nearly 150 people; Benazir's unexpected show of vehemence against Musharraf; the outbreak of the rebellion led by Maulana Fazlullah a.k.a. Maulana Radio in Swat; a worsening of the relations between the media and the government; Musharraf's decision on November 3 to impose emergency, suspend the Constitution, and impose a provisional constitution by decree; the ban on all television channels, except those run by the government; the protests against the state of emergency and the media curbs; the notification of the presidential election by the Election Commission; the Sharifs' return to Lahore on November 25 on a plane provided by the Saudi government; Musharraf handing over army command to Gen Ashfaq Pervez Kayani on November 28, and his induction into office as a civilian president on November 29. The crisis was over, I thought. How wrong I was!

While these events shook Pakistan, and drew the world's attention and concern, to me, in my own little world of Dawn and journalism, this meant writing an editorial a day in tiring and exceptionally nerve-racking circumstances with the deadline nearing. Writing an editorial a day was nothing new for me; but here the issue was the rapidity of events with which to cope. Often, I had to write two editorials, because by the time I was able to finish the one decided upon earlier in the day, the situation had changed dramatically by the evening, rendering the editorial obsolete and forcing me to write another one. The writing side those days was far below its strength. On September 21, Majeed retired, with Zubeida Mustafa taking over as leader page editor. This further depleted the writing side. Even though there were valuable colleagues like Irfan, Ayesha and Mona, the brunt of top editorials, especially those concerning political and geopolitical matters, had to be borne by me. Musharraf's decision to proclaim a state of emergency on November 3, the results of the presidential elections and most of the judgments I have referred to above came in the afternoon or some time late in the evening, and consequently the editorials had to be written in a hurry to meet the deadline.

"Written in a hurry" obviously sounds jarring, because a journalist is always in a hurry, and journalism, to repeat a cliché, is "literature in a hurry". But in this case it meant more than the usual hurry. Let us note that the reader just does not care whether you wrote in a hurry; he wants his time's worth. Besides, those who read editorials — according to a research — constitute less than two per cent of newspaper readership. But their educational level is high. In Pakistan, English editorials are read by policymakers, the elite, the intellectuals, the business class and diplomats and (more frighteningly) fellow journalists! For that reason, the level of argument and language must have a certain standard and adequately convey the paper's views on a given issue to the reader in a limited number of words. In the seventies, when I began writing, there used to be two editorials, the last one spilling over to the next column and giving a bad look to the leader page. The wordage for the two editorials was slightly over 1,200. In the late nineties, Dawn started having three editorials daily. Zubeida was the "man" behind this change. There were solos, too, especially on the federal budget in June each year, and on some big events, besides the usual "solos" on December 31 and January 1, one devoted to a comment on international affairs and the other to domestic developments, each consisting of slightly over 1,200 words. The solos which I wrote in the first decade of the 21st century, and which I remember, included those on 9/11 and the suicide bombing of the American Consulate in Karachi on June 14, 2002. The word scheme for the three editorials was 550 for the first one; 370 for the second and 300 for the third. Often there were variations and adjustments, and the first could only be 500 and the second and third bigger. But on average the first had 550 words. Thus the challenge during the March-December crisis referred to above was to cram all your thoughts — what Dawn thought of a given issue — in 550 words and in the time available to you.

Normally, the editorial conference was supposed to begin at 11am. With Majeed as boss, people started coming to the meeting at 11:30; sometimes even later. A cup of tea was served, and often the serious talk of deciding three topics for the editorials gave way to the staff members' domestic matters. Besides the usual pleasantries and concerns about someone having regular bouts of flu or the kids' problem at school, the talk was gossip pure and simple. Often I came out of the meetings at 12:30pm and had hardly written a meaningless sentence or two before it was time for lunch. So editorials for me really began at 1.30pm. By 3.30 my first draft would be ready, and I would "switch off", as I used to say, not the computer but myself. After doing some other work, reading newspapers, attending to email or perhaps barging into a colleague's room to exchange notes and have another cup of tea I would return to the editorial, improve language, check facts, marshal new arguments, prune or add and then finalise it to hand it over to Majeed at around 4.30pm. It was seldom that I was asked to write an editorial again in the evening.

When Tahir Mirza became editor in 2004, there was a change in policy, for he insisted we make a comment that very day for the editorial to appear the next day. For the life of me I could not understand why quality must be sacrificed for the sake of a hurried comment. The editor and the majority were against me. My stand for a well-informed comment appeared weak because our competitors — The News, The Nation and Daily Times — commented the same day. I just could not understand why there had to be a dull, lack-lustre and insipid comment. I still remember the editorial — written not by me — about Zafrullah Khan Jamali. The prime minister had resigned, and we had to write an editorial that very day, and the leader was written by a very competent man. However, the readers must have felt cheated the next day, for it was a comment for the sake of comment and contained absolutely nothing that could be called worthwhile, much less pungent and biting. Editorials in the other papers, too, were equally dull and wishy-washy. If I were asked to write an editorial on Jamali's resignation, it would have been equally hollow. The day after Jamali's resignations, the newspapers were full of inside stories about the events leading to his resignation, the history of other prime ministers being forced to resign if not dismissed, and some useful information about some of Jamali's decisions, good and bad. The point to be emphasised in the editorial was missing: it was after decades that a prime minister had not been hounded, he and his family not arrested, tortured and humiliated and a list of his alleged wrongdoings and lurid stories and white papers about his acts of malfeasance not accompanied his ouster from office. The last prime minister to leave office gracefully and allowed to live in peace ever after was Sir Malik Firoz Khan Noon, who was ousted in the Ayub-Mirza coup in October 1958. Bhutto had been hanged, and Mohammad Khan Junejo sacked under the Constitution's article 58-2b by Ziaul Haq, who came on TV to read a long charge-sheet against him and his ministers. Benazir and Sharif were dismissed twice, but Jamali faced no charges of corruption and was allowed to leave office in peace.

On the afternoon of March 9, 2007, Majeed told me that the CJ had been sacked. That was not true, for what 'Mush' did was to call the CJ to his office and hand him the Reference that accused the CJ of malfeasance. The editorial on this humiliation of the Chief Justice (even though this was not the first time in Pakistan's history) appeared "normally". The CJ was summoned by Musharraf to his "camp office" in Rawalpindi on March 9, which was a Friday. The news was carried in Saturday's paper, and my solo, consisting of 1,239 words and entitled "A big blow to the judiciary" appeared in Sunday's issue.

"With the Chief Justice of Pakistan having become 'non-functional'," the editorial said "another sordid chapter has been added to the judiciary's chequered history. Ghulam Mohammad began the process of destroying the foundations of Pakistan's constitutional and democratic structure, but he is not known to have interfered with the judiciary. That the Sindh Chief Court tried to undo the dissolution of the Constituent Assembly in October 1954 showed that the judiciary till then had acted independently. However, the Federal Court then came to his rescue with the notorious 'Doctrine of Necessity' that has since held the ground.... As years wore on, the judiciary more or less acquiesced in its role as a subservient institution whose duty was to legitimise every authoritarian ruler's assumption of power, even if he acquired it by means of a military coup, and to uphold all his actions which often were in utter violation of the fundamentals of law and constitutional propriety.... That is how the Doctrine of Necessity became an intrinsic part of Pakistan's constitutional jargon, for, instead of being forgotten as a one-time exception, this doctrine has been exploited by the generals, who often found — barring some exceptions — willing allies ... [in] the judiciary.

"Generals Ayub, Zia and Musharraf all overthrew elected governments. While the Noon ministry, which Ayub and Iskander Mirza combined to dislodge by a coup, was not directly elected, it had, nevertheless, enjoyed a majority in the assembly and had ... constitutional status, but Zia and Musharraf overthrew governments which had come to power through general elections. Once in power, they de-fanged the courts by appointing yes men to the apex judiciary so as to ensure uninterrupted legitimisation of all their actions. Zia was in a class by himself. He not only got rid of five judges of the Supreme Court, he also sacked Chief Justice Mohammad Yaqoob Ali. Zia also made no secret of his fascist bent of mind by declaring publicly that the 1973 Constitution was a scrap of paper which he could tear up any time. The Provisional Constitution Order and the Revival of the Constitution Order were not at all what their imposing titles suggested; they were instruments of manipulation to perpetuate his rule which he had assumed initially for 90 days to hold elections. Finally, the Constitution he left behind ... had been stripped of its parliamentary character, all powers were concentrated in his person, and like Gen Musharraf today, he continued to remain both army chief and president till his death....

"... Now coming to Friday's episode, one is appalled to see the photograph of a general in uniform calling the country's Chief Justice to his 'camp office' as if the latter were a 'suspect' in a case of embezzlement, thus stripping him of the dignity to which he was entitled ... by virtue of the office he held. Chief Justice Iftikhar Mohammad Chaudhry was then not allowed to return to his office and was 'escorted' home. Gen Musharraf has made a reference against him to the Supreme Judicial Council, and the media has published a list of the alleged acts of malfeasance by Mr Justice Chaudhry. Since the charges are sub judice and commenting on them would constitute 'contempt', one cannot but take note of the background against which the Chief Justice was made 'non-functional' and the 'judicial activism' that came to be associated with his name since he became chief justice in June 2005. More important, it is difficult to avoid the suspicion that some of his verdicts had irked the government and for that reason it did not wish an independent Chief Justice to be in office at a time when the apex court could be called upon to decide vital constitutional issues in the light of continued reports that President Musharraf will retain the two offices and that the existing assemblies will re-elect him as president for another term.... While SJC will, no doubt, decide upon the case whose outcome will have profound consequences for the future course of law and constitution in Pakistan, the nation is appalled that those who impose accountability on others and imprison politicians are accountable to no one. Is not the nation justified in wondering why the men in khaki consider themselves above accountability? He who seeks justice must come with a clean hand is an old axiom. The generals seek to dole out justice to others, but they themselves are not prepared to present themselves before an impartial, civilian tribunal to defend their actions. It is for this reason that, since Zia's days, the word 'accountability' has acquired a strange connotation because it is hard to dispense with the notion that the military uses the shibboleth of accountability to persecute the regime's political enemies through what can be called inquisition courts.

"A larger question is Pakistan's image. The government has been very keen to project a soft image for Pakistan, and there is no doubt that this country gets bad press abroad, often because the good here does not make news, while terrorism, honour killings and gang rapes regularly hit world headlines. But then the nature of the regime in power is a major factor in giving the country a good or bad image. Friday's treatment of the Chief Justice is hardly the episode that will cast Pakistan in a better image abroad. In fact, it will have a negative impact on the world and add to the impressions abroad that Pakistan is just another Muslim country where the ruler's word is the law." From what I know the editorial was well received by all, including people sympathetic to Musharraf. Many believed that the Chief Justice's conduct was not above board, but the method the General had chosen was shocking.

A source of utmost concern for all right thinking Pakistanis about this time was the continued occupation of the Lal Masjid (red mosque) by people for whom the word militants would be a gross understatement, for their activities had turned them into outright criminals and later rebels. Led by two brothers, Ghazi Abdul Rashid and Abdel Aziz, they represented that phenomenon in which every Tom, Dick and Harry in Pakistan thought he had the right to "spread good and suppress evil" (amr bil-ma'aroof wa nehi anil munkar). Iqbal quotes Mishkaat (a collection of the sayings of the Holy Prophet) to emphasise that everyone does not have the right to preach, because the results could be counterproductive and even lead to chaos. I have dwelt on this question in detail in Chapter 14, but I have no doubt in my mind that the Lal Masjid phenomenon betrayed the essentially low intellectual calibre of most Pakistani ulema and their total failure to grasp the implications of their way of preaching and its impact on society. Most appallingly, they seemed to have condoned — and in some cases encouraged — violence to achieve their aim of giving Pakistan an Islamic "system". Often violence has been glorified and considered a form of jihad. While the non-political ulema were often harmless, the discredit for turning Islam into a fitna — public mischief — went to the politicised ulema. Every political party has the right to pursue its aims by means which promote its interests, so long as the method adopted to advance its political cause does not hurt the state itself. The movement launched against Bhutto in March 1977 by the PNA, the nine-party alliance, had the support of secular elements, including men like retired Air Marshal Asghar Khan and Abdul Wali Khan. But the manpower, organisation, and motivation had largely come from three religious parties, the Jamaat-i-Islami, headed then by Mian Tufail Mohammad, the Jamiatul Ulema-i-Islam, led by Mufti Mahmood, and the Jamiatul Ulema-i-Pakistan, headed by Maulana Shah Ahmad Noorani. This was perhaps for the first time that the religious parties had truly discovered their strength — a strength not reflected in their miniscule presence in parliament. This is not to say that the religious parties had not resorted to violence and strikes earlier. But the PNA movement was unprecedented in character, more so because the industrial class, hurt by Bhutto's sweeping nationalisation programme, funded the agitation generously. This combination of secular financial power and "religious" organisation and manpower rocked Pakistan and led to the fall of an elected government and the establishment of military dictatorship.

The Lal Masjid crisis hit world headline when on January 3, 2007, the girl students of Hafsa Madressah occupied a government library as a protest against the proposed demolition of mosques built illegally in the Islamabad area. What moral values and Islamic injunctions guided them one does not know, but millions the world over began seeing a new and horrible image of Muslim women. This image wasn't one of women wearing hijab or even a shuttle-cock burqa that covered a woman from head to toe; compared to the Hafsa girls those were normal females. No, clad in robes and hoods and carrying sticks, those brainwashed Hafsa girls seemed to take a leaf out of the KKK's book of terror and, except for cross burning and lynching, seemed in spirit and action closer to the white supremacists in the US than to the normal Muslim female that has existed worldwide for a millennium and a half. On March 3, Hafsa commandos, led by Umme Hassan, wife of Abdel Aziz, raided an apartment building, broke into the house of a woman alleged to be a whore, beat her and her two daughters up and abducted them. The most unfortunate part of the story was that the Hafsa girls got away with it, and the Lal Masjid brigade got the right signal. From now on, the issue was clear: who ran the government in Islamabad —Musharraf or the two misguided brothers for whom fanatic was an understatement. They had already been harassing shopkeepers in Islamabad's Blue Area, warning them to stop selling entertainment CDs and other "obscene" stuff, and threatening to destroy their shops. On May 18, their commandos — this time boys — abducted four policemen. Four days later three more cops were taken prisoner, and on June 22 they raided a Chinese-run massage parlour, claiming that it was a brothel, and kidnapped six Chinese nationals, and later released them "because China is Pakistan's friend". The charge that it was a brothel turned out to be totally false.

As I wrote in a signed article in Dawn's issue of May 23 a "baffling and disappointing" phenomenon of the Lal Masjid affair was that civil society was quiet, "notwithstanding some murmur here and there." Even though I have never been V. S. Naipaul's admirer, I quoted his theory that that converts — especially Iranians, South Asians and the Malay stock — suffered from neurosis. To them, according to Naipaul, nothing is sacred "except the sands of Arabia". "As we can clearly see," I wrote, "to the Lal Masjid warriors, even the mosque is not sacred because it stands on a non-Arabian soil. The threat to carry out suicide attacks in which innocent human beings will be atomised seems to certify the correctness of Naipaul's theory that to converts nothing is sacred." I then compared the Lal Masjid brothers to "David Koresh, the crackpot 'saviour' who shut himself up in his compound in Waco, Texas." I was then in Washington DC and saw the live coverage of the crackdown ordered by Attorney General Janet Reno after a 51-day stand-off. "Tanks opened holes in the walls, helicopters opened up with machine guns and the compound was burnt down, with flames shooting 75 feet into the sky. There were nearly 80 dead, including Koresh, his followers, in trance or under his spell, 22 children and two pregnant women." Reno's excessive use of force, I wrote, "was criticised, but by and large the entire American nation heaved a sigh of relief because Koresh and his evil cult had no followers, and no one went about burning buses in L.A. and D.C. This is not the case here, for the Aziz-Rasheed brothers — and Zille Huma's killer – are not without admirers, and even those who have reservations about the Lal Masjid duo's modus operandi are hoping for a crackdown so as to make propaganda capital out of it." (Zille Huma, Punjab's Social Welfare the Minister, was shot dead by a fanatic on February 20, 2007, because she was not wearing a hijab). I said: "The question, however, is: is this abnormal way of enforcing Sharia something that only the government should tackle? If the authorities fail to sweep off the lot, is the government alone the loser and not society itself? The problem with this kind of reasoning is that it can be misunderstood and interpreted as an attempt to justify governmental inaction. The law enforcement agencies' options are limited. They cannot open up with artillery or fire teargas shells, for this exactly is what the Lal Masjid, the Taliban and their supporters are hoping and praying for. The mosque can be stormed, with some casualties on both sides, but the ultimate triumph will be that of the Taliban supporters, to whom a crackdown on the sacred precincts of the mosque will give a resounding propaganda victory — proof that it is only the Taliban and their types who can protect mosques. In such a scenario, the stand-off at Lal Masjid may come to an end, but the crackdown will translate itself into more power and more votes for the 'neurotic' religious right. Worse still, such a crackdown could create fissures in the establishment and in the army, both of which are not without Taliban sympathisers, with consequences that are too frightful to visualise." I then pleaded for a national consensus on the issue: "A crackdown on the Lal Masjid cultists will be possible only if there is a national consensus behind it. However, given the fractious nature of our politics, with political differences turning into animosities, such a consensus is out of the question. There is no doubt many NGOs, including women's rights groups, have demonstrated against the Lal Masjid-Hafsa politburo, and it goes without saying that Aziz-Rasheed brothers' criminal acts — abductions, attacks on shops and threats of suicide bombings — have not exactly been commended by many religious groups and parties. The MMA's component parties belong to Deobandi, Barelvi, Ahl-i-Hadees and Jafria schools, and none of them has approved the Lal Masjid gang's actions. But the criticism lacks depth and sincerity, for one obvious reason: all opposition parties are thoroughly enjoying the government's predicament. The government's dilemma is: if it does not act, it stands accused of failing to enforce its writ even in the federal capital; if it comes down hard on the two brother maulanas and their acolytes, the repercussions will shake the government, as if it is not already shaking. More important, the media, which today is chiding the government for failing to enforce its writ, will be the first to condemn the crackdown. (Just visualise TV images showing cops running berserk in the mosque and chasing and beating up nice 'Islamic' boys). That is how the media the world over is. What the political parties and civil society in general fail to realise is that if the Lal Masjid clerics succeed in appearing as victims of a governmental crackdown the problem will not go away, because it is the next government — and civil society — which will be faced with a similar, and perhaps greater and wide-ranging fitna (the Quranic term for public mischief). The entire strategy of the two brothers is focussed on one point — dare the government into rash action. The more they provoke the authorities, the more diffident the government becomes... What they want is a military crackdown. There is no doubt they will lose the first round, and the authorities will evict the brainwashed lot from the mosque, but in the long run it is they and not the government or civil society that will be victorious. If there is to be a crackdown it must have the nation's support. This can be obtained through parliament, provided the government and the opposition adopt a united stance. However, in the present circumstances neither the government nor the opposition nor society's liberal sections — angry with the government over the CJ affair and the May 12 killings — would be willing to unite to crush a menace that one day could engulf the entire country."

On July 3 the Lal Masjid commandos burnt down a section of the Environment Ministry building close to the mosque and snatched arms from some security personnel. This was perhaps the proverbial last straw on the camel's back, and the government finally launched the long-delayed crackdown. After opening up with machine guns and mortars, the army halted the operation to let those who wanted to get out leave in safety. As women fled, Abdel Aziz was caught while trying to flee after wrapping himself in a burqa. Rashid was killed, and the final death was 93, and there were no women and children.

In Dawn's editorial of July 5, entitled "An end at last", I criticised both the Lal Masjid's fanatic leadership and the government. It said: "... First the chiefs of the Lal Masjid rebellion: in what way have the brothers Rasheed and Ghazi advanced the cause of Islam which was supposed to be the aim behind the 'government' and the 'court' they had set up in the sacred precincts of the mosque? Does Islam approve of crime — raids on homes, kidnapping, attacks on shops and defiance of the law of the land — to enforce Sharia? Did the raid by girl commandos on the home of a woman of ... ill repute abolish prostitution throughout the country? Is asking young boys and girls to take the law into their own hands the best way of teaching them Islam and making them good Muslims? Did not the Holy Prophet (PBUH) say that the best Muslim was one from whose hands and tongues other Muslims were safe? Did the self-deluded clerics of the Lal Masjid conform to this Hadith? Did it not occur to them that no government — Islamic or otherwise, democratic or dictatorial, civilian or military — would tolerate the defiance of its writ for long and that sooner or later the government was bound to act, especially after the nationals of a friendly country like China had been kidnapped?

"Now the government. If it had to bare its teeth, should it have waited for six long months to do so? Were not the Lal Masjid militants encouraged in their criminality by the government's kowtowing to the religious right? Did not the invitation to the Imam of Kaaba and the help sought from him for defusing the Lal Masjid crisis betray the government's will to act? Should foreign help be sought for solving domestic problems, no matter how grave? The government must also let the people know about the role of the secret agencies in this case and their incompetence, if not complicity in the affair. Why did the law enforcement agencies fail to prevent the smuggling of arms and stocks of fuel into the mosque? Why were not non-lethal methods — like cutting off supplies and sequestering the mosque — adopted to tire out the brainwashed lot inside?

"... The Lal Masjid brothers are guilty of blackmail, murder, vandalism, trespass and kidnapping. If they surrender or are captured alive, they must be given the benefit of a fair trial in an open court. The crimes they have committed are a blot on the fair names of the ulema. That is not how the great ulema produced by South Asia — Shah Waliullah, Maulana Maudoodi, Ahmad Raza Khan Barelvi, Shabbir Ahmad Usmani and others — ever asked their followers to behave. Regrettably, the government found itself isolated because neither the MMA leadership nor the secular parties categorically condemned the Lal Masjid brigade. It is now for the Pakistani people to decide whether they want the kind of Islam that Iqbal and Jinnah stood for or the intolerant, obscurantist brand being preached and practised by bigoted semi-literates."

In another editorial written on July 15, entitled "Sharia at gunpoint" I again criticised the delay on the government's part in launching the crackdown. It said: "...[T]he Aziz-Ghazi duo had left the government with no other option. The only regret is that an operation that should have been carried out in January, when the Hafsa girls occupied the children's library, took place in July. This six-month gap was utilised by the militants holed up in the mosque to strengthen their position and convey their perverted philosophy to the people through the media. Let not the same mistake be repeated, for what is going on in Fata and the NWFP calls for an immediate and firm response. Incidents such as Saturday's suicide attack in North Waziristan that killed at least 18 soldiers cannot be tolerated. The reaction among sections of tribesmen in Bajaur, Battagram and Swat does not reflect the consensus in Pakistan on the Lal Masjid stand-off. Many people have criticised the mistakes made by the intelligence agencies and security forces before and during the operation and regretted the loss of innocent lives. But by and large there is unanimity on the despicable methods adopted by the two brothers to blackmail the nation and the government.

"In the NWFP, too, the reaction to the entire episode has by and large been positive, but sections of tribesmen under the Taliban influence have vowed revenge. Their fanaticism is evident from the fact that they do not really care who gets killed or injured or maimed. Their quarrel is with the government, but they would not mind killing innocent people when their suicide bombers blow themselves up in public places. Those who want to enforce Sharia at gunpoint deserve to be tackled with the full force of the state. Their violence and the coverage they get in the media may give an impression that they are about to take over Pakistan; actually, they are in a small minority. As the Lal Masjid affair shows, no religious scholar or madressah management has approved of the criminality perpetrated by the two brothers. Barring the MMA, which is a political alliance that misses no opportunity to flay the government, most ulema have either criticised the Lal Masjid leadership or stayed aloof. No one of any consequence has supported the Lal Masjid clerics.

"What we are witnessing in parts of the Frontier is merely a continuation of the anti-government movement launched by pro-Taliban tribesmen since the American attack on Afghanistan and Islamabad's decision to join the war on terror. The Lal Masjid affair has come in handy for them. While talks and tact must be part of the strategy to pacify the area, the fanatics led by clerics should be told that force will be met with force, and they will be responsible for the loss of innocent lives. They must be told bluntly that Sharia cannot be imposed through force, and the people of Pakistan will resist any such attempt. Unfortunately, the acute differences between the government and the opposition have emboldened the militants..."

Meanwhile, Musharraf was getting desperate and wanted to be elected before he called a general election. Hints from his advisers had made it clear that he would seek his re-election from the outgoing assemblies. This was outrageous, and the opposition acted with understandable fury and the media denounced it. On September 18, Pirzada informed the Supreme Court that "if elected" Musharraf would discard his uniform and be a civilian head of state. The "if elected" caveat contained both an assurance of his intentions and a warning to the opponents that, if pressed too hard, Musharraf could take extra-constitutional steps to get the controversial election going. Nevertheless, Dawn took notice of this editorially in its issue of September 19. Entitled "If elected..." my editorial said: "... The substantive paragraph of the letter given to the apex court by Syed Sharifuddin Pirzada needs to be reproduced. It said, 'If elected for a second term as president, General Pervez Musharraf shall relinquish charge of office of chief of army staff soon after election and before taking oath of office as president.' What happens if he is not elected? Will Gen Musharraf, in that case, continue to remain the army chief and breathe down the necks of the president and the prime minister? The letter also does not clear up another major issue: will the president seek re-election by the existing assemblies or by those that will come into being as a result of the parliamentary elections due later this year? The letter to the Supreme Court assumes that there is no bar on a government employee from seeking a political office within two years of retirement. This is an issue on which the apex court has yet to give a ruling.

"One wishes President Musharraf had shown a bit more confidence in himself. Notwithstanding his current rating, the earlier part of his rule saw some positive developments that included a consistently high rate of economic growth and the partial success of the normalisation process with India; and — barring some unsavoury incidents — he has allowed the press to operate freely. Also, let us accept, the opposition is hopelessly divided, and its leaders — some of them with a long history of mutual recriminations — are working at cross purposes. Under the circumstances, it would have been in the fitness of things if he had decided to fight re-election as head of state after discarding his uniform rather than doing so 'if elected for a second term'.

"It is time the president made it clear that he would seek re-election from the new assemblies. It looks absurd that the assemblies which themselves have a life of five years should give Gen Musharraf a decade. A transparent presidential election will set the pattern for the parliamentary elections, but it is a matter of concern that we still have no trace of an interim set-up...

"The time for manipulating the Constitution and for weird legal contrivances is gone. The people of Pakistan want unadulterated democracy — democracy as is understood the world over."

The opposition here made a colossal tactical mistake, for it went to court to challenge Musharraf's right to contest a presidential election while being the army chief. After all, the opposition and the press had been demanding for years that Musharraf discard his uniform and be a civilian head of state. He was doing precisely this, and going to court merely meant putting obstacles in the way of what the opposition itself wanted. On September 28 a Supreme Court bench headed by Justice Bhagwandas rejected six-to-three the opposition's petitions on technical grounds, saying it was not "maintainable" under clause (3) of article 184 of the Constitution. Thus, without saying what it thought of Musharraf's right to contest a presidential election while being the army chief at the same time, the short order read out by Justice Bhagwandas said:: "For reasons to be recorded later, as per majority view of 6 to 3, the petitions are held to be not maintainable within the contemplation of Article 184(3) of the Constitution (court's original jurisdiction under the fundamental rights). As per minority view of Justice Rana Bhagwandas, Justice Sardar Muhammad Raza Khan and Justice Mian Shakirullah Jan, all these petitions are held to be maintainable under Article 184(3) and hereby accepted. As per majority view these petitions are hereby dismissed as not maintainable."

The judgment was good news for Musharraf after a series of disappointments that included the Supreme Court's decision of July 20 restoring Iftikhar as Chief Justice. The opposition and anti-Musharraf lawyers reacted negatively. There were shouts of "Shame! Shame!" when the judgment was announced, with Abdul Hamid Khan, a constitutional expert and author, attacking the integrity of the six of the judges by saying, "The verdict proves that a majority of the judges, known for their links with the establishment, have stuck to their affiliations".

Noting the opposition's disappointment with the judgment, Dawn warned the pro and anti-government forces not to act rashly or do anything that could derail the democratic process — a bit of advice that unfortunately was not followed. Entitled A little less foggy, my editorial of September 29 said "... what follows Friday's judgment is going to be crucial in the context of the orderly holding of the presidential election. All along, the two sides have to keep one aim in view — the democratic process must be advanced. The post-judgment scenario is both a challenge and an opportunity for the government and its opponents. By their epic struggle this summer, the lawyers made a major contribution to the cause of the judiciary's independence and rule of law. This struggle must be pursued relentlessly, but in a way that does not cause a setback to constitutionalism or give an opportunity to extra-constitutional forces to queer the pitch for democracy. In one go, let us accept, Pakistan cannot make up for the 60 years it has lost in terms of democratic evolution..."

The opposition went to court again, asking that the presidential election scheduled for October 6 be stayed, because by virtue of being the army chief he had no right to contest the presidential election — a plea slightly different from the earlier petitions, which had challenged his right to hold two offices. The Supreme Court gave a decision that was odd. While it refused to stay the presidential election, the court ruled that the vote should go ahead, but the results of the election be not notified. That hardly served to clarify the issue. As Dawn's editorial of October 6, entitled Whose victory?, said: " It is now a matter of opinion whether Friday's short order on the presidential election today has served to remove the political uncertainty that has surrounded the nation since the July 20 decision on the CJ's case. The government's euphoria over the Supreme Court's refusal to stay the presidential election has been dampened by the accompanying caveat that the results of the polling will not be notified till the apex court makes its decision known on the merit of the case. That only postpones the outcome of the current bout of politico-judicial battles. Last week's six-three judgment dismissing the petitions challenging President Pervez Musharraf's right to contest the presidential election was based on technical grounds; it did not go into the merit of the case. The position remains unchanged even after yesterday's Supreme Court judgment, which was unanimous. The opposition must have felt disappointed, though a flicker of hope must still be there, since the apex court is still to give its opinion on what after all is the issue — whether a general can contest the presidential election. Profound and arcane they may be, the implications of the Seventeenth Amendment have served President Musharraf eminently well. What is more, sections of the opposition — the MMA to be specific — supported it and thus made the Legal Framework Order part of the Constitution. For that reason, the opposition leaders would be too naïve if they thought that the courts would give them what they failed to get for themselves on the floor of parliament or on the streets.

"The en bloc resignations by the MMA-led opposition will now make no difference to the outcome of the election, since the ruling coalition has enough votes to make candidate Musharraf win without the results being officially notified. With the PPP on board, the electoral process is now moving forward. The opposition, too, legitimised the presidential election by putting up Mr Wajihuddin Ahmed as its candidate, Mr Amin Fahim's candidacy being little more than the PPP's show of me-tooism…"

Finally the presidential election was held on October 6 and Musharraf, as expected, won. Noting that results of the election have been "announced and not notified," the editorial said President Pervez Musharraf was "one step nearer to another five-year term, provided the Supreme Court does not disqualify him. The result of Saturday's poll was never in doubt. While the MMA-led opposition boycotted the election, the PPP chose to adopt an ambivalent position. Mr Amin Fahim, the PPP candidate, never formally announced his retirement, and the party abstained from voting; … Mr Wajihuddin Ahmad's presence in the race — symbolic in the beginning — became incongruous when his supporters resigned from the electoral college. As a result it was a walk-over for the incumbent who won 354 of the weighted votes with Mr Wajihuddin getting a handful. President Musharraf then thanked God for his 'great victory', and Law and Parliamentary Affairs Minister Sher Afgan Niazi declared everything about the election to be 'constitutional, legal, moral and legitimate'. That, however, is his opinion, and it is for the judges to decide what they think about it.

"The nation will now wait with bated breath for the Supreme Court's verdict which could, if the 10 judges so decide, upset the general's applecart. Oct 17 is incidentally the date for the next hearing, and not for the judgment. If the hearing drags on, one does not know how long the nation will have to wait in suspense for the outcome of what is basically a power struggle devoid of ethics and morality on either side. This must be emphasised because the government machinery has all but come to a halt since the March reference against the CJ. Since then, one event after another has rattled the nation. And there is more to go. The May 12 killings, the storming of Lal Masjid, the judgment restoring the CJ to his office, the verdict in favour of the Sharifs' 'inalienable right' to return, the opposition's petitions against President Musharraf's right to contest the election, and Friday's 'yes, but' verdict, besides the brute display of power by the government's coercive apparatus...

"This looks like an unending crisis in which the two sides seem utterly indifferent to the people's welfare. The lack of popular response on Saturday to the opposition's strike call shows the people's contempt for both sides. If on the one side they see a general using every trick up his sleeve to stay in power, on the other side they watch with dismay a fragmented opposition groping in the dark for a worthwhile strategy that could make the people believe that there was an opposition that offered a feasible alternative..."

On October 18, 2007, Benazir returned to Pakistan from her second exile. It was perhaps the first Bhutto spectacle where I was absent as a spectator. There was one obvious reason: I was feeling my age. When her father first came to Karachi after resigning as foreign minister on his famous train journey; when he came to Karachi start his election campaign in 1970, when he addressed his first election rally at Nishtar Park, when he spoke again to a massive crowd at Nishtar Park in January 1972 after becoming the chief martial law administrators in those days when voices in India were calling for "finishing the job"; again when he spoke to a relatively small crowd at the same Nishtar Park when the language riots had served to reduce his following in Karachi, which still had a majority of the Urdu-speaking people; again when he came to Karachi by train after being released by Zia from captivity at Murree in 1977, I was there. Never as a journalist but as a "people". And when

Benazir came to Karachi in 1986 — after getting at Lahore a reception which some say even her father never got — I was there in the crowd at Jinnah's mausoleum. But October 2007 was different. Gone were the happy birds of youth. Gone were the days when I could be on my feet the whole day, and a cup of tea and a cantaloupe would be enough for a lunch that could serve me well into midnight. Then I could drink a glass of water from an Irani restaurant or have a bowl of chholay without worrying about hepatitis-B. In 2007 I must have absolutely hygienic food, bottled water, perpetual shade if not an air-conditioned room, some rest, if not on a couch then at least in my office chair, and a perpetual reminder, as if by God: you have very little time left, so make the best use of it. Standing on the roadside and waiting for a Bhutto procession to pass: was this the best way of serving the Bhutto cause in old age? Wouldn't I be serving the Bhutto cause more effectively if I passed those hours in my newspaper office, poring over books and newspapers, surfing the internet, collecting facts and figures, working on my book, and writing an editorial or an article that could be of better use to the only cause dear to me: Pakistan?

I watched Benazir's return on TV in my office at Haroon House, when the Emirates plane carrying her landed at the Karachi airport at about 1 pm. Later, at night at home, I watched the PPP revelry up to 11pm. I seldom go to bed before midnight, but I do not know why on the night between Thursday and Friday (October 18-19) I chose to sleep off at 11.30pm. Razia was surprised. Here was a Bhutto extravaganza and I was going to bed! When I woke up at 1.30am, Nasir told me about the twin blasts and the death of 132 people. Selfish as it may sound to the reader, my first thought was whether the editorial which I would be asked to write the next day would contain words that would convey in 550 words the nation's true feeling on carnival turned into carnage. I was appalled that the PPP advisers and the brains behind the procession that moved at a snail's pace should have discarded the basic minimum security precautions needed for Benazir's protection, especially when intelligence had forewarned of an attempt on her life.

There was division in the writing staff the next morning. The younger ones, among them Mona Khan and Ayesha Azfar, opposed crticising the PPP on this score. Their position was that the nation had to stand up to the terrorists, that no one should display cowardice, and that Benazir was right in standing on the top of the truck while the crowd below pushed and jostled. My argument was that there were better ways of standing up to the terrorists, and that a demonstration of raw courage that could turn out to be costly in terms of death and destruction was not suited to the occasion. Musharraf was fighting terrorism in his own way. He could be criticised for any number of reasons, but he took necessary precautions when he moved. Even in the heat of battle, he is a bad soldier who throws his life away. The PPP advisers had let Benazir discard the bullet-proof glass screen, and her procession took almost 12 hours to reach Karsaz, the place where the suicide bomber struck. Abbas, the editor, was then in Islamabad, and I took brief from him on the telephone. He seemed to side with the younger lot and said the Dawn editorial should make it clear that the nation should stand up to the terrorists, that the election campaign should proceed normally when electioneering began, and that under no circumstances should the government attempt to curtail political activity because of the terror threat. I had lost, and the resulting editorial was mediocre stuff, but it retained my criticism of the crawl. Entitled Standing up to terror, the editorial in the issue of October 20, 2007, said in part: "...Benazir Bhutto and her party may have their quota of denigrators, but no one can deny that the throngs that greeted her and the festive atmosphere that prevailed in the nation's biggest city on that fateful night also served to highlight a value system in which bigotry, intolerance and oppression under cover of religion have no place. We salute those who lost their lives, we share the grief of the women rendered widows, we lament the loss of breadwinners for scores of families, and we agonise over the fact that many of the injured will pass their lives as physically disabled. But their sacrifices have not gone in vain, for they have conveyed a definite message loud and clear to the terrorists: the people of Pakistan will not bow down to terror. No matter what the cost in terms of casualties and human suffering, we have as a nation demonstrated to the people of the world watching the drama on Karachi's streets that their resolve to stand up to terror remains unimpaired. The terrorists may kill and maim and destroy, but the Pakistani people have made their choice clear: they stand their ground and reject fanaticism that thrives on human blood. By standing on the top of the truck all along and showing her face to those present along the route and to the millions glued to TV sets worldwide, Ms Bhutto, no doubt, showed courage, more so because her enemies had threatened to kill her. But it must be asked of the PPP leaders, was the ... crawl necessary?"

Even though Musharraf had won the presidential election, the court had ordered that the results of the election be not notified. Once again the opposition went to court, pleading with the court to declare his election null and void. The court proceedings dragged on and Musharraf appeared impatient and unsure — unsure whether the court's verdict would go in his favour. Even though the 11-man bench was headed by Mr Justice Javed Iqbal, Musharraf's nemesis — Iftikhar Chaudhri — had returned on July 20 as Chief Justice. Musharraf was unhappy with the Supreme Court's decision on "disappearances". The court had acted with vigour and asked that those who had "disappeared" must be traced and given freedom. The government had two versions on the disappearance: one, several of those "disappeared" were terrorists, with confirmed involvement in acts of terror. The government wanted time to prosecute them and to get as much information from them as possible. Two, many of the young men who had disappeared had left their homes without informing their parents to join the Taliban and other terrorist groups. In several of his speeches, Musharraf hinted that if the "transition to democracy" were halted by those opposed to him he could impose martial law, and that would be counterproductive for those who wanted a return to democratic rule. Inaugurating the Peshawar-Islamabad motorway Musharraf alleged that some elements were trying to derail the third phase of the on-going political process but that he was determined to go ahead.

Taking note of the president's warning, Dawn's editorial of November, entitled, President's warning, said he "issued a stern warning to terrorists, no doubt, but a perusal of the speech would make it clear that he did not have the terrorists in mind when he spoke of the threat to the democratic process. One wishes the president were a bit more specific. While there is no doubt that acts of terror and what is going on in Swat — virtual rebellion against the state — pose a threat not only to democracy but to society itself, one expects the military-led government to stand firm and stick to the election schedule notwithstanding any political developments or court verdicts.

"What causes concern are periodic statements from ruling party bigwigs hinting at measures that could delay the general election. PML leaders are on record having said that the life of the assemblies could be extended by a year or perhaps there could be emergency rule. The latter possibility was serious enough to prompt Washington into warning Islamabad against any measures that could cause a setback to the democratic process. Since the Supreme Court's July 20 judgment that held the reference against the Chief Justice illegal, the government's attitude toward the judiciary has been a mixed bag. While it accepted the decision in the CJ's case with good grace, its implementation of the judgment on the Sharifs' right to return is at the moment being examined by the Supreme Court. As for the judgment due shortly on the constitutionality of the presidential election held on Oct 6, the government has no choice but to accept it.

"It will cause chaos and lead to consequences that cannot be predicted at this stage if a negative decision by the Supreme Court evokes from the military a response other than that of unconditional compliance. President Musharraf's pledge to the Supreme Court to shed uniform ('if elected') was conditional. What happens if the court rules against him? Will he continue as army chief and president and then prolong what has been an intolerable status quo for the nation? The president is right that some elements are trying to derail the democratic process, but he must make sure that the military he represents is itself not going to do anything that will block the movement toward what he calls the third phase of the political process."

Rumours were rife that a state of emergency was a distinct possibility and the corps commanders had given their approval to the Chief to go ahead. On November 3 Musharraf struck, imposed a state of emergency, held the Constitution in abeyance and promulgated by decree a provisional constitution. All the good work done over the eight years was lost. "SO we are back to square one. Back to Oct 12, 1999" as Dawn's editorial of November 4 said. My original headline to the editorial was "Musharraf's second coup". Majeed approved it and Abbas liked it, but perhaps Abbas liked it too much, for he chose this to be the headline for the lead story. So the headline for my editorial was changed to Another move toward absolutism. "All the gains over the years have gone down the drain", it said. "All this talk about the forward thrust towards democracy, about the impending 'third phase' of the political process and the lip service to the sanctity of judiciary turned out to be one great deception. The people have been cheated. In a nutshell, one-man rule has been reinforced, and there is no light at the end of the tunnel — a tunnel that is dark and winding with an end that is perhaps blocked. The reports about emergency rule were denied umpteen... times by President Pervez Musharraf and Prime Minister Shaukat Aziz. The denials were bogus. From now on it would simply be a waste of newspaper space and channel time if ever a denial by this government is printed or aired.

"In a sense this is Gen Pervez Musharraf's second coup. Just as Ziaul Haq assumed all powers for himself twice — first in 1977 in what was a classical coup d'etat and in 1988 by using powers under article 58-2b of the Constitution —Musharraf has followed suit with some difference. In his second coup, Zia sent Junejo packing; in this second Musharraf coup, the Constitution has been held in abeyance and Prime Minister Shaukat Aziz and his ministers will continue to function. But his rule is now absolute, and civil society and democracy have received a blow. The general had not addressed the nation till the writing of these lines. All private channels had gone off air, and only the state-controlled PTV released the proclamation of emergency order which spoke of the 'visible ascendancy in the activities of extremists' as the reason for imposing the emergency. Frankly, not even the most naïve amongst us would buy this line. In what way does the proclamation of emergency help in prosecuting the war on terror?

"Already, the president enjoys all the powers that a ruler could possibly hope to amass. He is Chief of the Army Staff, he is president and he is supreme commander of the armed forces. What more power does he want? After all, for crushing the militants he will use those very military and paramilitary forces which are already doing the job — the Frontier Constabulary, the Frontier Corps, the army, the Rangers, and the plethora of intelligence agencies about whose incompetence now no one has any doubts. We state emphatically what has forced Gen Musharraf to declare emergency are the doubts about the outcome of the Supreme Court's judgment on his right to contest the presidential election. No one is going to accept what he is going to tell us, neither the people of Pakistan nor the aid-givers. Despite public declarations to the contrary, the voices demanding him 'to do more' may be the only ones not unhappy with these developments as they would expect him to deliver more effectively. But we ask: can a general who does not enjoy the people's mandate really carry the nation along and fight the terrorists alone?"

The order justifying the promulgation of emergency gave several reasons for the president's action: one, "visible ascendancy in the activities of extremists and incidents of terrorist attacks"; two some of the judges were working "at cross purposes" with the executive and the legislature in the fight against terrorism, "thereby weakening the government and the nation's resolve and diluting the efficacy of its actions to control this menace". Three, this had created a situation where it was no more possible to govern the country according to the basic law, and "the Constitution provides no solution for this situation". It said "... (T)here has been increasing interference by some members of the judiciary in government policy, adversely affecting economic growth, in particular," adding that there was "constant interference in executive functions." The order blamed the judiciary for having "weakened the writ of the government." The police force had been "completely demoralized" and the intelligence agencies had been "thwarted in their activities and prevented from pursuing terrorists." While "some hard core militants, extremists, terrorists and suicide bombers, who were arrested and being investigated were ordered to be released," it said "the persons so released have subsequently been involved in heinous terrorist activities, resulting in loss of human life and property. Militants across the country have, thus, been encouraged while law enforcement agencies (were) subdued."

The text of the proclamation said: "WHEREAS there is visible ascendancy in the activities of extremists and incidents of terrorist attacks, including suicide bombings, IED explosions, rocket firing and bomb explosions and the banding together of some militant groups have taken such activities to an unprecedented level of violent intensity posing a grave threat to the life and property of the citizens of Pakistan;

"WHEREAS there has also been a spate of attacks on state infrastructure and on law-enforcement agencies;

"WHEREAS some members of the judiciary are working at cross purposes with the executive and legislature in the fight against terrorism and extremism, thereby weakening the government and the nation's resolve and diluting the efficacy of its actions to control this menace;

"WHEREAS there has been increasing interference by some members of the judiciary in government policy, adversely affecting economic growth, in particular;

"WHEREAS constant interference in executive functions, including but not limited to the control of terrorist activity, economic policy, price controls, downsizing of corporations and urban planning, has weakened the writ of the government, the police force has been completely demoralized and is fast losing its efficacy to fight terrorism and intelligence agencies have been thwarted in their activities and prevented from pursuing terrorists;

"WHEREAS some hard-core militants, extremists, terrorists and suicide bombers, who were arrested and being investigated, were ordered to be released. The persons so released have subsequently been involved in heinous terrorist activities, resulting in loss of human life and property. Militants across the country have, thus, been encouraged while law-enforcement agencies subdued;

"WHEREAS some judges by overstepping the limits of judicial authority have taken over the executive and legislative functions;

"WHEREAS the government is committed to the independence of the judiciary and the rule of law and holds the superior judiciary in high esteem, it is nonetheless of paramount importance that the honourable judges confine the scope of their activity to the judicial function and not assume charge of administration;

"WHEREAS an important constitutional institution, the Supreme Judicial Council, has been made entirely irrelevant and non est by a recent order and judges have, thus, made themselves immune from inquiry into their conduct and put themselves beyond accountability;

"WHEREAS the humiliating treatment meted to government officials by some members of the judiciary on a routine basis during court proceedings has demoralised the civil bureaucracy, and senior government functionaries, to avoid being harassed, prefer inaction;

"WHEREAS the law and order situation in the country as well as the economy have been adversely affected and trichotomy of powers eroded;

"WHEREAS a situation has thus arisen where the government of the country cannot be carried on in accordance with the Constitution and as the Constitution provides no solution for this situation, there is no way out except through emergent and extraordinary measures;

"AND WHEREAS the situation has been reviewed in meetings with the prime minister, governors of all four provinces, and with Chairman of Joint Chiefs of Staff Committee, Chiefs of the Armed Forces, Vice-Chief of Army Staff and Corps Commanders of the Pakistan Army; NOW, THEREFORE, in pursuance of the deliberations and decisions of the said meetings, I, General Pervez Musharraf, Chief of the Army Staff, proclaim Emergency throughout Pakistan.

"2. I, hereby, order and proclaim that the Constitution of the Islamic Republic of Pakistan shall remain in abeyance. This Proclamation shall come into force at once."

While placing the Constitution in abeyance and promulgating the PCO, the order proclaiming the emergency said the country would be governed "as nearly as may be" possible in accordance with the Constitution.

Immediately after the state of emergency was declared, Musharraf dismissed Iftikhar and appointed Abdul Hamid Dogar as the new Supreme Court Chief Justice. Iftikhar, who had been made non-functional on March 9 and was reinstated by a Supreme Court order on July 20, was now out of the apex court for the second time. He would have to wait 16 more months before he would return to the Supreme Court in triumph. A majority of the judges of the Supreme Court and the four High Courts either did not take the oath under the provisional constitution or were not invited to do so. Of the SC's 19 judges only three – Justice Muhammad Nawaz Abbasi, Justice Faqir Muhammad Khokhar and Justice M Javed Buttar – took the oath. While in Sindh, 23 of the 27 High Court judges, including Chief Justice Sabihuddin Ahmad, refused to swear by the provisional constitution, the biggest was surprise was in Balochistan where all the five High Court judges agreed to fall in line. Of Punjab High Court's 31 judges, only 13 took the oath, while in Peshawar only five of the 13 High Court judges agreed to stay on.

However, there was one extraordinary development. Before they went home, seven of the Supreme Court judges declared the PCO illegal. Anticipating some trouble, the judges had not gone home, and finally when Emergency was declared, they overturned it, restrained all army and civilian officers from obeying orders flowing from the

PCO, asked the President and the Prime Minister to refrain from taking actions which went against the independence of judiciary and told all judges not to take a fresh oath under the PCO. Those who overturned the Emergency proclamation were, besides Iftikhar, Rana Bhagwandas, Javed Iqbal, Mian Shakirullah Jan, Nasirul Mulk, Raja Fayyaz and Ghulam Rabbani. The brief two-page order, whose copies were made available to the media, said: "We feel that the government has no ground or reason to take extra-constitutional steps, particularly for the reasons being published in newspapers that a high-profile case is pending and is not likely to be decided in favour of the government, although the matter is still pending."

One immediate effect of the imposition of emergency was the loss of fundamental rights for the citizens, because the Constitution's article's 9, 10, 15, 16, 17, 19, and 25 guaranteeing these rights were suspended. Simultaneously, the General issued two ordinances that drastically curtailed the freedom of the press and threatened action against the media if it printed or broadcast matter which "defames or brings into ridicule the head of state, or members of the armed forces, or executive, legislative or judicial organ of the state". The publication of a newspaper violating these guidelines could be suspended for a period of up to 30 days and in the case of TV channels a three-year jail term or Rs 10 million in fine or both. The Press, Newspapers, News Agencies and Books Registration Ordinance, 2002, was amended, with a new section (5-A) prohibiting the publication of any material that consisted of photographs of suicide bombers, terrorists (except required by the law-enforcement agencies for the purpose of investigation), bodies of victims of terrorist activities, statements and pronouncements of militants and extremist elements and any other thing, which may, in any way, promote aid or abet terrorist activities or terrorism, or their graphic and printed representation based on sectarianism and ethnicity or racialism. Besides the usual warning for publishing anything that may hurt "the ideology of Pakistan or the sovereignty, integrity or security of Pakistan", the amendment restrained the press from printing or any material likely to incite violence or hatred or create inter-faith disorder or be prejudicial to the maintenance of law and order.

The amendments made to Section 20 of the Pakistan Electronic Media Regulatory Authority, 2002, restrained TV channels from broadcasting video footage of suicide bombers, terrorists, bodies of victims of terrorism, statements and pronouncements of militants and extremist elements "and any other act which may, in any way, promote, aid or abet terrorist activities or terrorism". The channels were also warned not to host or propagate any opinion in any manner prejudicial to the ideology of Pakistan or sovereignty, integrity or security of Pakistan or to telecast programmes that incite violence or hatred or any action prejudicial to maintenance of law and order. Also banned were TV discussions which were sub judice or "anything which is known to be false or baseless or is mala fide or for which there exist sufficient reasons to believe that the same may be false, baseless or mala fide".

The proclamation of the Emergency was followed by a crackdown on political activists and leaders of the legal community. Besides Iftikhar and several judges who were put under house arrest, those rounded up included Aitazaz Ahsan, Ali Ahmed Kurd and Munir Malik, human rights activist and lawyer Asma Jehangir, Imran Khan, Sindhi 'nationalist' leaders Dr Qadir Magsi and Rasool Bux Palijo, and Baloch 'nationalist' leader Mahmood Khan Achakzai, besides members of the Balochistan Nationalist Party.

On November 4, Shaukat Aziz dropped the hint that the general election could be postponed. Dawn took up the issue and criticised the prime minister and Musharraf himself harshly. Entitled "No delay in polls", the editorial of November 6 said: "... [T}he continuation of a state of ambiguity since March 9 has served to put the nation in limbo. Now delaying the polls will only intensify the political confusion. The implications of the judgments delivered by the Supreme Court before Nov 3 may be behind us to the extent they concerned the dual office issue, but the gravity of the larger political and constitutional crises prevailing at the moment is independent of those judgments.

In his speech to the nation following the enforcement of the state of emergency, President Pervez Musharraf spoke of the problems that had led him to take this extreme action, and they included, besides judicial activism, the law and order situation created by terrorists and religious extremists, who were challenging the state's writ. It is not clear in what way a postponement of the general election will help the government crush the insurgency in Fata and Swat.

"The insurgents are an uncompromising lot. Besides a loose commitment to the enforcement of Sharia, they have no precise goals, and often it appears they are waging war on Pakistan's state apparatus because there is no other way in which they can make themselves felt. They are well armed, the mountainous terrain and the porous border with Afghanistan help them, their supply lines are intact, and that is the reason why they have shown extraordinary resilience and tenacity. In a nutshell, their ability to fight on is independent of the government's constitutional nostrums. On the other hand, the military-led government will now be hard put to show results and convince the world and the Pakistani people that the enforcement of emergency had paid dividends and helped it make gains against the militants. This appears doubtful.

"By coming down hard on the liberal elements in society, the military has denied itself a source of strength in the war on the religious extremists. The round-up of politicians, leading lawyers and human rights activists will cast the regime in a negative image, and the world would not be wrong in coming to the conclusion that the generals had used the war on terror as a ploy to strengthen their stranglehold over the country. Because of the gravity of the situation we demand that the emergency be lifted at the earliest, the government should give a deadline within which the purposes for which the emergency was proclaimed will be achieved, that notwithstanding the curbs on the media, political activity will not be curtailed, and the general election will be held as originally planned — in January next. Only a government deriving a popular mandate can pull Pakistan out of the bog and maintain its unity and integrity."

On November 11, Musharraf addressed his first press conference after the imposition of emergency, announced that the general election would be held in the first week of January 2008 and blamed the judges — most of whom had quite the Supreme Court after refusing to take an oath under the PCO — for paralysing government. On November 22, the reconstituted Supreme Court, now headed by Abdul Hamid Dogar, dismissed the last of the petitions challenging Musharraf's election as president and paved the way for the General to become Pakistan's President. Twenty-five days after he imposed emergency, Musharraf shed what he used to call his "skin" — his army uniform. This he did at a sombre ceremony at the Pakistan Hockey Ground close to the General Headquarters. It was the first ever public ceremony of the change of command. On November 28 more than eight years after the Generals ousted Nawaz Sharif in a coup — when Musharraf himself was midway between Colombo and Karachi — the commando General finally quit the army after serving it for 46 years, nine as its chief, and handed the baton of the Chief of the General Staff to the man he had chosen to replace him — Ashfaq Parvez Kayani. Tearful, Musharraf said: "Although I would not be in uniform tomorrow, my heart will continue to beat [with] it as it has been my family since I joined it at the age of 18. It is a sad moment for me to bid farewell to the army after serving it for 46 years. This is life, and every good thing has to come to an end." The next day, Musharraf took the oath of office as President of Pakistan, the oath being administered by Chief Justice Abdul Hamid Dogar at a President House ceremony attended among others by Generals and diplomats and a caretaker prime minister. The country was now having a caretaker prime minister whose task it was to organise the general election. However, instead of a neutral prime minister with a neutral cabinet, Musharraf had chosen a PML-N-Q leader, Muhammedmian Soomro, to preside over the general election.

As I sat down to write this very chapter after I had returned from my usual evening walk, I thought I should check my email. It contained a BBC news alert, saying there was a bomb blast at Benazir's rally. Nothing more. I dashed to the room after next and turned on TV. The headline of a Pakistani channel said Benazir had been injured. How serious nobody knew. I turned to the BBC and the headline said "Bhutto critical". I thought I should go into the Editor's room. Zubeida was already there, and soon Afshan Suboohi, Business editor, walked in. She said Benazir was dead. Nobody believed her. She said something had pierced her throat. Abbas went on to do some explaining — I think hoping against hope — that she was in a bullet-proof vehicle, and at best if a bomb had blown a hole in it a pellet or two might have been lodged there. I thought Abbas was right. Afshan said she had received a phone call from a friend — not a doctor — at the Rawalpindi General Hospital where Benazir had been rushed. He told her she was dead. Within minutes all channels had reported that Benazir, the Muslim world's first woman prime minister, was dead. I had checked the email at 5.15. By 5.25pm her death was confirmed. Officially, she was pronounced dead at 6.16pm. Her death meant that three of Zulfiqar Ali Bhutto's four children had met violent death. Including the father, this was the fourth violent death of one of the world's best known political families. Bhutto was executed on April 4, 1979; Shahnawaz, younger of the family's two sons, was found dead in his apartment in French Riviera on July 18, 1985, while the eldest son, Murtaza, was shot dead in Karachi as his car headed toward his Clifton home on September 20, 1996. This happened at a time when his sister was prime minister. Only Sanam remained. Mother Nusrat was still alive, though ill, and lived in Dubai.

We were all devastated. For a few minutes Abbas, Zubeida and I remained dumb, the enormity of the event refusing to sink into our heads. We avoided eye contacts, for we were on the verge of becoming emotional. Why? I asked. Why must it be Pakistan again? And why must it be a Bhutto? Who had killed her? What was her crime? From his mountain fastness somewhere in Waziristan, Baitullah Masood had denied on the eve of her arrival in Karachi that he had pledged to kill her. He might have denied his involvement in Benazir's murder, but he could not deny the Baitullah family's involvement in the murder of a Chinese engineer. What was that Chinese engineer's fault? — that he was working on a dam whose waters would have brought some land under cultivation, created new jobs for the area's Pakthoons and produced more food for men, women and children of Pakistan. Of Pakistan. That was the provocation. The Chinese engineer must be killed because he was working for Pakistan's good, and that was what the Baitullah brothers and their supporters would not tolerate. His idea of introducing Shariat was to do everything possible to wreck Pakistan. Old enmity. He and the people he drew inspirations from had not forgiven Jinnah for creating Pakistan. This was the same philosophy which the Lal Masjid rebels had displayed, and they had supporters in Pakistan's religious establishment. As I have written elsewhere, this was a manifestation of the philosophy which the religious parties had espoused for long in Pakistan. You are either for Islam or for Pakistan; you cannot be for both. If they had expressed their philosophy earlier — when the state was strong and anti-national elements masquerading as religious divines had not infiltrated Pakistan's state structure — they would have been lynched by the people. As the state grew weaker, parties, groups, media men, "Islamist" army officers, bureaucrats and elements espousing this philosophy entrenched themselves in Pakistan's state structure. So long as Zia was alive, he had them under his control and used them for his own witch-hunting purposes. His concept of promoting the Islamic cause was simple: if you can help me destroy the PPP you are a good Muslim, you are the right people to enforce the Islamic "system" and I need you. It was this kind of human stuff that ran the plethora of intelligence agencies under him, and they used money and the state's resources with criminal indifference to all moral values only to advance their and their master's cause. In this process some great scoundrels ran key Pakistani institutions. Many of these crooks had no qualms of conscience about using government money and facilities to advance their partisan propaganda which they deluded themselves into believing that it was Islamic. The political period between Zia's death and Nawaz Sharif's ouster by Musharraf (1988-1999) was one of political chaos. Benazir and Nawaz Sharif replaced each other twice in a manner that was strictly speaking constitutional but in reality conspiratorial. It was during this period that two religious parties, the Jamaat-i-Islami and the Jamiatul Ulema-i-Islam (Maulana Fazlur Rahman's faction) ran foreign policies independent of the foreign office. The militias which these parties ran had been kept on leash by the Zia-led ISI. However, with Zia gone, these parties and militias discovered their strength in the chaotic 1988-1999 period. In addition to fighting the war in Afghanistan, recruiting Pakistani boys for fighting on the Taliban's side in Afghanistan, and using Pakistani territory for training and indoctrination, these militias defied the weak Benazir and Sharif governments. Yet in this defiance, there was no hostility toward Pakistan. The real break between the Foreign Office and the Musharraf-led army on the one side and the religious parties on the other came on September 11, 2001, when Islamabad joined the war on terror. No government worth its salt could have taken any other decision. I have written about 9/11 and Islamabad's foreign policy options elsewhere in this book. Here, I am merely pointing out that the blind hatred which the religious parties, the Taliban and Al Qaeda developed for Musharraf ultimately took the form of hostility toward the state of Pakistan itself.

Cumulatively, most political religious parties, especially the JI, must take full responsibility for the rise of terrorism, for the JI through its propaganda machinery and the "Islamist" Generals through the use of state funding and government apparatus condoned and even encouraged acts of terrorism directed at the state and people of Pakistan. The Lal Masjid rebels' criminal deeds — abduction, including those of Chinese nationals, murder, arson and open mutiny — received no condemnations from these elements that during the Zia regime virtually ruled the country and shamelessly used Pakistan's official — and to me sacred — resources for advancing partisan propaganda.

In its issue of December 29, Dawn published on its back page the English translation of a conversation between Baitullah Mehsud and another militant, a certain Maulvi Saab. The conversation, which took place on Friday, a day after Benazir's assassination, was in Puhsto, and the English translation by AFP, the French news agency, was based on the Urdu version given by the Ministry of the Interior:

Maulvi Sahib (MS): Assalaam Aleikum.

Baitullah Mehsud (BM): Waleikum Assalaam.

MS: Chief, how are you?

BM: I am fine.

MS: Congratulations, I just got back during the night.

BM: Congratulations to you. Were they our men?

MS: Yes they were ours.

BM: Who were they?

MS: There was Saeed, there was Bilal from Badar and Ikramullah.

BM: The three of them did it?

MS: Ikramullah and Bilal did it.

BM: Then congratulations.

MS: Where are you? I want to meet you.

BM: I am at Makeen (a town South Waziristan tribal region), come over, I am at Anwar Shah's house.

MS: OK, I'll come.

BM: Don't inform their house for the time being.

MS: OK.

BM: It was a tremendous effort. They were really brave boys who killed her.

MS: Mashallah. When I come I will give you all the details.

BM: I will wait for you. Congratulations, once again congratulations.

MS: Congratulations to you.
BM: Anything I can do for you?

MS: Thank you very much.

BM: Assalaam Aleikum.

MS: Waaleikum Assalaam.

Again an editorial had to be written. My nerves were shattered. I had already written one on a Karzai-Musharraf meeting in Islamabad. The leader page had already been made up and it contained, besides the Karzai editorial, the one I had written about Lebanon's presidential crisis. Who cared now for Karzai or for a presidential crisis in another land? The leader page was ready to go to press, and it was too late to disturb it. I suggested we have an editorial on the front-page, a short one, say less than 400 words, and convey our views on one of the biggest tragedies foisted on Pakistan. Normally, it has never been Dawn's policy — barring those Altaf days — to put an editorial on page one. Abbas agreed, and I began writing one. Given the pressure, the grief, the all-enveloping gloom and with reports of violence coming from all over Pakistan, and the chances of reaching home slim, I sat down to begin it. It was difficult to gather thoughts or even to place fingers on the keyboard. After all, as Abbas said, "we are journalists up to a point". We were not machines. I wrote whatever I could and gave it to Abbas. As it appeared on page one on the morning of December 28 it was hardly mine. Abbas improved it, and Zubeida gave her own input. Abbas never sat still in his chair and kept moving between the news room and city room, making phone calls to Islamabad, talking to the reporters who had been at Liaquat Bagh, and monitoring the reports of rioting throughout the country, the situation in Karachi especially, the mobs burning any target that was good enough. Every now and then he took a look at the editorial and kept improving it. I think it was ready near midnight. The beginning wasn't very impressive, but given the enormity of the crime, its implications for Pakistan, and the personality of the leader Pakistan had been deprived of, the best of writers would have not come up to everyone's expectations. On the whole it came on very well, and I think I should share its extracts with the reader. Entitled "A dream snuffed out", it said: "...Among sinking hearts, an emptiness, and doom and gloom many questions will need to be answered. Did she die because she was a woman politician swimming against the tide of obscurantism? Did she die because she was in the process of staging a comeback after being dismissed twice on charges of corruption and misconduct? Did she die because she represented the aspirations of millions of her supporters — supporters so committed that they refused to blame the party leadership for many unfulfilled dreams? The reception accorded to her as she returned home, ending years in exile on October 18, was a demonstration of such selfless dedication by several hundred thousand supporters. More than 150 people, mostly PPP activists, died in the bombing aimed at her that night in Karachi. Her supporters knew very well she was the target and yet thronged each venue she appeared at. Such was their bond... She died literally yards from where Liaquat Ali Khan was felled by an assassin's bullet and probably a mile from where her father, Zulfikar Ali Bhutto, had his life snuffed out by the hangman's noose. We know nothing about Liaquat Ali Khan's murder and very little about Z.A. Bhutto's killing beyond what his supporters say was a judicial murder.

"No amount of condemnation will compensate for the sense of loss that fills millions of hearts across the land today. We can't even begin to imagine the grief of her family who have been robbed of the jewel in their crown... she kept her father's political legacy alive in a male-dominated society. He had championed the popular cause and had given a sense of dignity to the common man in Pakistan. Benazir Bhutto had the mettle to do the same. The repercussions of her murder will continue to unfold for months, even years. What is clear is that

Pakistan's political landscape will never be the same, having lost one of its finest daughters."

Reports coming from all over Pakistan were disturbing, and I thought I should go out to see what it was like. I went to the nearest Irani restaurant, Khairabad, where I have been eating for more than three decades, and it was closed. Traffic jams had cleared, but the area presented the sight of a town under curfew. Reports, often exaggerated, made it clear I would not be able to drive home. Gulbadin, my faithful driver, told me driving was hazardous. All public and private transport had gone off roads. Hundreds of thousands of people and their vehicles were caught in traffic jams throughout Karachi. Many saw their cars turned into ashes. My own niece, Dr Uzma, Qaiser's daughter, was caught in a traffic jam in Malir as a mob went about burning just about everything. She and her husband abandoned the car, picked up their children, one of them an infant, and sought refuge in a nearby home. Razia was getting worried about how I would return. Sikki had reached home, but Faisal was in his office and was in contact with me. Everybody, however, agreed it was too dangerous to step out, and one must stay where one was, even if this meant passing the night at one's office. Railway stations were being burnt, tracks had been pulled out, signalling systems destroyed, even ambulances and fire engines attacked and in some cases set on fire. Worldwide, stock markets fell, oil prices went up, European securities sank, and investors were nervous. Such was the impact of BB's assassination the world over.

At this hour, with my nerves shattered, Ayesha came to my room and asked me whether I would do a piece on Benazir for the annual supplement. "In this mayhem, in this chaos, in the midst of this tragedy?" I asked. Her deadline was mid-day the next day, and it was already 10.30pm. She was most persistent, and it seemed there was no getting away with it. Normally, each year I do a piece on the Middle East for Dawn's annual supplement, which we call Year-Ender. For that reason, I take notes on the Middle East throughout the year, and sometimes wrote whole paragraphs which I knew would not be outdated by the time the year ended. Thus writing the Middle East piece was quite easy. But to produce an article for the Year-Ender in a matter of hours and on a tragedy that had stunned the world and personally devastated me was a daunting task. It required ideas and language that did justice to the subject. A journalist must, of course, be ready to get going any time, anywhere at the shortest possible time while guns boom. But here I am not talking about news reporting but about a comment.

The problem basically was not the newsman but the Pakistani in me. I remember how, as a school boy, I reacted to the news of Liaquat Ali Khan's assassination at the same park where Benazir fell 56 years later. The date was October 16, 1951, and Razi broke the news to me some time late in the evening that the prime minister was dead. I was tense, and I remember asking Razi and Abbo, "Liaquat has been murdered. But there is no danger to Pakistan itself. Is there?" This was the natural reaction of a boy who had been forced to leave his country, Hyderabad, one fine morning after he was roused from his bed and told to pack up because the enemy army was approaching. I have never forgotten this trauma, and my assessment of parties, leaders, personalities and governments — their foreign and security policies, especially — has invariably had this perspective. I also judged my editors through this prism, and I regret to say many of them disappointed me. To my query that dark evening — dark literally and figuratively — because electricity had till then not reached PIB Colony where we lived — Abboo and Razi assured me that, yes, the prime minister had been murdered, but there was no danger to Pakistan itself. I slept soundly that night. Throughout my life, I now realise, two parallel streaks have run in me: Abboo's proclivity for poetic pessimism and Ammi's pragmatism. I have struggled with both, and ultimately on each occasion Ammi's pragmatism prevailed. Once again, on December 27, 2007, as news of disturbances, rioting and arson came from all over Pakistan, I had the same sense of foreboding I had as a school boy that dark, dark night in 1951. Emotionally devastated and physically exhausted, I, nevertheless, was able to assess the situation by asking myself the same question which I had asked Abbo and Razi 56 years ago: "There is no danger to Pakistan, is there?" There was none. There would be repercussions of the murder, and at best the elections might be postponed (they were), and there may be continued instability for Pakistan, but that was hardly new. The country had been unstable since March 9, and I did not see any possibility of things getting any worse once the rioting was over and calm returned. How strange that in such moments I must make Berlin April 1945 and the German people as my reference point. Different people, different culture and a different history, no doubt, but a wonderful people, whose main characteristic like the Turks is resilience. Being nearer in time they can be a source of inspiration to any nation. My decades of reading about Germans and Germany had steeled me for that occasion. What was there to be so pessimistic about? Was there a Der Fuhrer about to commit suicide? Was there a break-out from Haroon House, with tearful secretaries saying goodbyes, cyanide capsules in hands, artillery shells falling on the Dawn office, and enemy tanks in the streets of Karachi? I looked out the window. Traffic had disappeared, and even though the recently built barracks within the compound of Jinnah Court had partly blocked my view of Dr Ziauddin Ahmad Road the scene was one of serenity. No clouds of smoke, no fire raging, no sounds of explosions, only a stray vehicle speeding through the deserted road every now and then. Things weren't so bad after all, I said to myself, and began banging on the keyboard. Aisha had won. Grief was there. But life must go on. Journalism must go on. By midnight I had half finished the article, when the van was ready to take me home.

The drive, which daily took me anything between 60 and 70 minutes on the way back home, was this time over in 25 minutes. The Pakhtoon driver, Mohabbat Khan, drove the van at a minimum of 90mph through the kind of Karachi I had never seen before. Like millions of other Karachiites, I had been witness to countless disturbances, ethnic riots, sectarian trouble and bomb blasts, besides those awful days in the early '90s when Karachi was almost Beirut. But even under a curfew, there was some traffic on the main roads and some life in back streets.

One could see police and army trucks, media vehicles and company vans having curfew passes taking essential staff for radio, TV, water, gas, electricity, railways and airports. But that night on December 27, 2007, Karachi was a ghost town, for I had never seen such a sight before, with not a soul in sight.

As we learnt later, the police and Rangers had been ordered off streets, because the authorities did not wish the angry protesters and looters to clash with the police and Rangers and turn the occasion into an anti-government demonstration. All that I saw on the streets were the hulks of burnt-out cars, buses, trucks and vehicles of all sorts. At the NIPA Chowrangi we counted 71 vehicles put to the torch, with the air thick with the smell of burning tyres. What was the fun in attacking and burning un-related targets — people and shops and factories that had nothing to do with the crime at Rawalpindi and who might in fact be mourners? A plastic factory fell victim to crowd frenzy, killing six people. I reached home at 0030. The next day, grief-laden fear and tension created a feeling that seemed to stifle me. The office van came to me pick me up at about 12 noon. On the way it took more staff members, and I reached Haroon House at 1.30pm when the Friday prayer in the Rangers' Mosque was coming to a close. I missed it. I had no editorial for me that day, for I had to comply with Aisha's order for the obituary on BB. I had written half of it the previous evening, worked at home in the morning while waiting for the van and finally finished it by 4pm. I was not sure whether it shaped, but Aisha was delighted, so was Abbas. The heading that I had suggested — She had come to be assassinated — was overruled in favour of what Aisha came up with — Death has left on her only the beautiful' from poet Thomas Hood. It was a 1,500-word piece, and the last few lines read: "...The gap she leaves behind is not only emotional; it is very much a political challenge for Pakistan. Will it then be Pakistan's destiny to be led by midgets and regional status politicians claiming to be national leaders? There is something in Sindh's soil — its water, its air, its history, its culture, its farms and fields, its Sufi traditions and its uniquely Sindhi character — that produces men and women of extraordinary charisma. Not for Sindh to produce mini-leaders of provincial status. Forget the giants like Jinnah, Bhutto and Benazir. Even Junejo, Ziaul Haq's protégé, showed in no unmistakable terms that the people of Sindh have some built-in flair for politics. With Jinnah, Bhutto and Benazir it was more than political brilliance; it was a charisma that few have possessed outside Sindh. The Daughter of the East [name of Benazir's book] will live on not only in history books but in the hearts and minds of millions of people the world over. A century will pass but there will be no other Benazir Bhutto." The article appeared in the annual number appearing on January 1, 2008, and I felt disappointed that it was not put on Dawn's internet edition.

In the late afternoon, I had my usual walk. I had stopped going to the park opposite, for two reasons: first, the volume of traffic had increased so much that it was difficult to cross in safety; two, they had started charging an entry fee. While the fee was only nominal, it broke my walk's momentum: I had to stop, give the money, obtain a ticket and, in case I did not give them the exact change, wait for the City Government man to return the change. This was too much of a bother. So I started taking a walk in the cricket ground of the D. J. Science College situated next to the Rangers' Headquarters. This way I did not need to cross the road or waste time on the entry fee. That day — December 28 — if I wanted I could have crossed the road blindfolded. Also, there was no one to charge the entrance fee, because no City official was there, and the park was full of boys — mostly Pakhtoons — playing cricket. It seemed they either did not know or perhaps did not care that Pakistan was burning. I was wrong. They knew every bit of what was happening to their country, but by playing cricket and not taking part in burning and destroying they were serving Pakistan. I wished everyone played cricket, — played any game — had sex, but refrained from burning and killing and destroying. I was sure that in the eyes of God the sight of a man fornicating in the quiet of his room was less offensive than that of a man who went about killing and burning and destroying. This was my philosophy of the day. If you did not kill, did not burn, did not destroy, did not paralyse a city and did not make the life of fellow citizens miserable, then you were an angel. You were serving Pakistan the way no one else was. Losses to the economy stemming from the two days of disturbances were estimated by the Karachi Chamber of Commerce and Industry at Rs 80 billion in Karachi alone (Dawn Business Section, January 6, 2007). One can only guess what the figure would be for the entire country.

After the walk I sat down on a bench and watched and brooded. It was a typical Karachi winter sky: sapphire blue without a trace of cloud and hardly any wind. The sun was going down, and its yellow rays fell on the buildings around, especially on the wall that separated the park from Governor House. It had recently be re-painted and gone from light to turmeric yellow. Sadness had settled on everything. I drew heart from the fact that it wasn't the first time that I was in that park with a sad heart. No matter what the tragedy, I was able to pull through — even triumph. All those tragedies weren't personal. I had sat in that park when Bhutto was murdered and I had wondered whether Pakistan would be able to stand it. Yes, Pakistan was not only able to survive, 19 years later, thanks to Bhutto, Pakistan became a nuclear power. Twenty-eight years later his daughter was murdered, and I wondered whether Pakistan would be able to absorb the shock. Bhutto's murder had not led to any public disturbances. Such was the tyranny imposed on Pakistan by Ziaul Haq, by the criminal and corrupt generals around him, by the "religious" parties supporting him, and by that section of the press which was bootlicking Ziaul Haq that no outpouring of public grief was possible. Musharraf was hardly a dictator. The press was free. While Zia murdered and flogged his opponents, Musharraf let his enemies bask in the false glory of standing up to him. While criticising Zia risked prison, flogging, property forfeiture, torture and even death, lampooning Musharraf in the wildest of terms meant fun, fame and a sense of importance out of proportion to the intrinsic worth of the criticism or of the critic himself. The disturbances in the wake of BB's murder were spontaneous, but so weak had Pakistan's coercive apparatus become by then that riots and arson often appeared fun. I had also been there at the park when

America attacked Afghanistan in the wake of 9/11 and some parties had begun their anti-government campaign. Would the campaign rock Pakistan? Would it bring the country to a halt? Would there be a military coup, and a pro-Taliban government take over, making America have a go at Pakistan while India gloated? Nothing of the sort happened. Now Benazir was gone, the country was burning, and few had any idea what the future held for my country. I was convinced: no matter what the tragedy, Pakistan would come through, for this nation had shown resilience few nations were capable of demonstrating. The greatest guarantee of Pakistan's survival, continued progress and the inevitable march toward greatness is one undeniable truth: the people of Pakistan want to live as a nation and are prepared to die for it, no matter what the quality of their leadership and media. Period. The issue is closed and no more open to discussion.

***

On February 18, 2008, I cast what could be my last vote. The polling station was housed in a school with a catchy English name. I had told my family to go to the polling station individually because one never knew if there would be an act of terrorism. Gulbadin came to pick me up and I drove to the polling station, located in a street off Abul Hasan Ispahani Road about five minutes' drive from my home. At the polling station there was no chaos, and no rush, though there were more women then men. I suppose the women had been herded to the polling station by MQM workers. The presiding officer gave me two ballot papers after applying the indelible ink to my right thumb. But there was no privacy, no booth, no curtains. I couldn't care less if the MQM watched. I voted for the PPP candidates for the National and Sindh Assemblies. So strong are party and political loyalties of an average Pakistani voter that I just did not know, and did not care to know, who the candidates for the National and Sindh Assemblies were. I just stamped the Arrow, the

PPP's election symbol. (Faisal Raza Abidi, the candidate for the National Assembly I voted for, lost to an MQM man). It was over in 10 minutes. Sikki went to the polling station only to destroy his ballot paper. He could be quite cynical at times. He just wanted to make sure no one misused his unused vote. So he banged the stamp on as many candidates as possible to disqualify his vote. Later in the evening, as I watched TV for the results, the Muslim League (Nawaz faction) appeared ahead of the PPP. Unhappy, I made a thoroughly unnecessary call to Abbas, for he must have been amused by my lack of nerves. I do not know what his true sentiments were and whether he was concerned over what then appeared to be the PML-N lead. To me he said, "What matters is a two-thirds majority" (the PPP and the PML-N taken together, so that they could amend the Constitution and remove the changes made by Musharraf). My concerns were misplaced, because most of the early results were coming from urban Punjab, where the Sharifs were strong. By midnight, the picture had changed and the two parties appeared running neck and neck as results of voting in remote villages became available. When I got up at 5.30 in the morning, the PPP was in the lead. It was to maintain that lead till the end. Once again Bhutto had won from his grave. "The PPP is finished!" God alone knows how many times I have heard this phrase from the PPP baiters each time the PPP government was thrown out. Each time, the "finished" party rose like a phoenix.

~~~~~~~~~

On January 1, 2009, Ayesha became the youngest person to be Dawn's op-ed editor after Zubeida called it a day. A graduate in international relations from the London School of Economics, Ayesha had joined Dawn in 1990 after a brief stint with Star. Zubeida had developed some problems with her eyesight. Once she entered my room, and even though I was present she left without noticing my presence. It was then that I realised the acuteness of her problem: she could not see on the periphery, had stopped driving long ago, crossing roads was hazardous and she missed steps when going down. I was sorry to see her keep the white cane. Along with Majeed and me she was part of AAK's kitchen cabinet, and I recall with fondness the countless lunches and dinners and parties we all had; the brainstorming sessions, which stretched for hours when the "line" on a crucial editorial had to be decided, when ideas were to be pooled and writers short-listed for special supplements on national days, like December 25, Jinnah's birthday, August 14, Pakistan's independence day, March 23, the Republic Day , and such special occasions as the 50th and 60th anniversaries of Dawn's founding, We all worked in what AAK called "a spirit of healthy competition" – working, gossiping, discussing and, yes, that which is inevitable in a such a long relationship, quarrelling, over an unprecedented three decades. AAK, it goes without saying, was the prima donna. Long after he had retired and even after his death we continued to consider ourselves part of the team. Zubeida's career in Dawn was glorious and spanned 34 years, and as I have said earlier the weekly Books and Authors I consider to be her major contribution to Dawn.

I suffered a sense of personal loss when Majeed retired after half a century of association with the Dawn group. No two staff members were so close to each other as Majeed and I were. Majeed put himself to work daily with a lion's heart, poring over editorials – three every day, six on weekends, besides articles and columns for op-ed pages – and never seemed to tire. He was truly Dawn's unknown soldier because he remained unknown to the readers, for nobody ever read the by-line of a man who for decades edited and gave shape to the chaotic ideas and language of countless contributors, some of whom eventually turned into recognised columnists. "Churchill must be turning in his grave", he often said when he wrestled with some horribly written copy. The semantics of the English language, he once remarked, were beyond the subcontinentals, and suggested that the UN pass a binding resolution making it illegal for Pakistanis and Indians to write in English. Often

Majeed took a load of copies home and edited them while sweating profusely in candle light in Karachi's sweltering and humid nights without the benefit of a fan much less air-conditioning as the city suffered one of its power outages. He stayed on in the office even when the day's work was over, and the joke made the rounds that once he returned home in the afternoon but his family refused to recognise him. It is a measure of his commitment to work that even after retirement he has continued to come to the Dawn office. Majeed has suffered many tragedies in life, including the fact that his daughter became a widow at a young age. But I never found Majeed mean and petty and revengeful against anyone, and I never detected malice in his character, nor did I ever find him shouting at someone – something, as I have said earlier, is my yardstick for judging a man. The reason for his retirement lay, again, in a failing eyesight, but regretfully Majeed seemed to have developed resistance against treatment. His colleagues believed his eyes could have been saved if he followed treatment. Instead, to our horror, each time there was an appointment with an eye specialist he would make some excuse to dodge it and turn up at the office and keep working over endless cups of tea. At least five years before retirement he had begun using the magnifying glass to read and edit, and by the time he retired he could only read headlines with the help of the magnifying glass. For a man who had been used to reading all his life this was a tragedy. In fact I could gather the depth of his agony when he told me one day that television for him had become radio. He was a ruthless slave driver as far as I was concerned, and made me write five editorials in a week sometimes for months. I would have rebelled, if someone else were to do this. He briefed and briefed and briefed, and often turned up in my room late in the afternoon as I was busy finalising the editorial. There he would brief me again, and it goes without saying he was a Dawn man to the core and seldom deviated from policy even if he personally thought differently. Ignoring the eyesight, he has otherwise maintained good health.

17

BROTHER ARABS

ONE UNFORTUNATE FEATURE OF Pakistan's external relations has been its flawed Arab policy, flowing from romantic absurdities and a failure to grasp the essentially secular nature of the Arab mind. Based on assumptions that were derived from a distorted perception of Middle Eastern history, Pakistan's Arab policy has been a colossal failure, especially during the first two decades. It was too simplistic to succeed, and it did not take into account the Arabs' historical experience and their concept of religion — which is quite secular in character and different from South Asian Islam, marked as the latter is by the imprints left on its followers by the geographical confines of the subcontinent, by their interaction with the Hindu majority over more than a millennium, and by a shallow interpretation of the texts by the clergy. Most South Asians, even educated ones, translate this interpretation into daily life in a way that is often antithetical to Islam and makes Arabs wonder and hide their smile. To the people of the new Muslim state that came into being in August 1947, Pakistan's birth was an event of cosmic proportions, an occasion for the world Muslims to rejoice. The world's largest Muslim country — Pakistanis kept repeating — had come into being, and this was bound to herald a new era for the world in general and the Muslim world in particular. If any Muslim did not share Pakistanis' euphoria over the birth of their country and over the partition of India he was at best a bad Muslim, at worst, pro-India, the ultimate epithet which a Pakistani can hurl at an enemy. Great disappointment was in store for them, for the Arabs were indifferent to Pakistan's birth, and in some cases adopted an attitude that bordered on concealed hostility.

There were some exceptions, of course. During the pre-oil period, the rulers of Hejaz received plentiful doses of monetary aid from South Asian Muslims, especially from the Hyderabad State, and the founder of modern Saudi Arabia, Ibn Saud, was fully aware of the sentiments that the subcontinent's Muslims had for the Guardian of the Two Holy Places, no matter whether he was Hashemite or Saudi. Similarly, some Palestinian leaders like Amin el-Husseini, who had been in contact with the subcontinent's Muslims because of the conflict with the European settlers and needed political and monetary support, were beholden to them for their passion for Palestine's cause. As a student of Class VIII at Bahadur Yar Jang High School, Karachi, I remember seeing Amin el-Husseini make a surprise visit to our class. He had blue eyes on an apple-red face and worn a black robe. The year was 1949, and the Palestinian leader must obviously have visited Pakistan to meet the leaders of the young nation. However, barring these exceptions, the vast majority of Arab leaders and peoples from the Gulf to the Atlantic showed no special enthusiasm for Pakistan. To them the birth of Pakistan was an event to the extent that it announced the end of British rule, and "India" became free.

What our foreign policymakers failed to grasp during Pakistan's formative phases was how the Arabs tended to view the West and how their view of non-Arab Muslims was characterised by their historical experience, which in some cases was hurtful. Throughout their history, the Arabs have interacted with basically two non-Arab Muslim peoples — the Iranians and the various Turkic peoples. With both, their experience has been adversarial and unhappy. The Arab caliphate conquered Iran in the seventh century and gave it a new religion, a new script, new legends and new heroes — all Arab. More than a millennium would pass before there would be a stirring of Iranian nationalism, and even then those — the Safavids — who would finally give the Iranian people a state of their own and evoke pride in the pre-Islamic Persian glory would themselves be Turkic. With the Turks of all brands — Seljuk, Mamluk, Taimurid and Ottoman — the Arab experience has been horrible. In 861, the Abbasid army's Turkish soldiers murdered Mutawakkil, the last great Abbasid caliph, and captured power. From then on the greater part of the Arab world would be under the rule of various Turkish dynasties until the end of World War I. This is, of course, a simplification of Middle Eastern history, for the Abbasid caliphate lasted till 1258 when the Mongols sacked Baghdad, but during these four centuries the caliphs were merely puppets in the hands of Central Asian soldiers of fortune who had made the Middle East their playground. There were times when some Abbasid caliphs — actually kings — asserted themselves, but by and large the Middle East remained under the sway of various Turkish dynasties till the Ottoman Empire collapsed in 1918.

Corruption, misrule and excesses characterise rule by all dynasties during days of decline. So was the case with the Ottomans. The peace and prosperity which the Arabs initially enjoyed under the Ottomans gradually vanished as the Ottoman Empire began its long and painful decline from the 17th century onward. Two events — the stunning success of the Wahhabi uprising in the Arabian peninsula and Napoleon's military victory in Egypt — exposed Turkey's military weakness and made the Arabs think. While the question for the maritime powers, Britain and France especially, was how to check the Russian advance toward Constantinople and how to dispose of the empire's Arab provinces, for the Arabs themselves the main question was their own future in a post-Ottoman Middle East. The various constitutional schemes worked out to tame the Sultan-Caliph during the nineteenth century and turn the empire into an Arab-Turkish enterprise never had a chance of success. Sultan Abdul Hamid II (1876-1909) added to the frustration of all his subjects, including the Turks themselves, when he suspended the constitution, abolished the assembly and set up a police state. The Young Turks got rid of Abdul Hamid but did little to address Arab grievances. No wonder, the initial Arab reaction to European overtures during World War I was enthusiastic. The decision by Hussein bin Ali, the Sharif of Mecca, to ally himself with the British during World War I showed the extent of anti-Turkish feelings among the Arabs and highlighted their naivety when he made himself believe that the British would make him the head of a mighty Arab empire east of the Suez if the Hashemites allied themselves with the Allies and revolted against the Ottomans. The Sykes-Picot pact and the Balfour declaration ended the Arabs' brief honeymoon with the European victors of the war.

Ignoring the Crusades and all that they stood for, there is no doubt that the French and British behaviour in the aftermath of World War I, the occupation of Syria, Iraq and Palestine as a 'mandate' from the League of Nations, and the occupation of the entire North African Arab coastal belt from Egypt to Morocco by Britain, France and Italy, revived among the Arabs with greater intensity the memories of a millennium of conflict with peoples across the Mediterranean. This conflict began with a clash with a Constantinople-based "European" power — the Byzantine Empire — in the 7th century during the reign of Second Caliph Umar, when the Arabs wrested Syria, Palestine and Egypt from the empire. Subsequently, the Umayyads took Arab power into the heart of Europe in France via the Iberian Peninsula. The "secession" of Spain from the Arab empire after the Abbasid seized power in the middle of the eighth century; the rise of the Fatimids as a naval power in the Mediterranean; the Christian Reconquista and finally the Crusades: all along these centuries the Arab was involved in conflict with Christian Europe — the godfather of what today we call the West, a term that developed during Europe's colonial expansion. In sharp contrast, the experience of the Muslims of South Asia has been limited and Hindu-specific. Their heroes are those Central Asian and Turco-Afghan warriors who defeated Hindu kings in battles and created one Muslim empire after another over a period that lasted from the eighth century to 18th century. No wonder, Pakistanis should choose to name their missiles after these Central Asian and Afghan heroes — Ghaznavi (after the man who conquered that part of South Asia which is more or less today's Pakistan (997-1030), Ghauri, the first Muslim sultan to take Delhi in 1192; and Abdali, whose victory at the battle of Panipat in 1757 broke Marahtta power. There is one bizarre phenomenon, though. The first Muslim general on a military expedition to India was Arab — Muhammad bin Qasim, whose victory secured Sindh and southern Punjab for the Umayyads. But, while the Pakistanis consider him their hero, Mohammd bin Qasim hardly finds a mention among Arab legends. In fact, given the dimensions of the victories by other Arab conquerors against the Sassanid and Byzantine empires, and the push further into North Africa, Europe and Central Asia by Okba bin Nafay, Tariq bin Ziyad, Musa bin Nusair and Qutaybah bin Muslim and their impact on world history, bin Qasim gets a footnote in Arab history.

South Asian Muslims view world history through their own limited experience and expect such a cosmopolitan people as the Arabs to do the same. To the former, history revolves round an eternal conflict between Muslims and infidels, and to them there is no greater and "better" infidel than the Hindu. While they do share the Arabs' view of Christian Europe, they are shocked when they see Arabs utterly indifferent to — and even unaware of —the Hindu being an infidel. To the Arabs the Hindus are infidels like the Chinese and Japanese, and the Arabs see no reason why they should waste their time and energy trying to annihilate the Hindus. That was the reason why Pakistan's foreign policy in the first two decades ran into serious trouble with Arab governments and remained facile for a couple of decades until the Pakistan Foreign Office seemed to have come of age and developed a maturer understanding of the harsh world of geopolitics if not of the Arab mind.

The basic problem was a two-way misunderstanding: while Pakistan could not understand why the Arab governments were not categorically and zealously supporting it on the Kashmir issue and other problems with India, most Arab leaders could not fathom why Pakistan had chosen to join Western military pacts. Way back, as a college student, I heard an Arab friend tell me, "We can understand Turkey joining Nato and other Western military pacts; we can also understand why Iran chose to be part of the Baghdad (later Cento) Pact. But for the life of me I cannot understand why Pakistan has chosen to become a member of these pacts." Even though on Pakistani soil, he was looking at the issue from an Arab point of view and was guilty of the same ignorance which Pakistanis often showed. Like most Arabs my friend had little knowledge of South Asian history and could for that reason be forgiven. But Pakistanis claim they know Arab history and yet they failed to see the vast difference in the attitudes, prejudices and preferences of the two peoples.

The misfortune was that Pakistan's entry into the US-led military pacts coincided with the rise of Arab nationalism, led by Gamal Abdel Nasser. It was an angry nationalism and for obvious reason anti-Western, and since the Cold War was at its peak, the Arab nationalists had no choice but to draw closer to the Communist world, from which the nationalist Arab camp received unqualified diplomatic support, besides economic and military aid. Let us not go here deeply into the difference between European and American policies toward Arab nationalism. But, briefly, we can note that the end to the tripartite aggressions against Egypt in the aftermath of the nationalisation of the Suez Canal by Nasser in 1956 would not have been possible if America had not reacted very negatively. President Eisenhower was angry with Britain, France and Israel because he had not been informed of the plans — conspiracy, to be more specific — to attack Egypt, and Israel would not have quit the Sinai Peninsula if Eisenhower had not put his foot down. In fact, there was a surprising degree of understanding between Washington and Moscow on the tripartite aggression. In the fifties, the colonial powers were successful in getting American sympathy for their cause by equating Arab nationalists with communists. However, by the time John F. Kennedy moved into the White House, America appeared to have realised that men like Nasser, Iraq's Abdel Karim Kassim, Syria's strongman Shukri al-Kuwatli, and a Lebanese like Saeb Salam were anything but communist, and that the only force which could take on the communists and check Soviet influence in the Middle East was Arab nationalism. While these differences were there, America shared the colonial powers' categorical commitment to Israel's security, and that served to erode whatever tacit admiration the Arab nationalist camp had for Washington. To quote my Arab friend again, the British and French had used their bases in the Middle East to attack Egypt, and thus the removal of the Western bases from the Arab world and from such Western allies as Turkey and Iran, and the overthrow of the regimes tolerating these bases or providing new ones to Western powers, became two major foreign policy goals for the Arab nationalist regimes.

As a student and ultra-nationalist imbued with love for Pakistan, I hated Nasser for what I perceived to be his hostile attitude toward Pakistan, and it was much later that I realised Nasser's greatness and the contribution he had made to the awakening of the Arab world and the position which Arab nationalism came to occupy in the larger Afro-Asian struggle against European colonialism. What drew him away from Pakistan and closer to India was the former's membership of US-led military pacts. Pakistan was a member of the Baghdad Pact (later named Cento – the Central Treaty Organisation) whose other members were Iran, Iraq, Turkey and Britain, the US being a member only of Cento's military committee. Pakistan was also a member of the South-East Asian Treaty Organization (Seato), besides having a bilateral military alliance with the US. After the 1956 tripartite attack on Egypt, Pakistan also adhered to the Eisenhower Doctrine. This way Pakistan became what Henry Kissinger called America's most "allied ally". By virtue of its membership of Seato and Cento, Pakistan linked the two pacts to Nato, because Nato-member Turkey was also in Cento. This gave rise to a myth – the foremost among the myth-makers being American journalists in those mad, mad, anti-commie days – that Pakistan was the sole and key link in the global chain of Western military pacts defending the "free world" against the evil that communism was. Many Pakistanis, including me, took this nonsense seriously. The Arab nationalist camp could not understand why Pakistan had joined these "imperialist" military pacts. "Imperialism", "imperialist" and "imperialists" were then the shibboleths the Afro-Asian and Latin American leaders made full use of to attack and deride America and its allies whenever the opportunity arose. No wonder Nasser drew closer to India because Nehru, along with Nasser, Soekarno, Nkrumah and Tito, was one of the leaders of the non-aligned movement, which despite its innocuous-sounding name was pro-Soviet in orientation

The big break with Nasser came with the Suez affair. Nasser nationalised the Suez Canal in July 1956 to raise money for the Aswan Dam, which the US, unhappy with Nasser's modest arms deal with Czechoslovakia in October the previous year, had declined to fund. For Britain and France – and Israel – larger issues were involved. Britain was still a power in the Middle East. Iraq and Jordan were virtually under its occupation, its troops guarded the Suez Canal, and Britain had had a stake in its military presence in the oil-bearing Gulf region. Besides guarding its oil interests, Britain also wanted to ensure against the spread of Arab nationalist ideas, with a tinge of socialist rhetoric, which Nasser was keen to spread throughout the Arab world. What helped Nasser was the anti-Western wave sweeping the Arab world since the establishment of Israel and the forced expulsion of the Palestinians from their soil. For France, the main problem was Algeria, where insurgency was gaining in strength, encouraged by Cairo's Voice of the Arab radio and the arms which the Algerian fighters received from Egypt. France thus wanted to get rid of Nasser, whom the British and French press began referring to as a mini-Hitler. Worse still, Ben-Gurion had developed nuclear ambitions for Israel and offered intelligence on Algerian guerillas in return for French military aid and nuclear technology. (The full account of Israeli-French nuclear collaboration is given in Michael Karpin's book Bomb in the Basement).

It was around this time that I began hearing a bit of intellectual rubbish from Pakistani intellectuals, especially those with a religious bent of mind — Arab nationalism was a Christian Arab idea! Not only that: they also discovered Michel Aflaq as the villain of the piece who purportedly propounded and nurtured such a pernicious idea as Arab nationalism. Educated in France, Aflaq was no doubt an intellectual and a prolific writer, but he never had on the Arab world the impact the Pakistani critics of Arab nationalism would have us believe. With Salah Bitar he co-founded the Baath Party in 1945, but his aim was to give a socialist colour to Arab nationalism. Neither Syria, where he was born, nor Iraq, where he had an admirer in Saddam Hussein and where he died and had a Muslim burial, gave him much importance, except to the extent that the Baath Party's Syrian and Iraqi chapters exploited his name. On the whole Aflaq — who outlived Nasser — operated on the periphery of politics in Iraq and Syria at a time when a giant like Nasser was the icon of millions of Arabs and was recognised as such by the world, especially his enemies. Before the attack on Egypt, Anthony Eden reacted with anger that it was nonsense to say that all he wanted was a solution to the problem created by Nasser's nationalisation of the canal. He said, "But what's all this nonsense about isolating Nasser, of 'neutralising' him as you call it? I want him destroyed, can't you understand?" (Peter Mansfield, The Arabs, p 294). The fact was that Arab nationalism was neither a Christian fabrication nor a socialist conspiracy; and Arab Christians played no role in the rise and spread of nationalism, except to the extent that Christians are part of the Arab world, with substantial populations in Lebanon, Syria, Iraq and Egypt. To that extent they played their full part in the nationalist fervour that began earnestly in mid-19th century. However, those who laid the foundations of Arab nationalism — in some cases perhaps without realising what they were doing —were not only not Christian, they were arch conservative Muslim, and at least one of them was not even an Arab: he was a Turco-Albanian, Mehmet Ali Pasha, Egypt's Ottoman governor.

In 1798, Napoleon landed in Egypt with a force of 15,000, occupied Alexandria, and — even though Nelson had destroyed the French fleet at Abu Qir — went on to take Cairo after what is known as the Battle of the Pyramids. He had mighty plans — to take Jerusalem, occupy Syria, fight his way through Anatolia, and then cross the Bosporus to make the Sultan-Caliph sign what Napoleon said would be the ultimate in his conquests — the Peace of Constantinople. A renegade Mamluk general, Ahmad Jazzar, stood in his way. Ottoman Syria's virtually independent and ageing governor, Jazzar made Napoleon suffer his first defeat with the help of the English navy that appeared off Acre. Napoleon, who remembered Jazzar till his death, lifted the siege and went home. This was an event that made the Arabs think. Till then the Sultan-Caliph's forces had been losing battles to his enemies in Europe; this time Turkey lost to a European general on its home ground. This sent a message not only to Europe but to the Sultan's own subjects, especially Arab.

Already, by the end of the 18th century, the combination of Saudi temporal power and the teachings of Mohammad bin Abdul Wahhab had thrown the Arabian Peninsula into chaos and unleashed a movement that the Ottomans had found difficult to control. Mohammad Ibn Saud, a sheikh with his base at Diriyah, some 40 miles from Uyaynah, where Abdul Wahhab was born, gave protection to him and consolidated the alliance by having his son marry Abdul Wahhab's daughter. This "marriage between religion and the sword", as Philip K Hitti puts it, changed the Arabian Peninsula's history and was to profoundly affect Muslims thought throughout the world. The two focussed on wiping out anything that even remotely resembled idolatry, and this led to the destruction of graves and tombs venerated by many, especially the Shias. Ibn Saud died in 1765, by which time only a small portion of the peninsula had come under Saudi rule. It was, however, the astonishing military successes of Ibn Saud's son, Abdel Aziz I, that brought the entire Arabian Peninsula, and even areas beyond it, under Saudi rule. In 1798, about the time that Napoleon was in Egypt, the Turkish Sultan took notice of the challenge to his authority in the holy land and sent a force to crush the Saudis, but, astonishing as it may sound, the Ottomans were unable to put down the rebellion. This was an entirely new development and shook the Arabs from their slumber. The Arabs now realised that it was not the French, the Russians or Hapsburg alone who could defeat the Ottomans; even they themselves had the power to humble the Turks. The Arab imagination had been fired — and there was no "Christian" Michel Aflaq on the horizon.

Continued military triumphs won admiration for Abdel Aziz from neighbouring tribes and chieftains, enabling him through a series of alliances to extend his control to Oman, Qatar and Bahrain. Now he felt he was strong enough to foray into mainstream Ottoman territory, invaded Iraq, conquered Karbala in 1801 and massacred its Shia population. A year later, in a further blow to Ottoman power and prestige, Abdul Aziz's Bedouin army took Mecca and in 1804 it captured Madina. Preoccupied with the war in Europe, the Sultan had not paid full attention to the situation on the Najd plateau, where Turkish rule was generally lax and relied mostly on the goodwill of friendly tribes, whom it sometimes paid to maintain peace. However, Hejaz was a different matter, for the loss of the two of Islam's holiest cities and the massacre of the Sultan's Shia subjects at Karbala meant that the challenge to his authority had assumed the form of a full-fledged rebellion. Ultimately it was left to Mehmet Ali Pasha and his sons — Tusun and Ibrahim — to crush the Wahhabi revolt. Ibrahim captured Diriyah, razed it to the ground and sent Saudi chief, Abdullah bin Saud, in chains to Constantinople, where he was executed.

A controversial figure, Mehmet Ali Pasha like all empire builders was brave, ruthless and duplicitous. A skilful diplomat he both obeyed and defied the two governments that mattered to him — at Constantinople and London. He re-took Egypt for the Sultan-Caliph in the wake of Napoleon's departure, and the victories he secured over the Wahhabis added to his prestige. After differences with the Sultan and the Whitehall in the wake of the Greek war of independence, the Pasha's army under his son Ibrahim inflicted a series of defeats on the Ottomans, captured Syria and entered Anatolia. He could have marched on and taken Constantinople had not the Ottomans' worst enemy, Russia, come to the Sultan's help. The Pasha then went on to take Hejaz,

Yemen and Sudan. He would have formally announced himself Sultan-Caliph, because both Mecca and Medina were in his domain, but the combined pressure by European powers, especially Britain, forced him to vacate all Ottoman territories and confine himself to Egypt, whose Vali he was eventually recognised. It was as Egypt's virtual sultan that the Pasha came into his own. What helped him was the Egyptian people's disgust with the centuries of Mamluk rule. He won the Egyptians' sympathy by his economic reforms, which included cleaning the Nile canals, adding a million acres to agriculture and introducing the cultivation of long-staple cotton. This way he was able to win over the new class of prosperous small landlords, besides securing the support of the ulema and the leaders of the trading community. Conscious that he could not trust the remnants of Ottoman officers in the army and administration, because to them he was a rebel against the Sultan, the Pasha began recruiting Egyptians in his army. This helped in no small measure in giving the Egyptians a sense of participation in governance, with the Arabs in other Ottoman territories envying Egypt. Also having an impact on the social scene was the printing industry. Even though it was Napoleon who had set up Egypt's first printing press, it was during the Pasha's regime that the printing presses got going in Egypt. He also paid attention to higher education, setting up medical and engineering colleges. He remained what he was — a blonde from Albania who had once served the Ottoman Sultan, but the vicissitudes of his career, Egypt's "opening" during his regime (1805-48), and the reforms he introduced contributed in no small measure to the rise of Egyptian, and subsequently, Arab nationalism.

More than six decades after the Pasha's death, the focus of the struggle for Arab freedom and dignity would move from Egypt to Hejaz. Sultan Abdul Hamid II had called Hussein bin Ali, the Sharif of Mecca, over to Constantinople, made him one of his advisers and given the Hashemite chief due protocol. There was one condition, though: he should stay within the confines of the Ottoman capital, because the Sultan-Caliph suspected his loyalty. The Young Turks, idealists, energetic, and, as was proved later, jingoists, made him abdicate and disregarding the sultan's warning allowed the Sharif to return to his beloved Hejaz. The correspondence between the Sharif and Sir Henry McMahon, Britain's High Commissioner in Egypt during World War I, is a matter of history. British apologists have insisted till this day that the promises made to the Hashemites in the Hussein-MacMahon correspondence excluded Palestine and that there was no betrayal of the Arab cause. Ignoring here both this controversy and the occupation of Syria, Iraq and Palestine by Britain and France as a League of Nations 'mandate', we can only note what is germane to our discussion — that the banner of revolt against the Ottomans for Arab freedom was raised not by a Christian army led by Aflaq (who was then six years old) but by one of the Arab and Muslim world's most august and revered families, the Hashemites, who had been the Guardians of the Two Holy Places since the early 13th century.

Subsequent developments preceded Pakistan's birth by three decades: the Balfour Declaration was issued in 1917 and European Jews began settling in Palestine; the Syrians' attempt to proclaim a republic was crushed by France; Prince Faisal, the Sharif's third son, was proclaimed King of Iraq; Ibn Saud descended from Najad to capture Hejaz and drive the Hashemites out; Britain de-linked the East Bank from Palestine and in its magnanimity proclaimed Abdullah, the Sharif's second son, king of Transjordan. Thanks to Britain, the Sharif not only had his dreams shattered, he had to say farewell to the Hashemites' home base. Britain's refusal to support the Sharif militarily against Ibn Saud was based on reasons that are a classical example of British sophistry. It was not a question of supporting one of Britain's war-time allies, the British said; the conflict had religious overtones. While Ibn Saud represented a new and fiercely puritan version of Islam, that of the Sharif was the traditional and liberal Islam. Taking sides in a dispute between the two would mean taking sides in a purely religious controversy among the Muslims, and that might not go well with His Majesty's Muslim subjects, including those in India. The truth was that, as far as the Allies were concerned, the Sharif had outlived his utility. To undermine him, Britain had already given international recognition to Ibn Saud by opening talks for demarcating the border between British-occupied Iraq and Ibn Saud's territories. Abandoned, the Sharif went to Cyprus and later to Amman, the capital of his son's newly created kingdom, where he died in 1931.

One can here grasp the anger which must have gripped the Arab world. The Ottoman Empire would have lost anyway, even if sections of the Arabs had not revolted against it. Let us also note, though, that not all Arabs trusted the Allies, and Arab regiments were part of the Ottoman army and took part in battles, including that in Gallipoli. But the sense of betrayal among the Arabs was the greater because not only had they not been rewarded for making common cause with the Allies against fellow Muslims, they had been double-crossed, with Palestine handed over to the Zionists, and Iraq and Syria placed under a League of the Nations 'mandate'. The anger was coupled with the shame that they had chosen to revolt against the Turks in wartime. The Arab revolt was, and is still, viewed by South Asian Muslims in an altogether different light. While the Hashemites take pride in unfurling the banner of freedom, the Muslims of South Asia merely saw it as an act of treachery, without realising that the Ottoman empire was ripe for collapse, and that all non-Turkish minorities had for long been planning for the day when the empire founded by Orhan in the 14th century would pass into history. Hassan bin Talal, onetime Jordan's crown prince, said of the revolt: "The vision of my great-grandfather, Sharif Hussein, was of a United States of Arabia, in which the historical and cultural particularities of all its regions and peoples would be recognised and respected. Arab renaissance to him meant a covenant with the poor and the marginalised in realising all their inalienable rights" (Dawn February10, 2009).

There were many reasons why the Muslims of South Asia had a special and emotional regard for the Turks. With their own Turkish (Mughal) Empire destroyed and they themselves living under the raj in a Hindu majority country, the Ottoman Empire to them appeared the last remaining symbol of Turkish-Muslim glory. It had to survive and deserved to be protected and cherished at all costs by all the world's Muslims — a view which, as we have seen above, was not shared by the Arabs and Kurds. The futile and unrealistic attempts by them to save the Caliphate foundered on the rock of Kemal Ataturk's realism but, nevertheless, showed their attachment to the Ottomans and to the concept of pan-Islamism. Turkey's estrangement with the Arabs after the end of the World War I, its European orientation, and after World War II its membership of the North Atlantic Treaty Organisation served to alienate it further from an Arab world in whose eyes the West was the principal enemy. It was in this post-World War II world that Pakistan threw in its lot with the West, the US especially, as it sought security and made the fundamental mistake, as pointed out in earlier pages, of assuming Arab friendship.

The Arabs have no concept of pan-Islamism as a political concept. They do recognise Islamic brotherhood as a religious concept, but no Arab statesman has seriously pursued 'Islamic unity' a la Jamaluddin Afghani as a viable political strategy. From a geographical point of view also, only the Arab world, spread across two continents and lying under Europe's underbelly, can serve as a fulcrum for Muslim unity. Neither Pakistan, nor, say, Indonesia close to down under can serve as an axis round which the Islamic world can revolve. The Arabs think, and I believe rightly, that they alone have in them that spark that can attract the rest of the Muslim world, even though the Arabs form only 20 per cent of the world's Muslim population. Their role in history has been more than that of empire builders. Strange as it is, only those areas, with the sole exception of the Iberian peninsula, have till this day a Muslim majority which were conquered by the Arabs, while the vast regions conquered by non-Arabs, especially the various branches of the Turkic peoples, have been 'lost'. In South Asia, Balochistan, Sindh and the NWFP still have a Muslim majority since the Arabs took these areas in the seventh century. But, with the exception of Bengal, the entire India conquered during what is called the sultanate period has till this day retained a

Hindu majority. Even Delhi, which remained the seat of Muslim power for six and a half centuries, had a Hindu majority till the British finally dislodged the Muslims from power. Even Punjab had to be partitioned in 1947, because it did not have a Muslim majority. We see the same phenomenon in Eastern Europe and the Balkans, where Ottoman rule in some cases lasted over half a millennium — as in Greece and Bulgaria. But with the exception of thin Muslim majorities in Albania and Kosovo, the entire Balkan Peninsula has been 'lost'.

What we Pakistanis fail to realise is that for the Arabs, Islam is part of the Arab being — whether it is thinker-politician Michel Aflaq, freedom fighter George Habbash or novelist Amin Malouf —, that for them Islam is something non-controversial, and that they do not believe in talking about Islam, a Pakistani speciality which amuses and sometimes annoys the Arabs. In private gatherings Pakistanis have often attempted to carry coals to Newcastle and tried to enlighten the Arabs on Islam. This was especially true of the fifties and sixties when Arab nationalism was anathema to Pakistani clerics, who lectured their Arab friends on the divinely ordained unity of the People of the Books, and how as good Muslims it was their duty to help the Christian West dam the rising wave of Godless communism (and by implication be Pakistan's allies against Hindu India). This concept of the "eternal" unity of the people of the books was repudiated by Pakistani ecclesiastics in 2001 after America attacked and destroyed the "Islamic" Taliban government of Afghanistan. The Arabs are too sophisticated to stage such a somersault. They view geopolitics as it should be viewed — a phenomenon which resembles Hobbes's state of nature: a war of all against all, in which all states try to advance their national interests, notwithstanding emotional sympathy for a given state. Even English-speaking and "Christian" America, Canada, Britain, Australia and New Zealand do not see eye to eye on all issues because of differences in geographical locations and clashing interests. To expect the Arab countries to turn themselves into a political entity and to view Pakistan's problems as their own is to repudiate the fundamental principles of geopolitics and show gross immaturity of political judgment. The Arab retains his fiercely independent outlook and self-respect despite the vicissitudes of history and doesn't suffer from any sense of inferiority. One obvious reason for this self-confidence is that, barring the Maghreb states, no Arab country has languished under colonial rule the way Muslims of South Asia have. The Arabian peninsula never experienced European rule, while such important Arab countries as Iraq and Syria — Balad al-Shaam, which includes Lebanon and Palestine — were under British and French occupation for hardly two decades. Both were occupied by Britain and France in the aftermath of World War I, and both moved toward freedom after World War II. Similarly, Libya was taken by Italy in 1913, and became free after WWII. Egypt was occupied by Britain in 1882, but even in this occupation Egypt retained its traditional administrative and legal structure, with its own flag, laws, currency and language in a treaty relationship of the kind Hyderabad State had with Britain. All along these decades Arabic continued to be the state language in all Arab countries. In sharp contrast, the British takeover of India was total, for the 'native' laws and Persian as court language disappeared and English came to occupy a hold on the South Asian mind in a way that has persisted till this day. While attachment to their language is one of the biggest sources of pride for the Arabs, the continued and forced use of English for the Muslims and Hindus of South Asia has served to instil inferiority complex in them and belittle them in their own eyes. A South Asian, whether Hindu or Muslim, considers it a great personal misfortune that "I cannot speak English like an Englishman".

A greater diversity in approach stems from South Asia's geographical location and the South Asians' first contact with the angrez — an omnibus term that originally meant Englishman but which has often been used for any European or white man. The nations of the Middle East have interacted with peoples across the Mediterranean since the dawn of history. Whether it was Roman Africa or the Umayyad, Abbasid and Ottoman times, or the modern colonial era with the British and the French calling the shots, peoples on the Mediterranean's southern, eastern and northern shores have continued to interact in war and peace — more in peace than in war as is generally assumed. Given the common Mediterranean skin and its various shades, it becomes a matter of opinion who is an angrez. The break-up of the Mediterranean's "cultural unity" is often bemoaned by Western historians, because the rise of Islam seemed to have made a permanent cleavage between the Mediterranean's northern shores on the one hand and the southern and eastern shores on other. Yet the interaction among Mediterranean nations continued, for the peoples of Asia Minor, Anatolia, Syria, Lebanon, Palestine, Egypt, Tripolitania, Cyprus, Greece, Malta, Sardinia, Algeria, Morocco, Tunis, Spain, southern France and Italy seemed to disregard geopolitical power equations when it came to trade. For this reasons peoples in these countries retain a liberal outlook, believe in free intermingling with all races, and are open to cultural assimilation. You only have to row a boat to reach the other side. Today, in spite of the tensions in the eastern Mediterranean region, board a ferry going, say, from Latakia to Sicily via Cyprus and take a look at the passengers' faces to realise that such a concept as angrez doesn't exist. The Mediterranean with the varied topography of its sacred hinterland where civilisation began, the minarets and the spires, the imams and the clergy, the Star of David, the winter rains and the abundance of vineyards and orchards with their loads of grapes, figs, pomegranates, apples, pears, olives and citrus, and the women's long dress with scarves often worn by both Muslim and Christian women — all represent a normal phenomenon that has continued for the millennia irrespective of political considerations. Wars only served to increase the fusion of races and cultures and helped create the Mediterranean type. This was not the case with the people of Bengal and Madras, who saw the angrez with his leper skin for the first time when he came in his boat from a distant island. He had circumvented the African coast, sailed across the Indian Ocean and the Bay of Bengal and come ashore to find a totally different land. The people were black skinned, the climate was hot and humid, and food habits were different, so were clothes and dwellings, and among the Muslims the thing called purdah, which to quote Marmaduke Pickthall is "neither of Islamic nor of Arabian origin" This was the mystic and exotic East in juxtaposition with the West, where the angrez had come from. For the Arab, East and West do not exist. He is part of both and for that reason has a cosmopolitanism that is reflected in his statecraft and daily life. Pakistanis criticise and regard as Western many traits in Arab culture, especially those with regard to dress and women, without realising that the Arabs are co-sharers of certain aspects of Mediterranean culture and Hellenic civilisation. .

The Arabian Peninsula may be isolated geographically. But once the Arabs burst out of it in the seventh century, they found themselves at the crossroads of three continents and many civilisations. The people they ruled and mixed with were as varied culturally, ethnically and racially as one can expect in an empire that stretched from Sindh to Spain. Subsequently, this empire broke up into several pieces. But the experience they had with subject peoples — and others — left an everlasting impression on the Arab mind, history, culture and race. The most pertinent point to note is that, in this empire, which reached its geographical peak during the time of Hisham bin Abdul Malik (724-743), the Arabs, according to Glubb Pasha, constituted one per cent of the population. This population included Sindhis, the Baloch, Afghans, Central Asian Turks, Persians, Kurds, Armenians, Greeks, Berbers, black Africans, Venetians and Genoese, Sicilians, Corsicans and Sardinians, Spaniards, Portuguese and Frenchmen, besides a host of nationalities with which they came in contact through commerce and war on land and sea — virtually all European nationalities, Chinese, Malays and Hindus. To this interaction was added fresh experience in the form of Crusades, which lasted nearly two hundred years and whose theatre of operation was not confined to Palestine as is generally assumed. The Crusades were more than wars and battles. Their net effect was a cultural and racial intermixture of the European and Middle Eastern peoples on an unprecedented scale. The Middle Eastern peoples here were not only Arabs but also Turks and Kurds, and the descendants of such ancient races as the Hebrews, Persians, and Armenians. Also to operate on Arab territory were the Mongols and (for nearly a thousand years) a bewildering variety of Turkic tribes. Constant intercourse with these peoples gave the Arab people an outlook that was cosmopolitan and liberal; and a mind that was open to new ideas and forms. It accepted whatever it considered good in others. It also made Arabs extremely secular in matters of statecraft, for the Umayyad and Abbasid states had no choice but to rely on Jews, Greeks and Persians to look after finance and administration. The greater effect of this mix was on an intellectual plane, for the Arabs could not have salvaged the lost treasure of Greece and Rome and set up institutions of learning if they had not had a secular vision, more so because their religion itself visualised a secular society.

Over the centuries, the Arab personality also underwent a physical change. What does an Arab look like? Initially — and there is a lot of vagueness in this "initially" — the Arab belonged to the peninsula and, with his aquiline nose, looked the stereotype of a Semite. Within a few centuries, this had given way to a variety of racial types. Now an Arab was anyone who spoke Arabic. A Caucasian blond in Beirut, a swarthy Semite in Oman or an African type in Darussalam all belonged to the universal Arab nation if he spoke Arabic. This universality in Arab experience is in direct contrast with the experience of the Pakistani (or South Asian Muslim) personality that has throughout history operated within the "box" that is the Subcontinent. The Subcontinent too, has had its exposure to foreign elements, but this has been entirely different from the Arab experience. Unlike the Arab situation, foreigners have come to the subcontinent and (with the exception of the British) settled down here. This coming was not matched by a "going." In other words, the South Asian experience of foreigners has been mostly in the form of a one-way traffic — invaders and conquerors coming from abroad. What was missing was interaction on a footing of equality with non-South Asians. While this has not exactly made the South Asian Muslims xenophobic, they have certainly over the centuries come to view foreigners (both Muslim and non-Muslim) as a higher, conquering breed. Worse, since many (though not all) Muslim invaders came to the subcontinent on desperate rescue pleas by native Muslims, the South Asian Muslims have continued to look to foreign Muslims as their trouble-shooters. Such stories as Muhammad bin Qasim's reaction to the pleas by Muslim women and children held hostage by Raja Dahar; or the Marahtta excess during the post-Aurangzeb era which prompted a punitive expedition by Ahmad Shah Abdali, and the like have had a profound impact on the psyche of South Asian Muslims. Centuries have passed but this attitude has not changed. They continue to look to Muslim powers outside the Indo-Pakistan subcontinent as saviours who would dash to South Asia on a mercy plea by native Muslims. Unfortunately, the Arabs have no special interest in the non-Arab Muslim world, because, as C. W. Smith puts it in his Islam in Modern History, the Arabs are "uninterested in and virtually unaware of Islamic greatness after the Arab downfall." For the Arabs, he says, "in 1258 (the fall of Baghdad)...Islamic history virtually came to an end."

Another problem is the very word 'Muslim'. This word stands on its own and doesn't' need the crutches of an external anti-thesis as we Pakistanis believe. Again, they are victims of history and have made no effort to rise above the past. An Arab, a Turk or an Iranian may be a Muslim but he doesn't look at the world through that prism. History and the modern world recognise them as such because of the languages they speak. In the subcontinent, a Muslim in Punjab or Sindh or Bengal and the rest of the subcontinent spoke the same language as his Hindu or Sikh neighbour. For that reason his identity throughout history has been 'Muslim'. While a problem in Syria or Azerbaijan is a Syrian problem or an Azerbaijanian problem, in the subcontinent there was no other way of describing it except as a Muslim problem. If Algerians are being massacred, one would speak of Algerians being killed, but in South Asia there could be only one description — a Muslim massacre. Here we see a similarity with Bosnian Muslims. The Muslims of Bosnia speak the same Serbo-Croat language as their Christian compatriots. But when the war began in 1989 the international media spoke of "Muslims" being massacred, because there was no other way in which the community that was being targeted by the other could be identified. Suddenly the non-Christian citizens had discovered their Muslim identity and separateness. On the Muslims of South Asia, the word 'Muslim" has an electrifying effect. Unlike a Saudi or Iraqi or Uzbek, the Muslim of South Asia has always thought of himself as having no other identity, and even though Pakistan is now 61 years old, Pakistanis still think they are Muslim first. They waste their time on endless academic discussions which revolve round the absurd question: where do I take inspiration from — from the sands of Arabia or from the ruins of Moenjodaro? The Saudi has no such problem. He is a Saudi, an Arab and a Muslim all at the same time and he sees no contradiction in this. Pakistanis are lost and bewildered.

Think for a moment of a Sri Lankan Christian who develops an excessive hatred of the Japanese because they attacked "us Christians at Pearl Harbour on December 7, 1941". While an American may appreciate this gesture of support, he must be wondering what Sri Lanka has to do with the Japanese and Pearl Harbour. The Sri Lankan would then develop a sense of betrayal if he found the Americans were not at his beck and call. The same is more or less true of the Arabs, who are surprised — though sometimes pleasantly — that Pakistanis take Arab problems so seriously. Yasser Arafat expected world Muslim support for the Palestine cause, but when one of Pakistan's leading intellectuals, Eqbal Ahmad — a friend of Edward Said's — protested to Arafat's purported sell-out of Jerusalem in the Declaration of Principles signed in Washington in September 1993 Arafat asked him in what way this concerned him. Eqbal Ahmad wrote this in an article for Dawn, but I regret to say I am unable to locate it. Arafat loved Pakistan, but one doesn't know how Eqbal worded his question and what exactly was Arafat's answer, especially because the PLO leader had problems with English. But the 'incident' only serves to strengthen my argument that Pakistanis are unable to understand the Arab mind, because their approach is awkward, simplistic and unrealistic.

Here I recall what a stir — though of a wrong kind — I made at a gathering of intellectuals from all over the world at Amman in April 2009. The occasion was the first-ever meeting of the West Asia North Africa (WANA) forum, His Royal Highness Hassan bin Talal's brainchild. Its aim is to counter "the sentiments of rage" in the area by identifying and sharing human concerns in the region and charting "the possibilities of the future for the well-being of all people in WANA". After HRH's presidential address, and speeches among others by former Finnish President and Nobel Prize Winner Martti Ahtisaari on the opening day, the delegates broke up into three panels — economy, environment and social. Since I am an expert at nothing, I chose to sit on the social panel, praying that I would not be called upon to speak at a gathering where some of the world's leading Arab and Western academics and intellectuals were present. I was astonished at the quality of Arab intellectuals, several of them teaching at American and European universities. Like Pakistan's, the Arab image stands grossly distorted and will take time for correction. There was very little time for interaction, and the entire proceedings were businesslike and exacting. But whatever little chance I had of talking to Arab academics and intellectuals made me acutely conscious of the inadequacy of my own personality. The panel was in fact a brainstorming session where experts in their respective fields were in the process of recommending proposals to regional policymakers for implementation. The moderator was Baker al-Hiyari, Deputy Director at the Royal Institute for Inter-Faith Studies, Jordan, and the speakers included such personalities as Syrian woman scholar Dr Seteney Shami, who is Programme Director at the Social Science Research Council, New York; Dr Shafeeq Ghabra, Professor of Political Science at the Kuwait University; Prof. Juho Saari, Professor of Sociology at the University of Eastern Finland, Prof. Sultan Barakat, Director of Post-War Reconstruction and Development at the University of York, and Prof. Volker Perthes, Director of the German Institute for International and Security Affairs, Berlin. Dear me! I should have kept quiet, and I might have. But, unfortunately and to my embarrassment, every participant was asked to give his views on the speeches made and recommendations being prepared. And lo! Patriotism got hold of me, and I spoke quite a bit of nonsense that included the eternal Pakistani complaint that the Arabs didn't care a fig for Pakistan. I would have been less audacious if I had restricted myself to this 'complaint'; no, I went on to say that, to the Arabs, Islamic, not merely Arab, history; ended in 1258; that they were utterly indifferent to the cultural contributions to the world of Islam by non-Arab empires like Ottoman, Safavid and Mughal, that the Arabs were self-centred — yes, I used that word —; that the Arabs wanted all non-Arab Muslims to be with them on the Palestine issue, but they themselves wouldn't be with the latter, and so on. I wouldn't say the participants were flabbergasted, but they were most certainly surprised, because I hadn't bothered to speak on the social panel's agenda but harangued the audience on what to them was extraneous matter. Unknown to me Hassan had sneaked in and heard me.

"Professor Siddiqi, (what an ego trip for me!) I think you are wrong", he said. "I am half-Turkish on Mother's side". The Hashemite prince then referred to her in-laws' Calcutta connections and spoke in good humour of the subcontinent being "my susraal". Susraal is subcontinental for the parents' home of one's wife. Susraal also refers to in-laws collectively. What His Royal Highness failed to realise how much I felt disappointed because the one sentence I wanted to hear from him he never uttered "Princess Sarvath is Pakistani!" Here I wouldn't here attach much importance to a dialogue the Iraqi Air Force chief had with Pakistan's Ambassador in Baghdad, Aslam Khattak. Abdel Karim Kassem, the Iraqi strongman who had overthrown the Hashemite monarchy in July 1958, had all nightclubs closed and the girls sent to Beirut. Ahmad Soekarno, unapologetically candid about his admiration for female beauty, came on a visit to Baghdad and made it known that he wanted to have cabaret entertainment. The Iraqi state had to oblige his Indonesian guest, the girls were brought from Beirut and the performance staged. The Iraqi air force chief was livid and told Khattak, "I am sure a Muslim like Nehru would never have done such a thing." When Khattak told him that Nehru was a Hindu, who worshipped idols, he replied, "Oh, brother, I know you people hate India, (but) for God's sake don't tell me that Nehru is not a Muslim!" (Mohammad Aslam Khan Khattak, A Pathan Odyssey, p 128-29). One need not attach too importance to the incident. An Iraqi air for chief could be as ignorant as an American Congressman, but Ambassador Khattak summed up his view of the Arab personality when he said "the emphasis Pakistan placed on religion did not exist among these (Arab) people" (ibid p 222). According to Khattak, some Arabs also thought the partition of India was a diabolical British plot, like the partition of Palestine.

An instance of the Pakistani people's naivety on the Indo-Arab relations came in September 1956 when Nehru visited Saudi Arabia. As the Saudi monarch welcomed the Indian prime minister at the Riyadh airport, some people raised the slogan Merhaba Rasool al-Salam. The crisis that followed in Pakistan-Saudi relations was an indication both of our lack of knowledge of Arabic and of our people's unjustified sensitivity to normal diplomatic relations between India and the Arab world. The Pakistani anger stemmed from the use of the word rasool. The Pakistani ulema — whose knowledge of Arabic, with some honourable exceptions, is extremely poor — thought the word had only one meaning: prophet. The problem was worsened by a Western wire agency, which translated Merhaba Rasool al-Salaam into "Welcome O Prophet of Peace!" There was a furore in Pakistan, the Press reacted negatively, and a delegation of the Jamiatul Ulema-i-Pakistan went to the Saudi Embassy in Karachi to "lodge a protest", as the agency report on Dawn's front page said, though I have no doubt in my mind they must have returned not only satisfied but highly embarrassed when the Saudis must have enlightened them on the meaning of rasool. Nevertheless, the public furore forced the Saudi Embassy to issue a clarification, which Dawn published on page one in its issue of September 27, 1956. The clarification said: "The Saudi Arabian Embassy in Pakistan regret[s] to note the incorrectness of the Arabic phrase into English by correspondents who seem to ignore the

ABC of the Arabic language. It is, therefore, incumbent on the Embassy to clarify that the Arabic word 'rasool' means 'messenger' and not at all 'prophet'."

This did not satisfy Dawn's fiery editor, Altaf Husain, to whom devotion to Pakistan was almost a religion. In his editorial entitled "Vain Expectations", published in the same issue, Husain showed extreme disgust with the use of the word rasool by the Saudis but at the same time appealed to the people of Pakistan to realise that their support to Muslim countries was a one-way traffic and they better adopt a more realistic attitude. The editorial made a mention of some of King Farouk's remarks making fun of Pakistan. I had heard about these remarks by the Egyptian king several times but wasn't sure whether they were factoid or fact. The Dawn editorial confirmed it.

Commenting on the Saudi clarification with regard to the word 'rasool', the Dawn editorial said: "Most Muslims in this country know what the literal meaning of the word rasool is but they also know that it has acquired a sacred connotation since the advent of the prophet whom the Kalmia describes as Mohammad-ur-Rasool Allah – Mohammad the Messenger of God. It is more than strange that in the rich vocabulary of the Arabic language King Saud and his Court could not find any other slogan to tell their people to shout in honour of the illustrious visitor from Hindu Bharat. Besides, it is the Prophet of Islam who is looked by Muslims throughout the world as the Prophet or Messenger Peace, because through him God propagated Islam, the religion of peace."

In what was considered an unprecedented attack by a Pakistani newspaper on the founder of modern Saudi Arabia, the editorial referred to the anti-Muslim pogroms that were then going on India and said these facts were brought to the king's notice "but all that he has done is to authorise his Ambassador in Karachi to issue vague assurances in the most general terms, deliberately evading any specific reference to the subject matter ... And, to cap it all, he has welcomed in his own Capital at this precise moment the head of the ... [Indian] Government in a manner which belies the assurances of the Saudi Arabian Embassy in Karachi". This way, said the paper, "His Majesty is doing the very opposite of helping his brethren (in ...India) in every possible way"

Pointing out that from its very inceptions Pakistan had been working for the unity of the Muslim world, the editorial said "regardless of its own interests", Pakistan earned "ill will and suspicion instead of appreciation and it became increasingly manifest that most of other Muslim Governments did not share the same enthusiasm for Islamic unity, and some of them were plainly jealous of Pakistan who, they wrongly thought, was trying to set itself up as the leader of the Muslim world... Egypt is perhaps the best illustration. Ridiculing the Islamic stand taken by Pakistan, King Farouk is once reported to have joked with his courtiers: 'Don't you know that Islam was born on August 14, 1947?' There was a time when Egypt, as a member of the Security Council, refused to give its vote to a resolution on Kashmir which six non-Muslim members were prepared to support and it was only after weeks of begging and diplomatic approaches that the essential seventh vote of Egypt was secured. The present [Nasser's] regime has shown no better friendliness towards this country. The other day the Egyptian Embassy in Karachi denied a report published in a Syrian newspaper which has quoted President Nasser as saying that Suez was as dear to Egypt as Kashmir was to [...India]. Yesterday, a local contemporary quoted extensively from .. [an Indian] journal to whose correspondent also President Nasser appears to have said the same thing. Only a direct contradiction from Mr Nasser himself –and not from Egyptian diplomats far from Cairo – will now convince anybody that the statement thus twice attributed to him by newspapers of two different countries was really unfounded." The editorial then advised the people of Pakistan to "calmly and dispassionately take all these bitter truths into consideration and restrain to some extent their vain expectations from the so-called Muslims world". In the same issue, the paper carried on page one a cartoon – drawn by Altaf's son, Ajmal, – which showed Nasser fishing in the Suez Canal and hobnobbing with an Indian girl (Nehru in a sari) with his back toward Pakistan (a girl) showing her heart with the words "Love for Egypt".

It is significant that in his book, The Philosophy of the Revolution, Nasser gave his idea of Egypt's place in the world by placing his country at the centre of three concentric circles. The first, inner circle was the Arab world, and there is no doubt he correctly visualised Egypt as the heart of the Arab world for reasons of its geography, history and culture. The second circle represented Africa, which was then engaged in anti-colonial liberation struggles, and Cairo was host to the headquarters of no less than a dozen African revolutionary movements. The third circle was Islamic. He said he drew strength from this circle, but Pakistan was missing from the Muslim countries he mentioned. It was in subsequent editions that Pakistan was included. However, all this did not stop Dawn from taking a passionately pro-Egyptian line when a few days later Israel, Britain and France attacked Egypt.

Written by Altaf, Dawn's editorial of Nov 1, 1956, was put on the front page and was titled "Hitler reborn". It said in part: "News at midnight tells of Anglo-French bombing of Egypt officially announced. It tells of Prime Minister Eden boasting of this heroic feet. It tells of Eden not only refusing to call Israel the aggressor despite the fact of its unprovoked invasion of Egypt, but suggesting that 'cumulatively' Egypt was the aggressor. It tells of Anglo-French justification of their defiance of the United Nations... It tells – and this is the happiest part of it – of the US officials saying that President Eisenhower and Secretary Dulles view the British-French venture as 'a desperate and dangerous gamble which seems certain to fail'. It tells of American feeling that the actions of its allies will 'galvanise the Muslim World and spur it into a crusade-type holy war that will involved Britain and France from the Atlantic to the Persian Gulf'. It tells, in fact, that in the middle of the twentieth century enlightened countries like Britain and France have suddenly turned the clock back by several hundred years, unwritten much of what has since been written in the book of human civilisation, and decided to act as self-chartered libertines with the gun and the bomb killing and conquering the weak like cowards. And so, this is the 'second Elizabethan age' of which so much was talked when Britain's young Queen ascended the throne!

"It is not our custom to print an editorial on the front page; but when Britain produces a Hitler who throws his own country's honour and all cherished moral, human and international values which it has itself fostered in the past, out of the windows of the Houses of Westminster into the Thames, and proceeds to shed innocent Muslim blood to dye red the Nile, opening a new and unbelievable chapter of perfidy and violence in the history of the human race – a little editorial custom is a small thing to disregard for the sake of proclaiming without losing a single day what the people of Pakistan feel...".

The Pakistani people, it said, were asking: "Is this not the rise once again of bigoted and perverted Christendom against the world of Islam in alliance with the Jews? Is this not a threat poised against Muslims from the Atlantic to the Pacific? Does it not make a mockery of the Pacts we have entered and turn our hopes in them into dupes and our satisfaction at them into sands in our mouths? What is our Government going to do about it? Prime Minister Suhrwardy is back and the people expect to learn today – repeat TODAY – the answer to the last question." The most remarkable thing about this editorial was that at the end it said within parenthesis "Earlier written editorial on page 5." I can visualise Altaf turning up at the Dawn office late in the evening, demanding to see the editorial, hitting the ceiling in rage, and then dictating an editorial right there and then.

Nearer in time — the year is 2002 — we get another instance of the Arab psyche, for what was involved was not a diplomatic issue but a massacre that shocked the world. The man who presided over this slaughter was Narindra Modi, Chief Minister of the Indian state of Gujarat. He belonged to the Bharatiya Janata Party, to which also belonged Indian Prime Minister A. B. Vajpayee. The massacre left at least 2,000 Muslims dead, and international observers and Indian's own human rights associations held Modi responsible for the slaughter. It was confirmed that the state machinery was involved in the massacre, and it was done with Modi's approval and knowledge. Yet not a single Arab country bothered to take up the issue with the Vajpayee government.

All Arab government took refuge behind a ready-made excuse: the riots were India's domestic affair, and no country could interfere in another country's internal matters. The excuse is untenable. In the first place, a violation of human rights — and one on such a colossal scale — cannot be ignored and shoved under the rug simply because it is a given country's internal matter. The international community has time and again spoken its mind and taken action whenever human rights violations crossed all limits of civilized behaviour – as in Indian-occupied Kashmir, the West Bank and Gaza, Bosnia, Kosovo, Rwanda and East Timor, and more recently in Iraq and Afghanistan. The international community not only condemned these barbaric violations of human rights; it acted decisively in some cases, like taking armed action, as against Serbia by the Clinton administration, and making the UN move and hold a plebiscite to signal mankind's determination not to remain indifferent to human suffering caused by ethnic or religious prejudices. From this point of view, the Arab countries had every right to express their horror over the grisly events in Gujarat and to register their protest with New Delhi over the state government's complicity in what Arundhati Roy called "a meticulously planned pogrom against the Muslim community.... under the benign gaze of the state and, at worse, with active state collusion." The rioters, she said, had "trucks loaded with thousands of gas cylinders, hoarded weeks in advance, which they used to blow up Muslim commercial establishments. They had not just police protection and police connivance, but also covering fire."

If riots were India's internal matter, why did some European countries disregard this diplomatic shibboleth and express their concern to the Indian government? Besides, if Arab countries did not find it prudent to criticise India individually, why could not the Arab League follow the example of the European Union? In the wake of the Gujarat massacre, the European Union (a "Christian club") came up with a declaration which was not made public. But it was prepared by the EU's own fact-finding mission and carried fifteen signatures, including those of diplomats from Belgium, Britain, France, Italy and Spain. The most sensational aspect of the EU report was that part which referred to "the carnage in Gujarat" as "a kind of apartheid" and said it "has parallels with Germany of the 1930s." The declaration, whose copy the Indian Express managed to have access to, believed the massacre in Gujarat was led by Vishwa Hindu Parishad and other extremist Hindu parties. Besides the EU mission, diplomats from the British, Dutch and German missions in New Delhi visited Gujarat and prepared reports on the pogrom. These reports were made available to some Indian newsmen, making the Indian External Affairs Ministry spokesman, Nirupama Rao, allege that some foreign missions were playing "a partisan role" by leaking their reports to the Press. While India considered all "leaks" as constituting "foreign interference", what it felt hurt most about was the Finnish rebuke, which came not in the form of a leaked report but as an interview by its Foreign Minister. Talking to the Indian Express, Finnish Foreign Minister Ekki Tuomioja said the riots in Gujarat were "of great concern to us." That was why the EU meeting at Luxembourg took notice of it. He added, "The pictures of the carnage are very disturbing." Shocking as it is, no Arab or Muslim diplomat stationed in India bothered to visit Gujarat to acquaint himself with the situation there and see the extent to which the state machinery had swung into action to help the rioters in the massacre of Muslims and the destruction of their property. Instead, it was left to Western diplomats to visit Ahmadabad and Baroda and compile reports for their governments.

The gist of the German report, which referred to the attacks on Muslims as "surgical strikes," was carried by the Hindustan Times, and asserted that Hindu extremist organizations carried lists of Muslim establishments to be attacked. The "lists" part of the report appears credible because it says some Hindu establishments were also vandalised for violating the VHP's code of conduct, which forbids Hindus from having a business relationship with Muslims. The Dutch report also confirmed the widespread belief that the Modi government failed to protect the minority community, that the Muslims were specifically targeted, and that the police abetted in attacks on Muslims. Astonishingly, even visiting

Western diplomats found it fit to "interfere" in India's internal matters — if reminding a government of its basic duty towards protecting the life and property of its citizens constitutes "interference." First, visiting Swiss Foreign Minister Joseph Deiss went on record as saying he had conveyed his country's concern over the "tragic" events in Gujarat both to his Indian counterpart and to Prime Minister Vajpayee. Next came Stephanie Dion, the visiting Canadian Minister for Inter-governmental Affairs, who said she was "eager to participate in a peace march" — as proposed by Indian Defence Minister George Fernandes. Dion also appealed to "all people of goodwill" to take part in the rally to establish peace in Gujarat. Another visitor, Australian Foreign Minister Alexander Downer, was not that blunt, but he did discuss the Gujarat situation with his Indian counterpart, as confirmed by India itself. No Arab diplomat based in New Delhi bothered to "discuss" the Gujarat carnage with the government, much less visit the Ahmadabad area, where Indian sources put the number of mosques and shrines, including the grave of Wali Dakhani, one of Urdu's earliest poets, destroyed at over 400. The Christian nations have not set up an organisation on the pattern of the Organisation of Islamic Conference, because they know it would be foolish to expect Norway, Bolivia, South Africa and the Philippines to have common defence and foreign policies. But whenever there is anti-Christian frenzy in India and Hindu fanatics attack churches and kill members of the Christian minority ambassadors from North America and Europe take up the issue with New Delhi and pressure it to improve conditions for India's Christians. That in no way contradicts their commitment to secularism.

One can go on arguing endlessly whether the Arab countries' attitude towards the Gujarat pogrom constituted, in the ultimate analysis, a reflection on Pakistani diplomacy. If the Arabs chose to keep mum over what was happening in Gujarat, then perhaps there was some basic flaw in our policy toward the Arabs and some gaucherie in the way we approached them. In sharp contrast, Indian diplomacy had been sophisticated and been able to blunt any Pakistani bid to win over the Arab countries' sympathy on religious grounds. India's secular approach has had a greater success with the Arabs than Pakistan's crude appeals to religious sentiments. The Arabs, like their religion, are secular in outlook, but this single truth has never been taken into consideration by us Pakistanis. This was the reason the Indian argument — that the British partitioned India in advance of the partition of Palestine to justify their action — appealed to the Arabs. India also pointed out to the Arabs the purported contradiction in Pakistan's approach to the two issues. While the Pakistanis upheld India's partition on religious grounds and considered it a triumph for them, they opposed the same principle in Palestine. To the Arab intellectuals, leaders, diplomats and journalists – most of whom shockingly oblivious of South Asia's history – this made sense.

Ghada Karmi, for instance, is a crusader for the Palestinian cause. She once worked in Pakistan and has visited the country on lecture tours. Her book In Search of Fatima makes fascinating reading, beginning with her childhood in Palestine, the family's flight, their stay in London, the 1967 war, her disillusionment with her "dishonest English" life, which came down in pieces as she came across the deep-seated hatred of the Arabs among the English, including her husband.. She found British Jews singing Israel's national anthem at weddings and clicking glasses in toasts "To Israel!" Nasser's nationalization of the Suez Canal threw the Britons into paroxysms of anger, followed by euphoria over the Israeli victories in 1956 and 1967. Her marriage ended in a divorce within four years. This led to her rediscovery of herself as a Palestinian. During her visit to Karachi in 2003, I 'complained' to her against the Arab attitude, especially the fact that the Arabs made little difference between Pakistan and India. Ghada gave several explanations, including her belief that the Arabs had been "colonised by Western civilisation at a very, very deep level". From this emerged, she said, "their lack of awareness of and concerns for non-Arabs and their problems, like Kashmir." (Two-state policy will fail, interview with Dawn, May 18, 2003). She, too, was like them, she said, until she saw the monuments of Islamic glory in South Asia. "Lahore is glorious with its Mughal monuments", so were the Muslim monuments like Taj Mahal and others she saw on a visit to India. But, she added, "it has never occurred to the Arabs to visit these places and take pride in what, indeed, is our common Islamic heritage. The only places the Arabs visit are Europe and America, because the Arabs think that is where the solution to all problems lies. Worse, they seem to despise their own institutions." If one talked to the Arabs these days, she said, many of them would tell you, "Bring back the Ottoman Empire, and I am one of them." Two years later, when there was talk of Pakistan recognising Israel, Ghada wrote that such a recognition would shock the Arab world, especially Palestinians because "Pakistanis have a special place in the hearts of all Palestinians precisely because of their sincerity, devotion and fellow feeling. They are in a unique category among other Muslims, seen as 'semi-Arabs', closer in fact than many 'full Arabs'. No one forgets Pakistan's generosity to Palestinians in their worst times, the number of students educated in Pakistani universities, the warm welcome and support for a cause which won them no friends in the West" (Ghada Karmi, Pakistan and Israel: a Palestinian view, Dawn, September 30, 2005). She quoted a letter in The Jerusalem Post by "the Canadian Coalition of Democracies" which begged Israel not to establish diplomatic relations with Pakistan. Written by Indian expatriates in Canada it appealed to Israel not to "betray" India by forging closer relations with Pakistan, because Israel and India shared many common values, including the war on 'Islamic terrorism'.

Yet Ghada herself has never written a line in support of the Kashmiris, who I suppose fall in the category of 'semi-Arabs'. In an article, entitled Arafat symbolizes the Palestinians' struggle, written a week before Arafat died, Ghada included India among Islamic countries. Eulogising Arafat's services to the Palestinian cause Ghada wrote: "Unlike other Arab leaders, he cultivated non-aligned and Islamic countries, like India and Pakistan (the last Indian BJP government was an aberration), and was a well-loved figure there" (Dawn, November 4, 2004). This is hardly different from what the Iraqi air chief said, who could perhaps be forgiven for his ignorance, for one doesn't know what his educational level was, but Dr Ghada Karmi is a well-informed political activist and author of several books.

Here I recall a remark by one of my journalist friends, Asim Ghani, about the Palestinian issue. A self-confessed atheist, Asim said he did not consider Palestine "an issue" in which he would take sides, because "I consider Palestine my personal tragedy". I asked why he sympathised with the Palestinians when he was not a believer. He replied that he might not be a believer but anyone who considered himself a human being could not be indifferent to the tragedy of the Palestinian people. Besides, he said, he was a product of Pakistan's Muslim society. Yes, this 'Muslim and semi-Arab society' is more Arab than the Arabs. I too have often felt that my feeling for Palestine was hardly different from Asim's. At the same time I have wondered if any Arab agonises over the fate of the Kashmiri people. Ghada and the Iraqi air force chief, with full respects to them, should not necessarily be considered the true spokespersons for the Arabs with regard to their feeling toward Pakistan, for we cannot forget that among those who gave their lives at Kargil in 1999 for Kashmir's freedom were Arab commandoes. In fact, a Jordanian was chief of the commandos. Their bravery was unparalleled, as confirmed by an Indian diplomat. G. Parthasarathy, Indian High Commissioner for Pakistan in Islamabad, visited the Dawn office in the aftermath of the Kargil affair for a chat and gave us the audio cassette which allegedly recorded the conversation which Pervez Musharraf, then army chief, had on the phone from Beijing with fellow generals in Pakistan, and which according to the Indians gave them an indication of the ethnic variety of the Muslim commandos taking part in the Kargil operation. Parthasarathy admitted that the mujahideen fought bravely and none of them was captured because they preferred death to surrender. That Arabs were among these heroes should not be forgotten.

Whatever the Arab attitude one, nevertheless, has to recognise that the concept of Ummah, an international community that transcends borders, has always existed among all Muslim peoples. The concept is based on the legends of early Islamic history, the persecution of the believers by the pagan merchants and tribal chiefs, the sufferings of the Holy Prophet and his companions, the fortitude they showed during their mission, his conduct in daily life — the only prophet whose life has been recorded by history in detail — , the Holy Prophet's peaceful entry as a victor in a city where he had been persecuted for 13 years, the amazing victories attending Muslim arms during the seventh and eighth centuries, and the rituals which Muslims throughout the world perform in Arabic constitute an unbreakable bond of unity and spiritual oneness among Muslims worldwide. This is something we can build upon so long as we take a pragmatic view of the harsh realities of geopolitics. No Muslim state, with the sole exception of Pakistan, will sacrifice its national interests for the sake of another Muslim country. Pakistan must note this. Most Pakistanis would deny it, but I believe that like many other nations, especially great powers, Pakistanis, too, have tried unabashedly to exploit Islam to advance their national interests. The greatest example of national aggrandisement under cover of noble slogans was set by European colonial powers, and later the United States. Both Britain and France led themselves to believe that they were on a civilizing mission, and that the conquest of Afro-Asia by Britain and France – and later in a restricted sense by Holland and Belgium – was in the interest of the conquered people. The United States pursued the same policy during the cold war, and is still doing it today, to advance its geopolitical and economic interests in the world, especially in the Middle East, under shibboleths that varied. During the cold war it was to save the world from "the communist danger" that America interfered brazenly in other nations' internal affairs, fomented trouble against pro-Soviet, pro-Chinese or even neutral regimes, and helped organise coups and assassinations to remove pro-communist dictators. At the same time it did everything possible with massive doses of military and economic aid to consolidate the power of dictators and monarchs if they were on the side of the 'free world'. After 9/11, the Bush administration began using the war on terror to tighten its stranglehold on many countries, especially those in the Middle East, and then attacked Iraq to overthrow and ultimately hang Saddam Hussein. The attack was launched without a second Security Council resolution, even though Dr Hans Blix, Swedish head of the UN Monitoring, Verification and Inspection Commission, had reported that there were no weapons of mass destruction in Baathist Iraq. Yet America (and Britain) chose to attack Iraq because it was in Israel's interest to destroy a regime which it thought posed the greatest threat to its security.

As noted, Pakistanis have often been angry with the Arabs, but they forget that Islam is in Arab blood; Islam to them is non-controversial, and they have no reasons like Pakistanis to flaunt their adherence to it or to prove to the world that they are good Muslims. Ultimately, the Pakistanis' complaint against the Arabs stems from the latter's perceived failure to help Pakistan vis-à-vis India. This is a very narrow and selfish use of Islam for national purposes, and Pakistanis are no less guilty than the other powers of using a noble idea in the pursuit of chauvinist aims.

The only way Muslim nations can help each other is to develop themselves economically, acquire science and technology, liberate women from the days of jahiliya in which many Muslim societies, including Pakistani, have trapped them, create societies that accept pluralism, allow a free flow of information, and give the minorities a chance to contribute to their nations' cultural growth, for all minorities, unless persecuted, contribute to the mainstream — like Jews in the heyday of Arab civilisation and in the West today and Christians in the Arab world. The aim of the Holy Prophet of Islam was to establish a just society free from exploitation and oppression. Powerful Muslim nations can this way help each other without needing a formal alliance or multinational grouping like the OIC. The Arabs, or for that matter any other foreign groups of Muslims, are not going to view Pakistan solely from the prism of a common religion. For that reason, any Turkish,

Iranian or Pakistani problem is not an Arab problem and cannot evoke Arab support on the plea that it is an Islamic issue. To understand the true Arab attitude to Islamic causes, let us note the reason why the Arabs agreed to the Second Islamic Summit Conference at Lahore in 1974. The conference was not organized by Z. A. Bhutto for the sake of a theory called Islamic unity. The call for the summit conference was given by him in the aftermath of the Ramazan war (October 1973), and its purpose was to mobilize Islamic support for the Arab cause. Only a dullard of an Arab would have refused to go to such a conference.

Let Pakistan develop itself. It has the necessary means, natural resources, hard-working people and skilled manpower to develop itself and create an egalitarian and prosperous society. While it is absurd to try to find scapegoats for our failure to make an economic and scientific breakthrough, the truth must be admitted: we have no choice but to divert a major part of our resources to Pakistan's defence. India has left us with no choice. This argument — security concerns — applies to the Arab world only marginally. For instance Syria, Egypt, Lebanon and Jordan can justify their military spending because of all that Israel has done and will continue to do. But that still doesn't explain why countries like Saudi Arabia, Libya, Algeria and oil-sheikhdoms like the UAE and Oman haven't developed technologically in spite of huge oil resources. On the other hand, Pakistan, in spite of having no oil, has made considerable technological progress, especially that which is relevant to defence. Stupid liberals in Pakistan have often been cynical and wondered why Pakistan had to build nuclear weapons and manufacture rockets, tanks and submarines and — in cooperation with China— jet fighters, while there was widespread poverty. The answer is simple: Pakistan, as said earlier, had no choice.

If the Arab world failed to develop a military-industrial complex, one could say that Israel's backers — America and the European Union — would not let the Arab world do so. But what has stopped the Arab world from acquiring non-military technology? Surely if the American wouldn't allow Saudi Arabia and Libya or the UAE to build the sinews of war, these countries could at least have acquired sophisticated, non-military technology, given the immensity of the oil wealth with them. They at least could have made themselves self-sufficient in food, but as we know the Arab world's food import bill alone runs into several million dollars a day.

Postscript

Some developments that have made many events mentioned in the book obsolete need to be corrected. This also holds good for the many ups and downs in my own little life. But first the nation:

- The most shocking and blood curdling event which shook not just Pakistan but the world was the Taliban's attack on the Army Public School, Peshawar, and the massacre of 132 students and their woman principal on December 16, 2014. The greater tragedy was there were people who justified the Taliban's murder of the innocent souls and called it a jihad.

- When I cast my vote in the 2008 elections, I thought it was the last time I was voting. In 2013, for the first time in the post-Zia period, an elected government completed its five-year tenure, and once again I had my left thumb smeared with indelible ink to exercise my right as a citizen of Pakistan on May 22, 2013. The result was a disappointment for Imran Khan. The 'captain', who claimed that his party came second, chose the role of an agitator to stage a sit-in that lasted 126 days without achieving any of his aims. The Peshawar massacre came in hand as an excuse for the charismatic Khan to call off the sit-in.

- After sixteen years, the Supreme Court of Pakistan announced its verdict in the Asghar Khan case on October 19, 2012. Paragraph 13 of the judgment said:

> Late Ghulam Ishaq Khan, the then President of Pakistan, General (R) Aslam Baig and General (R) Asad Durrani acted in violation of the Constitution by facilitating a group of politicians and political parties, etc., to ensure their success

against the rival candidates in the general election of 1990, for which they secured funds from Mr. Younus Habib. Their acts have brought a bad name to Pakistan and its Armed Forces as well as secret agencies in the eyes of the nation. Therefore, notwithstanding that they may have retired from service, the Federal Government shall take necessary steps under the Constitution and Law against them.

No action has been taken against them till this day.

- I have repeatedly mentioned the Constitution's article 58-2b because three Presidents used it to dismiss elected Prime Ministers and dissolve the National Assembly. However, no President can do so again because article 58-2b was abolished by the Eighteenth Amendment in April 2010. The man behind the consensus was the PPP's Raza Rabbani.

- Maulana Abdul Aziz, the chief cleric of Lal Masjid, has been acquitted in all the cases registered against him.

- Dawn had a change in stewardship, with Zaffar Abbas replacing Abbas Nasir as Editor in 2010. Nasir left for greener pastures in Europe. This book mentions Zaffar as a reporter in The Star (since then closed) and as Dawn Islamabad's Resident Editor. His contribution has so far included a radical alteration of Dawn's layout. I also received, through him what can be called my life's last 'promotion': I became Dawn's first Readers' Editor in June 2014.

- Two tragedies have occurred in the Dawn family M.A. Majid dies on December 20, 2012. He used to make me write as many as six editorials a week, and he enjoyed it when I called him my slave driver. Another tragedy was the murder of a brilliant young journalist, Murtaza Rizvi, on April 19, 2012. Author, journalist, linguist and Dawn Lahore's Resident Editor, Murtaza and I had passed two delightful 'boys nights out' in Lahore when I was on my way to Tehran in October 2006. His knowledge of literature, art and politics was amazing, so was his speed of writing, for he managed to write a book on Pakistan's politics within three months while on vacation in Bangkok. His British publishers liked the book and commissioned him for a new one before he died. A brilliant career was cut short.

- Another extraordinary friend I lost was Kaleem Omar, my colleague at The Star. As Reema Abbasi wrote of him, Omar "pursued investigative reporting and Audrey Hepburn with almost equal interest, and his obituary for Telly Savalas became so popular that it eventually found its way to the actor's widow." His death left an unfinished 300-segment poem that he lovingly referred to as 'A Troubadour's Life', and his books of English poetry --Wordfall and Pieces of Eight -- received "rave reviews" in international publications. Reema Thought Kaleem was always "captive to his own heart and died of it."

- At the familial level, on June 3, 2014, Qamar Jahan, my elder sister, died at my Gulshan home. The tragedy of her death also ended a tragedy, for it put an end to a schizophrenic life that tormented her and the family all her life. Amazing as it appears, despite becoming a shizo coupled with paranoia when she was in her twenties, she continued to be a working woman – efficient typist and stenographer – till the age of sixty. May God give peace to a life that never knew happiness.

- Among the cousins who are no more in this world was Assad Rafi, killed in a traffic accident in New York. He was a friend more than a cousin, and the evenings we passed together when we were young and in a Karachi where life was peaceful have always lived in my memory. He had developed liver cirrhosis while in the US, and I wondered whether I would ever be able to see him. In 2012 he came to Karachi with his wife Irfana, and Razia and I dined with them at PC in the dining hall the overlooks Sherpao Garden. By a strange coincidence Shabnam, on a visit from Bangladesh, was at a dinner there, so we four had a good look at a heroine we had been crazy about in our youth. She had still retained the looks of her youth. Assad had almost recovered from cirrhosis and was going shopping a day before Eid when, apparently under sedation, he lost control and the car hit a pole.

- Of the gang of four of I have mentioned in the book, Baughty was the first to go. He had moved away from the chaos of Soldier Bazaar to the quiet and green splendour of the Malir army base. I met him a few weeks before the final parting, and found him cool and composed, waiting to embrace death. He had a disdain for dietary restraint, and ultimately it was complications from diabetes that got him.

- On July 28, 2017, Nawaz Sharif the first Pakistani prime minister to be disqualified for hiding financial facts. The Supreme Court's five-man bench said he was neither Ameen (truthful) nor Sadiq (honest). He has stepped down and filed a revision appeal with the apex court.

APPENDIX I
KASHMIR RESOLUTION 3

RESOLUTION 47 (1948) ON THE INDIA-PAKISTAN QUESTION SUBMITTED JOINTLY BY THE REPRESENTATIVES OF BELGIUM, CANADA, CHINA, COLUMBIA, THE UNITED KINGDOM AND UNITED STATES OF AMERICA AND ADOPTED BY THE SECURITY COUNCIL AT ITS 286TH MEETING HELD ON 21 APRIL 1948. (DOCUMENT NO. S/726 DATED 21 APRIL 1948).

THE SECURITY COUNCIL

Having considered the complaint of the Government of India concerning the dispute over the State of Jammu and Kashmir, having heard the representative of India in support of that complaint and the reply and counter complaints of the representative of Pakistan,

Being strongly of opinion that the early restoration of peace and order in Jammu and Kashmir is essential and that India and Pakistan should do their utmost to bring about cessation of all fighting,

Noting with satisfaction that both India and Pakistan desire that the question of the accession of Jammu and Kashmir to India or Pakistan should be decided through the democratic method of a free and impartial plebiscite,

Considering that the continuation of the dispute is likely to endanger international peace and security,

Reaffirms its resolution 38 (1948) of 17 January 1948;

Resolves that the membership of the Commission established by its resolution 39 (1948) of 20 January 1948, shall be increased to five and shall include, in addition to the membership mentioned in that Resolution, representatives of ....and..., and that if the membership of the Commission has not been completed within ten days from the date of the adoption of this resolution the President of the Council may designate such other Member or Members of the United Nations as are required to complete the membership of five;

Instructs the Commission to proceed at once to the India sub-continent and there place its good offices and mediation at the disposal of the Governments of India and Pakistan with a view to facilitating the taking of the necessary measures, both with respect to the restoration of peace and order and to the holding of a plebiscite by the two Governments, acting in co-operation with one another and with the Commission, and further instructs the Commission to keep the Council informed of the action taken under the resolution; and, to this end, Recommends to the Governments of India and Pakistan the following measures as those which in the opinion of the Council and appropriate to bring about a cessation of the fighting and to create proper conditions for a free and impartial plebiscite to decide whether the State of Jammu and Kashmir is to accede to India or Pakistan.

A — RESTORATION OF PEACE AND ORDER

1. The Government of Pakistan should undertake to use its best endeavours:

   (a) To secure the withdrawal from the State of Jammu and Kashmir of tribesmen and Pakistani nationals not normally resident therein who have entered the State for the purposes of fighting,

and to prevent any intrusion into the State of such elements and any furnishing of material aid to those fighting in the State;
(b) To make known to all concerned that the measures indicated in this and the following paragraphs provide full freedom to all subjects of the State, regardless of creed, caste, or party, to express their views and to vote on the question of the accession of the State, and that therefore they should cooperate in the maintenance of peace and order.

2. The Government of India should:

(a) When it is established to the satisfaction of the Commission set up in accordance with the Council's Resolution 39 (1948) that the tribesmen are withdrawing and that arrangements for the cessation of the fighting have become effective, put into operation in consultation with the Commission a plan for withdrawing their own forces from Jammu and Kashmir and reducing them progressively to the minimum strength required for the support of the civil power in the maintenance of law and order;
(b) Make known that the withdrawal is taking place in stages and announce the completion of each stage;
(c) When the Indian forces shall have been reduced to the minimum strength mentioned in (a) above, arrange in consultation with the Commission for the stationing of the remaining forces to be carried out in accordance with the following principles:
   (i) That the presence of troops should not afford any intimidation or appearance of intimidation to the inhabitants of the State;
   (ii) That as small a number as possible should be retained in forward areas;
   (iii) That any reserve of troops which may be included in the total strength should be located within their present base area.

3. The Government of India should agree that until such time as the plebiscite administration referred to below finds it necessary to exercise

the powers of direction and supervision over the State forces and policy provided for in paragraph 8, they will be held in areas to be agreed upon with the Plebiscite Administrator.

4. After the plan referred to in paragraph 2(a) above has been put into operation, personnel recruited locally in each district should so far as possible be utilized for the re-establishment and maintenance of law and order with due regard to protection of minorities, subject such additional requirements as may be specified by the Plebiscite Administration referred to in paragraph 7.

5. If these local forces should be found to be inadequate, the Commission, subject to the agreement of both the Government of India and the Government of Pakistan, should arrange for the use of such forces of either Dominion as it deems effective for the purpose of pacification.

B — PLEBISCITE

6. The Government of India should undertake to ensure that the Government of the State invite the major political groups to designate responsible representatives to share equitably and fully in the conduct of the administration at the ministerial level, while the plebiscite is being prepared and carried out.

7. The Government of India should undertake that there will be established in Jammu and Kashmir a Plebiscite Administration to hold a Plebiscite as soon as possible on the question of the accession of the State to India or Pakistan.

8. The Government of India should undertake that there will be delegated by the State to the Plebiscite Administration such powers as the latter considers necessary for holding a fair and impartial plebiscite including, for that purpose only, the direction and supervision of the State forces and police.

9. The Government of India should at the request of the Plebiscite Administration, make available from the Indian forces such assistance as the Plebiscite Administration may require for the performance of its functions.

10. (a) The Government of India should agree that a nominee of the Secretary-General of the United Nations will be appointed to be the Plebiscite Administrator.

    (b) The Plebiscite Administrator, acting as an officer of the State of Jammu and Kashmir, should have authority to nominate the assistants and other subordinates and to draft regulations governing the Plebiscite. Such nominees should be formally appointed and such draft regulations should be formally promulgated by the State of Jammu and Kashmir.

    (c) The Government of India should undertake that the Government of Jammu and Kashmir will appoint fully qualified persons nominated by the Plebiscite Administrator to act as special magistrates within the State judicial system to hear cases which in the opinion of the Plebiscite Administrator have a serious bearing on the preparation and the conduct of a free and impartial plebiscite.

    (d) The terms of service of the Administrator should form the subject of a separate negotiation between the Secretary-General of the United Nations and the Government of India. The Administrator should fix the terms of service for his assistants and subordinates.

    (e) The Administrator should have the right to communicate directly, with the Government of the State and with the Commission of the Security Council and, through the Commission, with the Security Council, with the Governments of India and Pakistan and with their representatives with the Commission. It would be his duty to bring to the notice of any or all of the foregoing (as he in his discretion may decide) any circumstances arising which may tend, in his opinion, to interfere with the freedom of the Plebiscite.

11. The Government of India should undertake to prevent and to give full support to the Administrator and his staff in preventing any threat, coercion or intimidation, bribery or other undue influence on the voters in the plebiscite, and the Government of India should publicly announce and should cause the Government of the State to announce this undertaking as an international obligation binding on all public authorities and officials in Jammu and Kashmir.

12. The Government of India should themselves and through the Government of the State declare and make known that all subjects of the State of Jammu and Kashmir, regardless of creed, caste or party, will be safe and free in expressing their views and in voting on the question of the accession of the State and that there will be freedom of the Press, speech and assembly and freedom of travel in the State, including freedom of lawful entry and exit.

13. The Government of India should use and should ensure that the Government of the State also use their best endeavour to effect the withdrawal from the State of all Indian nationals other than those who are normally resident therein or who on or since 15th August 1947 have entered it for a lawful purpose.

14. The Government of India should ensure that the Government of the State releases all political prisoners and take all possible steps so that:

(a) all citizens of the State who have left it on account of disturbances are invited and are free to return to their homes and to exercise their rights as such citizens;

(b) there is no victimization;

(c) minorities in all parts of the State are accorded adequate protection.

15. The Commission of the Security Council should at the end of the plebiscite certify to the Council whether the plebiscite has or has not been really free and impartial.

C — GENERAL PROVISIONS

16. The Governments of India and Pakistan should each be invited to nominate a representative to be attached to the Commission for such assistance as it may require in the performance of its task.

17. The Commission should establish in Jammu and Kashmir such observers as it may require of any of the proceedings in pursuance of the measures indicated in the foregoing paragraphs.

18. The Security Council Commission should carry out the tasks assigned to it herein.

(The resolution was passed without a negative vote, Belgium, Columbia, Ukraine and the USSR abstaining.)

The Security Council's Third Resolution is significant in that it virtually amounts to the world body's indictment of India. In Part (A), the resolution makes two demands on Pakistan, vide sub-paragraphs (a) and (b), makes one demand (paragraph 5) on both Pakistan and India, and makes 17 demands on New Delhi. Submitted to the Security Council by Belgium, China, Canada, Columbia, the UK and the USA, the document give us an idea of how the UN's Resolution 47 (1948), adopted by the UN's executive arm at its 286th meeting on April 21, 1948 (Document No S/726) made it clear which party stood in the way of a Kashmir solution.

APPENDIX II
TASHKENT DECLARATION JANUARY 10, 1966: TEXT

THE PRIME MINISTER OF INDIA and the President of Pakistan, having met at Tashkent and having discussed the existing relations between India and Pakistan hereby declare their firm resolve to restore normal and peaceful relations between their countries and to promote understanding and friendly relations between their peoples. They consider the attainment of these objectives of vital importance for the welfare of the 600 million people of India and Pakistan.

(i) The Prime Minister of India and the President of Pakistan agree that both sides will exert all efforts to create good neighbourly relations between India and Pakistan in accordance with the United Nations Charter. They reaffirm their obligation under the Charter not to have recourse to force and to settle their disputes through peaceful means. They considered that the interests of peace in their region and particularly in the Indo-Pakistan subcontinent and indeed, the interests of the peoples of India ad Pakistan were not served by the continuance of tension between the two countries. It was against this background that Jammu & Kashmir was discussed, and each of the sides set forth its respective position.

TROOPS' WITHDRAWAL

(ii) The Prime Minister of India and the President of Pakistan have agreed that all armed personnel of the two countries shall be withdrawn not later than 25 February 1966 to the positions they held prior to 5 August 1965, and both sides shall observe the cease-fire terms on the cease-fire line.

(iii) The Prime Minister of India and the President of Pakistan have agreed that relations between India and Pakistan shall be based on the principle of non-interference in the internal affairs of each other.

(iv) The Prime Minister of India and the President of Pakistan have agreed that both sides will discourage any propaganda directed against the other country and will encourage propaganda which promotes the development of friendly relations between the two countries.

(v) The Prime Minister of India and the President of Pakistan have agreed that the High Commissioner of India to Pakistan and the High Commissioner of Pakistan of India will return to their posts and that the normal functioning of diplomatic missions of both countries will be restored. Both Governments shall observe the Vienna Convention of 1961 on Diplomatic Intercourse.

TRADE RELATIONS

(vi) The Prime Minister of India and the President of Pakistan have agreed to consider measures towards the restoration of economic and trade relations, communications as well as cultural exchanges between India and Pakistan, and to take measures to implement the existing agreement between India and Pakistan.

(vii) The Prime Minister of India and the President of Pakistan have agreed that they will give instructions to their respective authorities to carry out the repatriation of the prisoners of war.

(viii) The Prime Minister of India and the President of Pakistan have agreed that the two sides will continue the discussions of questions relating to the problems of refugees and eviction of illegal immigrations. They also agreed that both sides will create conditions which will prevent the exodus of people. They further agree to discuss the return of the property and assets taken over by either side in connection with the conflict.

SOVIET LEADERS THANKED

(ix) The Prime Minister of India and the President of Pakistan have agreed that the two sides will continue meetings both at highest and at other levels of matters of direct concern to both countries. Both sides have recognized the need to set up joint Indian-Pakistani bodies which will report to their Governments in order to decide what further steps should be taken.

(x) The Prime Minister of India and the President of Pakistan record their feelings, deep appreciation and gratitude to the leaders of the Soviet Union, the Soviet Government and personally to the Chairman of the Council of Ministers of the USSR for their constructive, friendly and noble part in bringing about the present meeting which has resulted in mutually satisfactory results. They also express to the Government and friendly people of Uzbekistan their sincere thankfulness for their overwhelming reception and generous hospitality.

They invite the Chairman of the Council of Ministers of the USSR to witness this declaration.

| Prime Minister of India | President of Pakistan |
| Lal Bahadur Shastri | Mohammed Ayub Khan |

Tashkent, January 10, 1966

APPENDIX III
SIMLA AGREEMENT, JULY 2, 1972: TEXT

1. The Government of India and the Government of Pakistan are resolved that the two countries put an end to the conflict and confrontation that have hitherto marred their relations and work for the promotion of a friendly and harmonious relationship and the establishment of durable peace in the subcontinent, so that both countries may henceforth devote their resources and energies to the pressing task of advancing the welfare of their peoples.

In order to achieve this objective, the Government of India and the Government of Pakistan have agreed as follows:

(i) That the principles and purposes of the Charter of the United Nations shall govern the relations between the two countries;
(ii) That the two countries are resolved to settle their differences by peaceful means through bilateral negotiations or by any other peaceful means mutually agreed upon between them. Pending the final settlement of any of the problems between the two countries, neither side shall unilaterally alter the situation and both shall prevent the organization, assistance of encouragement of any acts detrimental to the maintenance of peaceful and harmonious relations;

(iii) That the prerequisite for reconciliation, good neighbourliness and durable peace between them is a commitment by both the countries to peaceful co-existence, respect for each other's territorial integrity and sovereignty and non-interference in each other's internal affairs, on the basis of equality and mutual benefit;

(iv) That the basic issues and causes of conflict which have bedevilled the relations between the two countries for the last 25 years shall be resolved by peaceful means;

(v) That there shall always respect each other's national unity, territorial integrity, political independence and sovereign equality;

(vi) That in accordance with the Charter of the United Nations they will refrain from the threat of use of force against the territorial integrity or political independence of each other.

2. Both Governments will take steps within their power to prevent hostile propaganda directed against each other. Both countries will encourage the dissemination of such information as would promote the development of friendly relations between them.

3. In order progressively to restore and normalize relations between the two countries step by step, it was agreed that:

(i) Steps shall be taken to resume communications, postal, telegraphic, sea, land including border posts, and air links including overflights.

(ii) Appropriate steps shall be taken to promote travel facilities for the nationals of the other country.

(iii) Trade and cooperation in economic and other agreed fields will be resumed as far as possible.

(iv) Exchange in the fields of science and culture will be promoted.

In this connection delegations from the two countries will meet from time to time to work out the necessary details.

4. In order to initiate the process of establishment of durable peace, both the Governments agree that:

 (i) Indian and Pakistani forces shall be withdrawn to their side of the international border.
 (ii) In Jammu and Kashmir, the line of control resulting from the cease-fire of December 17, 1971 shall be respected by both sides without prejudice to the recognized position of either side. Neither side shall seek to alter it unilaterally, irrespective of mutual differences and legal interpretations. Both sides further undertake to refrain from the threat or the use of force in violation of this Line.
 (iii) The withdrawals shall commence upon entry into force of this Agreement and shall be completed within a period of 30 days thereof.

5. This Agreement will be subject to ratification by both countries in accordance with their respective constitutional procedures and will come into force with effect from the date on which the Instruments of ratification are exchanged.

6. Both Governments agree that their respective Heads will meet again at a mutually convenient time in the future and that, in the meanwhile, the representatives of the two sides will meet to discuss further the modalities and arrangements for the establishment of durable peace and normalization of relations, including the questions of repatriation of prisoners of war and civilian interests, a final settlement of Jammu and Kashmir and the resumption of diplomatic relations.

(Zulfikar Ali Bhutto)	(Indira Gandhi)
President,	Prime Minister
Islamic Republic of Pakistan	Republic of India

Simla, the 2nd July, 1972

Index

A

A big blow to the judiciary (editorial), 483
A dream snuffed out (editorial), 517
A Holocaust is Not an Accident (editorial), 271
A little less foggy (editorial), 495
A victory not notified (editorial), 496
Aaj (Urdu monthly), 258; two-volume history of Karachi, 258
Aali, Jameeluddin: wrote second Islamic Summit Anthem, 173
Abbas, Mahmoud, 328, 329
Abbas, Zaffar: frontpage piece for *Dawn*, 230; gave *Dawn* a new layout in December 2013, 182
Abbasi, Justice Muhammad Nawaz, 507
Abbasi, Khaqan: dies in Ojhri Camp incident, 227
Abbasi, Nazir: death in custody, 230
Abbasi, Reema, 433
Abdul Aziz I: Shia population massacre at Karbala 1539
Abdul Hamid II, Sultan, 540
Abdul Wahhab, Mohammad bin, 589
Abdullah bin Saud: taken in chains to Constantinople, 539
Abdullah, Shaila, 260
Abdullah, Sheikh: against Kashmir's accession to Pakistan, 133; arrest, 140; ego, in jail, 134; meeting with Ayub Khan, 134; released, 134
Abidi, Agha Hasan, 112
Abidi, Raza Ali, 83
Abu Ali Hasan ibn Ali Tusi, see Nizamul Mulk
Abu Bakr, Sebi ben, 193
Abu Hanifa, Imam, 450
Abu-Nidal Organisation, 365

Accountability, 291, 485, 506
Achakzai, Mahmood Khan, 509
Ackerman, Gary, 387
Action Against Racism Group, 197
Adam, Siddik, 112
Adeel, 196, 200, 201; National Bank of Pakistan (London branch), 201; re-do family history, 201
Afaq, Mohammad, 47
Afghan: issue, 236; peddler, 264; refugees, 257, 291, 330; resistance, 217, 222; War, 206, 239, 243, 248, 250, 288, 291, 304, 431, 439, 443, 464, 472
Afghanistan: votes against Pakistan for a UN membership, 141; Soviet Union invades, 174, 255, 261, 311; British role in, 196; anti-Soviet jihad, 249; Wakhan corridor, 254; Soviet withdrawal, 288, 342, 508, 520; Saudi Arabia and the UAE ended their ties, 460; hostility towards Pakistan, 514; NWFP should be incorporated into Afghanistan 467; Bush administration's attack, 470; inter-twined geopolitically and economically with Pakistan, 475; India has a major economic and intelligence presence in, 522; Taliban government of, 596; human rights violations, 609

Aflaq, Michel, 537, 539, 544
AFP (Agence France-Presse), 145, 515
Afridi, Rahmat, 275
Afro-Asian conference in Bandung, Indonesia (1955), 107
Afro-Caribbean Association, 198
Aga Khan III, 97, 258
Aga Khan: Foundation, 254, 457; National Council for Pakistan, 257; Rural Support Programme, 254, 255
Ahmad Shah (last Qajar king), 206
Ahmad, Abdul Ghafoor, 211, 262
Ahmad, Afaq, 38
Ahmad, Asrar, 64
Ahmad, Brigadier Imtiaz (called Billa), 230, 231
Ahmad, Chief Justice Sabihuddin, 507
Ahmad, Eqbal: protest against Declaration of Principles, 550
Ahmad, Haseen, 62
Ahmad, Hassan, 25
Ahmad, Ibtisam, 17, 31, 110
Ahmad, Irfan, 467
Ahmad, Javed, 285
Ahmad, Khawaja Nisar, 214
Ahmad, Niaz, 255
Ahmad, Qazi Hussain, 473
Ahmad, Rashid, 143
Ahmad, Saghiruddin, 58
Ahmad, Sami, 110, 184

Ahmad, Shamim, 17, 31, 114
Ahmad, Sultan, 66
Ahmad, Tanvir, 301
Ahmed, SyedJaffer, 141
Ahmed, Wajihuddin, 497
Ahsan, Aitzaz, 509
Aideed, Mohammad Farah, 359, 360
Akhbar-e-Jahan, 76
*Akhbar-e-Khawatee*n, 125
Akhtar, Hassan, 110
Akhtari Begum scandal, 72–73
Akhund, Iqbal, 160
Akram, Wasim, 200
Al Aqsa mosque: burning (on August 21, 1969), 145
Al Murtaza, 146
Al Qaeda, 514
al-Assad, Hafez, 172, 177
Albright, Madeleine, 334
Aleemi, Akmal, 277
Alfred P. Murrah Federal Building, 412
Ali, Ahmad, 84
Ali, Chaudhry Muhammad, 18, 52, 87
Ali, Habib, 83
Ali, Hamdan Amjad, 76
Ali, Jam Sadiq, 76, 234, 423
Ali, Mehrunnisa, 141
Ali, Mohammad Ashraf, 214
Ali, Mohsin, 61, 113
Ali, Muazzam, 46, 47, 53, 59; Aslam Ali (brother), 60, 61; Ghazanfar (nephew), 46; Muhtaram Ali (brother), 60; Owais Aslam Ali (nephew), 61
Ali, Pir Mahfooz, 113
Ali, Wajid, 112
Aligarh University, 201, 240, 264
All Pakistan Newspaper Employees' *Ad Hoc* Committee, 155
All Quiet on the Western Front, 34
Allahabadi, Akbar, 205
Allenby, Sir Edmund, 196
Al-Motamar al-Alam al-Islami (World Muslim Congress), 514
al-Nahyan, Sheikh Zayed bin Sultan, 172
Alvi, Ataur Rahman, 112–113
Alvi, Saleem, 62
American Brat, An, 260
American(s): aid to Israel, 371; aid, 55; anti-communist propaganda, 55-6; books on journalism, 41; commitment to the anti-Soviet resistance, 243; Consulate in Karachi attacked (2002), 480; leaders, 55; money laundering, 376; multiracial character, 278; newspapers, 42; presence in all news organisations in Pakistan, 54; recognise the reality of a multicultural, multiracial milieu, 278; scholars, 274

Amin, Hafizullah, 462

Amin, Nurul, 143

Amir, Ayaz: columnist, Dawn, 242; joins the PML-N, 242; quits politics and returns to writing, 243; rejoins the Muslim League, 243; wins a seat in the National Assembly from Chakwal, 243; writes for The News, 243

Ammi (mother), 52, 70, 88, 108, 120, 244, 269, 519; asthmatic attack, 245; at New Delhi, 5; call-up notice, 33; death, 243, 244, 269, 270; HCS (Hyderabad Civil Service) officer, 28; importance of higher education, 7; Razia (niece), 77, 81, 98; tower of strength, 71; Zaheer (brother), 81

Amrit Bazar Patrika (Calcutta), 121

An American Witness to India's Partition, 466

An end at last (editorial), 490

Andrews, Robert E., 393

Anjam, 64

Anjuman-e-Tarraqi-e-Urdu, 80

Another move toward absolutism (editorial), 503

Ansari, Jamil/Jameel, 10, 19, 144, 159

Anti-Americanism: a fad the world over, 474

APMSO (All Pakistan Mohajir Students Organisation), 260, 261, 270, 423

APNEC (All Pakistan Newspaper Employees' Confederation), 155; press release, 213

APP (Associated Press of Pakistan), 6, 46, 68, 236, 241, 273, 295

Arab News, 289

Arab(s), 167, 172, 360, 343; anti-colonial struggle, 176; anti-Turkish feelings, 532; anti-Western, 534; cannot evoke Arab support on the plea that it is an Islamic issue, 566; cause, 169; concept of religion, 529; countries, 172; country not languished under colonial rule, 545; double-crossed, 542; empire, 195; freedom banner raised by the Hashemites, 542; had the power to humble the Turks, 539; head of government or state, 173; India's secular approach, 561; indifferent to Pakistan's birth, 529; intelligentsia, 176; involved in conflict with Christian Europe, 532; Islam is non-controversial, 565; Islam is part of the Arab being, 544; Israel war (1948-49), 332; mind, 174; nationalism,

438, 534, 535, 536, 537, 540; nationalist regimes, 535; no perception of pan-Islamism as a political concept, 543; no special interest in the non-Arab Muslim world, 549; Pakistan's crude appeals to religious sentiment, 569; have a cosmopolitan, liberal outlook, 546; personality underwent a physical change, 598; provinces, 196; reasons why agreed to Second Islamic Summit Conference at Lahore, 566; secular in matters of statecraft, 548; secular in outlook, 568; states, 202; the Hindus are infidels like the Chinese and Japanese, 533; the word "Muslim", 550; think partition of India a diabolical British plot, like the partition of Palestine, 561; two-way misunderstanding with Pakistan, 533; unity, 167; view of the West, 557; world, 167, 193, 196, 340

Arabs, The, 566

Arafat Symbolises the Palestinians' Struggle (article), 562

Arafat, Yasser: Battle of Karameh (1967), 18; second Islamic Summit, 172; signing of the Declaration of Principles, 328, 330, 603; Interim Agreement on the West Bank and the Gaza (also called Oslo II), 331; sovereign Palestinian state, 332; Camp David summit, 334, 335; "concessions" Barak offered, 334; Jenin massacre, 335; under virtual arrest, 338; resorted to diplomacy and an unsuccessful guerilla war to put the Palestinian issue on the world's frontpages, 438; death, 335

Arif, General K.M., 224

Aristide, Jean-Bertrand, 324

Armitage, Richard, 464, 465

Armstrong, Karen, 445

Arnett, Peter, 393

Arora, C.K., 372

Arshad, 297, 298, 341

Article 58(2-b), 86, 87, 231, 237, 305, 482, 503, 529, 552

As Dawn Saw It, 260

Ashir, Mohammad, 10, 54, 425

Ashir, Uzair, 16

Ashrawi, Hanan, 331, 367

Asif Jah, 78; establishes state of Hyderabad, 78; receives recognition and title of Nizam, 78; writes peace treaty, 78

Askari, Mohsin, 191

Asmi, Saleem, 13, 254, 443

Ataturk, Kemal, 485, 543

Atlantic Monthly, The, 337
Atwood, Brian, 373
Ausdreau, Sergeant George F., 281
Awami League, 143, 151, 231
Ayub Khan: Pakistan's First Military Ruler, 107, 132
Azad Kashmir, 139, 254; October 8, 2005, earthquake, 33, 457
Azadi: Kashmir's Freedom Struggle, 370
Azam, Nuzaira, 297
Azfar, Ayesha, 433, 500, 621; caught trying to flee in a burqa, 490; Umme Hassan (wife), 487
Aziz, Shaukat, 503, 503, 509

B

Baath Party, 537
Babar, Maj.-Gen. Naseerullah Khan, 233, 235
Badruddin, S.G. M., 253, 426
Baig, Iqbal, 396
Baird, Zoë, 320
Bakhtiar, Taymour, 207
Balfour Declaration, 196, 532, 541, 582, 593
Baloch, Liaquat, 234, 473
Baloch: nationalists, 106; Students Organisation, 261
Balochistan, 29, 97, 186, 213, 475; Nationalist Party, 509

Bangkok, 200, 203, 249
Bangladesh, 7, 21, 28, 136, 144, 163, 179, 180, 192, 276, 309, 469, 477
Bangladesh: A Legacy of Blood, 7
Barak, Ehud, 332
Bari, M.A., 167
Barlas, Safdar, 268
Barna, Minhaj, 62; London correspondent, 155; APNEC chief, 155
Bashir, Mohammad, 112
Basic Democrats, 104, 105
Baughty, 76, 156, 157, 158; death, 582
Bazm-e-Adab (literary club), 62
Bazy, Jimmy, 197
Beg, Dr. Abdul Qayyum, 108
Beg, General Mirza Aslam, 224, 231, 236, 368, 394; appointed Vice-Chief of the Army Staff with the rank of a full General, 224; confesses to his crime, 232; founder of FRIENDS, 233; heroin smuggling, 234; Mehrangate scandal, 234, 235
Begin, Menachem, 310, 328
Bell, Tom, 198
Ben-Gurion, David, 536
Bennett, Lansing, 304
Bereuter, Doug, 397
Bey, K.Murad, 174
Beyond the Cayenne Wall, 260

Bhagwandas, Justice Rana 495; head, Supreme Judicial Council, 478

Bharatiya Janata Party, 138, 557

Bhashani, Maulana Abdul Hamid Khan, 151

Bhoshan, Bharat, 372

Bhutto, Benazir, 30, 102, 223, 224, 227, 239, 265, 302, 357, 375, 392, 457, 478, 479, 500, 517, 522; a joint Press conference with Bill Clinton, 273, 348, 414; address to the US Congress, 358; aftermath of her assassination, 518; anti-Benazir alliance, 396; appears on Larry King Live, 400, 401; as Defence Minister, 358; assassination, 357, 518; at Johns Hopkins University, 400; at Simla, 138; becomes the Islamic world's first woman Prime Minister, 229, 274; biggest spy game, 231; bombing of her procession in Karachi (2007), 479, 548; conditions for becoming prime minister, 236; *Dawn* editorial on her death, 554; denounces Pressler amendment, 409, 474; dismissed by President Farooq Ahmad Khan Leghari (1996), 384; Election 1993, 384; F-16s issue, 387; first dismissal, 88, 234, 421; Hazrat Bal issue, 385; idea of suicide, 357; interview by NBC, 302, 303; interview to the *International Herald Tribune*, 407; ISI chief's confession, 230; Mehrangate scandal, 233, 234, 236; not bow down to terror, 501; obituary, 521; offers to sign the Nuclear Non-proliferation Treaty, 399; on Kashmir, 389, 390, 397; on nuclear issue, 385; refused sword symbol, 232; returns to Pakistan from first exile, 247; returns to Pakistan from second exile (2007), 498; second dismissal, 95, 262 shocking behaviour, 358 solitary confinement, 358 speech at Los Angeles World Affairs Council, 409; *The Star*'s policy on wedding, 268, 269; visits America (June 1989), 357; visits America as leader of the Opposition (1993), 357, 365; visits America as Prime Minister (March-April 1995), 357; visits Harvard University, 358; wedding 269, 272; women's issues, 425

Bhutto, Zulfiqar Ali, 93, 508, 512, 529, 560; abolishes the "gazetted" condition, 416; arrested (November 13, 1968),

146; Ayub's martial law Cabinet, 111; considers Afghanistan; most important geopolitically for Pakistan, 475; demand Kohinoor diamond's return to Pakistan, 200; dismisses the Balochistan government, 186; Election campaign (1970), 60; files affidavit to challenge his detention under the Defence of Pakistan Rules, 136; as Foreign Minister, 115; government, 169, 173, 183; hanged, 148–166; as Information Minister, 60, 187; Islamic socialism, 149; July 1977 coup, 61; land reforms (1972), 256; last speech in the National Assembly, 461; leads procession from Rawalpindi to Pindi Gheb, 146; making Pakistan a nuclear power, 312; nationalisation programme, 166, 165, 187, 473, 486; oil crisis, 200; ouster, 263; personality and policies, 186; plans underground railway system for Karachi, 45; popularity, 205; presidential address, Lahore Summit (1974), 174, 175; rallies, 151; RCD, 202; released from detention, 210; resigns as Foreign Minister, 112; Second Islamic Summit Conference (Lahore, 1974), 172, 566; speech on Kashmir Issue, UN Security Council (September 22, 1965), 102, 122; speech to the General Assembly (September 28, 1965), 115, 125, 127, 479; Tashkent secret, 149; tore up own speech instead of Polish resolution, 160, 161; tumultuous welcome at Lahore, 132; undertook train journey, 210; view of the popular anti-Ayub agitation, 136

Biden, Joe, 365
bin Laden, Osama, 290, 372, 412
Binnori madressah, 441
Bizenjo, Mir Ghous Bakhsh, 469
BlackWings, 260
Blackburn, 196, 198; Asians, 199
Blair, Tony, 196
Blix, Dr.Hans, 565
BOAC (British Overseas Airways Corporation), 53; Comet 4-A, 53, 54, 57
Bogra, Mohamed/Mohammad Ali, 87, 107, 156
Bokhari, Ashfak, 457; Amna Batool (niece), 457
Bokhari, Javed/Jawaid, 46, 60, 61, 259
Bokhari, Syed Ataullah Shah, 467
Bokhari, Tayyab, 46, 52
Bomb in the Basement: How Israel went Nuclear and what

that means for the World, The, 536

Bombay, 6, 8, 24, 239; terrorists attack (November 26, 2008), 139

Bonaparte, Napoleon: military victory in Egypt, 531; Siege of Acre of 1799, 537

Boucher, Richard, 303, 371

Boudiaf; Mohamed, 366

Boumedienne, Houari, 172

Boys Will Be Boys, 260

Brady Bill (Brady Handgun Violence Prevention Act), 346

Brady Sarah, 346

Brady, James, 346

Breyer, Judge Stephen, 322

Britain: faithful ally of Bush administration, 196; homes and building, 195; Labour government, 118; race relations, 197; refusal to support the Sharif of Mecca militarily against Ibn Saud, 541

British: annexation of Sind by, 4; arrogance, 41; books on journalism, 37; colleagues, 41; Commonwealth, 96; crafted bureaucratic system, 28; created a race problem (South Africa, America, Australia), 199; era politicians, 18; era, 43; Firms in Karachi (Volkert, Forbes, Campbell, Ralli, Sasson, Graham), 8; genocide, 199; government, 26, 88, 95; humane and sophisticated, 196; in practice close to Islam, 196; India, 85; Indian Army, 41; nationality, 7; news agency, 6; newspapers, 6, 39; owned newspapers, 23; paramountcy, 117; parliamentary norms, 90; Press, 6; raj, 9; role in Iran, Afghanistan, Malaya, Gulf, Zanzibar, Oman, 196; Press, 242; rule, 8, 28; ruled Bengal, 21; theories advanced by publicists, 78; troops, 4

Brown Amendment, 375

Brown, General, 280, 286

Brown, Hank, 375

Brown, Sherrod, 393

Burhani, Ismail, 74

Burney, I.H., 41, 168

Burney, Naushaba (née Hussain), 37

Burton, Dan, 387

Bush, George H.W., Sr. (41st President, 1989-1993), 217; does not issue the certification required under the Pressler law, 312, 397, supported the return of President Aristide, 324; NRA member, 345; Pakistani and American officials sign a series

of agreements, 358; Richard Nixon, 381; administration, 336, 337
Bush, George W., Jr. (43rd President, 2001-2009), 319, 338, 375; military package pledged to Musharraf, 384; attacks Taliban Afghanistan (2001), 517; determined to destroy the Taliban government, finds a willing ally in India, 473; war on terror, 565
Buttar, Justice M. Javed, 501
Bux, Pir Ilahi, 63

C

Caffery, Jefferson, 91
Cairo, 46, 58, 60, 176, 333
Calcutta, 27, 28, 29, 52
Canadian Coalition of Democracies, 562
Carter, Jimmy, 251, 294; brought Israel and Egypt to the table, 333; Camp David accords (1978-79), 333, 347; denounced as anti-Semitic, 251; hated Ziaul Haq's dictatorship, 310; imprisonment wall, 334; strong human rights agenda, 310; view of Israel's intentions and the prospects of peace, 336
Case of Exploding Mangoes, A, 260

Castro, Fidel, 49
Cawthorn, Sir William, 96
CENTO (Central Treaty Organization), 60, 534, 535
Chapter from Memory, A, 246
Charlie Wilson's War, 311
Chattha, Hamid Nasir, 410
Chaudhri, A.T., 426
Chaudhry, Chief Justice Iftikhar Muhammad, 477, 484, 555; accused of malfeasance by Musharraf, 482; made "non-functional" by the Presidential Reference, 478; put under house arrest, 509; out of the apex court for the second time, 507; returns as Chief Justice, 511
Chaudhry, Fazal Ilahi, 172, 180
Chaudhuri, Niraj C., 199
Cheema, Umar, 232
Cheney, Dick, 338, 358
Chhapra, Abdul Hamid, 155, 214
China, 9, 18, 101, 109, 133, 139, 181, 254, 288, 299, 308, 381, 394, 469
Christopher, Warren, 329, 370, 374
Chundrigar, Ismail Ibrahim (I.I.), 89; resigns, 98
Church of Scientology, 248
Churchill, Winston, 227
CIA, 58, 207, 217, 292, 327, 341, 366; aid to the mujahideen,

310, 311; conducting the war in Afghanistan, 226, 227

Clemenceau, Georges, 120

Clerics: attitude towards sculpture, dance, music, 449 focusing on inanities, 452; have no concept of essential attributes of a modern state, 452; political, 480, 485, 486; refuse to study works of classical age Islamic scholars, 450; regard sacrosanct the subcontinental Muslims' customs and practices, 448; two categories, conventional and political 436; victims of their own clichés and rhetoric, 451

Clinton, Bill: administration, 323, 396, 409; American objectives for South Asia, 400; anti-gun law, 346; Attorney General nomination, 322; calls for a Kashmir settlement, 317; Camp David (2000), 332; campaign to tighten gun control, 345; favourably inclined towards Pakistan, 359; first nomination of a Supreme Court judge by a Democratic President in twenty-six years, 322; five-hour visit to Islamabad, 382; foreign policy, 337; joint Press conference with Benazir, 273; Kashmir issue, 348; Monicagate, 316, Narasimha Rao's visit, 384, 385, 386, 387, 388, 389, 390; National Rifle Association, 345;, Pakistan taken off the "watch list", 369, Presidency,318; Progress toward Regional Proliferation in South Asia (report), 361; release the F-16s to Pakistan, 405; Rose Garden Press conference, 360; signing of the Declaration of Principles, 328; Sikh rights, 364; Somalia, 323; strong anti-crime agenda, 343; the insulting way in which the Americans and Israelis treated Arafat, 334; The Washington Times launches a smear campaign, 342; too much of a Zionist to be neutral, 365; wanted to install Aristide back in power, 333

Clinton, Hillary Rodham, 345

Cobbler's Holiday or Why Ants Don't Wear Shoes, The, 260

Cold War, 17, 48, 50, 135, 405, 534, 564

Combined Opposition Parties (COP), 105, 215; leadership, 108

Communist(s), 63, 64, 107, 215, 230; dogma, 472; Karachi peace

committee, 72; manifesto, 517; movement, 20, 43; world, 585

Communist: Party of India (CPI), 63; Party of Pakistan (CPP), 230
Composite Dialogue (January 2004), 138
Condit, Gary, 363
Congress for Cultural Freedom, 49
Conservative Party, 198
Constitution 1956, 90, 94
Constitution 1973, 86, 222
Council Muslim League, 151
Courier Mail, 11
Cowasjee, Ardeshir, 235, 242; pathological hatred of the Bhuttos, 243
Creveld, Martin van, 177
Cricket, 20, 53, 54; the Ashes, 54
Crile, George, 311
Crime: news, 50; reporting, 50
Crocodiles are Here to Swim, The, 369
Cromer, Earl of (Evelyn Baring), 199
CSP (Civil Service of Pakistan), 28, 30, 33

D

Dacca/Dhaka, 3, 21, 45, 72
Dada, Kasim, 112
Dadabhoy, Abdul Qadir, 76, 158, 178
Daily Express (London), 12

Daily News, 17, 31, 144, 145, 247
Daily Telegraph, 11
Darling, Frank, 304
Darra Adamkhel tribal factories, 264
Darut Tarjuma (Translation Bureau), 79
Daughter of the East, 357, 522
Daultana, Mian Mumtaz, 151
Dawn: a new layout (December 2013), 182; About Ourselves (editorial), 27; advertisement-news ratio, 168; bomb blast at office (March 31, 1975), 185, 186; *Books and Authors* (weekly), 241; conversion into a daily, 22; cricket coverage, 54; *Dawn Magazine* column "Of People", 242; Dawn Magazine, 268, 270, 285, 287, 294; *Dawn Overseas Weekly* (DOW), 183, 184, 277, 278; Delhi staff, 26; *Economic and Business Review,* 61, 143, 252, 253; editorial on the Mehran Bank scandal, entitled "Our Secret Godfathers" (April 25, 1994), 234; editorial on the results of the referendum, 220; editorials, letters to the Editor, astrology box, 167; fiftieth anniversary supplement (July 29, 1997), 183; fifty years'

supplement, 26; Fire in *Dawn* office (headline), 27; follows the Muslim League policy, 23; Friday Feature becomes a fortnightly feature, 622; Friday Feature, 182; Gambols strip, 12; house style, 15; Internet edition, 278; Islamabad edition, 241; journalists in the sixties, 10; Launches Lahore edition, 253; layout unprofessional, 193; leader page, top article, middle article, 167; Looking back (article), 183; *Magazine*, 46, 183, 202; management willing to pay "interim relief", 153; name controversy, 22; new offices at Haroon House, 147; office fire (1961) 27; offices attacked and burnt, 25; overcomes financial crisis, 252; Pakistan Zindabad! (headline), 25; policy, 21; popularity, 25; publishes a picture with a factually wrong caption (1989), 423; publishes long poem by Elsa Kazi and Pamaiz Shami, 93; Republic Day celebrations, 90; Republic Day 91; shift work, 11, 12; stylebook, 13; Summit Bureau, 173; Referendum and After (editorial, December 24), 221; support for Pakistan's pro-Western foreign policy, 63; The New Cabinet (editorial), 89; trade union activity in, 47; visits by Diplomats to exchange ideas, 433; weekly; founded October 1941, 22; *Young World,* 246; Yusuf Haroon (chief editor, April 13, 1966, to April 5, 1967), 158

Dayan, Moshe, 176, 177

Declaration of Principles, 328, 330, 550

Deir Yassin massacre, 18

Deiss, Joseph, 560

Delphi, 27, 249

Democratic Action Committee: general strike, 146

Democratic Party convention, 249

Desai, Anita, 260

Descent into Chaos: How the War against Islamic Extremism is being Lost in Pakistan, Afghanistan and Central Asia, 450

Desert Fox, The, 11

Deserter's Tale, The, 343

Diem, Ngo Dinh, 309

Dinshaw, E.A., 112

Dion, Stéphane Maurice, 560

Dixon, Sir Owen, 123

Doctrine of Necessity: becomes intrinsic part of Pakistan's constitutional jargon, 483

Dogar, Justice Abdul Hamid, 507, 511
Douglas-Home, Alec, 106
Downer, Alexander, 560
DPA (Deutsche-Presse Agentur), 145
Dubai Chalo (PTV play), 416
Dubai, 93, 416; phenomenon, 134, 416, 418; workers, 415
Duffy, Michael T., 355
Dulles, John Foster, 607
Durand Line, 20, 276, 462, 467, 475,
Durrani, General Asad, 231, 232, 233, 235, 236, 391, 392; affidavit about Mehrangate money distribution, 233; Mehrangate scandal, 233
Dyer, R.E.H., 199

E

Earth Times, The (New York), 261
Earthscan (London-based NGO), 203, 248
East Pakistan, 3, 6, 37, 40, 87, 94, 132, 141, 143, 151, 153, 160, 163, 187, 213, 225, 231, 284, 394, 414, 415, 426, 469, 477; military crackdown in March 1971, 7, 159, 160; youth alienated, 187
Ebrahim, Fakhruddin G.: appointed Governor of Sindh, 270; decision to deploy Rangers outside the Karachi University's perimeter, 271; refused to take the oath under the Provisional Constitution Order promulgated by Ziaul Haq's decree in 1981, 271
Echo, 193, 194
Eden, Anthony, 91, 537
Egypt, 46, 180, 195, 333
Eighth Amendment, 306
Einstein, Albert, 299
Eisenhower, Dwight D., 41, 91, 283, 308, 381, 534, 556; Doctrine, 535
Ejaz, Ali, 416
Elections: (1958), 52; (1970), 187; (1977) rigged, 211; (1985), 217, political parties barred from taking part, 261; (1988), 234, 236, 237; (1990), 233, 237, 525; (1993), 384; (2008), 524; results, 525; (2009), 258; (2013), 289
el-Husseini, Amin, 18; visit to Pakistan, 317
Elkholy, Abdo A., 248
Enayatullah, Anwar, 246
Encyclopaedia Britannica, 79
Engineer, Asghar Ali, 248
England, 8, 54, 201
En-lai, Zhou (Chou En-lai) 107, 308
Enterprise (weekly), 37

Esposito, John, 248, 453
Europe, 49, 200, 252
European colonialism, 49
Evening Star, 10, 11, 12, 28, 50, 144, 146, 161, 168, 268; Star Weekend (Saturday magazine), 268, 269

F

F-16s, 311, 313, 373, 374, 375, 387, 390, 400, 405, 409
Face-veil, 449
Facts Are Facts: The Untold Story of India s Partition, 515
Fahd, King, 70; Prince, 91
Fahim, MakhdoomAmin, 497
Fai, Ghulam Nabi, 364
Faisal, King, 172; assassinated, 180
Faiz, Faiz Ahmad, 183, 240, 260, 370, 425
Fareedi, Sibte Farooq, 110
Farid, Sibte Farooq, 58
Farooqi, Muqeemuddin, 63
Farooqi, Musharraf Ali, 260
Faruqi, Mahmood Azam, 213, 262
Faruqi, Salman, 76
Faruque, Ghulam, 113
Faruqui, Justice A.S., 153
Father (Abbu) see Siddiqi, Muhammad Abdullah
Fayyaz, Justice Raja, 555
Fazlullah, Maulana (a.k.a. Maulana Radio): leads rebellion in Swat, 479
Feldman, Herbert, 142
Fernandes, George, 560
Fernandez, Walter, 7
Ferraro, Geraldine, 250
Fisk, Robert, 338
Foot, Michael, 17
For Life, Peace and Justice, 247
Ford, Gerald, 383
Foreign Assistance Act (called the Peace, Prosperity and Democracy Act, 1994), 373
Foreign Assistance Act 1961, 312
Fourth Estate, The, 369
Franco, Francisco, 220
Freedom of Information Act, 295
Freeman, Ivor, 198
Freier, Shalhevet, 299
Friedman, Thomas L., 339
FRIENDS (Foundation for Research on National Development and Security), 233
From Crisis to Crisis, 142
From Memory, 95
From Mutiny to Mountbatten, 22
Frontier Post, 275

G

Gabol, Abdul Sattar, 187
Gaddafi, Muammar, 189, 193
Gandhi, Indira, 134, 138

603

Gandhi, Mohandas Karamchand, 87, 466, 468
Garhi Khuda Bux, 216
Gauhar, Altaf, 107, 132, 166, 425; Ayub's Information Secretary 132; and Sheikh Abdullah, 133; book 113; Dawn editor 239; government pressure, 166; in jail, 183; turns against Bhutto 132
Gazdar, Hashim, 74
Geneva accords, 217, 224, 226, 228
Geometry of God, The, 260
Ghalib, Mirza, 205, 429
Ghani, Asim, 563
Ghauri, S.R., 110, 113
Gilgit-Baltistan, 254, 255, 256; referred to as the Crescent of Hope, 256 ; Swiss-style democracy, 257
Gilman, Benjamin, 396, 398
Ginsburg, Ruth Bader, 322
Give Us Back Our Onions, 369
Glenn, John, 303
Globe, 11
Glorious Koran, 449
Gokal, Abul Hasan, 247
Goldberg, Jeffrey, 337
Goralski, Robert, 41
Gore, Al, 407
Government of India Act 1935, 88
Graham, Frank P., 124, 125

Grand Mosque, Mecca: seizure by anti-Saudi radicals, 310
Green Card, 44, 93, 342, 428, 429, 430, 431
Guardian, The, 218, 249
Guinier, Lani, 322
Guinness Book of World Records, 103
Gujarat massacre (2002): Arab countries' attitude towards pogrom, 560; diplomats from Switzerland, Canada, Australia went on record conveying concern over the "tragic" events, 560; Dutch report; 559; European Union declaration, 558; extremist Hindu parties led the massacre, 559; Finnish rebuke, 559; foreign missions' reports on the pogrom, 559; German report, 559; human rights associations held Modi responsible for the slaughter, 557, 558; ignored by Arab countries, 558; no Arab or Muslim diplomat stationed in India bothered to visit Gujarat, 559; Western diplomats compiled reports for their governments, 559
Gul, Lt-Gen. Hamid, 230, 231, 236; confession to Benazir Bhutto, 230; Mehrangate scandal, 233, 234

Guns of Navarone, The, 15
Gwadarport, 97

H

Habib, Younus, 233, 235
Habibullah, Mian, 386
Hafiz, 205, 429
Hafizullah, 282
Hafsa
Hafsa Madressah: commandos, 487; girls, 487; girl students occupy government library, 487
Haider, Osman, 76
Hamas, 365
Hamid, Mohsin, 260
Hamidullah, Muhammad, 80
Hamilton, Lee, 338, 387, 388, 396, 398
Hanif, Mohammed, 260
Hans Blix Commission report, 464
Haq, Maulvi Abdul, 80
Haq, Ziaul, 30, 40, 61, 81, 86, 105, 163, 180, 211, 214, 215, 216, 218, 220, 229, 231, 239, 240, 242, 271, 292, 306, 310, 358, 460, 482, 522; a hang Bhutto Cabinet, 213; afraid of a sudden aid freeze by America, 226; allows religious parties to turn Pakistan into a recruiting/ training ground for the Afghan War, 261; amends 1973 Constitution, 86; amends the Political Parties' Act, 231; angry about issues where he was vulnerable, 224; announces a referendum, 217; announces elections, 217; article 48 (5-b), 231; article 58 (2-b), 231, 237; assumed all powers for himself twice (1977, 1988), 503; bureaucracy, 270; Cabinet, 214; continuation of dictatorship, 223; *coup d'état,* 142, 263; death, 30, 217, 243, 299; destroyed the Pakistani film industry, 267; develops ingenious method of bribing legislators, 229; dictatorship, 163, 252, 314; era, 230; funeral, 173; Generals in Suzuki controversy, 224; government, 317; held election in 1985, 209; Islamic character, 216; Islamic government, 174; and Junejo, 224; key American ally, 217; lacked a political base, 223; last visit to Britain, 226; lied brazenly, dishonest and a flatterer, 216; military dictatorship, 427 never expected Benazir's triumphal return, 223, 224; no concept of human dignity, 215; patronised Sindhi nationalist parties, 261; postpones the election, 212; promises to hold elections

605

within ninety days, 209; Provisional Constitution Order 1981, 271; punishments can be used as a form of entertainment, 209; Referendum Order, 1984, (President's Order 11 of 1984), 218; referendum, 218, 219, 220, 221; regime, 30, 229; rule, 73; sacks Chief Justice Mohammad Yaqoob Ali, 484; fascist bent of mind, 484; sacks Junejo and dissolves National Assembly, 228; scraps plans for underground railway system for Karachi, 45; screening in bureaucracy, 21, 29; *Shubkhoon* (night attack), 209; swept the grave of Bhutto's father, 216; tension with Junejo, 224, 228; tyranny, 180, 358, 471; Umra, 216

Haqqani, Irshad Ahmad, 212, 403; *Jang column* (January 17, 2002), 212

Haroon House, 147, 160, 161, 185, 245, 301, 413, 423, 430, 499, 520, 521; siege of, 423

Haroon, Amber, 269

Haroon, Haji Sir Abdullah, 63

Haroon, Hameed, 268, 423

Haroon, Mahmoud, 223; policy on Benazir's wedding, 272

Haroon, Saeed, 187

Haroon, Yusuf, 158, 233

Haroons, 183, 187

Harriman, W. Averell, 109

Hart, Gary, 249, 250

Hasan, Mumtaz, 112

Hasan, Wajid Shamsul, 273

Hasan/Hassan, Khalid, 277, 276, 369, 370

Hashmi, Khawar Naeem, 213, 214

Hassan bin Talal, 70, 542, 551

Hassan, Ahmad, 22, 31, 47, 50, 53, 62, 431; arrest, 47

Hassan, Bilal, 143

Hassan, Mubashir, 167

Hassan, Munawwar, 262

Hassan, Zawwar, 110

Hawai Adda, 69, 70

Hayauddin, Major General Mian, 58

Hazrat Bal Shrine, 385

Headquarters of Martial Law Administrator, Zone A, (Punjab): press release, 213

Heisenberg, Werner, 80

Heitink, J.G, 461

Hekmatyar, Gulbuddin, 393, 475, 518

Helms, Jesse, 323, 324, 325, 326, 327, 328

Heroin Plan by Top Pakistanis Alleged (lead story), 391

Hersh, Seymour, 462

Hinchey, Maurice D., 394

Hinduism, 449
Hindustan Times, 559
Hisam, Zeenat, 258
History of Israel: from the Rise of Zionism to Our Time, A, 177
Hitler reborn (editorial), 556
Hitti, Philip K., 538
Ho Lung, 91
Hobbes, Thomas, 57; state of nature, 57, 90, 544
House Republican Task Force on Terrorism, 353
Hubbard, Sergeant, 287
Hughes, Sergeant, 284
Hume, Brit, 322
Hurriyet, 83, 168
Husain, Altaf, 2, 10, 47, 144, 215, 425, 554; Ainul Muluk (penname), 24; "Ayub and COP" (editorial), 215; anti-British activity, 21; British government employee, 24; China supporter, 181; 'Dar-el-Islam' (weekly column, The Statesman), 24; Director of Public Information, Calcutta, 24; hated communists and leftists, 47; : "Hitler reborn" (editorial), 556; Khan Bahadur Syed Ahmadullah (father), 21; meeting with Jinnah, 26–7; offer of *Dawn*'s editorship, 24; Press Adviser, Government of India, Delhi, 24; Shahed (penname), 24; 'Through the Muslim Eyes' (fortnightly column, The statesman), 24; Zeba Zubair (daughter), 22

Hussain, Abida: ambassador to US, 330, 335, 336; reaction to Benazir's NBC interview, 302, 303; hostility to Benazir, 304; resigns as ambassador, 304, 305; joins PPP, 304; diplomatic idiom, 305, Senator's *faux pas*, 304; views on Ghulam Ishaq Khan, 305; receives Mehrangate money, 232, 233

Hussain, Altaf: Aligarh-Qasbah Colony massacre 265; "buy useful things" speech, 265; enters hospital, 422; interview by author 265; leaves for London, 467 made use of the ethnic clashes in Karachi to turn MQM into a mass organization in southern Sindh, 265; Mohajirs' Supermo, 292; Nine Zero, 421; receives Mehrangate money, 258; released from prison in 1987, 264; Sohrab Goth procession 265. See also MQM

Hussain, Anwar (aka Annoo Bhai), 2
Hussain, Dr. Mahmood, 264
Hussain, Fida, 259
Hussain Lalarukh, 247

Hussain, Marjorie, 111
Hussain, Qazi, 263
Hussain/Hussain, Irfan, 242; adopts the penname Mazdak, 243; wrote for Dawn as Afzal Hussain, 243
Hussein bin Ali (Sharif of Mecca), 540; Abdullah, second son, King of Transjordan, 541; decision to ally himself with the British during World War I, 532; Prince Faisal, third son, King of Iraq; 541; vision of a United States of Arabia, 542
Hussein, Maisoon, 246
Hussein, Saddam, 34, 278, 416, 537, 565
Hussein-McMahon correspondence, 196
Hutton, Len, 201
Hyderabad State, 78, 260; Indian occupation of, 201; mini-Islamic world, 80; Trust, 305
Hye, Professor Shamsul, 63

I

Ibn Saud, Mohammad, 538; died, 562; founder of modern Saudi Arabia, 554; his son marries Abdul Wahhab's daughter, 538; "marriage between religion and the sword", 538; receives international recognition, 542
Ibn Taymiyyah, 450
Idrees, Kunwar, 242; saved Benazir by turning her residence into a sub-jail, 243
If elected... (editorial), 493
Iftikharuddin, Mian, 240
Ignatius, Michael, 5
IJI (Islami Jamhoori Ittehad), 232
IJT (Islami Jamiat-e-Tuleba), 99; attack on the offices of Urdu daily, Jang, 266; educational institutions meant for "enforcing" the Islamic "system, 270; focus on girls for an Islamic "system", 291; misbehaved with Dr. Mahmood Hussain, 264; wage war on *"fahhashi"* on the campuses, 263
Ikramullah, M., 96
Ilyas, Mohammad, 213
Imroze (Urdu daily), 63
In Search of Fatima, 561
In the Arena: A Memoir of Victory, Defeat, and Renewal, 336, 337, 338, 422
In the City by the Sea, 260
In the Line of Fire, 473
India(n): invasion of Goa (1961), 7; Muslims in, 22; partition of, 9; post-British, 22; theories advanced by British publicists,

78; Government, 114, 130; forcible annexation of Jammu and Kashmir, 127; Kashmir policy, 134; takes the Kashmir issue to the UN, 121; propaganda, 128; secularism, 131; High Commissioner, 101; Civil Service (ICS), 28; exclusive use of three eastern rivers (Beas, Sutlej and Ravi), 143; attacks Pakistan on (November 3), 144; India-China war (1962), 101, 181;

Indian occupied Kashmir, 99, 101, 116, 139, 254; films, 280; Army, 83, 110, 117, 119, 343, ; Navy, 102; nuclear programme, 385; nuclear test in May 1974, 310; a major economic and intelligence presence in Afghanistan, 475; Hazrat Bal issue, 385; Prithvi and Agni missiles, 362; National Congress, 24, 88; Indian Parliament, 121; terrorist attack on Indian Parliament (December 13, 2001), 138; Indian-occupied Kashmir, 393

Indian Express, 559

Indonesia, 204, 249; Communist Party, 151; massacre in 1965-66, 170

Indus: river, 143; Waters Treaty (1960), 143

Indyk, Martin, 334

Internal Revenue Service, 342
International terrorism, 371, 393
Invisible Writings, 434
Inzamam-ul-Haq, 246
Iqbal, Afzal, 271
Iqbal, Brigadier S.M. A., 432
Iqbal, Dr Mohammad, 264, 430; views on ijtihad, 453
Iqbal, Justice Javed, 501
Iqbal, Rana Nayyar, 214
Iran, 177, 208, 366, 488; conquered by the Arab Caliphate, 543; Pahlavi Iran, 207; Islamic, 229; Islamic revolution, 180, 462; stirring of Iranian nationalism, 531; war, 188
Iraq, 206, 247, 343, 365
Ishteyaque, S. M., 109
ISI (Inter-Services Intelligence), 217; heroin smuggling, 234; made IJI, 232; political cell, 234; pulls out its operatives and lifts over 1,000 Taliban fighters out of the Kunduz area, 462
Islahi, Amin Ahsan, 262
Islam and Theocracy, 447, 453
Islam in Modern History, 549
Islam the Straight Path, 453
Islam, 20, 24, 30, 40, 167, 196, 241, 254, 393, 478, 491, 531; envisaged a classless society,

452; militant, 371; reduced to an ideology, 149
Islam, Ghayurul, 65, 253, 426
Islamic: fundamentalism, 372; ideology, 150, 229; bomb, 314; society, 490; state, 236; system, 242, 500, 518; terrorism, 562; ummah, 202, 564; unity, 582; values, 219; world, 410
Islamisation, 30, 218
Islamism and Democracy in India, 468
Islamist(s), 420; militias, 217
Ismaili, 97, 258; community: significant contribution in the fields of education and healthcare, 258
Ismay, Lord, 119
Israel Lobby and US Foreign Policy, The, 336
Israel, 174, 176, 177, 178, 251, 294, 310, 311, 315, 328, 330–338, 366, 534, 536, 556, 562, 566; accepts Security Council Resolution 242 (French version), 177; lobby in the US, 336, 337; nuclear force, 177; withdrawal from the occupied territories, 177
Israeli(s), 176, 329, 330, 353; settlements, 127; soldiers, 138
ISSB (Inter-Services Selection Board), 98

J

Jabbar, Khawar, 143
Jabir, Rafiq, 113
Jackson, Jesse, 249
Jafar, Mahdi, 167, 174
Jafar/Jaffar, Mahdi, 12, 110
Jafri, Iqbal Ahmad, 213, 214
Jahangir, Asma, 509
Jalalpuri, Saeed Ahmad, 467
Jalil, Abdul, 112
Jam Saqi trial, 230
Jamaat-e-Islami (JI), 18, 99, 104, 105, 149, 174, 213, 234, 236, 261, 270, 467, 472, 486, 514; anti-PPP stance, 144; close allies of capitalist and feudal classes, 150; drags Indonesia massacre into the election campaign, 151; fascism latent in the party's philosophy, 262; *Führerprinzip*, 262; government registers a case of high treason against six JI leaders, 472; has internal democracy, 262; jihad against "atheistic communism", 150; leadership orders its cadres to take precautionary measures, 152; mid-term election, 236; must take full responsibility for the rise of terrorism, 514; party structure, 262; philosophy, 240; planned massacre by the

"socialists" of "Islam-loving people", 152; reproduce in Urdu cheap anti-communist USIS propaganda literature, 150; Shoora (consultative body), 262; socialist phobia, 153; spirit behind the PNA movement, Bhutto's ouster, and Ziaul Haq's coup d'état, 263; student wing (the Islami Jamiat-e-Tulaba), 263; supported by some powerful media barons, 151; war on *fahhashi*, 263

Jamal, Akhtar, 169

Jamal, Lateef Ebrahim, 60

Jamal, Yusuf, 76

Jamali, Tufail Ahmad, 64; *GarTu Bura Na Maanay* (column in Imroze), 65

Jamali, Zafrullah Khan, 482

Jamiat-e-Ulema-e-Islam (JUI-F), 473

Jamiatul Ulema-e-Islam (Maulana Fazlur Rahman's faction), 514

Jamiatul Ulema-e-Islam, 514

Jamiatul Ulema-e-Pakistan, 553

Jamil, Jalbi, 84

Jan, Justice Mian Shakirullah, 495, 508

Jan, Justice Sajjad Ahmed, 153

Jang group, 20, 36, 83, 161

Jang, Bahadur Yar, 264

Jarring, Gunnar V., 123, 124

Jatoi, Ghulam Mustafa, 60, 233, 386, 387, 388, 389

Jauhar, Mohammad Ali, 264

Javeri, Tapu, 260

Jazzar, Ahmad, 538

Jerusalem Post, The, 562

Jerusalem, 178, 179, 196, 333, 335, 336, 562

Jinnah on World Affairs, 141

Jinnah, Fatima, 105, 262; election symbol candle, 106

Jinnah, Mohammad Ali (Quaid-e-Azam), 2, 3, 18, 20, 21, 22, 23, 24, 25, 36, 43, 63, 78, 80, 87, 88, 105, 133, 134, 186, 245, 261, 262, 370, 410, 468, 472, 520, 522; close associates, 18; newspaper boss, 25; correspondence with world leaders, 141; leadership, 410

Johnson, David, 396

Johnson, Lyndon B., 308, 344; administration, 101, 145

Jones, Paula, 250, 316

Joseph, Pothan, 22, 25

Journalism/ Journalists, 17, 26, 39, 48; benefits of career in, 29; lessons in, 38; journalists regarded as a spy in all dictatorships, 203; journalists flogged during the rule of the PNA Cabinet, 213

Junagadh, 80, 141

611

June 3 plan, 81, 87

Junejo, Mohammad Khan, 30, 40, 217, 233, 261, 271, 278, 482; government, 261; clash with Zia over the Afghan War, 217; advises Zia to give up Army Chief post and become a civilian President, 223; annoys Zia, 223, 248; tensions developing with Zia, 227, 228; calls a meeting of Opposition leaders, including Benazir Bhutto, 227; Chauhar Harpal (Rawalpindi) clash, 227; decides to act against those responsible for the blast at Ojhri Camp, 228; freed the Press, 251; visits the US, 231; gives an off-the-record briefing to the media on the Afghan war and the Geneva accords, 224; joins the Muslim League, 242; orders the administration not to interfere with Benazir's arrival, 223; proceeds on a tour of China, South Korea and the Philippines, 228; replaces Yaqub Khan with Zain Noorani as Foreign Minister, 224; refuses an extension to General Rahimuddin, 224; retires General K. M. Arif, 248; appoints Mirza Aslam Beg as Vice-Chief of the Army Staff with the rank of a full General, 224; sacked and the National Assembly dissolved, 228; taken into "protective custody", 228

K

Kabir, Humayun, 24
Kadri, Sibghatullah, 197
Kalashnikov, Mikhail, 20
Kalat, Khan of, 141
Kamal, Ajmal, 258
Kamal, Lateef, 83
Kansi, Mir Aimal, 304, 307, 314, 341, 359, 365, 366
Karachi Union of Journalists, 64
Karachi University (KU), 36, 38, 39, 40, 43, 46, 62, 94, 158; agitation against typing and shorthand, 39; annual convocation falls victim to violence by the IJT, 264; campus gun battles between armed student groups, 264; Journalism course, 37, 38; Journalism Department/Department of Journalism, 37, 39; new campus, 54, 59, 75; Princess Street campus, 59; (teachers): Barkat Warsi, 75; C. A. Salahuddin, 75; Professor Ilyas Ahmad, 75

Karachi: Christian or Goan district, 43; commuting in, 43;

currency dealers, 44; federal capital, 52, 62; increase in population following Partition, 43; life in apartment buildings, 43; literary scene, 19; mass transit system, 45, 46; monsoon rains in, no power breakdowns in the late fifties, 43; Pathan middle class, 19; Pax Britannica days, 8; Pizza Hut burnt, 57, 56; red light district, 2; sea breeze, 43, 52; summer in, 5; trams, 44, 45; tram system, 45; underground railway system, 45; urban renewal scheme, 44; winter in, 4; no paper published during journalists' strike, 154; ethnic riots began in April 1985, 265; freely available arms and ammunition, 264; gun battles between different student groups, 269; prone to mob violence, 225; virtual destruction of educational atmosphere, 270 communities (Baloch, 10; Christian, 3; Goans, 4, 7, 10; Gujrati-speaking, 3; Makranis, 4; Parsis, 7, 10; Sindhis, 3, 10; Urdu-speaking, 3); Karachi Goan Association, 4, 7; Karachi Press Club, 14, 16, 64, 66, 153; memories of, 14,

Kardar, Abdul Hafeez, 200

Kargil affair, 563

Karimjee, Mohammed Ali, 157

Karmal, Babrak, 462

Karmi, Ghada, 561, 562, 563; Arabs "colonised by Western civilisation at a very, very deep level", 561; never written a line in support of the Kashmiris, 562; "Pakistan and Israel: a Palestinian View" (Dawn, September 30, 2005), 614; visit to Karachi in 2003, 562

Karpin, Michael, 536

Karzai, Hamid, 475

Kashmir Holocaust, 370

Kashmir, 21, 80, 85, 99, 105, 109, 116, 118, 119, 122, 128, 129, 130, 131, 132, 133, 134, 139, 140, 141, 177, 195, 254, 304, 317, 345, 351, 353, 354, 355, 364, 368, 370, 390, 395, 401, 406; chronology of the dispute, 116 ff.; civilian population massacre in Poonch, 117; Instrument of Accession, 117; issue, 563; landmark agreements, 138; Pakhthoon tribesmen, 117; plebiscite, 88, 108, 115, 116, 118, 120, 121, 122, 123, 124, 130, 131, 133

Kashmir's Exclusion from Indian Democracy (article), 140

Kassem, Abdel Karim, 552

Kasuri, Khurshid Mehmud, 139
Kayani, General Ashfaq Parvez, 479; succeeds Musharraf as Chief of Army Staff, 507
Kazi, Elsa, 103
Kazim, Safia, 296, 297, 302, 404
Keddie, Nikki, 248
Kennedy, John F., 534
Key, Joshua, 343
Khairi, Habib Wahabul, 235
Khalistan, 364
Khambatta, Jal Framji, 7; Armaity (daughter), 9; Assistant Manager, Karachi Race Club, 9; Jer (wife), 9; office etiquette, 9; Yokohama Special Bank, 8, 9
Khan Justice Sardar Muhammad Raza, 495
Khan Sahib, Dr., 95; ministry dismissed, 74
Khan, Abdul Ghaffar (aka Frontier Gandhi), 87, 211, 262, 466
Khan, Abdul Hamid, 495
Khan, Abdul Wali, 151, 186, 211, 466, 468, 426, 486; gives NAP a pro-Moscow orientation, 469
Khan, Ahmad Ali (AAK), 10, 26, 69, 156, 161, 163, 164, 166, 181, 183, 184, 186, 187, 188, 225, 241, 242, 243, 246, 248, 249, 252, 253, 261, 266, 267, 274, 278, 292, 421, 425; belonged to "Partition generation", 239; Dawn Editorship, 174, 184; discontinues Ayaz Amir's column, 242; exclusive interview of Bhutto for Dawn, 187; fighting for Press freedom, 242; first meeting with Bhutto, 149; freelance writers he encouraged, 242; held hostage by MQM workers, 423 hurt by Bhutto's attitude, 187; kitchen cabinet, 526; launches *Dawn Overseas Weekly (DOW)*, 183; leftist, 181; member of the Communist Party, 181; National Press Commission,183; obituary, 166; opposes formation of a multi-class trade union, 156; personality, 247, sets up a *Dawn* Summit Bureau, 173
Khan, Air Marshal Asghar, 141, 211, 212, 249, 486; moves the apex court on a human rights petition, 233; petition (HRC 19/96), 233
Khan, Akhtar Hameed, 62
Khan, Amanullah, 110, 113
Khan, Azhar Ali, 109
Khan, Dr. A. A., 249
Khan, Dr. Abdul Qadeer, 312
Khan, Dr.Ikram U., 395
Khan, Dr. Mahmood Hussain, 36
Khan, Fatehyab Ali, 38; *amicus curie* in Bhutto's trial, 76

Masooma Hassan (wife), 76
Khan, Gauhar Ayub, 106
Khan, Ghulam Ishaq, 231, 305, 367, 368, 237; cartoon, 237; dismisses Benazir Bhutto government (1990), 86, 237; dismisses Nawaz Sharif government (1993), 86, 237; attempts to create a new political alliance to defeat Benazir, 232; resigns (1993), 405
Khan, Hakim Ajmal, 264
Khan, Hakim Taj Mohammad, 63
Khan, Imran, 200, 509
Khan, Inamullah, 174
Khan, Khan Abdul Jabbar see Khan Sahib, Dr.
Khan, Liaquat Ali, 25, 26, 28, 130, 131, 292; assassination, 564
Khan, Lt.-Gen. Ghulam Jilani, 255
Khan, Masudullah, 214
Khan, Maulvi Tamizuddin, 86
Khan, Mazhar Ali, 183, 240; Marxist, 198
Khan, Mir Osman Ali (last Nizam), 78
Khan, Mohammad Ayub, 39; Abdul Hameed (Rawalpindi Polytechnic student) is killed in police clash, 146; anti-communist strongman, 108; appoints a commission to go into the question of a new capital, 225; asks General Yahya Khan to take over, 135; authoritarianism system, 106; basic democracy, 104, 106; Cabinet, 60; calls for China's admission to the United Nations, 108; Chief Martial Law Administrator, 39, 95; Constitution of 1956 abrogated and martial law promulgated, 95, 142; *coup d'état*, 157; Decade, 108; decision to agree to a ceasefire, 106; decision to build a new capital, 106; election symbol flower, era, 64, 164; *Friends, Not Masters*, 113; government, 106, 234; government's fury fell on the house of the Haroons, 159; Great Decade of Development and Reform, 134, 142; Hashim fires two shots at Ayub, 146; industrialisation, 107, 414; meeting with Sheikh Abdullah, 150; offers to sign a no-war pact with India without a Kashmir settlement, 149; *Outlook* (weekly magazine), 37; Pakistan-China border delineated, 107; Presidential election, 105, 106; radio and television address (March 25, 1969), 135; RCD, 202; rebuilding of the ancient Silk Route, 108;

referendum,104, 105; refugee rehabilitation, 73; regime, 30, 40, 210; resignation in March 1969, 104, 135; revolt, 159; screening in bureaucracy, 30; skill at diplomatic manoeuvring, 107; system, 45, 73; Tashkent Declaration, 115, 143; Working Journalists' (Conditions of Service) Ordinance, 153

Khan, Mohammad Daud, 507, 508

Khan, N.D., 427, 428

Khan, Nasrullah, 211

Khan, Nazakat Ali,296

Khan, Prince Aly, 97

Khan, Prince Karim Aga, 107, 284

Khan, Qamruddin Qilich 278, see Asif Jah 78

Khan, Qayyum, 20, 52

Khan, Roedad, 136

Khan, Sahibzada Yaqub, 224, 236, 404

Khan, Sardar Amir Azam, 60

Khan, Sarfaraz, 169

Khan, Sir Syed Ahmad, 264, 438

Khan, Tikka, 219

Khan, Uzma Aslam, 260

Khan, Yahya, 135, 136, 143, 159, 308, 382; abrogates 1962 Constitution, 136, 143; assumption of power, 143; Ayub hands over power, 135-6;

Legal Framework Order, 143; orders military crackdown in East Pakistan, 159; principle of parity discarded,143; screening in bureaucracy 14-29

Khanna, Meher Chand, 91

Khar, Ghulam Mustafa, 169, 233

Kharal, Mohammad Khalid, 146

Khattak, Anwar, 396

Khattak, Mohammad Aslam Khan, 553

Khayyam, Omar, 206, 429

Khokhar, Justice Faqir Muhammad, 507

Khomeini, Ayatollah Ruhollah Moosavi, 173

Khou, Philip, 193

Khrushchev, Nikita, 13

Khuda ki Basti, 62

Khuhro, Ayub: creates Sindh Muslim League, 51; quits mainstream Muslim League, 51

Khulna: newsprint factory, 163

Khurshid, Dr Abdul Salam, 174

Khusro, Amir, 205

Khwaja, Akhtar Hussain, 64

Kidwai, Azim, 246

Killed by UN peacekeepers (editorial), 360

King, Larry, 231

Kissan Mazdoor (Peasants' andWorkers') Party, 75

Kissinger, Henry, 177, 278, 308,

309, 310, 382, 535
Kitchener, Herbert, 199, 142
KJWB (Karachi Joint Water Board), 84, 85, 279, 280, 281, 288, 429,
Knesset (legislative branch of the Israeli government), 332
Koestler, Arthur, 434
Kohat, 82, 98
Korei, Ahmad, 334
Koresh, David, 321, 488
Kozyrev, Andrei, 330
Kuala Lumpur, 46, 249
Kurd, Ali Ahmed, 509
Kureishi, Omar, 246, 62

L

Lafontant, Roger, 326
Lahore Press Club, 169
Lal Masjid (Red Mosque), 485, 492; army crackdown on July 478; Aziz-Rashid brothers, 488, 489; Aziz-Rashid brothers: criminal acts, 489; clerics succeed in appearing as victims, 489; commandos burn down a section of the Environment Ministry building, 489; -Hafsa politburo, 489; incident, 300, 335; militants, 510; phenomenon, 486, 489; rebellion, 490, 502; rebels, 514; standoff, 492

Landmark in a Paper's Odyssey (article), 26
Law of Return, 332
Lawrence of Arabia, 250
Lawrence, Sergeant, 283, 284
Leader, The, 50, 83, 145
League of Nations, 196, 532, 541,
Lebanese Hezbollah, 365
Legal Framework Order, 143, 159
Leghari, Farooq: dismisses Benazir Bhutto government (1996), 86; cartoon, 237
Letters to Uncle Sam, 370
Lewinsky, Monica, 250, 293
Lewis, Bernard: Catholic Church ideology, 150
Lewis, S., 65
Lippmann, Walter, 33, 36, 171
Livingston, Robert, 397
Lloyd, Selwyn, 96
Locke, John, 74
Lodhi, Maleeha: ambassador to US, 304, 372, 397
London: blasts (7/7), 34
Los Angeles Times, 289
Ludhianvi, Maulana Yusuf, 441; assassination aftermath, 477

M

M-249, 23
Macmillan, Harol, 101
Madani, Hussain Ahmad, 467, 473

617

Magsi, Dr. Qadir, 509
Maharaja of Kashmir (Hari Singh), 116, 141; flees capital, takes refuge in Jammu, 117; signs Instrument of Accession to India, 117
Maheu, René, 168
Mahmood, Arif, 260
Mahmood, Fazal, 201
Mahmood, Mufti, 211, 486
Mahvi, MasoodAli, 201
Majeed/Majid,M. A., 23, 34, 526, 527; death, 563
Majlis-i-Shoora (Consultative Assembly), 217
Makhdooms, 201
Makhdoomzadgan-e-Fatehpur: the brood ofMakhdooms from Fatehpur, 201
Making of the President, 344
Malihabadi, Josh, 80
Malik, Munir, 509
Malik, Qayyum, 37
ManjalIqbal, 188
Mansfield, Peter, 537
Mansoor, Jaffer, 58
Mansoori, Shafi, 186
Mansuri, G.M., 268
Manto, Saadat Hasan, 370
Mao Zedong, 49, 252
Maqbool, Lt.-Gen. Khalid, 236
Marker, Jamsheed, 28
Marri, Humayun, 234

Martial Law, 33, 39, 95, 248, 261, 459; lifted on January 1, 1986, 223; Regulations (5 and 33), 213; Regulations (24 and 55), 74
Mascarenhas, Neville Anthony, 5, 6; Yvonne Gertrude D'Souza (wife), 7, 5, 6
Mashhadi, Rukhsana, 246
Mashriq, 113
Massacre at Waco, Texas, 1993, 321
Masseruah, Abdul Salam, 412
Massey, Reginald, 260
Matri, Inqilab, 60
Matter of Detail, A, 260
Maududi, Maulana Syed Abul Ala, 174, 261, 467, 486, 489; death, 186
Mazur, Suzan, 389
McCollum, Bill, 395
McCurry, Mike, 315, 370, 371
McMahon, Sir Henry, 541
McNaughton, A. G. L., 123
McVeigh, Timothy, 411
Mearsheimer, John J., 336, 337
Meatless Day, 260
Meenai, Salman, 31, 164, 182
Mehran Bank scandal, 233, 234, 236; list of beneficiaries, 258
Mehsud, Baitullah, 457, 515; conversation a day after Benazir's assassination, 515
Mehsud, Hakeemullah, 457

618

Melbourne Age, 11
Memon, Yousaf, 234
Memory Lane to Jammu, 370
Menderes, Adnan, 91
Menezes, Donald, 5
Menon, Krishna, 85, 116, 122, 463
Metzenbaum, Howard, 366
Miandad, Javed, 200
Middle East, 17, 205, 565
Mikoyan, Anastas, 91
Mikulski, Barbara A., 368
Miller, Keith, 54
Milli Yekjehti Council, 442
Mir, Mir Taqi, 172
Mirani, Aftab Shahban, 273
Mirza, Iskander, 39, 87, 89, 92, 93, 95, 142, 426; abrogates 1956 Constitution and promulgates martial law, 95; acting Governor-General, 87; controlled democracy, 104; elected Pakistan's first President, 93; signs the
proclamation of the Islamic Republic of Pakistan, 90; signs 1956 Constitution, 995
Mirza, Tahir, 276, 426; becomes editor in 2004,
MMA (Muttahida Majlis-e-Amal), 497, 496; boycott presidential election, 497; disapproved Lal Masjid gang's actions, 489; do not condemn the Lal Masjid brigade, 491
Mob Paralyses Karachi (lead story), 443
Mob violence, 443, 445
Modi, Narendra: government failed to protect the minority community, 559; massacre in Gujarat, 559
Mohajir, 265, 421, 466
Mohammad, Bakhshi Ghulam, 140
Mohammad, Fateh, 214
Mohammad, Ghulam (GM), 483; appoints Mohamed Ali Bogra as Prime Minister, 87; dismisses Prime Minister Nazimuddin's government, 86; dissolves Constituent Assembly, 85; Maulvi Tamizuddin Khan challenges dissolution of the Constituent Assembly, 86
Mohammad, Hanif, 260
Mohammad, Khan, 217
Mohammad, Mian Tufail 211, 486
Mohammad, Sufi, 456
Molotov, V.M., 91
Mondale, Walter, 249, 291
Monteiro, Noel, 7
Moore, Arthur, 24
Morning News, 3, 5, 6, 17, 31, 32, 51, 61, 108, 109, 144, 202, 223
Morning Star, 198

Mosaddegh, Mohammad, 485
Moshe Dayan, 177
Mossadegh, Ahmad, 207
Moth Smoke, 260
Mother *see* Ammi
Mountbatten, Lord Louis, 85, 88, 108, 116, 117, 119, 141, 195, 199
MQM Haqiqi (Authentic), 421
MQM, 152, 270; anti-Benazir demonstrations in Washington and in Los Angeles, 411; attitude toward the Press, 298; dissidents form MQM Haqiqi, 421; Mehrangate scandal, 234; Nawaz Sharif launches army crackdown, 467; split down the middle over extortion racket, 421; workers "boycott" Dawn (1991), 423
Mubarak, Hosni, 200
Mug's Game, A, 369
Mughals: administrative system, 79; contribution to India, 86
Mujahid Force, 77, 99
Mujahid, Sharif Al, 37, 174
Mujib, General, 266
Mukhtar, Maulana Habibullah, 441
Mulk, Justice Nasirul, 555
Mullahism, 448
Muneer, K.M., 112
Munir, Justice Mohammad, 93

Murad, Aslam, 74
Musharraf, Pervez, 87, 139, 220, 384, 473, 477, 479, 493, 510; announces general election in the first week of January 2008, 511; appoints Abdul Hamid Dogar as the new Supreme Court Chief Justice, 507; becomes civilian President, 223; confesses that the referendum was anything but fair, 320; cooperates with America in the war on Afghanistan, 463; crackdown on political activists and leaders of the legal community, 509; desperate to seek re-election from outgoing Assemblies, 493; election as President for a second term, 479, 493, 494; first Press conference after the imposition of Emergency, 511; government, 106, 574; hands over army command to General Ashfaq Parvez Kayani, 479; imposes a state of emergency, 503; Kargil operation, 563; lawyers' protests against the humiliation of the Chief Justice, 478; Opposition asks scheduled presidential election be stayed, 496; Opposition challenges his right to hold two offices, 496; Opposition plead to court to declare Musharraf's

election null and void, 501; pledges to shed his uniform ("if elected"), 502; Presidential Reference against Chief Justice Iftikhar Muhammad Chaudhry, 478; reasons for imposing emergency, 504; re-inserts article 87 in the Constitution, 118,237; requests for ISI operatives in Kunduz, 462; resignation (2008), 477; retaliation by the Taliban in the form of suicide bombings, 478; sacks Chief Justice Iftikhar Muhammad Chaudhry (2007), 477, 484; Seventeenth Amendment, 496; sheds his army uniform, 511; signs joint statement with Vajpayee (January 6, 2004), 138; takes the oath as President of Pakistan, 511; unhappy with the Supreme Court's decision on "disappearances", 501

Mushtaq, Mohammad, 186

Music, 19

Muslim countries, 174, 92

Muslim League, 3, 8, 22, 23, 51, 52, 87, 164, 223, 242

Muslim, The (Islamabad), 13

Mustafa, K.G., 153

Mustafa, Zubeida, 184, 233, 240, 241, 480, 512, 516, 525 *Books and Authors*, 241; problems with her eyesight, 525 takes over as leader page editor, 480; writer on international affairs and foreign policy, 241

Mutawakkil (last great Abbasid-Caliph), 531

Muttahida Ulema Council: declares suicide bombings"*haram*", 456

My Political Struggle, 212

Myers, Dee Dee, 322

Myths of Zionism, The, 199

N

Naeemi, Maulana Dr. Sarfaraz: assassinated, 456

Naipaul, V.S., 487

Nakai, Mohammad Arif, 410

NAP (National Awami Party), 151, 186, 466, 469; Baloch wing breaks away to form Pakistan National Party, 469

Napier, Charles James, 199

Naqvi, Jamal, 230

Naqvi, Maniza, 260

Naqvi, Sarwar, 304, 367, 372

Narayan, Jayaprakash, 126

Nasir, Abbas, 230

Nasiri, Nematollah, 207

Nasser, Gamal Abdel, 556, 537, 438, 534, 535, 536

National Accountability Bureau 236

National Front, 196, 198; race relations policy and peaceful intentions, 197
National Liberation Front, 18
National News Publications (Pvt) Ltd, 113
National Party, 196; supporters, 197
National Press Trust, 58, 64, 112, 154, 223, 276; trustees, 112; Commission, 183
Nationalisation, 148
NATO (North Atlantic Treaty Organization), 17, 49, 534, 535
Nawa-e-Waqt, 154
Nazimuddin, Khwaja, 6, 86, 105; Chief Minister of Bengal, 24
Nehru, Jawaharlal, 5, 80, 85, 87, 96, 107, 553, 555; arrests Sheikh Abdullah, 134; obsession with Kashmir, 139; orders the invasion of Hyderabad state, 78; orders invasion of Kashmir, 117; promises plebiscite in Kashmir, 115, 116, 118, 120; reiterates commitments to UN resolutions, 335, 108, 123, 333; telegram to Liaquat Ali Khan,118; telegram to Prime Minister Clement Attlee, 118; wriggles out of the plebiscite commitment, 122
Netanyahu, Benjamin, 332

New Delhi, 46, 88, 109, 134, 139, 141
New York Times, The, 37, 315
NewYork, 249, 250
News, The, 233
Newsweek, 60
Niaz, Anjum, 258, 259, 260
Niazi, Sher Afgan, 497
Niazi, Zamir, 31
Nichols, Beverley, 26
Night of the Generals, The, 14, 15, 16
Nishtar, Sardar Abdul Rab, 20
Niven, David, 15
Nixon, Richard, 145, 308, 384, 382, 168; administration, 309; death, 383; seeks a negotiated settlement with Hanoi, 143
Nizams of Hyderabad, 79; flowering of Muslim culture, 79; institutes of learning, 79-; patronised men of learning/ wisdom from north India, 79
Nizamul Mulk, 78, 206; established madressahs, 78; *Siyasatnama*, 78
No delay in polls (editorial), 509
Noble, Allan, 91
Noel-Baker, Philip, 119
Non-Aligned Movement, 536
Non-cooperation movement (1922-23), 63

Noon, Sir Malik Feroz Khan, 39, 87, 482, 90, 95, 96; appoints Prince Aly Khan as Pakistan's ambassador to the United Nations, 97; gives Gwadar's 300 Hindus Pakistani nationality, 96; purchases Gwadar from Muscat for Pakistan, 96; receives letter from Iskander Mirza, 95

Noor Jahan, 206

Noorani, Maulana Shah Ahmad, 486

Noorani, Shah Ahmad, 211

Noorani, Zain, 224

Nooruddin, Khwaja, 6, 113

North-Western Frontier Province (NWFP), 20, 29, 87, 88, 186, 254, 141, 466, 472; plebiscite, 87; referendum 1947, 416

O

O City of Lights, 370

O'Leary, Hazel Reid, 350, 406

O'Toole, Peter, 250, 293,

OIC (Organization of the Islamic Cooperation), 565; first Islamic summit at Rabat, Morocco (September 22-25), 146; second Islamic Summit (Lahore, February 22-24), 172, 566

Oil crisis, 184, 200; prices rise, 415

Ojhri: ammunition depot (Faizabad) blast, 227, 228, 227, 271; inquiry, 272

Omar, Kaleem: death, 563

One Unit, 51, 89

Orangi Pilot Project, 62

Osmania University, 71

Ottoman Empire, 196, 531, 542, 562

Our Bones are Scattered: The Cawnpore Massacres and The Indian Mutiny of 1857, 79

Outlook, 37

Ovais, S.M., 174

Ozal, Turgut, 403

P

Pagaro, Pir (Syed Shah Mardan Shah-II), 233

Pahlavi, Mohammad Reza Shah (Shah of Iran), 173, 177; cast Iran in his own image, 207; Corporal Reza (father), 173; establishes secret police Savak (*Sazman-i-Amniyet va Ittilaat-i-Kishver*), 207; Pahlavi, 206, 207; spends $100 million on a festival held at Persepolis (*Takht-e-Jamshid*), 207

Pakhtoon Students Federation, 264

Pakhtoonistan, 20, 88, 461, 467, 475; Moscow becomes an avowed champion, 461

623

Pakhtoons, 420; community, 414
Pakistan & Gulf Economist, 76
Pakistan Annual, 23
Pakistan Army, 98, 103; liberates part of Kashmir, 119; surrenders (December 16, 1971), 144
Pakistan Electronic Media Regulatory Authority, 2002: Section 20 amended, 509
Pakistan Federal Union of Journalists (PFUJ), 62, 64, 65, 153, 154, 155; improving the standards of journalism, 64; Journalists' strike called off, 154; organised Pakistani journalists on trade union lines, 64; referendum for the journalists' strike, 153
Pakistan Peoples Party (PPP), 30, 143, 144, 146, 148, 150, 152, 187, 209, 211, 261, 273, 304; alliance with PML-J, 410; election 1993, 384; election 2008, 511; election symbol, 231; Foundation Meeting Document No.4, 148; government (1971-77), 60; government's curbs on the Press, 187; land reforms 1972, 256; nationalisation policies, 187; obtains a majority in November 2009 elections to the Gilgit-Baltistan Legislative Assembly, 258; rallies, 219; rule, 495; scuffle with MQM workers, 396
Pakistan Times, The (Lahore), 11, 37, 113, 181, 183, 187, 213, 223, 240, 266, 276, 277
Pakistan: A Dream Gone Sour, 136
Pakistan: aid suspended in October 1990, 304; America's "most allied ally", 101, 108, 132, 461; American alliance, 181; ban on alcohol (1977), 7; beginning of the polarisation of politics and society, 150; brutalisation of society, 209; bureaucracy, 29, 30, 31; Chhamb-Jaurian area, 101 compulsions and motives in training and arming the Taliban, 468; corporate sector, 112; Cricket team, 259; criminalisation of politics, 261; diplomatic relations with the Taliban's Afghanistan, 463; end of "dominion status" under the British Commonwealth, 90; ethnicity on the rise, 261; first general election held on the basis of adult franchise, 143; flawed Arab policy, 529; Foreign Office, 80, 533; High Commission, New Delhi, 5; ideology of, 40, 218, 229; Information Ministry, 58; intelligence services, 5; Kahuta

uranium enrichment plant, 236; Karakoram Highway (KKH), 119, 108, 255; Kashmir policy, 393; Keamari Company, 109, 110, 99, 101; membership of the US-led military alliances, 63; nationalism, 92; not responsible for 9/11, 506; nuclear issue, 303; on "watch list" of terrorism, 307, 313, 359; Pakistan Ex-servicemen's Association, 232; Pakistan Institute of International Affairs, 76, 111; Pakistan Institute of Labour Education and Research (PILER), 259; Pakistan Management Corporation (PMC), 61; Pakistan Press Commission recommends formation of a Wage Board, 153; PASRO (Pakistan Army Supplementary Reserve of Officers), 103; plan to purchase M-1 1 missiles from China, 394; plebiscite in Kashmir, 118, 124; Potohar plateau, 106, 225; quits Commonwealth, 192; quota system, 28; recognises Bangladesh as a sovereign nation, 180; recognising Israel, 562; Rehabilitation Ministry, 73; religious right, 470, 489, 491; Republic Day celebrations, 90, 91,100, 101; role of militant organisations in domestic politics, 217; screening in bureaucracy, 29, 30; self-determination" for the people of Kashmir instead of a plebiscite, 124, 125; Stand-Still Agreement with Maharaja of Kashmir, 116, 117; taken off the "watch list" on the terrorism list, 369; traditional, secular left, 465; transfer of capital from Karachi to Islamabad, 226; Twenty-Two Families, 148; urban planning, 225; Urdu-speaking middle class, 29; war with India (1960), 27; war with India (1965), 77; war with India(1971), 179, 338; wins the only gold in hockey at Los Angeles Olympic Games, 251; world's biggest irrigation systems, 143

Pakistan: The Enigma of Political Development, 248

Pakistani American Political Action Committee, 395

Pakistani Bride, The, 260

Pakistani: Goan(s), 5, 7; civilians, 18, 34; eating habits, 53, 61; film industry, 267; in a position of authority, 41; mob violence, 440, 445; nation, 20; officers emulating the British, 41; soldiers and defence installations, 18; Women/girls hijab, 420

Palestine Islamic Jihad, 365
Palestine Liberation Organisation, 328
Palestine, 20, 185, 251, 330, 365, 337, 530, 541, 553, 563, 532
Palestine: Peace Not Apartheid, 251, 335
Palestinians, 195, 330, 334; Diaspora, 18; issue, 8, 18, 22; refugees, 18
Palijo, Rasool Bux, 509; joins the NAP, 469
Pandit, Vijay Lakshmi, 121
Parbhani, 26, 44, 78, 80, 85
Parthasarathy, G: visit to Dawn office, 563
Partition, 25, 41, 60, 88, 108, 129, 133, 201, 239, 259, 262, 264, 291, 296; holocaust, 26, 85, 201, 240, 271
Pasha, Muhammad Ali, 547; higher education, 540; Egypt's virtual sultan, 540; printing presses, 540; victories over the Wahhabis, 539
Pataudi, Sher Ali Khan, 168
Patel, Dorab, 210
Patel, Vallabhbhai, 85
Pathan Odyssey, A, 553
Patton, George S., 41
Payami, Akhtar, 241
Peace Corps, 49

Peck, Gregory, 14
Peled, Benyamin, 177
Pell, Claiborne, 323, 338
Pelosi, Nancy, 319
Pentagon, 316, 375
Peres, Shimon, 328, 329
Perry, William, 374, 406
Persian, 205, 207
Phillips, David, 388, 466
Philosophy of the Revolution, The, 556
PIA, 58, 253; first airline from the free world to fly to China, 58; hijacking of a plane by Al Zulfiqar (1981), 230; inaugural flight (Boeing 2013) to Cairo crashes (1965), 65-6, 58; service to Shanghai, 108
Pickthall, Marmaduke, 80, 449, 547
Pieces of Eight, 547
Pincher, Chapman, 12
Pingar, Abdul Sattar, 76, 187; Rafat Tabani (wife), 157
Pioneer (Lucknow), 11
Pir of Manki Sharif, 63
Pirzada, Abdul Hafeez, 167, 233
Pirzada, Sharifuddin, 478, 493
PML-J, 410
PML-N, 237, 535; election 1993, 384; election 2008, 524
PNA (Pakistan National Alliance), 212, 262, 486; ruse to postpone

elections, 211; movement, 212, 240, 265, 503, 536

Polish resolution, 160

Powell, Colin: first Press conference after 9/11, 463; September 12 phone call to Musharraf, 473

Powell, Enoch, 197

PPA (Pakistan Press Association), 46, 48, 50, 51, 53, 59, 60, 61, 62, 76, 126, 240, 322, 295: CENTO anti-subversion funds, 60; launch of (1956), 60; mode of reception of news, 51

PPI (Pakistan Press International), 46, 61, 154, 214, 268 Prashad, Maharajah Sir Krishna, 79

President's warning (editorial), 502

Press in Chains, 31

Press, 6, 16, 46, 159, 163, 215, 234, 242, 273, 288, 300; aftermath of journalists' strike, 153; censorship, 39; debate about tram tracks, 45; decline in the journalists' role in Press industry trade unionism, 64; form a vertical union embracing all industry workers, 64; freedom, 240; frightened into submission or consisted of zealous Zia supporters, 220; harshly criticizes frisking and the Rangers' deployment, 271; industry's worst financial days, 163; Journalists' countrywide strike, 64, 453; Journalists' failed strike (1970), 62, 154; Journalists' strike (reasons), 154; Journalists' strike called off, 154; Musharraf curtails freedom, 556; non-journalist staff, 154; opposed to Sheikh Mujib's Six Points, 160; Press and Publications Ordinance (1963), 40; structural change in the trade union movement, 152; Working Journalists' (Conditions of Service) Ordinance, 153

Press, Newspapers, News Agencies and Books Registration Ordinance, 2002: amended, with a new section (5-A), 508

Pressler Law/Amendment, 217, 307, 312, 373, 387, 395, 397, 399, 400, 405, 406, 409, 474, 357, 374

Pressler, Larry, 303, 312, 313, 400; letter to Bill Clinton, 273, 313

Progressive writers, 19; left-leaning, 240

PTV, 51, 173, 232, 266, 277, 416,

Pugwash Council, 299

Punjab, 45, 59, 92, 116, 173, 212, 225, 236, 276, 364; Punjab Assembly chamber, 173; Punjab

Union of Journalists (PUJ), 64, 65; Punjabi bureaucracy, 45; Provincial Assembly, 227
Punjabi Students Organisation, 264
Purdah system, 449
PurLBalraj, 139, 140

Q

Qadir, Manzur, 107
Qadri, Maulana Asadul, 174
Qizilbash, Nawab Muzzafar Ali, 74
Question Time, 369
Quinn, Anthony, 14, 15
Quit India movement, 24
Quran, 35, 105; Surah Al-Kahf (The Cave), 35; Surah Al-Baqra, 179; veiling of all women or their seclusion, 449
Qureshi, Fazal, 46, 60, 61
Qureshi, Moeen, 38, 411

R

Rabbani, Justice Ghulam, 508
Rabbani, Raza, 621
Rabin, Yitzhak, 328, 329, 330, 331, 332
Radcliffe, Sir Cyril, 141
Radio Pakistan, 12, 19, 38, 48, 51, 69, 77, 92, 110, 297
Rafaqat, Lt.-Gen., 233

Rafi, Assad, 623
Rafsanjani, 366
Rahimuddin, General, 224
Rahman, I.A., 426
Rahman, Maulana Fazlur, 473
Rahman, Mufti Muneebur, 456; against the Taliban and suicide bombings, 456
Rahman, Sheikh Mujibur, 151, 179; assassinated, 180; invited to Lahore Summit, 174
Rahman, Sheikh Omar Abdul, 314
Rahman, Sherry: Star Weekend, 268
Rahmarullah, S., 174
Raipuri, Akhtar Hussain, 80
Raja, 188, 189
Ramay, Hanif, 169, 170, 172
Rammal, Anwar, 255
Ramzan war (October 1973), 415, 566
Rangers, 271, 521
Rao, Narasimha, 348, 349, 350, 351, 352, 355, 388,
Rao, Nirupama, 559
Rape of Bangladesh, The, 7
Raphel, Arnold, 317
Raphel, Robin, 317, 318, 353, 364, 389
Rashid, Ahmed, 462
Rashid, Ghazi Abdul (Lai Masjid), 485; killed, 490
Rawalpindi, 227, 271, 272; jail, 146

Ray, Siddharta Shankar, 363, 374
Raza, Syed Hashim, 174
Razaee, Mohammad Ali, 366
Razia: 98, 201, 259, 314, 376, 404, 434, 499, 518; arrives in Delhi en route to Pakistan, 5, 108; attends Benazir-Clinton joint press conference, 375; betrothal, 189; emergency nationality, 5; life in America, 339; Zaheer (father), 81
Razwy, Akhtar Adil, 11, 144, 147, 183, 268, 429
RCD (Regional Cooperation for Development), 202
Read, John Kingsley, 196
Reagan, Ronald, 217, 220, 250, 249, 311, 312, 346, 384
Reconstruction of Religious Thought in Islam, 451, 453
Red Shirts, 20
Referendum Order, 1984, (President's Order 11 of 1984), 218
Rehman, General Akhtar Abdur, 231
Reluctant Fundamentalist, The, 260
Remarque, Erich Maria, 34
Reno, Janet, 320, 346, 488
Reports on Kashmir by United Nations Representatives, 123, 124, 125

Republican Party (RP), 89
Requiem for an Unsung Messiah, 260
Return of the Onion, The, 369
Reuters, 6, 145, 473
Rizvi, Absar, 46
Rizvi, Murtaza: death, 512
Rizvi, Sajid, 202
Rizwan, Badar, 297
Robinson, William P., 344
Rohan, Michael Dennis, 145
Rohrabacher, Dana, 387, 397
Roline, Sophie, 167
Roosevelt, Franklin D., 421
Rose, John, 199
Rosen, Steven, 337
Ross, Dennis, 334
Rousseau, Jean-Jacques, 74
Rowlands, Don, 193
Roy, Arundhati, 249, 260, 558
Roy, Raja Tridev, 143
Rubaiyat, 429
Rubinstein, Alvin Z., 248
Rushdie, Salman, 260, 366, 443
Russell, Bertrand, 17, 299
Russell-Einstein Manifesto, 299
Russia, 17, 35, 78, 120

S

Saadat, Anwar, 91, 451; assassinated, 188; Camp David, 333, 347; recommends inviting

Sheikh MujiburRahman to the second Islamic Summit, 197; second Islamic Summit, 172; succeeds in unfreezing the Israel issue, 177; wins back the Sinai, 438
Saadi, 205, 468
SAARC (South Asian Association for Regional Cooperation), 402
Sabzvari, 99
Sachar, Howard M., 177
Sadequain, 206
Sadequain: The Holy Sinner 1954-1987, 286
Sadeque, Najma, 246
Saeed, Farrukh, 275
Saffron Dreams, 260
Said, Edward, 381
Said, Farida MunaverJahan, 260
Salahuddin, Ghazi, 83, 244; "Karachi Diary", 241, 433
Saleem, Khalid, 388
Salt and Saffron, 260
Samdani, Zafer, 275, 277, 266; obituary note, 276
Sanaullah, 83, 84
Sandys, Edwin Duncan, 109
Sanneback, N. H., 283
Sarajevo Saturdays, 260
Sarbanes, Paul, 328, 316
Sarvath, Princess, 552
Sarwar, Sehba, 260
Satanic Verses case, 443

Saudi Arabia, 91, 173, 216, 420
Savak (Iranian secret police), 230; burning of Rex Cinema in Abadan, 208
Sawyer, Thomas, 387
SEATO (South East Asia Treaty Organization), 307, 535
Section CaseAgainst Security DetenusGazdar, MuzaffarulHaq, Burhani and Murad (newsitem), 74
Sehbai, Shaheen, 241, 404
Sentinel, The, 50
Separate electorates, 89
attack on TwinTowers, 460; attacks onAmerica, 433; Pakistan joins thewar on terror, 493
Shafi, Mohammad, 65
Shah Nawaz, 112
Shah, Huzoor Ahmad, 50
Shah, SajjadAli, 235
Shahab, Qudratullah, 136
Shahabnama, 136
Shaikh, Nasir A., 112
Shajie, Abdul Rab, 38
Shakoor, M.A., 64
Shami, Parwaiz, 93
Shamsie, Kamila, 260
Shamzai, Mufti, 441; assassination aftermath, 490
Shao-chi, Liu, 132
Sharia at gunpoint (editorial), 492
Sharif, Maqbul, 276

Sharif, Nawaz, 30, 86, 87, 233, 234, 235, 237, 239, 265, 278, 302, 304, 305, 306, 360, 367; abolishes article 384,390, 404, 410,511,514; addresses Mohajir crowd (1991), 421; pledges to build a mass transit system for Karachi, 421; anti-Benazir demonstrators, 404; arrival in Islamabad from London anddeportation to Saudi Arabia, 478; decides to get rid of the Chief Justice SajjadAli Shah, 235; dismissal (1993), 95; drug deals to pay for covert military operations, 391; election 1993, 422; launches army crackdown on the MQM, 393; publicly announces Pakistan possesses nuclear weapons, 410; Punjab's Chief Minister, 453; resigns (1993), 405; returns to Pakistan (2007), 525; right to return, 332; second term as Prime Minister (1997), 235; storms the Supreme Court,235

Sharif, Omar, 14, 15, 250
Sharon, Ariel, 34, 332, 338
Shastri, LalBahadur, 115
Shattuck, John, 356
Shaukat, 83
Shehki, Mohammad Ali, 273
Sheikh, Abdul Quddoos, 109, 155

Shervani, Afzal (aka AfzalAhmad), 38, 62
Sherwani, Latif Ahmad, 174
Shia, 258; mosque bombed, 56; procession, 19; state, 278
Siachen glacier, 361
Sibtain, Syed Mohammad, 76
Siddiqi, Ahmed Razi, 67, 76, 84, 88, 568, 569; Ayub government's pressure for vote, 105; elected Basic Democrat, 44;in Aurangabad, 81;inpolice, 48;Marxistleanings, 104; military
scientist-wife, 104; personality,40, 80; ties with Jamaat-e-Islami, 115; trainee-pilot, 62
Siddiqi, Dr. Raziuddin, 28, 79
Siddiqi, Manzoor, 1
Siddiqi, Mazheruddin, 447, 452
Siddiqi, Meher, 88
Siddiqi, Muhammad Abdullah, 33, 76, 88, 84, 223, 568, 569; Deputy Collector of Parbhani, 26; poetic pessimism, 77; Hyderabad state, 78; Nizam's bureaucracy, 71; grief, 71; moves to Razi's home, 244; Osmania University hockey captain, 71, 244; well versed in Persian and wrote poetry, 205; favourite poet Amir Khusro, 205; reaction to Eid greetings, 269; death, 259, 267

Siddiqi, Qaiser, 88; Jahan, 260; marriage, 189; witness to bogus voting during Zia's referendum, 243
Siddiqi, Qamar, 119; death, 563; Jahan, 260; schizophrenic coupled with paranoia, 623
Siddiqi, Shaukat, 62
Siddiqi, Zuhair, 426
Sidhwa, Bapsi, 260
Siegel, Mark, 367
Simla agreement (July 2, 1972), 138, 348, 350
Sind/Sindh: government, 36; Muslim League, 52; Union of Journalists (SUJ), 64, 65
Singapore, 46, 249
Singh, Jaswant, 463; offers America bases in India for the US air force, 463
Singh, Manmohan, 116
Sinha, Yashwant, 139
Smith, C.W., 549
Soekarno, Ahmad, 151, 552
Soofi, Syed Mohammad (*Musawat*, Karachi), 214
Soomar/Sumar, A. K., 64, 112
Soomro, Muhammad Mian, 511
South Asia: race-conscious area, 199
South Korea, 107, 193
Sovereignty: Islamic and Modern, 75

Soviet Union, 261, 311, 320, 461; invades Afghanistan, 174; invasion, 254; Soviet-American *détente*, 58; Soviet-Chinese ideological polemics, 17
Splintered Mirror, The, 260
Srinagar, 131; airport, 117
Stalin, Joseph, 72
Standing Conference of Pakistani Organisations (United Kingdom), 197
Standing up to terror (editorial), 500
Star, The, 225
State of Islam: Culture and Cold War Politics in Pakistan, The, 468
Statesman, The, 17, 24, 25; 'Muslim Jehan' by "Musafir" (column), 24
Stevenson, Adlai, 383
Stinger heat-seeking missile, 227
Story of a Widow, The, 287
Story of My Life, 176
Story of Noble Rot, The, 260
Straits Times, 194
Studer, Captain Magnus P., 281
Suboohi, Afshan, 512
Suez Canal, 176; nationalisation, 148, 187, 427, 486
Suharto, 534, 537
Suhrawardy, HuseynShaheed, 87; resigns at the President's request, 89

Suleman, Syed M., 174
Suleri, Sara, 260
Suleri, Z. A. (editor, *The Times of Karachi*), 60, 62
Sun, The, 114, 132, 144, 157, 161, 163, 164, 165, 191, 194, 195, 208, 213, 218, 247, 262
Sunday Times, The (London), 6
Sunde, Arne Toralf, 145
Sunni, 257; processions, 19; suicide-bomber, 56
Supreme Court of Pakistan:announces verdict in theAsghar Khan case, 621; caseunder Article 184(3) of theConstitution, 233; decisionthat every Pakistani had an"inalienable right" to return toPakistan, 478; declaresreference against the ChiefJustice illegal, 502; dismisses petitions challenging Musharraf's election as President, 511; gives the go-ahead to Presidential election but results not be notified by the Election Commission, 479; judges declare the Provisional Constitution Order 2007 illegal, 555; judgment restoring Iftikhar as Chief Justice, 524; Mehrangate scandal case pending, 261; refuses to stay the presidential election but the results of the election not be notified, 501; rejects the Opposition's petitions, 494; restores Iftikhar as Chief Justice, 495; stormed by Nawaz Sharif's goons, 235

Supreme Judicial Council, 484
Swat, 40, 185, 259, 340, 456, 510
Swisher, Clayton E., 333
Sykes-Picotpact, 196, 532
Symington amendment (1976), 312
Syrians, 176, 177

T

Talbot, Phillips, 87, 466
Talbott, Strobe, 349, 374
Taliban Pass into History (editorial), 505
Taliban, 263, 501, 514, 544; Afghanistan, 493; attacks Army Public School, Peshawar and massacre 132 students (December 16, 2014), 620; barbaric philosophy, 471; blew up the International Islamic University, Islamabad 2009, 457; brand of Islam, 518;
government of Afghanistan, 544; Islamic government, 472; military activity in the Federally

Administered Tribal Areas, 478; military activity, 225; murdered innocent children and call it jihad, 620; philosophy, 471; seize parts of Swat, 471

Talibanism, 458

Taraki, Nur Ahmad, 462

Tarbela: Dam, 160; affair, 143; issue, 181

Tareen, Ameen, 38, 62

Tashkent, 149; Declaration, 111, 115, 122, 123, 138, 143,

TASS (Soviet news agency), 63

Tehran Journal, 202

Tehran, 46, 202, 204; airport, 204,

Thatcher, Margaret, 226,

Theory and Practice of Socialism, 470

Third World, 49, 251; countries, 49, 53

Thomson Foundation (TF), 189

Time (magazine), 44

Times of Karachi, The (ToK), 1, 6, 27, 38, 60, 61, 62,

Times, The (London), 2, 6, 60

Tiwari, S.N., 356,

Toor, Saadi, 468

Torricelli, Robert, 387, 390

Truth About Camp David: the Untold Story About the Collapse of the Middle East Peace Process, The, 333

Tuomioja, Erkki, 559

Turkey, 202, 204, 216, 251, 254,

Two-state policy will fail (interview), 561

U

UN (United Nations), 49, 97, 102, 108, 118, 120, 121, 122, 124, 129, 131, 299, 360; appoint representatives for Kashmir, 123; Declaration of Human Rights, 299; General Assembly, 125; peacekeepers, 360, 361; resolutions, 130, 115; Security Council, 109, 120, 135, 160, 177, (passes resolution for a plebiscite to decide Kashmir's future), 120, (passes resolution reaffirming the principle of a plebiscite for Kashmir), 124, (report by Gunnar V. Jarring), 124, (statements by Frank P. Graham), 124, (Resolution 211), 103, (Resolution 47), 120, (Resolution 242), 177, 333, 335

UN Monitoring, Verification and Inspection Commission, 565

UNCIP (United Nations Commission for India and Pakistan), 115, 129; resolutions of 13 August 1948 and 5 January1949, 115, 120, 123, 124, 129,

UNESCO (United Nations Educational, Scientific and Cultural Organization), 55
Unicorn and The Dancing Girl, The, 370
United Arab Emirates, 172, 416
UPI (United Press International), 163
Urdu, 223, 266; -speaking community, 264
US (United States of America), 55, 58, 119, 193, 195, 201, 251, 276, 277; aid to Pakistan, 239; Congress, 251; funded anti-Soviet jihad in Afghanistan, 249
US Embassy: Karachi (later Consulate), 62; Islamabad, burnt, 339
USIA (United States Information Agency), 55
USIS (United States Information Service), 48; anti-communist propaganda, 49; press releases (three categories), 49; propaganda against the USSR, 50; white communists, 50; yellow communism, 56, 66
Usmani, Khwaja Muzaffarul Haq, 74
Usmani, Maulana Taqi, 467
Usmani, Shareef Kamal, 83

V

Vajpayee, A. B.: agrees to Indo-Pakistan composite dialogue, 138; Gujarat riots (2002), 608; visits Islamabad to attend SAARC Conference (January 4-6, 2004), 138
Valibhai, Najmuddin, 112
Verdict on India, 142; "Dialogue with a Giant" (chapter on Jinnah), 26
Verrall, Richard, 197
Vietcong's Tet offensive (January 31, 1968), 145
Vishwa Hindu Parishad, 559

W

Wage Board, 153, 155; first award, 153; second award, 153; "interim relief, 153,
Wall Street Journal, 341,
Walt, Stephen M., 336,
WANA (West Asia North Africa) forum, 551
Ward, Andrew, 79
Warsaw Pact, 17
Warsi, Barkat, 164
Washington Post, The, 234, 278, 302, 391, 406
Washington Times, The, 394

635

Watergate scandal, 309, 381, 388,
Wattoo, Manzoor Ahmad, 410
West Pakistan, 51, 103, 160, 187, 259, 284; High Court, 158
Western Mail, 193, 194
Where Reason and Religion Clash (article), 34
White, Theodore S., 344
Whose victory? (editorial), 544, 545
Wilde, Oscar, 195
Wilder, L. Douglas, 379
Wilson, Harold, 101
Wirth, Timothy E., 371
Wisner, Frank, 373, 374
WMD (Weapons of Mass Destruction), 196, 363, 464, 565
Wood, Kimba, 320, 321, 322
Woolsey, James, 365, 366, 367
Wordfall, 622
Wordsworth, William Christopher, 27
Working Journalists' (Conditions of Service) Ordinance, 153
World Bank, 57, 135
World Trade Centre, 290, 314, 372, 412
World Trade Organisation, 350

Y

Yahya, Ahsan, 164, 246, 247

YomKippur War (October 1973), 176, 200
Young Communists, 198
Young, Desmond, 11
Yousuf, Ramzi, 314, 408
Yusuf, 83

Z

Zahedi, MJ., 185
Zaheen, Tariq, 299
Zaheer, 81
Zaheer, Mahdi, 173
Zaidi, Bushra, 265
Zaidi, Nisar, 213, 214
Zaki, Akram, 372
Zaman, Hameed, 110,111; Rasheeda (wife), 110, 111
Zardari, Asif Ali, 273, 368, 370
Ziauddin, Mohammad, 241
Zille Huma, 488
Zionist Israel, The, 177
Ziring, Lawrence, 248
Zubair, Khwaja Mohammad, 17
Zubairi, Hamid, 25
Zubairi, Mohammad Ahmad, 10, 16,
Zubairi, Yameen, 295, 296, 297, 299, 302, 304.

INDEX

Printed in Poland
by Amazon Fulfillment
Poland Sp. z o.o., Wrocław